Windows Vista
The Definitive Guide

William R. Stanek

O'REILLY

· Taipei · Tokyo

Windows Vista: The Definitive Guide
by William R. Stanek

Published by O'Reilly Media, Inc., 1005 Gravenstein Highway North, Sebastopol, CA 95472.

O'Reilly books may be purchased for educational, business, or sales promotional use. Online editions are also available for most titles (*safari.oreilly.com*). For more information, contact our corporate/institutional sales department: (800) 998-9938 or *corporate@oreilly.com*.

Editor: Jeff Pepper	**Indexer:** Julie Hawks
Production Editor: Rachel Monaghan	**Cover Designer:** Karen Montgomery
Copyeditor: Audrey Doyle	**Interior Designer:** David Futato
Proofreader: Rachel Monaghan	**Illustrators:** Robert Romano and Jessamyn Read

Printing History:

February 2007:   First Edition.

ISBN-10: 0-596-52800-0
ISBN-13: 978-0-596-52800-3
[C]

Table of Contents

Part II.   Mastering Your Data and Digital Media

Part IV. Managing and Supporting Windows Vista

Part V. Advanced Tips and Techniques

Preface

Welcome to *Windows Vista: The Definitive Guide*. As the author of 63 books, I've always wanted to write the kind of how-to book that anyone—regardless of his or her skill level—could read from cover to cover and walk away with a wealth of knowledge about the subject at hand. O'Reilly is the first publisher to let me write a computer book for anyone and everyone in my own unique style, and the result is the book you hold in your hands, which I truly hope you agree is one of the best all-around guides to Windows Vista on the market.

As the author of two other Windows Vista books and a user of Windows Vista since its earliest beginnings, I bring a unique perspective to this book—the kind of perspective you can gain only after working with a product for several years. Long before there was a finished product called Windows Vista, there was a beta product, and before that there was an alpha product that most people outside of Microsoft don't even know existed. From these early beginnings, the final version of Windows Vista slowly evolved until it became the finished product that is available today.

As you've probably noticed, there's more than enough information about Windows Vista on the Web. There are tutorials, reference sites, discussion groups, and more to help make it easier to use Windows Vista. However, the advantage to reading this book instead is that all of the information you need to learn Windows Vista is organized in one place and presented in a straightforward and orderly fashion. This book has everything you need to customize Windows Vista, master your digital media, manage your data, and maintain your computer.

But wait, there's more, because there are plenty of other Windows Vista books available. Other books introduce and simplify Windows Vista, or provide quick starts or step-by-step guides, or promise to teach even dummies how to use Windows Vista. In this book, I don't pretend anyone is a dummy and I don't just teach you the steps you need to follow; I teach you how features work, why they work the way they work, and how to customize them to meet your needs. You'll also learn why you may want to use certain features of the operating system and when to use other features to resolve any problems you are having. In addition, this book provides tips, suggestions, and examples of how to optimize your computer for performance, not just appearance. This book won't just teach you how to configure your computer—it'll teach you how to squeeze out every last bit of power and how to make the most out of the features and programs included in Windows Vista. It'll also teach you how to take advantage of the latest features, such as Windows ReadyBoost.

Also, unlike many other books on the subject, this book doesn't focus on a specific user level. This isn't a lightweight beginner book or a book written exclusively for developers or administrators. Regardless of whether you are a beginner, power user, or seasoned professional, many of the concepts in this book will be valuable to you. And you'll be able to apply them to your computer regardless of which edition of Windows Vista you are using.

How This Book Is Organized

Rome wasn't built in a day, and this book wasn't intended to be read in a day, a week, or even 21 days. Ideally, you'll read this book at your own pace, a little each day as you work your way through all the features Windows Vista has to offer. This book is organized into 5 parts and 29 chapters. The chapters are arranged in a logical order, taking you from the simplest tasks to the more advanced ones. The tasks you'll perform the most and will get the most benefit from are right up front. The tasks you'll perform less often but will find extremely important for maintaining your computer come later. Paul Marquardt contributed to the chapters in Part IV and wrote Chapter 25.

In Part I, *Setting Up, Customizing, and Tuning Windows Vista*, you'll find everything you need to set up, customize, and optimize Windows Vista's core features.

Chapter 1, *Getting Started with Windows Vista*
> Provides details on getting started with Windows Vista. You'll learn about the various editions of the product, upgrade options, starting and using Windows Vista, and critical changes from earlier releases of Windows.

Chapter 2, *Optimizing Windows Vista's Interface*
> Focuses on optimizing the user interface in Windows Vista. You'll also learn about new features, including live thumbnails, Windows Flip, Windows Flip 3D, Windows Sidebar, and gadgets.

Chapter 3, *Fine-Tuning Windows Vista's Appearance and Performance*
> Provides tips and techniques for fine-tuning Windows Vista's appearance and performance. You'll also learn how to personalize Windows Vista.

Chapter 4, *Installing, Configuring, and Maintaining Software*
> Discusses installing and configuring the software, and includes extensive details on how software installation has changed and the features you can use to manage the software once it's installed.

Chapter 5, *Customizing Your Computer's Hardware Devices*
Discusses installing and configuring hardware, and includes extensive details on how hardware installation has changed and the features you can use to manage hardware once it's installed.

Part II, *Mastering Your Data and Digital Media*, explores everything you need to know to take control of the data and media stored on your computer.

Chapter 6, *Mastering Windows Explorer and Searching Your Computer*
Examines the changes and new features in Windows Explorer, including new navigation and search options. You'll also learn how to optimize the search features of the operating system.

Chapter 7, *Navigating the Web with Internet Explorer 7*
Discusses Internet Explorer 7, the new browser version included with Windows Vista. You'll learn tips and techniques for making the most of the powerful new features of the browser, and you'll learn how to protect your computer and your data while surfing the Web.

Chapter 8, *Creating Your Media Library with Windows Media Player*
Details how to use Windows Media Player 11 to build a media library. You'll learn how to rip and burn audio CDs as well as data CDs and DVDs. You'll also learn how to make the most of your music, pictures, videos, and recorded TV shows.

Chapter 9, *Capturing and Managing Your Digital Pictures and Videos*
Shows you how to capture, organize, and manage digital pictures and digital videos using Windows Photo Gallery. You'll learn how to optimize and organize your collection, how to create slide shows, and how to burn CDs and DVDs to create copies of your pictures and videos.

Chapter 10, *Making Video DVDs and Movies*
Since Windows Vista is the first version of Windows with built-in support for burning DVDs, this chapter explores the ins and outs of making video DVDs and movies using Windows DVD Maker and Windows Movie Maker.

Chapter 11, *Securing and Sharing Your Data*
Explains how to secure your data by setting access permissions, and how to share your data. As Windows Vista includes a completely new set of file sharing options, experienced users will want to read this chapter closely to learn about the new sharing options and how they are best used.

Chapter 12, *Setting Up Printers, Scanners, and Fax Machines*
Teaches you how to set up and configure printers, scanners, and fax machines.

Chapter 13, *Making the Most of Your Computer's Accessories*
Explores the wealth of accessories included with Windows Vista, including the Snipping Tool, Windows Speech Recognition, Mobility Center, Sticky Notes, Windows Journal, and more.

Part III, *Connecting and Networking*, examines everything you need to know to get connected and network your computer.

Chapter 14, *Setting Up Your Network*
Describes how to set up a home or small-office network and how to configure Transmission Control Protocol/Internet Protocol (TCP/IP)—the primary networking protocol used by Windows Vista.

Chapter 15, *Protecting Your Computer with Windows Defender and Windows Firewall*
Explores computer security and the features included in Windows Vista to protect your computer and your data while you are connected to the Internet. You'll learn about viruses, spyware, malware, and the programs used to protect your computer from them: Windows Defender and Windows Firewall.

Chapter 16, *Using Windows Mail, Calendars, and Contacts*
Explains how to use Windows Mail, Windows Calendar, and Windows Contacts.

Chapter 17, *Mastering Dial-Up, Broadband, and On-the-Go Networking*
Teaches you everything you need to know to master dial-up, broadband, and on-the-go networking.

In Part IV, *Managing and Supporting Windows Vista*, you'll learn the techniques you can use to manage access to and support Windows Vista.

Chapter 18, *Managing User Accounts and Parental Controls*
Focuses on user and group accounts, and discusses parental controls.

Chapter 19, *Managing Disks and Drives*
Provides tips for installing, partitioning, formatting, and mounting disks. You'll also learn about data compression and encryption.

Chapter 20, *Handling Routine Maintenance and Troubleshooting*
Provides a one-stop shop for everything you need to know to perform routine maintenance and begin troubleshooting.

Chapter 21, *Getting Help and Handling Advanced Support Issues*
Zeros in on advanced support issues to help you diagnose and resolve tough problems.

In Part V, *Advanced Tips and Techniques*, you'll learn about Windows Vista's most advanced features.

Chapter 22, *Installing and Running Windows Vista*
While not everyone will need to install Windows Vista from scratch, this chapter tells you how to perform a standard installation and an upgrade installation.

Chapter 23, *Exploring the Windows Boot Environment*
Explores the new boot environment used by Windows Vista. You'll learn about boot configuration data and how to view or edit it. You'll also learn how to manage the boot sector and install a previous version of Windows on a computer running Windows Vista.

Chapter 24, *Understanding Windows Vista Security Changes*
> Examines the security changes in Windows Vista as compared to Windows XP.

Chapter 25, *Mastering Windows Media Center*
> Explores installing and configuring Windows Media Center. The chapter also provides a detailed guide to mastering Windows Media Center once you have it up and running. As you'll see, getting Windows Media Center to work can be a challenge, even for a seasoned professional.

Chapter 26, *Using Group Policy with Windows Vista*
> Explains all about using Group Policy with Windows Vista and the important changes to Group Policy.

Chapter 27, *Navigating Windows Vista Policy Changes,* and Chapter 28, *Navigating Internet Explorer 7 Policies*
> These chapters provide an overview of new policies for Windows Vista.

Chapter 29, *Desktop Tips and Tricks with Keyboard Shortcuts*
> Provides a handy reference for using the wealth of keyboard shortcuts that are available in Windows Vista.

Who Should Read This Book

Is this book for you? That depends:

- If you've seen Windows Vista and want to upgrade from an earlier release of Windows, this book is for you.
- If your home computer includes Windows Vista and you want to learn about the operating system, this book is for you.
- If you are using Windows Vista at work and you want to learn about the operating system, this book is for you.
- If you are a developer or administrator and want to learn about Windows Vista, this book is for you.
- If you are an information manager and want to learn about Windows Vista, this book is for you.

If you've never seen a computer before, but you've heard that Windows Vista is really neat, this book isn't for you. You'll need a more general book about computing before you are ready to use this book.

What You Need Before You Start

There are hundreds of books on the market that explain how to get started with computers, the Internet, and other technologies related to computers. This book isn't one of them. I'm assuming that if you're reading this book, you already have a working knowledge of computers and the Internet. If you don't have a computer at home, that's fine, but you should have previously used a computer at work or at a library. You should also have some knowledge of how operating systems work and how to use a browser to surf the Web. If you know what the Start button is and what Internet Explorer is, you're in good shape—please read on!

Conventions Used in This Book

Within this book, I'll use the following typographical conventions:

constant width
> Indicates code terms, command-line text, and command-line options.

constant width bold
> Indicates values that should be typed literally.

constant width italic
> Indicates variables and user-defined elements.

italics
> Indicates URLs and introduces new terms.

I'll also use the following elements:

Notes to provide additional information or highlight a specific point.

Warnings to provide details on potential problems.

Other Resources

No single magic bullet exists for learning everything you'll ever need to know about Windows Vista. While some books are offered as all-in-one guides, there's simply no way one book can do it all. With this in mind, I hope you'll use this book as it is intended to be used—as a comprehensive, but by no means exhaustive, guide. Plenty of other great Windows Vista books are available—and I've even written a few of them. So as you set out to learn and truly master Windows Vista, I hope you'll keep this in mind.

Also, your current knowledge will largely determine your success with this or any other Windows Vista book. As you encounter new topics, take the time to practice what you've learned and read about. Seek out further information as necessary to get the practical, hands-on knowledge you need.

Throughout your studies, I recommend that you regularly visit Microsoft's Windows Vista site (*http://www.microsoft.com/vista*) and Microsoft's support site (*http://support.microsoft.com*) to stay current with the latest changes in the operating system. To help you get the most out of this book, there's a corresponding web site at *http://www.williamstanek.com/vista*. This site contains information about Windows Vista, updates to the book, and updated information about Windows Vista.

How to Contact Us

The good folks at O'Reilly and I tested and verified the information in this book to the best of our ability, but you may find that features have changed (or even that we have made—gasp!—mistakes!). To make this book better, please let us know about any errors you find, as well as your suggestions for future editions, by writing to:

O'Reilly Media, Inc.
1005 Gravenstein Highway North
Sebastopol, CA 95472
800-998-9938 (in the U.S. or Canada)
707-829-0515 (international/local)
707-829-0104 (fax)

You can also send us messages electronically. To be put on the mailing list or request a catalog, send email to:

info@oreilly.com

There is a catalog page for this book, which lists errata, examples, or any additional information. You can access this page at:

http://www.oreilly.com/catalog/9780596528003

To ask technical questions or comment on the book, send email to:

bookquestions@oreilly.com

For more information about O'Reilly, please visit:

http://www.oreilly.com

For more information about the author, please visit:

http://www.williamstanek.com

You are welcome to send your thoughts to me at *williamstanek@aol.com*. If you contact me about features that you'd like to know more about, I'll try to either update my web site or add the information to the next edition of the book. Thank you.

Safari® Enabled

 When you see a Safari® Enabled icon on the cover of your favorite technology book, that means the book is available online through the O'Reilly Network Safari Bookshelf.

Safari offers a solution that's better than e-books. It's a virtual library that lets you easily search thousands of top tech books, cut and paste code samples, download chapters, and find quick answers when you need the most accurate, current information. Try it for free at *http://safari.oreilly.com*.

Acknowledgments

Increasingly, I find myself trying to do things in fundamentally different ways than they've been done before. For this book, I had the crazy idea that I could get everything I've learned about Windows Vista over the past five years into a single volume that was not only clear and concise but also straightforward and easy to use, giving you, the reader, maximum value and maximum learning potential. With that in mind, I spent a great deal of time planning the approach I would take, and tapped into my previous experience writing two other Windows Vista books before I wrote this one.

During the many long months of writing this book, I continued to refine that approach, focusing the content and zeroing in on everything I thought would be of value as you set out to learn and master Windows Vista. I hope that as a result of all my hard work the book you hold in your hands is something unique. This isn't a 300-page introduction or a 1,500-page all-in-one reference. This is a relentlessly focused and comprehensive 950-page guide to what you truly need to know to master Windows Vista as a user.

Over the course of this project, I've worked with many different people at O'Reilly, but none was as helpful or instrumental to the writing process as Jeff Pepper. Not only did Jeff believe in me, but he also believed in my vision for this project every step of the way. Whenever an obstacle arose during the writing process, Jeff was there to help and to ensure that I had everything I needed to complete the work. I'd like to thank Audrey Doyle for her careful editing of the book. Audrey also provided helpful comments that made the review process easier. Others at O'Reilly that I've worked with during this project include John Osborn, Sara Peyton, Mark Brokering, and Laurie Petrycki. At the early stages of this project, I also worked with Preston Gralla. If our luck holds and the stars are aligned correctly, Preston and I will be speaking at events together about Windows Vista.

Paul Marquardt contributed to the chapters in Part IV and wrote Chapter 25. At the time I wrote this book, Paul was working at Dell as a PC support technician; previously he worked with the Oklahoma Department of Human Services as a senior systems administrator. If Dell has realized what an asset Paul is, he's likely been promoted. If not, he probably has a permanent position in IT management where his skills will be put to good use.

O'Reilly has an extensive editing and review process. Chris Crayton was the chief technical reviewer of the book. He reviewed the book from start to finish, and it was a great pleasure to work with him. Chris plans to share the book with his students. We also received very helpful reviews from Jim Schlotter and John Vacca. Thank you!

Thanks also to the literary agency, Studio B. David Rogelberg and Neil Salkind are great to work with. An extra-big thank you goes to Neil for helping out during this project. It's hard to believe we've been working together for 10 years. It has been a pleasure having you as my nonfiction agent.

Hopefully, I haven't forgotten anyone, but if I have, it was an oversight. Honest. ;-)

PART I

Setting Up, Customizing, and Tuning Windows Vista

CHAPTER 1

Getting Started with Windows Vista

I'll give you the bad news right up front: Windows Vista isn't what you think it is. While Windows Vista *is* the latest release of the Windows operating system for personal computers, it *isn't* what it seems. Windows Vista does look a lot like its predecessors, albeit with a cleaner, more inviting interface. If you have a powerful computer, you might also be enjoying Windows Vista's new Aero glass interface— or not. Regardless, you'd be hard-pressed not to notice all the eye candy Windows Vista presents, and this may lead you to believe the operating system is little more than new veneer for the same old software. Nothing could be further from the truth—and in this chapter, I'll show you why. I'll start by helping you get to know Windows Vista and its various editions. After discussing how to start and use Windows Vista, I will introduce some of the new ways you can work with this powerful operating system.

For the sake of this book, I'll assume you are fairly familiar with the Windows operating system and have worked previously with Windows 98, Windows Me, Windows 2000, or Windows XP. If that description fits you, read this chapter to learn about the key changes in Windows Vista that will affect you the most. If you already have some experience with Windows Vista, some of the material here may be familiar to you, but I recommend that you read the chapter anyway because some of the subtler changes in the operating system have the biggest impact on your computer. Also, keep in mind that because I'm assuming you have prior experience with a Windows operating system, I won't discuss computing basics, such as what a keyboard is or what a mouse is.

Getting to Know Windows Vista

From top to bottom, Windows Vista is dramatically different from earlier versions of Windows. Windows Vista is the first version of Windows in which the user experience changes based on your computer hardware. The experience a computer can deliver depends on whether it is Windows Vista Capable or Windows Vista Premium Ready:

- A Windows Vista Capable computer will deliver the core experience. To be Windows Vista Capable, a computer must have an 800 MHz or faster processor, 512 MB of RAM, a graphics processor that is DirectX 9-capable, and a CD-ROM drive. DirectX is a technology for enhancing a computer's multimedia capabilities, allowing more realistic 3D graphics and more immersive sound.

- A Windows Vista Premium Ready computer will deliver an enhanced experience. To be Windows Vista Premium Ready, a computer must have a 1 GHz or faster processor, 1 GB of RAM, an enhanced graphics processor with at least 128 MB of RAM that supports DirectX 9 graphics with a Windows Display Driver Model (WDDM) driver, at least a 40 GB hard drive with 15 GB of free space, a DVD-ROM drive, a sound card with audio outputs, and either a modem or a network card for connecting to the Internet.

 Some computers have graphics processors that share memory with the operating system. With shared memory, no additional graphics memory is required beyond the 1 GB of RAM.

Thanks to Microsoft's like-named logo programs with computer manufacturers, you'll find new computers have the Windows Vista Capable logo, the Windows Vista Premium Ready logo, or both. If your computer doesn't have one of these logos, it doesn't mean Windows Vista won't run on your computer. You can still install Windows Vista as long as your computer meets the Windows Vista Capable hardware requirements.

Other features of Windows Vista may require additional hardware. For example, to watch or record live TV, your computer needs a tuner.

Navigating Windows Vista Editions

Continuing the trend started with Windows XP, Windows Vista combines the previously separate home and business products into a single product family. Unlike Windows XP, Windows Vista editions aren't organized by hardware type or processor architecture. Instead, Windows Vista comes in several distinctly different editions, including:

- Starter
- Home Basic
- Home Premium
- Business
- Enterprise
- Ultimate

Each edition has a different set of features. Windows Starter Edition is a budget edition for emerging markets. Windows Vista Home Basic and Home Premium are the standard editions for home users, and as such, they include various home entertainment features. Windows Vista Business and Enterprise are the standard editions for business users, and as such, they include various business and management features. Windows Vista Ultimate is for those who want the best of both home and business features.

You can quickly determine which version of Windows Vista you are using by clicking Start → Control Panel and then clicking Get Started with Windows under System and Maintenance. As Figure 1-1 shows, this starts the Welcome Center. The Welcome Center also runs at startup automatically, unless you clear the "Run at startup" checkbox.

Figure 1-1. Getting started using the Welcome Center

When working with the various Windows Vista editions, keep the following in mind:

- While Windows XP had a separate edition for Media Center, Windows Vista includes Media Center as a standard feature. Both Home Premium and Ultimate include Media Center.

- While Windows XP had a separate edition for Tablet PCs, Windows Vista includes support for Tablet PCs as a standard feature. Home Premium and higher editions all support Tablet PCs.

- While Home Basic and Home Premium both include home entertainment features, only Business, Enterprise, and Ultimate include the features necessary to join a Windows domain.

- While Home Basic supports many of the same features as Home Premium, it doesn't support the new Aero interface (which you'll learn about in Chapter 2).

If you purchased a new computer or you work in an office where a new computer was delivered to you, Windows Vista was probably installed for you, and you only had to turn on your computer and click a few buttons to get your computer up and running. Because of this, you probably didn't have much of a choice as to which version of Windows Vista was installed. Thanks to new Windows Vista features, your edition choices are more open than you may think, however, so don't skip ahead just yet.

If you're installing Windows Vista yourself or are upgrading your computer from an earlier version of Windows, you can pick which version to install and can install or upgrade to Windows Vista, as discussed in Chapter 22 of this book. You can purchase an upgrade copy of Windows Vista for earlier releases of Windows. You can upgrade Windows 2000 or Windows XP to a corresponding or better edition of Windows Vista by buying and installing an upgrade copy of Windows Vista. With upgrade copies, you have two general upgrade options:

In-place upgrade
   With an in-place upgrade, you perform an upgrade installation of Windows Vista and retain your applications, files, and other settings as they were in the previous edition of Windows.

Clean install
   With a clean install, you replace your previous edition of Windows with Windows Vista and do not retain applications, files, and other settings. While you must reinstall all applications, you can retain files and other settings by running Windows Easy Transfer, prior to installing Windows Vista. After the installation is complete, you need to run Windows Easy Transfer again to reload your files and settings.

As Table 1-1 shows, the version of Windows you are running largely determines your options for using upgrade copies of Windows Vista. The in-place upgrade option means that a clean install option also is available, but not vice versa. For earlier versions of Windows, you must purchase and install a full (nonupgrade) copy of Windows Vista.

Table 1-1. Using upgrade copies of Windows Vista

Operating systems	Windows Vista editions				
	Home Basic	Home Premium	Business	Enterprise	Ultimate
Windows 2000	Clean install	Clean install	Clean install	Clean install	Clean install
Windows XP Home	In-place upgrade	In-place upgrade	In-place upgrade	In-place upgrade	In-place upgrade

Table 1-1. Using upgrade copies of Windows Vista (continued)

Operating systems	Windows Vista editions				
	Home Basic	Home Premium	Business	Enterprise	Ultimate
Windows XP Professional	Clean install	Clean install	In-place upgrade	In-place upgrade	In-place upgrade
Windows XP Professional x64	Clean install	Clean install	Clean install	Clean install	Clean install
Windows XP Media Center	Clean install	In-place upgrade	Clean install	Clean install	In-place upgrade
Windows XP Tablet PC	Clean install	In-place upgrade	In-place upgrade	In-place upgrade	In-place upgrade

Unlike earlier releases of Windows, your choices for which edition of Windows Vista your computer runs don't end with the installation process. You can upgrade from the basic editions to the enhanced editions. To do this, you use a Windows Anytime Upgrade, as discussed in the "Upgrading Your Windows Vista Edition" section of Chapter 22. Once you've completed the edition upgrade, your computer will have all the features and capabilities of the new edition.

Starting and Using Windows Vista

Whether you are running a Home, Business, or Ultimate edition of Windows Vista, the core features of the operating system are the same. This means that on a home computer, an office workstation, or a mobile computer, you'll have the same standard set of features and you'll work with Windows Vista in the same way.

When you first start using Windows Vista, you should do the following:

1. Log on and finalize the installation.
2. Perform essential configuration tasks.
3. Review your computer's configuration and activate the operating system.

I discuss these tasks in the sections that follow.

Logging On and Finalizing the Installation

When you start Windows Vista, you know it's a different kind of operating system from earlier versions of Windows. During installation, you are prompted to create a local machine account. This account is created as a computer administrator account. When the operating system starts, you can log on using this account and you'll see the Welcome Center, shown previously in Figure 1-1.

If you purchased a new computer with Windows Vista already installed, you'll have to complete a mini-setup the first time you start your computer. As part of the mini-setup, you'll need to finalize the operating installation. The procedure you'll need to perform will be similar to the following:

1. When prompted, choose your country or region and your keyboard layout. Click Next.

2. You must next create a local machine account that will be created as a computer administrator account. Enter a username. Type and then confirm a password. Enter an optional password hint and then choose a picture for the account. Click Next.

3. Type a computer name and select a desktop background. Click Next.

4. Select a Windows Update option for the computer. Usually, you'll want to use the recommended settings to allow Windows Vista to automatically install all available updates and security tools as they become available. Choose Ask Me Later only if you want to disable Windows Update.

5. Setup displays the date and time settings. Make changes as necessary and then click Next.

6. If a network card was detected during setup, networking components were installed automatically. Because of this, you'll next need to configure each detected network connection:

   a. Depending on the type of location and connection, click Home for a home network, Work for a network in a workplace, or Public Location for a public network. Windows Vista will then configure networking as appropriate for this location.

   b. If there are multiple networks, you'll see a prompt for each network. You can configure each detected network in a different way.

7. Click Start. Windows Vista will then check the computer performance and assign a performance rating. When the operating system starts, you'll see the Welcome Center.

Performing Essential Configuration Tasks

The Welcome Center provides an overview of the system and quick access to key configuration tasks. The version of the Welcome Center you see depends on whether your computer is part of a home network or a business network. On a home network, your computer will operate in a workgroup configuration. On a business network, your computer will operate in a domain configuration.

The tasks you can perform from the Welcome Center include:

Connect to the Internet

Click the Connect to the Internet task and then click Connect to the Internet in the main panel to set up an Internet connection. Use this option to connect to a wireless router or to connect using a password-protected account over DSL or a dial-up or cable modem. See Chapters 14 and 17 for detailed information on networking.

View computer details

Click "View computer details" and then click "Show more details" to view basic information about your computer, including details on the Windows Vista edition, service packs installed, and your computer's performance rating. I discuss fine-tuning your computer's performance in Chapter 3.

Transfer files and settings

Click "Transfer files and settings" and then click "Start Windows Easy Transfer" to transfer user accounts, files and folders, program settings, Internet settings, and email settings from your old computer. For the transfer, you can use CDs, DVDs, Universal Serial Bus (USB) flash drives, external hard drives, network folders, or a Windows Easy Transfer cable.

Add new users

Click "Add new users" and then click "Add user accounts" to configure user accounts for each person that will log on locally to the computer. To learn more about managing user account settings, see Chapter 18. This option is available only when your computer is not part of a Windows domain. For domain computers, you manage user accounts in a slightly different way. See Chapter 18 for details.

Connecting your computer to the Internet is one of the essential tasks you'll need to perform to finalize the initial setup of your computer. As Figure 1-2 shows, the Connect to the Internet option can help walk you through the configuration of an Internet connection in three specific scenarios:

- If your computer has a wireless adapter and you need to connect to a wireless router or a wireless network, you can use this option to configure your connection. In the Welcome Center, click the Connect to the Internet task and then click Connect to the Internet. This starts the Connect to the Internet Wizard. On the "How do you want to connect?" page, click Wireless. If there are no configured devices or networks to select on the "Select a network to connect to" page, click "Set up a connection or network" and follow the prompts.

- If you are using DSL or a cable modem that requires a username and password, you can use this option to configure your connection. In the Welcome Center, click the Connect to the Internet task and then click Connect to the Internet. This starts the Connect to the Internet Wizard. On the "How do you want to connect?" page, click Broadband (PPPoE). After you provide the required username and password, select the "Remember this password" checkbox and then click Connect.

- If you are using a dial-up modem or ISDN, you can use this option to configure your connection. In the Welcome Center, click the Connect to the Internet task and then click Connect to the Internet. This starts the Connect to the Internet Wizard. On the "How do you want to connect?" page, click Dial-up. Enter the dial-up phone number, provide the required username and password, and then select the "Remember this password" checkbox. Click Connect.

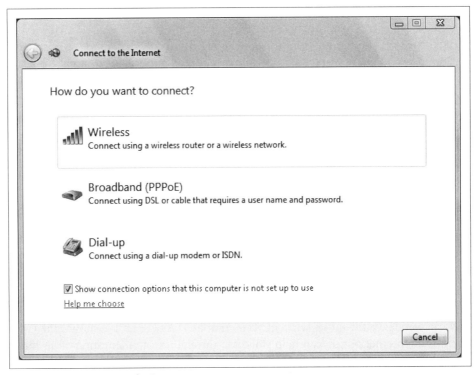

Figure 1-2. Connecting to the Internet

If your computer is configured as part of a home or business network that is already connected to the Internet, you don't need to use the Connect to the Internet option—simply make sure your computer has the proper configuration for its network adapter.

Most home networks and business networks use dynamically assigned network configurations. As this is the default configuration for Windows Vista, you typically do not need to change your network settings as long as your computer's network adapter is connected properly to the network.

If your computer's network adapter isn't connected to the network via a network cable, connect the network cable now. Your computer will then configure its networking settings and should also detect that it is on a network. You'll then be prompted for the type of network. Once you've specified whether you are using a home, work, or public network, your computer will update its configuration for this network location.

Reviewing and Activating Your Computer

In the Welcome Center, the View Computer Details task is selected by default. Because you are just getting started with Windows Vista, you'll probably want to click Show More Details to access the System console and view additional information about your computer. As Figure 1-3 shows, the System console provides links for performing common tasks and a system overview in four basic areas:

Windows edition
> Lists the operating system edition and service packs. To protect your computer and optimize performance, you'll want to ensure that your computer is running the latest service pack. With Windows Vista, you can install service packs and other product updates automatically as part of Windows Update. To learn more about Windows Update, see Chapter 20.

System
> Lists the processor, total memory, and performance rating of your computer. Your computer's performance rating was computed automatically during finalization of the installation. The Windows Experience Index is calculated based on the processor speed, total memory, graphics processor, and hard disk transfer rate. To learn more about updating your computer's performance rating and techniques for improving your computer's performance, see Chapter 3.

Computer name, domain, and workgroup settings
> List the computer name, description, domain, and workgroup details. All computers are members of either a workgroup or a domain, and this membership affects how you can configure the computer and the options available. To learn more about making your computer a member of a workgroup or domain, see Chapter 20.

Windows activation
> Lists the computer's product ID and activation status. If your computer is using a retail version of Windows Vista, it must have a product key and you must activate the operating system using this product key. In Windows Vista, the product key provided during installation is what determines the operating system version and features that are installed. When you upgrade your Windows Vista edition, you are essentially buying a new product key and telling Windows Vista to unlock and install the additional features of this edition. See Chapter 22 for details on upgrading Windows Vista editions.

Windows Vista performs activation and uses product keys differently than Windows XP. By default, Windows Vista requires activation over the Internet. In the System console, activate the operating system by clicking "Activate Windows now" under "Windows activation" and then clicking "Activate Windows online now" in the Windows Activation dialog box. Your computer then checks your Internet connection and attempts to activate the operating system. If this process fails, you'll need to resolve any issues that are preventing your computer from connecting to the Internet and then click "Activate Windows online now" again.

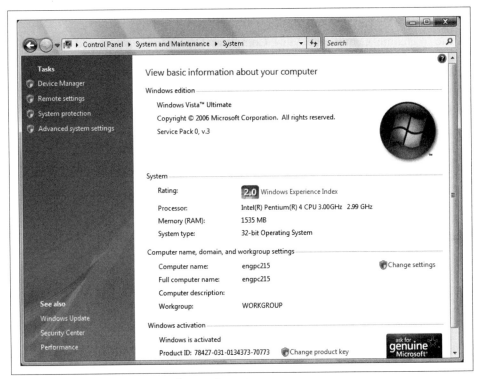

Figure 1-3. Viewing the computer's basic information

Unlike with Windows XP, you can easily change your computer's product key with Windows Vista. You may need to change your product key to comply with your license agreement. For example, you may already have a computer running on your network with the current single-computer product key. In the System console, click "Change product key" under Windows Activation. In the Windows Activation window, shown in Figure 1-4, enter the product key. You do not need to enter the dashes in the product key. When you click Next, the product key will be validated. You'll then need to reactivate Windows Vista over the Internet.

Working with Windows Vista

From startup to shutdown, Windows Vista is different from its predecessors—and these differences go far beyond the gadgets and other gizmos in Windows Vista's highly designed interface that I discuss in Chapter 2. If you want to truly know how Windows Vista works and what makes it tick, you need to dig under the hood.

Windows Vista is the first truly hardware-independent version of Windows. Unlike earlier releases of Windows, Windows Vista doesn't boot from an initialization file. Instead, the operating system uses the Windows Boot Manager to initialize and start the operating system. The Boot Manager is a key component of Windows Vista's

Figure 1-4. Changing your product key

extensive boot environment. You'll learn all about the Boot Manager and the boot environment in Chapter 23; here's what you need to know right now:

- The boot environment dramatically changes the way the operating system starts. Microsoft created the boot environment to resolve several prickly problems related to boot integrity, operating system integrity, and firmware abstraction.

- The boot environment is loaded prior to the operating system, making it a pre-operating system environment. As such, you can use the boot environment to validate the integrity of the startup process and the operating system itself before actually starting the operating system.

- The boot environment is created as an extensible abstraction layer that allows the operating system to work with multiple types of firmware interfaces without requiring the operating system to be specifically written to work with these firmware interfaces. Rather than updating the operating system each time a new firmware interface is developed, the firmware interface developers can use the standard programming interfaces of the boot environment to allow the operating system to communicate as necessary through the firmware interfaces.

Currently, Basic Input Output System (BIOS) and Extensible Firmware Interface (EFI) are the two prevalent firmware interfaces for computers. Firmware interface abstraction makes it possible for Windows Vista to work with BIOS-based and EFI-based computers in exactly the same way, and this is one of the primary reasons why Windows Vista achieves hardware independence.

The other secret ingredient for Windows Vista's hardware independence is Windows Imaging Format (WIM). Microsoft distributes Windows Vista on media using WIM disk images. Here's what you need to know about WIM right now:

- WIM uses compression and single-instance storage to dramatically reduce the size of image files. Using compression reduces the size of the image in much the same way as ZIP compression reduces the size of files. Using single-instance storage reduces the size of the image because only one physical copy of a file is stored for each instance of that file in the disk image.

- Because WIM is hardware-independent, Microsoft can use a single binary for each supported architecture: one binary for 32-bit architectures and one binary for 64-bit architectures. If you work at a company that creates disk images of various computer configurations, you can use this technology to reduce the number of disk images you must maintain.

The final secret ingredient for Windows Vista's hardware independence is modularization. Windows Vista uses modular component design so that each component of the operating system is defined as a separate independent unit or module. As modules can contain other modules, various major features of the operating system can be grouped together and described independently of other major features. Because modules are independent from one another, you can swap modules in or out to customize the operating system environment. Modularization has many benefits:

- Thanks to modularization, you can more easily add features to the operating system. Instead of having to go through a lengthy add or remove component process as with earlier releases of Windows, with Windows Vista you can easily turn features on or off. If you click Start → Control Panel → Programs and then click "Turn Windows features on or off," you can quickly and easily select features to add or remove using the Windows Features dialog box, shown in Figure 1-5. Insert the Windows Vista media when prompted.

- Thanks to modularization, Windows Vista is language-independent. Some languages are included with your version of Windows Vista. Others you need to purchase separately and install. You can add or remove language packs as easily as you can Windows features. If you click Start → Control Panel and then click Change Display Language under Clock, Language, and Region, you can quickly and easily install and uninstall language packs. Click the Install/Uninstall Languages button to launch the Install or Uninstall Display Languages Wizard, shown in Figure 1-6, and follow the prompts to add or remove language support. You'll need to insert the Windows Vista or language pack media when prompted.

Figure 1-5. Adding and removing features simply by turning them on and off

Logging On, Switching, Locking, Logging Off, and Shutting Down

No tour of getting started with Windows Vista would be complete without discussing logging on, switching, locking, logging off, and shutting down. If you're an experienced Windows user, you may be tempted to skip this section, but please don't. Skim this section instead, because some of the changes aren't immediately obvious.

Logging On to Your Computer

Windows Vista displays the logon screen at startup. The way the startup screen works depends on whether you are at home or at the office:

- At home, you'll see that all standard user and administrator accounts you've created on the computer are listed on the startup screen. To log on, you click the account name. If the account is password-protected, you must click the account name, type the account password, and then click the arrow button.

- At the office, Windows Vista displays a blank startup screen after startup. You must press Ctrl-Alt-Delete to display the logon screen. By default, the last account to log on to the computer is listed in *Computer\username* or *domain\username* format. To

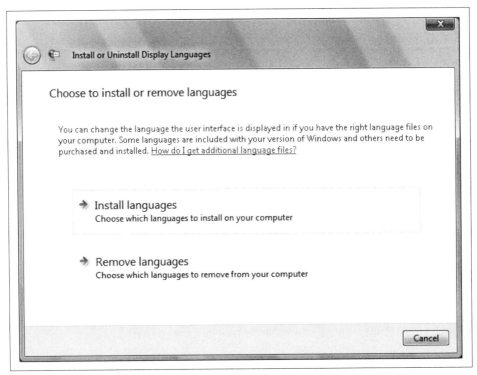

Figure 1-6. Adding and removing language support

log on to this account, you type the account password and then click the arrow button. To log on to a different account, click the Switch User button and then click "Log on as another user." Type the username and password, and then click the arrow button.

When working at the office, you can specify the domain and the account name using the format *domain\username*, such as enigma\williams. If you want to log on to the local machine, you type .*username*, where *username* is the name of the local account, such as .\williams.

Switching Users

If multiple people use your computer, you can easily switch users by pressing Ctrl-Alt-Delete and then clicking the Switch User button. At home, the logon screen is displayed, as with startup. At the office, a blank startup screen is displayed and you must press Ctrl-Alt-Delete again. Another way to switch users is to click Start, click the Options button to the right of the power and lock buttons, and then click Switch User.

Locking Your Computer

You can lock your computer by pressing Ctrl-Alt-Delete and then clicking the Lock This Computer option. You can also lock the computer by clicking Start and then clicking the Lock button. The Lock button is a blue button with a picture of a lock on it. The way you unlock your computer depends on whether you are at home or at work:

- At home, a lock screen is displayed with the name of the user who is logged on. Clicking the account name or picture allows you to log back on as that user. If a password is required for the account, you'll need to enter the password before logging on.

- At the office, a lock screen is displayed with the name of the user who is logged on. If you want to log back on as the user, you must press Ctrl-Alt-Delete and then enter the user's password.

Logging Off Your Computer

When you are finished using your computer, you can log off or shut down. You can log off your computer by pressing Ctrl-Alt-Delete and then clicking the Log Off option. You can also log off by clicking Start, clicking the Options button to the right of the power and lock buttons, and then clicking Log Off.

 A running program may prevent logoff. If so, the Log Off dialog box is displayed and the programs currently running on the computer are listed. If one of the currently running programs is causing a problem with logoff, an explanation of the problem is displayed below the program name. You can then cancel the logoff or continue. Cancel the logoff if you want to save your work and exit a program. Continue the logoff if you are sure you have saved your work.

Turning Off Your Computer

When it comes to turning off and shutting down, Windows Vista isn't like earlier releases of Windows. In Windows Vista, turning off a computer and shutting down a computer are separate tasks. By default, when you turn off a computer running Windows Vista, the computer enters sleep mode. When entering sleep mode, the operating system automatically saves all work, turns off the display, and enters a low-power-consumption mode with the computer's fans and hard disks stopped. The state of the computer is maintained in the computer's memory. When the computer wakes from sleep mode, its state will be exactly like it was when you turned it off.

You can turn off a computer and enter sleep mode by clicking the Start button and then clicking the power button on the Start menu. To wake the computer from the sleep state, you can press the power button on the computer's case or a key on the computer's keyboard. Moving the mouse also wakes the computer.

You can turn mobile computers off and on by closing and opening the lid. When you close the lid, the laptop enters the sleep state. When you open the lid, the laptop wakes up from the sleep state.

There are, however, a few gotchas with the power button and the sleep mode. The way the power button on the Start menu works depends on the following:

System hardware
> For the power button to work, the computer hardware must support sleep mode. If the computer hardware doesn't support the sleep state, the computer can't use the sleep state and turning off the computer powers it down completely.

System state
> For the power button to work, the system must be in a valid state. If the computer has installed updates that require a reboot or you've installed programs that require a reboot, the computer can't use the sleep state and turning off the computer powers it down completely.

System configuration
> For the power button to work, sleep mode must be enabled. If you've reconfigured the power options on the computer and set the power button to the Shut Down action, the computer can't use the sleep state and turning off the computer powers it down completely.

You can determine exactly how Windows Vista is configured by clicking Start and looking at the power button icon. An amber power button, depicting a shield with a line through the top of it, indicates that the computer will turn off and enter low-power sleep state. A red power button, depicting a shield with a line in the middle of it, indicates that the computer will shut down and completely power off.

 When working with sleep mode, it is important to remember that the computer is still drawing power and that you should never install hardware inside the computer or connect devices to the computer when it is in the sleep state. The only exception is for external devices that use USB or IEEE 1394 (FireWire) ports. You can connect USB and FireWire devices without shutting down the computer.

Regardless of your computer's power button configuration, you can power it down completely by using the Shut Down option. Shutting down the computer is the only way to ensure that the power to the computer is turned off. To shut down your computer, click Start, click the Options button to the right of the power and lock buttons, and then click Shut Down. You can also shut down your computer by pressing Ctrl-Alt-Delete and then clicking the red power button in the lower-right corner of the window.

CHAPTER 2

Optimizing Windows Vista's Interface

Everything that connects you—the user—to the computer is collectively referred to as the *user interface*. The basic elements of the user interface include the desktop, Start menu, taskbar, windows, dialog boxes, and wizards. These basic elements remain in Windows Vista, and you'll be able to work with them in much the same way as you have previously. Many other aspects of the user interface in Windows Vista have been revised, however, making this the most sweeping overhaul of the user interface in the history of Windows. Because of the massive changes, you'll find that you have to learn new ways of performing common tasks, and you'll discover much that is new.

The user interface has two key aspects: appearance settings and user profile settings. Appearance settings determine the color schemes, screen resolution, and sizing for window text, buttons, and icons. User profile settings determine where user files are located and what interface preferences are used.

Like earlier releases of Windows, Windows Vista's default appearance settings work well. With the introduction of automated screen sizing, screen resolution, and window sizing, appearance settings typically are optimized right at the start, making it easier to work with the operating system. Because a one-size-fits-all recipe would be very boring, Windows Vista gives you many choices about the appearance and behavior of your desktop, Start menu, taskbar, and other interface elements.

Your interface customizations are stored in your user profile. Because each user of your computer has a separate user profile, you are able to customize the desktop to meet your unique needs without affecting the interface settings of other users. This means your preferred settings will be remembered and restored each time you log on to your computer, and so will the preferred settings of any other users.

Customizing Windows Vista's Desktop

The enhanced user interface in Windows Vista is visually stunning, and a key component in the interface is the desktop. As you'll discover in this section, you can work with the desktop and its related features in many new and exciting ways. If you're familiar with earlier releases of Windows, you may be tempted to skip this section, but don't—there are a lot of new features and new ways you can work with the desktop.

Getting Around the Desktop

As Figure 2-1 shows, the desktop has standard features, but you can customize it with additional features as well. Standard desktop features include the Start menu, the taskbar, and the notification area.

Figure 2-1. Windows Vista desktop with Aero glass

Programs or folders you open appear on the desktop in separate windows. You can arrange open program and folder windows on the desktop by right-clicking an empty area of the taskbar and then selecting one of the following viewing options:

Cascade Windows
> Arranges the open windows on the screen so that they overlap, with the title bar remaining visible

Show Windows Stacked
> Resizes the open windows and arranges them each in a portion of the screen

Show Windows Side by Side
> Resizes the open windows and stacks them side by side

If you right-click an empty area of the taskbar and then select Show the Desktop, Windows Vista minimizes all open windows and displays the desktop. If you later right-click an empty area of the taskbar and select Show Open Windows, Windows Vista restores the minimized windows to their previous states.

In addition to opening program and folder windows, you can store files, folders, and shortcuts on the desktop. Any file or folder you save on the desktop appears on the desktop. Any file or folder you drag from a Windows Explorer window to the desktop stays on the desktop. You can add a shortcut to a file or folder to the desktop by following these steps:

1. Click Start and then click Computer.
2. Use the Windows Explorer window to locate the file or folder you want to add to the desktop.
3. Right-click the file or folder.
4. On the shortcut menu, point to Send To and then select Desktop (Create Shortcut).

You can add system icons to the desktop, too. By default, the only system icon on the desktop is the Recycle Bin. You can add or remove system icons by completing the following steps:

1. Right-click an empty area of the desktop and then select Personalize.
2. In the left pane of the Personalization window, click Change Desktop Icons under the Tasks heading.
3. Click Customize Desktop. This opens the Desktop Icon Settings dialog box, as shown in Figure 2-2.
4. Add or remove the Computer, Control Panel, Internet Explorer, Network, and User's Files icons by selecting or clearing the related checkboxes.
5. Click OK.

Figure 2-2. Adding and removing desktop icons

Once you've added an icon to the desktop, you can work with it using the techniques summarized in Table 2-1. If you no longer want an icon or shortcut on the desktop, right-click it and select Delete. When prompted, confirm the action by clicking Yes.

Table 2-1. Working with desktop icons

Desktop icon	Usage
Computer	Double-clicking the Computer icon opens a window where you can access hard disk drives and devices with removable storage. Right-clicking the Computer icon and selecting Manage opens the Computer Management console. Right-clicking the Computer icon and selecting Map Network Drive allows you to connect to shared network folders.
Control Panel	Double-clicking the Control Panel icon opens the Control Panel, which provides access to system configuration and management tools.
Internet Explorer	Double-clicking the Internet Explorer icon opens Internet Explorer to your default home page. Right-clicking the Internet Explorer icon and then selecting Start Without Add-ons starts Internet Explorer without using browser extensions or other add-ons.
Network	Double-clicking the Network icon opens a window where you can access the computers and devices on your network. Right-clicking the Network icon and selecting Map Network Drive allows you to connect to shared network folders.
Recycle Bin	Double-clicking the Recycle Bin icon opens the Recycle Bin, which you can use to restore deleted items or permanently remove items. Right-clicking the Recycle Bin icon and selecting Empty the Recycle Bin permanently removes all items in the Recycle Bin.

Getting Around the Start Menu

The Start button is the gateway to your computer's menu system. Clicking the Start button displays the Start menu. You can also display the Start menu by pressing the Windows logo key on your keyboard.

The Start menu allows you to run programs, open folders, search your computer, get help, and more. As with Windows XP, the Start menu in Windows Vista has two views:

Standard
> The standard Start menu is the default view and provides easy access to programs, folders, and search.

Classic
> The classic Start menu is an alternative view that provides the look of the Start menu in Windows 2000 and earlier releases of Windows.

In most cases, you'll want to use the standard Start menu rather than the classic Start menu, because the standard Start menu includes enhancements that make it easier to access programs and folders on your computer. It is also more customizable.

 For the purposes of the discussion in this section, I'll assume you are using the standard Start menu. You can switch between the standard and classic Start menus at any time by right-clicking the Start button and then selecting Properties. In the Taskbar and Start Menu Properties dialog box, the Start Menu tab is selected by default. Click Start Menu to use the standard Start menu, or click Classic Start Menu to use the classic Start menu. Click OK to apply the settings.

The standard Start menu in Windows Vista is organized differently than in Windows XP. See Figure 2-3 for an example of the standard Start menu in Windows Vista.

The standard Start menu has four key areas:

Programs list
> The programs list in the left pane displays recently used programs and programs that have been pinned to the Start menu.

Common folders and features
> The common folders and features options in the right pane provide quick access to the folders and features used most often.

Control buttons
> The control buttons in the lower portion of the right pane include the Power, Lock, and Options buttons used to control the state of the computer.

Search box
> The Search box in the lower portion of the left pane allows you to search your entire computer for files, folders, or programs.

I discuss these Start menu features in the sections that follow.

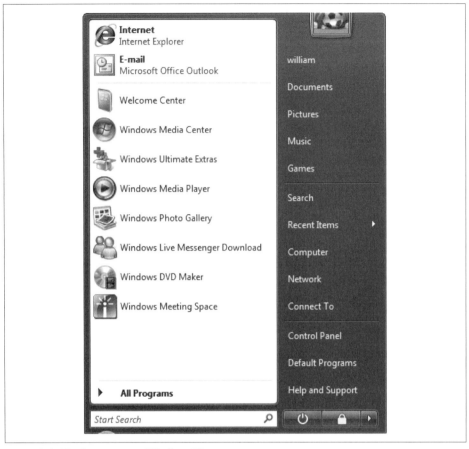

Figure 2-3. The Start menu in Windows Vista

Navigating and customizing the programs list

The Start menu's left pane displays recently used programs and programs that have been pinned to the Start menu. In the default configuration, Internet Explorer and your default mail program are pinned to this list, and up to eight recently used programs are displayed as well. You can customize the programs list by pinning additional items to the Start menu and by changing the number of recently used programs to display.

Programs pinned to the Start menu are listed in the uppermost section of the programs list. Pinning programs to the Start menu provides quick access to your favorite programs. You can pin a program to the Start menu by following these steps:

1. Click the Start button.
2. Navigate the menu to the program's menu entry.
3. Right-click the program's menu entry.
4. On the shortcut menu, select Pin to Start Menu.

If you no longer want a program to be pinned to the Start menu, you can unpin it by following these steps:

1. Click the Start button.
2. Right-click the program on the Start menu.
3. Select "Remove from this list."

On the Start menu, recently used programs are listed in the lower portion of the programs list. You can remove a program from the recently used list by right-clicking it and then selecting "Remove from this list." This won't, however, prevent the program from being added to the list in the future.

You can customize the programs list by completing the following steps:

1. Right-click the Start button and then select Properties.
2. In the Taskbar and Start Menu Properties dialog box, the Start Menu tab is selected by default. Click Customize. Set the "Number of recent programs to display" option to an appropriate value.
3. The "Show on Start menu" options control the way web browsers and email programs are listed on the Start menu:
   a. Use the drop-down list provided to select the web browser you want to show on the Start menu. If you don't want to show a browser on the Start menu, clear the Internet link checkbox.
   b. Use the drop-down list provided to select the email programs you want to show on the Start menu. If you don't want to show an email program on the Start menu, clear the E-mail link checkbox.
4. Click OK twice.

Navigating common folders and customizing the listed features

The Start menu's right pane provides access to commonly used folders and features. While at first glance it may seem that this part of the Start menu is similar to the Start menu in Windows XP, this is deceiving because there are major changes in the locations accessed by these buttons.

In Windows XP, your documents are stored by default in personal folders under *%SystemDrive%\Documents* and *Settings\%UserName%*. Your personal folder contains a My Documents folder, which in turn contains other folders, such as My Pictures and My Music. Windows XP also has folders named My Computer, My Recent Documents, and My Network Places.

 Windows Vista has many environment variables, which are used to refer to user-specific and system-specific values. *%SystemDrive%* and *%UserName%* refer to the SystemDrive and UserName environment variables, respectively. Often, I'll refer to environment variables using this syntax: *%VariableName%*.

In Windows Vista, these familiar folders don't exist. The only way your computer may have references to these folders is if you performed an in-place upgrade of the operating system. In this case, your main profile folder may include shortcuts to the locations where these folders were stored when your old settings were migrated. Generally, these shortcuts would point to locations under *%SystemDrive%\Windows.old.*

In Windows Vista, your documents are stored by default in personal folders under *%SystemDrive%\Users\%UserName%*. As Figure 2-4 shows, your personal folder contains the following folders:

Contacts
> The default location for storing your contacts for use in your mail programs

Desktop
> The default location for storing your desktop configuration

Documents
> The default location for storing your word processing documents

Downloads
> The default location for storing programs and data you've downloaded from the Internet

Favorites
> The default location for storing your Internet favorites

Links
> The default location for storing your Internet links

Music
> The default location for storing your music files

Pictures
> The default location for storing your pictures

Saved Games
> The default location for storing your saved game data

Searches
> The default location for storing your saved searches

Videos
> The default location for storing your video files

Knowing this, you can put the Start menu's common folder options into perspective. From top to bottom, the option buttons are as follows:

Current User
> Shows your logon name. Clicking this option opens your personal folder.

Documents
> Opens the Documents folder within your personal folder in Windows Explorer.

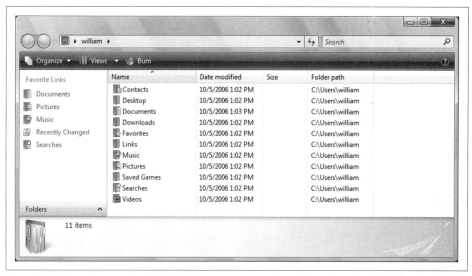

Figure 2-4. Navigating your personal folders

Pictures
> Opens the Pictures folder within your personal folder in Windows Explorer.

Music
> Opens the Music folder within your personal folder in Windows Explorer.

Games
> Opens the Microsoft Games folder in Windows Explorer.

Search
> Opens a local computer search in Windows Explorer. You can use this for advanced searches.

Recent Items
> Provides a menu view that lists recently opened files.

Computer
> Opens the Computer view in Windows Explorer. This allows you to access hard disk drives and devices with removable storage.

Network
> Opens the Network Explorer. This allows you to browse the computers and devices on your network.

Connect To
> Runs the Connect to a Network Wizard for connecting to wireless networks.

Control Panel
> Opens the Control Panel, which provides access to system configuration and management tools.

Default Programs
> Displays the default programs in the Control Panel. This lets you choose the programs that Windows Vista uses by default for documents, pictures, and more.

Help and Support
> Displays the Help and Support console. This lets you browse or search help topics.

You can add features to the Start menu's right pane using the Customize Start Menu dialog box. Right-click the Start button and then select Properties. In the Taskbar and Start Menu Properties dialog box, click the Customize button on the Start Menu tab. In the Customize Start Menu dialog box, select or clear options as appropriate and then click OK twice.

Features you can add include:

Administrative Tools
> Displays the Administrative Tools menu or window. This lets you access your computer's administrative tools.

Favorites
> Displays your favorite links as a menu. This lets you quickly access favorite locations.

Printers
> Displays the Printers window. This lets you access currently configured printers.

Run
> Displays the Run dialog box. This lets you run commands.

 While you may have used the Run options previously, you'll find the Search box to be much easier to work with. Not only can you use the Search box to open and run commands quicker, but you can also run commands with fewer clicks.

Navigating the control buttons and customizing the power configuration

Below the common folder and feature buttons on the Start menu's right pane, you'll find your computer's control buttons. Here's what these buttons do:

Power
> Puts the computer in sleep mode or shuts it down, depending on the system configuration

Lock
> Locks the computer so that a logon screen is displayed

Options
> Displays the following additional options: Switch User, Log Off, Lock, Shut Down, and Restart

As discussed in Chapter 1, your computer's power configuration determines how the power button works. Windows Vista has three power plans, which you can use to automatically manage the way your monitor, hard disks, and computer as a whole enter standby, sleep, or hibernation mode. Power plans also control other power settings. The standard power plans are:

Balanced
> This plan uses a balanced approach to managing power and is the default.

High Performance
> This plan optimizes the computer for performance by allowing it to consume as much power as needed.

Power Saver
> This plan optimizes the computer to conserve power by allowing it to more quickly turn off the monitor, hard disks, and computer to conserve power.

Power plans have basic settings and advanced settings. The basic settings control when the display is turned off and when the computer enters sleep mode. The advanced settings control all other power configuration options. You can select a power plan to use with the Power Options utility in the Control Panel. Click Start, and then click Control Panel. In the Control Panel, click the Additional Options link and then click Power Options. Specify the power plan to use by selecting it under the Preferred Plans heading.

You also can use power configuration settings to control the way in which the power button and the "Password protection on wakeup" feature work. In the default configuration, pressing and holding a computer's power button shuts down the computer. Pressing a portable computer's sleep button or closing the lid turns it off and puts it in sleep mode. By default, all power plans use the "Password protection on wakeup" feature to ensure that when your computer wakes up from sleep mode, no one can access your computer without first entering a password to unlock the screen.

You can configure power buttons and "Password protection on wakeup" options by following these steps:

1. Click Start, and then click Control Panel.

2. In the Control Panel, click the System and Maintenance link and then click Power Options.

3. In the left pane, click the "Choose what the power button does" link. This displays the "Define power buttons" page in the Control Panel, as shown in Figure 2-5.

4. Use the "When I press the power button" list to specify whether the computer should shut down, sleep, or hibernate when the power button is pressed.

5. Use the "Password protection on wakeup" options to specify whether the computer requires a password on wakeup.

6. Click "Save changes."

Figure 2-5. Configuring your computer's power buttons

Navigating the Search box

Below the Start menu's programs list in the left pane, you'll find the Search box. The Search box allows you to quickly search your computer or the Internet. You can work with the Search box using the following techniques:

- To use the Search box, simply click the Start button and type your search text (see Figure 2-6). Search results are displayed in the left pane of the Start menu. Click on a result to run a program or open a folder or file.

- To clear the search results and return to the normal view, click the Clear button to the right of the Search box, or press the Escape key.

> You don't need to click in the Search box before you begin typing. Just type your search text and you'll see any matching results.

Your computer uses the Windows Search service to perform the search. This service searches the entire computer using the search text you provided. As discussed in detail in Chapter 6, the Windows Search service matches the search text to words that appear in the title of any program, file, or folder and returns any matches found. For locations you've indexed, the Windows Search service also searches the contents of text-based documents and file properties. You can customize the way search works by using the Indexing Options utility in the Control Panel, and by setting indexing options in the Folder Options utility in the Control Panel.

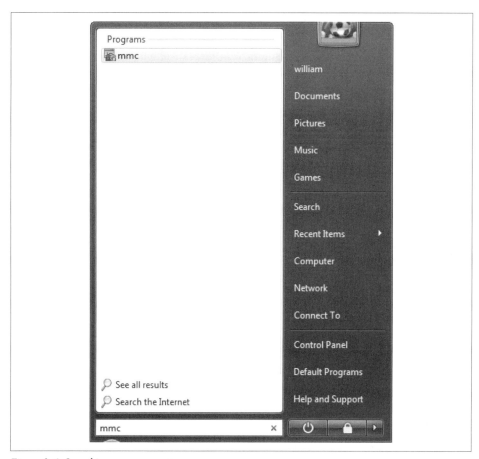

Figure 2-6. Searching your computer

Getting Around the Taskbar

The taskbar in Windows Vista has several key features:

Start button
Displays the Start menu, as previously discussed

Quick Launch Toolbar
Displays quick-access buttons for programs

Program buttons
Provide access to running programs

Notification area
Displays system notifications and the current time

Each area has feature enhancements. The sections that follow discuss the enhancements for the Quick Launch Toolbar, program buttons, and the notification area.

Navigating and customizing the Quick Launch Toolbar

You'll find the Quick Launch Toolbar to the right of the Start button. The Quick Launch Toolbar is displayed by default in Windows Vista with two buttons:

Show/Hide the Desktop
> Shows the desktop by hiding all open windows, or unhides the desktop and shows open windows

Switch Between Windows
> Displays the Flip 3D view for switching between open windows

You can work with the Quick Launch Toolbar in several ways. If the toolbar is currently displayed and you want to hide it, right-click an open area of the taskbar, point to Toolbars, and then select Quick Launch. Simply repeat this procedure if the toolbar is hidden and you want to display it.

A new feature in Windows Vista is the ability to easily add any program to the Quick Launch Toolbar. To customize the toolbar by adding programs, follow these steps:

1. Click the Start button.
2. Find the program you want to be able to quickly access in the menu.
3. Right-click the program's menu item.
4. On the shortcut menu, select Add to Quick Launch.

To remove a program from the toolbar, right-click its icon and then select Delete. This removes the program's button from the toolbar.

Navigating and customizing taskbar buttons

The taskbar displays buttons for open programs that allow you to open their windows. You'll find taskbar buttons to the right of the Start button and the Quick Launch Toolbar.

You can customize taskbar behavior using the Taskbar Appearance options found on the Taskbar tab of the Taskbar and Start Menu Properties dialog box (see Figure 2-7). To display this dialog box with the Taskbar tab selected, right-click an open area of the taskbar and then select Properties. Once the dialog box is displayed, select or clear options as preferred and then click OK.

Table 2-2 details how you can use the options provided to customize taskbar behavior. By default, all the options are selected except Auto-Hide the Taskbar.

Figure 2-7. Customizing the taskbar

Table 2-2. Options for customizing the taskbar

Taskbar option	When selected...	When not selected...
Lock the Taskbar	Locks the taskbar in place to prevent accidental moving or resizing.	Allows you to move the taskbar to dock it to other sides of the screen and to resize the taskbar to display fewer or more rows of buttons.
Auto-Hide the Taskbar	Allows the taskbar to automatically hide when you aren't using it and display only when you move the cursor over it.	Ensures that the taskbar is always displayed on the desktop (though not necessarily on top of other windows).
Keep the Taskbar on Top of Other Windows	Ensures that the taskbar, when active, is always displayed on top of other windows.	Allows other windows to be displayed on top of the taskbar when it is not active.
Group Similar Taskbar Buttons	Groups similar taskbar buttons by type.	Ensures that each program has its own button.
Show Quick Launch	Displays the Quick Launch Toolbar.	Hides the Quick Launch Toolbar.
Show Window Previews (Thumbnails)	Displays window preview thumbnails when you move the pointer over taskbar buttons.	Disables display of window preview thumbnails.

One of the more significant taskbar enhancements in Windows XP was the introduction of program grouping. Rather than display a button for each program, the taskbar groups similar buttons by default. Grouping buttons saves room on the taskbar and makes sure that in most cases, you don't need to expand the taskbar to find the buttons for open programs. For example, if you open six different folders in Windows Explorer, these items would be grouped together under one taskbar button. Clicking the taskbar button would then display a pop-up dialog box with an entry for each window, allowing you to select the grouped window to open.

Windows Vista introduces several significant enhancements to the taskbar. These enhancements are:

- Live thumbnails
- Windows Flip
- Windows Flip 3D

When you move the mouse pointer over a taskbar button (and Show Windows Previews is enabled), Windows Vista displays a live thumbnail of the window, showing the content of that window. Figure 2-8 shows an example of a live thumbnail. If the content in the window is being updated, such as with a running process or active video playback, the thumbnail continuously updates to reflect the live state of the window. If the preview is for grouped taskbar buttons, Windows displays a thumbnail of the most recently started window and makes the thumbnail appear to include a group of windows.

Figure 2-8. A live thumbnail

When you press Alt-Tab, Windows Vista displays a flip view containing live thumb-nails of all open windows. Because the thumbnails are live views, they continuously update to reflect their current state regardless of the type of content. Figure 2-9 shows an example of a flip view. You can work with a flip view using the following techniques:

- Pressing Alt-Tab and then holding Alt keeps the flip view open.
- Pressing Tab while holding the Alt key allows you to cycle through the windows.
- Release the Alt key to select the current window and bring it to the front.
- Alternatively, select a window and bring it to the front by moving the mouse pointer over the thumbnail and clicking.

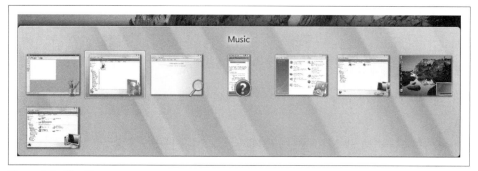

Figure 2-9. The flip view

When you press the Windows logo key and the Tab key, Windows Vista displays a 3D flip view. This 3D flip view provides a skewed 3D view of all open windows. Because the 3D window views are live, the windows continuously update to reflect their current state regardless of the type of content. Figure 2-10 shows an example of a 3D flip view. You can work with a 3D flip view using the following techniques:

- Pressing the Windows logo key + Tab and then holding the Windows logo key keeps the 3D flip view open.
- Pressing the Tab key while holding the Windows logo key allows you to cycle through the windows.
- Release the Windows logo key to select the current window and bring it to the front.
- Alternatively, select a window and bring it to the front by moving the mouse pointer over the thumbnail and clicking.

Figure 2-10. The 3D flip view

Navigating and customizing the notification area

You'll find the notification area on the far-right side of the taskbar. As Figure 2-11 shows, the notification area is divided into two sections:

- An area for normal notification icons, such as those used by programs you've installed
- An area for system notification icons, such as those for the network, power, volume, and clock controls

Figure 2-11. Viewing system and program notifications

Notifications for programs and the operating system behave in different ways:

- Generally, if you move the pointer over a program notification icon and then click, you'll see a shortcut menu (provided one is available).
- Generally, if you move the pointer over a program notification icon and then double-click, you'll open the related program or window.

- Generally, if you move the pointer over a system notification icon, you'll see a status window that provides information about the notification.
- Generally, if you move the pointer over a system notification icon and click, you'll see a control window that provides information about the notification and allows you to configure the related feature.

You can use the system notification icons as summarized in Table 2-3.

Table 2-3. Working with system notification icons

System notification icon	Moving pointer over the icon…	Clicking the icon…
Network	Displays the network to which you are connected and the current access configuration, such as Local Only.	Adds shortcut links to the control window. Use the Connect to a Network link to configure wireless network connections and the Network and Sharing Center link to manage your network configuration.
Volume	Shows the current system volume and speaker configuration.	Allows you to adjust the computer volume or mute the sound entirely. Click the Mixer link to display mixing options for application sound.
Clock	Displays the day of the week, date, and year.	Displays a calendar view of the current month and a clock depicting the current time. Browse other monthly calendars using the buttons provided. Click Change Date and Time Settings to modify the computer's date and time.

You can customize the way notifications work using the dialog boxes shown in Figure 2-12. Use the Taskbar and Start Menu Properties dialog box to configure general options, and the Customize Notification Icons dialog box to configure specific notifications.

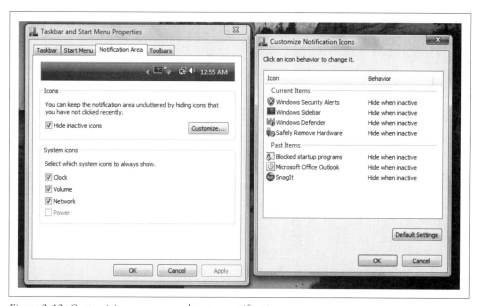

Figure 2-12. Customizing program and system notifications

You can configure program notification behavior by completing the following steps:

1. Right-click an open area of the taskbar and then select Properties.
2. In the Taskbar and Start Menu Properties dialog box, click the Notification Area tab.
3. To always display program notification icons, clear the "Hide inactive icons" checkbox, click OK, and skip the remaining steps.
4. To hide inactive notification icons, as per the default configuration, select the "Hide inactive icons" checkbox and then click Customize to display the Customize Notification Icons dialog box.
5. Notification icons are listed by name and behavior. Click in the Behavior column to set the icon's behavior as "Hide," "Show," or "Hide when inactive."
6. Click OK twice.

You can configure system notification behavior by completing the following steps:

1. Right-click an open area of the taskbar and then select Properties.
2. In the Taskbar and Start Menu Properties dialog box, click the Notification Area tab.
3. The System Icons panel options control which notification icons are displayed. To display an icon, select its checkbox. To hide an icon, clear its checkbox.
4. Click OK.

Using Gadgets and Windows Sidebar

Gadgets and sidebars are new features in Windows Vista. A gadget is a small application designed to perform a very specific function, such as providing a desktop calendar or virtual notepad. You can add gadgets directly to the desktop or to a view pane called Windows Sidebar. You can add Windows Sidebar to the left or right side of the desktop; its sole purpose is to make it group your desktop gadgets.

Inspecting Your Computer's Gadgets

Windows Sidebar and several default gadgets are displayed on the right side of the desktop in most installations. The sidebar has a fixed size, allowing it to display several gadgets in a vertical column. If you add more gadgets to the sidebar than can fit in one column, additional columns are added to the sidebar and you can navigate the columns of gadgets using the small arrow buttons at the top of the sidebar, as shown in Figure 2-13. To the left of the small arrow buttons, you'll find the Add Gadget button. Clicking this button displays the Gadget Gallery dialog box, as also shown in Figure 2-13.

Figure 2-13. Working with your computer's gadgets

The Gadget Gallery shows all the gadgets that are available on your computer. When multiple pages of gadgets are available, you can navigate the pages using the Previous and Next Page buttons provided in the upper-left corner of the window. You can also use the Search box to search for gadgets by name. As you type your search text, the list of gadgets is automatically filtered to include only those gadgets matching the search text you entered.

In the lower-left corner of the Gadget Gallery window, you'll find a Show details/ Hide details button used to show or hide a Details Pane. Clicking a gadget with the Show Details Pane expanded displays the gadget details, which include the gadget name, version, and description. Double-clicking a gadget adds it to the uppermost position on the first sidebar column.

You can visit Microsoft's Gadget Gallery on the Internet by clicking either of the links provided. Some gadgets are updated automatically when new versions become available as part of the standard Windows Update process. Other gadgets you must update manually by downloading the desired gadget update.

Windows Vista comes with several standard gadgets that provide a variety of functions. Before discussing how to work with the sidebar and manage gadgets, let's take a closer look at the gadgets you'll use the most.

The Feed Headlines gadget displays data from selected Really Simple Syndication (RSS) feeds that have been configured in Internet Explorer. RSS feeds can contain news headlines, lists, and other information.

Using the Calendar gadget

Anyone who likes to keep a calendar on her desk to show the day of the week and day of the month will love the Calendar gadget. This gadget displays a desktop calendar that you can dock to the sidebar or drag around the desktop.

You can work with the gadget in a variety of ways. As the leftmost view in Figure 2-14 shows, the current day and date are displayed by default. If you click the calendar, you can view the current month. You can view other months in the calendar using the right-facing and left-facing arrow buttons.

Figure 2-14. Navigating the Calendar gadget views

To display the day and date view for a particular entry, simply click it. The tab in the lower-left corner and the color of the view indicate that you are not viewing the current day and date. You can return to the current day and date view by clicking the tab in the lower-left corner of the calendar.

Using the Clock gadget

Anyone who likes wall clocks or dislikes the bland system clock will like the Clock gadget. This gadget displays an analog clock with hour and minute hands by default (see Figure 2-15). Moving the mouse pointer over the clock and clicking shows the digital time with hour, minutes, and seconds.

The Clock gadget is one of several gadgets that have configurable properties:

- You can change the clock face to any one of the eight standard clock faces.
- The clock time zone you use can be different from that used by the computer clock.
- The clock can have a name, which is useful if you use a time zone other than the one you are in.
- The clock can have a second hand, though its movement can be rather distracting.

Figure 2-15. Working with the Clock gadget

To change the time zone or modify other options, right-click the Clock gadget and then select Options. You can then use the dialog box shown in Figure 2-15 to set the clock options.

Using the Contacts gadget

Windows Vista includes a contact management program called Windows Contacts. As discussed in Chapter 16, you can use Windows Contacts to create and manage personal or business contacts as well as groups of contacts. The Contacts gadget provides quick access to these contacts (see Figure 2-16).

The default view provides an alphabetical list of your contacts. You can use the slider provided to browse contacts, or you can use the Search box to search for contacts by name. As you type your search text, the list of contacts is automatically filtered to include only those contacts matching the search text you entered. When you find a contact you want to view, you can click the entry to view the details for that contact, including the contact's email address and phone number.

Figure 2-16. Working with the Contacts gadget views

Two tabs are provided on the left side of the Contacts gadget. Clicking the top tab displays the contacts list. Clicking the bottom tab displays the detailed entry for the currently selected contact.

Using the CPU Meter gadget

Having problems with a slow or unresponsive computer, or like being able to see what's going on with your computer? If so, you might want to start using the CPU Meter gadget. This gadget displays the current percentage utilization of the computer's CPU and memory as a series of gauges (see Figure 2-17). The large gauge shows the CPU utilization; the small gauge shows the RAM utilization.

Figure 2-17. Working with the CPU Meter gadget

Similar to a tachometer in a car, the CPU and RAM gauges show high utilization in yellow and red. The gauges are handy if you are experiencing performance problems and are wondering what is happening with your computer.

Generally, if either gauge peaks into yellow or red usage, the computer may become sluggish and slow to respond because of the high utilization of its resources. If both gauges peak into yellow or red usage, or either gauge is at 98 percent utilization or higher, your computer may become extremely sluggish or unresponsive to your requests.

Windows Vista includes some great new features to resolve performance issues, which I will discuss in Chapter 3.

Using the Weather gadget

Anyone stuck in a cubicle without a window or wanting to know about the weather in some far-off place will like the Weather gadget. This gadget provides an overview of the weather at a particular location courtesy of the weather provider configured for your computer. The default weather provider is MSN. Using this gadget, you can tell at a glance whether it is sunny, cloudy, snowing, or raining (see Figure 2-18). You can also see the outside temperature.

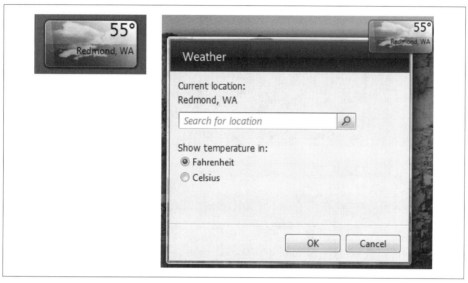

Figure 2-18. Using the Weather gadget

You can work with the gadget in several ways. You can set the location for which you want to view the weather, which is great if you are currently in Ohio but your heart and mind are in Colorado, where you're heading for vacation. You can also specify whether to display the temperature in degrees Fahrenheit or degrees Celsius.

To change the location of your weather reports or the way temperature is displayed, right-click the Weather gadget and then select Options. You can then use the dialog box shown in Figure 2-18 to set the weather options.

Using the Stock gadget

Anyone who tracks securities, companies, or indexes in the stock market will like the Stock gadget. This gadget provides an overview of the major stock market indexes by default (see Figure 2-19). In the United States, the major indexes are the Dow Jones Industrial Average ($INDU), the NASDAQ Composite Index ($COMPX), and the S&P 500 Index ($INX). Quotes are provided by the default quote provider with a 20-minute delay. The default quote provider is IDC Comstock.

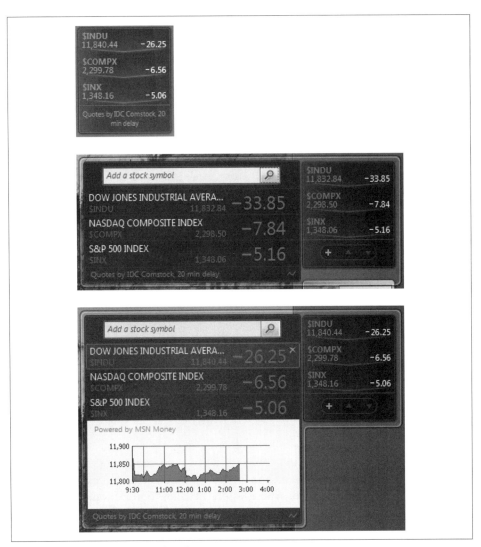

Figure 2-19. Navigating the Stock gadget views

You can work with the Stock gadget in several ways. By default, the Stock gadget displays details on three tracked stocks at a time, in a vertical column. The most recently tracked stocks are listed first. If you move the mouse pointer over the gadget, you'll see a control panel with several buttons. You can use the Scroll Up and Scroll Down buttons to navigate through the summary details for the stocks you are tracking.

You can change the position of a stock in the list by clicking its entry and dragging it slowly up or down. Using this technique, you can move a tracked stock from the bottom of the list to the top or from the top of the list to the bottom.

If you move the mouse pointer over a stock entry, a delete button is displayed in the upper-right corner. Click the delete button to stop tracking the stock.

All publicly traded securities, companies, and indexes have a stock symbol. If you want to add a security, company, or index, follow these steps:

1. Move the mouse pointer over the Stock gadget.

2. Click the "Add a stock symbol" button. This displays the second view of the Stock gadget, as shown in Figure 2-19.

3. In the Search box, enter the stock symbol for the security, company, or index you want to track and press Enter. If the stock is found, the stock is added to the list of tracked stock symbols, and you'll get quotes for it automatically.

If you want to view all of your tracked securities, companies, and indexes, move the mouse pointer over the Stock gadget and click the "Add a stock symbol" button. To view a graph of the stock, move the mouse pointer over the stock entry and click. Be careful not to click the stock name, as this opens the stock's MSN page in Internet Explorer.

Using the Currency gadget

Anyone who converts money from one currency to another will like the Currency gadget. This gadget converts currency using the current market rate, allowing you to see at a glace how much your money is worth in another currency.

The default currency provider for this gadget is MSN Money. The Currency gadget is handy for anyone traveling to a foreign country or working in a country and getting paid in a currency other than the one to which he is accustomed.

As Figure 2-20 shows, the Currency gadget has two entries. The first entry sets the amount of a specific currency you want to convert and the second entry is the value in the specified currency. Using this feature you can, for example, convert 10 U.S. dollars into euros or 10 euros into U.S. dollars.

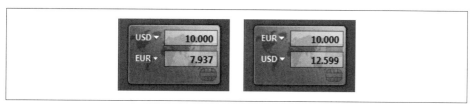

Figure 2-20. Using the Currency gadget

Using the Notes gadget

Anyone whose monitor or desk has yellow sticky notes stuck to it will like the Notes gadget. This gadget provides a notepad into which you can type notes, such as "Pick up milk after work" or "Call Mom at 5 p.m."

The default view of the Notes gadget shows the currently selected note in your note-pad (see Figure 2-21). When you move the mouse pointer over the Notes gadget, you'll see a control panel that allows you to navigate the note stack and add or remove notes. The position of the current note in the note stack is also displayed. For example, if the position is 1/2, you are viewing the first note in the stack and the stack has two notes in all.

Figure 2-21. Navigating your sticky notes

You can navigate the note stack using the Previous and Next buttons. You can add and remove notes using the Add Note and Remove Note buttons, respectively. To add a new note to the top of the stack, click the Add Note button. To remove the currently displayed note, click the Remove Note button.

Your notes are tracked only as long as the Notes gadget is open or saved as part of the sidebar state. If you close the Notes gadget by right-clicking the gadget and selecting Close Gadget, all your notes are cleared out. This means the next time you open the Notes gadget, you'll start with a new note stack.

Using the Slide Show gadget

Anyone who has pictures stored on her computer that she wants to view while working will like the Slide Show gadget. This gadget displays pictures from a selected folder as a continuous slide show where pictures rotate at a specified interval (see Figure 2-22).

Moving the mouse pointer over the Slide Show gadget displays a control panel that allows you to pause the slide show or play the slide show. You can also navigate to the previous and next pictures using the Previous and Next buttons. The View button opens the currently displayed picture in Windows Photo Gallery. You'll learn more about Windows Photo Gallery in Chapter 9.

By default, pictures in the computer's sample pictures are displayed in the slide show. Right-click the Slide Show gadget and select Options, and you can modify the Folder setting to use any preferred folder by following these steps:

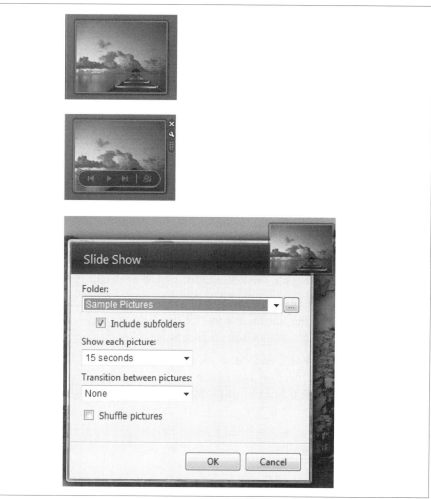

Figure 2-22. Working with the Slide Show gadget

1. Open the Slide Show Options dialog box by right-clicking the Slide Show gadget and selecting Options.

2. If you want to use your Pictures folder, click in the Folder list and select Pictures. To use another folder, click the Browse button to display the Browse for Folder dialog box. Use the Browse for Folder dialog box to locate and select the folder you want to use, and then click OK.

3. To include subfolders of the selected folder, select the Include Subfolders checkbox.

4. Click OK.

You can customize the way the slide show works by following these steps:

1. Open the Slide Show Options dialog box by right-clicking the Slide Show gadget and selecting Options.

2. Use the "Show each picture" list to set the duration to show each picture. You can set the duration using preset intervals, from five seconds to five minutes.

3. Use the "Transition between pictures" list to set the transition to use when changing to a new picture. If you don't want to use transitions, select None. Otherwise, select the desired transition, such as Fade.

4. By default, pictures are displayed in alphabetical order. To shuffle pictures rather than display them in order, select the "Shuffle pictures" checkbox.

5. Click OK.

Managing Windows Sidebar

Whether Windows Sidebar is displayed by default depends on your computer's configuration. Typically, though, the sidebar is displayed by default.

When the sidebar is displayed, you can add or remove gadgets and work with available gadgets. To close the sidebar and free up the desktop space it uses, right-click an open area of the sidebar and then select Close Sidebar.

When the sidebar is closed, you can work with it using the Windows Sidebar notifications icon in the notification area of the taskbar. Click the icon to open the sidebar. Right-click the notification icon to display a shortcut menu with the following options:

Open
  Opens Windows Sidebar

Bring Gadgets to Front
  Brings all open gadgets to the front so that you can view and work with them

Add Gadgets
  Opens the Gadgets Gallery dialog box so that you can add gadgets

Properties
  Displays the Windows Sidebar Properties dialog box

Exit
  Closes and exits Windows Sidebar

Figure 2-23 shows the Windows Sidebar Properties dialog box. You can use this dialog box to control the sidebar using the following options:

Start Sidebar when Windows starts
  Select this checkbox to have the sidebar start when Windows starts. Clear this checkbox if you do not want the sidebar to start when Windows starts.

Sidebar is always on top of other windows
> Select this checkbox to ensure that the sidebar is always on top and other windows are resized around it. Clear this checkbox to allow other windows to be displayed on top of the sidebar.

Display Sidebar on this side of screen
> Use the Left and Right options to specify whether the sidebar is displayed on the left or right side of the screen.

Display Sidebar on monitor
> Use the selection list to specify on which monitor the sidebar should be displayed. This option works only if you have multiple monitors connected to your computer.

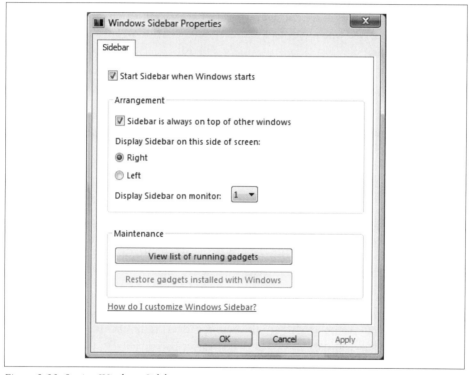

Figure 2-23. Setting Windows Sidebar properties

If you want to close and exit the sidebar, complete the following steps:

1. Right-click the Windows Sidebar notification icon and select Exit. You are then prompted to confirm that you want to exit the sidebar.

2. As shown in Figure 2-24, a checkbox is provided for controlling whether the sidebar starts when Windows Vista starts. Select or clear this option as appropriate.

3. Confirm that you want to exit the sidebar by clicking Exit Sidebar.

Figure 2-24. Exiting the sidebar

When you exit the sidebar, the sidebar and all open gadgets are closed regardless of whether any of the gadgets are docked to the sidebar or are floating on the desktop. To restart the sidebar and open your gadgets, click Start → All Programs → Accessories → Windows Sidebar.

Managing Your Computer's Gadgets

You can work with gadgets in a variety of ways. You can detach gadgets from the sidebar and move them around the desktop by right-clicking a gadget and selecting Detach from Sidebar. Once you've detached a gadget, you can click and drag to move it to different locations on the desktop. To put the gadget back on the sidebar, right-click the gadget and select Attach to Sidebar.

You can display a detached gadget on top of all other windows by right-clicking the gadget and selecting Always on Top. Once you've moved the gadget to the top, right-clicking the gadget and selecting Always on Top a second time clears the setting and makes the gadget work like any other window—it can be brought to the front when in use or put to the back when not in use.

Every gadget has an opacity setting that controls whether you can see through it. Since the default opacity setting is 100 percent, you can't see through gadgets by default. If you want to be able to see through a gadget, right-click it, point to Opacity, and then select the desired opacity. The lower the opacity setting is, the more translucent the gadget will appear to be and the better you'll be able to see what's behind it. The higher the opacity setting is, the less translucent the gadget will appear to be and the less you'll be able to see what's behind it.

You can add gadgets to Windows Sidebar by following these steps:

1. Click the Add Gadgets button at the top of the sidebar. This opens the Gadget Gallery dialog box.

2. In the Gadget Gallery dialog box, double-click each gadget you want to add to the sidebar.

3. To find additional gadgets, click the "Get more gadgets online" link.

You can remove a gadget from Windows Sidebar or the desktop by right-clicking it and selecting Close Gadget. When you are working with many gadgets, you'll find that the View Gadgets dialog box comes in very handy. You can display and work with this dialog box by completing the following steps:

1. Right-click the Windows Sidebar notification icon and select Properties. This displays the Windows Sidebar Properties dialog box.

2. Click "View list of running gadgets." This opens the View Gadgets dialog box, as shown in Figure 2-25.

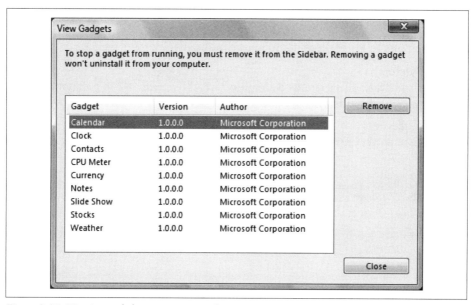

Figure 2-25. Viewing and closing running gadgets

3. In the View Gadgets dialog box, each running gadget is listed by name, version, and author. To remove a gadget from the sidebar or the desktop, select it by clicking it and then click Remove.

If for some reason the computer's default gadgets were removed or modified, you can restore the gadgets installed with Windows Vista by following these steps:

1. Right-click the Windows Sidebar notification icon and select Properties. This displays the Windows Sidebar Properties dialog box.

2. Click "Restore gadgets installed with Windows."

3. When prompted, confirm the action.

Customizing Menus and the Control Panel

As you've seen, the desktop has many customizable features. You also can customize your computer's menus and Control Panel, and this section shows you how to do it.

Navigating and Customizing Your Computer's Menus

When you want to work with programs installed on a computer, you'll use the All Programs menu, as with earlier releases of Windows. When you click the Start button and then click All Programs, you'll see a list of programs installed on the computer, followed by a list of folders.

Depending on the system configuration, the programs you'll see include:

Default Programs
> Opens the Default Programs dialog box, which you can use to configure default programs and features, as discussed in Chapter 4

Internet Explorer
> Opens Internet Explorer, which you can use to browse the Web, as discussed in Chapter 7

Windows Calendar
> Opens Windows Calendar, which you can use to manage appointments and tasks using a calendar, as discussed in Chapter 16

Windows Contacts
> Opens Windows Contacts, which you can use to manage personal and business contacts, as discussed in Chapter 16

Windows Defender
> Opens Windows Defender, which you can use to protect your computer from malware, spyware, and other malicious programs, as discussed in Chapter 15

Windows DVD Maker
> Opens Windows DVD Maker, which you can use to burn DVDs, as discussed in Chapters 8, 9, and 10

Windows Mail
> Opens Windows Mail, which you can use to send and receive email, as discussed in Chapter 16

Windows Media Center
> Opens Windows Media Center, which you can use to manage home entertainment options for pictures, videos, movies, TV, and music, as discussed in Chapter 25

Windows Media Player
> Opens Windows Media Player, which you can use to view pictures, play music, and play videos, as discussed in Chapter 8

Windows Movie Maker
  Opens Windows Movie Maker, which you can use to make movies, as discussed in Chapter 10

Windows Photo Gallery
  Opens Windows Photo Gallery, which you can use to view and manage digital images, as discussed in Chapter 9

Windows Update
  Opens Windows Update, which you can use to keep your operating system up-to-date, as discussed in Chapter 20

The folders under the All Programs menu have also changed. The changes to the menu may take awhile to get used to. Still, once you get used to the changes, navigating the menus will be fairly painless. The top-level folders are:

All Programs → Accessories
  Provides access to the most commonly used accessories, including the Calculator, Command Prompt, Connect to a Network Projector, Notepad, Paint, Remote Desktop Connection, Snipping Tool, Sync Center, Windows Explorer, and Windows Sidebar.

  Out of all the new accessories, the Snipping Tool is my favorite. You can use it to capture portions of a screen and then save, annotate, or share the captured snippet. By default, the Snipping Tool always captures portions of the screen to the clipboard, making snippets available in other programs as well.

All Programs → Accessories → Ease of Access
  Provides access to the accessibility tools, such as the Ease of Access Center, Magnifier, Narrator, On-Screen Keyboard, and Windows Speech Recognition. The Ease of Access Center provides a central console for managing accessibility options.

  Windows Speech Recognition is one of the most powerful new accessories. With the help of a microphone, this accessory allows you to train your computer to recognize your voice. You can then dictate and control your computer by voice.

All Programs → Accessories → System Tools
  Provides access to commonly used system tools, such as Backup, Disk Cleanup, System Information, System Restore, and Windows Easy Transfer. Windows Easy Transfer replaces the Files and Settings Transfer Wizard in Windows XP.

  Also includes Internet Explorer (No Add-ons), which is a protected version of Internet Explorer without browser extensions or other add-ons. You can use this version of Internet Explorer to protect your computer from potentially malicious web sites and programs.

All Programs → Games
  Provides access to Microsoft games installed with the operating system. The games available depend on the edition of Windows Vista you are using.

All Programs → Maintenance

Provides access to maintenance tools, including the Backup and Restore Center, Help and Support, Problem Reports and Solutions, and Windows Remote Assistance.

All Programs → Startup

Lists programs that are set to start up automatically when you log on. This doesn't mean these are the only startup programs for your computer. You may configure other programs for automatic startup, as discussed in Chapter 4.

Windows Vista manages menus in different ways than earlier Windows releases. By default, menus are sorted alphabetically automatically as you add, change, or remove menus and menu items. Windows Vista highlights newly installed menus and programs, and opens submenus when you pause on them with the mouse pointer. Windows Vista also allows you to view shortcut menus and use drag-and-drop on the desktop and within menus.

You use the settings in the Customize Start Menu dialog box to control how Windows Vista manages its menus. Knowing this, you can customize your computer's menus by following these steps:

1. Right-click the Start button and select Properties. This opens the Taskbar and Start Menu Properties dialog box.

2. On the Start menu, click Customize. This displays the Customize Start Menu dialog box.

3. Click the Use Default Settings button to restore the operating system default settings. Or use the following options to customize your menus:

   Enable context menus and dragging and dropping

   Select this option to allow shortcut menus to be displayed and to allow dragging and dropping. Clear this option to prevent shortcut menus from being displayed and to prevent dragging and dropping.

   Highlight newly installed programs

   Select this option to highlight menus and menu items for newly installed programs. Clear this option to disable newly installed program highlighting.

   Open submenus when I pause on them with the mouse pointer

   Select this option to open submenus when you pause on them with the mouse pointer. Clear this option to require clicking a submenu to expand it and view its contents.

   Sort all programs menu by name

   Select this option to sort the menu automatically by name. Clear this option to show newly installed menus and menu items last.

4. Click OK to save your settings.

Navigating and Customizing the Control Panel

Clicking the taskbar's Start button and then clicking Control Panel displays the Control Panel. You can also display the Control Panel in any Windows Explorer view by clicking the leftmost option button on the Address bar and selecting Control Panel. As with Windows XP, the Control Panel in Windows Vista has two views:

- Category Control Panel view, shown in Figure 2-26, is the default view and provides access to system utilities by category, utility, and key tasks. Category Control Panel view is also referred to simply as Control Panel.

Figure 2-26. Using Category Control Panel view

- Classic Control Panel view, shown in Figure 2-27, is an alternative view that provides the look and functionality of the Control Panel in Windows 2000 and earlier versions of Windows. With Classic Control Panel view, each Control Panel utility is listed separately by name.

Because Category Control Panel view provides quick access to frequent tasks, it is the view you will use most often. With this view, the Control Panel opens as a console on which 10 categories of utilities are listed. For each category, there's a top-level link and under this are several of the most frequently performed tasks for the category.

Clicking a category link provides a list of utilities in that category. For each utility listed within a category, there's a link to open the utility and under this are several of the most frequently performed tasks for the utility.

In Category Control Panel view, all utilities and tasks run with a single click. The left pane of the console has a link to take you to the Control Panel home page, links for each category, and links for recently performed tasks. Not only is this very efficient, but also it's very easy to use.

Figure 2-27. Using Classic Control Panel view

Because menu options and Control Panel options open with a single click by default, you might want to configure your computer to use single-click to open items such as documents as well. This may help you avoid confusion as to whether you need to click or double-click. When you have single-click open configured, pointing to an item selects it.

You can configure single-click open by completing the following steps:

1. Click the Start button and then click Control Panel.

2. In the Control Panel, click Appearance and Personalization.

3. Under Folder Options, click Specify Single- or Double-click to Open.

4. In the Folder Options dialog box, select Single-Click to Open an Item (Point to Select) and then click OK.

Once you have everything set to open with a single click, you hopefully will find that working with the Control Panel and Windows Explorer is much more intuitive.

CHAPTER 3

Fine-Tuning Windows Vista's Appearance and Performance

Never before has there been a release of Windows in which appearance and performance were so closely tied together. However, not only is the way Windows Vista looks and behaves integral and inseparable, but also you must often make a careful trade-off between the two to achieve the desired result. Because of this, fine-tuning Windows Vista's appearance and performance is often a balancing act, especially if you want your computer to remain responsive under the widest circumstances possible.

Of the many interlinked appearance and performance features, the ones over which you have the most control are:

- Experience scoring
- Account controls
- Personalization settings
- Performance options

In this chapter, you'll learn how to fine-tune these features while maintaining the balance between appearance and performance.

Balancing Appearance and Performance

Since Windows Vista has a scalable user experience, there needed to be a way to determine the capabilities of a computer. The solution Microsoft developed was to capture a performance baseline based on specific performance metrics during installation of the operating system.

Getting Your Windows Experience Index Score

During installation, Windows Vista assigned your computer a Windows Experience Index. This index is a relative rating of your computer's capabilities with regard to its:

- Processor
- Physical memory (RAM)
- General graphics
- Gaming graphics
- Primary hard disk

 The "general graphics" and "gaming graphics" component titles are misnomers; more appropriate titles would be "general graphics" and "multimedia graphics." *Graphics* is meant to reflect overall performance for Windows interfaces. *Gaming graphics* is meant to reflect performance for graphics-intensive applications, such as 3D business applications and 3D games.

To assign the Windows Experience Index, Windows Vista determines:

- The number of processors installed on your computer and the processor type
- The number of calculations per second your computer's processor can perform
- The total amount of physical memory installed on your computer
- The number of memory operations your computer's memory can perform
- The total amount of graphics memory installed on your computer
- The data transfer rate of your computer's primary hard disk

These performance metrics help Windows Vista determine the relative performance of your computer. You can view your computer's Windows Experience Index and the related subscores by completing the following steps:

1. Click Start and then click Control Panel.
2. In the Control Panel, select System and Maintenance.
3. Click Performance Information and Tools.
4. As shown in Figure 3-1, your computer's performance scores are listed by component in the Performance Information and Tools console.

Understanding Your Windows Experience Index Score

Your computer's base score is determined by the lowest subscore. The computer being rated in Figure 3-1 has a Windows Experience Index base score of 2.5. The base score can help you determine the type of software programs you can run on the computer. The base score also determines the level of scaled performance Windows Vista delivers. Certain operating system features will work only when your computer meets the minimum base score requirements, and the use of certain other features, such as high display resolutions with Aero glass or themes on multiple displays, will have a severe impact on your computer's performance.

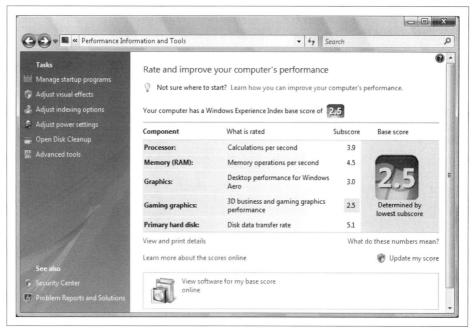

Figure 3-1. Viewing your computer's performance scores

Most current computers will have a base score of between one and five. The Windows Experience Index is designed to scale as computer technology advances. Thus, while current computers have top scores in the 5s and 6s, tomorrow's computers may have top scores in the 9s and 10s.

Table 3-1 provides an overview of what the base scores mean. If you want to improve your computer's base score, you can upgrade the hardware component responsible for the low score. For example, if gaming graphics is your lowest score, you could upgrade your graphics card to improve your rating. Don't do this, however, without first consulting the performance details to determine exactly how the component is configured currently.

Table 3-1. Understanding your computer's Windows Experience Index score

Base score	What the score means	Description of experience
1.0 to 1.9	Degraded user experience	You can use the computer for general computing, word processing, and music playback. The computer probably isn't suited for more advanced tasks, such as gaming or multimedia. The user experience will be severely limited.
2.0 to 2.9	Reduced user experience	You can use the computer for general computing, business applications, basic gaming, and basic multimedia. The computer probably isn't suited for more advanced tasks, such as multiplayer or 3D gaming and advanced multimedia. The user experience will be limited.

Base score	What the score means	Description of experience
3.0 to 3.9	Basic user experience	You can use the computer for general computing, advanced business applications, expanded gaming, and expanded multimedia. The computer probably isn't suited for advanced gaming, such as multiplayer 3D gaming, or advanced multimedia, such as recording and playing HDTV.
4.0 to 4.9	Full user experience	You can use the computer for advanced computing, advanced business applications, advanced gaming, and advanced multimedia. The computer can use all the new features of Windows Vista with full functionality. Aero glass will display higher resolutions while achieving good performance, and using themes on multiple monitors shouldn't impact performance.
5.0 and higher	Superior user experience	You can use the computer for the most demanding tasks, including those that are both graphics-intensive and processor-intensive. The computer can use all the new features of Windows Vista with full functionality. Aero glass will display higher resolutions while achieving good performance, and using themes on multiple monitors shouldn't impact performance.

Improving Your Windows Experience Index Score

In the Performance Information and Tools console, you can view detailed performance and configuration information by clicking "View and print details." As Figure 3-2 shows, the configured details are provided for each hardware component being tracked and you can print this information for future reference by clicking "Print this page." For this computer, gaming graphics has the lowest subscore. By examining the details, you can see the key reason for this is that the video card has only 128 MB of dedicated graphics memory. Thus, while 526 MB of graphics memory is available, 398 MB is coming from shared system memory and only 128 MB is dedicated. This means the computer is borrowing 398 MB of RAM from the physical memory available, leaving less physical memory available for applications and the operating system.

If you installed a new graphics card with 512 MB or more of dedicated RAM on the computer, the graphics and gaming graphics subscores would increase substantially. You could then have Windows Vista recalculate the performance scores by clicking "Update my score." Windows Vista would then begin rating your computer by evaluating the performance of each tracked hardware component. When this process is completed, each component is listed with an appropriate subscore and the computer's new base score is listed in the Performance Information and Tools console. The rating process can take several minutes to complete.

The scores are meant to be helpful guidelines, and you can squeeze extra performance out of your computer in a variety of ways, but typically, this extra performance comes at a direct sacrifice to the way Windows Vista looks and behaves. For example, if your computer's base score is low because of graphics/gaming graphics, you can improve overall performance by turning off graphics-intensive features of the operating system, such as Aero glass, visual effects, live thumbnails, backgrounds, and themes.

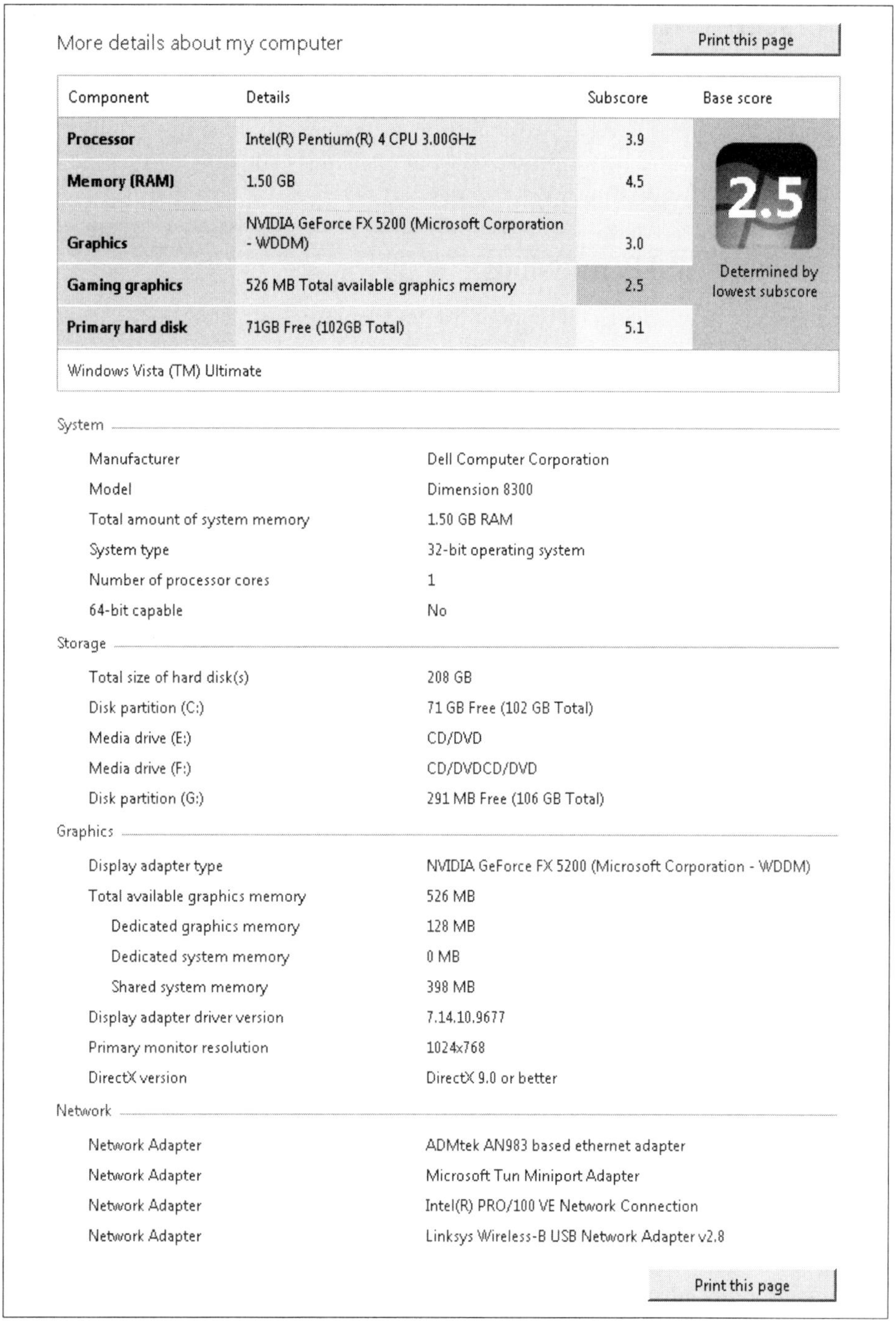

More details about my computer

Print this page

Component	Details	Subscore	Base score
Processor	Intel(R) Pentium(R) 4 CPU 3.00GHz	3.9	
Memory (RAM)	1.50 GB	4.5	**2.5**
Graphics	NVIDIA GeForce FX 5200 (Microsoft Corporation - WDDM)	3.0	
Gaming graphics	526 MB Total available graphics memory	2.5	Determined by lowest subscore
Primary hard disk	71GB Free (102GB Total)	5.1	

Windows Vista (TM) Ultimate

System

Manufacturer	Dell Computer Corporation
Model	Dimension 8300
Total amount of system memory	1.50 GB RAM
System type	32-bit operating system
Number of processor cores	1
64-bit capable	No

Storage

Total size of hard disk(s)	208 GB
Disk partition (C:)	71 GB Free (102 GB Total)
Media drive (E:)	CD/DVD
Media drive (F:)	CD/DVDCD/DVD
Disk partition (G:)	291 MB Free (106 GB Total)

Graphics

Display adapter type	NVIDIA GeForce FX 5200 (Microsoft Corporation - WDDM)
Total available graphics memory	526 MB
Dedicated graphics memory	128 MB
Dedicated system memory	0 MB
Shared system memory	398 MB
Display adapter driver version	7.14.10.9677
Primary monitor resolution	1024x768
DirectX version	DirectX 9.0 or better

Network

Network Adapter	ADMtek AN983 based ethernet adapter
Network Adapter	Microsoft Tun Miniport Adapter
Network Adapter	Intel(R) PRO/100 VE Network Connection
Network Adapter	Linksys Wireless-B USB Network Adapter v2.8

Print this page

Figure 3-2. Viewing your computer's configuration details

Understanding User Account Control and Its Impact on Performance

User Account Control (UAC) is a collection of features designed to improve your computer's security and better protect it from malicious programs. UAC fundamentally changes the way Windows Vista works.

User Accounts and Permissions

Windows Vista has two general types of user accounts:

- Standard user accounts
- Administrator user accounts

As we'll discuss in Chapter 18, standard users can perform any general computing tasks, such as starting programs, opening documents, and creating folders, as well as any support tasks that do not affect other users or the security of the computer. Administrators, on the other hand, have complete access to the computer and can make changes that affect other users and the security of the computer.

Unlike earlier releases of Windows, Windows Vista makes it easy to determine which tasks standard users can perform and which tasks administrators can perform. You may have noticed the multicolored shield icon, shown in Figure 3-3, next to certain options in Windows Vista's windows, wizards, and dialog boxes. This is the Permissions icon. It indicates that the related option requires administrator permissions to run.

Figure 3-3. The Permissions icon, which indicates that the related option requires administrator permissions to run

Permission and Consent Prompting

In Windows Vista, regardless of whether you are logged on as a standard user or as an administrator, you see a UAC prompt whenever you attempt to perform a task that requires administrator permissions. The way the prompt works depends on whether you are logged on with a standard user account or with an Administrator account.

If you are logged on with a standard user account, you are prompted to provide administrator credentials, as explained here and shown in Figure 3-4:

- At home, the prompt lists each local computer Administrator account by name. To proceed, you must click an account, type the account's password, and then click OK.

- At the office, the prompt shows the logon domain and provides username and password boxes. To proceed, you must enter the name of an Administrator account, type the account's password, and then click OK.

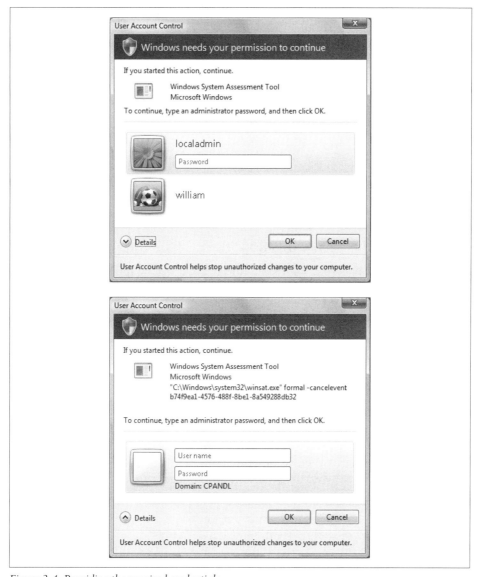

Figure 3-4. Providing the required credentials

If you are logged on with an Administrator account, you are prompted for consent to continue, as shown in Figure 3-5. The consent prompt works the same whether you are at home or at the office.

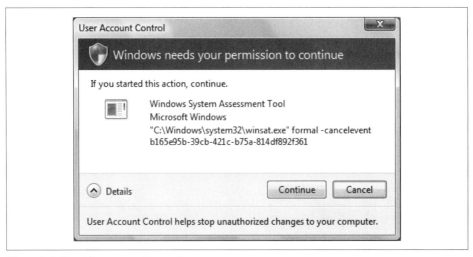

Figure 3-5. Providing consent to continue

Elevation and the Secure Desktop

The process of getting a user's approval prior to running an application in administrator mode and prior to performing actions which change system-wide settings is known as *elevation*. Elevation enhances security by reducing the exposure and attack surfaces of the operating system. It does this by providing notification when you are about to perform an action that could impact system settings, such as installing an application, and eliminating the ability for malicious programs to invoke administrator privileges without your knowledge and consent.

Prior to elevation and display of the UAC prompt, Windows Vista does several things in the background. The key thing you should know is that Windows Vista switches to a secure, isolated desktop prior to displaying the prompt. The purpose of switching to the secure desktop is to prevent other processes or applications from providing the required permissions or consent. All other running programs and processes continue to run on the interactive user desktop—only the prompt itself runs on the secure desktop.

Elevation, permission/consent prompts, and the secure desktop are the key aspects of UAC that affect you the most. As you can see, they have a measurable impact on the way Windows Vista works. Due to these UAC features:

- User accounts are not used in the same way as they are in Windows XP.
- Applications do not run in the same way as they do in Windows XP.
- Most configuration tasks are not performed in the same way as they are in Windows XP.

While these features have a far-reaching impact on the way you use Windows Vista, they enhance security and provide your computer with better protection from malicious programs. If you use these features as they are intended to be used, your computer will be protected from many types of malicious programs.

Turning UAC On and Off

To your own detriment, and I mean that quite literally, you can disable UAC and all its related features on a per-account basis. Rather than completely disabling UAC, you can enable and disable individual features through policy settings. As we'll discuss in Chapter 18, you can find these policy settings under *Security Settings\Local Policies\Security Options*.

At home, you can turn UAC on and off for your account by following these steps:

1. Click Start and then click Control Panel.
2. In the Control Panel, click the User Accounts heading and then click User Accounts again.
3. On the User Accounts page, click "Turn User Account Control on or off."

 When you click "Turn User Account Control on or off," you are prompted for permissions or consent, as discussed previously. Because this is an inherent part of the user interface and a feature that you can enable or disable, I will not mention each time the prompt is displayed. Rather, I will assume that you provide the permissions or consent as required.

4. To disable UAC, clear the "Use User Account Control" checkbox. To enable UAC, select the "Use User Account Control" checkbox. Click OK.
5. When prompted, click "Restart now" or "Restart later" as appropriate. You will need to restart your computer for this change to take effect.

At the office, you cannot turn UAC on and off using this technique. While you may be able to configure individual UAC features through policy settings, these features will more than likely be set so that you cannot configure them.

Understanding Windows Vista Personalization

As you've seen, many factors can affect your computer's appearance and performance, including your hardware components and account controls. The way you achieve a balance between appearance and performance, however, is largely through the trade-offs you make when applying personalization settings, and it is personalization settings that largely determine your experience.

Personalization Settings

In Windows Vista, you can access personalization settings by clicking Start → Control → Appearance and Personalization → Personalization. As Figure 3-6 shows, this displays the Personalization page in the Control Panel. The available personalization settings are:

Windows Color and Appearance
Sets the user experience level and color scheme for your computer.

Desktop Background
Controls the desktop background colors and pictures used.

Screen Saver
Controls the screensaver and when it displays.

Sounds
Controls the system sounds used by Windows Vista.

Mouse Pointers
Controls the mouse pointers used by Windows Vista.

Theme
Sets the theme used by Windows Vista. A *theme* is a collection of appearance settings that includes the desktop background, sounds, and mouse pointers used by Windows Vista.

Display Settings
Controls monitors used by Windows Vista, their display resolutions, and their refresh rates. Also allows you to extend your desktop onto a second monitor.

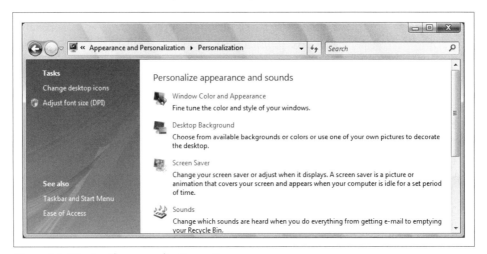

Figure 3-6. Viewing the personalization options

User Experience Levels

The user experience level is the foundation on which your personalization settings are based. Table 3-2 provides an overview of each user experience level.

Table 3-2. Understanding the user experience levels

User experience level	Can be used with...	Provides...
Windows Classic	Any Windows Vista edition; any Windows Vista Capable computer	The look and feel of Windows 2000 while retaining the functionality improvements in Windows Vista. You'll find a refined Start menu and streamlined Explorer windows, both with integrated search.
Windows Standard	Any Windows Vista edition; any Windows Vista Capable computer	Adds slightly improved performance, gradients, and shading to the Windows Classic experience.
Windows Vista Basic	Any Windows Vista edition; any Windows Vista Capable computer	Adds improved performance and enhanced reliability to the Windows Standard experience. Supports the new Windows Display Driver Model (WDDM) to enable smooth window handling, increase stability, and reduce glitches, such as relics and slow screen refreshes while moving user interface elements. Supports Windows Flip. Supports transparent glass for Windows Sidebar only.
Windows Aero	Windows Vista Home Premium edition or higher; any Windows Vista Premium Ready computer	Builds on the Windows Vista Basic experience. Adds Aero glass, transparency for all windows, live taskbar thumbnails, and Windows Flip 3D.

Each user experience level builds on and includes the features of the preceding level(s). If your computer has a low subscore for processor, physical memory, general graphics, gaming graphics, or any combination thereof, you may want to use the Windows Classic or Windows Standard experience level to improve your computer's performance. Figure 3-7 shows the look and feel of Windows Standard. Windows Classic and Windows Standard offer similar user experiences. Generally speaking, if you reduce the overhead associated with drawing gradients and shading, you can use the Windows Classic experience and you won't notice much difference.

If your computer has an average to high score for processor, physical memory, general graphics, gaming graphics, or any combination thereof, you may want to use the Windows Vista Basic or Windows Aero experience level to improve your computer's appearance. Windows Vista Basic and Windows Aero offer very similar user experiences. Figure 3-8 shows the look and feel of Windows Vista Basic.

Because of the previously listed feature differences among the various experience levels, you'll see related differences in the interface. Two rather subtle changes you'll need to watch out for have to do with the Quick Launch Toolbar and the Window Color and Appearance page. For the Quick Launch Toolbar, keep the following in mind:

Figure 3-7. Viewing the standard experience level

- When you are using Windows Classic or Windows Standard, the "Switch between windows" button is displayed but disabled.

- When you are using Windows Vista Basic, the "Switch between windows" button displays Windows Flip view.

- When you are using Windows Aero, the "Switch between windows" button displays Windows Flip 3D view.

For Windows Color and Appearance settings, keep the following in mind:

- When you are using Windows Classic, Windows Standard, or Windows Vista Basic, you can set the user experience level and color scheme, but you cannot mix colors or configure transparency settings. This is why clicking Windows Color and Appearance opens the Appearance Settings dialog box rather than the Windows Color and Appearance page in the Control Panel.

- When you are using Windows Aero, you can use the Windows Color and Appearance page in the Control Panel to change the color of windows, set color intensity, mix colors, and enable or disable transparency. To display the Appearance Settings dialog box so that you can set the user experience level and color scheme you must click the "Open classic appearance properties for more color options" link.

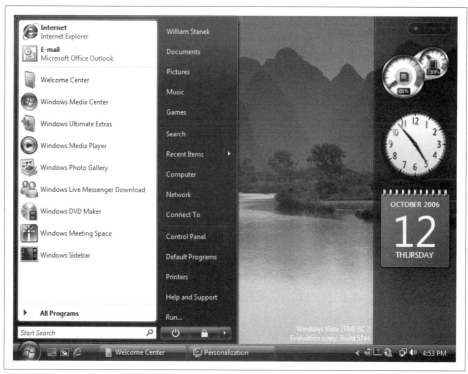

Figure 3-8. Viewing the enhanced experience level

Personalizing Windows Vista

From fine-tuning your window colors and experience level to choosing your desktop backgrounds, screensavers, sounds, mouse pointers, themes, and display settings, you can personalize Windows Vista in many different ways. Navigating this maze of options can be tricky, especially when you want to achieve robust performance while maintaining a desired look and feel. Even experienced users often neglect the basics of this essential balancing act, so you may be tempted to skip this section. But don't.

Fine-Tuning Your Window Colors and Experience Level

Aero gives the user interface a highly polished, glassy look. When you use Aero, you can set the glass color, intensity, and transparency. Several default colors are available, including graphite, blue, teal, red, orange, pink, and frost. By selecting a color and then using the "Color intensity" slider, you can create softer or bolder colors. By enabling transparency, you make it possible to see through parts of windows, menus, and dialog boxes. You can also create the exact color you want using Hue, Saturation, and Brightness color mixers. The one feature sorely missing is a way to enter numeric color values, which would allow you to use standard colors from color palettes.

Of these many Aero settings, the transparency setting is the biggest resource hog. If your computer has a low to middling score for its processor, physical memory, general graphics, or gaming graphics, you might want to disable this feature to achieve better performance.

Optimizing Aero glass

When you are using Windows Aero, you can configure the glass color, transparency, and intensity by completing the following steps:

1. Click Start and then click Control Panel.
2. In the Control Panel, click Appearance and Personalization and then click Personalization.
3. On the Personalization page, click Window Color and Appearance.
4. As shown in Figure 3-9, select one of the base colors available. Do this to save time even if you want to use the color mixer.
5. To enable transparency, select the "Enable transparency" checkbox. To disable transparency, clear the "Enable transparency" checkbox.
6. Use the "Color intensity" slider to control the intensity of the color. Move the slider to the left to soften the color. Move the slider to the right to make the color bolder.
7. If you want to adjust the color, click the "Show color mixer" button and then use the Hue, Saturation, and Brightness sliders to achieve the desired color.
8. Click OK to save your color settings.

Changing the experience level and appearance effects

By default, Windows Vista uses the highest experience level your computer is capable of. If you want to change the experience level, complete the following steps:

1. Click Start and then click Control Panel.
2. In the Control Panel, click Appearance and Personalization and then click Personalization.
3. On the Personalization page, click Window Color and Appearance.
4. If you are using Aero, click "Open classic appearance properties for more color options."
5. On the "Color scheme" list, shown in Figure 3-10, choose the desired experience level. If you choose an option other than Windows Aero, Windows Vista Basic, Windows Standard, or Windows Classic, you'll be using a modified color scheme for the Windows Classic experience level.
6. Click OK to save your settings or continue with the next procedure.

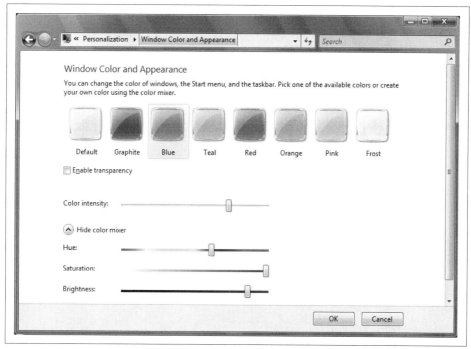

Figure 3-9. Setting the window color and appearance

While you are working with the Appearance Settings dialog box, you may want to set appearance effects for screen fonts, shadows under menus, and display of window contents while dragging:

1. In the Appearance Settings dialog box, click the Effects button. This displays the Effects dialog box, shown in Figure 3-11.

2. By default, Windows Vista smoothes the edges of screen fonts to make them easier to read. Typically, this is the desired behavior. For CRT monitors, you'll want to use the Standard setting. For LCD monitors, you'll want to use the ClearType setting.

3. Displaying shadows under menus adds somewhat to the overhead when drawing menus. To help conserve your computer's resources, you can disable this feature by clearing the "Show shadows under menus" checkbox.

4. Showing window contents while dragging can use a considerable amount of system resources, especially when dragging large or graphics-intensive windows. To help conserve your computer's resources, you can disable this feature by clearing the "Show windows contents while dragging" checkbox.

5. Click OK twice to save your settings.

Figure 3-10. Choosing the experience level

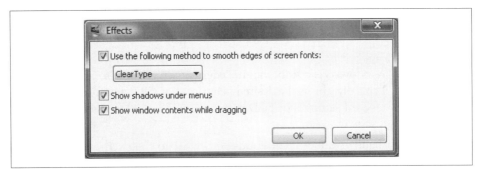

Figure 3-11. Configuring additional effects

Choosing Your Desktop Background

The Windows desktop can display a solid background color or a picture as Windows wallpaper. Windows Vista provides a fairly large set of ready-to-use background images that you can use as wallpaper.

On your computer's hard drive, these default background images are stored in the *%WinDir%\Web\Wallpaper* folder. If you examine the properties of these images, you'll see that each has a keyword tag. Windows Vista uses the keyword tag to group these images into named sets.

You can create background images to use as Windows wallpaper as well. You must create these background images as *.bmp*, *.gif*, *.jpg*, *.jpeg*, *.dib*, or *.png* files. If you add images in these formats to the *%WinDir%\Web\Wallpaper* folder and add a tag to each image, the images will be available as part of the Windows wallpaper and organized into the named sets according to your keyword tags. Although working with images and applying keyword tags to images are discussed in Chapter 9, the key thing you need to know in terms of adding new wallpaper or even using your own images from a different location is that you should optimize every background image you use. If you don't do this, you risk seriously impacting your computer's performance.

In case you're wondering why this may be so, let me tell you the cautionary tale of an experienced pro (me) who added a picture of his kids to the desktop background and suddenly found his computer's performance was moderately degraded. This is what happened:

> My digital camera takes high-resolution pictures—most do these days—and its pictures are about 4 MB in size, on average. By adding an unedited picture to the desktop background, I was forcing the operating system to swap in 4 MB of extra data every time the operating system displayed the desktop.
>
> Now you may be thinking, "4 MB is no big deal; my computer has gigabytes of RAM." Well, the problem wasn't system memory (RAM) but graphics memory. Most computers use both dedicated and shared graphics memory. The dedicated memory on most computer video cards is relatively meager, in contrast to shared memory, which is part of RAM, so swapping in and out 4 MB is a big deal. Also, the image was sized at 3,072 x 2,304 pixels when the screen size I was using was 1,600 × 1,200 pixels. This means that not only did the graphics card have to manage this large picture, but also Windows Vista had to resize the image to fit on the screen.
>
> The solution to the problem was fairly simple: I opened the image in my photo editor, resized it to 1,600 × 1,200 pixels, and saved the resized image with a new name to the Pictures folder in my profile. The resized image was 1 MB, and my computer was much happier.

If you examine the default images Windows Vista uses for wallpaper, you'll find that most are less than 2 MB in size. In fact, the Vista images, some of the most visually stunning wallpaper images, are the most highly optimized. You'll find that they are available at a standard screen ratio of 1,600 × 1,200 and with a widescreen ratio of 1,600 × 900.

You can set the background for the desktop by completing the following steps:

1. Right-click an open area of the desktop and then select Personalize.
2. On the Personalization page in the Control Panel, click Desktop Background. This displays the Desktop Background page, as shown in Figure 3-12.

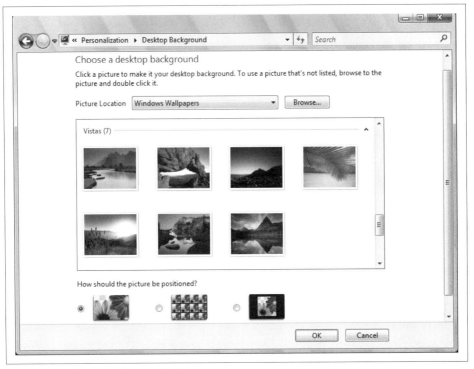

Figure 3-12. Choosing a desktop background

3. Use the Picture Location pull-down menu to specify where to look for the picture you want to use, or click Browse to select a location. The default locations are as follows:

Windows Wallpapers
    Displays the wallpaper images in the *%WinDir%\Web\Wallpaper* folder.

Pictures
    Displays the images in your Pictures folder.

Sample Pictures
    Displays the images in your Sample Pictures folder.

Public Pictures
    Displays the images in your computer's Public Pictures folder.

Solid Colors
    Allows you to choose from more than 50 background colors, or create your own background color by clicking More and then using the Color dialog box to select or mix your color.

4. Once you've located the image or color you want to use, click it to select it.

5. If you are using a background image, use the "How should the picture be positioned?" options to select a display option for the background. You have three display position options:

Fit to Screen
>Stretches or shrinks the image to fill the desktop background. This is a good option for photos and large images.

Tile
>Repeats the image so that it covers the entire screen. This is a good option for small images and icons.

Center
>Centers the image on the desktop background. Any area that the image doesn't fill uses the current desktop color.

6. When you are finished updating the background, click OK.

Choosing and Configuring Your Screensaver

Screensavers turn on when a computer has been idle for a specified period. Originally, screensavers were designed to prevent image burn-in on CRT monitors by displaying a continually changing image. With today's monitors, burn-in is not much of a problem, but screensavers are still around because they offer a different benefit today: the ability to password-lock your computer automatically when the screensaver turns on.

>Windows Vista performs many housekeeping tasks in the background when the computer is idle. These housekeeping tasks extend to creating indexes, defragmenting hard disks, creating whole computer backups and system restore points, and more. Because of this, you want to be more careful than ever when choosing a screensaver for your computer. So, while you can install your fancy fish-tank screensaver with the sharks and stingrays, you may do so at the expense of your computer being able to perform background tasks while you are away from your desk rather than while you are sitting at your desk.

Selecting a screensaver

You can configure your screensaver by performing the following steps:

1. Right-click an open area of the desktop and then select Personalize.

2. Click the Screen Saver link to display the Screen Saver Settings dialog box, shown in Figure 3-13.

3. Use the Screen Saver listbox to select a screensaver. Although you can install additional screensavers, the standard screensavers are:

    (None)
    >Turns off the screensaver.

    3D Text
    >Displays the time or custom text as a 3D message against a black background.

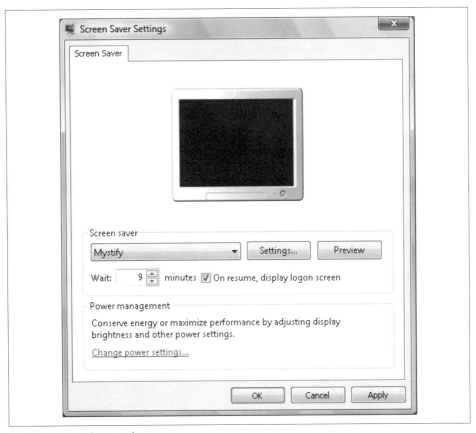

Figure 3-13. Configuring the screensaver

Aurora
> Simulates the lights of the aurora borealis against a black background.

Blank
> Displays a blank screen (i.e., a screen with a black background and no text or images).

Bubbles
> Displays multicolored bubbles floating across your desktop. The open windows and documents on the desktop remain visible.

Mystify
> Displays arcing bands of lines in various geometric patterns against a black background.

Photos
> Displays photos and videos from a selected folder as a slide show.

Ribbons

> Displays ribbons of various thicknesses and changing lines against a black background.

Windows Energy

> Displays the Windows logo and then changing lines of energy (similar to power lines) against a background that changes in hue from green to blue to purple.

Windows Logo

> Intermittently displays the Windows logo and arcing bands of lines against a black background.

(Other)

> If you've installed a screensaver program on your computer, you'll typically see options for the additional screensavers this program provides. Be careful with some of these, as they can require a substantial amount of system resources to maintain, preventing your computer from effectively performing background housekeeping tasks.

4. To password-protect the screensaver, select "On resume, display Welcome screen." Clear this option only if you do not want to use password protection.

5. Use the Wait box to specify how long the computer must be idle before the screensaver is activated. A reasonable value is between 10 and 15 minutes.

6. Click OK.

Customizing the 3D Text and Photos screensavers

Two of the standard screensavers deserve additional discussions: 3D Text and Photos. With these screensavers (and likely any custom screensavers you install), clicking Settings displays a dialog box that allows you to customize the screensaver. To customize the 3D Text screensaver, follow these steps:

1. In the Screen Saver Settings dialog box, select 3D Text as the screensaver and then click Settings. This displays the 3D Text Settings dialog box shown in Figure 3-14.

2. You can display the current time or a custom message as 3D text. To display the current time as 3D text, select Time. To display a custom message as 3D text, select Custom Text and then type your message.

3. Click Choose Font. Use the Font dialog box to set the font to use for the 3D text. The default font is Tahoma.

4. Use the Resolution slider to control the display resolution of the text. The higher the resolution, the more processing power required to draw and move the message.

5. Use the Size slider to control the size of the text.

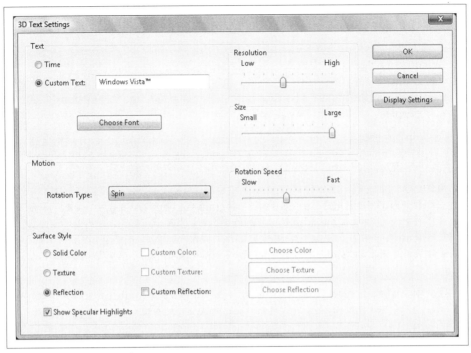

Figure 3-14. Configuring the 3D Text screensaver

6. Use the Rotation Speed slider to control the speed at which the text moves and rotates on the screen. The faster the rotation, the more processing power required to draw and move the message.

7. Use the Rotation Type listbox to select the type of rotation to use, such as spin or tumble. If you set the rotation type to None, you can turn off rotation and reduce the amount of processing power required to draw and move the message.

8. Use the following Surface Style options to configure the way the 3D text looks:

Solid Color

Displays the text in a solid color. Click Custom Color and then click Choose Color to display the Color dialog box. Choose the color to use and click OK.

Texture

Displays the text with a textured surface. Click Custom Texture and then click Choose Texture to display the Choose Custom Texture dialog box. You can use any bitmap (*.bmp*) image as the texture. Once you find a *.bmp* image to use, click Open.

Reflection

Displays the text with a reflective surface. Click Custom Reflection and then click Choose Reflection to display the Choose Custom Reflection dialog box. You can use any bitmap (*.bmp*) image as the texture. Once you find a *.bmp* image to use, click Open.

9. Click OK to save your settings and then click OK to use this screensaver.

The Photos screensaver is my favorite of all the screensavers. Not only does it display a slide show of photos and videos, but it can also make collages, photo albums, photo stacks, and more. Several filtering options are available as well, and I recommend you use these options, because they can save you from potential embarrassment if the wrong pictures are accidentally displayed. For example, using Windows Photo Gallery, which is discussed in Chapter 9, you can add keyword tags to images and then in the Photos screensaver, you can display only photos with certain tags, such as those having Family or Kids tags. Photo Gallery also allows you to assign a star rating to photos as an indicator of quality. In the Photos screensaver, you could use this feature to display only your best five-star photos.

 To make the most of the Photos screensaver, your computer must have a graphics processor that is DirectX 9- and WDDM-capable. If your computer's graphics processor doesn't support these features, you won't be able to select themes that control how images are displayed and rotated.

You can customize the Photos screensaver by following these steps:

1. In the Screen Saver Settings dialog box, select Photos as the screensaver and then click Settings. This displays the Photos Screen Saver dialog box shown in Figure 3-15.

2. If you are using Windows Photo Gallery, you can make all your Photo Gallery pictures available by selecting "Use all pictures and videos from Photo Gallery." You can then filter these photos using the following options:

   With this tag
   Enter the keyword tags of photos you want to display. Windows Vista will only display photos with these tags. Separate multiple keywords with a comma or semicolon.

   With this rating or higher
   Select "Any rating" to display photos with any star rating. Select another star rating to display photos with that rating or higher.

   Don't show items tagged
   Enter the keyword tags of photos you don't want to display. Separate multiple keywords with a comma or semicolon.

3. If you want to use photos and videos from a specific folder rather than the Photo Gallery, you can choose "Use pictures and videos from" and then click Browse to select the folder to use. The default folder is your Pictures folder.

4. Use the options on the "Use this theme" list to choose how images are displayed and rotated. The options you may prefer include:

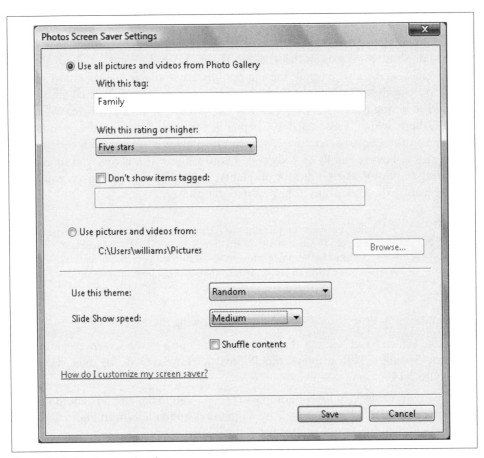

Figure 3-15. Configuring the Photos screensaver

Album

Creates a photo album from the photos and rotates the pages of the album according to the slide show speed.

Collage

Creates a photo collage from the photos and changes the collage according to the slide show speed.

Frame

Displays the photos as framed pictures and changes the framed pictures according to the slide show speed.

Stack

Displays the photos as a photo stack with each photo slightly offset so that you can see the edges of pictures below the topmost picture. Changes the photos in the stack according to the slide show speed.

Glass
> Displays the photos as though they are behind glass, and changes the photos according to the slide show speed.

Random
> Chooses a display option randomly.

5. Use the options on the "Slide Show speed" list to set the speed of the slide show. The options are Slow, Medium, and Fast.

6. Normally, photos are displayed in alphanumeric order. If you want to shuffle the photos and display them in random order, select the "Shuffle contents" checkbox.

7. Click Save and then click OK.

Choosing Your System Sounds

Windows Vista plays sounds in response to a wide variety of events, such as when you log on, when you open or close programs, or when you type an asterisk. Programs you install, such as America Online, can have their own sounds as well. You can configure all of these sounds and manage them collectively using sound schemes. A sound scheme is simply a set of sounds that you want to use together.

Windows Vista has two standard sound schemes: No Sounds, which turns off all program sounds except the Windows Startup sound played when you log on; and Windows Default, which is configured to use the standard Windows sounds.

Selecting a sound scheme

You can configure your system to use an existing sound scheme by completing the following steps:

1. Right-click an open area of the desktop and then select Personalize.

2. Click the Sounds link to display the Sound dialog box with the Sounds tab selected, as shown in Figure 3-16.

3. Use the Sound Scheme listbox to choose the sound scheme to use.

4. Click OK to save your settings.

Customizing your sound scheme

You can configure your system to use a customized sound scheme by completing the following steps:

1. Right-click an open area of the desktop and then select Personalize.

2. Click the Sounds link to display the Sound dialog box with the Sounds tab selected, as shown in Figure 3-16.

3. In the Program list, sounds are organized according to the program to which they relate and the related event that triggers the sound. To preview a sound for a particular event, select the event in the Program list and then click the Test button.

Figure 3-16. Configuring your computer's system sounds

4. To change the sound for an event, select the event in the Program list and then use the Sounds list to choose an available sound. You can also click Browse to select other sounds available on the system. The sound files must be in Microsoft *.wav* format.

5. To save a changed sound scheme, click Save As, type a name for the scheme in the field provided, and then click OK.

6. Click OK to close the Sounds dialog box.

Choosing Your Mouse Pointers

In Windows, the innocuous mouse pointer has many faces, and each face tells something about the current way you are using the mouse pointer. The three types of mouse pointers you see the most are the Normal Select pointer, the Text Select pointer, and the Link Select pointer. You can configure the appearance of these and other types of mouse pointers and manage them collectively using pointer schemes. A *pointer scheme* is simply a set of mouse pointers that you want to use together.

Windows Vista has more than 20 standard pointer schemes. The schemes you'll use the most are:

(None)

This doesn't turn mouse pointers off. Instead, it uses nondescript pointers.

Windows Aero

The standard pointers used with the Windows Aero experience. Also comes in large and extra-large options.

Windows Black

Inverts the pointer colors so that black backgrounds are used instead of white backgrounds. Also comes in large and extra-large options.

Windows Standard

The standard pointers used with the Windows Standard user experience. Also comes in large and extra-large options.

 If you're tired of the standard black-on-white or white-on-black pointers, you might want to try the 3D-Bronze scheme. It's one of my favorites, as it adds a dash of color to the pointer—and makes it easier to see the pointer against a white background, such as when you are typing in Microsoft Word.

Selecting a mouse pointer scheme

You can configure your system to use an existing pointer scheme by completing the following steps:

1. Right-click an open area of the desktop and then select Personalize.

2. Click the Mouse Pointers link to display the Mouse Properties dialog box with the Pointers tab selected, as shown in Figure 3-17.

3. Use the Scheme listbox to choose the pointer scheme to use.

4. Click OK to save your settings.

Customizing your mouse pointer scheme

You can configure your system to use a customized pointer scheme by completing the following steps:

1. Right-click an open area of the desktop and then select Personalize.

2. Click the Mouse Pointers link to display the Mouse Properties dialog box with the Pointers tab selected, as shown in Figure 3-17.

3. In the Customize list, pointers are organized according to their type. To change a pointer, select the pointer and then click Browse. This opens the Browse dialog box with the Cursors folder selected. Choose the cursor pointer to use and then click Open.

4. To save a changed pointer scheme, click Save As, type a name for the scheme in the field provided, and then click OK.

5. Click OK to close the Mouse Properties dialog box.

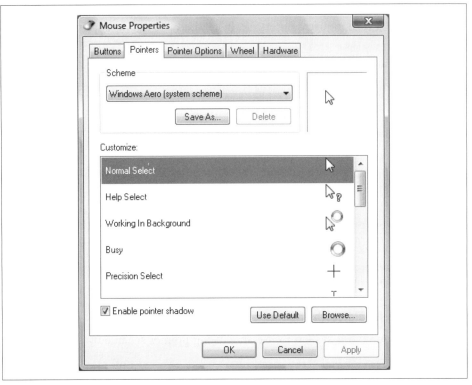

Figure 3-17. Configuring your computer's mouse pointers

Choosing and Managing Your Themes

Desktop themes are combinations of the visual and audio elements Windows Vista uses to set the appearance of menus, icons, backgrounds, screensavers, system sounds, and mouse pointers. The default themes your computer uses are based on the user experience level.

Saving your customized settings

As you customize the backgrounds, screensavers, system sounds, and mouse pointers your computer uses, you modify the default theme; you can then save these modified settings together as a new theme by following these steps:

1. Right-click an open area of the desktop and then select Personalize. In the Personalization console, click Theme.

2. In the Theme Settings dialog box, shown in Figure 3-18, click Save As and then use the Save As dialog box to save the theme. Theme definition files end with the *.theme* file extension. Unless deleted in the future, the custom theme will appear as an option in the Theme listbox.

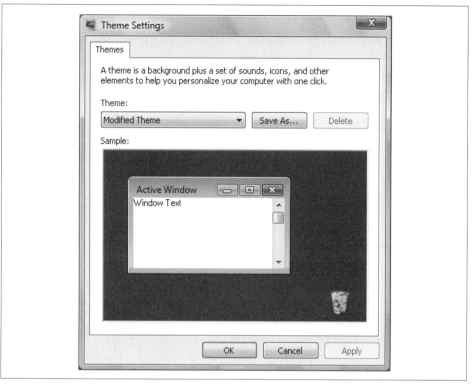

Figure 3-18. Saving your settings as a theme

Applying a saved theme

In addition to any custom themes you create, several default themes are available, including the Windows Vista theme used when you choose the Windows Vista Basic or Windows Aero experience, and the Windows Classic theme used when you choose the Windows Standard or Windows Classic experience.

You can apply a default or saved theme by completing these steps:

1. Right-click an open area of the desktop and then select Personalize. In the Personalization console, click Theme.

2. Use the Theme list to select the theme you want to use. If you want to use a theme saved to an alternative location, select Browse and then use the Open Theme dialog box to select the *.theme* file that contains the saved theme.

3. The Sample Pane provides a preview of the theme's appearance. If the theme appears as you expected, click OK. Otherwise, select a different theme and then click OK.

Configuring Your Monitors

Windows Vista automatically configures your monitor settings the first time you log on. Windows does this by choosing the best display settings for your monitor. The optimized settings include:

Screen resolution

Determines how much information is displayed on the screen, measured horizontally and vertically in pixels. Low resolutions, such as 640×480 or 800×600 pixels, fit fewer items on the screen but those items appear larger. High resolutions, such as 1,280×1,024 or 1,600×1,200, fit more items on the screen but those items appear smaller. Clarity typically is determined by the dots per inch (dpi) being displayed. Generally, the higher the dpi, the better the text and on-screen elements will look. However, if you set the screen resolution too high, you might affect the supported refresh rate and color options, which could reduce clarity as well.

Refresh rate

Controls the frequency at which the screen is redrawn. To get the best possible display, you'll want to be sure you use as fast a refresh rate as possible. If the refresh rate is set too low, the screen can flicker, which can cause eyestrain and headaches. To reduce or eliminate flicker, you'll want the refresh rate to be at least 72 hertz.

Color

Controls the number of color bits associated with each pixel. To get the best possible display, you'll want to use at least 32-bit color. With 24-bit color, you won't see most of Windows Vista's visual effects. With 16-bit color, the edges of interface elements may appear to be jagged rather than smooth.

Your computer's video card and monitor together determine the screen resolution, refresh rates, and colors that you can use. Generally, you'll want to use the highest quality setting that is mutually supported. Most monitors have a base or native resolution, which is the resolution that the monitor was designed to display best.

Proper display depends on your computer using accurate information about your graphics card and monitor. Depending on which graphics card and monitor models Windows Vista thinks you have, different driver files are installed. These drivers determine which display resolutions, colors, and refresh rates are available and appropriate for the system. If the graphics card and monitor aren't detected and configured properly, Windows Vista won't be able to take advantage of their capabilities.

Your display settings can be less than optimal for many reasons. Sometimes Windows Vista doesn't detect the device, and a generic device driver is used. At other times, Windows Vista detects the wrong type of device, such as a different model, in which case the device will probably work but some features won't be available, or worse, incorrect (and incompatible) options will be available.

Setting the screen resolution and color quality

You can set the screen resolution and color quality by completing the following steps:

1. Right-click an open area of the desktop and then select Personalize.
2. Click Display Settings. This opens the Display Settings dialog box, as shown in Figure 3-19.

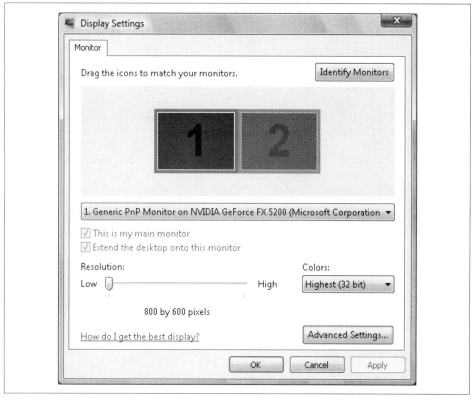

Figure 3-19. Configuring the screen resolution and colors

3. On a system with multiple monitors or graphics cards, click 2 to configure settings for the second monitor.
4. Use the Resolution slider to set the display size, such as 1,600×1,200 pixels.
5. Use the Colors listbox to select a color quality, such as Highest (32 bit).
6. Click OK.

Setting the refresh rate

You can set the refresh rate for a monitor by completing the following steps:

1. Right-click an open area of the desktop and then select Personalize.

2. Click Display Settings. This opens the Display Settings dialog box.

3. On a system with multiple monitors or graphics cards, click 2 to configure settings for the second monitor.

4. Click Advanced Settings.

5. On the Adapter tab, click "List all modes." The "List all modes" dialog box shows the refresh rates supported by the selected monitor. Click OK.

6. On the Monitor tab, use the "Screen refresh rate" list to set the desired refresh rate.

 If you clear the "Hide modes that this monitor cannot display" checkbox, Windows Vista will display refresh rates that exceed the capabilities of the monitor and graphics card. Select these additional hidden modes only when you know for sure that your monitor and graphics card support a particular mode, such as may be the case when you are using a generic driver. Keep in mind that running the computer at a higher refresh rate than it supports can damage the monitor and video adapter.

7. Click OK twice to save your settings.

Customizing multiple-monitor configurations

If multiple monitors are connected to your computer, you can designate one monitor as the primary and the other as the secondary monitor. You can also extend the desktop onto your second monitor. To configure options for multiple monitors, complete the following steps:

1. Right-click an open area of the desktop and then select Personalize.

2. Click Display Settings. This opens the Display Settings dialog box.

3. If multiple monitors are configured, select the monitor you want to work with. Monitor 1 is the primary monitor. Monitor 2 is the secondary monitor.

4. By default, the primary monitor is assumed to be on the left and the secondary monitor on the right. Because of this, when you move the mouse pointer off the right edge of the primary monitor, the mouse pointer appears on the left side of the secondary monitor. If you want the monitor on the right to be the primary monitor, you can reverse this order by clicking 2 and dragging to the left. Now when you move the mouse pointer off the left edge of the primary monitor, the mouse pointer appears on the right side of the secondary monitor.

5. To extend the desktop onto your secondary monitor's display, select the "Extend the desktop onto this monitor" checkbox.

6. Click OK.

Setting the monitor or graphics card driver

If the monitor or graphics card shown in the Display Settings dialog box does not match the one you are using, you should visit your computer manufacturer's web site and obtain the proper driver. Typically, you can do this by accessing the manufacturer's support page and entering the serial number or model of your computer. Most computer manufacturers maintain drivers for a number of years and provide updates for these drivers as they become available.

 In most cases, you'll download a zipped file containing the drivers you need. To extract the files from the ZIP, you'll need to right-click the *.zip* file and then select Extract All. After you select a destination folder, click Extract.

You install monitor and graphics card drivers using separate procedures. To specify the monitor driver to use, follow these steps:

1. Right-click an open area of the desktop and then select Personalize.

2. Click Display Settings. This opens the Display Settings dialog box.

3. On a system with multiple monitors or graphics cards, click 2 to configure settings for the second monitor.

4. Click Advanced Settings.

5. On the Monitor tab, click Properties.

6. In the Driver tab, click Update Driver. This starts the Update Driver Software Wizard.

7. Click "Browse my computer for driver software."

8. Click Browse to select a search location. Use the Browse for Folder dialog box to select the start folder for the search, and then click OK. Because Windows Vista searches all subfolders of the selected folder automatically, you can select the drive root path, such as C, to search an entire drive.

9. Click Next. Click Close when the driver installation is completed.

To specify the graphics card driver to use, follow these steps:

1. Right-click an open area of the desktop and then select Personalize.

2. Click Display Settings. This opens the Display Settings dialog box.

3. On a system with multiple monitors or graphics cards, click 2 to configure settings for the second graphics card.

4. Click Advanced Settings.

5. On the Adapter tab, click Properties.

6. In the Driver tab, click Update Driver. This starts the Update Driver Software Wizard.

7. Click "Browse my computer for driver software."

8. Click Browse to select a search location. Use the Browse for Folder dialog box to select the start folder for the search, and then click OK. Because Windows Vista searches all subfolders of the selected folder automatically, you can select the drive root path, such as C, to search an entire drive.

9. Click Next. Click Close when the driver installation is completed.

Optimizing Performance

In addition to the previously discussed features, you can fine-tune your computer's performance by setting these performance options:

- Visual effects
- Application performance
- Virtual memory
- Memory protection
- ReadyBoost

The sections that follow discuss each performance option in turn.

Fine-Tuning Visual Effects

The Windows Vista interface has many graphical enhancements including visual effects for menus, toolbars, windows, and the taskbar. Because displaying these visual effects can require substantial system resources, Windows Vista lets you optimize the way visual effects are used. You can optimize for appearance or for performance. You can also customize the settings or let Windows Vista choose the best configuration.

The visual effects available are:

- Animate controls and elements inside windows
- Animate windows when minimizing and maximizing
- Enable desktop composition
- Enable transparent glass
- Fade or slide menus into view

- Fade or slide ToolTips into view
- Fade out menu items after clicking
- Show preview and filters in folder
- Show shadows under menus
- Show shadows under mouse pointer
- Show thumbnails instead of icons
- Show translucent selection rectangle
- Show window contents while dragging
- Slide open combo boxes
- Slide taskbar buttons
- Smooth edges of screen fonts
- Smooth-scroll list boxes
- Use a background image for each folder type
- Use drop shadows for icon labels on the desktop
- Use visual styles on windows and buttons

You can configure Windows performance by completing the following steps:

1. Click Start and then click Control Panel.
2. In the Control Panel, click the System and Maintenance category heading link.
3. Click Performance Information and Tools.
4. Under Tasks, click "Adjust visual effects." This opens the Performance Options dialog box shown in Figure 3-20.
5. On the Visual Effects tab, you have the following options for controlling visual effects:

    Let Windows choose what's best for my computer
    Enables the operating system to choose the performance options based on the hardware configuration. For a newer computer, this option will probably be identical to the "Adjust for best appearance" option because of its hardware and performance capabilities.

    Adjust for best appearance
    Enables all visual effects for all graphical interfaces.

    Adjust for best performance
    Disables all visual effects.

    Custom
    Allows you to enable or disable the visual effects options individually.

6. Click OK to apply your settings.

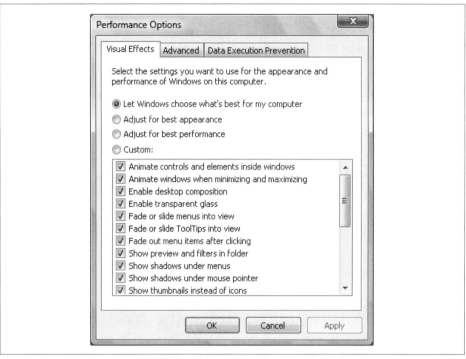

Figure 3-20. Optimizing visual effects

Fine-Tuning Application Performance

Application performance determines the relative priority of applications being run by users and those being run by the operating system. Unlike earlier releases of Windows, Windows Vista does a much better job of prioritizing, and as a result, background processes and housekeeping tasks have less impact on performance. Because of this, the default configuration for application performance, which gives scheduling priority to applications you are running, is typically what you'll want to use. The only time you may want to change this behavior is if you are using a computer running Windows Vista as a server. For example, if you were using a computer as a printer server or web server, you would probably want to change the scheduling priority settings.

You control application performance by completing the following steps:

1. In the Control Panel, click the System and Maintenance category heading link.

2. Click Performance Information and Tools.

3. Under Tasks, click "Adjust visual effects." This opens the Performance Options dialog box.

4. On the Advanced tab, shown in Figure 3-21, select "Background services" to optimize performance for a computer you are using as a server. Otherwise, select Programs to optimize performance for a computer you use to run applications, such as Microsoft Word.

5. Click OK.

Figure 3-21. Setting the processor scheduling options

Fine-Tuning Virtual Memory

Your computer uses virtual memory to extend the amount of available RAM by writing physical memory (RAM) to disks through a process called *paging*. With paging, Windows Vista writes a set amount of RAM, such as 1,834 MB, to the disk as a paging file, where the operating system can access it from the disk when needed in place of physical memory.

Windows Vista writes paging files to disk drives as a file named *pagefile.sys*. Windows Vista creates an initial paging file automatically for the drive containing the operating system. By default, other drives don't have paging files, so you must create these paging files manually if you want to use them.

As with many other aspects of performance, Windows Vista does a much better job than its predecessors do of automatically managing virtual memory. Typically, Windows Vista will allocate virtual memory at least as large as the total physical memory installed on the computer. This helps to ensure that paging files don't become fragmented, which can result in poor system performance.

You can also manually manage virtual memory. If you do this, you'll typically want to use a fixed virtual memory size. You fix the size of the virtual memory by setting the initial size and the maximum size to the same value, and this in turn prevents fragmentation.

> In most cases, I recommend setting the total paging file size so that it's twice the physical RAM size on the system. For instance, on a computer with 1,024 MB of RAM, you would ensure that the "Total paging file size for each drive" setting is at least 2,048 MB. If your computer has more than 2 GB of RAM, however, you'll probably want to set the paging file size so that it's the same size as the physical memory.

You can manually configure virtual memory by completing the following steps:

1. In the Control Panel, click the System and Maintenance category heading link.
2. Click Performance Information and Tools.
3. Under Tasks, click "Adjust visual effects." This opens the Performance Options dialog box.
4. On the Advanced tab, click Change to display the Virtual Memory dialog box shown in Figure 3-22. The following information is provided:

   Drive [Volume Label] and *Paging File Size (MB)*
   Show the current configuration of virtual memory. The dialog box lists each volume with its associated paging file (if any). The paging file range shows the initial and maximum size values of the related paging file.

   Paging file size for each drive
   Provides information on the currently selected drive and enables you to set its paging file size. "Space available" indicates how much space is available on the drive.

   Total paging file size for all drives
   Provides a recommended size for virtual RAM on the system and shows the amount currently allocated.

5. By default, Windows Vista manages the paging file size for all drives. If you want to configure virtual memory manually, clear the "Automatically manage paging file size for all drives" checkbox.
6. In the Drive listbox, select the disk volume you want to work with.
7. Select "Custom size" and then enter an initial size and a maximum size.
8. Click Set to save the changes.
9. Repeat steps 6–8 for each disk volume you want to configure.
10. Click OK. If prompted to overwrite an existing *pagefile.sys* file, click Yes.

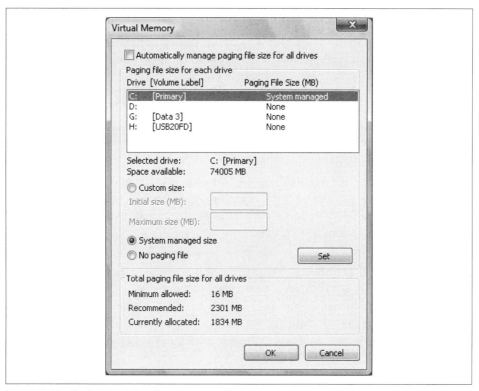

Figure 3-22. Configuring virtual memory

11. If you updated the settings for a paging file that is currently in use, you'll see a prompt explaining that you need to restart the system for the changes to take effect. Click OK.

12. Click OK twice to close the open dialog boxes. You'll see a prompt asking if you want to restart the system. Click Restart.

You can have Windows Vista automatically manage virtual memory by following these steps:

1. In the Control Panel, click the System and Maintenance category heading link.

2. Click Performance Information and Tools.

3. Under Tasks, click "Adjust visual effects." This opens the Performance Options dialog box.

4. On the Advanced tab, click Change to display the Virtual Memory dialog box shown in Figure 3-22.

5. Select the "Automatically manage paging file size for all drives" checkbox.

6. Click OK twice to close the open dialog boxes.

Fine-Tuning Data Execution Prevention

Data Execution Prevention (DEP) is a memory protection technology. Your computer uses DEP to mark all memory locations used by applications as nonexecutable unless the location explicitly contains executable code. If an application attempts to execute code from a memory page marked as nonexecutable, the processor can raise an exception and prevent it from executing. This behavior is designed to thwart a malicious program, such as a virus, from inserting itself into areas of memory. By allowing only specific areas of memory to run executable code, DEP protects your computer from many types of self-replicating viruses.

You can implement DEP via hardware or software. Hardware-based DEP is more robust because you can extend it to any program or service running on the computer. Software-based DEP is less robust because it typically works best when protecting Windows programs and services.

32-bit versions of Windows support DEP as implemented by Advanced Micro Devices Inc. (AMD) processors that provide the no-execute page-protection (NX) processor feature. Such processors support the related instructions and must be running in Physical Address Extension (PAE) mode. 64-bit versions of Windows also support the NX processor feature.

You can determine whether your computer hardware supports DEP by completing the following steps:

1. In the Control Panel, click the System and Maintenance category heading link.
2. Click Performance Information and Tools.
3. Under Tasks, click "Adjust visual effects." This opens the Performance Options dialog box.
4. Click the Data Execution Prevention tab. As Figure 3-23 shows, the lower portion of this tab lists the DEP support available.

Once you've accessed the Data Execution Prevention tab, you can configure the way DEP works using these options:

Turn on DEP for essential Windows programs and services only
    Enables DEP only for the operating system services, programs, and components. This is the default and recommended option for computers that support execution protection and are configured appropriately.

Turn on DEP for all programs except those I select
    Enables DEP for the operating system, as well as all programs and services you are running.

Because some programs won't work with or will become unstable with software-based DEP, you may find that you have to add exceptions when you enable DEP for all programs. Click Add to specify programs that should run without execution protection. In this way, execution protection will work for all programs except those you have listed.

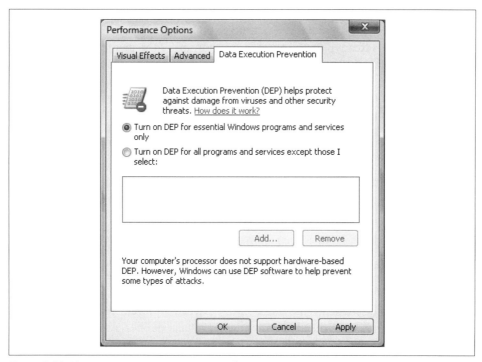

Figure 3-23. Viewing your computer's DEP configuration

Using ReadyBoost to Enhance Performance

Windows Vista uses your computer's disk drives for paging files and system cache. Because reading from and writing to a disk is significantly slower than reading from and writing to physical memory (RAM), this can cause performance bottlenecks that make your computer seem sluggish or unresponsive. To reduce the performance impact related to reading and writing the system cache, Windows Vista introduces Windows ReadyBoost.

Windows ReadyBoost is a feature that lets you extend the disk-caching capabilities of the computer's main memory to a USB flash device. Using flash devices for caching allows the operating system to make random reads faster by caching data on the USB flash device instead of your computer's disk drives. Windows Vista can read flash devices up to 1,000 percent faster than physical disk drives, significantly boosting the overall performance of your computer.

The types of USB flash devices you can use with Windows ReadyBoost include:

- USB 2.0 flash drives
- Secure Digital (SD) cards
- CompactFlash cards

Further, these devices must be at least 512 MB or larger and have sufficiently fast flash memory. Because some flash devices have both slow and fast memory, you may find that Windows ReadyBoost can use only a portion of the memory on the device. Windows Vista can use an amount of flash memory equal to twice the amount of physical memory (RAM) on the computer. Therefore, if your computer has 1 GB of RAM, you could use up to 2 GB of memory on a flash device to boost your computer's performance.

When Windows ReadyBoost is enabled, Windows Vista uses the USB flash device primarily for caching that uses random input/output and small, sequential input/output rather than large, sequential input/output. This is because the memory on USB flash devices is better suited to random I/O and small, sequential input/output than large, sequential I/O.

Because USB flash devices are meant to be portable, Windows Vista adds protections to prevent the sudden removal of a USB flash device from crashing the computer and to prevent reading of any sensitive data written to the flash device. To allow a USB flash device to be removed at any time, Windows Vista ensures that all data writes are made to the hard disk first and then copied to the flash device. This eliminates the potential for data loss when removing a flash device. To prevent reading of sensitive data, Windows Vista encrypts all data written to a flash device so that it can be used only with the computer on which it was originally written.

Enabling Windows ReadyBoost

You can enable Windows ReadyBoost by completing the following steps:

1. Insert a USB flash device into a USB 2.0 or higher port.

2. The AutoPlay dialog box should be displayed automatically. If you always want to use the device with Windows ReadyBoost when inserted, select the "Always do this…" checkbox.

 Windows Vista should display the AutoPlay dialog box automatically. If it doesn't, you've probably selected the "Always do this…" checkbox previously. You can clear a previous selection by clicking Start → Default Programs. On the Default Programs page in the Control Panel, click "Change AutoPlay settings." On the AutoPlay page, scroll down to the bottom of the page. Click "Reset all defaults" and then click Save. Remove the USB flash device and then reinsert it to display the AutoPlay dialog box.

3. If the flash memory performs at a sufficiently high speed, Windows Vista will display a "Speed up my computer" option in the AutoPlay dialog box. Select the "Speed up my system using Windows ReadyBoost" option.

4. Windows Vista extends the computer's physical memory to the device. The default configuration enables Windows ReadyBoost to reserve all available space on the device for boosting system speed.

If you previously inserted a flash device and declined to use Windows ReadyBoost, you can enable ReadyBoost by completing the following steps:

1. Click Start and then click Computer.
2. Right-click the USB flash device in the Devices with Removable Storage list and then choose Properties.
3. Click the ReadyBoost tab, as shown in Figure 3-24.

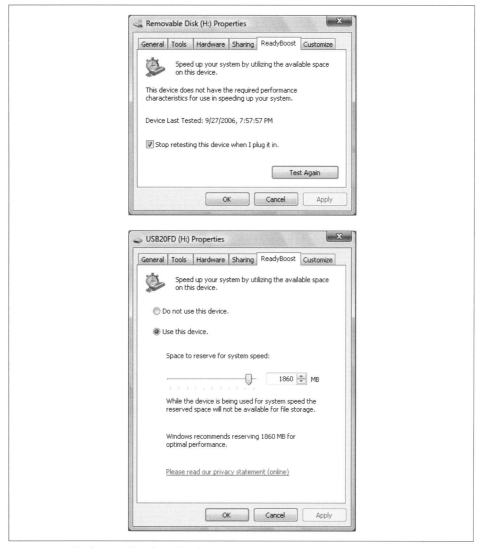

Figure 3-24. Configuring Windows ReadyBoost

4. If a similar flash device was previously determined to be incompatible with ReadyBoost, you'll need to click Test Again.

5. If the device is compatible, click "Use this device" to enable ReadyBoost.

6. Use the "Space to reserve for system speed" slider or combo box to set the amount of space to use with ReadyBoost. If you reserve less than the total amount of space available, you can use the free space for your personal files and data.

7. Click OK.

Configuring Windows ReadyBoost

Windows ReadyBoost does not have to use all available space on the USB flash device. You can also configure a specific amount of space to reserve for files and data. To do this, complete the following steps:

1. Click Start and then click Computer.

2. Right-click the USB flash device in the Devices with Removable Storage list and then choose Properties.

3. Click the ReadyBoost tab, as shown in Figure 3-24.

4. Use the "Space to reserve for system speed" slider or combo box to set the amount of space to use with ReadyBoost.

5. Click OK.

Ejecting a ReadyBoost device

You can safely remove a USB flash device that uses ReadyBoost at any time. Because Windows Vista writes to disk first and then copies data to the device, no data is lost and there is no negative impact on your computer. However, when you remove the device, your computer's performance level returns to its normal, nonboosted state. You can safely remove a USB flash device by completing these steps:

1. Click Start and then click Computer.

2. Right-click the USB flash device in the Devices with Removable Storage list and then choose Eject or Safely Remove.

CHAPTER 4

Installing, Configuring, and Maintaining Software

Most modern software and game programs have automated setup processes, making it easy to install and run your programs. Resolving problems if automated setup fails or if a program does not run as expected is not so easy, however, which is why you need a strong understanding of how software installation works and the techniques you can use to diagnose and resolve any problems you encounter.

Software Installation: What's Changed

Compared to earlier releases of Windows, the processes of installing, configuring, and maintaining software and game programs work differently in Windows Vista. Primarily, this is because of changes to:

- The way accounts are used
- The way User Account Control (UAC) works
- The removal of the Add/Remove Programs utility
- The way application access tokens are used
- The way applications write to the system locations

Unlike earlier releases of Windows, Windows Vista has only standard user accounts and administrator accounts. When you log on to Windows Vista, you use one type of account or the other, removing the gray area between these two types of accounts that was previously available through the Power Users group. In Windows Vista, the Power Users group is included only for backward compatibility, and you should use it only when you need to resolve compatibility issues.

In Windows Vista, software installation, configuration, and maintenance are processes that require elevated privileges. Because of this, only administrators can install, configure, and maintain software. As discussed in Chapter 3, elevation is a feature of UAC. Because of UAC, Windows Vista is able to detect software installation. When Windows Vista detects a software-installation-related process, it prompts for permission or consent prior to allowing you to install, configure, or maintain software on your computer.

Windows Vista does not include an Add/Remove Programs utility. Instead, it relies completely on the software and game programs themselves to provide the necessary installation features through a related Setup or Autorun program.

 Most programs created for Windows 95, Windows 98, Windows Me, Windows 2000, and Windows XP use *setup.exe* programs. Programs created for Windows Vista and later versions of Windows can use *autorun.exe* programs, particularly if those programs use current versions of Windows installers. For simplicity's sake, I'll refer to both Setup and Autorun programs as Setup programs.

Windows Vista also provides new architecture guidelines for software and game programs that fundamentally change the way software access tokens are used and the way software programs write to system locations. These changes are so far-reaching that software not specifically designed to support the new architecture guidelines is considered legacy software. This means there are two general categories of software that you can use with Windows Vista:

- Windows Vista-compliant applications
- Legacy applications

Any software written specifically for Windows Vista's new architecture guidelines is considered a compliant application and can be certified as compliant with Microsoft. Applications certified as compliant have the Windows Vista-compliant logo. Applications written for Windows Vista have access tokens that describe the privileges required to run and perform tasks. Windows Vista-compliant applications fall into two general categories:

Administrator user applications
    If an application requires elevated privileges to run and perform tasks, it is considered an administrator user application. Administrator user applications can write to system locations of the registry and filesystem.

Standard user applications
    If an application does not require elevated privileges to run and perform tasks, it is considered a standard user application. Standard user applications should write only to nonsystem locations of the registry and filesystem.

Any application written for an earlier version of Windows is considered a legacy application. Legacy applications run as standard user applications and in a special compatibility mode that provides virtualized views of file and registry locations. When a legacy application attempts to write a system location, Windows Vista gives the application a private copy of the file or registry value. Any changes are then written to the private copy, and this private copy is in turn stored in the user's profile data. If the application attempts to read or write to this system location again, it is given the private copy from the user's profile.

Software Installation: What You Need to Know

The more you understand about software installation, the better prepared you'll be to resolve problems you may encounter. Generally, the installation process starts when you trigger the AutoPlay or Autorun process. AutoPlay or Autorun in turn starts the software application's Setup program. Setup is a program responsible for managing the installation process. Part of the installation process involves validating your credentials and checking the software's compatibility with Windows Vista.

AutoPlay

AutoPlay options determine how Windows Vista handles files on CDs, DVDs, and portable devices. You can configure separate AutoPlay options for each type of CD, DVD, and media your computer can handle.

With software and games, you have the following AutoPlay options:

Install or run program
  Uses the program's Autorun file to start installing or running the program automatically.

Open folder to view files using Windows Explorer
  Opens Windows Explorer so that you can browse the CD or DVD.

Take no action
  No action is taken when Windows Vista detects the CD or DVD. You must manually start the installation process.

Ask me every time
  Displays the AutoPlay dialog box, which prompts you for an action to take, as shown in Figure 4-1.

You can configure AutoPlay options for software and games by completing the following steps:

1. Click Start → Default Programs.
2. On the Default Programs page in the Control Panel, click Change AutoPlay settings.
3. As shown in Figure 4-2, use the Software and Games list to set the default AutoPlay option to use.
4. Click Save to save your settings.

Autorun

When AutoPlay is enabled, Windows Vista checks for a file named *Autorun.inf* when you insert a CD or DVD into a CD or DVD drive. For software applications and games, this file identifies the Setup program and related installation parameters that should be used to install the software or game.

Figure 4-1. Selecting the Autorun or Setup option to install or run a program

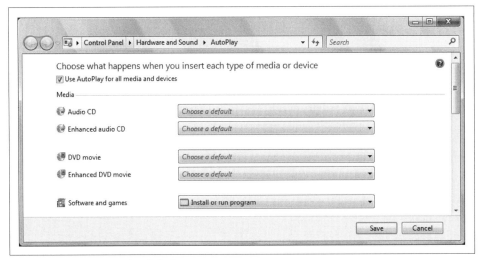

Figure 4-2. Setting AutoPlay defaults

As *Autorun.inf* is a text-based file, you can view its contents in any standard text editor, such as WordPad or Notepad. Most *Autorun.inf* files are similar to the following example:

```
[autorun]
OPEN=SETUP.EXE
ICON=SETUP.EXE,1
SHELL=OPEN
DisplayName=Microsoft Encarta 2007
```

When AutoPlay triggers this *Autorun.inf* file, Windows Vista opens a file named *Setup.exe* when the CD or DVD is inserted into the CD or DVD drive. Because *Setup.exe* is a program, Windows Vista runs this program. The *Autorun.inf* file also specifies an icon to use, the status of the shell, and the program's display name.

Although you'll usually find that an *Autorun.inf* file opens and then runs a Setup program, this isn't always the case. When AutoPlay triggers this *Autorun.inf* file, Windows Vista opens a file named *Default.htm* in Internet Explorer:

```
[autorun]
OPEN=Autorun\ShelExec default.htm
```

As long as AutoPlay is enabled, you can retrigger the AutoPlay and Autorun processes by opening and then closing the drive bay.

Application Setup

With Windows Vista, only administrators can install software. This means you must either install software using an account with administrator privileges, or provide administrator permissions when prompted. Administrator privileges are required to change, repair, and uninstall software as well.

Most software applications have a setup program that uses Windows Installer, InstallShield, or Wise Install. The job of the installer program is to track the installation process and make sure the installation completes successfully. If the installation fails, the installer is also responsible for restoring your computer to its original state by reversing all the changes the Setup program has made. While this works great in theory, you can encounter problems, particularly when you are installing older programs. Older programs won't have and won't be able to use the features of the latest versions of installer programs, and as a result, they sometimes are unable to uninstall a program completely.

Because a partially uninstalled program can spell disaster for your computer, you should protect yourself by creating a System Restore checkpoint prior to installing any software or game. By creating a restoring point, as discussed in Chapter 21, you can be sure that you can fully recover your computer to the state it was in prior to installing the software or game. This way, if you run into problems, you'll have an effective recovery strategy.

Before installing any software or game, you should do the following:

- Check whether it is compatible with Windows Vista. You can determine compatibility in several ways. You can check the software packaging, which should specify whether the program is compatible or provide a Microsoft Windows Vista logo. Alternatively, you can check the software developer's web site for a list of compatible operating systems.

- Check the software developer's web site for updates or patches for the program. If available, download the updates or patches prior to installing the software and then install them immediately after completing the software installation. Some software programs, such as Adobe Creative Suite and Microsoft Office, have automated update processes that you can use to check for updates after installing the software. In this case, after installation, run the software and then use the built-in update feature to check for updates or patches.

To avoid known compatibility issues with legacy applications, Windows Vista includes an automated detection feature known as the Program Compatibility Assistant. If the Program Compatibility Assistant detects a known compatibility issue when you run a legacy application, it notifies you about the problem and provides possible solutions for resolving the problem automatically. You can then allow the Program Compatibility Assistant to reconfigure the application for you. While the Program Compatibility Assistant is helpful, it can't detect or avoid all compatibility issues. You may have to configure compatibility manually, as discussed in the "Configuring Compatibility for Other Software" section, later in this chapter.

 You should not use the Program Compatibility Assistant or the Program Compatibility Wizard to install older virus detection, backup, or system programs. These programs may attempt to modify your computer's filesystems in a way that is incompatible with Windows Vista, and this could prevent Windows Vista from starting.

Diagnosing a problem you are having as a compatibility issue isn't always easy. For deeper compatibility issues, you may need to contact the software developer's technical support staff. Some issues even support staff may not be able to resolve without time to study the problem. Consider the following:

- When a computer manufacturer shipped computers with Windows XP, many recently purchased computers experienced infrequent "red screen" crashes. In contrast to blue screen crashes, which typically are related to operating system or hardware components, software drivers can cause a red screen crash. This problem was eventually pinpointed to an incompatibility between the firmware Basic Input Output System (BIOS) the computer was using and the software driver for certain graphics cards with a new 3D graphics feature. To resolve the problem, the computer's firmware BIOS and graphics card driver both needed to be updated.

- When a software manufacturer shipped a new version of its application suite, many recently purchased computers experienced problems starting and running the applications. After an automated update process had run, users were told their product licenses were invalid. This problem eventually was pinpointed to an incompatibility between the license-validation feature used by the application and the hard disk configuration being used by some customers. To resolve the problem, the software developers had to create an application path that let the license-validation feature work with hard disks that were mirrored.

In both examples, the compatibility issues were the direct result of technological innovation. In the first example, graphics cards implementing new 3D graphics features caused an unforeseen incompatibility with the computer's firmware. In the second example, computers increasingly began shipping with mirrored hard disks, a feature that was previously used primarily on servers, and the license-validation feature was unable to recognize and validate the software applications across the mirrored disks.

Installing and Running Your Software

Whether you are using your computer to create Word documents, view photos, or send email, you are running software that handles these tasks for you. Windows Vista's job is to provide a framework for you to install, configure, and run your software.

Installing Software

Unlike earlier releases of Windows, Windows Vista doesn't provide a tool for adding, reconfiguring, or removing software. Instead, it relies on the software itself to provide these features through a Setup program.

Most of the time installing and running your software using its Setup program is easy, and you can install your software from a CD or DVD by following these steps:

1. Insert the media disk into your computer's CD or DVD drive.

2. If Windows Vista displays the AutoPlay dialog box, click Run Setup.exe or a similar option under Install or Run Program. When Setup starts, follow the prompts to install the software, and skip the remaining steps.

3. If Windows Vista doesn't display the AutoPlay dialog box, click Start → Computer. In the Computer window, double-click the CD or DVD drive.

4. If Windows Vista detected the software's Setup program (using *Autorun.inf*), you are then prompted for permission or consent to run the Setup program.

5. If Windows Vista doesn't detect the software's Setup program, the contents of the disc are displayed in Windows Explorer. Double-click Setup.exe.

6. When Setup starts, follow the prompts to install the software.

7. Most software applications have a setup program that uses Windows Installer, InstallShield, or Wise Install. If the installation fails and the software has an installer, follow the prompts to allow the installer to restore your computer to its original state. Otherwise, exit Setup and then try rerunning Setup to either complete the installation or uninstall the program.

You can run installed software by selecting the software's menu option or double-clicking its desktop shortcut. If you run into problems installing or running the software, be sure to read the sections of this chapter titled "Configuring Software Availability," "Configuring Compatibility for MS-DOS or 16-Bit Software," and "Configuring Compatibility for Other Software."

However, not all programs have distribution media discs. If you download a program from the Internet, it'll probably be in a ZIP or self-extracting executable file, and you can install the program by following these steps:

1. Start Windows Explorer.

2. Extract the program's setup files using one of the following techniques:

   - If the program is distributed in a *.zip* file, right-click the file and select Extract All. This displays the Extract Compressed (Zipped) Folders dialog box. Click Browse, select a destination folder, and then click OK. Click Extract.

   - If the program is distributed in a self-extracting executable file, double-click the *.exe* file to extract the setup files. You'll see one of several types of prompts. If you're prompted to run the file, click Run. If you're prompted to extract the program files or select a destination folder, click Browse, select a destination folder, and then click OK. Click Extract or OK as appropriate.

3. In Windows Explorer, browse the setup folders and find the program's *Setup.exe* file. Double-click Setup.exe to start the installation process.

4. When Setup starts, follow the prompts to install the software. If the installation fails and the software used an installer, follow the prompts to allow the installer to restore your computer to its original state. Otherwise, exit Setup and then try rerunning Setup to either complete the installation or uninstall the program.

Configuring Software Availability

Most software programs written for Windows 2000 or later are made available automatically to all users on a computer. This occurs because the software writes to areas of the registry and filesystem available to all users, and because the software makes its program shortcuts available to all users. During installation, some software programs prompt you to choose whether you want to install the software for all users or only for the currently logged-on user. Other programs—typically older programs written for Windows 98 or earlier—install themselves only for the current user.

For software that requires per-user configurations, you can make the software available to multiple users by completing the following steps:

1. Log on to the computer using an account that should have access to the program.

2. Install the software using its Setup program.

3. Repeat this process for each user.

For software that doesn't require per-user configuration, you can make the software available to all users on your computer by completing the following steps:

1. Log on as the user who installed the program.

2. Right-click the Start button and select Explore. This starts Windows Explorer with the currently logged-on user's Start Menu folder selected.

3. Under Programs, right-click the folder for the program group or the shortcut you want to work with and then select Copy.

4. Right-click the Start button and select Explore All Users. This starts Windows Explorer with the Start Menu folder for all users selected.

5. Right-click Programs and then select Paste. The program group or shortcut should now be available to all users of the computer.

6. Repeat steps 2–5 as necessary to copy all the related program groups and short-cuts for the software application.

You can make a program available only to you rather than to all users by completing these steps:

1. Log on using your account.

2. Right-click the Start button and select Explore All Users. This starts Windows Explorer with the Start Menu folder for all users selected.

3. Select Programs, right-click the folder for the program group or shortcut that you want to work with, and select Cut.

4. Right-click the Start button and select Explore. This starts Windows Explorer with your Start Menu folder selected.

5. Right-click Programs and then select Paste. The program group or shortcut should now be available only to you.

6. Repeat steps 2–5 as necessary to copy all the related program groups and short-cuts for the software application.

 Moving the software's program group or shortcuts doesn't prevent other users from running the program; it simply hides the program from other users. They may still be able to start the software from Windows Explorer.

Configuring Compatibility for MS-DOS or 16-Bit Software

Windows Vista cannot run MS-DOS or 16-bit programs that require direct access to your computer's hardware or that require 16-bit drivers. Windows Vista can run only MS-DOS or 16-bit programs that don't require direct access to your computer's hardware and that don't require 16-bit drivers.

When you run an MS-DOS or 16-bit program, Windows Vista performs some compatibility tasks automatically. Under MS-DOS and 16-bit filesystems, filenames and directory names are restricted to eight characters with a three-character file extension, such as *Chapter3.txt*. This naming convention is often referred to as the 8.3 file-naming rule or the standard MS-DOS file-naming rule. MS-DOS and 16-bit folder paths are similarly restricted. On the other hand, the filesystems used with Windows Vista support long filenames with up to 255 characters. To help ensure that MS-DOS and 16-bit applications are compatible with your computer, Windows Vista translates between long and short filenames to ensure that your computer's filesystems are protected when an MS-DOS or 16-bit program modifies files and folders.

Windows Vista runs these MS-DOS and 16-bit programs using a virtual machine that mimics the 386-enhanced mode used by the original operating systems for which these programs were developed: Windows 3.0 and Windows 3.1. Unlike earlier Windows releases, Windows Vista runs multiple MS-DOS and 16-bit programs within a single virtual machine. Although each program is managed using a separate thread, all the programs share a common memory space. As a result, if one MS-DOS or 16-bit program fails, it usually means others running on the computer will fail as well.

You can help prevent one 16-bit or MS-DOS program from causing another to fail by running it in a separate memory space. Although running a program in a separate memory space uses additional memory, you'll usually find that the program is more responsive. Another added benefit is that you'll be able to run multiple instances of the program—as long as all the instances are running in separate memory spaces.

To configure a 16-bit or MS-DOS program to run in a separate memory space, complete the following steps.

1. Right-click the program's shortcut or menu option and then select Properties. This opens the program's Properties dialog box.
2. On the Shortcut tab, click the Advanced button. This displays the Advanced Properties dialog box.
3. Select the "Run in separate memory space" checkbox.
4. Click OK twice to close all open dialog boxes and save the changes.

Configuring Compatibility for Other Software

Windows Vista warns you if you try to install a program with a known compatibility issue and opens the Program Compatibility Assistant to help you resolve the problem. Sometimes, however, a program won't install or it will install but won't run, and you won't know why. To get the program to install or run you'll need to adjust its compatibility settings, and Windows Vista provides two ways of doing this:

- Using the Program Compatibility Wizard to configure compatibility settings for you
- Editing a program's compatibility settings yourself

Although both techniques work the same way, the Program Compatibility Wizard is the only way you can change compatibility settings for programs that are on shared network drives, CD or DVD drives, or other types of removable media drives. The capability to work with various types of media allows the Program Compatibility Wizard to install programs that otherwise would not install.

Running the Program Compatibility Wizard

The Program Compatibility Wizard is similar to the Program Compatibility Assistant. The key differences between the two are:

- Windows Vista runs the Program Compatibility Assistant automatically when you try to install a program with a known compatibility issue.
- The Program Compatibility Wizard is a feature that you can use if you suspect a compatibility issue is preventing you from installing or running a program.

You can start and use the Program Compatibility Wizard by completing the following steps:

1. Click Start → All Programs → Accessories and then select Program Compatibility Wizard. If this option is not available, click Start → Help and Support. In the Help and Support console, type **Program Compatibility Wizard** into the Search box and then press Enter. Click Start the Program Compatibility Wizard or a similar option and then click the "Click to open the Program Compatibility Wizard" link.

2. Read the welcome message and then click Next. As shown in Figure 4-3, specify how you want to locate the program you would like to run with compatibility settings. You can:

    Choose from a list of programs
    Typically, you'll use this option if you are configuring compatibility for a program you installed but which won't run or runs with errors. If you choose this option and click Next, Windows Vista searches your computer for all program executables and allows you to choose one of the programs it finds.

    Use the program in the CD-ROM or other removable media drive
    Typically, you'll use this option to help you install or run a program on a CD or DVD. If you choose this option and click Next, Windows Vista lets you configure compatibility options for the program in your computer's CD or DVD drive.

    Locate the program manually
    Typically, you'll choose this option if neither of the other options works, and you want to browse files and folders to find the program you want to work with. If you want to use this option, click Next and then click Browse. You can then use the Please Select Application dialog box to locate the program's executable file, which can be an *.exe*, *.com*, *.pif*, *.cmd*, *.bat*, or *.lnk* file.

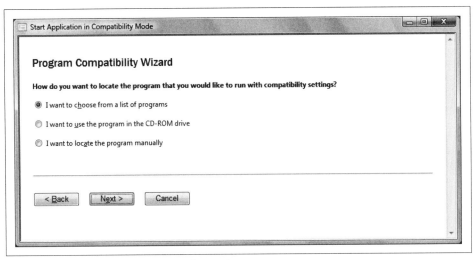

Figure 4-3. Specifying how you want to locate the program

3. Choose the operating system for which the program was designed and then click Next. When running the program, Windows Vista will simulate the environment for the operating system you choose. As Figure 4-4 indicates, the choices are:

- Windows 95
- Windows NT 4.0 with Service Pack 5
- Windows 98/Windows Me
- Windows 2000
- Windows XP with Service Pack 2

4. Choose the required display settings and then click Next. If you are trying to run a game, a multimedia program, or any other program that requires specific display settings, you'll need to specify the required display settings. As shown in Figure 4-5, these options are:

256 colors
   Restricts your computer to 8-bit, 256-color video display when running the program. This setting is often required with games, multimedia, and educational software developed for Windows 95/Windows 98.

640 x 480 screen resolution
   Resizes the screen to 640×480 pixels when you run the program. This setting is often required with games, multimedia, and educational software developed for Windows 95/Windows 98.

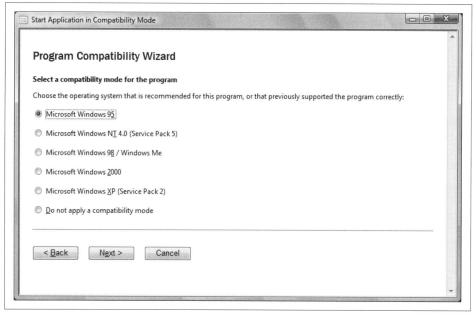

Figure 4-4. Specifying the operating system for which the program was developed

Disable visual themes

Turns off themes and user experience settings while running the program to allow text on the program's menus and buttons to display without modification. Use this option if you have problems reading or accessing menus and buttons within the program and you want the program to use Windows Vista Basic experience settings.

Disable desktop composition

Turns off desktop composition while running the program to prevent conflicts, such as those that may occur when your desktop background uses colors in one way and the program uses colors in another way. Use this option to correct problems with the display, and particularly with the way the program uses colors.

Disable display scaling on high DPI settings

Turns off scaling when your monitor uses a display setting with a high number of dots per inch (dpi). Use this option if the program's windows appear to be stretched and you want them to appear normally.

By selecting "256 colors," 640×480 Screen Resolution, or both, you are restricting the video display. This can help with programs that have problems running at higher screen resolutions and color depths. You can also disable themes, desktop compositing, and display scaling on high dpi settings.

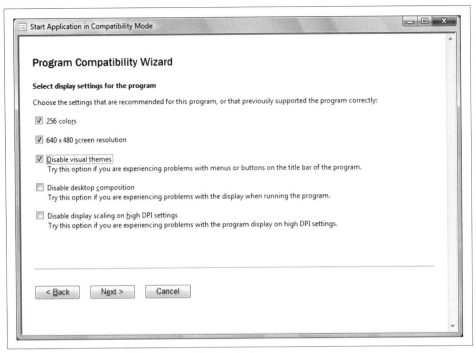

Figure 4-5. Setting compatibility options for the display

5. Many programs developed for earlier versions of Windows need to run with elevated privileges to function properly. If you suspect this is the case with the program you are configuring, and you are logged on using an Administrator
account, select the "Run as administrator" checkbox.

> If you are not logged on as an administrator, you will not be able to
> select the "Run as administrator" checkbox. Instead, when you finish
> configuring compatibility options, right-click the program's menu
> item or shortcut and then select Properties. In the Properties dialog
> box, click the Compatibility tab, select the "Run this program as an
> administrator" checkbox, and then click OK. The program will then
> always attempt to run elevated privileges and prompt you for permis-
> sion or consent as appropriate. If the "Run this program as an admin-
> istrator" checkbox is dimmed, you are not logged on as an
> administrator. You can work around this by clicking the "Show set-
> tings for all users" button and providing credentials when prompted.
> You will then be able to configure compatibility options for all users
> and select the "Run this program as an administrator" checkbox.

6. Click Next twice. The wizard will then run the program to test the compatibility settings. When this process finishes, you are prompted to specify whether the program worked correctly. You have three options:

Yes, set this program to always use these compatibility settings
> Click this option if the program runs correctly and you want to use the compatibility settings you configured.

No, try different compatibility settings
> Click this option if the program doesn't run correctly and you want to change the compatibility settings starting with step 3.

No, I am finished trying compatibility settings
> Click this option if the program doesn't run correctly and you want to exit the wizard rather than trying to use different compatibility settings.

 If your computer's display settings are reset, don't panic. Click Start → Control Panel. In the Control Panel, click Adjust Screen Resolution under Appearance and Personalization. Click the Display Settings dialog box and drag it up so that you can see the OK, Cancel, and Apply buttons. Drag the Resolution slider to the right, choosing an appropriate higher resolution. The colors should adjust upward automatically. Click OK. If these settings improve the display, click Yes when prompted to save the settings. If necessary, access the Display Settings dialog box again to fine-tune your display settings.

7. Click Next. Choose whether to send compatibility data to Microsoft. Click Next and then click Finish to exit the wizard.

Setting compatibility options manually

Rather than using the Program Compatibility Wizard, you can manually configure compatibility settings. This is handy if you want to edit the settings after you configured them using the wizard.

You can set compatibility options manually by completing the following steps:

1. Right-click the program's shortcut icon and then select Properties.

2. Select the Compatibility tab, as shown in Figure 4-6. You cannot run programs that are part of the Windows Vista operating system in compatibility mode. Because of this, the options are unavailable for built-in programs.

3. By default, compatibility options you set are for yourself only. If you want to set compatibility options for all users, click the "Show settings for all users" button, and provide consent or credentials when prompted. You will then be able to configure compatibility options for all users.

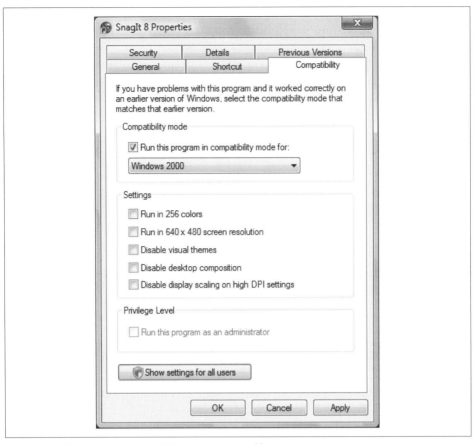

Figure 4-6. Choosing the compatibility options to enable

4. Select the "Run this program in compatibility mode for" checkbox and then use the selection menu to choose the operating system for which the program is designed.

5. Optionally, use the options in the Settings panel to restrict the video display settings for the program. Select 256 colors, 640×480 screen resolution, or both, as required.

6. Optionally, disable themes, desktop compositing, display scaling on high dpi settings, or all three, as required.

7. Select the "Run as administrator" checkbox if you want the program to run elevated.

8. Click OK. Double-click the shortcut to run the program and test the compatibility settings. If you still have problems running the program, you might need to modify the compatibility settings again.

Managing Software Once It's Installed

Installing software is only one part of software management. Often after you install software, you'll need to make configuration changes to your computer or the software itself. You may want files of a certain type to open in the software when you click or double-click the files in Windows Explorer. You may need to reconfigure, repair, or uninstall the software. Alternatively, you may need to resolve problems with the way the software starts or runs. I discuss all of these tasks in the sections that follow.

Assigning Default Programs

When you install productivity applications, such as Microsoft Word or Adobe Photoshop, the installation process may configure your computer so that certain types of files automatically open in the application when you click or double-click it in Windows Explorer. The installation process may also configure your computer so that when you insert media containing music, video, or pictures, the media is opened and played automatically using a particular application.

Associating an application with particular file types and running an application for certain types of media are separate features. You make files with a specific extension or type open in a specific program by associating the file extension or type with the program. You make media on CDs, DVDs, or portable devices open and play in a particular program by making a program the default for AutoPlay.

You configure file associations and default programs either only for yourself or globally for all users of your computer. Your individual default settings override global default settings. For example, you might want Apple iTunes to be your default audio player, but the global default for all users could be set to use Windows Media Player.

Setting your default programs

You can configure your default programs by completing the following steps:

1. Click Start and then click Default Programs.
2. Click "Set your default programs."
3. As shown in Figure 4-7, select a program you want to work with from the Programs list.
4. If you want the program to be the default for all the file types and protocols it supports, click "Set this program as default" and click OK. Skip the remaining steps.
5. If you want the program to be the default for specific file types and protocols, click "Choose defaults for this program."
6. As shown in Figure 4-8, select the file extensions and protocols for which the program should be the default.
7. Click Save.

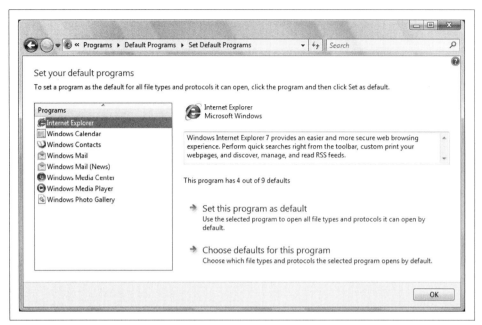

Figure 4-7. Selecting the program you want to work with

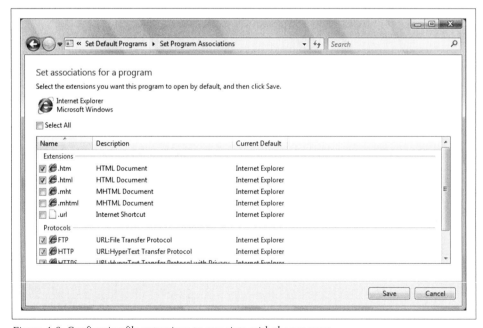

Figure 4-8. Configuring file extensions to associate with the program

Setting global default programs

You can configure global default programs—default programs for all the users of your computer—by completing the following steps:

1. Log on to your computer using an account with administrator privileges.

2. Click Start and then click Default Programs. Click Set Program Access and Computer Defaults.

3. As shown in Figure 4-9, choose a configuration from one of the following options:

    Microsoft Windows

    Sets the currently installed Microsoft Windows programs as the defaults for web browsing, sending and receiving email, playing media files, instant messaging, and Java Virtual Machine support.

    Enables access to other programs. If you've installed other programs, you can configure your computer to use the currently installed program for a particular task. For example, if you installed Microsoft Office, Microsoft Outlook is configured automatically for use as your default email program. To change this, you would click the "E-mail program" list and choose Windows Mail or another program.

    Non-Microsoft

    Sets the currently installed non-Microsoft Windows programs as the defaults for web browsing, sending and receiving email, playing media files, instant messaging, and Java Virtual Machine support.

    Removes access to Microsoft Windows programs if you've configured non-Microsoft Windows programs as the defaults. For example, if you installed Mozilla as your web browser and set this as the default, the Non-Microsoft option removes access to Internet Explorer.

    Custom

    Enables you to choose programs as the defaults for web browsing, sending and receiving email, playing media files, instant messaging, and Java Virtual Machine support.

    Each program available to use as a default has a related "Enable access to this program" checkbox. If you clear this checkbox, you remove access to the program when a viable alternative is installed.

4. Click OK to save your settings.

Reconfiguring, Repairing, or Uninstalling Software

Once you install software, you can manage its installation using the Programs and Features page in the Control Panel. More than any other version of Windows, Windows Vista takes advantage of the features of the installer program used with your software. This means you'll have more configuration options than you otherwise would.

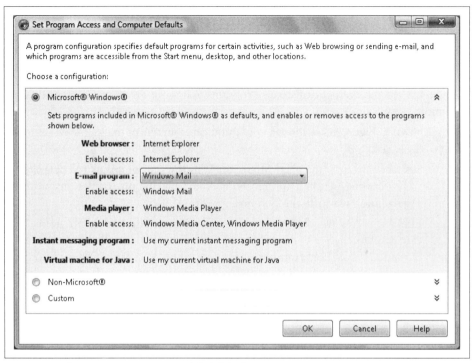

Figure 4-9. Choosing your computer's global defaults

For example, previously, most software allowed you to rerun Setup to uninstall the program but didn't necessarily allow you to rerun Setup to change or repair the software. Windows Vista surfaces these features to make it easier to manage your software.

You can use the Programs and Features page to reconfigure, repair, or uninstall software by following these steps:

1. Click Start → Control Panel.

2. In the Control Panel, click Uninstall a Program under Programs.

3. In the Name list, click the program you want to work with and then select one of the following options on the toolbar:

   • Change, to modify the program's configuration

   • Repair, to repair the program's installation

   • Uninstall, to uninstall the program

   • Uninstall/Change, to uninstall or change a program with an older installer program

Viewing and Managing Currently Running Programs

Software Explorer is a handy tool for working with your computer's programs. You can start Software Explorer by clicking Start → All Programs → Windows Defender. On the Windows Defender toolbar, click Tools → Software Explorer.

As shown in Figure 4-10, you can use Software Explorer to view and manage your computer's currently running programs and processes by selecting Currently Running Programs on the Category list. In the Name list, Software Explorer lists programs by name according to the software publisher. The process ID number of the main process under which the program is running follows the program name.

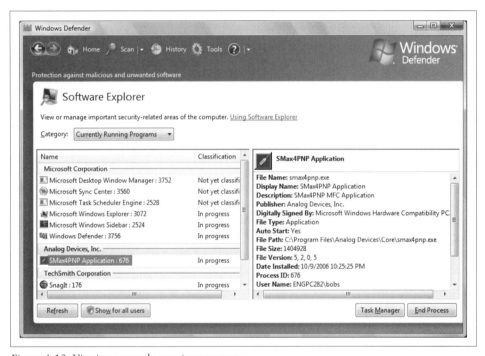

Figure 4-10. Viewing currently running programs

You can use Software Explorer to work with your running programs in several ways. You can view details about a running program's configuration by clicking the program in the left pane. Table 4-1 provides an overview of the summary details provided for running programs.

Table 4-1. An overview of configuration details for running programs

Configuration aspect	Description
Auto Start	Lists whether the program is configured as a startup program
Classification	Lists the classification of the executable file as either permitted or not permitted
Date Installed	Lists the date and time that the file was installed
Description	Lists a description of the application
Digitally Signed By	Lists the company that digitally signed the program's executable file
Display Name	Lists the application name that Windows Vista uses
File Name	Lists the executable filename
File Path	Lists the complete file path to the executable file
File Size	Lists the size of the executable file in bytes
File Type	Lists the type of file listed in the File Name field, such as whether a file is an application file or an application extension file
File Version	Lists the version and revision numbers of the executable file
Process ID	Lists the ID number of the main process under which the program is running
Publisher	Lists the company that published the software
Ships with Operating System	Lists whether the executable file ships with the operating system
User Name	Lists the name of the user or system account under which the program is running

You can also use Software Explorer to stop a program, which may be necessary, for instance, if a program is not responding and you want to quit the program. While you can view and work with currently running programs you started, you must have administrator permission to view and work with running programs started by other user or system accounts. To view currently running programs for other users and the operating system, click "Show for all users." When prompted, provide consent or credentials. You'll then be able to view and work with all running programs and processes.

When you select a program or process in the left pane, you can terminate the process by clicking End Process and then clicking Yes when prompted to confirm the action. When you click the Task Manager button, Windows Vista opens Task Manager. You can also open Task Manager by pressing Ctrl-Alt-Delete.

As Figure 4-11 shows, Task Manager has two tabs for working with running programs:

Applications
> Lists applications you are currently running by name and status, such as Running or Not Responding. To exit a program, click the program in the Task list and then click End Task.

Processes
> Lists all programs and processes you are running on the computer by image name, your username, and resource usage. To stop a process, click the process and then click End Process.

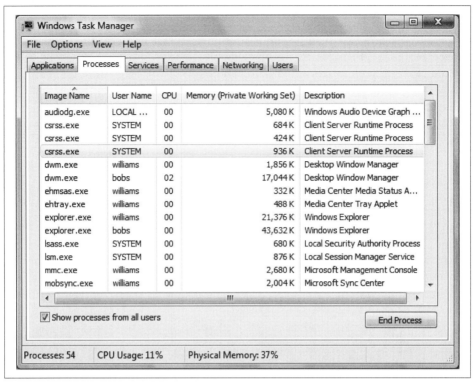

Figure 4-11. Accessing processes in Task Manager

By default, Task Manager's Processes tab shows only your running processes. To see running processes for all users, you must click "Show processes from all users" and provide consent or credentials when prompted. You'll then see all processes running on the computer. You will also be able to right-click processes and select from an extended list of management options, including:

Open File Location
> Opens the folder containing the executable file for the process in Windows Explorer

End Process Tree
> Stops the process and all dependent processes

Create Dump File
> Creates a memory dump file for the selected process

Properties
> Opens the Properties dialog box for the executable file

Viewing and Managing Startup Programs

Some software programs you install, such as antivirus or backup software, are configured as startup programs. As the name implies, startup programs run in the background and start automatically when you log on. You can view the currently configured startup programs using Software Explorer. Software Explorer also allows you to enable, disable, or remove startup programs.

Viewing your startup programs

You can open Software Explorer and view your startup programs by completing the following steps:

1. Click Start, click All Programs, and then click Windows Defender.

2. On the Windows Defender toolbar, click Tools and then click Software Explorer.

3. In Software Explorer, the Startup Programs option is selected in the Category list by default. When you click a program in the left pane, details about the program's configuration are displayed in the right pane, as shown in Figure 4-12.

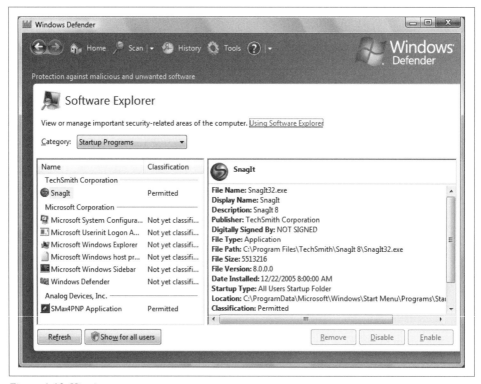

Figure 4-12. Viewing your startup programs

Table 4-2 provides a summary of the configuration details for startup programs.

Table 4-2. Overview of configuration details for startup programs

Configuration aspect	Description
Classification	Lists the classification of the executable file as either permitted or not permitted
Date Installed	Lists the date and time that the file was installed
Description	Lists a description of the application
Digitally Signed By	Lists the company that digitally signed the program's executable file
Display Name	Lists the application name that Windows Vista uses
File Name	Lists the executable filename
File Path	Lists the complete file path to the executable file
File Size	Lists the size of the executable file in bytes
File Type	Lists the type of file listed in the File Name field, such as whether a file is an application file or an application extension file
File Version	Lists the version and revision numbers of the executable file
Location	Lists the folder path where the startup program shortcut was created, or the Run registry key value
Publisher	Lists the company that published the software
Ships with Operating System	Lists whether the executable file ships with the operating system
Startup Type	Lists how you have configured the program to start automatically, such as whether the startup program is in the Startup folder for all users or is in your personal Startup folder
Startup Value	Lists the options or parameters passed to the program at startup

Enabling, disabling, and removing your startup programs

You can configure startup programs for your account specifically or for all users on your computer, depending on whether you installed a program only for your use or for all users. You have three options for managing startup programs. You can:

Disable automatic startup
> If you don't want a program to start automatically when you log on, you can disable it. A disabled startup program will no longer run on startup.

Enable automatic startup
> If you previously disabled a startup program, you can change this by enabling the program to run at startup.

Remove
> If you no longer need a startup program or you want to prevent it from being enabled in the future, you can remove it.

 Before you remove a startup program, you should first disable it. You should then restart your computer and determine whether there is any negative impact on your computer.

While you can enable, disable, and remove startup programs from your account and you may not need administrator permissions, you must have administrator permissions to manage startup programs configured for other, or all, users on your computer.

You can enable, disable, and remove startup programs by following these steps:

1. Click Start, click All Programs, and then click Windows Defender.

2. On the Windows Defender toolbar, click Tools and then click Software Explorer.

3. In Software Explorer, the Startup Programs option is selected in the Category list by default. Click a startup program in the left pane.

4. If the program is configured as a startup program for your account, you can enable, disable, or remove it using the option buttons provided.

5. If the program is configured as a startup program for another user or for all users, the Remove, Disable, and Enable buttons will be dimmed so that you cannot select them. Before you can use these options, you must click "Show for all users," and then provide consent or credentials when prompted.

6. If you are disabling or removing a startup program, you will need to confirm this when prompted by clicking Yes.

Viewing and Managing Network-Connected Programs

As Figure 4-13 shows, you view programs that are connecting to the local area network (LAN), the Internet, or both by selecting the Network Connected Programs option on the Category list in Software Explorer. In the Name list, programs are listed by name according to the software publisher. The process ID number of the main process under which the program is running follows the program name.

You can use Software Explorer to work with your network-connected programs in several ways. You can view details about a network-connected program's configuration by clicking the program in the left pane. The details provided for Winsock service providers include similar details to running programs. Additional details you'll see include:

Foreign Address
Lists the remote Internet Protocol (IP) address and port number being used by a particular protocol (if any)

Local Address
Lists the local IP address and port number being used by a particular protocol (if any)

Protocol
Lists the Transmission Control Protocol/Internet Protocol (TCP/IP) being used by the program

State
Lists the state of the port being used, such as whether it is listening for incoming requests

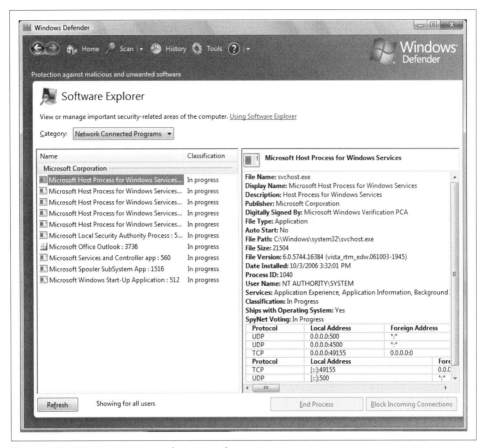

Figure 4-13. Viewing your network-connected programs

You can also use Software Explorer to stop or block incoming connections to a network-connected program. While you can view and work with network-connected programs you started, you must have administrator permission to view and work with network-connected programs started by other user or system accounts. To view network-connected programs for other users and the operating system, click "Show for all users." When prompted, provide consent or credentials. You'll then be able to view and work with all network-connected programs.

When you select a program or process in the left pane, you can terminate the process by clicking End Process and then clicking Yes when prompted to confirm the action. When you select a program and then click Block Incoming Connections, you can prevent network users from connecting to the program.

Viewing and Managing Local Service Providers

In Software Explorer, you view programs that are acting as local service providers for Winsock by selecting the Winsock Service Providers option in the Category list. In the Name list, Software Explorer lists Winsock providers by name according to the software publisher. The program name is followed by or includes the protocol the provider uses, such as TCP/IP.

When you select a local service provider, you can view that program's configuration details in the right pane (see Figure 4-14). The details provided for Winsock service providers include similar details to running programs. Additional details you'll see include:

LSP Type
> Lists the type of provider, such as Transport Provider

GUID
> Lists the Globally Unique Identifier (GUID) of the provider

Special Path
> Lists the device path the program is using for Winsock communications, if applicable

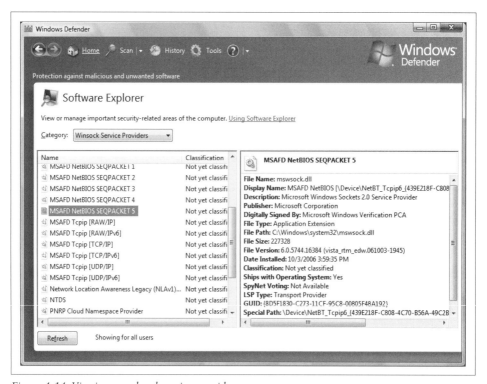

Figure 4-14. Viewing your local service providers

While you can view and work with local service providers started under your user account, you must have administrator permission to view and work with local service providers started by other user or system accounts. To view local service providers for other users and the operating system, click "Show for all users." When prompted, provide consent or credentials. You'll then be able to view and work with all local service providers.

Adding and Removing Windows Features

In earlier versions of Windows, you use the Add/Remove Windows Components option of the Add or Remove Programs utility to add and remove operating system components. In Windows Vista, operating system components are considered Windows features that can be turned on and off rather than added and removed.

Table 4-3 provides a complete list of available Windows features and their uses. The table also denotes the default on or off state for Windows Vista editions that support the feature.

Table 4-3. Windows features

Windows feature	Description	Default configuration
ActiveX Installer Services	Enables the ActiveX Installer Services, which you can use to install software based on policy settings.	Off
Games	Enables the games included with the operating systems. You can select the Games option to install all available games, or expand the Games node to select individual games. Games available include Chess Titans, FreeCell, Hearts, Inkball, Mahjong Titans, Minesweeper, Purble Place, Solitaire, and Spider Solitaire.	On
Indexing Service	Windows Vista uses the Windows Search service for content indexing and property caching of documents. If you are using your computer to provide web server services, you can enable Indexing Services for backward compatibility with search features used in your web pages.	Off
Internet Information Services	Windows Vista includes Internet Information Services 7. You can use this option and its related sub-options to configure FTP, web, and application services.	On for partial subset
Microsoft .NET Framework 3.0	Enables .NET Framework 3.0, a comprehensive framework for client-server communications over a network. Some features in the operating system require the related XPS viewer. If you install applications that require the Windows Communication Foundation APIs, you can enable the related options.	On for XPS Viewer
Microsoft Message Queue (MSMQ) Server	Enables a server service that allows queuing for web applications.	Off

Table 4-3. Windows features (continued)

Windows feature	Description	Default configuration
Print Services	Enables network printing services. Use Internet Printing Client to enable your computer to use HTTP to connect to a web print server. Use LPD Print Service to enable your computer to work as a Line Printer Daemon and Remote Line Printer client. Use LPR Port Monitor to enable your computer to print to TCP/IP printers connected to a Unix server.	On for Internet Printing Client
Remote Differential Compression	Enables your computer to transfer the differences between two objects over the network. This option is used primarily with Group Policy and domain configurations to reduce network bandwidth usage.	On
Removable Storage Management	Enables management and cataloging of removable media. Also allows you to operate automated removable media devices, such as a tape library device.	Off
RIP Listener	Enables your computer to listen to route updates sent by routers that use Routing Information Protocol Version 1 (RIPv1).	Off
Services for NFS	Enables your computer to participate in file sharing using the Network File Sharing (NFS) protocol. Use Client for NFS if your office network has NFS shares.	Off
Simple TCPIP Services	Enables simple TCP/IP services, such as echo and daytime. These services may open your computer to attack and are not recommended for use with Windows Vista.	Off
SNMP Feature	Enables Simple Network Management Protocol (SNMP) agents that monitor the activity of network devices and create reports of this activity. Use Windows Imaging Format (WMI) SNMP Provider only if you are an administrator who uses SNMP administration tools for monitoring network activities.	Off
Tablet PC Optional Components	Enables optional components normally used with Tablet computers including the Input Panel, Snipping Tool, Sticky Notes, and Windows Journal.	On for Tablet PCs
Telnet Client	Enables your computer to connect to other computers using Telnet.	Off
Telnet Server	Enables your computer to receive Telnet connections from other computers.	Off
TFTP Client	Enables your computer to connect to other computers using TFTP.	Off
Windows DFS Replication Services	Enables your computer to replicate files to other computers and in this way keep your offline files in sync.	On
Windows Fax and Scan	Enables your computer to send, receive, and manage faxes, and to scan and manage documents.	On

Table 4-3. Windows features (continued)

Windows feature	Description	Default configuration
Windows Meeting Space	Enables Windows Meeting Space, which you can use for collaboration and virtual meetings.	On
Windows Process Activation Service	Installs the .NET environment, configuration APIs, and process model for the Windows Process Activation Service.	On
Windows Ultimate Extras	Installs the extra programs for Windows Ultimate Edition.	On

You can turn Windows features on and off by following these steps:

1. Click Start → Control Panel.

2. In the Control Panel, click Programs.

3. Click "Turn Windows features on or off." This displays the Windows Features dialog box, as shown in Figure 4-15.

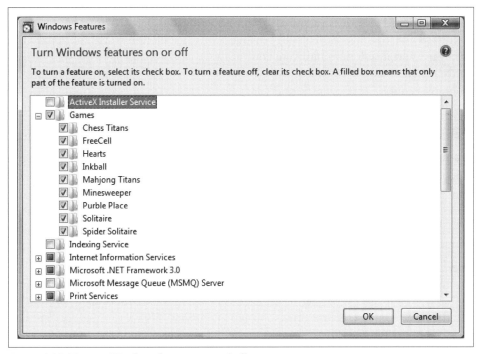

Figure 4-15. Turning Windows features on and off

4. To turn features on, select feature checkboxes. To turn features off, clear feature checkboxes.

5. When you click OK, Windows Vista reconfigures components as appropriate for any changes you've made. You may need your original installation media.

CHAPTER 5

Customizing Your Computer's Hardware Devices

One of the most frustrating aspects of working with computers is that just about every computer has different hardware devices. Even computers from the same manufacturer may have different motherboards, disk controllers, video cards, and network adapters. Like its predecessors, Windows Vista has an extensive list of compatible hardware devices and also supports Plug and Play. Helping you navigate your hardware options, understand how hardware installation works, optimize your hardware, and install new hardware is what this chapter is all about. As you'll learn, hardware has changed considerably in the past few years and there are many important new options.

Hardware Installation: What's Changed

Hardware installation from Windows XP to Windows Vista hasn't changed much. What has changed significantly since Windows XP was introduced is the array of options when it comes to hardware devices. Whether you are installing new hardware in your existing computer or getting acquainted with the types of hardware available for a computer you've recently purchased, it's important to consider your options carefully. All computers can use two types of hardware:

Internal hardware devices

Internal hardware devices are devices you install inside your computer. Typically, you'll need to power down and unplug your computer, and then remove the computer case before you can install an internal device.

External hardware devices

External hardware devices are devices you connect to your computer. Because you don't have to open your computer's case to connect external devices, you typically don't need to power down or unplug your computer before installing an external device.

The bulk of the message-board posts I see regarding hardware relate to the following:

- Which type of internal device is the right choice?
- Which type of external device is the right choice?

You'll find answers to these questions in the sections that follow.

Which Type of Internal Device Is the Right Choice?

When it comes to internal devices, the right type of device to use is typically the device your computer is designed to work with. Most current computers use internal devices with one of the following interfaces:

EIDE

Enhanced Integrated Drive Electronics (EIDE), also called Parallel ATA (PATA), devices have been the standard in the home computer industry for many years. Although EIDE is still in wide use at the time of this writing, you may find that some newer computers don't have EIDE input ports. To add support for EIDE devices, you can install a PCI EIDE controller card.

SATA

Serial ATA (SATA) devices are becoming increasingly popular. As of the time this book was written, most motherboard manufacturers include SATA input ports on their boards. Because SATA cables are significantly smaller than EIDE cables, this results in less clutter inside your computer and improved airflow for better cooling. While some older computer system motherboards don't have SATA input ports, you can install a PCI SATA controller card to add support for SATA drives.

You can use Windows Vista with both EIDE and SATA hardware devices, and it doesn't really matter to the operating system which type of device you use. Your computer, on the other hand, must be configured specifically to work with EIDE, SATA, or both. If you don't know whether your computer has EIDE or SATA ports on the motherboard, you can look at the type of cables being used inside your computer. As Figure 5-1 shows, EIDE cables and SATA cables are very different.

Figure 5-1. Comparing EIDE and SATA cables

There are some feature differences between EIDE and SATA that you should know about. Most EIDE devices support a maximum data transfer rate of 100 Mb per second and allow two devices to be connected per cable. Most EIDE devices have a 10-pin jumper block, which configures whether the device is being used in a single device or Primary (Master)/Secondary (Slave) configuration. The pins on the jumper block are also used to configure cable selection settings.

Most SATA devices have a maximum data transfer rate of 150 or 300 Mb per second and allow only one device to be connected per cable. Most SATA devices have an 8-pin jumper block and there are no Primary (Master)/Secondary (Slave) configurations.

Which Type of External Device Is the Right Choice?

You connect external devices to your computer rather than installing them inside your computer. This makes external devices easier to install and means you can attach most external devices without having to reboot your computer. It's not so easy, however, to understand the various and similar-looking interfaces available with external devices. Most current computers use external devices with one of the following interfaces:

Universal Serial Bus (USB)

USB 2.0 is the industry-standard peripheral connection for most Windows-based computers. This connection transfers data at a maximum rate of 480 Mb per second, with sustained data transfer rates usually from 10 to 30 Mb per second. The actual sustainable transfer rate depends on many factors, including the type of device, the data you are transferring, and the speed of your computer. Each USB controller on your computer has a fixed amount of bandwidth, which all devices attached to the controller must share. If your computer's USB port is an earlier version—USB 1.0 or 1.1—you can use USB 2.0 devices, but the transfer rates will be significantly slower. To add support for USB 2.0 devices, you can install a PCI USB 2.0 controller card.

FireWire

FireWire, also called IEEE 1394, is a high-performance connection standard for most Windows-based computers. This interface uses a peer-to-peer architecture in which peripherals negotiate bus conflicts to determine which device can best control a data transfer. FireWire has several configurations, including FireWire 400 and FireWire 800. FireWire 400, also called IEEE 1394a, has maximum sustained transfer rates of up to 400 Mb per second and is suitable for hard drives, digital video, professional audio, high-end digital cameras, and home entertainment devices. FireWire 800, also called IEEE 1394b, has maximum sustained transfer rates of up to 800 Mb per second and is suitable for the high-speed connection and bandwidth required for multiple-stream, uncompressed digital video and high-resolution digital audio. To add support for FireWire devices, you can install a PCI FireWire controller card.

Although you can use Windows Vista with both USB and FireWire hardware devices, your computer must be configured specifically to work with USB, FireWire, or both. Most computers have USB, FireWire, or both ports that are accessible in the front of the computer as well as additional USB, FireWire, or both ports accessible from the back of the computer. You'll also find that newer monitors have USB, FireWire, or both ports to which you can connect devices as well. Figure 5-2 shows the types of cable connectors and ports that are used with USB and FireWire.

Figure 5-2. Matching up USB and FireWire options

When working with USB, there are some important things to know. First, USB 1.0, 1.1, and 2.0 ports all look alike. To determine which types of USB ports your computer has, refer to the documentation that came with it. This documentation should list the types of USB ports and their locations. With an older computer, you will typically find USB 1.0 ports. Other computers may have a mixture of USB 1.1 and USB 2.0 ports. For example, your computer's high-end or professional-quality sound/video card may have a USB 2.0 port, while the rest of the USB ports on your computer are using USB 1.1.

Newer computers will typically have USB 2.0 ports. Newer LCD monitors will have USB 2.0 ports to which you can connect devices as well. When you have USB devices connected to a monitor, the monitor acts like a USB hub device. As with any USB hub device, all devices attached to the hub share the same bandwidth, and the total available bandwidth is determined by the speed of the USB input to which the hub is connected on your computer.

 If you don't know the version of your computer's USB ports and you don't have documentation for your computer, don't worry. I'll tell you about some tricks you can use to determine the USB version of your computer's ports a little later in this chapter, in the section titled "Viewing Installed Hardware."

When working with FireWire, there are some important things to know as well. First, FireWire 400 and FireWire 800 ports and cables have different shapes, making it easy to tell the difference between them—if you know what you're looking for. With that said, FireWire 400 ports and cables look exactly like early versions of FireWire that were implemented prior to the finalization of the IEEE 1394a and IEEE 1394b specifications.

Early FireWire implementations, which I'll call standard FireWire (as opposed to the FireWire, FireWire 100, or FireWire 200 designation), have a different number of pins on their connector cables and a different number of connectors on their ports. Because of this, you can tell standard FireWire and FireWire 400 apart by looking closely at the cables and ports. If you look closely at standard FireWire cables and ports, you'll see four pins or four connectors. If you look closely at FireWire 400 cables and ports, you'll see six pins or six connectors. FireWire 400 cables may also be slightly thicker than standard FireWire cables (because they have more wires and require more shielding than standard FireWire).

When you are purchasing an external device for your computer, you'll also want to consider how easy it is to connect the device to different systems. Although just about all Windows-based computers have USB 1.0 or higher ports, not all computers have FireWire ports. Because of this, if you are purchasing an external device for use at home and at the office, you may want to get a device that supports USB. For a bit more money, you also may be able to get a device with a dual interface that supports USB 2.0 and FireWire 400, or a triple interface that supports USB 2.0, FireWire 400, and Fire-Wire 800. A device with dual or triple interfaces will give you more options.

Hardware Installation: What You Need to Know

Each hardware device installed on your computer has an associated device driver. The device driver tells the operating system how to use the hardware abstraction layer (HAL) to work with the related hardware device. The HAL in turn performs the low-level communications with the hardware device. When you install a hardware device through the operating system, you are essentially telling the operating system about the device driver it uses, and this is what allows the operating system to work with the device.

When you are installing hardware devices and working with device drivers, you need to know:

- Where the operating system stores device drivers
- How the operating system validates device drivers
- When the operating system checks for driver updates

You'll find answers to these questions in the sections that follow.

Where Does the Operating System Store Device Drivers?

Windows Vista has an extensive library of device drivers, which are maintained in the driver store. You'll find the driver store in the *%SystemRoot%\System32\DriverStore* folder. Within the driver store, you'll find subfolders with localized driver information for each language component configured on the system. For example, for localized U.S. English driver information, you'll find a subfolder called *en-US*.

The driver store also has a file repository containing nearly ten thousand files that support tens of thousands of different devices. The file repository is located in the *%SystemRoot%\System32\DriverStore\FileRepository* folder. The purpose of the file repository is to be the main storage location for device drivers. As you install updates and service packs for the operating system, you may also be updating or changing driver information files in the file repository.

Microsoft has certified every device driver in the driver store to be fully compatible with Windows Vista. These drivers are also digitally signed by Microsoft to ensure their authenticity. When you install a Plug and Play hardware device, Windows Vista checks the driver store for a compatible device driver. If a device driver is found, Windows Vista automatically installs the device.

In the file repository, device drivers are organized by device class. In the various sub-folders, you'll find *.inf* and *.sys* files for each device driver. You may also find *.man* and *.dll* files for drivers.

All device drivers have an associated Setup Information file, which ends with the *.inf* extension. The *.inf* file is a text file containing detailed configuration information about particular classes of devices or a related set of devices. As an example, the *msmouse.inf* file has driver information for logical serial mouse and logical PS/2 mouse devices from Microsoft (see Figure 5-3).

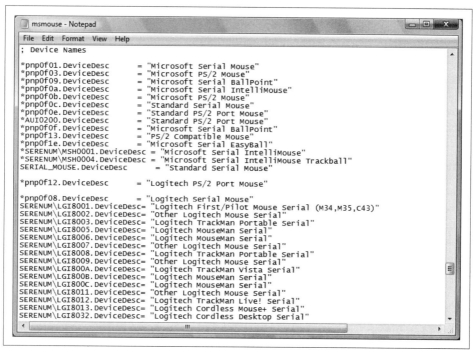

Figure 5-3. Viewing the devices associated with the driver file

The driver information file specifies the basic configuration settings for the HAL and identifies any source or linked library files that the device should use. Source files have the *.sys* extension. Linked library files have the *.dl* extension. Some drivers also have associated component manifest (*component.man*) files. Component manifest files are written in eXtensible Markup Language (XML). They include details on the driver's digital signature and can include Plug and Play information used by the device to configure itself automatically.

All drivers installed on the operating system have a source *.sys* file in the *%SystemRoot%\System32\Drivers* folder. Within the Drivers folder, you'll find subfolders with localized driver source files for each language component configured on the system. For example, for localized U.S. English driver source files, you'll find a subfolder called *en-US*.

Following this, the key folders used with drivers on a computer localized for U.S. English are:

- *%SystemRoot%\System32\DriverStore*
- *%SystemRoot%\System32\DriverStore\en-US*
- *%SystemRoot%\System32\DriverStore\FileRepository*
- *%SystemRoot%\System32\Drivers*
- *%SystemRoot%\System32\Drivers\en-US*

When you install a device driver, the driver is written to a subfolder of *%SystemRoot%\System32\Drivers* and configuration settings are stored in the registry. The driver's *.inf* file is used to control the installation and write the registry settings. If the driver doesn't already exist in the driver store, it does not already have an *.inf* file or other related files on the system. In this case, the driver's *.inf* file and other related files are written to a subfolder of *%SystemRoot%\System32\DriverStore\ FileRepository* when you install the device.

How Does the Operating System Validate Device Drivers?

Microsoft validates drivers using compatibility testing. Every device driver in the driver store is included because it passed extensive testing by the Windows Hardware Quality Lab. Once a device driver has been tested, Microsoft makes it possible to authenticate drivers by digitally signing them to prevent them from being tampered with. Because any changes to a signed driver void the digital signature, you can be sure that any device driver digitally signed by Microsoft is valid and authentic. Further, any device driver with a valid digital signature signed by Microsoft should not cause your system to crash or become unstable.

Drivers can also be digitally signed by their manufacturers. When a manufacturer digitally signs a driver, the manufacturer is giving proof of the driver's authenticity but not necessarily that it is 100 percent compatible with Windows Vista. Still, as with drivers signed by Microsoft, any changes to a device driver signed by a manufacturer invalidate the digital signature, giving you a clear indication that a device driver has been tampered with.

Because unsigned drivers have been neither validated nor authenticated, they are much more likely than any other device driver or program you've installed to cause the operating system to freeze or your computer to crash. This is why Windows Vista warns you by default when you try to install a device with an unsigned device driver. You can also configure Windows to eliminate this warning or to prevent unsigned drivers from being installed.

Unlike Windows XP, you can only manage device driver settings through Group Policy. In Group Policy, you can configure device-driver-signing settings using the "Code signing for device drivers" policy (see Figure 5-4). This policy is located in *User Configuration\Administrative Templates\System\Driver Installation*. When you enable this policy, you can specify the action to take as Ignore, Warn, or Block. These settings are used as follows:

Ignore
Allows you to install any unsigned driver without having to see and respond to a warning prompt

Warn
Prompts you each time to continue with the installation of an unsigned driver or to stop the installation

Block
Prevents you from accidentally or purposefully installing unsigned driver software

You'll learn more about Group Policy in Chapter 26.

How Does the Operating System Obtain Driver Updates?

As you'll learn in Chapter 20, Windows Vista uses a feature called Windows Update to keep the operating system, its components and services, and related Microsoft software up to date. You can configure Windows Update to obtain updates for device drivers. If you do this, Windows Vista checks for driver updates as part of the normal update process.

Because Windows Update only updates device drivers included with the operating system, any devices you've installed that have their own device drivers are not necessarily updated in this way. Still, driver information files do contain information about particular classes of devices or related sets of devices, so it is possible that as manufacturers introduce new models of hardware devices, support for these newer devices will be added through the update process. This is one of the reasons why when you connect a new device, Windows Vista checks for a matching driver automatically using Windows Update.

Figure 5-4. Setting the desired code signing option

As long as your computer is connected to the Internet when you install a new device, this check is automatic and transparent. If you don't want Windows Vista to check for drivers automatically, or you want Windows Vista to notify you before checking for drivers, you can change the default Windows Update Driver settings by completing the following steps:

1. Click Start and then click Control Panel.

2. In the Control Panel, click System and Maintenance and then click System.

3. On the System page, click Change Settings under Computer Name, Domain, and Workgroup Settings. Or click Advanced System Settings in the left pane.

4. In the System Properties dialog box, click the Hardware tab and then click the Windows Update Driver Settings button.

5. As shown in Figure 5-5, select the desired update setting. The options available are:

    • Check for drivers automatically (recommended)

    • Ask me each time I connect a new device before checking for drivers

    • Never check for drivers when I connect a device

6. Click OK to save your settings.

Figure 5-5. Configuring the desired update driver setting

Learning About Your Computer's Hardware Devices

Computers can have all sorts of hardware devices installed in and connected to them. Keeping track of all these components and their related device drivers without a little help would be nearly impossible, and that's where Device Manager comes in handy. You'll use Device Manager to learn about your computer's hardware components and the device drivers they use.

Viewing Installed Hardware

Device Manager is your window to the hardware components installed on your computer. You can access Device Manager and view all the hardware devices installed on your computer by completing the following steps:

1. Click Start and then click Control Panel.

2. In the Control Panel, click System and Maintenance.

3. Scroll down and then click Device Manager.

As Figure 5-6 shows, Device Manager's default view shows the devices installed in or connected to your computer by device type. If you expand a device type node, such as DVD/CD-ROM devices, you'll see the actual hardware components that are installed. The device list shows warning symbols if there are problems with a device:

- A yellow warning symbol with an exclamation point indicates a problem with a device.
- A red *X* indicates a device that the user or administrator improperly installed or disabled for some reason.

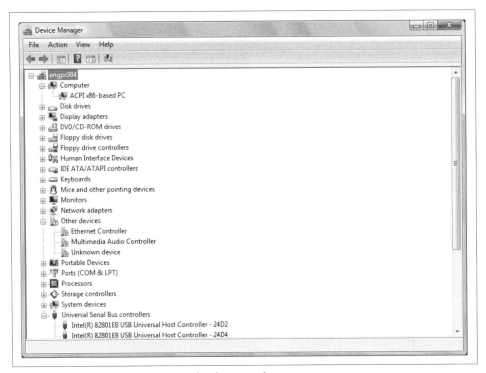

Figure 5-6. Reviewing your computer's hardware configuration

The options on the View menu allow you to change the way devices are listed. The View menu options include:

Devices by type
 Displays devices by the type of device installed, such as disk drives or display adapters. This is the default view.

Devices by connection
 Displays devices by the type of connection. For example, you may see the base node for the computer as ACPI Multiprocessor PC or ACPI x86-based PC. If you expand this, you'll see the ACPI connections and a connection for the computer's hardware bus, such as PCI Bus. If you then expand the PCI Bus connection, you'll see all the hardware connected to the PCI bus.

Resources by type
 Displays the status of allocated resources by resource type and type of device using a resource. Resource types are direct memory access (DMA) channels, input/output (I/O) ports, interrupt requests (IRQ), and memory addresses.

Resources by connection
Displays the status of all allocated resources by connection type rather than device type.

Show hidden devices
Displays non-Plug and Play devices as well as devices that have been physically removed from the computer but haven't had their drivers uninstalled.

Getting to Know Your Computer's Hardware Devices

Since working with the various device types is straightforward but not always intuitive, let's look at the primary types of devices and how they are used. After reading this section, you'll know more about the ways you can work with and customize your computer's devices. Customizing your computer's keyboard, mouse, and audio settings is covered next.

Disk drives

When you select Disk Drives in Device Manager, you'll see a list of the physical hard disks installed in the computer by type, such as USB or ATA. If you right-click a disk, select Properties, and then click the Policies tab, you'll see an important configuration option regarding the disk's write-caching optimization (see Figure 5-7). Any removable disk, such as a USB disk, should be optimized for quick removal. Any fixed disk, such as an ATA disk, should be optimized for performance. These are the default and standard configurations.

Figure 5-7. Viewing the disk driver settings for caching and safe removal

Display adapters

When you select Disk Drives in Device Manager, you'll see a list of graphics cards (display adapters) installed in the computer by manufacturer and model, such as NVIDIA GeForce FX 5200. If the device supports Windows Display Driver Model (WDDM), which is a requirement for Windows Vista Premium Ready computers, this should also be listed (in most cases).

DVD/CD-ROM drives

When you select Disk Drives in Device Manager, you'll see a list of the DVD/CD-ROM drives installed in the computer by manufacturer, type, and model. For DVD drives, if you want to know the type of read/write disks your computer supports, this is the place to check. The disk name should list DVD+RW if the DVD-ROM drive can burn to DVD+R discs, DVD-RW if the DVD-ROM drive can burn to DVD-R discs, or DVD+-RW if the DVD-ROM drive can burn to DVD+R and DVD-R discs.

Another tricky feature when burning DVD discs is the region code. Most DVDs are encoded to play in specific regions. In the United States, your DVD player is most likely set to work with Region 1-encoded discs. If you move to another country because of deployment, transfer, or whatever, you may find that you need to change the region code on your computer's DVD-ROM drive. You can do this by right-clicking the DVD-ROM drive in Device Manager, selecting Properties, and then clicking the DVD Region tab, as shown in Figure 5-8. On the DVD Region tab, select a country or geographic region and then click OK.

 You can change your DVD-ROM drive only a limited number of times—as per the "Changes remaining" value. When the "Changes remaining" value reaches zero, you cannot change the region even if you reinstall Windows or move the DVD drive to a different computer.

Human interface devices

When you select Disk Drives in Device Manager, you'll see a list of the general-purpose input devices that are configured specifically as human interface devices, including mouse devices, trackballs, and keyboards. These devices are also listed under their specific device type.

IEEE 1394 bus host controllers

When you select Disk Drives in Device Manager, you'll see a list of the IEEE 1394 host controllers installed in your computer. You won't see this entry if your computer doesn't support IEEE 1394.

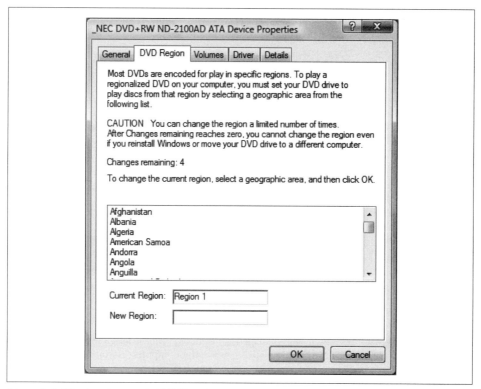

Figure 5-8. Viewing the encoded DVD region

Keyboards

When you select Disk Drives in Device Manager, you'll see a list of the keyboards connected to the computer. Most keyboards have a power management setting that allows you to wake the computer by pressing a key. You can control this configuration by right-clicking the keyboard device, selecting Properties, and then clicking the Power Management tab, as shown in Figure 5-9. If you don't want to allow the device to wake the computer, clear the "Allow this device to wake the computer" checkbox.

Mice and other pointing devices

When you select Disk Drives in Device Manager, you'll see a list of the mouse, trackball, and other pointing devices connected to the computer. Most pointing devices have a power management setting that allows you to wake the computer by moving the device.

Figure 5-9. Setting the desired power management configuration

You can control the power management configuration by right-clicking the pointing device, selecting Properties, and then clicking the Power Management tab. If you don't want to allow the device to wake the computer, clear the "Allow this device to wake the computer" checkbox. Otherwise, this checkbox should be selected so that you can use the device to wake the computer.

> When I'm using power management options, I find it much more efficient to use only the keyboard to wake the computer. If you turn off the Wake the Computer setting for other input devices, this will prevent you from accidentally waking the computer by bumping the mouse or trackball.

Monitor

When you select Disk Drives in Device Manager, you'll see a list of the general type of monitor connected to your computer. If your computer's monitor has power management settings, you control these as discussed in Chapter 3.

Network adapters

When you select Disk Drives in Device Manager, you'll see a list of the network adapters installed in or connected to your computer. If your computer has IEEE 1394 ports, you should see a related entry for each port. Your computer's Ethernet card and wireless adapters should also be listed.

Most network adapters have a power management feature that allows the operating system to turn them off to save power. Although you can also configure power management settings to wake the computer if the device becomes active, you should rarely do so because this setting may cause the computer to periodically wake to refresh its network state. It may also cause a laptop to turn on when you don't want it to; this may allow someone to attempt to connect remotely to your computer when you think it is off and safe.

For network adapters, you can control the power management configuration by completing the following steps:

1. In Device Manager, right-click the network adapter, select Properties, and then click the Power Management tab, as shown in Figure 5-10.

2. If you want to allow the computer to turn off this device to save power, select the "Allow the computer to turn off this device to save power" checkbox. Otherwise, clear this option to ensure that the device isn't turned off to save power.

3. If you don't want to allow the device to wake the computer, clear the "Allow this device to wake the computer" checkbox. Otherwise, this checkbox should be selected so that you can use the device to wake the computer.

4. Click OK.

Figure 5-10. Optimizing the power management settings as appropriate

Sound, video, and game controllers

When you select Disk Drives in Device Manager, you'll see a list of the audio codecs, game ports, audio cards, audio drivers, video cards, video codecs, and video drivers installed in your computer by manufacturer, model, and type. By viewing the available devices, you can determine what type of sound and video cards are installed. If your computer has an integrated sound card, video card, or both, this is listed as part of the device name as well.

System devices

When you select Disk Drives in Device Manager, you'll see a list of all the hardware components related to your computer's motherboard and system bus. If you want to determine whether your computer supports ACPI or has a PCI bus, this is the place to look.

If your computer seems to be losing track of time when you power it off, and you suspect there is an issue with your computer's CMOS clock (which runs on battery), System Devices is the place to look.

Typically, a computer's CMOS battery will last 7 to 10 years or more. You can check your computer's CMOS clock by completing the following steps:

1. In Device Manager, select "System CMOS/real time clock" and then select Properties.
2. On the Details tab, shown in Figure 5-11, select "Current power state," "Power data," or a similar power setting to determine the current power state of the CMOS clock.
3. If power settings information is provided, your clock is most likely working fine.
4. If you are unable to obtain this information when you select "Current power state," "Power data," or a similar power setting, you may need to replace the battery for the CMOS clock.

USB controllers

When you select Disk Drives in Device Manager, you'll see a list of all the USB devices installed in your computer, including controllers and hubs as well as some types of connected devices. Host controllers are listed by manufacturer, model, and type. The model and type details should also specify the USB version supported. For example, if you see entries for USB Universal Host Controller and USB2 Enhanced Host Controller, you'll know your computer has USB 1.0/1.1 ports and USB 2.0 ports.

Viewing and Managing Device Information

Each hardware device installed in or connected to your computer has a driver file associated with it. You view and manage devices using Device Manager. If you right-click a device entry, you'll have device management options similar to the following:

Properties
    Displays the Properties dialog box for the device

Uninstall
    Uninstalls the device and its drivers

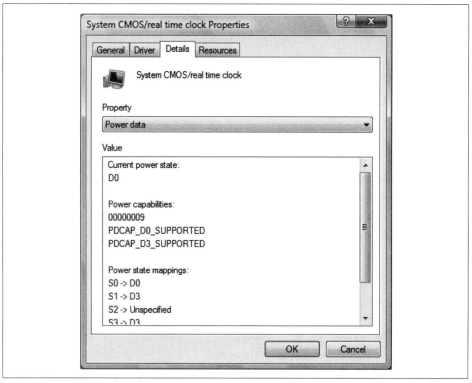

Figure 5-11. Checking the CMOS clock

Disable
    Disables the device but doesn't uninstall it

Enable
    Enables a device if it's disabled

Update Driver
    Starts the Hardware Update Wizard, which you can use to update the device's driver

Scan for Hardware Changes
    Checks the hardware configuration and determines whether there are any changes

Using a device's properties information, you can view the location of its driver file and related details. Right-click the device you want to work with and then select Properties. In the Properties dialog box, click the Driver tab and then click Driver Details to display the Driver File Details dialog box.

As Figure 5-12 shows, the Driver File Details dialog box provides the following information:

Driver files
    Lists the full file path to all driver files used by the device.

Provider
    Lists the manufacturer of the driver.

File version
    Lists the version of the driver files.

Digital signer
    Lists whether and by whom the driver is signed. Drivers signed by Microsoft Windows are standard system drivers.

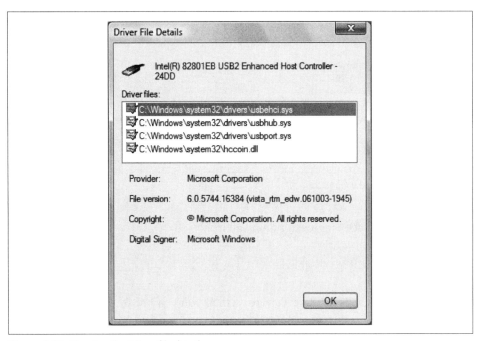

Figure 5-12. Viewing the driver file details

Customizing Your Computer's Input Devices, Regional Settings, and Date/Time

Of all the devices connected to your computer, the ones you use the most are the computer's keyboard and mouse. If you're like me, you may also use your computer audio devices about as often. Because you spend so much time working with these devices, you may want to customize their settings for the way you work, and this section will show you how.

Optimizing Your Keyboard Settings

Day in and day out you probably tap away at your keyboard without giving much thought to the way it works. To get the most out of your computer, however, you really should take a few minutes to optimize your keyboard settings.

Configuring your computer's keyboard

You can view and configure your computer's keyboard settings by completing the following steps:

1. In the Control Panel, click Hardware and Sound and then click Keyboard. This displays the Keyboard Properties dialog box shown in Figure 5-13.

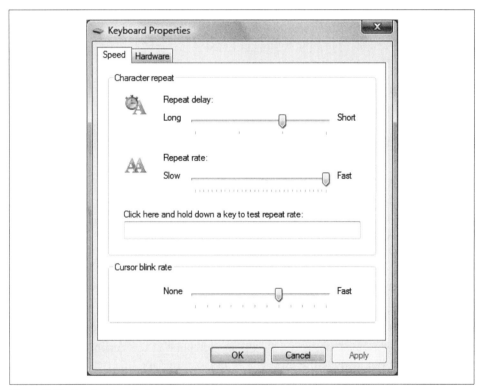

Figure 5-13. Configuring the keyboard settings

2. Use the "Repeat delay" slider to configure the delay for repeating characters when you hold down a key. There are four repeat delay intervals, with Long providing the longest repeat delay and Short providing the briefest repeat delay. If you are a novice typist or a person with a physical disability, you might want to set the repeat delay to Long to reduce the likelihood of accidentally repeating keys. If you work in data entry and frequently fill rows with the same character by pressing and holding a key, you may want to set the repeat delay to Short.

---

3. Use the "Repeat rate" slider to configure how quickly characters repeat when you hold down a key. The default repeat rate is Fast. If you have a problem with sticky keys or want to reduce the likelihood of excessively repeated characters, you can set a slower rate by moving the Repeat Rate slider to the left.

4. Click in the field provided to test the repeat delay and repeat rate you've selected.

5. Use the "Cursor blink rate" slider to configure the rate at which the cursor blinks. If you find the blinking cursor annoying, set the cursor blink rate to None. If you sometimes have trouble finding the cursor, you may want to set the blink rate a little faster than normal to help you see it.

Configuring the device driver for your keyboard

All keyboards have device drivers that you can manage. To view or work with your keyboard's drivers, complete the following steps:

1. In the Control Panel, click Hardware and Sound and then click Keyboard.

2. On the Hardware tab, click Properties.

3. In the Keyboard Properties dialog box, click the Driver tab.

4. Using the buttons provided, you can view driver details, update drivers, roll back drivers, and uninstall drivers as necessary.

Configuring your programmable keyboard

If your computer has a programmable IntelliType keyboard from Microsoft, you'll find several additional tabs in the Keyboard Properties dialog box, including Key Settings and Zooming. You can use the options on these tabs to update the type of keyboard, reassign keys, and control zoom settings.

Updating the keyboard type. To update the type of IntelliType keyboard, complete the following steps:

1. In the Control Panel, click Hardware and Sound and then click Keyboard.

2. On the Key Settings tab, you'll see the model name of the keyboard as currently assigned in bold. Move the mouse pointer over the Update… entry to the right of the model name to display a clickable Update button.

3. When you click the Update button, the Update Keyboard dialog box is displayed.

4. Flip your keyboard over and read the keyboard model, such as Microsoft Natural Ergonomic Keyboard 4000.

5. In the Keyboard Model list, select your keyboard model and then click OK twice.

Reassigning keys. To reassign keys on an IntelliType keyboard, complete the following steps:

1. In the Control Panel, click Hardware and Sound and then click Keyboard.

2. On the Key Settings tab, the current key assignments are listed by name and action, such as Starts America Online or Not Assigned. Click the key name you want to reassign and then click Edit.

3. You'll see one of several Reassign A Key dialog boxes. The simplest lets you choose a program to run. For primary programmable keys, such as Mail, you'll have several options:

   Start a program
   Choose this option and then use the selection list provided to choose a related program to start. For example, with Mail you might see options for America Online, Outlook, Windows Mail, and Hotmail.

   Choose from a list of commands
   Choose this option and then click Next. Select the command to perform, such as Copy (Ctrl-C), and then click Finish.

   Start a program, Web page, or file
   Choose this option and then click Next. Click Browse to select a program or file to open and then click OK. Or type a browser path to open a web page. Click Finish.

   Disable the user of this key
   Choose this option and then click Finish to disable the key.

4. Click OK.

Configuring the zoom key. To configure zooming on an IntelliType keyboard, complete the following steps:

1. In the Control Panel, click Hardware and Sound and then click Keyboard.

2. On the Zooming tab, use the Zooming slider to select a zooming speed.

3. To disable zooming, clear Enable Zooming. Otherwise, select this option to enable magnification using the zoom key.

4. To disable accelerated zooming, clear Enable Accelerated Zooming. Otherwise, select this option to enable faster zooming by pressing and holding the zoom key.

5. Click OK.

Optimizing Your Mouse Settings

You use the mouse pointer, trackball, or other input device every time you work with your computer, but have you taken the time to optimize the way it works? Probably not, because the mouse, like the keyboard, is another hardware component we tend to take for granted. Let's fix this by taking a few minutes to optimize your mouse.

Configuring your computer's mouse settings

You can optimize your computer's mouse settings by completing the following steps:

1. In the Control Panel, click Hardware and Sound and then click Mouse. This displays the Mouse Properties dialog box shown in Figure 5-14.

Figure 5-14. Configuring the mouse settings

2. If your mouse is on the left side of your keyboard rather than the right side, you're probably left-handed and may want to switch the primary and secondary mouse buttons by selecting "Switch primary and secondary buttons." With the buttons switched, the right button is for clicking and the left button displays the shortcut menu. As a result, wherever you are instructed to right-click something, you would actually need to left-click it.

3. Use the "double-click speed" slider to adjust the way your computer recognizes a double-click. If you move the slider to the left you increase the likelihood of your computer recognizing a double-click whether you double-click fast or slow. If you move the slider to the right you decrease the likelihood that your computer will recognize double-clicks with longer pauses between clicks. Double-click the folder provided to test your settings. If the test folder doesn't open and close as expected, change the settings until you get the desired effect.

4. Select "Turn on ClickLock" to select or drag without having to hold down the mouse button. With ClickLock on, briefly press the mouse button to set the lock, move the mouse without holding the button to drag, and then release the click lock by clicking the mouse button again.

5. On the Pointer Options tab, use the Motion slider to set the pointer speed. In most cases, you'll want a relatively fast pointer. To allow the pointer to zip across the screen, move the slider all the way to the right. To ensure that the pointer doesn't appear bouncy by increasing pointer precision, select "Enhance pointer precision." Enhancing pointer precision also lets you easily make small, precise pointer movements even when the pointer speed is set all the way to Fast.

6. Select "Automatically move pointer to the default button…" to have the pointer automatically move to the default button in a dialog box.

7. Select the "Display pointer trails" checkbox if you sometimes have trouble seeing the pointer, and then use the slider to adjust the length of the pointer trail. If you have trouble seeing the pointer sometimes and don't like pointer trails, select "Show location of pointer when I press the Ctrl key instead."

8. Select "Hide pointer while typing" to hide the pointer (and get rid of an annoying distraction) while typing.

9. Click the Wheel tab.

10. By default, most computers scroll three lines at a time when you move the mouse wheel one notch. You can use the "Vertical scrolling" options to set the number of lines to scroll, or select "One screen at a time" to configure the mouse wheel so that one notch scrolls a screen at a time.

11. If you have a mouse wheel with a tilt feature, you can use this to scroll left and right a specified number of characters at a time. By default, the mouse horizontally scrolls three characters at a time. Enter a different Horizontal Scroll in the combo box provided, if desired.

12. Click OK to apply your settings.

Configuring the device driver for your mouse

All input devices, including mouse and trackball devices, have associated device drivers that you can manage. To view or work with your input device's driver, complete the following steps:

1. In the Control Panel, click Hardware and Sound and then click Mouse.
2. On the Hardware tab, click Properties.
3. In the Mouse Properties dialog box, click the Driver tab.
4. Using the buttons provided, you can view driver details, update drivers, roll back drivers, and uninstall drivers as necessary.

Optimizing Your Audio Settings

Most computers these days have sound cards as well as built-in, attached, or separately connected speakers. Your computer may also have an audio input device such as a microphone. Windows Vista handles sound a bit differently than its predecessors. In Windows Vista, you can configure the computer's main volume and the volume for running applications separately. By default, the volume level for running applications is set relative to the main volume. Because of this, if you increase or decrease the main volume, the volume of running applications is increased or decreased as well relative to its initial value.

Controlling your computer's master volume and application volume

You can control the master volume and application volume for your computer using the following steps:

1. Click the Volume icon in the System Tray to display the Volume control.
2. With the Volume control displayed, you can adjust the main volume as necessary and the volume of running applications will be adjusted as well.
3. To adjust the volume for running applications, click Mixer and then use the Applications sliders to adjust the volume of running applications that have programmable audio input levels.

 The main volume must always be at least as high as the application volume. If you increase the volume of an application past the main volume level, you will increase the main volume as well.

Setting audio playback levels

For more advanced control of audio devices, you can use the Sound utility. In the Sound utility, playback and recording levels for sound are controlled separately. You can set the output levels for audio playback by completing the following steps:

1. In the Control Panel, click Hardware and Sound and then click Sound.

2. On the Playback tab, double-click the audio playback device you want to configure. This displays a Properties dialog box.

3. On the Levels tab, you can work with the main controls as follows:

    a. Use the slider to set the desired playback volume.

    b. To mute the device, click the sound button to the right of the slider. To unmute the device, click the sound button again.

    c. To adjust the speaker balance, click the Balance button, drag the L and R sliders as appropriate to set the desired balance between the computer's left and right speakers, and then click OK.

4. Click OK to save the settings.

Setting up your speakers

To set up your speakers, complete the following steps:

1. In the Control Panel, click Hardware and Sound and then click Sound.

2. On the Playback tab, select the audio playback device you want to configure and then click Configure. This displays the Speaker Setup Wizard.

3. On the Choose Your Configuration page, use the "Audio channels" list to select the speaker setup that is most like your computer's configuration. You can use the options available as follows:

    Mono
    Select this option if your computer has a single speaker (or you want all your speakers to be used as mono speakers).

    Stereo
    Select this option if your computer has one left speaker and one right speaker.

    Quadraphonic
    Select this option if your computer has two pairs of speakers: front-left, front-right, rear-left, and rear-right.

    5.1 Surround
    Select this option if your computer has surround sound with front-left, front-right, rear-left, rear-right, and center speakers.

4. Test the configuration by clicking the Test button. Click any individual speaker depicted to test its playback. Click Next when you are ready to continue.

5. If you previously selected 5.1 Surround, you'll see the Customize Your Configuration page next. As necessary, disable the center, subwoofer, rear speaker pair, or any combination thereof by clearing the related checkboxes. Click any speaker to test it. Click Next to continue.

6. On the Select Full-Range Speakers page, you can fine-tune the configuration. Select Front Left and Right to get more dynamic range out of your speakers (if this is supported). If you have speakers with limited dynamic range, clear the Front Left and Right, the Surround Speakers, or both checkboxes to reduce the dynamic range of the selected speakers.

7. Click Next and then click Finish.

Setting playback quality

To configure playback quality settings for your speakers, complete the following steps:

1. In the Control Panel, click Hardware and Sound and then click Sound.

2. On the Playback tab, double-click the audio playback device you want to configure. This displays a Properties dialog box.

3. On the Advanced tab, use the Default Format selection list to set the sample rate and bit depth to use. In most cases, the default setting is 16-bit, 44,100 Hz CD Quality sound.

Setting audio recording levels

To set the input levels for audio recording, follow these steps:

1. In the Control Panel, click Hardware and Sound and then Sound.

2. On the Recording tab, double-click the audio recording device you want to configure. This displays a Properties dialog box.

3. On the Levels tab, use the slider provided to set the recording volume as appropriate. If a Balance button is provided, click the Balance button, drag the L and R sliders as appropriate to set the desired balance, and then click OK.

4. Some microphones have a MIC Boost option that is used to boost the microphone's input volume. On the Custom tab, select MIC Boost to boost the microphone volume.

5. Click OK to save your settings.

Setting audio recording quality

To configure the default recording quality, complete the following steps:

1. In the Control Panel, click Hardware and Sound and then click Sound.

2. On the Recording tab, double-click the audio recording device you want to configure. This displays a Properties dialog box.

3. On the Advanced tab, use the Default Format selection list to set the sample rate and bit depth to use. In most cases, the default setting is 2-channel, 16-bit, 44,100 Hz CD Quality sound.

4. Click OK to save your settings.

Optimizing Your Computer's Regional and Language Settings

In a global-connected world, you may often find yourself working in another country or working with a computer from another country. If this is the case, you may want to adjust the computer's regional settings, language settings, or both.

Regional settings control the default units of measurement, currency, and date formatting. By specifying that you are in a particular region of the world, you choose all the appropriate settings for that region. To configure regional settings, complete the following steps:

1. In the Control Panel, click Clock, Language, and Region and then click Regional and Language Options.

2. On the Formats tab, use the "Current format" list to select a country or region, as shown in Figure 5-15. The Examples area should now display the formatting standards for the selected region.

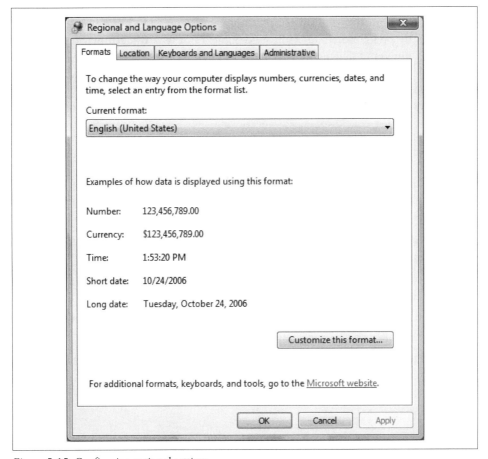

Figure 5-15. Configuring regional settings

3. To customize these settings, click "Customize this format" and then use the Customize Regional Options dialog box to modify the basic number, currency, time, and date settings for the region. When you are finished, click OK to close the Customize Regional Options dialog box.

4. Some software and services provide you with local information, such as news and weather. On the Location tab, you can use the selection list provided to set either the current location or the location for which you want to get local news and weather information.

5. On the Keyboards and Languages tab, click "Change keyboards." In the "Text services and input languages" dialog box, use the "Default input language" selection list to set the default input language to use with the keyboard.

6. If the computer has multiple input languages, a language bar is docked to the taskbar by default so that you can choose the input language. You can use the options on the Language Bar tab to control whether and how the language bar is displayed.

7. If the computer has multiple input languages, you can shift among input languages by pressing Left-Alt-Shift by default. On the Advanced Settings tab, you can set hot keys for switching among input languages and hot keys to switch to a specific input language as well. Under "Hot keys for input languages," select the desired Action, such as "To English (United States) – US," and then click Change Key Sequence. In the Change Key Sequence dialog box, select the Enable Key Sequence checkbox, select the desired key sequence, such as Ctrl-0, and then click OK.

8. Click OK to save these settings.

You can easily change the display and input languages for Windows Vista. Some languages are included with your versions of Windows Vista. Other languages you need to purchase and install.

To configure support for additional display and input languages, complete the following steps:

1. In the Control Panel, click Clock, Language, and Region and then click Regional and Language Options.

2. On the Keyboards and Languages tab, click "Install/uninstall languages."

3. Click "Install languages."

4. Select the languages to install or click Browse to locate the folder that contains the language files.

5. Click Next and then click Finish.

Optimizing Your Computer's Date and Time Settings

Your computer should always be set to the current date and time. If it isn't, you may have problems with misfiled documents or correspondence. Incorrect time settings could also cause you to miss appointments or meetings.

Setting your computer's date and time

You can manually set your computer's date and time by completing the following steps:

1. On the desktop taskbar, click the clock in the System Tray and then click "Change date and time settings." This displays the Date and Time Settings dialog box.

2. To change the date and time, click "Change date and time." Use the options shown in Figure 5-16 to set the system date and time as appropriate, and then click OK.

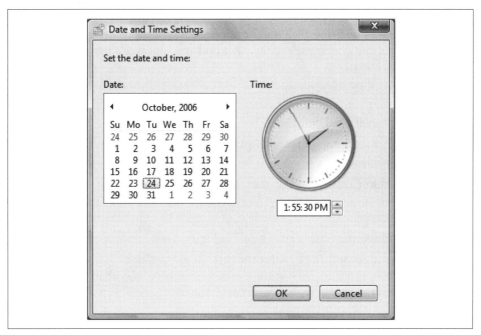

Figure 5-16. Setting the system time

3. To change the time zone, click Change Time Zone. Use the options shown in Figure 5-17 to set the time zone for the computer. Some time zones within the United States and abroad use daylight saving time. If you select a time zone where this is applicable, you'll be able to select the "Automatically adjust clock for Daylight Saving Time" checkbox. Use daylight saving time or clear this checkbox so that daylight saving time is not used.

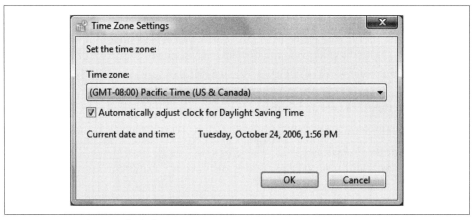

Figure 5-17. Configuring daylight saving time

4. When you configure your computer to use daylight saving time, the Date and Time dialog box tells you the date and time when daylight saving time starts and ends, as well as how the click will be adjusted. If you want to be reminded one week before this occurs, select the "Remind me one week before this change occurs" checkbox.

5. Click OK to save your settings.

Displaying time in additional time zones

You can configure your computer to display time in up to three time zones by completing the following steps:

1. On the desktop taskbar, click the clock in the System Tray and then click "Change date and time settings." This displays the Date and Time Settings dialog box.

2. Click the Additional Clocks tab, shown in Figure 5-18.

3. To configure a second clock, select the first "Show this clock" checkbox. Use the related selection list to choose the desired time zone and then type a display name for this time zone, such as **West Coast Time**.

4. To configure a third clock, select the second "Show this clock" checkbox. Use the related selection list to choose the desired time zone and then type a display name for this time zone, such as **Paris Time**.

5. Click OK to save your settings.

Once you've configured additional clocks, moving the pointer over the clock icon in the System Tray displays the time in each configured location. The computer's default system time is listed as Local Time.

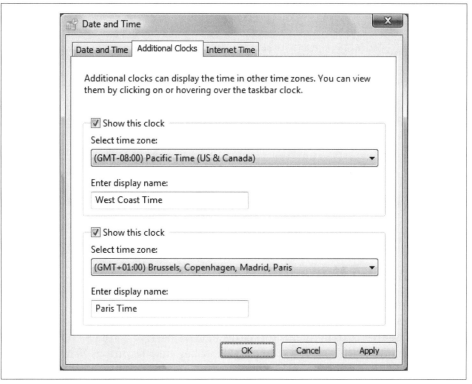

Figure 5-18. Displaying additional clocks

Keeping your computer's clock synchronized

To keep system time in close synchronization with world time, you'll want to use Internet time. At the office, Internet time is probably configured automatically by your organization's administrators.

At home, you can enable or disable Internet time by completing the following steps:

1. On the desktop taskbar, click the clock in the System Tray and then click "Change date and time settings." This displays the Date and Time Settings dialog box.

2. Select the Internet Time tab and then click "Change settings." This displays the Internet Time Settings dialog box, as shown in Figure 5-19.

3. To enable Internet time, select "Synchronize with an Internet time server" and then select the time server you want to use. Several default time servers are listed, including *time.windows.com* and *time.nist.gov*. You can select one of these or type in the fully qualified domain name of another time server to use.

4. To disable Internet time, clear the "Synchronize with an Internet time server" checkbox.

5. To update and synchronize the computer time, click "Update now."

6. Click OK to save your settings.

Figure 5-19. Configuring Internet time

Installing and Managing Hardware

When it comes to installing and managing hardware, Windows Vista is in many ways much smarter than earlier releases of Windows. As discussed previously, this is partly because the setup programs for hardware devices have gotten better and partly because Windows Vista itself has improved. A key new feature in Windows Vista that makes hardware installation and management easier is hardware diagnostics. Hardware diagnostics is a part of the top-to-bottom diagnostics framework discussed in Chapter 21.

Getting Available but Not Configured Hardware to Work

Thanks to hardware diagnostics, Windows Vista automatically detects and tries to help you resolve issues with hardware components. If you installed Windows Vista on your computer, you may have found that certain hardware devices weren't automatically configured during installation. In many cases, hardware diagnostics will detect available but not configured hardware and then use the automatic update framework to retrieve required drivers the next time Windows Update runs.

The update process is subject to several caveats. You must enable Windows Update and configure it to allow retrieval of drivers and driver updates by completing the following steps:

1. Click Start and then click Control Panel.

2. In the Control Panel, click System and Maintenance and then click Windows Update.

3. In Windows Update, click the Check for Updates link in the Tasks pane.

When drivers become available, you must install them. Windows Update does not install drivers or driver updates automatically. To install downloaded drivers and driver updates, follow these steps:

1. Click Start and then click Control Panel.

2. In the Control Panel, click System and Maintenance and then click Windows Update.

3. In Windows Update, click Check for Updates in the left pane and then click "View available updates."

4. On the "View available updates" page, you can review the available updates.

5. Optional updates, such as those for device drivers, may not be selected for installation automatically. To ensure that an update is installed, select the related checkbox, as shown in Figure 5-20.

6. When you click Install, Windows Vista will create a restore point prior to installing device drivers. If necessary, you can use this restore point to recover the system, as discussed in Chapter 21. Windows Vista will then install the updates.

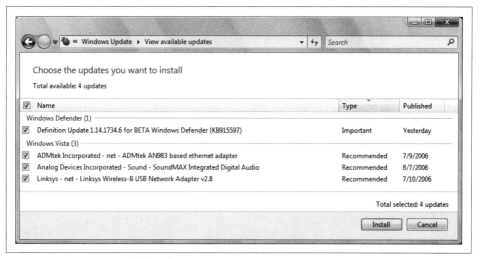

Figure 5-20. Viewing available updates

Once you've installed the driver for a device, Windows Vista should both detect the hardware and install the device automatically. If Windows Vista detects the device but isn't able to install the device automatically, it starts the Found New Hardware Wizard to help you through the installation process. In the Found New Hardware Wizard, click "Locate and install driver software (recommended)" to continue with the installation. The Driver Software Installation component will then search for preconfigured drivers and should find the driver that you've just made available to complete the installation.

Installing New Hardware Devices

Plug and Play is a technology that makes it possible for the operating system to detect the device type and automatically install a device using device drivers available on the computer or by prompting for required drivers. Most newer hardware devices are Plug and Play-compatible. This makes it much easier to install new hardware devices. With compatible internal devices, you typically will need to:

1. Run the device's setup program.
2. Shut down and unplug the computer.
3. Insert the device into the appropriate slot or connect it to the computer.
4. Restart the computer.
5. Let Windows Vista automatically detect and install the device.

With compatible external USB or FireWire devices, you will typically need to:

1. Run the device's setup program.
2. Insert the device into the appropriate slot or connect it to the computer.
3. Let Windows Vista automatically detect and install the device.

However, not all devices have or need setup programs. For example, with USB memory keys, all you need to do is insert the device into the appropriate slot and Windows Vista will detect and install it.

If Windows Vista detects but isn't able to install a device automatically, it starts the Found New Hardware Wizard. You can use this wizard to complete the installation by following these steps:

1. In the Found New Hardware Wizard, click "Locate and install driver software (recommended)" to continue with the installation.
2. The Driver Software Installation component will then search for preconfigured drivers. If it doesn't find one, it will prompt you to insert the disk that came with the hardware device.
3. If you have an installation disk for the device, insert the disc, follow the prompts to complete the installation, and skip the remaining steps. If you don't have an installation disk, click "I don't have the disk. Show me other options" and then follow the remaining steps in this procedure.
4. Click "Browse my computer for driver software" and then click Browse to select a search location.
5. Use the Browse for Folder dialog box to select the start folder for the search, and then click OK. All subfolders of the selected folder are searched automatically.
6. When you click Next, the wizard will search for and install any appropriate driver. If the wizard can't find an appropriate driver, you'll need to obtain one and then manually install the device driver as discussed next, in "Installing and Maintaining Device Drivers."

If Windows Vista doesn't detect the device and you've connected it properly, you may be working with an older non-Plug and Play device. You can complete the installation of a non-Plug and Play device by completing the following steps:

1. Click Start and then click Control Panel.
2. In the Control Panel, click Classic View and then double-click Add Hardware.
3. In the Add Hardware Wizard, read the introductory message and then click Next.
4. If you choose "Search for and install the hardware automatically" and then click Next, the wizard searches for and attempts to automatically detect the new hardware. When the search is complete, any new devices found are displayed, and you can select one.
5. If you choose "Install the hardware that I manually select from a list" and then click Next, or if no new devices are found in the automatic search, you'll need to select the hardware type. Select the type of hardware, such as Imaging devices or Printers, and then click Next. Scroll through the list of manufacturers to find the manufacturer of the device and then choose the appropriate device in the right pane.
6. Once you complete the selection and installation process, click Next. Confirm that you want to install the hardware by clicking Next again.
7. Click Finish. Your computer's new hardware should now be available.

Installing and Maintaining Device Drivers

Device drivers are the low-level workhorses of the operating system. They are responsible for making the appropriate calls to the HAL. Any inappropriate calls made by device drivers can cause system-wide problems that are difficult to trace back to the device drivers themselves. This can occur because when a device driver makes bad calls, these bad calls often cause other problems, such as service failures or improper read/write operations, which in turn can lead to fatal stop errors or data corruption.

Because device drivers are so important to proper system operation, it is crucial to periodically check for updates to your computer's drivers and apply driver updates as appropriate. While Windows Update provides a way to check for updates to drivers included with the operating system, you can't rely exclusively on Windows Update. As discussed previously, you need to check the available updates periodically to see if there are optional updates for drivers that you may want to install. For other driver updates, you'll need to check the support pages at the web site for your computer's manufacturer.

As driver updates become available, you'll need to determine whether you want to install the updates. If you've been having problems with a device or other system problems, you probably will want to install the driver updates. Keep in mind that in some cases, you may need to restart your computer to finalize the driver update. If you experience problems after installing or updating a driver, you roll back the driver to its previous version, as discussed in the next section, "Rolling Back Device Drivers."

You can install and update device drivers using Device Manager. Click Start and then click Control Panel. In the Control Panel, click System and Maintenance and then click Administrative Tools. In Administrative Tools, double-click Device Manager. In Device Manager, right-click the device you want to manage and then select Update Driver. This starts the Update Driver Software Wizard, as shown in Figure 5-21.

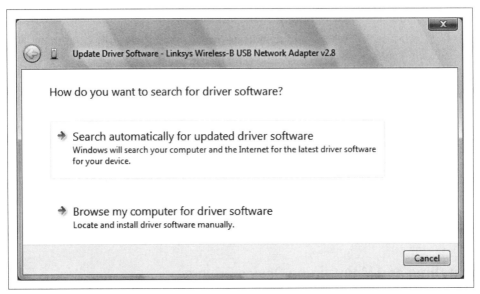

Figure 5-21. Updating the driver software

You can now search for the driver using one of the following techniques:

- Perform automatic search of Windows Update web site and your computer.
  1. Click "Search automatically for updated driver software" to have Windows Vista search your computer and the Internet for the latest driver for the device.
  2. If Windows Vista finds a more recent driver than the one currently installed, it will install the driver. If Windows Vista does not find a more recent version of the driver, it will keep the current driver.
  3. Click Close.
- Perform search of your computer in locations you specify.
  1. Click "Browse my computer for driver software" and then click the Browse button if you want Windows Vista to search only your computer or if you want to locate the device driver manually.
  2. Use the Browse for Folder dialog box to select the start folder for the search and then click OK. All subfolders of the selected folder are searched automatically.

3. Windows Vista will search the location you've specified for the latest driver for the device, and install the driver if found. If it does not find a more recent version of the driver, Windows Vista will keep the current driver.

4. Click Close.

- Choose the driver to install.

    1. Click "Browse my computer for driver software" and then click "Let me pick from a list of device drivers on my computer" to select the driver to install based on the type of hardware device.

    2. Select the appropriate hardware type, such as Imaging devices or Printers, and then click Next.

    3. Scroll through the list of manufacturers to find the manufacturer of the device, and then choose the appropriate device in the right pane.

    4. If the manufacturer or device you want to use isn't listed, insert your device driver disk into the floppy drive or CD-ROM drive, and then click the Have Disk button. Follow the prompts. Afterward, select the appropriate device.

    5. After selecting a device driver through a search or a manual selection, click Next to continue.

    6. If the wizard can't find an appropriate driver, you'll need to obtain one and then repeat this procedure.

    7. Click Close.

Rolling Back Device Drivers

Sometimes you may find that installing a device or a device driver has the unintended consequence of causing your computer to fail to start up. If this occurs, don't panic. You should be able to recover your computer using the Last Known Good Configuration or Safe Mode, as discussed in Chapter 21. You will then need to roll back the device driver or recover the computer to a previous restore point.

You may want to roll back a device driver for other reasons as well, such as when you are experiencing problems with the device or the device isn't working as you expected after updating the device driver. To roll back a device driver, follow these steps:

1. Click Start and then click Control Panel.

2. In the Control Panel, click System and Maintenance.

3. Scroll down and then click Device Manager.

4. In Device Manager, right-click the device you want to manage and then select Properties. This opens the Properties dialog box for the device.

5. Click the Driver tab and then click "Roll back driver." When prompted to confirm the action, click Yes.

6. Click Close to close the driver's Properties dialog box.

Keep in mind that if the driver file hasn't been updated, a backup driver file won't be available. Because of this, the "Roll back driver" button will be disabled and you will not be able to click it.

Enabling, Disabling, Removing, and Uninstalling Hardware Devices

The USB and FireWire devices you'll work with the most are the ones with removable storage, such as USB memory keys, digital cameras, and external disk drives. These USB and FireWire devices are meant to be portable and easily connected and disconnected. To disconnect and remove a device with removable storage, complete the following steps:

1. Close any Windows Explorer views accessing data on the device.

2. Close any open document, picture, or other media file saved on the device.

3. Click Start and then click Computer. This displays the Computer console, a special view of Windows Explorer.

4. Under Devices with Removable Storage, you'll see a list of devices with removable storage, as shown in Figure 5-22.

5. Right-click the device you want to disconnect and then select Safely Remove.

6. Remove the device or disconnect its cable.

Figure 5-22. Viewing devices with removable storage

You can reconnect the device later simply by plugging the device back in or connecting its cable to the appropriate port on your computer.

You can remove other devices that you no longer need as well. For printer devices connected via a serial or parallel port, you can simply disconnect the cable and then disable or remove the software printer associated with the hardware printer device, as discussed in Chapter 12.

For internal devices, you will need to shut down and unplug your computer, and then remove the device from the computer. When you restart the computer, Windows Vista should detect the configuration change and uninstall the drivers for the device.

In some cases, when you remove a device you'll need to tell Windows Vista this by uninstalling the device in the operating system. When you uninstall a device, Windows Vista removes the driver association for the device but doesn't prevent the device from being detected if it isn't physically removed.

If you want to prevent a device from being used but don't want to physically remove it, as may be the case for internal devices, you can disable the device. When you disable a device, Windows Vista prevents the device's drivers from loading and in this way blocks access to the device. Since a disabled device has no associated drivers, you can be sure that the disabled device isn't causing problems with your computer.

You can uninstall a device through the operating system by completing the following steps:

1. In Device Manager, right-click the device you want to work with and then select Uninstall.
2. In the Confirm Device Uninstall dialog box, shown in Figure 5-23, select "Delete the driver software for this device" if you want to prevent Windows Vista from automatically reinstalling the device.
3. Click OK.

Figure 5-23. Confirming that you are uninstalling the device

You can disable a device through the operating system by completing the following steps:

1. In Device Manager, right-click the device you want to work with and then select Disable.

2. When prompted to confirm the action, as shown in Figure 5-24, click Yes.

3. If you later want to enable a previously disabled device, you can do so by right-clicking the device in Device Manager and then selecting Enable.

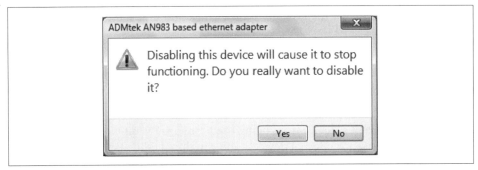

Figure 5-24. Confirming that you want to disable the device

Troubleshooting Hardware

Windows Vista's comprehensive diagnostics framework can detect and diagnose automatically many common problems with hardware devices. When Windows diagnostics detects a problem, Windows Vista displays a Problem Reports and Solutions balloon telling you there is a problem. If you click this balloon, Windows Vista should open the Problem Reports and Solutions console, which can help you resolve the problem.

If you suspect a device isn't working properly, you can check Device Manager to verify whether the device is working properly. For malfunctioning devices, you'll find an error status code and a suggested resolution for this error status code on the General tab of the device's Properties dialog box. In Device Manager, right-click the device you want to work with and then select Properties to view the error details.

You can resolve most hardware device problems by reinstalling the device driver. You can reinstall the driver for a device with a warning or error status by completing the following steps:

1. Click Start and then click Control Panel.

2. In the Control Panel, click System and Maintenance.

3. Scroll down and then click Device Manager.

4. In Device Manager, right-click the device you want to work with and then select Properties.

5. In the Properties dialog box, click the Reinstall Driver button.

6. Perform the driver reinstallation using one of the techniques discussed in "Installing and Maintaining Device Drivers," earlier in this chapter.

You can also uninstall the drivers and let Windows Vista reinstall the current versions of the driver files from the driver store. To do this, right-click the device in Device Manager and then select Uninstall. In the Confirm Device Uninstall dialog box, click OK but do not select the "Delete the driver software for this device" checkbox. If reinstalling the device driver doesn't work, check to make sure the device is properly connected. You may need to disconnect and reconnect the device.

If you are still unable to get the device to work properly, visit the device manufacturer's web site and check for alternative versions of the device driver. Sometimes an older version of a device driver is more stable than the latest version.

PART II

Mastering Your Data and Digital Media

CHAPTER 6

Mastering Windows Explorer and Searching Your Computer

When it comes right down to it, regardless of what you use your computer for, its most important function is to make it possible for you to create and store documents, pictures, music, videos, and other files. Thanks to Windows Vista's extensive interface enhancements, you have many new options for working with your files and searching your computer. To get the most out of these new features, you need to master Windows Explorer and Windows Search, which is exactly what this chapter is all about.

Windows Explorer: What's Changed

You might not have realized it before, but the Control Panel, My Computer, and My Network Places as used in earlier versions of Windows were simply different faces for Windows Explorer that allowed you to view and work with the features of your computer in different ways. While these various faces for Windows Explorer weren't tightly integrated previously, Windows Vista corrects this so that Windows Explorer behaves more like a console or browser shell, and its many faces are now all well integrated so that you always have similar functionality and features.

As you start working with the new Windows Explorer, you should know right away that Microsoft renamed My Computer and My Network Places as Computer and Network. One of the key reasons for this change was to simplify the naming and make them easier to reference. Microsoft also renamed My Documents, My Pictures, My Music, and My Videos as Documents, Pictures, Music, and Videos.

As Figure 6-1 shows, Microsoft gave Windows Explorer a complete makeover that includes:

- A new Address bar to replace the old one
- A Search box for fast searches
- A new menu bar to replace the old one
- New layout and view panes to replace the Explorer bars
- New options for previewing folders and files

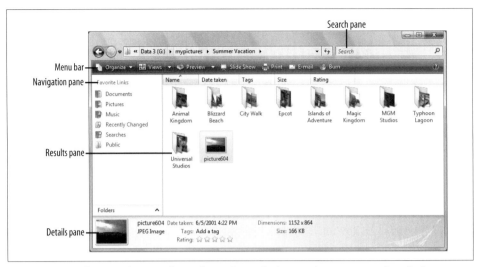

Figure 6-1. Windows Explorer's enhanced interface, which is much easier to work with than previous releases of Windows

As also shown in Figure 6-1, Windows Explorer organizes information according to a specific layout setting that includes several standard view panes, including a Navigation Pane for making quick selections and a Results Pane for viewing the folders and files stored in a selected location. Unlike summary details provided in earlier releases of Windows, the current version of Windows Explorer provides visual summaries of the types of content in your folders when you are working with certain views. A folder containing pictures will show a thumbnail graphic for some of those pictures stacked within the folder graphic. A folder containing documents will show a preview of those documents within the folder graphic.

When you select an item, you'll see details about that item in the Details Pane. The details listed depend on the type of item.

For disk drives, you'll see a visual summary of space used. You'll also see drive designator, filesystem type, free space, and total size (Figure 6-2).

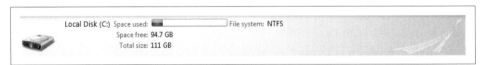

Figure 6-2. Summary for a disk drive

For devices with removable storage, you'll see drive designator and filesystem type (Figure 6-3).

Figure 6-3. Summary for a removable storage device

For shortcuts, you'll see folder name, creation date, last modified date, and size. If the shortcut is within a shared folder, you'll see details regarding how the related folder is shared (Figure 6-4).

Figure 6-4. Summary for a shortcut

For folders, you'll see folder name and last modified date. If the folder is shared, you'll see details regarding how the folder is shared (Figure 6-5).

Figure 6-5. Summary for a folder

For pictures, you'll see filename, file type, the date the picture was taken, the picture's width and height dimensions, and file size. You'll also see tags and ratings associated with the picture (Figure 6-6).

Figure 6-6. Summary for a picture

For music and audio books in Windows Media Player-supported formats, you'll see album cover, filename, file type, and size. You'll also see the artists' names, album name, genre, play time (length), rating, and year produced (Figure 6-7).

Figure 6-7. Summary for an audio file

For movies and videos in Windows Media Player-supported formats, you'll see a preview of the first frame, filename, date modified, date created, and size (Figure 6-8).

Figure 6-8. Summary for a video file

Navigating Your Computer with the Address Bar

The ubiquitous Address bar appears at the top of Windows Explorer and all its related views. Because you see the Address bar so much, you may take it for granted and not get the most out of its new features. Let's fix that by taking a closer look at what the Address bar offers.

Accessing Locations on Your Computer

The Address bar displays your current location as a series of links separated by arrows. This allows you to determine the current location on your computer, on your network, or on the Internet. File and folder locations aren't the only types of locations you can navigate using these features. You can also navigate Control Panel categories and network devices.

In the example shown in Figure 6-9, the location is:

    Computer → Local Disk (C:) → Users → williams

This tells you that the absolute path followed to get to the current location is *C:\Users\williams*.

Figure 6-9. The address path, which lists the current location

In some cases, you might also see a relative or abbreviated path, such as may happen when you follow a shortcut or browse to a path that cannot be fully depicted on the Address bar. As shown in Figure 6-10, a relative or abbreviated path is indicated by the left-pointing double-angle character (<<). In this example, the location is:

    « mypictures → Summer Vacation → Islands of Adventure

This tells you that the relative or abbreviated path of the current location is *mypictures\Summer Vacation\Islands of Adventure*.

Figure 6-10. The address path providing a relative location

When you are working with network paths in the Network view of Windows Explorer, as shown in Figure 6-11, you'll have quick access to network locations and shared resources on remote servers. Click the Network entry in the path to display a list of remote computers and network resources. Click the name of a remote computer or network resource to list its shared resources.

Figure 6-11. Working with network resources

Here are the features of the Address bar, from left to right:

Forward/Back buttons
> The Forward and Back buttons allow you to navigate locations you've already visited. Similar to when you are browsing the Web, the locations you've visited are stored in a location history, and you can browse the location history by clicking the Forward and Back buttons.

Recent Pages button
> The Recent Pages button provides a drop-down list of recently accessed locations. You can jump to a recently accessed location quickly by clicking the Recent Pages button and then clicking the desired location. Because the recently accessed locations are limited to the current session, only locations you've accessed since starting Windows Explorer are listed.

Address Path button
> The Address Path button shows the absolute or relative path you are currently accessing and provides options for working with this path. As discussed next, the Address path includes a Location Indicator icon, a Path Selection list button, Location Path entries, and a Previous Locations button.

Refresh button
> The Refresh button refreshes the view. Clicking the Refresh button displays any updates to contents in the selected location.

Out of all these features, the one you'll work with the most is the Address path. The Address path has four key components, and from left to right, they are:

Location Indicator icon

The Location Indicator icon depicts the type of resource you are currently accessing. You'll see different icons, including those for disk drives, folders, virtual folders, and so on. Clicking the Location Indicator icon shows the actual path or location, such as *C:\Users\Williams\Pictures*. Although you cannot click the path a second time to restore the original view, you can double-click the icon to view the same drop-down list provided by the Previous Locations button.

Path Selection list button

The Path Selection list button provides access to the available base locations. Selecting a base location allows you to quickly access a key Windows Explorer view, such as Control Panel, Computer, or Desktop.

Location Path entries

The Location Path shows the absolute or relative path to the current location. You can access a folder anywhere along the path that's displayed by clicking the link for that folder. You can access a subfolder of any folder displayed by clicking the arrow to the right of the folder. This displays a list of all folders in the selected folder, and you can access one of these folders by clicking it.

Previous Locations button

This provides a drop-down list of locations you've accessed which can include file locations, network drive locations, and web addresses. Unlike the Recent Pages button, the locations listed can include locations opened in previous Windows Explorer or Internet Explorer sessions. You can jump to a recently accessed location quickly by clicking the Previous Locations button and then clicking the desired location.

Using Selected Paths to Quickly Navigate Your Computer

Base locations accessible via the Path Selection list button are important because they allow you to access key locations on your computer with the click of a button. Clicking the Path Selection list button is the easiest way to access and navigate base locations. The base locations available are:

Current user

Selecting this base location accesses your personal folder in Windows Explorer (see Figure 6-12). Depending on your selection, the taskbar may be updated to include these additional options: Open, for opening a selected folder or file; Share, for sharing a selected folder or file; Burn, for burning a selected folder or file to CD or DVD; and Previous Versions, for accessing a previous version of a selected folder or file. When you select a file, you'll also see Print, E-mail, Slide Show, and Preview options.

Figure 6-12. Accessing your documents, pictures, and other files

Computer

Selecting this base location accesses your computer's hard disk drives and devices with removable storage (see Figure 6-13). Depending on your selection, the taskbar may be updated to include these options: "System properties," for accessing the System console in the Control Panel; "Uninstall or change a program," for opening the Installed Programs console in the Control Panel; "Map network drive," for mapping a shared folder on a computer; and Properties, for accessing a selected item's Properties dialog box.

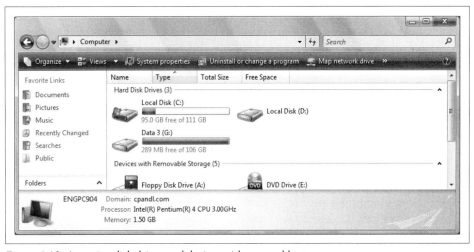

Figure 6-13. Accessing disk drives and devices with removable storage

Control Panel

Selecting this base location accesses the Control Panel in Windows Explorer (see Figure 6-14). You can then work with Control Panel options using Category or Classic view. The Control Panel doesn't have a menu bar, but it does have an Address bar and Search box. Using the Search box, you can quickly find Control Panel tools and task links.

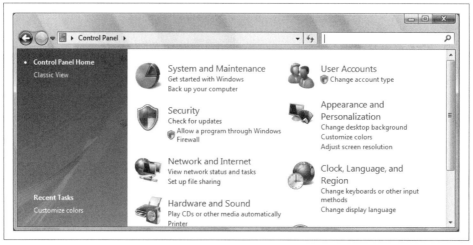

Figure 6-14. Accessing the Control Panel

Desktop

Selecting this base location accesses the desktop in Windows Explorer (see Figure 6-15). This allows you to view and work with all the shortcuts, files, and folders stored on the desktop. When you select files or folders, you'll have the same options as when you are working with your personal folder or any other folder. Use this view to help you clean up the clutter on your desktop or to find items on a cluttered desktop.

Network

Selecting this base location accesses the base page for the computers and devices on your network (see Figure 6-16). Depending on your selection, the taskbar may be updated to include these additional options: Search Active Directory, for when you are at the office and want to find available resources; Network and Sharing Center, for configuring network sharing and printing options; Add a printer, for adding a printer; and Network Center and Connect to a Network icons on the taskbar, to provide quick access to these features.

Figure 6-15. Accessing items stored on the desktop

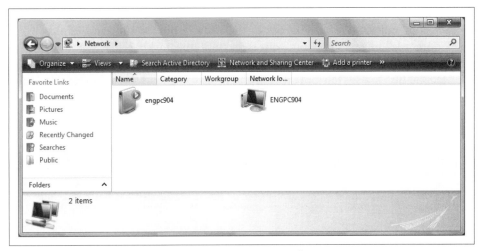

Figure 6-16. Accessing computers and devices on your network

Public

Selecting this base location accesses the base page for publicly shared files on your computer (see Figure 6-17). Depending on your selection, the taskbar may be updated to include these additional options: Open, for opening the selected folder or file; Sharing Settings, for configuring sharing options for your computer; and Burn, for burning a selected folder or file to CD or DVD.

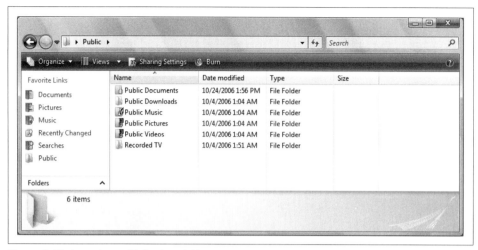

Figure 6-17. Accessing publicly shared files on your computer

Recycle Bin

Selecting this base location accesses the Recycle Bin in Windows Explorer (see Figure 6-18). Depending on your selection, the taskbar may be updated to include these options: "Empty the Recycle Bin," for permanently deleting all Recycle Bin items; "Restore all items," for restoring all Recycle Bin items to their original locations; and "Restore item," for restoring a selected item to its original location.

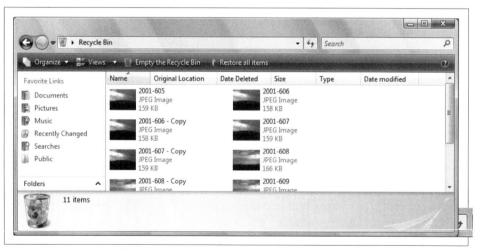

Figure 6-18. Accessing deleted items on your computer

Searching Your Computer

In the "Navigating the Search box" section of Chapter 2, I discussed using the Start menu Search box. The Search box in Windows Explorer is similar. However, there are some important differences and many additional advanced options.

Searching Your Computer: The Essentials

The Search box, shown in Figure 6-19, is provided in all views of Windows Explorer. This means you can search Control Panel, Network, Computer, Desktop, Public, and Recycle Bin locations.

Figure 6-19. The Search box, for searching for files and folders

The way the Windows Search service performs a search depends on where you are searching. A general search works like this: the Windows Search service matches the search text to words that appear in the title of any file or file folder, the properties of any indexed file or folder, and the contents of indexed documents. The automatic indexing of selected files and folders is a key feature of Windows Vista that improves the search results and helps to speed up the search process.

With Windows Explorer, you must click in the Search box prior to typing your search text. This means a basic search requires two steps:

1. In Windows Explorer, access the start location for your search.
2. Click in the Search box and then enter the search text.

The Windows Search service is the operating system feature that performs the search. Once the Windows Search service completes a search in the selected location, it automatically begins another search if you enter additional search text or if you change the search text. You can stop a search in progress at any time by clicking the Stop button—the red *X* on the right side of the Address bar. You can repeat a search by clicking the Refresh button.

With the Computer view of Windows Explorer, you can use the Search box to search your entire computer, including all disk drives and all devices with removable storage. To do this, follow these steps:

1. Click Start and then click Computer.
2. Click in the Search box and then enter the search text.

With other views of Windows Explorer, the Windows Search service does not perform a whole computer search. Instead, it searches only the selected location and its subnodes. This means if you were to search the *C:\Documents* folder, the Windows Search service would search *C:\Documents* and all its subfolders. It would not search other folders or other locations.

As Figure 6-20 shows, results are returned to the Results Pane in Windows Explorer and the Address bar is updated to reflect that you are viewing search results. The search results themselves are listed by name, date modified, file type, folder, authors, and tags. If you click the Location Indicator icon on the left side of the address path, you'll see the actual search text passed to the Windows Search service. See "Searching Your Computer: Save Search Options," later in this chapter, for details on saving searches so that you can run them again in the future.

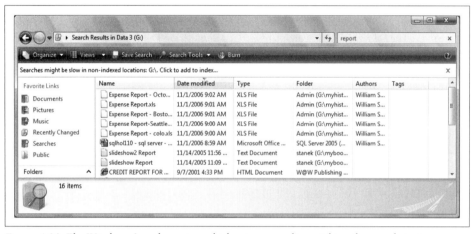

Figure 6-20. The Windows Search service, which returns results matching the search text

As you've seen, the basics of searching for files and folders are fairly straightforward. To improve your search results, however, you need to use the advanced search options and features built into Windows Vista. These additional advanced features include:

- Search options, for fine-tuning the search results
- The Search Pane, for filtering search results by document type
- Advanced Search, for performing advanced searches using multiple filters
- Indexing options, for managing which files and folders are indexed
- Save Search, for saving advanced search criteria for future searches

I discuss these advanced search features in the sections that follow.

Searching Your Computer: Search Options

Search options control the way the Windows Search service searches your computer. By default, Windows Search searches indexed locations and nonindexed locations in different ways:

- In indexed locations, the Windows Search service searches filenames and contents. This means it will look for matches to your search text in filenames and folder names, file properties and folder properties, and the actual textual contents of files.

- In nonindexed locations, the Windows Search service searches filenames only. This means it will look for matches to your search text only in filenames and folder names. It will not look for matches to your search text in file and folder properties, or in the actual textual contents of files.

By default, Windows Search searches subfolders of a selected location and allows partial matches. Thanks to partial matching, the Windows Search service matches your search text to part of a word or phrase rather than to whole words only. This allows you to search for *picture* and get matching results for *pictures*, *pictured*, *my picture*, *my pictures*, and so on.

You can customize the search options for your computer by completing the following steps:

1. If you have a Windows Explorer window showing search results, click Search Tools on the menu bar and then select Search Options. Otherwise, click Start and then click Control Panel. In the Control Panel, click Appearance and Personalization and then click Folder Options. Finally, select the Search tab in the Folder Options dialog box.

2. As shown in Figure 6-21, you can then use the Search tab options in the Folder Options dialog box to configure search options. To restore the default search options, discussed previously, click Restore Defaults, click OK, and then skip the remaining steps.

3. On the "What to search" panel, select the options that best describe what you want to be searched. To have the Windows Search service always search filenames and contents, select "Always search file names and contents (might be slow)." To have the Windows Search service always search filenames only, select "Always search file names only."

If you select either "Always search" option, you force the Windows Search service to ignore whether a folder is indexed when searching. This does not mean that indexes won't be used, however. When indexes are available, the Windows Search service will use them. When indexes aren't available, the Windows Search service will not be able to use indexes to speed up the search process, and this can result in extremely slow searches.

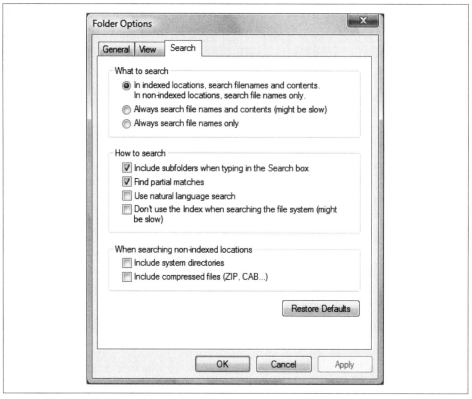

Figure 6-21. Configuring the search options

4. On the "How to search" panel, use the following options to configure how searches work:

Include subfolders when typing in the Search box
When selected, the Windows Search service searches the selected location and all subnodes of the location. This lets you search entire drives or complete folder structures. When not selected, the Windows Search service searches only the selected location and does not search subnodes of the location.

Find partial matches
When selected, the Windows Search service returns results for partial matches as well as whole-word matches. When not selected, the Windows Search service performs whole-word searches only.

Use natural language search
When selected, the Windows Search service allows you to enter search text as a question you might ask someone else. For example, you could enter the question, "Where is the Music folder?" and the Windows Search service

would know that you are looking for a folder named Music or folders containing music. When not selected, the Windows Search service uses all the text you enter for matching, as discussed previously.

Don't use the index when searching the file system
When selected, the Windows Search service ignores indexes that might be available to help speed up the search process. This forces the Windows Search service to examine the current state of files and folders, but it can be extremely slow. When not selected, the Windows Search service uses indexes to speed up the search process if indexes are available.

5. On the "When searching non-indexed locations" panel, specify whether the Windows Search service includes system locations, compressed files, or both when searching nonindexed locations.

6. Click OK to save your search options.

Searching Your Computer: Basic Search Filters

Sometimes you won't know the exact name of a resource you are looking for. Instead, you may know only the type of resource, such as whether you are looking for a document, picture, or music file. Or you may know that what you're looking for isn't a document, picture, or music file. In these cases, you can use the Search Pane to narrow your results using search filters.

You'll find the following default search filters:

All
Returns all results matching your search text and the current search options. This is the default search filter.

E-mail
Filters the search results so that only email messages are included in the search results.

Document
Filters the search results so that only document files are included in the search results.

Picture
Filters the search results so that only picture files are included in the search results.

Music
Filters the search results so that only music files are included in the search results.

Other
Filters the search results so that email, document, picture, and music files are excluded from the search results.

Want to know a secret? A little-known fact is that these same basic search filters are available with Windows Explorer, the Start menu, and other search boxes in Windows Vista. To use these filters with other Search boxes, simply type one of the following filter names into the Search box: e-mail, document, picture, music, video, or movie. For example, if you click Start and then type **music** into the Search box, you'll see a list of all the music on your computer. If you have a lot of music, you'll then need to click See All Results to get an expanded view of the search results.

When you are performing searches, you can use basic search filters by completing the following steps:

1. In Windows Explorer, access the start location for your search.

2. Click in the Search box and enter the search text.

3. Click Search Tools on the menu bar and then select Search Pane. This adds the Search Pane above the menu bar (see Figure 6-22).

4. On the Search Pane, click the button for the basic search filter you want to use, such as Document.

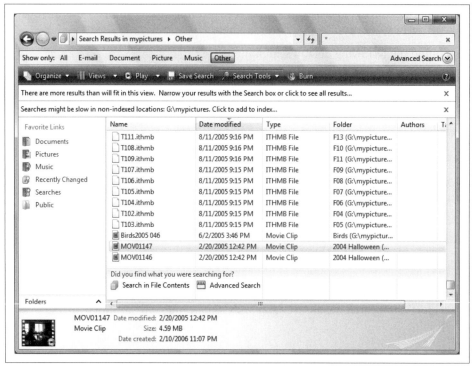

Figure 6-22. Using the Search Pane to filter the search results

In Figure 6-22, note that the Windows Search service provides several warning messages:

- The first warning explains that there are too many results to fit in this view. Because the Windows Search service returns only the first 5,000 matching results, you'll see this warning whenever there are more than 5,000 items in the search results. In this case, you will typically want to try to narrow your search by entering more specific search text in the Search box. You can, however, click the warning text and then select "Show all results" to force the Windows Search service to display all matching results.

- The second warning explains that searches might be slow because you are searching nonindexed locations. If you don't want to see this warning in the future, click the warning text and then select "Don't show this message again." If you frequently search this location, you can speed up future searches by clicking the warning text and then selecting "Add to index." See also "Indexing Your Computer for Faster Searches," for details on customizing the list of indexed locations.

When you know the type of file you are looking for but not necessarily the name, you can enter a wildcard character to start your search. In the example shown in Figure 6-22, I didn't know the name of the file I was looking for or even part of it, so I entered * as a wildcard character to match any name. Since I also knew I wasn't looking for an email, document, picture, or music file, I selected Other on the Search Pane to narrow the search results. This achieved the desired results, because the movie clips I was looking for were listed in the search results. Since these particular movie clips were *.mpg* files, I could also have searched for *.MPG.

Searching Your Computer: Advanced Search Filters

Basic search filters allow you to search your computer quickly for specific types of files with filenames matching specific search text. Basic search filters are, in most cases, fairly efficient, but they may not be efficient enough to help you pinpoint a specific file. This is where advanced search filters come into the picture. When you want to perform a thorough search based on multiple criteria, you'll want to use an advanced search. With an advanced search, you can:

- Set the start location as part of the search criteria.
- Search for files created, modified, or both within specific date ranges.
- Search for files with specific file sizes.
- Include hidden and system files in search results.
- Search for files containing specific tags.
- Search for files created by specific authors.

You can perform an advanced search by completing the following steps:

1. Click Start and then click Search. This displays the Search Results view in Windows Explorer (see Figure 6-23).

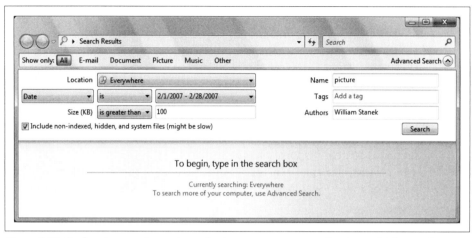

Figure 6-23. Performing an advanced search when you want to search using multiple search parameters

2. Click the Advanced Search button and then use the Location list to select the start location for the search. The options available include:

Everywhere
Search all local hard drives, devices with removable media, and connected network shares.

Indexed locations
Search all indexed locations.

Computer
Search all local hard drives and devices with removable media.

Local hard drives
Search all local hard drives.

Choose search locations
Search specified locations.

When you elect to choose search locations, the "Choose search locations" dialog box is displayed. The initial locations are the base locations discussed previously, as well as Offline Files, for searching offline file locations; Microsoft Office Outlook, for searching saved messages; and Search Folders, for selecting saved searches to include in the search. If a node can be expanded, you'll see an open triangle to the left of the location name. Click this to expand the location. For example, you could expand Computer and then expand Local Disk (C:) to select a folder on the C: drive.

3. Use the Date options if you want to search based on specific date-related criteria. Three selection lists are associated with date-based searches:

   a. Use the first selection list to set a date range for the search. Your options for setting date ranges include Date, for searching on the creation and modification date; Date Created, for searching on the creation date only; and Date Modified, for searching on the last modification date only.

   b. Use the second date-related list to specify how dates are used in your search. Your options are "any," for searching for any date; "is," for searching for a specific date or inclusive dates; "is before," for searching for a date prior to a specified date; and "is after," for searching for a date occurring after the specified date.

   c. Click the third selection list to display a calendar view for selecting a specific date to use with your "is," "is before," or "is after" search criteria. With the "is" search criteria, you can set an inclusive date range by clicking the start date and dragging the pointer to the desired end date.

4. Use the Size options to search based on specific size criteria. If you choose an option other than "any," you can set specific size values for the search using "equals," "is less than," and "is greater than." Then set the file size, in kilobytes (KB), that files returned in the search must be equal to, less than, or greater than.

5. To set the full or partial filename to match, enter the desired search text in the Name text box.

6. To search for files containing a specific tag, enter the tag that a file must have in order to be listed in the search results.

7. To search for files created by or modified by specific users, enter the username with which a file must be associated in order to be listed in the search results.

8. Click Search to begin your search. As with other types of searches, the search results are listed in the Results Pane.

Searching Your Computer: Save Search Options

Whenever you perform a search, Windows Vista updates the menu bar in Windows Explorer to include a Save Search button. Clicking this button allows you to save your search criteria so that you can rapidly perform an identical search in the future. Windows Vista saves your search criteria as a search folder.

Search folders are new for Windows Vista. They have a blue icon with a magnifying glass, as shown in Figure 6-24.

Figure 6-24. A search folder

When you access a particular search folder, the Windows Search service either retrieves the cached results of your previous search or performs a new search using the search criteria. The result is a list of matching files and folders that appear to be in the selected folder. The folder actually does not contain any files or folders, however. The folder's only actual (physical) content is the associated search string.

Within your profile folder is a folder named Saved Searches. Saved Searches contains the default search folders created when you installed Windows Vista as well as any search folders you've created. The default search folders include:

Recent Documents
    A list of documents you've opened or created in the past few days

Recent E-mail
    A list of email messages sent or received within the past few days

Recent Music
    A list of music you've opened or worked with in the past few days

Recent Pictures and Videos
    A list of pictures and videos you've viewed or worked with in the past few days

Recently Changed
    A list of files you've modified in the past few days

Shared by Me
    A list of files and folders you've shared on your computer

Recent E-mail is one of the more interesting of the default search folders. This search folder searches for email messages that are saved on your computer and returns a list of recently sent or received messages. When you click a message in the Results Pane, the message contents are shown in the Preview Pane, as shown in Figure 6-25. When you select an email message in the Recent E-mail folder, messages are listed by:

From names
    Who sent the message

Subject
    The message subject

Date received
    The date the message was sent or received

To names
    To whom the message was sent

Size
    The size of the message

Folder path
    The mail profile associated with the message

Importance

The relative importance of the message

Flagged status

Whether the message was flagged

 With Windows Mail (which is included with Windows Vista) and Microsoft Office Outlook, you can save email messages on your computer in a *.pst* or *.ost* file. The Recent E-Mail folder is designed to search these related folders only.

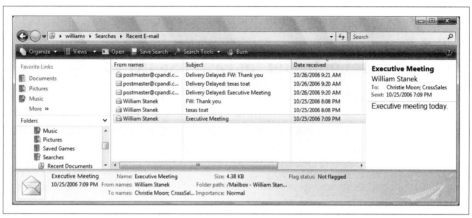

Figure 6-25. Search results for email messages, which provide additional details and previews

You can create your own search folder by completing the following steps:

1. Perform your search as discussed previously.

2. Click Save Search on the menu bar.

3. In the Save As dialog box, shown in Figure 6-26, type the name of the search folder in the "File name" text box. Be as descriptive as possible to make it easier to determine exactly what the search folder does.

4. Click Save to create the search folder.

Like the default search folders, search folders you create are stored by default in your Saved Searches folder. You run the related search again later by accessing Saved Searches and then accessing your virtual folder. While you cannot edit search folders to update the search criteria, you can delete a search folder, configure the desired search criteria, and then save the new search using the old search folder name.

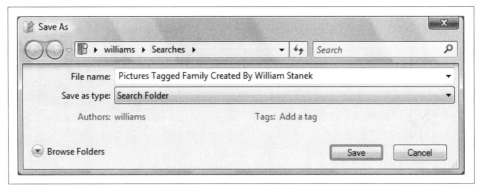

Figure 6-26. Saving the search parameters as a search folder

Indexing Your Computer for Faster Searches

In addition to performing searches, the Windows Search service is also responsible for indexing your computer. You tell the Windows Search service about locations that should be indexed by designating them as searched locations. Once you've designated a folder as an indexed location, the Windows Search service is notified that it needs to update the related index whenever you modify the contents of the folder.

You can manage the indexing of your computer's files and folders in several ways. You can:

- Add or remove indexed locations.
- Specify file types to include or exclude.
- Optimize file properties for indexing.
- Rebuild indexes if you suspect problems.

The sections that follow discuss these indexing options.

Adding or Removing Indexed Locations

The Windows Search services indexes the following locations by default:

Microsoft Office Outlook
This means that if you installed Microsoft Office Outlook, your mail saved on your computer will be indexed for fast searching.

Offline files
This means that if you configured offline files, as discussed in Chapter 11, all offline file folders will be indexed for fast searching.

Start menu

This means that the Start menu and all related menu options are indexed for fast searching.

Users

This means that your personal folders and the personal folders of others who log on to your computer are indexed for fast searching.

 Your computer includes personal folders for the default user profile. These personal folders, saved in the *%SystemDrive%\Users\Default* folder, are excluded from indexing by default. This is the desired setting in most cases, as you don't want to index folders or files associated with the default user.

You can add or remove indexed locations by completing the following steps:

1. If you have a Windows Explorer window showing search results, click Search Tools on the menu bar and then select "Modify index locations." Otherwise, click Start and then click Control Panel. In the Control Panel, click System and Maintenance and then click Indexing Options.

2. As shown in Figure 6-27, the Indexing Options dialog box provides an overview of indexing on your computer, which includes the total number of items indexed and the current indexing state. The currently indexed locations are listed under Included Locations.

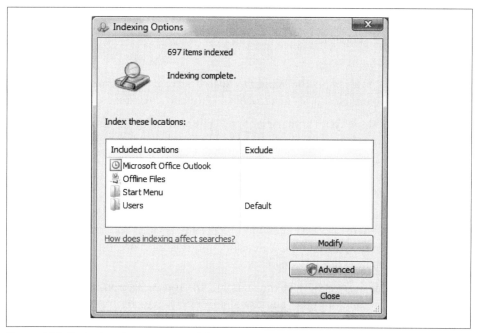

Figure 6-27. Reviewing the current search locations

3. In the Indexing Options dialog box, click Modify.

4. In the Indexed Locations dialog box, click Show All Locations (it's at the bottom of the dialog box).

5. In the Indexed Locations dialog box, shown in Figure 6-28, select locations to index, or clear checkboxes for locations you no longer want to index. The locations you can index include offline file folders, Microsoft Office Outlook, hard disk drives, and devices with removable storage. If a node can be expanded, you'll see an open triangle to the left of the location name. Click this to expand the location. For example, you could expand Local Disk (C:) to select a folder on the C: drive.

 System folders are excluded from indexing and are displayed dimmed to prevent them from being selected. If you enable indexing of the entire system drive, the following system folders are excluded automatically: Windows, ProgramData, and Program Files.

6. When you click OK to save your changes, the Windows Search service index adds locations and removes indexes for removed locations.

Specifying Files Types to Include or Exclude

From previous discussions, you know that the Windows Search service is designed to index:

- Filenames and folder names
- File and folder properties
- File and folder contents

What you don't know is *how* the Windows Search service determines which types of files and folders to index. It does so according to the file extension.

File extensions and file types go hand in hand. File type associations determine what type of data is stored in a file and how the file should be handled when opened. When you open most types of files, a helper application handles the display of the file. For example, when you open a document file with the *.doc* extension, Microsoft Office Word is used to display the document.

The Windows Search service uses the information that it knows about file types and file extensions to help it index files more efficiently. More specifically, Windows Vista assigns a file filter to each file extension, and this filter determines exactly how files with a particular extension are indexed.

Table 6-1 provides an overview of the standard file filters. As you install additional applications on your computer, additional file filters may be installed as well to improve indexing of related application files.

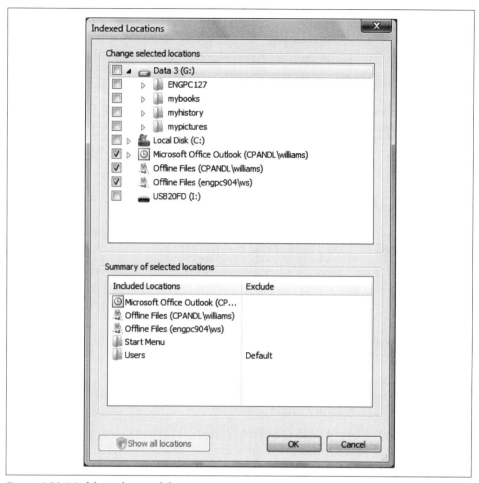

Figure 6-28. Modifying the search locations

Table 6-1. File filters used by the Windows Search service

Filter name	Filter description
HTML filter	This filter is designed to work with files formatted using Hypertext Markup Language (HTML). Since this filter recognizes HTML markup tags, you can use it to extract filenames, file properties, and file contents. Because this filter also understands <META> tags, you can also use it to extract meta tag properties within the <HEAD> </HEAD> tags of an HTML file.
Microsoft Office Document filter	This filter is designed to work with documents in Microsoft Office, including the documents for Word, Excel, and PowerPoint. Since this filter recognizes Office document formats, you can use it to extract text contents and properties unique to Office.
MIME filter	This filter is designed to work with email attachments formatted using the Multipurpose Internet Mail Extension (MIME) file format. For messages containing attachments, this filter helps the Windows Search service identify the associated file type so that the attachment's contents can be indexed appropriately.

Table 6-1. File filters used by the Windows Search service (continued)

Filter name	Filter description
Null filter	This filter is used with binary files and other nontext-based file formats. The Null filter retrieves only the filename and file properties. It does not filter the contents of a file.
Plain Text filter	This filter is designed to improve indexing of plain-text files and file types not registered for use with specific applications. It filters filenames, file properties, and file contents. This is the default filter, and it is not able to recognize any document formats. It handles files as a sequence of ASCII or Unicode characters.
XML filter	This filter is designed to work with files formatted using eXtensible Markup Language (XML). Since this filter recognizes XML markup tags, you can use it to extract filenames, file properties, and file contents. Because this filter also understands <META> tags, you can also use it to extract meta tag properties within the <HEAD> </HEAD> tags of an XML file.

You can specify file types that the Windows Search service should include or exclude when indexing files by completing the following steps:

1. If you have a Windows Explorer window showing search results, click Search Tools on the menu bar and then select Modify Index Locations. Otherwise, click Start and then click Control Panel. In the Control Panel, click System and Maintenance and then click Indexing Options.

2. In the Indexing Options dialog box, click Advanced to display the Advanced Options dialog box shown in Figure 6-29.

3. On the Index Settings tab, select the "Index encrypted files" checkbox if you want the Windows Search service to index files that have been encrypted. Selecting or clearing this option will cause the Windows Search service to completely rebuild the indexes on your computer.

4. If you want to improve indexing of non-English characters, select the "Treat similar words with diacritics as different words" checkbox. A diacritic is a mark above or below a letter that indicates a change in the way it is pronounced or stressed.

If you select "Treat similar words with diacritics as different words," you'll see a warning prompt stating that the Windows Search service will completely rebuild the indexes for indexed locations on your computer. The Windows Search service needs to rebuild the indexes completely to include previously ignored or substituted characters.

5. On the File Types tab, shown in Figure 6-30, each file extension and filter association is listed. If a file extension is selected, the Windows Search service includes files of this type when indexing. If a file extension is not selected, the Windows Search service excludes files of this type when indexing. Select or clear file extensions as appropriate.

Figure 6-29. Configuring advanced index settings

6. When you install new applications, those applications may register new filters with the Windows Search service and configure related file extensions to use these filters. This is the best way to add indexing functionality. If you want to add support for a particular file extension, type the file extension in the text box provided and then clicking Add New Extension.

7. To change the way files with a particular extension are indexed, select the file extension and then click either Index Properties Only or Index Properties and File Contents.

 Change the way indexing works for a file extension only when you are sure the indexing configuration you've chosen works. Generally speaking, you can always stop indexing the contents of a particular file type but rarely can you index the contents of a file type that isn't already being indexed. Trying to index the contents of a nontext-based file type can cause indexing problems.

8. Click OK to save your settings.

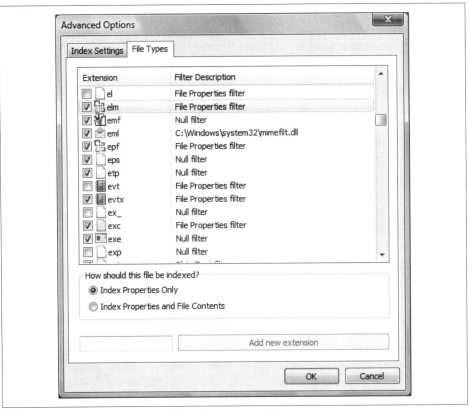

Figure 6-30. Controlling the types of files that are indexed

Optimizing File Properties for Indexing

As with file contents, the Windows Search Service indexes file properties to display search results of indexed files and folders faster. All files have properties associated with them and the type of file determines what the related properties are. Document files can have properties such as:

- Title
- Subject
- Tags
- Rating
- Categories
- Comments
- Authors
- Last Saved By

- Company
- Manager
- Data Last Saved

Photos and other types of image files can have special properties in addition to standard document properties, such as:

- Dimensions
- Width
- Height
- Horizontal Resolution
- Vertical Resolution
- Bit Depth
- Camera Maker
- Camera Model
- Exposure Time
- ISO Speed
- Focal Length

Music and other types of audio files can have special properties in addition to standard document properties, such as:

- Artists
- Album Artist
- Album
- Year
- Genre
- Length
- Bit Rate
- Producers
- Publisher

You can view and configure a file's properties by completing the following steps:

1. Right-click the file and then select Properties.
2. In the Properties dialog box, click the Details tab.
3. Click a property's entry to select it for editing, and then type the desired property value. Separate multiple values with a semicolon. For example, if you want to add tags to a file, you would click the Tags property, type the first tag, type a semicolon, type the second tag, and so on.
4. Click OK.

Although additional properties can be useful, sometimes you won't want this information to be saved with a file. For example, if you are publishing a file to a web site or sending a file to someone as an attachment, you might not want this additional, possibly sensitive information to be associated with the file. You can remove extended properties from a file by completing the following steps:

1. Right-click the file and then select Properties.

2. In the Properties dialog box, click the Details tab.

3. Click the Remove Properties and Personal Information link.

4. In the Remove Properties dialog box, select "Create a copy with all possible properties removed" to create a clean copy of the file.

5. When you click OK, the copy is created with the same filename as the previously selected file, and the suffix – *Copy* is added.

Resolving Indexing Problems

In order for you to perform searches, the Windows Search service must be running. It must also be running to index files. If you suspect you are experiencing a problem with searching or indexing, you should check the status of the Windows Search service. For details on how to work with and troubleshoot services, see Chapter 20.

Other problems you may experience with searching and indexing have to do with:

Corrupt indexes
> An indicator of a corrupt index is when your searches do not return the expected results or new documents are not being indexed properly.

Improper index settings
> An indicator of improper index settings is when your searches fail or the Windows Search service generates bad file errors in the event logs.

Index location running out of space
> An indicator of the index location running out of space is when indexing of new documents fails and there are out-of-disk-space reports in the event logs for the Windows Search service.

The Windows Search service does a good job of correcting some problems with indexes automatically. For other types of problems, you'll find error reports in the form of Windows events in the system event logs. You can correct most problems with searching and indexing by completing the following steps:

1. If you have a Windows Explorer window showing search results, click Search Tools on the menu bar and then select Modify Index Locations. Otherwise, click Start and then click Control Panel. In the Control Panel, click System and Maintenance and then click Indexing Options.

2. In the Indexing Options dialog box, click Advanced to display the Advanced Options dialog box shown in Figure 6-29.

3. If you suspect your computer's indexes are corrupt, click Rebuild. Windows Vista rebuilds the indexes on your computer by stopping, clearing out indexes, and then starting the Windows Search service. Indexes are similarly rebuilt whenever you restart your computer.

4. If you suspect improper index settings are causing problems, click Restore Defaults to restore the default indexing settings.

5. By default, the Windows Search service creates indexes in the *%SystemDrive%\ProgramData\Microsoft* folder. If the *%SystemDrive%* folder is low on disk space or if you want to try to balance the workload onto other hard disk drives, you may want to change the index location. To do this, click Select New on the Index Location panel. In the Browse for Folder dialog box, select the disk drive and folder in which the index should be stored and then click OK. The next time you restart your computer or the Window Search service, indexes will be created in the new location.

6. Click OK. In the Indexing Options dialog box, you can track the status of re-indexing files by watching the number of indexed items increase. The indexing status should also, but will not always, list Indexing in Progress.

CHAPTER 7

Navigating the Web with Internet Explorer 7

Back in the late 1990s, Internet Explorer became the top choice for browsing the Web by offering innovative features and being the best of its class. While other browsers from those heady, fast-paced days of the World Wide Web's early evolution have all but disappeared, Internet Explorer has continued. It now dominates the web browser market, but for a while it lost something special. Namely, it lost some of the cutting-edge innovation that made it the leader in the first place. With Version 7, though, Internet Explorer regains its place as a cutting-edge web browser with innovations worthy of applause.

Windows Vista includes Internet Explorer 7 as the default program for accessing web pages. Internet Explorer 7 is also available as a free download for anyone using Windows XP or Windows Server 2003. This newest version of Internet Explorer features a streamlined interface that increases the viewing area for web pages, tabbed browsing for easier navigation when you are viewing multiple web pages, and an extensive security shield that is designed to safeguard the integrity of your computer and protect your personal information.

Whether you are a novice or a pro, you'll find that Internet Explorer 7 is easier to work with than previous releases and that it offers more possibilities for customization and optimization. Before you race off to customize and optimize Internet Explorer 7, however, you should take a few minutes to get to know its new interface, as discussed in the first part of this chapter. You'll then be better prepared for the advanced discussion in the second part of this chapter, in which I cover new features and new ways of performing familiar tasks.

Getting Started with Internet Explorer 7

You can start Internet Explorer 7 by selecting Internet Explorer on the Start menu or by clicking Internet Explorer on the Quick Launch Toolbar. When you are browsing the Internet, Internet Explorer 7 runs in an enhanced security mode, called Protected Mode, by default. You can also start Internet Explorer 7 in a locked-down mode, called No Adds-ons Mode, by clicking Start → Accessories → System Tools →

Internet Explorer (No Add-ons). In this special, locked-down mode, Internet Explorer runs without ActiveX controls or browser extensions.

With Internet Explorer 7, Microsoft shows that it has clearly been listening to customers and watching the competition. As you can see in Figure 7-1, Internet Explorer 7 has a redesigned interface that maximizes web page display while reducing the toolbar size, uses tabs instead of separate windows, and features an integrated Web Search box.

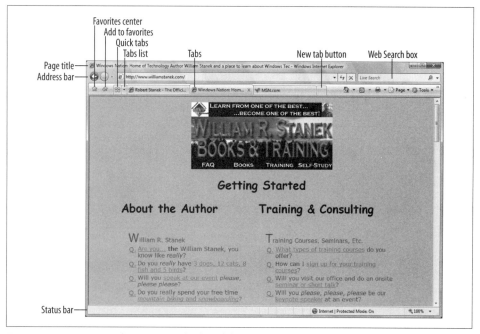

Figure 7-1. Internet Explorer 7's new look and feel

Tabbed browsing is the enhancement that has the most significant impact on the way you browse the Web. With tabbed browsing, you can open new browser pages in a separate tab rather than in a separate window. In this way, tabbed browsing helps you organize web pages so that you can easily navigate among them simply by clicking tabs. While Internet Explorer still allows you to open new windows by pressing Ctrl-N or selecting Page → New Window, you may not need to do this and may instead want to open a new tab.

Each Internet Explorer window can have up to eight pages open on separate tabs. You can open a page in a new tab in several ways. You can hold the Ctrl key while clicking a link to open the referenced page in a new tab. You can display a new tab by pressing Ctrl-T and then typing the desired web page address in the Address field. As Internet Explorer always displays the New Tab button to the right of the last tab in the line of available tabs, you can also click this button and then type the desired web page address in the Address field.

Internet Explorer gives you several options for working with tabs. You can change the order of tabs by clicking a tab and dragging it to the left or right until you reach the desired position. You can close a tab by right-clicking it and selecting Close. You can close all tabs except the current tab by right-clicking the tab and selecting "Close other tabs."

Whenever there are at least two tabs in use, a Quick Tabs preview and Tabs List button are added to the toolbar to the left of the tabs. Pressing Ctrl-Q or clicking the Quick Tabs button displays a thumbnail preview of all tabbed pages, as shown in Figure 7-2. To access one of the tabbed pages, you simply click the page's thumbnail. The Tabs List page displays a list of open web pages. To access one of these pages, you click its entry in the list.

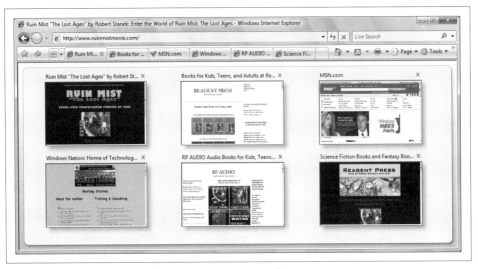

Figure 7-2. Using the Quick Tabs preview to navigate easily

Another new feature that you'll find especially helpful is the Favorites Center. You can access the Favorites Center by clicking the Favorites Center button on the toolbar or by pressing Alt-C. With the Favorites Center, shown in Figure 7-3, you finally have a single location to view and access the following:

Favorites
> Lists your favorite web pages. The Favorites view has a master favorites list that, by default, is organized in the order in which you add pages. You can rearrange page entries by clicking them and dragging them up or down in the list. You can organize favorites into folders as well for easy navigation and quick access. Simply click a folder to display the related list of favorites.

Feeds
> Lists Really Simple Syndication (RSS) feeds to which you've subscribed. RSS feeds can contain news headlines, lists, and other information provided by businesses or individuals.

History

Lists pages you've accessed by date and site. You'll find entries for the current day, day of the week, past week, and so on. If you click a date entry, you'll see folders for each site accessed on that date. Clicking a site entry shows the pages visited at the site. Clicking a page entry opens the page for viewing.

Figure 7-3. Using the Favorites Center to access favorites, feeds, and browser history

Getting Around the Web and Using Internet Explorer 7

Tabbed browsing, Quick Tabs, and the Favorites Center are just a few of the more obvious ways Internet Explorer has changed. Some of the subtler changes in Internet Explorer have to do with the toolbars and related options. As Figure 7-4 shows, Internet Explorer 7 has a Title bar, Address bar, Menu bar, Standard toolbar, and Status bar. The sections that follow discuss tips and techniques for working with these toolbars.

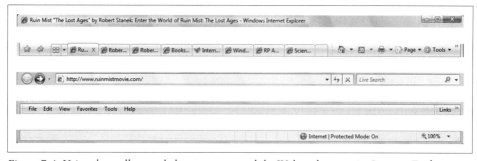

Figure 7-4. Using the toolbars to help you get around the Web and customize Internet Explorer

Navigating Web Page Addresses

Although in earlier releases you could move the Title bar and Address bar, you can no longer do so in Internet Explorer 7. In Internet Explorer 7, the Title bar and Address bar are fixed in place. The only time the Title bar and Address bar are not displayed is when you are in full-screen mode. You can turn full-screen mode on and off by pressing F11.

The Title bar shows the title of the current web page, followed by a description of the browser or a custom title if the browser Title bar has been customized through Group Policy settings. In Group Policy, you'll find the Browser Title policy setting for customizing the Title bar under *User Configuration\Windows Settings\Internet Explorer Maintenance\Browser User Interface* (see Figure 7-5).

Figure 7-5. The Title bar in Internet Explorer

 The Title bar is but one of many aspects of Internet Explorer that you can customize through Group Policy. You'll find more information on working with Group Policy in Chapter 27. For details on policies new to Internet Explorer 7, see Chapter 28.

The Address bar features Forward and Back buttons, an Address box, a Path History button, Refresh and Stop buttons, and a Web Search box (see Figure 7-6).

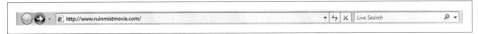

Figure 7-6. The Address bar in Internet Explorer

You can work with the Address box in a variety of ways. To access a page in the currently selected tab, you click in the Address box, type the web address, and then press Enter. Alternatively, you can press Alt-D to select the Address box and the previously entered web address without having to move the mouse and click. You can then type the desired web address and press Enter.

At the far-right side of the Address box is the Address History button, which depicts a down arrow. Clicking this button shows the addresses you've previously accessed from the browser history. You can then navigate to a previous address by selecting it. Alternatively, you can display the address history by pressing F4, use the up and down arrow keys to select a previous address, and then press Enter to browse to this address.

Another handy shortcut for working with web addresses is to type only the name of the web site you want to visit, and then press Ctrl-Enter to add the *http://www.* to the beginning and the *.com* to the end of the name. For example, if you entered **yahoo**, you could press Ctrl-Enter to create the address *http://www.yahoo.com*. You could then press Enter to browse to this address.

Searching the Web and Setting Search Providers

Internet Explorer 7 integrates a search feature directly into the browser window. To search the Web using the default search provider, click in the Web Search box, type your search text, and then press Enter or click the Search button. If you hold Alt while pressing Enter, you'll open the search in a new tab.

On most configurations of Internet Explorer 7, the default search provider is Live Search. Live Search is a search service provided by Microsoft, and not surprisingly, it has the most extensive search listings I've found anywhere—Google and Yahoo! included. You can add search providers to Internet Explorer 7 by following these steps:

1. In Internet Explorer 7, click the Search Options button to the right of the Search button.

2. On the shortcut menu, select Find More Providers.

3. On the Add Search Providers to Internet Explorer 7 page, you'll find a list of search providers. Click the search provider you want to add. This displays the Add Search Provider dialog box shown in Figure 7-7.

Add search providers only from sites you trust. Just because a site is listed as a provider, it doesn't mean the site is trustworthy or reliable. It simply means the site has built-in search facilities and the site owner sent Microsoft a provider file that can use those built-in search facilities.

4. To make the search provider your default for web searches, select the "Make this my default search provider" checkbox.

5. Click Add Provider.

You can have only one default search provider. If you make a particular provider your default, you'll use this provider anytime you type search text and then press Enter or click the Search button. To use an alternative search provider, type your search text, click the Search Options button, and then select the alternative provider.

Figure 7-7. Configuring additional search providers as alternatives

When you have configured multiple search providers, you can make a provider your default or remove a provider by completing the following steps:

1. In Internet Explorer 7, click the Search Options button to the right of the Search button.

2. On the shortcut menu, select Change Search Defaults.

3. In the Change Search Defaults dialog box, shown in Figure 7-8, you'll find a list of search providers you've configured for use.

4. To make a provider the default, click the provider in the Search Providers list and then click Set Default.

5. To remove a provider, click the provider in the Search Providers list and then click Remove.

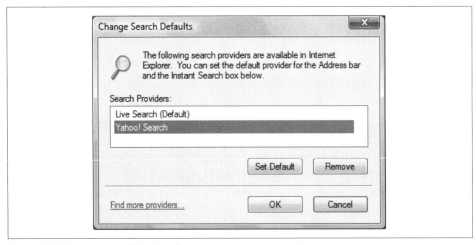

Figure 7-8. Setting a new default and removing a search provider

Working with Internet Explorer Menus and Toolbars

The Menu bar features the menus used in previous versions of Internet Explorer. You'll find File, Edit, View, Favorites, Tools, and Help menus (see Figure 7-9).

Figure 7-9. The Menu bar in Internet Explorer

In Internet Explorer 7, you can work with the Menu bar in several different ways. You can display the Menu bar by pressing the Alt key and then hide the Menu bar by pressing the Alt key again. You can turn on and lock the Menu bar by selecting Menu Bar on the Tools menu. Once you turn on and lock the Menu bar, you can no longer hide it by pressing the Alt key.

The Standard toolbar is the main toolbar in Internet Explorer 7. The Standard toolbar has a fixed position. The only time the Standard toolbar is not displayed is when you are in full-screen mode. Your only option for customizing the Standard toolbar is the resize slider to the right of the New Tab button. If you click this slider and drag to the right, you increase the area for tabs and decrease the area for option buttons. You can then display a shortcut menu with the hidden options by clicking the Expand (>>) button on the far right side of the Standard toolbar (see Figure 7-10).

Figure 7-10. The Standard toolbar in Internet Explorer

On the Standard toolbar, to the right of the New Tab button or on the Expand shortcut menu, you'll find the following options:

Home
Displays the page or pages you've configured for access when you start Internet Explorer or click the Home button.

Home Options
Displays a shortcut menu that allows you to select and manage home pages.

Feeds
Displays RSS feeds detected on the current page. This makes it possible to get updates about a page through RSS.

Print
Displays the Print dialog box, which allows you to print the current page.

Print Options
Displays a shortcut menu that allows you to select printing options, including Print Preview and Page Setup.

Page
> Displays a menu for managing windows and pages.

Tools
> Displays a menu for customizing the Internet Explorer interface and configuring security features.

Help
> Displays a menu with help options.

Research
> Displays or hides the Research Pane. You can use the Research Pane to look up words using available reference tools, such as a thesaurus.

You can use the options on the Page menu to edit, view, and save pages. Two important options that make it easier to view web pages and their contents are Text Size and Zoom.

The Text Size submenu provides options that let you resize the text in a web page relative to its original font size. You can use the Text Size options to resize text on a page by clicking Page, clicking Text Size, and then selecting the desired text size, such as Medium or Larger.

The Zoom submenu provides options that let you enlarge or shrink an entire web page and all its contents, including both images and text. You can quickly increase magnification by simultaneously pressing the Ctrl key and the + (plus sign) key on your numeric keypad. You can quickly decrease magnification by simultaneously pressing the Ctrl key and the – (minus sign) key on your numeric keypad. If you click Page and then click Zoom, you can select a desired zoom setting, such as 50 percent or 200 percent.

The Tools menu on the Standard toolbar provides access to Internet Explorer's safety and security features as well as other features. The options include:

Delete Browsing History
> Provides options for deleting cached browsing information, including temporary files, page history, cookies, saved passwords, and web form values.

Diagnose Connection Problems
> Starts network diagnostics for helping you determine the possible cause of connection and access problems.

Pop-up Blocker
> Provides options for managing the way pop-up blocking works. You can also enable and disable pop-up blocking.

Phishing Filter
> Provides options for managing the way phishing filters work. Malicious web sites use hidden forms and other phishing tactics to steal information you've previously entered into form fields, and phishing filters help to stop this from happening.

Manage Add-ons
Provides options for viewing and managing browser add-ons installed on your computer.

Work Offline
Configures Internet Explorer to work offline. When you are working offline, Internet Explorer attempts to retrieve pages you access from its offline browsing cache. If a page is available for offline browsing, Internet Explorer displays the page. Otherwise, Internet Explorer displays an error message.

Internet Options
Provides options for configuring Internet Explorer's settings. You can use the related dialog box to configure settings for security, privacy, content, connections, programs, and more.

Configuring Web Pages As Home Pages

One of my favorite new features in Internet Explorer 7 is the ability to have up to eight home pages. When you configure a web page as a home page, Internet Explorer opens the page anytime you start a new browser session or click the Home button. If you have more than one home page configured, Internet Explorer opens each page in a separate tab.

The Home Options button to the right of the Home button allows you to display and select from a list of home pages that you've configured. You can also use the options it provides to add, change, or remove home pages. You can add or change home pages by completing the following steps:

1. In Internet Explorer 7, click the Home Options button to the right of the Home button.

2. On the shortcut menu, select Add or Change Home Page. This displays the Add or Change Home Page dialog box shown in Figure 7-11.

Figure 7-11. Adding or changing your home page

3. Choose one of the following options and then click Yes to save your settings:

Use this webpage as your only home page
Removes any previously configured home pages and sets the currently selected web page as your only home page.

Add this webpage to your home page tabs
Adds the currently selected web page to the bottom of your home page tabs.

You can only have up to eight home pages. If you try to add a new home page and already have eight home pages, you'll see a warning prompt stating that you've already selected the maximum number of supported home pages. To add the web page as a home page, you'll need to remove at least one of the other home pages.

Use current tab set as your home page
Configures all the web pages you've opened in the current tab set as your home pages. Internet Explorer adds the pages in the order in which the tabs are open currently. You will not be able to change the order later.

Being able to add the current tab set as your home page can save you a great deal of time. To use this feature to your best advantage, open in separate tabs up to eight web pages that you visit frequently. To get the pages in the desired order, click and drag the related tabs into the desired positions. Once you have all the pages open and in the desired order, select Add or Change Home Page and then choose "Use current tab set as your home page."

You can remove home pages by completing the following steps:

1. In Internet Explorer 7, click the Home Options button to the right of the Home button.
2. On the shortcut menu, click Remove. This displays a new shortcut menu.
3. Click a page to remove it or click Remove All to remove all pages.
4. When prompted to confirm the action, click Yes.

Printing Web Pages Without Wasting Paper

Another of my favorite new features in Internet Explorer 7 is the new printing engine. Unlike earlier releases of Internet Explorer, the default printing option is to shrink the selected page to fit your default printer settings—this feature alone is extremely helpful. If you select the Print Options button to the right of the Print button and then select Print Preview, you can customize the print layout using the dialog box shown in Figure 7-12.

In Print Preview, four Adjust Margin guides are provided—one each for the left, right, top, and bottom margins. Not only do these guides show you visually where the margins are located, but you can also click a margin guide and drag left/right or up/down.

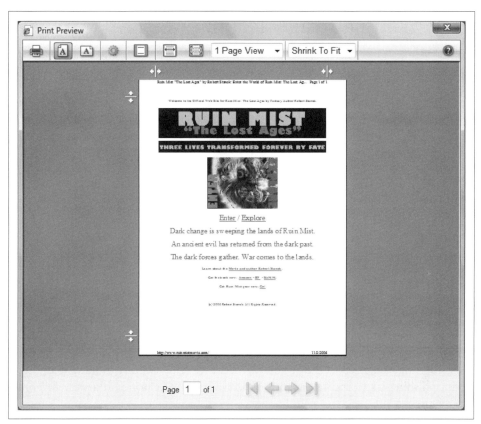

Figure 7-12. Using Print Preview to help you configure printing options

Table 7-1 summarizes the Print Preview options by listing the buttons on the top and bottom rows from left to right. The most important new option is the Change Print Size button, which lets you set the print size as a percentage of the actual page size. You can click the Change Print Size button and then select Shrink to Fit to ensure that a page prints properly.

Table 7-1. Print Preview options in Internet Explorer

Location/Option	Press to select	Description
Top row		
Print Document	Alt-P	Prints the document with the current settings.
Portrait	Alt-O	Changes the print orientation to portrait.

Table 7-1. Print Preview options in Internet Explorer (continued)

Location/Option	Press to select	Description
Landscape	Alt-L	Changes the print orientation to landscape.
Page Setup	Alt-U	Displays the Page Setup dialog box for configuring page size, paper source, headers, footers, and margins.
Turn Headers and Footers On or Off	Alt-E	Turns on or off the printing of headers and footers. You'll see headers and footers in the preview if they are turned on currently.
View Full Width	Alt-W	Resizes the page width so that it fills the preview window.
View Full Page	Alt-1	Resizes the print preview so that the full page is shown.
Show Multiple Pages	Alt-N	Allows you to select the number of print pages to preview simultaneously.
Change Print Size	Alt-S	Allows you to change the print size of the page. Use the print preview to determine how the web page will print. To ensure that the page prints properly with the margins you've selected, choose Shrink to Fit.
Bottom row		
Current Page	Alt-A	Allows you to specify which print page you want to preview.
First Page	Alt-Home	Allows you to view the first printed page.
Previous Page	Alt-left arrow	Allows you to go to the previous page in the print preview.
Next Page	Alt-right arrow	Allows you to go to the next page in the print preview.
Last Page	Alt-End	Allows you to view the last printed page.

Understanding Status Bar Indicators

The Status bar shows web addresses in links as well as the load progress and error status of the current page. When you are working with Internet Explorer 7, don't overlook important changes to the Status bar. On the right side of the Status bar, you'll find a phishing status indicator, an Internet security indicator, and a view magnifier (see Figure 7-13).

Figure 7-13. The Status bar in Internet Explorer

The phishing status indicator specifies the phishing status as it relates to the currently accessed site or page. When you are accessing most well-known or trusted sites, you'll typically see the phishing status indicator while a page is loading and the indicator will go away once the page is fully loaded. This doesn't mean that the phishing filter isn't active or available. If you click in the empty space to the immediate left of the Internet Security indicator, you can display all the standard phishing filter options. On some lesser-known web sites as well as on known phishing sites, the phishing status indicator may display a warning icon. Clicking this icon allows you to check the web site for phishing activities, report the web site, and configure phishing filter options.

The Internet security indicator specifies the current security zone and mode that Internet Explorer is using. Internet Explorer has separate security zones for Internet, Local Intranet, Trusted Sites, and Restricted Sites. When accessing sites in the Internet zone, Internet Explorer uses Protected Mode by default.

The View Magnifier icon shows the current Zoom setting. If you click the option button to the right of this icon, you can use Zoom settings to shrink or expand the textual and graphical contents of a web page. Shrink the page by selecting a zoom size smaller than 100 percent. Expand the page by selecting a zoom size larger than 100 percent.

Protecting Your Computer While Browsing

When you are browsing the Internet, Internet Explorer 7 runs in Protected Mode. This isolates it from other applications in the operating system and prevents add-ons from writing content in any location beyond temporary Internet file folders without explicit user consent. By isolating Internet Explorer from other applications and restricting write locations, Windows Vista prevents many types of malicious software from exploiting vulnerabilities on your computer. Protected Mode also restricts the way domains, web addresses, and security zones are used.

While Protected Mode is a key component in Internet Explorer's new comprehensive safety and security suite, many other safety and security features work together to protect your computer from malicious software. These additional security features include a pop-up blocker and a phishing filter. They also include privacy and content settings.

Viewing and Managing Add-Ons

Protected Mode limits the ActiveX controls and other add-ons that can run in Internet Explorer. Protected Mode also gives you better control over the add-ons that are installed and used by allowing you to view and manage add-ons in these unique categories:

Add-ons that have been used in Internet Explorer
> Lists all the add-ons that Internet Explorer has used since you installed your computer or the latest version of Internet Explorer

Add-ons currently loaded in Internet Explorer
> Lists the add-ons that Internet Explorer is currently using

Add-ons that run without requiring permission
> Lists the add-ons configured for use on your computer

Downloaded ActiveX controls (32-bit)
> Lists the add-ons you've downloaded from the Internet and configured for use

In the "Add-ons that run without requiring permission" list, you'll find default add-ons that are included with Internet Explorer or that you've downloaded through updates from Microsoft, as well as add-ons that you have installed and granted permission to run. For example, if you downloaded the ActiveX control for Flash and granted run permission to this control, you'll see it on the "Add-ons that run without requiring permission" list and the "Downloaded ActiveX controls (32-bit)" list. Although you can enable or disable any ActiveX controls and other add-ons, you can only delete ActiveX controls and other add-ons that you've downloaded.

You can view and manage ActiveX controls and other add-ons by completing the following steps:

1. In Internet Explorer, click Tools → Manage Add-ons → Enable or Disable Add-ons.

2. In the Show drop-down list, select the add-on category you want to view or manage (see Figure 7-14).

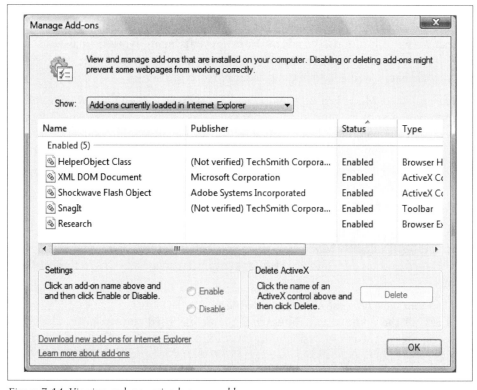

Figure 7-14. Viewing and managing browser add-ons

3. You'll then see a list of ActiveX controls and other add-ons in this category.

4. Click the add-on you want to work with.

5. To disable the add-on, click Disable to prevent the add-on from running in Internet Explorer.

6. To enable the add-on, click Enable to allow the add-on to run in Internet Explorer.

7. To delete the add-on if you previously downloaded it, click Delete. The add-on is then removed from Internet Explorer.

Understanding Web Address and Domain Restrictions

In Internet Explorer, the component responsible for parsing web addresses and determining domain name and location components is the Universal Resource Locator (URL) handler. URLs are simply the formal names of web addresses and other types of addresses that you can use to universally locate resources on the Internet. While the URL handler is extracting the domain name and location components from a web address, it performs several checks to ensure the validity of the web address and prevent possible URL parsing exploitations, such as URLs that attempt to run commands or URLs that perform suspect actions. These checks are new for Internet Explorer 7.

As part of its new features, Internet Explorer 7 supports both standard English domain names and internationalized domain names. English domain names are domain names represented using the letters A–Z, the numerals 0–9, and the hyphen. Internationalized domain names, also referred to as IDNs, are domain names represented using native language characters.

Unfortunately, as sometimes happens when new features are introduced, Internet Explorer's support for internationalized domain names makes it possible to create lookalike domain names for popular and trusted sites. For example, someone might create a site at *http://www.micrósoft.com* and if you didn't look really closely at the domain name, you could be fooled into believing you were accessing *http://www. microsoft.com*.

To help ensure that international characters aren't used to make a site seem like something it isn't, Internet Explorer implements international domain name antispoofing. International domain name antispoofing is designed to warn you against sites that could otherwise appear as known, trusted sites. Thanks to this feature, you'd receive a warning notification about possible spoofing if you clicked on a link to *http://www.micrósoft.com*.

Viewing and Managing Browsing History

As you browse the Web, Internet Explorer stores information about the pages you visit, the content of those pages, the information that web sites collect from you, and the information you provide while at web sites. This information is collectively referred to as your *browsing history*. Your browsing history includes:

Temporary Internet files
> Temporary Internet files are copies of web pages, images, and other related files.

Browser cookies
> Browser cookies store information about you collected by the web sites you visit.

History list
> The history list stores a list of web sites and pages you've visited according to the date accessed and the web address.

Form data
> Form data consists of information you've typed into online forms.

Passwords
> Passwords consist of passwords you've used when you signed into web sites that use forms-based authentication.

Internet Explorer stores copies of this information to improve your browsing experience. If you visit the same site or page later, Internet Explorer can use the data it has stored in its browser cache on your computer rather than having to reload the page and its contents over the Web. This data can also be used to reauthenticate you on web sites that require authentication and to provide information for automatically completing web forms.

Configuring temporary Internet file storage

With temporary Internet files, Internet Explorer can use copies of web pages, images, and other related files rather than having to download these files. This allows you to view pages faster on subsequent visits. You can control the way Internet Explorer stores copies of temporary Internet files by completing the following steps:

1. In Internet Explorer, click Tools → Internet Options. This displays the Internet Options dialog box.

2. On the General tab, click Settings under Browsing History. This displays the Temporary Internet Files and History Settings dialog box shown in Figure 7-15.

3. Configure how Internet Explorer uses stored data using the following "Check for newer versions of stored pages" options:

   Every time I visit the webpage
   > Select this option if you want Internet Explorer to check for a newer version every time you access a page. Here Internet Explorer will use a newer version when available and the cached version of the page otherwise.

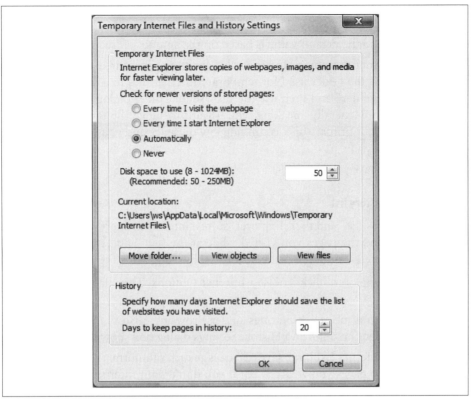

Figure 7-15. Configuring the way temporary Internet files are stored

Every time I start Internet Explorer

> Select this option if you want Internet Explorer to check for a newer version the first time you access a page during a browser session. Here Internet Explorer will use a newer version when available and the cached version of the page otherwise.

Automatically

> Select this option if you want Internet Explorer to check for a newer version the first time you access a page during a browser session, and to check for changes to images in a page according to the frequency with which they are changed. Here Internet Explorer will use a newer version when available and the cached version of the page otherwise. Internet Explorer will also check for newer images less frequently when images are changed infrequently.

Never

> Select this option if you want Internet Explorer to always use a cached version of a page if available. Here Internet Explorer will download a page only the first time you access it and will use the cached version of the page otherwise.

4. Use the "Disk space to use" combo box to set the amount of disk space reserved for temporary Internet files. The recommended space to reserve is from 50 MB to 250 MB and the default value is based on the amount of free space available.

5. By default, your temporary Internet files are stored in your user profile. If you want to move the folder used for temporary Internet files to a different location, click "Move folder" and then use the Browse for Folder dialog box to select the new location. Generally speaking, you'll want to move the temporary Internet files only if your primary disk is running low on space and you have another disk available.

6. Click OK to save your settings.

Configuring the history list

With the history list, Internet Explorer stores information about the date you accessed a site and the pages you visited while at the site. You can control the way Internet Explorer creates and uses the history list by completing the following steps:

1. In Internet Explorer, click Tools → Internet Options. This displays the Internet Options dialog box.

2. On the General tab, click Settings under Browsing History. This displays the Temporary Internet Files and History Settings dialog box shown in Figure 7-15.

3. By default, Internet Explorer saves 20 days' worth of information regarding web sites and web pages you've accessed. If you don't want Internet Explorer to create a history list, you can set the "Days to keep pages in history" box to 0. Otherwise, set the "Days to keep pages in history" box to the desired number of days to retain the browser history.

4. Click OK to save your settings.

Configuring AutoComplete settings for forms and passwords

AutoComplete settings control whether and how Internet Explorer stores web addresses, form data, and passwords. As you type web addresses in the Address bar, these addresses are listed according to the text you enter, allowing you to select an address in the history list. With form data, Internet Explorer stores the text you entered into online forms. When you fill out similar form fields later, Internet Explorer displays the data you previously provided so that you can select it rather than having to retype it.

With passwords, Internet Explorer stores the passwords you used when you signed into web sites that use forms-based authentication. When you visit a site again, Internet Explorer can use the password to reauthenticate you or provide the password for you after you enter your username.

You can control the way AutoComplete works by completing the following steps:

1. In Internet Explorer, click Tools → Internet Options. This displays the Internet Options dialog box.
2. On the Content tab, click Settings under AutoComplete. This displays the Auto-Complete Settings dialog box shown in Figure 7-16.
3. Use the following options to configure how AutoComplete works, and then click OK to save your settings:

    Web addresses
    > Select this option to save AutoComplete data for web addresses.

    Forms
    > Select this option to save AutoComplete data for form fields.

    User names and passwords on forms
    > Select this option to save AutoComplete data for usernames and passwords you enter.

    Prompt me to save passwords
    > Select this option to prompt you before saving a password. If you don't select this option, passwords are saved automatically.

Figure 7-16. Specifying the AutoComplete settings to use

Configuring the use of browser cookies

Internet Explorer stores in browser cookies the information about you that is collected by the web sites you visit. Web sites use cookies for a variety of reasons, such as tracking your preferences and storing information about items you've added to a shopping cart. When you access the same site later, the site can use the information stored in the cookie to enhance your browsing experience or obtain any necessary information about you.

Internet Explorer allows sites to store cookies on your computer based on where those sites are located. For sites on your local network and sites you've specifically designated as trusted, Internet Explorer accepts all cookies regardless of your privacy settings. For sites you've specifically designated as restricted, Internet Explorer blocks all cookies regardless of your privacy settings. When you are accessing sites on the public Internet that are configured as neither trusted sites nor restricted sites, you can manage the way cookies are used on the Privacy tab of the Internet Properties dialog box.

Internet Explorer relies on a web site's compact privacy policy to determine how the site uses cookies. The World Wide Web Consortium (W3C) has defined an official recommendation regarding web privacy, called the Platform for Privacy Preferences Project (P3P). P3P enables web sites to report their privacy practices in policy statements. Internet Explorer relies on what the site reports and cannot determine whether cookies are used as reported.

When working with cookies the two important terms to understand are *explicit consent* and *implicit consent*. Explicit consent means you have specifically opted to allow a site to collect personal information, such as when you accept a site's rules during sign-up. Implicit consent means you haven't opted out or told the site you don't want personal information to be collected. On the Privacy tab, you use the Settings slider to specify how cookies should be used. Privacy settings available include:

Block All Cookies
> Blocks all new cookies and ensures that web sites cannot read any existing cookies. Because Allow exceptions are ignored while this setting is selected, any sites you've configured as Allow exceptions are blocked as well.

High
> Blocks all cookies from sites that do not have a declared privacy policy regarding consent. It also blocks all cookies with a declared privacy policy stating that cookies gather information that could be used to contact you without your explicit consent.

Medium High
> Blocks cookies from sites other than the one you are viewing if they do not have a declared privacy policy statement regarding consent. It blocks cookies from other sites with a declared privacy policy stating that cookies gather information that could be used to contact you without your explicit consent. It also blocks cookies from the current site if there is a declared privacy policy statement specifying cookies gather information that could be used to contact you without your implicit consent.

Medium

The default privacy setting. Blocks cookies from sites other than the one you are viewing that do not have a declared privacy policy regarding consent. It restricts cookies from the current site and blocks cookies from other sites that have a declared privacy policy stating that cookies gather information that could be used to contact you without your implicit consent.

Low

Blocks cookies from sites other than the one you are viewing that do not have a declared privacy policy regarding consent. It restricts cookies from other sites that have a declared privacy policy stating that cookies gather information that could be used to contact you without your implied consent.

Accept All Cookies

Accepts all new cookies and allows web sites to read existing cookies. Because Block exceptions are ignored while this setting is selected, any sites you've configured as Block exceptions are allowed as well.

You can configure Internet Explorer's cookie settings by completing the following steps:

1. In Internet Explorer, click Tools → Internet Options. This displays the Internet Options dialog box.

2. On the Privacy tab, shown in Figure 7-17, use the Settings slider to set the desired privacy level for cookies.

3. To make an exception for a site rather than raise or lower your privacy setting, click the Sites button. Type the address of the web site in the field provided, and then click Allow or Block as appropriate. If you click Allow, cookies for the site will always be accepted. If you click Block, cookies for the site will always be blocked.

 You cannot make exceptions when you use the Block All Cookies or Allow All Cookies setting. With these settings, all cookies are always either blocked or allowed. There is no in-between or exception.

Clearing your browsing history

Occasionally, you may want to clear your browsing history. You may want to do this to prevent malicious individuals from getting your information or to maintain your privacy regarding web sites and pages you've visited. You may also want to do this if you are experiencing problems accessing a particular site or page, or to ensure that you are accessing the most recent version of a web site or page.

Figure 7-17. Configuring cookie settings for the Internet zone

To clear out your browsing history, complete these steps:

1. Close all Internet Explorer windows. Click Start → Control Panel → Network and Internet → Internet Options.

2. On the General tab, click Delete under Browsing History. This displays the Delete Browsing History dialog box shown in Figure 7-18.

3. Delete individual types of temporary Internet files by clicking the related buttons. When prompted, click Yes to confirm the action.

4. Click "Delete all" to clear out your entire browsing history, including temporary Internet files, cookies, the history list, form data, and passwords. When prompted, select "Also delete files and settings stored by add-ons" to delete temporary files and settings created by browser add-ons. Click Yes to confirm the action.

Blocking Pop Ups

Some web pages contain pop ups. A *pop up* is a subwindow that is displayed when you access a web page. Sometimes pop ups appear on top of the browser window; other times they appear under the browser window. Because most pop ups contain ads or are otherwise unwanted content, Internet Explorer blocks most types of pop ups it recognizes by default in all security zones, except the Local Intranet zone. This

Figure 7-18. Deleting your browsing history

means Internet Explorer uses the Pop-up Blocker when you are browsing sites on the public Internet, trusted sites, and restricted sites, but does not use the Pop-up Blocker when you access sites on your local network.

By default, when a pop up is blocked, Internet Explorer displays a message on the Information bar stating this. If you right-click the Information bar and select "Allow pop-up to display," Internet Explorer will display the pop up. Alternatively, if you right-click the Information bar and select "Allow all pop-ups for this site," Internet Explorer will configure the site as an Allowed Site, and all pop ups for the site will then be displayed.

You can enable or disable pop-up blocking by completing the following steps:

1. In Internet Explorer, click Tools → Internet Options. This displays the Internet Options dialog box.

2. On the Privacy tab, select the "Turn on Pop-up Blocker" checkbox to enable the Pop-up Blocker, or clear the "Turn on Pop-up Blocker" checkbox to disable the Pop-up Blocker.

With pop-up blocking enabled, you can configure the way the Pop-up Blocker works by completing the following steps:

1. In Internet Explorer, click Tools → Internet Options. This displays the Internet Options dialog box.

2. On the Privacy tab, select Settings under Pop-up Blocker. This displays the Pop-up Blocker Settings dialog box shown in Figure 7-19.

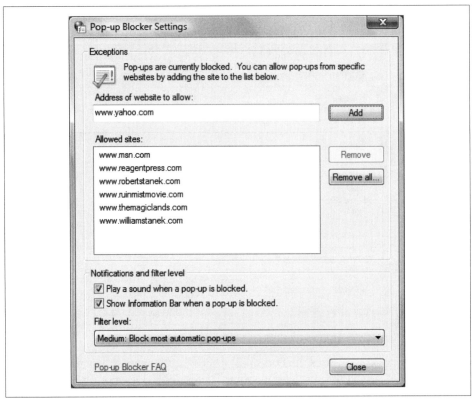

Figure 7-19. Configuring Pop-up Blocker settings

3. You can use these options to add or remove allowed sites:

   Add
   > To allow a site's pop ups to be displayed, type the address of the site in the field provided, such as **www.msn.com**, and then click Add. This site is then permitted to use pop ups regardless of Internet Explorer settings.

   Remove
   > To remove a site that is currently allowed to display pop ups, click the site address and then click Remove.

   Remove All
   > To remove all sites that are currently allowed to display pop ups, click Remove All. When prompted to confirm the action, click Yes.

4. To stop playing a sound when a pop up is blocked, clear "Play a sound when a pop-up is blocked."

5. To stop displaying an information message in the browser when a pop up is blocked, clear "Show Information Bar when a pop-up is blocked."

6. By default, most types of automatic pop ups are blocked when the Pop-up Blocker is enabled. You can use the following options of the Filter Level list to control the types of pop ups that are blocked:

   High: Block all pop-ups (Ctrl-Alt to override)
   > With this setting, Internet Explorer tries to block all pop ups. To temporarily override this setting, press Ctrl-Alt while clicking a link to open a page and its related pop up.

   Medium: Block most automatic pop-ups
   > With this setting, Internet Explorer tries to block pop ups most commonly used to display ads or other unwanted content. Some types of pop ups are allowed. To override this setting temporarily, press Ctrl-Alt while clicking a link to open a page and its related pop up.

   Low: Allow pop-ups from secure sites
   > With standard (HTTP) connections, Internet Explorer attempts to block pop ups most commonly used to display ads or other unwanted content. With secure (HTTPS) connections, Internet Explorer allows pop ups.

7. Click Close and then click OK to save your settings.

Protecting Your Computer from Phishing

Phishing is a technique whereby a site attempts to collect personal information about you without your knowledge or consent. Internet Explorer 7 has a phishing filter that is designed to warn you about potential phishing sites and known phishing sites. The warning is displayed on the Status bar as discussed previously.

The phishing filter is active by default for all security zones, except the Local Intranet zone. This means Internet Explorer uses the phishing filter when you are browsing sites on the public Internet, trusted sites, and restricted sites, but does not use the phishing filter when you access sites on your local network.

The phishing filter is always on by default. In Internet Explorer, you can turn off this feature by clicking Tools → Phishing Filter → Turn Off Automatic Website Checking. You can then manually check sites if desired by using the Check This Website option. If you suspect a site is collecting personal information without your knowledge or consent, you can report the site by using the Report This Website option. Keep in mind that you may have granted implied consent to a site when you signed up to use a site, or when you downloaded and installed a particular browser add-on or related Internet software.

Restricting Permissions Using Security Zones

Security levels and zones are important parts of Internet Explorer's security features. You can display security options for Internet Explorer by clicking Tools → Internet Options, and then clicking the Security tab in the Internet Options dialog box, as shown in Figure 7-20. The standard levels of security that you can use are:

High
> Appropriate for sites that might contain harmful content. With this security level, Internet Explorer runs with maximum safeguards and with less-secure features disabled.

Medium-high
> Appropriate for most public Internet sites. With this security level, Internet Explorer prompts you prior to downloading all potentially unsafe types of content and disables downloading of unsigned ActiveX controls.

Medium
> Appropriate only for trusted sites. With this security level, Internet Explorer prompts you prior to downloading most potentially unsafe contents and disables downloading of unsigned ActiveX controls.

Medium-low
> Appropriate only for sites on your internal network. With this security level, Internet Explorer disables downloading of unsigned ActiveX controls but downloads and runs most types of content without prompting.

Low
> Appropriate only for sites you know are trustworthy, such as secure internal sites. With this security level, Internet Explorer uses minimal safeguards, and downloads and runs most types of content without prompts.

Internet Explorer 7 uses security zones to help you restrict permissions according to where web sites are located and what you know about them. Each security zone is assigned a default security level. From most trusted to least trusted, the security zones are:

Local intranet
> This zone is used to configure security settings for sites on your local network. The default security level is Medium-low.

 Unlike earlier releases of Windows, Windows Vista can automatically detect when web sites are on your local network. Windows Vista does this by checking the network address of the web site and comparing it to the network address of your computer. Windows Vista also considers sites bypassed by the proxy server and network paths, such as Universal Naming Convention (UNC) paths, as being on the local network.

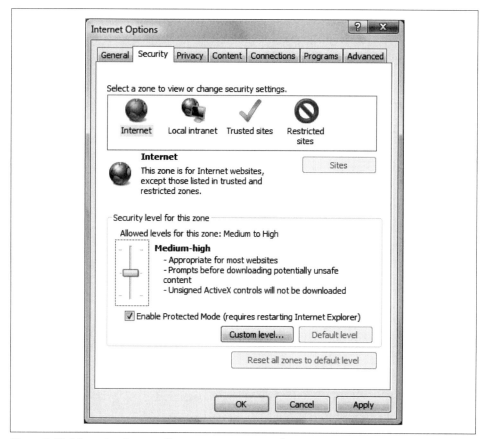

Figure 7-20. Managing the overall security on a per-zone basis

Trusted sites

This zone is used to configure security settings for sites that you explicitly trust and that are considered to be free of content that could damage or harm your computer. The default security level is Medium.

Internet

This zone is used to configure security settings for sites on the public Internet, and is used for all sites not placed in other zones. The default security level is Medium-high.

Restricted sites

This zone is used to configure security settings for sites that could potentially damage your computer. The default security level is High.

When you are working with the "Local intranet," "Trusted sites," and "Restricted sites" zones, you can specify the web addresses of sites that should be associated with these zones. With the "Local intranet" zone, you can also control the way Windows Vista detects sites on the local network.

Setting the security level for a zone

One way to modify the security level for a zone is to assign a new security level. With the "Local intranet" and "Trusted sites" zones, you can assign any desired security level. With the Internet zone, the only allowed security levels are Medium, Medium-high, and High. With the Restricted zone, the only allowed security level is High. You can also enable or disable Protected Mode on a per-zone basis. Protected Mode is enabled by default for all zones except the "Trusted sites" zone.

To configure the security level for a particular zone, follow these steps:

1. In Internet Explorer, click Tools → Internet Options. This displays the Internet Options dialog box.

2. On the Security tab, click the zone you want to work with.

3. To change the security level, move the "Security level for this zone" slider up or down to the desired level.

4. To enable Protected Mode for the zone, select the Enable Protected Mode checkbox. To disable Protected Mode for the zone, clear the Enable Protected Mode checkbox. Any changes you make to the Protected Mode settings require that you restart Internet Explorer for the changes to take effect.

5. To restore the default security settings for the selected zone, click the "Default level" button.

6. Click OK to save your settings.

To reset security for all zones, follow these steps:

1. In Internet Explorer, click Tools → Internet Options. This displays the Internet Options dialog box.

2. On the Security tab, click the "Reset all zones to default level" button and then click OK to save your settings.

Setting a custom security level for a zone

In addition to being able to assign a specific security level for a zone, you can also set a custom level by configuring the individual security settings summarized in Table 7-2. Generally, you want to set a custom level only to resolve a specific problem you are experiencing and should otherwise rely on the predefined security levels to achieve the desired results.

You can configure a custom security level for a particular zone by completing these steps:

1. In Internet Explorer, click Tools → Internet Options. This displays the Internet Options dialog box.

2. On the Security tab, click the zone you want to work with.

3. Click the "Custom level" button to display the Security Settings dialog box.

4. Use the individual security settings to specify how you want to handle potentially risky actions, files, programs, and downloads. With most settings your options may include:

Prompt
  Click Prompt to be prompted for approval before proceeding.

Disable
  Click Disable to skip prompting and automatically refuse the action or download.

Enable
  Click Enable to skip prompting and automatically accept the action or download.

5. Click OK to save your settings.

Table 7-2. Internet Explorer security settings and their meanings

Security category/setting	Description
.NET Framework	
Loose XAML	Controls the use of XAML documents that are formatted loosely (rather than strictly) according to their Document Type Definitions (DTDs).
XAML Browser Applications	Controls the use of XAML browser applications for viewing XAML documents within Internet Explorer.
XPS Documents	Controls the use of XML Paper Specification (XPS) formatted documents.
.NET Framework-reliant components	
Run components not signed with Authenticode	Controls the use of .NET Framework components that are not digitally signed.
Run components signed with Authenticode	Controls the use of .NET Framework components that are digitally signed.
ActiveX controls and plug-ins	
Allow previously unused ActiveX controls to run without prompt	Controls whether new ActiveX controls can run without first prompting for permission.
Allow scriptlets	Controls the use of scriptlets in web pages.
Automatic prompting for ActiveX controls	Controls whether you are automatically prompted each time before using ActiveX controls.
Binary and script behaviors	Controls the direct execution of binary executables and scripts, such as when you click links to an executable or script.
Display video and animation on a web page that does not use external media player	Controls whether embedded video and animation play in Internet Explorer.
Download signed ActiveX controls	Controls the downloading of signed ActiveX controls.
Download unsigned ActiveX controls	Controls the downloading of unsigned ActiveX controls.
Initialize and script ActiveX controls not marked as safe for scripting	Controls whether ActiveX controls not marked as safe for scripting can be modified or scripted based on the contents of a web page.

Table 7-2. Internet Explorer security settings and their meanings (continued)

Security category/setting	Description
Run ActiveX controls and plug-ins	Controls whether ActiveX controls and browser plug-ins run in Internet Explorer.
Script ActiveX controls marked for safe scripting	Controls whether ActiveX controls marked for safe scripting can be modified or scripted based on the contents of a web page. If you change this setting, you must restart Internet Explorer for the change to be applied.
Downloads	
Automatic prompting for file downloads	Controls whether Internet Explorer prompts you for file downloads.
File download	Controls whether Internet Explorer downloads files.
Font download	Controls whether Internet Explorer downloads fonts.
Enable .NET Framework setup	
Enable .NET Framework setup	Controls whether .NET Framework setup is enabled.
Miscellaneous	
Access data sources across domains	Controls whether scripts and other elements in a page can access data sources from other domains.
Allow META refresh	Controls whether automatic refresh or redirection of a page is allowed using the HTML META tag.
Allow scripting of Internet Explorer web browser control	Controls whether a web page can script the browser control directly.
Allow script-initiated windows without size or position constraint	Controls whether a script in a web page can open a window without size or position details.
Allow web pages to use restricted protocols for active content	Controls whether a web page can use restricted protocols with scripts and other types of active content.
Allow web sites to open windows without Address or Status bar	Controls whether a script in a web page can open a window without an Address or Status bar.
Display mixed content	Controls whether a web page can display content from both secure and unsecure sources.
Don't prompt for client certificate selection when no certificates or only one certificate exists	Controls whether Internet Explorer prompts you to select a client certificate when there is only one or no certificate available.
Drag and drop or copy and paste files	Controls whether Internet Explorer allows you to use drag and drop or copy and paste with web pages.
Include local directory path when uploading to a server	Controls whether Internet Explorer includes the full local directory path when you upload files to a remote server.
Installation of desktop items	Controls whether Internet Explorer allows items to be installed on the desktop.
Launching applications and unsafe files	Controls whether Internet Explorer allows other applications to be started and whether it allows unsafe files to be opened.
Launching programs and files in an IFRAME	Controls whether Internet Explorer allows other applications and files to be opened in an IFRAME.

Table 7-2. Internet Explorer security settings and their meanings (continued)

Security category/setting	Description
Navigate subframes across different domains	Controls whether Internet Explorer allows frames to come from multiple domains.
Open files based on content, not file extension	Controls whether Internet Explorer opens files based on the Multipurpose Internet Mail Extension (MIME) type or based on the file extension.
Software channel permissions	Sets the safety level for content pushed to the browser. You can set the safety level to High (recommended), Medium, or Low.
Submit nonencrypted form data	Controls whether Internet Explorer can submit nonencrypted (plain-text) form data to a web site.
Use Phishing Filter	Controls whether the phishing filter is enabled or disabled.
Use Pop-up Blocker	Controls whether the Pop-up Blocker is enabled or disabled.
User data persistence	Controls whether data you've entered is persistent when you open new browser windows.
Web sites in less privileged content zone can navigate into this zone	Controls whether web sites in a zone with a lower security level can redirect to web sites in a zone with a higher security level.
Scripting	
Active scripting	Controls whether Active scripting of web pages is allowed.
Allow programmatic clipboard access	Controls whether a script or other element in a web page can read what is copied to your computer's clipboard.
Allow Status bar updates via script	Controls whether a script or other element in a web page can update the Status bar.
Allow web sites to prompt for information using scripted windows	Controls whether a script or other element in a web page can display a prompt.
Scripting of Java applets	Controls whether a script or other element in a web page can script Java applets.
User authentication	
Logon	Controls the way user authentication works when you need to log on to a web site. The options are Anonymous Logon, Automatic Logon Only in Intranet Zone, Automatic Logon with Current User Name and Password, and Prompt for User Name and Password.

Configuring local intranet detection and sites

Windows Vista automatically detects sites on the local network according to their network address. If you experience problems with sites not being detected properly, you may want to disable automatic detection settings and allow only specifically included types of sites to be considered local sites. In addition to or instead of doing this, you can specifically identify a site as being on the local network.

To configure local intranet detection, specify local sites, or both, complete the following steps:

1. In Internet Explorer, click Tools → Internet Options. This displays the Internet Options dialog box.

2. On the Security tab, click the "Local intranet" zone and then click the Sites button. This displays the "Local intranet" dialog box, as shown in Figure 7-21.

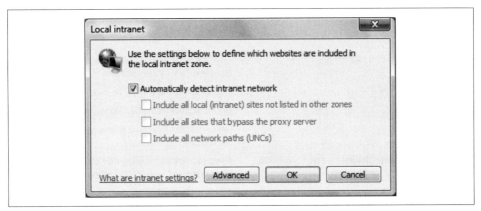

Figure 7-21. Configuring the way local network sites are used

3. If Windows Vista is unable to detect sites on the local network automatically, you may need to manually configure the intranet zone settings. To do this, clear "Automatically detect intranet network" and then specify sites to include. You can include local (intranet) sites not listed in other zones, sites that bypass the proxy server, and network paths (UNCs) by selecting the related checkboxes. To exclude a type of resource, clear the related checkbox.

4. To specify additional sites for the "Local intranet" zone or require secure verification using Hypertext Transfer Protocol Secure (HTTPS) for all sites in the "Local intranet" zone, click the Advanced button. This displays a new "Local intranet" dialog box with the following options:

   Add
   To add a site to the "Local intranet" zone, type the web address for a site and then click Add.

   Remove
   To remove a site from the "Local intranet" zone, click the web address and then click Remove.

   Require server verification (HTTPS:) for all sites in this zone
   To require secure verification for all sites in this zone using HTTPS, select this checkbox.

5. Click OK twice.

Configuring trusted sites

If you find that the normal security settings are too restrictive for a site that you explicitly trust and know to be free of content that could damage your computer, you can designate the site as a trusted site by completing these steps:

1. In Internet Explorer, click Tools → Internet Options. This displays the Internet Options dialog box.

2. On the Security tab, click the "Trusted sites" zone and then click the Sites button. This displays the "Trusted sites" dialog box, as shown in Figure 7-22.

Figure 7-22. Configuring trusted sites and related options

3. To add a site to the "Trusted sites" zone, type the web address for the site and then click Add.

4. To remove a site from the "Trusted sites" zone, click the web address and then click Remove.

5. To require secure verification for all sites in this zone using HTTPS, select the "Require server verification (HTTPS:) for all sites in this zone" checkbox.

6. Click OK to save your settings.

Configuring restricted sites

If you find a site that has offensive content or content that could damage your computer, you can designate the site as a restricted site by completing the following steps:

1. In Internet Explorer, click Tools → Internet Options. This displays the Internet Options dialog box.

2. On the Security tab, click the "Restricted sites" zone and then click the Sites button. This displays the "Restricted sites" dialog box, as shown in Figure 7-23.

Figure 7-23. Configuring restricted sites

3. To add a site to the "Restricted sites" zone, type the web address for the site and then click Add.

4. To remove a site from the "Restricted sites" zone, click the web address and then click Remove.

5. Click OK to save your settings.

 Keep in mind that designating a site as a restricted site doesn't stop you or anyone else from accessing the site. Instead, it establishes a higher level of security for the site.

Setting Advanced Internet Options

In the Internet Options dialog box, you'll find a wide variety of advanced settings on the Advanced tab. These advanced options allow you to fine-tune the way Internet Explorer works. Some advanced options can be set through other settings in the Internet Options dialog box, but they are provided on the Advanced tab so that you have a central location for managing settings.

Advanced settings are organized into several categories. The main categories are:

Accessibility
    Settings designed to improve ease of access

Browsing
    Settings that control the general way browsing works in Internet Explorer as well as the way web pages are displayed

HTTP 1.1
    Settings that control whether and how Internet Explorer uses HTTP 1.1

International
    Settings that control whether and how Internet Explorer displays and sends international domain names

Multimedia
    Settings that control how Internet Explorer works with pictures, sounds, animations, and ClearType text

Security
    Settings that control the way Internet Explorer uses various security and authentication technologies

Table 7-3 lists all the advanced options and details how they are used. Generally, you want to change advanced settings only to resolve a specific issue with the way Internet Explorer displays or accesses web pages. Otherwise, you should rely on the predefined settings. In Table 7-3, a setting is followed by a plus sign (+) if it is enabled by default and an asterisk (*) if you must restart Internet Explorer for a setting change to take effect.

You can configure advanced options by completing these steps:

1. In Internet Explorer, click Tools → Internet Options. This displays the Internet Options dialog box.
2. On the Advanced tab, select or clear individual advanced options to control the way Internet Explorer displays or accesses web pages. With most settings, select them to enable the setting and clear them to disable the setting.
3. Click OK to save your settings.

Some changes to advanced options may cause Internet Explorer to work differently than expected. If you experience unintended consequences because you have changed advanced options, you can restore the default configuration for advanced options by completing these steps:

1. In Internet Explorer, click Tools → Internet Options. This displays the Internet Options dialog box.
2. On the Advanced tab, click "Restore advanced settings."

Table 7-3. Internet Explorer advanced options and their meanings

Category/Setting	Description
Accessibility	
Always expand ALT text for images	Specifies whether the image size should expand to fit all of the alternate text when the Show Pictures checkbox is cleared.
Move system caret with focus/selection changes	Specifies whether to move the system caret whenever the focus or selection changes. Some accessibility aids, such as screen readers and screen magnifiers, use the system caret to determine which area of the screen to read or magnify.
Reset text size to medium for new windows and tabs+*	Specifies whether Internet Explorer resets the text size to Medium for new windows and tabs.
Reset zoom level to 100% for new windows and tabs+	Specifies whether Internet Explorer resets the zoom level to 100% when you open new windows and tabs.
Browsing	
Close unused folders in History and Favorites*	Specifies that when you open a folder in the Favorites bar, History bar, or Organize Favorites window, any folders opened previously will close.
Disable script debugging (Internet Explorer)+	Specifies whether you want to turn off your script debugger, if one is installed. Web site developers use script debuggers to test programs and scripts on their web pages.
Disable script debugging (Other)	Specifies whether you want to turn off your script debugger, if one is installed. Web site developers use script debuggers to test programs and scripts on their web pages.
Display a notification about every script error	Specifies whether to display the actual script errors when a page does not appear properly due to problems with its scripting. This feature is off by default, but it is useful to developers when testing web pages.
Enable FTP folder view (outside of Internet Explorer)+	Specifies whether to show FTP sites in folder view, which is similar to browsing folders in Windows Explorer. This feature might not work with certain types of proxy connections. If you clear this checkbox, FTP sites will display their contents in an HTML-based layout.
Enable page transitions+	Specifies whether, as you move from one web page to another, Internet Explorer fades out the page you are leaving and fades in the page to which you are going.
Enable personalized favorites menu	Keeps your Favorites list clean by hiding links that you haven't used recently, while still keeping other links easily accessible. You can view hidden links by clicking the down arrow at the bottom of the Favorites menu.
Enable third-party browser extensions+*	Specifies whether you want to enable features you installed for use with Internet Explorer that companies other than Microsoft may have created.
Enable visual styles on buttons and controls in webpages+	Specifies that you want the controls in web pages to use Windows display settings.

Table 7-3. Internet Explorer advanced options and their meanings (continued)

Category/Setting	Description
Enable websites to use the search pane*	Specifies whether web sites can use the Search Pane in Internet Explorer.
Force offscreen compositing even under Terminal Server*	Specifies that you want to force off-screen compositing even if you are running Terminal Server. This will eliminate the flashing you see with the compositing normally used by Internet Explorer running under Terminal Server; however, choosing this option might severely decrease the performance of Internet Explorer running under Terminal Server.
Notify when downloads complete+	Specifies whether to display a message at the end of a file download, to indicate that the download is complete.
Reuse windows for launching shortcuts (when tabbed browsing is off)+	Specifies that when you click a web link in an Internet-aware program, such as Office Outlook, and an Internet Explorer window is already open, the web page appears in the open browser window instead of opening a new window.
Show friendly HTTP error messages+	Specifies whether, when there's a problem connecting with an Internet server, to provide a detailed description with hints on how to correct the problem. If you clear this checkbox, you will see just the error code and the name of the error.
Underline Links	Specifies how you want links on web pages underlined. The options are Always, Hover, and Never. To underline all links, click Always. To not underline links, click Never. To underline a link when your mouse pointer is over the link, click Hover.
Use inline AutoComplete	Specifies whether you want Internet Explorer to complete entries when you type web addresses in the Address bar, based on entries you've used before.
Use most recent order when switching tabs with Ctrl+Tab	Specifies whether you want to view tabs in order of the most recently viewed tab when pressing Ctrl-Tab.
Use Passive FTP (for firewall and DSL modem compatibility)+	Specifies whether to use passive FTP, which does not require your computer to know its Internet Protocol (IP) address. Some network configurations will work only with passive mode turned on, and others will work only with passive mode turned off. This feature allows you to select which mode to use for compatibility with your network settings. Most network configurations will support both modes. The passive FTP mode is considered more secure.
Use smooth scrolling+	Specifies whether a special type of scrolling is used to display content at a predefined speed.
HTTP 1.1 settings	
Use HTTP 1.1	Specifies whether to attempt to use the HTTP 1.1 protocol when connecting to web sites. Some web sites still use HTTP 1.0, so if you are having difficulties connecting to a web site, you might want to clear this checkbox.

Category/Setting	Description
Use HTTP 1.1 through proxy connections	Specifies whether to attempt to use the HTTP 1.1 protocol when connecting to web sites by using a proxy server. Some web sites still use HTTP 1.0, so if you are having difficulties connecting to a web site through a proxy connection, you might want to clear this checkbox.
International	
Always show encoded addresses*	Specifies whether or not addresses should be displayed with UTF-8-encoded characters. UTF-8 is a standard that defines characters so that they are readable in any language. This enables you to view Internet addresses that contain characters from any language.
Send IDN server names+*	Specifies whether international domain names are sent to sites on the public Internet using UTF-8 encoding.
Send IDN server names for Intranet addresses*	Specifies whether international domain names are sent to sites on the local network using UTF-8 encoding.
Send UTF-8 URLs+*	Specifies whether to use UTF-8 encoding when exchanging web addresses that contain characters from any language.
Show Information Bar for encoded addresses+*	Specifies whether web addresses are displayed on the Information bar using UTF-8 encoding.
Use UTF-8 for mailto links*	Specifies whether mailto links in web pages use UTF-8 encoding rather than ASCII encoding.
Multimedia	
Always use ClearType for HTML*	Specifies whether ClearType is used for text in web pages.
Enable automatic image resizing+	Specifies that you want Internet Explorer to resize large images automatically so that they fit in the browser window.
Play animations in webpages+*	Specifies whether animations can play when pages are displayed. When this checkbox is cleared, you can still play an individual animation by right-clicking the icon that represents the animation and then clicking Show Picture.
Play sounds in webpages+	Specifies whether music and other sounds can play when pages are displayed.
Show image download placeholders	Specifies whether placeholders should be drawn for images while they are downloading. This allows items in the page to be positioned where they would appear when the images are fully downloaded. This option is ignored if the Show Pictures checkbox is cleared.
Show pictures+	Specifies whether images should be included when pages are displayed. When this checkbox is cleared, you can still display an individual image by right-clicking the icon that represents the graphic and then clicking Show Picture.
Smart image dithering+	Specifies whether you want Internet Explorer to smooth images so that they appear less jagged when displayed.

Table 7-3. Internet Explorer advanced options and their meanings (continued)

Category/Setting	Description
Printing	
Print background colors and images	Specifies whether you want Internet Explorer to print background colors and images when you print a web page. Selecting this checkbox might cause your printer to use a lot of ink.
Search from the Address bar	Specifies whether and where search results are displayed. The default option is to display the results in the main window.
Security	
Allow active content from CDs to run on My Computer*	Specifies whether active content from CDs opens automatically in Internet Explorer.
Allow active content to run in files on My Computer*	Specifies whether active content can run files on your computer.
Allow software to run or install even if the signature is invalid	Specifies whether software with an invalid digital signature can run or install.
Check for publisher's certificate revocation+	Specifies whether you want Internet Explorer to check a software publisher's certificate to see if it has been revoked before accepting it as valid.
Check for server certificate revocation+*	Specifies whether you want Internet Explorer to check an Internet site's certificate to see if it has been revoked before accepting it as valid.
Check for signatures on downloaded programs+	Specifies that you want Internet Explorer to verify the identity of programs you download. When you download programs, a dialog box will appear providing the information that Internet Explorer finds during the check.
Do not save encrypted pages to disk	Specifies whether secure, encrypted web pages are saved in your Temporary Internet Files folder. As these pages may contain sensitive personal information, you may not want to save encrypted pages on a shared computer.
Empty Temporary Internet Files folder when browser is closed	Specifies whether to clear the Temporary Internet Files folder when you close the browser.
Enable Integrated Windows Authentication+*	Specifies that you want to turn on Integrated Windows Authentication.
Enable memory protection to help mitigate online attacks (dimmed)	Specifies whether you want to enable memory protection to help protect your computer against online attacks. You can select this option only if your computer supports it.
Enable native XMLHTTP support+	Specifies whether support for XML HTTP is enabled.
Phishing Filter	Specifies the configuration of the phishing filter. The options are Disable Phishing Filter, Turn Off Automatic Website Checking, and Turn On Automatic Website Checking. The default setting is Turn On Automatic Website Checking.
Use SSL 2.0	Specifies whether you want to send and receive secured information through Secure Sockets Layer Level 2 (SSL 2.0), the standard protocol for secure transmissions. All secure web sites support this protocol.

Table 7-3. Internet Explorer advanced options and their meanings (continued)

Category/Setting	Description
Use SSL 3.0+	Specifies whether you want to send and receive secured information through Secured Sockets Layer Level 3 (SSL 3.0), a protocol that is intended to be more secure than SSL 2.0. Some web sites might not support this protocol.
Use TLS 1.0+	Specifies whether to send and receive secured information through Transport Layer Security (TLS), an open security standard similar to SSL 3.0. Some web sites might not support this protocol.
Warn about certificate address mismatch+*	Specifies whether Internet Explorer should warn you if the address (URL) in a web site's security certificate is not valid.
Warn if changing between secure and not secure mode	Specifies whether Internet Explorer should warn you if you are switching between Internet sites that are secure and sites that are not secure.
Warn if POST submittal is redirected to a zone that does not permit posts+	Specifies whether to warn you when information you enter on a web-based form is being sent to a web site other than the one you are currently viewing.

Troubleshooting Internet Explorer Problems

Internet Explorer has several built-in features for helping you resolve problems you may experience. If you are having problems accessing a web page or connecting to the Internet, you can initiate network diagnostics by selecting Diagnose Connection Problems on the Tools menu. As shown in Figure 7-24, Windows Network Diagnostics will then attempt to identify the problem. If the problem can be repaired automatically, you'll see a list of possible solutions. Click the solution to apply it.

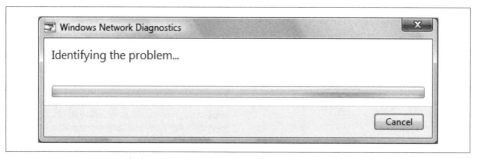

Figure 7-24. Using network diagnostics to identify problems

Sometimes a problem you are experiencing may be related to:

- The toolbars and add-ons you've installed
- The way you've configured the browsing history
- The security settings or security levels you've applied

- The advanced options you've configured for use
- The search providers and home pages you've configured for use

Rather than trying to troubleshoot each individual configuration area, Internet Explorer gives you a simple solution for resetting all Internet Explorer settings. The only settings not reset to their original default states are favorites, feeds, Internet connection options, Group Policy settings, and Content Advisor settings.

You can reset all Internet Explorer settings by completing the following steps:

1. In Internet Explorer, click Tools → Internet Options. This displays the Internet Options dialog box.

2. On the Advanced tab, click Reset under Reset Internet Explorer Settings.

3. When the warning dialog box shown in Figure 7-25 is displayed, click Reset.

Figure 7-25. Resetting Internet Explorer settings to resolve problems related to Internet Explorer configuration

When you exit all Internet Explorer windows and then restart Internet Explorer, all your Internet Explorer settings will be reset, and this should resolve any problems you're experiencing due to Internet Explorer configuration.

CHAPTER 8

Creating Your Media Library with Windows Media Player

To tell the truth, I've never been a big fan of Windows Media Player. It always seemed to me that the developers at Microsoft were more interested in the device's custom visual designs and background visualizations than what mattered most: creating an excellent media player that works like a media player should. With Windows Media Player 11, though, it's a different story. Microsoft has reduced the focus on custom visual designs (known as skins), streamlined the bloated menus, tightened up the interface, and completely reorganized the media library. The result is a media player that finally:

- Makes it easy to organize and find your media
- Supports all media types: music, pictures, videos, recorded TV, and other media
- Provides professional enhancements for music and video playback

So much has changed in Windows Media Player 11 that like Windows Vista itself, it seems more like a new program than the same old media player to which we've grown accustomed. Because of this, don't try to rip or burn CDs without first reading this chapter in its entirety. And whatever you do, don't give away your original CDs and DVDs just yet, because you're still going to need them.

Getting into Your Multimedia

Before you can get started with Windows Media Player 11, you're going to need to configure the player for first use. Afterward, you'll want to familiarize yourself with the interface and the supported media formats.

Configuring Windows Media Player for First Use

With Windows Media Player 11, navigating your media library is easier than ever—if you master the subtle changes in the interface. When you first start Windows Media Player by clicking Start → All Programs → Windows Media Player, you'll have to specify how Windows Media Player should be configured. As Figure 8-1 shows, you have two choices:

Express Settings

Configures the default settings you'll want to use most often. If you want to change the settings later, right-click the Library button and then select More Options. In the Options dialog box, select the Privacy tab. You'll have similar options as with step 2 of the Custom Settings procedure.

Custom Settings

Allows you to configure the settings to use. This gives you more control over the way Windows Media Player obtains and stores media information.

Figure 8-1. Choosing the initial settings for Windows Media Player

You can configure Windows Media Player to use express settings by clicking Express Settings and then clicking Finish. With express settings, Windows Media Player is configured as your default music and video player. Windows Media Player can download CD and DVD information from the Internet, obtain media usage rights automatically, and send anonymous usage information to Microsoft for the Customer Experience Improvement Program.

You can configure Windows Media Player to use custom settings by completing the following steps:

1. Select Custom Settings and then click Next. This displays the Select Privacy Options page shown in Figure 8-2.

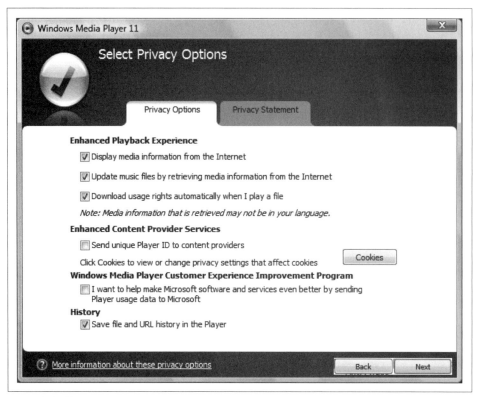

Figure 8-2. Choosing your privacy options

2. Use the following settings to configure your privacy settings and then click Next:

Display media information from the Internet
Select this option to allow Windows Media Player to try to obtain media information for the CDs and DVDs that you play. With music CDs, this allows Windows Media Player to retrieve the full details about the CD, including the album cover, album title, album artist, and song titles for each track. To obtain the media information, Windows Media Player sends the CD or DVD identifier to a database operated by your default online store or a Windows Media database. The online store or Windows Media database then sends the information back to your computer, where the information is stored. If your computer is offline, Windows Media Player stores the request for media information so that it can try to obtain the media information the next time you connect your computer to the Internet.

Update music files by retrieving media information from the Internet
Select this option to allow Windows Media Player to update music files by retrieving media information from the Internet. Windows Media Player can automatically obtain and update missing media information for music files that are added to or stored in your library, as long as the information is available.

Download usage rights automatically when I play a file
Select this option to allow Windows Media Player to acquire usage rights automatically for protected content when a file requires them. Usage rights allow you to use protected Windows Media-based files in a specific way. With a play right, you have the right to play the file. With a burn right, you have the right to burn the file to an audio CD. With a sync right, you have the right to sync the file to a portable device, such as an MP3 player. You cannot play, burn, or sync protected content if you do not have a license. In some cases, you may be required to pay for the license. In other cases, you may be required to complete a form before the content provider will issue the license to you.

Send unique Player ID to content providers
Select this option to allow Windows Media Player to send its unique identifier to web servers. The identifier identifies the player connection to a server and does not contain any personally identifiable information about you. Web servers typically use the identifier to monitor your connection, gather statistics, and provide access to content.

Cookies
Click this button to configure how cookies are used on your computer. Windows Media Player uses the cookie settings in Internet Explorer to communicate with other computers when playing streaming content and to communicate with the web sites that provide content to the player. Cookies also enable content providers to provide personalized services from their web sites. See "Configuring the use of browser cookies," in Chapter 7, for more information on cookies.

I want to help make Microsoft software and services even better by sending Player usage data
Select this option to send Microsoft anonymous information about the way you use Windows Media Player. Microsoft uses this information to improve future versions of Windows Media Player. Anonymous information about your hardware configuration and how you use related services is also sent to Microsoft.

Save file and URL history in the Player
Select this option to allow Windows Media Player to save lists of your most recently played files. These lists are used to allow you to navigate using the Forward and Back buttons and other similar options.

3. On the Customize the Installation Options page, use the checkboxes provided to specify whether to add a shortcut to the desktop, the Quick Launch Toolbar, or both. Click Next to continue.

4. On the Select the Default Music and Video Player page, you can set Windows Media Player as the default music and video player and then click Finish to complete the initial setup. Or, you can choose the file types that Windows Media Player will play. In this case, when you click Finish, the Set Program Associations dialog box is displayed, as shown in Figure 8-3. You will then need to:

   a. Select checkboxes for file types for which Windows Media Player should be the default.

   b. Clear checkboxes for file types for which Windows Media Player should not be the default.

   c. Click Save to save your settings and complete the initial setup.

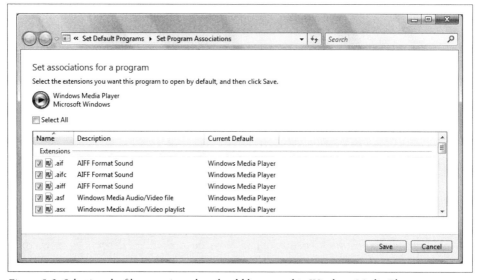

Figure 8-3. Selecting the file extensions that should be opened in Windows Media Player

Navigating Windows Media Player Menus and Toolbars

Windows Media Player 11 has a streamlined interface. Not only does this make working with Windows Media Player 11 more intuitive, but you'll also find that it is easier to organize your media. As Figure 8-4 shows, Microsoft gave Windows Media Player a complete makeover that includes:

A Navigation toolbar
   Provides browser-like Back and Forward buttons that let you navigate to pages you've viewed previously, as well as these Quick Access buttons: Now Playing, Library, Rip, Burn, and Sync. You'll also find Quick Access buttons for accessing and signing in to your default online store.

An Address toolbar

Allows you to navigate through the media available on your computer. It includes "Layout options" and "View options" buttons as well as a Search box and a "Show/Hide List pane" button.

A Controls toolbar

Provides basic controls for playing whatever is selected currently in Now Playing. The buttons are "Turn shuffle on/off," "Turn repeat on/off," "Stop," "Previous," "Play," "Next," "Mute," "Volume control," "View full screen," and "Switch to compact mode."

Figure 8-4. Using Windows Media Player 11 to view and manage your music, videos, pictures, and more

Using the Navigation toolbar

Like Windows Explorer, the Navigation toolbar includes Forward and Back buttons that allow you to access locations you've previously viewed. Clicking a Quick Access button on the Navigation toolbar allows you to access the main areas of Windows Media Player. You can:

- Click Now Playing to watch what's currently playing. With audio files, you'll see a visualization of the audio being played.
- Click Library to view and manage your media. You can also create playlists for your music.
- Click Rip to copy music from audio discs to your computer.
- Click Burn to create audio CDs and to create data discs on CD or DVD.
- Click Sync to synchronize your media to and from a portable device.
- Click Your Music Store to access your default online store.

If you right-click a Quick Access button or click the lower portion of a Quick Access button, you'll see an Options menu that provides additional related options.

Using the Address toolbar

As Figure 8-5 shows, Windows Media Player 11 has an address path similar to the one used in Windows Explorer. When you click library on the Navigation toolbar, the Address toolbar displays your current location as a series of links separated by arrows. This allows you to determine at a glance the current location within your media library.

Figure 8-5. The Navigation and Address toolbars in Windows Media Player 11

In the example shown in Figure 8-5, the location is:

```
Pictures → Library → All Pictures
```

The path portion of the toolbar has three key components. From left to right, they are:

Media Type icon
> This icon depicts the type of media you are currently working with. You'll see different icons for each type of media you can work with, including Music, Pictures, Video, Recorded TV, and Other Media.

Select a Category button
> This button provides access to the available media locations within your library. Selecting a media location allows you to access the last location you were viewing for that particular type of media within your library.

Location path entries
> The Location path shows the path to the current location within your media library. You can access folders anywhere along the path that's displayed by clicking the link for that location. You can access a subfolder of any folder location displayed by clicking the arrow to the right of the folder. This displays a list of all folders in the selected location, and you can access one of these folders by clicking it.

Media locations accessible via the Select a Category button are important because they allow you to access the last media locations you were working with for a particular media type. Clicking the Select a Category button is the easiest way to access and navigate media locations.

To the left of the Search box, you'll find the Layout Options and View Options buttons. Layout options allow you to:

- Show/Hide the Navigation Pane
- Show/Hide the List Pane
- Show/Hide Classic menus

View options allow you to switch among the following views:

Icon view
    Shows thumbnail icons for album covers or pictures without details

Expanded Tile/Tile view
    Shows thumbnail icons for album covers or pictures with details

Details view
    Shows details without thumbnail icons

In most cases, you'll want to use Expanded Tile or Tile view, as they give you a preview of the album cover or picture and all the related details. For each media type, you can customize the details listed in the related views by completing the following steps:

1. Using the Select a Media Category list, select the media category you want to work with, such as Music.
2. Click Layout Options and then click Choose Columns.
3. Select the columns to view. Clear the columns to hide.
4. Click OK to save your settings.

You can restore the original configuration by clicking Layout Options and then clicking Restore Columns.

Using the Search box

The Address toolbar also includes a Search box. You can use the Search box to quickly search for the media information associated with the currently selected type of media. The Search feature matches complete or partial words included in the media information.

You can search your media by completing the following steps:

1. Click in the Search box.
2. Type your search text.

Windows Media Player returns matches as you type. Click the Clear button to clear the search results.

Using the Navigation Pane

Regardless of which type of media you are working with, the primary navigation options in the Navigation Pane are the same. The only options that change are those associated with the Library node. Library node options change based on the type of media selected. Figure 8-6 shows as an example of the primary navigation options in the Navigation Pane on my computer.

Figure 8-6. The primary navigation options in Windows Media Player

In this example, the primary options are:

Playlists → Create Playlist
> Allows you to create a new playlist. After selecting this option, type the name of the playlist and then press Enter. The playlist will be displayed for editing and viewing in the List Pane, allowing you to drag and drop files onto the list.

Playlists → Your Playlist
> Allows you to edit an existing playlist by selecting it. The playlist will then be displayed for editing and viewing in the List Pane, allowing you to drag and drop files onto the list.

Now Playing
> Allows you to access Now Playing. You can control media being played with the Controls toolbar, regardless of whether you are accessing Now Playing.

Library
> Allows you to access a library of files related to a particular type of media. Library is the only node with subnodes that change based on the media type.

URGE
> Allows you to access the default online store, URGE. If you've configured a different online store, this will be accessible as well.

E: CD/DVD drive
    Provides access to the media loaded into the E: CD/DVD drive.

F: CD/DVD drive
    Provides access to the media loaded into the F: CD/DVD drive.

USB20FD
    Provides access to the MP3 player or other device with removable storage connected to the computer.

Your options will be slightly different depending on your default online store, the CD/DVD drives configured for your computer, and the devices you've connected. If your computer has multiple CD/DVD drives, you'll have an entry for each drive. If you've connected multiple devices with removable storage, you'll have an entry for each device.

Navigating your music library

Windows Media Player 11 supports playing music and sound files in the most popular formats. With Music, as shown in Figure 8-7, the Navigation Pane shows these primary views:

Recently Added
    Lists recently added music by artist and album name, with details for each song

Artist
    Lists your music by artist, number of songs, length, and rating

Album
    Lists your music by album, without song details

Songs
    Lists your music by artist and album name, with details for each song

Genre
    Lists your music organized into stacks by genre, such as alternative, country, pop, and rock

Year
    Lists your music organized into stacks by year recorded

Rating
    Lists your music organized into stacks by its rating

If you select Music → Library node, additional views are provided. These additional views are for contributing artist, composer, parental ratings, online stores, and folders.

Most music companies record audio CDs using audio encoding and Windows Media Player reads these files in CD audio (*.cda*) format. When you copy music from audio CDs (the process is called *ripping*), Windows Media Player stores the files on your hard disk using the default audio format and bit rate. The default audio format is Windows Media Audio, and the default bit rate is 128 kilobits per second (Kbps).

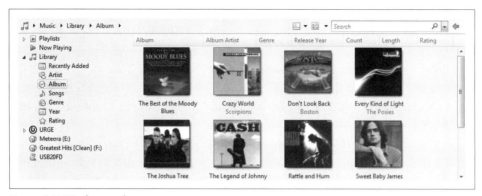

Figure 8-7. Working with your music

You can increase or decrease the default bit rate as appropriate. To get the best quality, you should increase the bit rate to 192 Kbps, which increases the size of the ripped files on your hard drive.

Table 8-1 provides an overview of the audio formats that Windows Media Player 11 supports. Some audio formats you can use for both audio and video. These formats, listed in Table 8-3, include professional and surround-sound formats that Windows Media Player can create and play.

Table 8-1. Audio formats supported by Windows Media Player 11

File type	File extensions
AIFF sound	.aif, .aifc, .aiff
AU sound	.au, .snd
AVI video	.avi
CD audio track	.cda
MIDI audio	.mid, .midi
MOD audio	.mod
MP3 audio	.mp3, .m3u
Real Media audio	.rmi
WAV audio	.wav
Windows Media Audio	.wma
Windows Media Audio shortcut	.wax

Navigating your picture library

Windows Media Player 11 supports viewing digital pictures from scanners and cameras. With Pictures, as shown in Figure 8-8, the Navigation Pane shows these primary views:

Recently Added
> Shows recently added pictures by date taken and filename

All Pictures
> Shows all your pictures by date taken and filename

Keywords
> Shows all your pictures organized into stacks by keyword

Date Taken
> Shows all your pictures organized into stacks by date taken

Rating
> Shows all your pictures organized into stacks by rating

Folder
> Shows all your pictures organized into stacks according to the folder in which they are stored on your hard drive

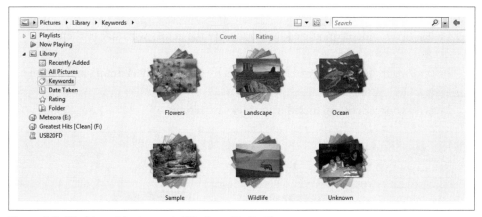

Figure 8-8. Working with pictures in Windows Media Player

Table 8-2 provides an overview of the picture formats Windows Media Player 11 supports. Because Windows Media Player is meant to be used with digital cameras and scanners and not with web images, it does not support some older file formats, such as GIF.

Table 8-2. Picture formats supported by Windows Media Player 11

File type	File extensions
Bitmap image	.bmp
JPEG image	.jpg, .jpeg, .jfif
PNG image	.png
TIFF image	.tif, .tiff
Word Perfect image	.wpg

You'll find that viewing pictures in Windows Media Player is similar to viewing pictures in Windows Photo Gallery. The two applications do in fact share subcomponents. However, Windows Media Player provides only basic features for viewing pictures and playing slide shows. Windows Photo Gallery, on the other hand, has extended viewing, editing, and slide show features.

Navigating your video library

Windows Media Player 11 supports playing videos with or without audio in the most popular formats. With Videos, as shown in Figure 8-9, the Navigation Pane shows these primary views:

Recently Added
    Lists recently added videos organized by letter of the alphabet and title

All Video
    Lists all your videos organized by letter of the alphabet and title

Actors
    Lists all your videos organized into stacks by the actors who star in them

Genre
    Lists all your videos organized into stacks by genre, such as drama and action

Rating
    Lists all your videos organized into stacks by rating

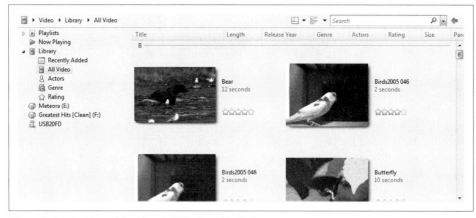

Figure 8-9. Working with videos in Windows Media Player

If you select the Video → Library node, additional views are provided. These additional views are for parental ratings, online stores, and folders.

Table 8-3 provides an overview of the video formats Windows Media Player 11 supports. Windows Media Player 11 supports a professional audio and video with audio format that allows you to use immersive surround sound if your computer has a multi-channel or high-resolution audio card. It also supports other related formats, which I've listed in the table as well.

Table 8-3. Video formats supported by Windows Media Player 11

File format/type	File extensions
Video formats	
DVD video	*.mpa, .m1v, .m2v, .mp2, .mp2v, .mpv2*
MPEG 1 and MPEG 2 video	*.mpe, .mpeg, .mpg*
Audio/Video format	
Windows Media Audio/Video Professional	*.asf, .wm, .wmv*
Recorded TV format	
Microsoft Digital Video Recorder	*.dvr-ms*
Additional supported formats	
Windows Media Audio/Video playlist	*.asx, .wpl, .wmx, .wvx*
Windows Media Player Skin File	*.wms*
Windows Media Player Skin Package	*.wmz*
Windows Media Download Package	*.wmd*
Windows Media Library	*.wmdb*

Navigating your recorded TV library

Windows Media Center records live TV in the Microsoft Digital Video Recorder (DVR-MS) format. You can play back recorded TV in Windows Media Center or in Windows Media Player. With recorded TV, as shown in Figure 8-10, the Navigation Pane shows these primary views:

Recently Added
Lists recently added TV shows organized by title

All TV
Lists all your recorded TV shows organized by date recorded

Series
Lists all your recorded TV shows organized into stacks by show/series

Genre
Lists all your recorded TV shows organized into stacks by genre, such as mystery, drama, and action

Actors
Lists all your recorded TV shows organized into stacks by the actors who star in them

Rating
Lists all your recorded TV shows organized into stacks by rating

If you select Recorded → Library node, additional views are provided. These additional views are for parental ratings, online stores, and folders.

Figure 8-10. Working with recorded TV in Windows Media Player

Playing Your Media

Once you've configured Windows Media Player 11, you can use it to play any audio or video file on your computer. If Windows Media Player is the default player for this type of file, you can launch the player and play the file simply by double-clicking it. With other types of supported files, you can right-click the file, select Open With, and then choose Windows Media Player as the program you want to use to open the file. While you can open and play media files using either of these techniques, doing so isn't the best or most constructive use of Windows Media Player. Instead, follow the techniques outlined in the sections that follow to get the most out of the player features built into Windows Media Player.

Using Now Playing with Media Added to Your Library

With media added to your library, you can select media to play in Now Playing simply by double-clicking an audio track, picture file, or video file. The way Now Playing works depends on the type of media:

- With an audio track, the related album or audio book starts playing, beginning with the audio track you selected and continuing according to the order of the tracks, or autoshuffling if you've turned on the autoshuffle feature.

- With a picture file, the related picture folder starts playing, beginning with the picture you selected and continuing with a slide show according to the order of the pictures, or autoshuffling if you've turned on the autoshuffle feature.

- With video or recorded TV files, the related video or TV folder starts playing, beginning with the video or show you selected and continuing with a slide show according to the order of the files, or autoshuffling if you've turned on the autoshuffle feature.

After you've selected the media you want to play, you can control playback using the Controls toolbar. The Controls toolbar is displayed in the lower portion of the main window, and there are two slightly different configurations of this toolbar.

Figure 8-11 shows an album being played. Below the visualization, you'll find the Controls Pane. The upper portion of the Controls Pane shows a progress indicator that graphically depicts how much of an audio or video track has played. To the right of the album or movie cover, Windows Media Player shows descriptive text that rotates among the album or movie title, the artists or actors, and the name of the current track.

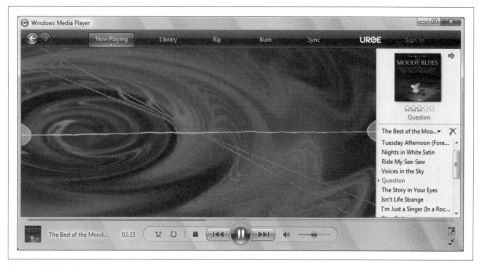

Figure 8-11. Playing your music

When working with all media types except movies, the List Pane allows you to select easily from among the available tracks or files, and the standard controls from left to right are:

Turn Shuffle On/Off
Toggles the shuffle feature on or off. When shuffle is on, Windows Media Player will play items in the current playlist in random order rather than in sequence.

Turn Repeat On/Off
Toggles the repeat feature on or off. When repeat is on, Windows Media Player will play the current playlist in its entirety and then play it again.

Pause
Pauses playing or displaying the current file.

Previous
Goes to the previous file. If you click and hold this button, you can rewind.

Play
Plays the current file.

Next
> Goes to the next file. If you click and hold this button, you can fast-forward.

Mute
> Mutes the sound.

Volume Control
> Adjusts the sound level.

View Full Screen
> Displays the player in full-screen mode, when allowed.

Switch to Compact Mode
> Displays the compact player with only the controls.

If you don't want to see the List Pane, you can hide it by clicking the Hide List Pane button, or by right-clicking Now Playing and then clearing the Show List Pane option. You can display the List Pane again by right-clicking Now Playing and then selecting the Show List Pane option.

Using Now Playing with Video DVDs Loaded into Your DVD Drive

You can play video DVDs loaded into your DVD drive by right-clicking Now Playing and then choosing the appropriate Play option, as shown in Figure 8-12. Windows Media Player starts playing the introductory materials, and then you'll see the DVD Start screen, which you can use to play the video, access specific episodes or chapters, view bonus material, or select an alternative language.

> Windows Media Player uses media information from the Windows Media database to display the movie title and information about the movie. If you aren't connected to the Internet and the required information wasn't previously downloaded into the Windows Media Player cache, you'll see the title "Unknown DVD."

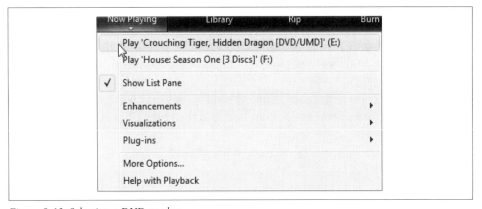

Figure 8-12. Selecting a DVD to play

When working with video DVDs, you'll see the modified Controls toolbar shown in Figure 8-13. Here, the first three buttons of the standard Controls toolbar are replaced with these two buttons:

DVD menu
Displays the DVD menu for selecting special features, getting DVD information, setting the video playback size, or viewing the video in full-screen mode.

Stop button
Stops playing the video. As with a DVD player, if you then click Play, play resumes from the beginning and you'll see promos and other introductory materials.

Figure 8-13. Playing a movie

Clicking the View Full Screen button or Full Screen option on the DVD menu displays the video in full-screen mode. You can exit this mode by pressing the Esc key. When a movie starts to play, you can skip the introductory materials by selecting the first movie track in the List Pane or by selecting the Root Menu option on the DVD menu.

On the DVD menu, you'll see a Special Features submenu that has these submenus:

Audio
Use this menu to choose an alternative language soundtrack. For example, with my *Crouching Tiger, Hidden Dragon* movie, I could listen to the movie in Chinese (Taiwan), English (United States), or French (France).

Set Video Size
Use this menu to set the default video size. By default, Windows Media Player is configured to fit the video to the player window on resize, allowing Windows Media Player to adjust the video size automatically if you change the size of the player window. You can also set a relative playback size within the window of 50 percent, 100 percent, or 200 percent.

All commercially produced DVDs are encoded with a unique code, similar to a bar code. Windows Media Player reads this code and sends it to a Windows Media database to obtain information about the DVD. This information is then stored in the Windows Media Player cache so that it is available the next time you play the DVD. If Windows Media Player doesn't download the DVD information automatically or you've recently connected your computer to the Internet, you can get the DVD information by completing the following steps:

1. Select "Get DVD information" on the DVD menu. You'll then see the "Find DVD information" dialog box shown in Figure 8-14.

2. In the "Find DVD information" dialog box, the information about the DVD should be displayed automatically. If it isn't, click Search and follow the prompts to select the correct DVD.

3. Once you have the right DVD information, you can customize any of the text entries associated with the DVD by clicking Edit, modifying the text entries as appropriate, and then clicking Next.

4. Click Finish to save the DVD information to the Windows Media Player cache.

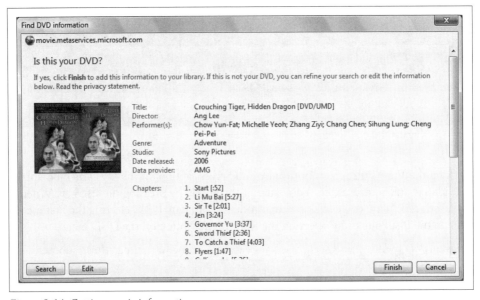

Figure 8-14. Getting movie information

Using Now Playing with Audio CDs Loaded into Your CD/DVD Drive

You can play audio CDs loaded into your CD/DVD drive by right-clicking Now Playing and then choosing the appropriate Play option, as shown in Figure 8-15. Windows Media Player starts playing the audio CD with Track 1. As with video DVDs, all commercially produced music CDs are encoded with a unique code. Windows Media

Player reads this code and sends it to a Windows Media database to display the album art, album title, artist, and song titles. This information is then stored in the Windows Media Player cache so that it is available the next time you play the music CD.

Figure 8-15. Selecting an audio CD to play

If you aren't connected to the Internet and the required information wasn't previously downloaded into the Windows Media Player cache, you'll see the title "Unknown CD." You can force Windows Media Player to refresh the media information by right-clicking Now Playing and then choosing the audio CD again. When working with audio CDs, you'll see the standard Controls toolbar.

With audio CDs, you can display visualizations. You can choose from among the many different types of visualizations available by right-clicking Now Playing, pointing to Visualizations, and then selecting a desired visualization on the Alchemy, Bars and Waves, or Battery submenu. Some of the visualizations are soothing, such as Battery → Event Horizon and Bars and Waves → Ocean Mist. Other visualizations are frenetic, such as Alchemy → Random and Bars and Waves → Scope.

To display the album art or audio book cover rather than a visualization, as shown in Figure 8-16, right-click Now Playing, point to Visualizations, and then select Album Art. You can turn off visualizations by right-clicking Now Playing, pointing to Visualizations, and then selecting No Visualization.

Enhancing Your Playback

Windows Media Player 11 includes several controls for enhancing audio and video playback. When you are working with Now Playing, you can display these controls by right-clicking Now Playing, pointing to Enhancements, and then selecting the custom control you want to use to enhance the playback. Once custom controls are displayed, you can navigate among them using the Forward and Back buttons to the left of the control name. You can close the controls by clicking the Close button (the red button with the X in the upper-right corner of the control window), or by right-clicking Now Playing, pointing to Enhancements, and then clicking Show Enhancements.

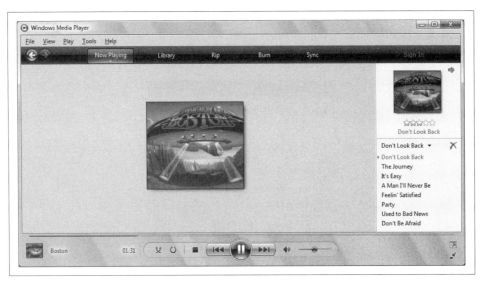

Figure 8-16. Using album art instead of visualizations

The Color Chooser control

You can control the colors Windows Media Player uses by using the Color Chooser control, shown in Figure 8-17. Select preset colors by clicking "Next preset," or use the Hue and Saturation sliders to create your own colors. Reset the colors to their original state by clicking Reset.

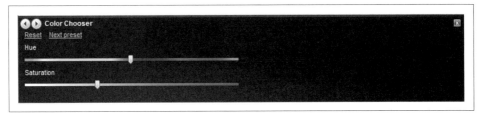

Figure 8-17. The Color Chooser control

The Crossfading and Auto Volume Leveling control

You can cross-fade audio tracks and reduce volume differences between songs using the Crossfading and Auto Volume Leveling control, shown in Figure 8-18. Crossfading gives you a smooth, gradual transition between songs on your playlist. When you turn on cross-fading, the volume at the end of a song fades out by gradually decreasing and the volume of the next song fades in and gradually increases. To enable and configure cross-fading, click "Turn on Crossfading" and then move the slider to select the amount of overlap time you want between the song ending and the song starting (if any).

If your songs play at different volume levels, you can have Windows Media Player normalize the volume for you so that you don't have to adjust it manually when a new song starts. To do so, click "Turn on Auto Volume Leveling." Both of these features work only with audio files that are in Windows Media or MP3 format and contain volume-leveling information. This information is added automatically when you rip audio into your media library.

Figure 8-18. The Crossfading and Auto Volume Leveling control

The Graphic Equalizer control

The Graphic Equalizer control, shown in Figure 8-19, helps you equalize audio playback for specific types of audio. To use the graphic equalizer, follow these steps:

1. If the graphic equalizer is turned off, click "Turn on" to enable Windows Media Player to equalize your audio playback.

2. The third link provided is for the Select Preset list. Clicking this option allows you to choose preset equalizer settings for Rock, Rap, Grunge, Metal, Dance, Techno, Country, Jazz, Acoustic, Folk, New Age, Classical, Blues, Oldies, and more.

3. After you select a preset, you can modify individual equalizer bands by using the sliders provided. To control how the sliders move in relation to one another, click one of the slider option buttons to the left of the equalizer.

Your changes are automatically saved to the Custom preset. To revert to the default settings, click Reset.

Figure 8-19. The Graphic Equalizer control

The Media Link for E-Mail control

You can send your friends a link to a short audio or video clip using the Media Link for E-Mail control, shown in Figure 8-20. To create a clip to send as a media link, follow these steps:

1. Use the Slow, Normal, Fast, Next Frame, or Previous Frame option to navigate to the desired starting point.

2. Click the Mark In link to mark the start of the clip.

3. As the audio or video plays, click the Mark Out link to mark the end of the clip.

4. Click "Send media link in e-mail" to open your default mail program and attach the media link to a new email message.

This feature doesn't send the actual clip. Instead, it sends a link to the clip on your computer. Because of this, the person to whom you send the link must have access to your network. For example, you could use this feature to send an audio or video clip to a friend at work when you are both on the same network.

Figure 8-20. The Media Link for E-Mail control

The Play Speed Settings control

The Play Speed Settings control, shown in Figure 8-21, allows you to slow down or speed up playback. For example, you might want to slow down an instructional video or audio so that you can follow along more closely, or you might want to skip through a boring video presentation by using a faster playback speed.

Playback speed is set to a numeric value where a play speed of 1.0 is the normal speed, anything less than 1.0 is a slower speed, and anything greater than 1.0 is a faster speed. To set the play speed, you can click the Slow, Normal, and Fast links. Or you can move the Play Speed slider to the desired play speed.

 With some videos, you can move forward or backward one frame at a time using the Next Frame and Previous Frame buttons. These buttons are displayed below the Play Speed slider.

Figure 8-21. The Play Speed Settings control

The Quiet Mode control

You can use the Quiet Mode control, shown in Figure 8-22, to reduce the difference between the loudest and softest sounds in a song. This feature works only with audio files that are in Windows Media Audio Pro or Windows Media Audio Lossless format. These formats contain volume-leveling information that is added automatically when you rip audio into your media library using either of these formats.

To enable and configure Quiet Mode, click the "Turn on" link and then specify the desired difference between loud and soft sounds by clicking either "Medium difference" or "Little difference." With "Medium difference," you'll get loud sounds that range up to 12 decibels (dB) above the average and soft sounds that range up to 12 dB below the average, so there'll be a smaller difference between loud and soft sounds as compared to when you are using a full dynamic range. With "Little difference," you'll get loud sounds that range up to 6 dB above the average and soft sounds that range up to 6 dB below the average, so there'll be the smallest difference between loud and soft sounds as compared to when you are using a full dynamic range.

Figure 8-22. The Quiet Mode control

The SRS WOW Effects control

You can use the SRS WOW Effects control, shown in Figure 8-23, to optimize bass, stereo, and other audio effects. SRS audio is a sound-enhancing technology, created by SRS Labs, Inc., to create high-quality immersive audio. You can turn on SRS WOW effects by completing the following steps:

1. Click the "Turn on" link.

2. Optimize the sound output for your speakers by clicking the Speakers link until it lists the appropriate type of speakers. The options are "Normal speakers," "Large speakers," and "Headphones."

3. Use the TruBass slider to specify the level of bass enhancement. Moving the slider to 0 turns off TruBass. The default setting is 50, for normal bass enhancement.

4. Use the WOW Effect slider to specify the stereo effect. Moving the slider to 0 turns off WOW Effect. The default setting is 50, for normal stereo effect.

 Because other audio settings on your computer can affect the volume and audio effects in Windows Media Player, you may find that you need to adjust the audio settings in Windows Vista rather than in Windows Media Player.

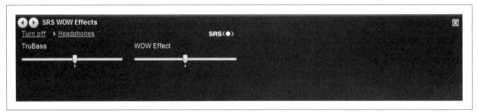

Figure 8-23. The SRS WOW Effects control

The Video Settings control

The Video Settings control, shown in Figure 8-24, helps you control video playback. You can set hue, saturation, brightness, and contrast using the sliders provided. To reset these values to their default state, click the Reset link. By default, Windows Media Player is configured to fit the video to the player window on resize, allowing Windows Media Player to adjust the video size automatically if you change the size of the player window. Using the "Select video zoom settings" list, you can fit the player to the video on start or set a relative playback size within the window of 50 percent, 100 percent, or 200 percent.

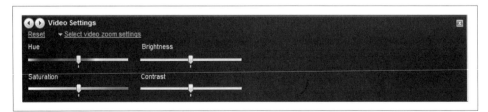

Figure 8-24. The Video Settings control

Building Your Media Library

Windows Media Player is designed to help you create and organize a media library. Your media library contains any folders you've added that contain media files, audio CDs you've ripped, and TV shows you've recorded. Within your library, your media is organized by category with separate areas for music, pictures, video, recorded TV, and other media and subcategories for artists, albums, songs, genre, year created, and so on. Windows Media Player adds all the media information automatically for audio CDs, movie DVDs, and recorded TV when your computer is connected to the Internet.

Because Windows Media Player handles most of the heavy lifting for you, building your media library is easy. All you need to do is add folders containing media files to your library, copy your audio CDs to your library, and let Windows Media Player handle the details. Using the built-in audio CD and data CD/DVD features, getting your media out of your library is just as easy. You can save copies of your music and other audio files to audio CDs, and you can save copies of your media to data CDs and DVDs. If you have an MP3 player or other device with removable storage, you can sync your media library to your device as well.

Adding Media Folders to Your Media Library

The easiest way to add media to your library is simply to move the media files to the appropriate personal folder. To add music or other audio to your library, simply copy or move the audio files to your Music folder. To add digital pictures to your library, simply copy or move the digital pictures to your Pictures folder. To add videos or recorded TV to your library, simply copy or move the video or TV files to your Videos folder.

Wondering how this works? Well, when you start Windows Media Player, the player checks your Music, Pictures, and Videos folders for any audio, picture, or video files you've added, and then updates your media library to reflect these changes automatically. You can have Windows Media Player add media from and monitor other folders in exactly the same way by completing the following steps:

1. In Window Media Player, right-click Library and then select Add To Library.

2. In the Add To Library dialog box, shown in Figure 8-25, the "My personal folders" option is selected by default under "Select the folders to monitor." This is why the player monitors your Music, Pictures, and Videos folders. If you want Windows Media Player to add media from and monitor your personal folders, shared media in the Public Music, Public Pictures, and Public Videos folder, and the personal folders of other users on the computer, select "My folders and those of others that I can access."

You can monitor files stored in another user's personal folders only if that person has shared the folder with you. For more information on folder sharing, see Chapter 11.

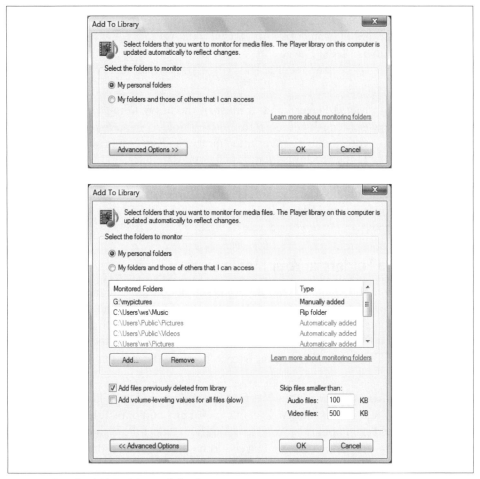

Figure 8-25. The Add To Library dialog box

3. Click Advanced Options to display a complete list of monitored folders and additional advanced options.

4. To monitor additional folders, click Add. In the Add Folder dialog box, select the folder to monitor and then click OK.

5. To stop monitoring a folder that you previously added, select the folder in the Monitored Folders list and then click Remove. Removing the folder tells Windows Media Player to stop monitoring the folder. The folder still exists on your disk drive.

6. To stop monitoring a folder that was added automatically, select the folder in the Monitored Folders list and then click Ignore. Ignoring the folder tells Windows Media Player to stop monitoring the folder.

7. If you've stopped monitoring folders or deleted files on the disk, the related media will still be displayed in Windows Media Player. To stop displaying files you've deleted or files that are in folders you are no longer monitoring, clear the "Add files previously deleted from library" checkbox.

8. By default, audio files smaller than 100 KB and video files smaller than 500 KB are not added to your media library. If desired, you can set different default values using the "Skip files smaller than" text boxes. To ensure that all audio and video files in monitored folders are added to the library, set the "Audio files" and "Video files" text boxes to zero.

9. When you click OK, Windows Media Player will search your computer and add or remove media as appropriate. In the Add to Library by Searching Computer dialog box, you'll see a report of the files found in monitored folders and the files added, as shown in Figure 8-26.

 Only the number of files listed as added is added to the library. If Windows Media Player has files in its library already, you'll see more files found than added.

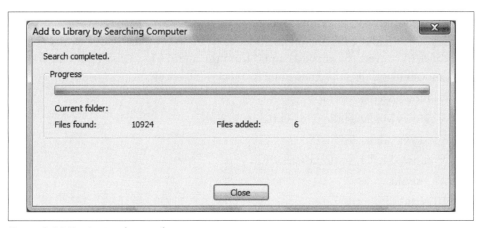

Figure 8-26. Reviewing the search report

Adding Media to Your Library When Played

By default, when you play an audio or video file on your computer or on the Internet, Windows Media Player adds the audio or video file to your library. Windows Media Player does not add audio or video that you play from removable storage devices or from shared network folders.

You can change the way Windows Media Player handles files you play by completing the following steps:

1. Right-click the Library button and then select More Options. This displays the Options dialog box.

2. In the Options dialog box, select the Player tab.

3. If you don't want audio or video files you play to be added to your media library, clear the "Add media files to library when played" checkbox. Otherwise, select this checkbox to add played files automatically to your library.

4. Click OK to save your settings.

Ripping Audio CDs into Your Media Library

With ripping, you copy tracks on audio CDs to your computer and store them as files. Before you start ripping audio CDs, you should:

- Learn about the audio formats that are available and then select a default audio format that best fits your quality needs and the type of audio CDs you work with the most.

- Configure the default ripping settings to specify how music is ripped and where music you've ripped is stored.

Choosing audio formats for ripping CDs

When you rip audio CDs, the audio codec in Windows Media Player works behind the scenes to convert the encoded audio from the audio CD to a standard file format that you can play. The audio encoding formats available are:

- Windows Media Audio
- Windows Media Audio with Variable Bit Rate
- Windows Media Audio Pro
- Windows Media Audio Lossless
- MP3 audio
- WAV audio

The sections that follow discuss how each audio format is used.

Windows Media Audio. The audio codec in Windows Media Player 11 is capable of ripping and playing audio files in Windows Media Audio format. Windows Media Audio is the default format and the default bit rate is 128 Kbps. You'll find that this audio format is best used with stereo recordings.

While other audio formats and bit rates are available, you may be surprised to learn that Windows Media Audio encoding is one of the most efficient audio encoding techniques available. In fact, as compared to MP3, Windows Media Audio delivers superior quality at a fraction of the bit rate. Because of this, Windows Media Audio should always be your first choice for audio encoding.

With Windows Media Audio, the audio codec samples audio at 44.1 or 48 kilohertz (kHz) using 16 bits. This offers quality sound at these bit rates:

48 Kbps
> With audio encoding at 48 Kbps, you get the smallest file sizes possible at a direct cost to sound quality. This encoding uses about 22 MB per CD.

64 Kbps
> With audio encoding at 64 Kbps, you get smaller file sizes and a small increase in sound quality. This encoding uses about 28 MB per CD.

96 Kbps
> With audio encoding at 96 Kbps, you get average file sizes and a modest increase in sound quality. This encoding uses about 42 MB per CD.

128 Kbps
> With audio encoding at 128 Kbps, you get large file sizes and a large increase in sound quality. This encoding uses about 56 MB per CD.

160 Kbps
> With audio encoding at 160 Kbps, you get larger file sizes and a larger increase in sound quality. This encoding uses about 69 MB per CD.

192 Kbps
> With audio encoding at 192 Kbps, you get the largest file sizes and the largest increase in sound quality. This encoding uses about 86 MB per CD.

Windows Media Audio with Variable Bit Rate. The audio codec in Windows Media Player 11 is capable of ripping and playing audio files in the Windows Media Audio with Variable Bit Rate format. This format is best used when you want to get the highest quality with stereo recordings.

Windows Media Audio with Variable Bit Rate enables you to record stereo and even higher-quality audio at smaller file sizes by automatically varying the encoding bit rate according to the complexity of the audio data. With Variable Bit Rate, the audio codec in Windows Media Player increases the bit rate to capture complex sections of the audio data and decreases the bit rate to maximize the compression of less complex sections. The result is compact, high-quality compression at these bit rates:

40 to 75 Kbps
> With variable audio encoding at 40 to 75 Kbps, you get the smallest file sizes possible at a direct cost to sound quality. This encoding uses about 18 to 33 MB per CD.

50 to 95 Kbps
> With variable audio encoding at 50 to 95 Kbps, you get smaller file sizes and a modest increase in sound quality. This encoding uses about 22 to 42 MB per CD.

85 to 145 Kbps

With variable audio encoding at 85 to 145 Kbps, you get average file sizes and a large increase in sound quality. This encoding uses about 37 to 63 MB per CD.

135 to 215 Kbps

With variable audio encoding at 135 to 215 Kbps, you get large file sizes and a substantial increase in sound quality. This encoding uses about 59 to 94 MB per CD.

240 to 355 Kbps

With variable audio encoding at 240 to 355 Kbps, you get the largest file sizes and the highest sound quality possible without using lossless encoding. This encoding uses about 105 to 155 MB per CD.

Windows Media Audio Pro. The audio codec in Windows Media Player 11 is capable of ripping and playing audio files in Windows Media Audio Pro. This format is best used when you want to record audio in 5.1- or higher channel surround sound. If you record audio in this format but play it back on a computer that doesn't have a sound card that supports surround sound, the multiple channels of audio are combined into two-channel stereo audio, ensuring that you always get the best playback experience.

Windows Media Audio Pro enables you to immerse yourself in multichannel surround sound at the same bit rate as stereo MP3 files. Windows Media Audio Pro also offers dynamic range control. During encoding, the maximum and average audio amplitudes are recorded as part of the encoding process. Using the Quiet Mode feature, you can configure playing to use full dynamic range, a medium difference range up to 12 dB above the average, or a minimal difference range up to 6 dB above the average.

With Windows Media Audio Pro, the audio codec samples audio at 44.1 or 48 kHz using 16 bits with stereo capabilities at 32 to 96 Kbps, and 20 bits with 5.1-channel surround at 128 to 256 Kbps. Although Windows Media Player cannot encode at higher rates, the player can play back at 48 kHz using 24 bits with 5.1- or 7.1-channel surround at rates up to 768 Kbps.

File sizes for Windows Media Audio Pro are similar to those for Windows Media Audio, with one exception. With Windows Media Audio Pro, you can rip audio at 32 Kbps, which uses about 14 MB per CD but offers low quality for music. However, you can use this low bit rate with spoken-word audio, such as a voice broadcast or audio book that contains no music, to achieve superior quality and highly compressed file sizes. At the supported stereo and higher rates, Windows Media Audio Pro offers a 1.5:1 to 2:1 compression savings over Dolby Digital 2.0, Dolby Digital 5.1, and DTS 5.1 surround sound.

Windows Media Audio Lossless. Windows Media Audio Lossless enables you to create a bit-for-bit duplicate of the original audio tracks so that no data is lost. You can use this format for archiving audio CD masters and preserving them exactly as they were created. With this audio format, the audio codec in Windows Media Player still performs compression, but this compression is mathematically lossless.

Because the audio codec increases the bit rate to capture complex sections of the audio data and decreases the bit rate to maximize the compression of less complex sections, Windows Media Audio Lossless offers a 2:1 to 3:1 compression savings over the original audio format. Thus, the variable, lossless rate of between 470 and 940 Kbps uses about 206 to 411 MB per CD.

Like Windows Media Pro, Windows Media Audio Lossless offers dynamic range control. During encoding, the maximum and average audio amplitudes are recorded as part of the encoding process. Using the Quiet Mode feature, you can configure playing to use full dynamic range, a medium difference range up to 12 dB above the average, or a minimal difference range up to 6 dB above the average.

MP3 audio. The audio codec in Windows Media Player 11 is capable of ripping and playing audio files in MP3 format. The Moving Picture Experts Group (MPEG) created standards for video and audio compression. MPEG-1 and MPEG-2 are standards for video compression. MPEG-3 or MP3 is the standard for audio compression. While MP3 is popular on the Internet, you may be surprised to learn that Windows Media Audio and related formats are actually the most used audio formats in the world at the time of this writing.

With MP3, the audio codec samples at these bit rates:

128 Kbps
> With audio encoding at 128 Kbps, you get the smallest file sizes possible at a direct cost to sound quality. This encoding uses about 57 MB per CD.

192 Kbps
> With audio encoding at 192 Kbps, you get average file sizes and a large increase in sound quality. This encoding uses about 86 MB per CD.

256 Kbps
> With audio encoding at 256 Kbps, you get large file sizes and a substantial increase in sound quality. This encoding uses about 115 MB per CD.

320 Kbps
> With audio encoding at 320 Kbps, you get the largest file sizes and the highest sound quality possible with MP3 encoding. This encoding uses about 115 MB per CD.

MP3 is best used when you want to be able to directly copy files to an MP3 player. However, keep in mind that some devices called MP3 players actually aren't MP3 players. For example, the Apple iPod actually uses MPEG-4 encoding and saves audio files with the *.aac* extension.

WAV audio. The audio codec in Windows Media Player 11 is capable of ripping and playing audio files in Microsoft WAV format. As WAV is lossless, you can use this format to create a bit-for-bit duplicate of the original audio tracks so that no data is lost. Unlike the Windows Media Audio Lossless format, however, the audio codec does not compress the audio data. Because there is no compression, WAV audio uses about 600 MB per CD. WAV is best used when you want to create archive masters that are the same size on disk as the original audio CD.

Configuring the default rip settings

You can configure the default rip settings by completing the following steps:

1. In Window Media Player, right-click Library and then select More Options.
2. In the Options dialog box, select the Rip Music tab, as shown in Figure 8-27.

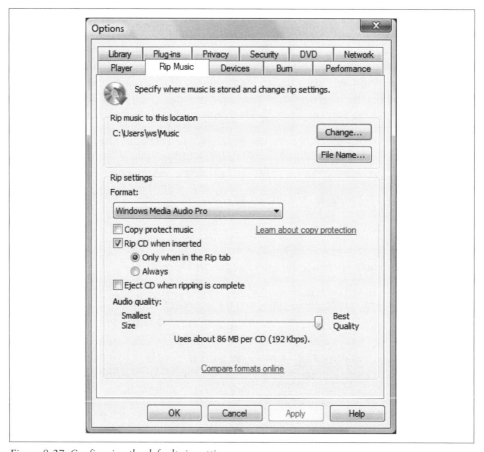

Figure 8-27. Configuring the default rip settings

3. Ripped files are automatically added to your media library and stored in the default folder for ripped music. The default folder for ripped music is your personal Music folder. You can change the Ripped music folder by clicking Change under "Rip music to this location." In the Browse for Folder dialog box, choose a storage folder for your music and then click OK.

4. Ripped audio files are named numerically according to the track number, followed by a space and the song title. You can change the default naming scheme by following these steps:

    a. Click File Name under "Rip music to this location."

    b. In the File Name Options dialog box, select the details you want to include in the filename, including the artist, album, track number, song title, genre, and bit rate.

    c. Select an item and then click Move Up or Move Down to arrange the detail order.

    d. Use the Separator list to specify the separator used between each detail item. You can choose a space, dash, dot, or underline.

    e. Use the preview text to double-check the filename, and then click OK to save your filename options.

5. For ripping, Windows Media Audio is the default format and the default bit rate is 128 Kbps. Use the Format list to select the desired format. Use the "Audio quality" slider to set the default bit rate.

6. By default, music you rip is not copy-protected. If you copy-protect the tracks you rip by selecting the "Copy protect music" checkbox, usage rights are required to play, burn, or sync the files.

7. By default, if you don't already have the audio CD in your library, Windows Media Player rips an audio CD when you insert it and then select the Rip tab. If you always want to rip audio CDs when you insert them, select Always instead of "Only when in the Rip tab." If you would rather start the rip process yourself on the Rip tab, clear the "Rip CD when Inserted" checkbox to turn off automatic ripping.

8. If you want to open the CD/DVD tray after ripping an audio CD, select the "Eject CD when ripping is complete" checkbox.

9. Click OK to save your settings.

Ripping audio CDs

Once you've configured the default rip settings, ripping an audio CD is easy. With automatic ripping, Windows Media Player rips the audio CD as soon as you insert it, and you don't have to do anything. With automatic ripping only when in the Rip tab, Windows Media Player rips the audio CD as soon as you insert an audio CD and then click the Rip tab on the toolbar. With manual ripping, you must insert the audio CD, click the Rip tab on the toolbar, and then click Start Rip.

With any of these options, you should connect to the Internet before Windows Media Player begins ripping the audio CD. This ensures that Windows Media Player can get the media information and name the ripped files as appropriate for the filename settings you've configured.

As shown in Figure 8-28, you can view the progress of the rip on the Rip tab. On the Rip tab, you can control the rip in a couple of ways:

• As Windows Media Player rips the audio CD, you can clear the checkboxes next to any songs that you don't want to rip.

• You can stop the rip process by clicking the Stop Rip button and then resume ripping by clicking the Start Rip button.

If your computer has multiple CD/DVD drives, you can rip multiple CDs simultaneously. Simply insert the audio CDs you want to rip and then start ripping. You can use the entries in the Navigation Pane to manage the rip process for each audio CD you are ripping. You'll find one entry for each CD/DVD drive.

Figure 8-28. Viewing the progress of the rip

After you've ripped an audio CD, you can select and play the ripped audio in your media library. If you weren't connected to the Internet when you ripped the audio CD, you can still add the media information. You can also edit the media information as necessary.

To get the media information for an audio CD, follow these steps:

1. Connect to the Internet.

2. Click the Library button and then click Album.

3. Right-click the album and then select "Find album info."

4. In the "Find album information" dialog box, shown in Figure 8-29, the information about the album should be displayed automatically. If it isn't, click Search and follow the prompts to select the correct album.

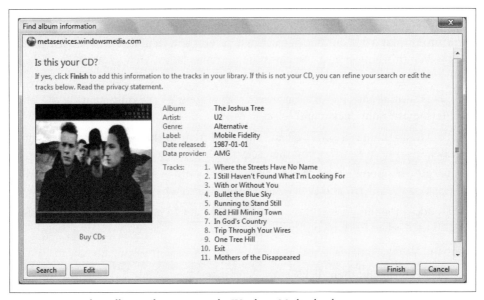

Figure 8-29. Finding album information in the Windows Media database

5. Once you have the right album information, you can customize any of the text entries associated with the album by clicking Edit, modifying the text entries as appropriate, and then clicking Next.

6. Click Finish to save the album information to the Windows Media Player cache.

If you already have the media information for an audio CD but want to check for updates or corrections, you can do so by completing these steps:

1. Connect to the Internet.

2. Click the Library button and then click Album.

3. Right-click the album and then select Update Album Info.

 With either technique, you will be prevented from getting media information if the "Update music files by retrieving media info from the Internet" option is not selected. To resolve this problem, right-click the Library button and click More Options. This displays the Options dialog box. On the Privacy tab, select the "Update music files by retrieving media info from the Internet" checkbox and then click OK.

Creating and Managing Playlists

Both the Navigation Pane and the List Pane have features for working with playlists. A *playlist* is a list of media files that you want to play together. Although you can mix and match media types as you see fit, you'll usually want to have separate playlists for pictures, music, and videos.

Creating and using playlists

At the far right of the Address toolbar is the Show/Hide List Pane button. Click this button to display your current playlist, where you can drag items to the list to add them. Click this button again to close the current playlist view. You can work with playlists in a variety of ways:

- To add an album, a stack, or an individual item as the only item on the Now Playing list, right-click it and select Play.
- To add an album, a stack, or an individual item to the Now Playing list, right-click it, point to Add To, and then select Now Playing.
- To add an album, a stack, or an individual item to an existing playlist, right-click it, point to Add To, and then select the playlist to which it should be added.
- To add an album, a stack, or an individual item to a new playlist, right-click it and then select Add to 'Untitled Playlist.'

Using the Navigation Pane, you can create a playlist by completing these steps:

1. Click Playlist and then click Create Playlist.
2. Type the name of the playlist and then press Enter.
3. The playlist will then be displayed for editing and viewing in the List Pane. Drag and drop files onto the list.
4. To change the order of individual items on the list, click an item and then drag up or down as appropriate.
5. To change the order of a group of files on the list, select the items and then drag up or down as appropriate.

Using the Navigation Pane, you can play items in a playlist by clicking the playlist and then pressing the Play button on the Controls toolbar. Alternatively, you can right-click the playlist and then select Play.

Editing playlists

Using the Navigation Pane, you can edit a playlist by completing these steps:

1. Click Playlist and then click the playlist you want to work with.
2. Drag and drop files onto the list.

3. To change the order of individual items on the list, click an item and then drag up or down as appropriate.

4. To change the order of a group of files on the list, select the items and then drag up or down as appropriate.

5. To save your changes, click Save Playlist.

Deleting Media and Playlists

You can easily delete an album, a playlist, or other media items from your media library by right-clicking the item and selecting Delete. By default, when you delete items, you'll see the dialog box shown in Figure 8-30, and you can specify whether to delete the selected item from the library only, or from the library and your computer.

Figure 8-30. Specifying the deletion technique

This dialog box also has a "Don't show this message again" checkbox. If you select this option, the default action you select will always be used when you delete items and you won't see this warning prompt again. You can still control the way deleting items works, however. To do this, right-click Library and then select More Options. On the Library tab, clear the "Delete files from my computer when deleted from library" checkbox if you want to delete items only from the library. Otherwise, select this checkbox to delete items from the library and your computer.

Burning Audio CDs and Data CDs or DVDs

Windows Media Player makes it easy to create your own custom CDs and DVDs. You can burn audio CDs as well as data CDs or DVDs. An audio CD is a CD that you can play in a standard CD player. A data CD or DVD is a disc that stores a copy of your media. With newer CD players, you may be able to play a data CD with Windows Media Audio (WMA), MP3, or WAV files.

To burn CDs or DVDs, your computer must have a readable/writable CD or DVD drive. If you aren't sure whether your computer has a readable/writable CD or DVD drive, you should look at the faceplate on the drive tray. A readable/writable CD or

DVD drive should have a large RW logo to indicate this, and under this logo it should state the supported format or formats. A CD burner can support CD-R, CD-RW, or both disc types. A DVD burner can support DVD-R, DVD+R, or both disc types. Most DVD burners also support CD-R, CD-RW, or both disc types.

Burning an audio CD

You can burn audio CDs in a standard audio format that can be used in most computers and CD players that play CD-R and CD-RW discs. Any audio files in your media library can be burned onto an audio CD, as can any audio files on your computer but not in your library, as long as they are in WMA, MP3, or WAV format. A standard CD-R and CD-RW disc can hold almost 80 minutes of audio. When burning audio CDs, it is important to keep in mind that Windows Media Player inserts two seconds between each song.

You can burn an audio CD by completing the following steps:

1. Click the Burn tab to select it. Next, right-click the Burn tab and then select Audio CD.

2. Insert a blank CD-R or CD-RW disc into your CD/DVD burner. As shown in Figure 8-31, you'll see details about the blank CD in the List Pane. If your computer has multiple disc burners and the burner you want to use is not the one selected, choose the one you want to use by clicking the Next Drive link in the List Pane.

 Although you can rip multiple CDs at a time, you can burn discs to only one burner drive at a time.

3. Add albums or songs from your media library by clicking and dragging them from the Details Pane to the List Pane to create a list of files to burn. If you need to clear the List Pane before beginning to build your burn list, click the button with the red X to clear the List Pane.

4. Windows Media Player calculates how many minutes and seconds of empty space remain on the disc after you add each song to the burn list, as long as you are working with songs in your media library. To add a song that is on your computer but not in your library, right-click the file and then click Add to Burn List, or drag the file to the List Pane.

5. If Windows Media Player is unable to determine the duration of songs added from files on your computer, it may not be able to calculate accurately how many songs can fit on the CD. To resolve this, right-click a song on the burn list and select Play to help Windows Media Player determine the correct duration of the song.

Figure 8-31. Burning an audio CD to create a custom mix up to 80 minutes in length

6. If you select more files than can fit on one disc, Windows Media Player can burn all of the files to multiple discs. Or you can create a data disc instead of an audio disc to fit more files on the disc. However, many CD players cannot play music burned to a data disc.

7. It is possible that the last song will not fit even if the total time exactly matches the CD length. This can occur because Windows Media Player inserts two seconds between songs when burning. If you want to burn only one disc in this session, remove files from the list until they all fit on one disc. Simply right-click a file you want to remove, and then click Remove from List. Removing files from the burn list will not delete the files from your media library.

8. In the burn list, drag files up or down to arrange them in the order you want them to appear on the disc. If you have chosen to burn more than one disc at once, make sure that files will be burned to the disc you want.

9. Click Start Burn. If you are burning multiple discs, insert a blank disc when the first one has finished burning, and then click Start Burn. Repeat this step until you have finished burning all of the discs. As a disc is burned, you can check its progress in the burn list.

To ensure a proper burn, you shouldn't try to perform any other actions on the computer while burning a disc. For example, the recording may be affected if you try to play music from your media library while burning a disc.

Burning a data CD or DVD

Burning data CDs and DVDs is different from burning audio CDs. Data CDs can store up to 700 MB of data. Single-sided single-layered data DVDs can store up to 4.7 GB of data. Your computer may also be able to burn double-sided single-layered or single-sided dual-layered DVDs that can store up to 9.4 GB of data, or double-sided dual-layered DVDs that can store up to 18.8 GB of data. Some DVD burners will let you burn to any format supported, and others can burn in only a specific format. Windows Media Player supports burning data discs to CD-R, CD-RW, DVD-R, DVD-RW, DVD+R, DVD+RW, and dual-layered DVD+R discs. Other formats are not supported, including DVD-RAM, DVD-Audio, and DVD-Video.

With data CDs and DVDs, you can burn any files in your library as well as any files on your computer. You can burn files in any format to create copies of your data. You can then use your data disc with your computer or other people's computers. On the other hand, if you burn the same type of media file, you can create discs that many newer CD and DVD players can read. If you create a data CD with albums and songs in WMA, MP3, or WAV format, any newer CD player that supports these formats can read and play the disc. Since data CDs can hold many more songs than audio CDs, you can create amazing, customized CDs. If you create a data CD with pictures in JPEG format, any newer DVD player that supports this format can read and play the disc as a slide show. Since data DVDs can hold an enormous number of JPEG images, you can create photo-album slide shows that run for hours.

You can burn a data CD or DVD by completing the following steps:

1. Click the Burn tab to select it. Next, right-click the Burn tab and then click Data CD or DVD.

2. Insert a blank disc into your CD/DVD burner. As shown in Figure 8-32, you'll see details about the blank CD or DVD in the List Pane. If your computer has multiple disc burners and the burner you want to use is not the one selected, choose the one you want to use by clicking the Next Drive link in the List Pane.

    Although you can rip multiple CDs at a time, you can burn discs to only one burner drive at a time.

3. Add pictures, albums, songs, videos, recorded TV, or other files from your media library by clicking and dragging them from the Details Pane to the List Pane to create a list of files to burn. If you need to clear the List Pane before beginning to build your burn list, click the button with the red X to clear the List Pane.

4. To add a file that is on your computer but not in your library, right-click the file and then click Add to Burn List, or drag the file to the List Pane. If you select more files than can fit on one disc, Windows Media Player can burn all of the files to multiple discs.

Figure 8-32. Burning a data CD or DVD to create copies of your media or to play in newer CD and DVD players

5. If you want to burn only one disc in this session, remove files from the list until they all fit on one disc. Simply right-click a file you want to remove, and then click Remove from List. Removing files from the burn list will not delete the files from your media library.

6. In the burn list, drag files up or down to arrange them in the order you want them to appear on the disc. If you have chosen to burn more than one disc at once, make sure that files will be burned to the disc you want.

7. Click Start Burn. If you are burning multiple discs, insert a blank disc when the first one has finished burning, and then click Start Burn. Repeat this step until you have finished burning all of the discs. As a disc is burned, you can check its progress in the burn list.

 To ensure a proper burn, you shouldn't try to perform any other actions on the computer while burning a disc. For example, the recording may be affected if you try to play music from your media library while burning a disc.

Syncing Your Media to MP3 Players and Other Devices

Windows Media Player allows you to sync your media easily to MP3 players and other devices with removable storage. To get started, you'll need to set up the device for syncing and then either manually sync your media or configure autosyncing using your playlists.

Setting up a device for syncing

You can configure an MP3 player or other device for syncing by completing the following steps:

1. Start Windows Media Player and then insert the device.

2. The first time you use the device you'll see the Device Setup dialog box shown in Figure 8-33. This dialog box shows the default name of the device and the remaining free space. In this example, the default name of the device was USB20FD and the device had 1.9 GB of free space.

3. Type a name for your device in the "Name your device" text box and then click Finish.

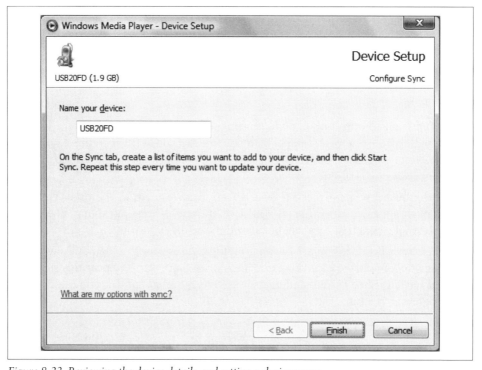

Figure 8-33. Reviewing the device details and setting a device name

You can now create a playlist to sync manually to the device, or sync existing playlists automatically. If a device is nearly full and you try to sync to it, you'll see the Manage Existing Files on Device page in the Device Setup Wizard, as shown in Figure 8-34. On this page, you can click the No option to leave the existing files on the device and sync to the remaining space available. Or you can click the Yes option to delete all digital media files on the device before syncing. Afterward, click Next and then click Finish.

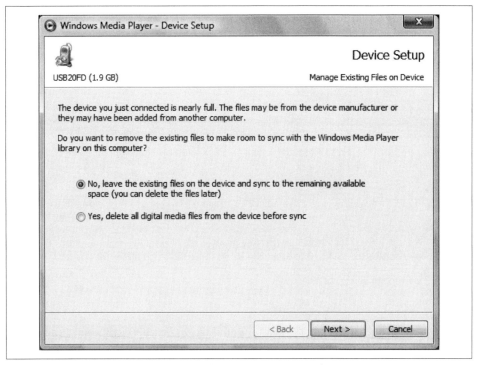

Figure 8-34. Managing existing files using the Device Setup Wizard

Syncing a device using manual playlists

You can create a playlist to manually sync to the device by completing the following steps:

1. Start Windows Media Player and connect your device.

2. On the Sync tab, create a list of items you want to add to the device by dragging albums or songs to the playlist on the List Pane, as shown in Figure 8-35. As you add items to the playlist, note the amount of free space remaining.

3. If you have connected multiple devices, you can switch among them by clicking Next Device.

4. When you've configured your playlist, click Start Sync to display the Sync Results page shown in Figure 8-36, and Windows Media Player will start the sync. Similar to when ripping audio CDs, you'll see the sync progress. You can stop the sync by clicking Stop Sync and then resume the sync by clicking Start Sync.

5. Repeat this procedure whenever you want to update the device manually in the future.

Figure 8-35. Creating your sync list

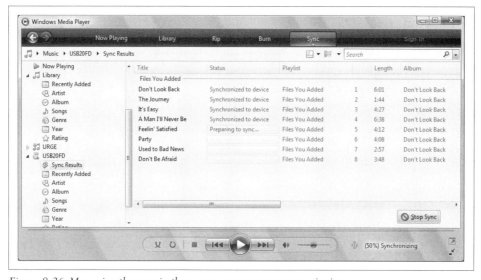

Figure 8-36. Managing the sync in the same way as you manage ripping

Syncing existing playlists automatically

You can configure automatic syncing for existing playlists by following these steps:

1. Start Windows Media Player and connect your device.

2. Right-click the Sync tab, point to the device on the shortcut menu, and then select Set Up Sync.

3. In the Device Setup dialog box, select the "Sync this device automatically" checkbox, as shown in Figure 8-37.

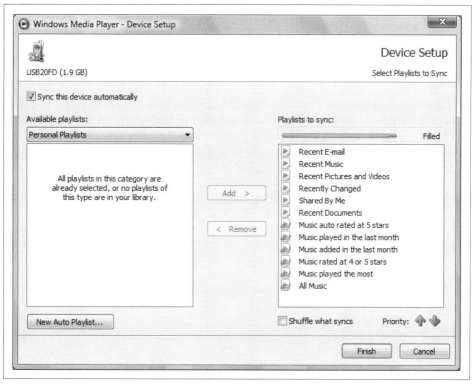

Figure 8-37. Selecting the playlists to sync automatically

4. On the "Available playlists" list, Personal Playlists is selected by default and all your personal playlists are configured for syncing.

5. If you select Sync Playlists on the "Available playlists" list, you can configure any of the following lists for syncing:

   - All Pictures
   - All Video
   - Pictures Rated 4 or 5 Stars
   - Pictures Taken in the Last Month
   - TV Recorded in the Last Week
   - Video Rated at 4 or 5 Stars

6. You can manage the list of playlists to sync in several different ways. You can:

   - Add a list that isn't selected by clicking it and then clicking Add
   - Remove a selected list by clicking it and then clicking Remove
   - Change the priority of a list by clicking it and then clicking the Up Priority or Down Priority button

7. If you have selected more media items than can fit on the device, you can select the "Shuffle what syncs" checkbox to shuffle the priority order each time you sync. This way you'll get different playlists each time.

8. When you click Finish, Windows Media Player will automatically sync with the device.

Each time you connect the device in the future, Windows Media Player will automatically sync with the device as well. To change the automatic sync configuration, repeat this procedure. To stop automatic sync, right-click the Sync tab, point to the device on the shortcut menu, select End Sync Partnership, and then click Yes when prompted to confirm. You will then need to add or remove files manually.

CHAPTER 9

Capturing and Managing Your Digital Pictures and Videos

Earlier releases of Windows include the Windows Picture and Fax Viewer for viewing digital pictures, performing basic editing, and playing slide shows using a series of pictures. Windows Vista includes a more full-featured program called Windows Photo Gallery. With Windows Photo Gallery, you can:

- View digital pictures and videos in any supported formats.
- Organize digital pictures and videos by tags, date taken, ratings, and folders.
- Touch up digital pictures by adjusting exposure and color, cropping, rotating, and so on.
- Print optimized versions of digital pictures at full-page or preset sizes.
- Play slide shows using a series of digital pictures.
- Burn CDs and DVDs to create copies of your pictures and videos.

Because Microsoft designed Windows Photo Gallery to coexist with Windows Media Player, you can use the same pictures and videos as those you're using with Windows Media Player. Any changes you make to picture and video properties in Windows Photo Gallery will be reflected in Windows Media Player when the media information updates, which typically happens automatically. The same is true for Windows Photo Gallery. If you make changes to picture and video properties in Windows Media Player, the changes will be reflected in Windows Photo Gallery when the media information updates.

Getting Started with Windows Photo Gallery

Windows Photo Gallery allows you to view, edit, organize, and share pictures and videos. You start Windows Photo Gallery by clicking Start → All Programs → Windows Photo Gallery. As Figure 9-1 shows, the main window has these key elements:

Navigation toolbar

Provides browser-like Back and Next buttons that let you navigate to pages you've viewed previously. It also has these Quick Access buttons: File, Fix, Info, Print, E-Mail, Burn, Make a Movie, and Open.

Navigation Pane

Provides quick access for organizing and displaying pictures and videos by type, tags, date taken, ratings, and folders.

Preview/work area

Displays thumbnail previews of pictures and videos when you select a particular category or type, and provides the main work area for when you are performing tasks such as fixing pictures.

Controls toolbar

Provides basic controls for manipulating a selected picture or video. You can change the default thumbnail size and the display size, rotate pictures clockwise or counterclockwise, begin and navigate a picture slide show, and delete selected items.

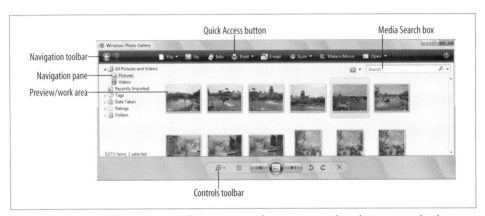

Figure 9-1. Using Windows Photo Gallery to view and manage your digital pictures and videos

Accessing Key Features

As Figure 9-2 shows, the Navigation toolbar includes Forward and Back buttons that allow you to access locations you've previously viewed. Clicking a Quick Access button on the Navigation toolbar allows you to access the main areas of Windows Photo Gallery.

Figure 9-2. The toolbars in Windows Photo Gallery

You can use the Navigation toolbar's Quick Access buttons as follows:

File
> Allows you to add folders, import images from cameras and scanners, and manipulate existing files.

Fix
> Allows you to edit a selected picture using Auto Adjust, Adjust Exposure, Adjust Color, Crop Picture, and Fix Red Eye options.

Info
> Displays an Information Pane for a selected picture or video that provides details about the related file.

Print
> Allows you to print selected pictures or the first frame of selected videos.

E-Mail
> Allows you to email selected pictures and videos.

Burn
> Allows you to create a DVD video using Windows DVD Maker. Only computers running Windows Vista Home Premium or Windows Vista Ultimate have Windows DVD Maker.

Make a Movie
> Opens the selected pictures and videos in Windows Movie Maker so that you can make a movie. Only computers running Windows Vista Home Premium or Windows Vista Ultimate have Windows Movie Maker.

Open
> Allows you to open selected pictures or videos in another program, such as Microsoft Office Picture Manager or Microsoft Paint.

Searching and Browsing Pictures and Videos

The Navigation Pane, shown as a separate panel on the left side of Windows Photo Gallery, and the Quick Search box, shown in the top-right corner of Windows Photo Gallery, provide quick access for organizing and displaying pictures and videos by type, tags, date, ratings, and folders. As Figure 9-3 shows, the Navigation Pane includes several top-level categories and subcategories. Selecting a category or subcategory displays related pictures, videos, or both.

You can use the Navigation Pane categories as follows:

All Pictures and Videos
> Under the All Pictures and Videos category are Pictures and Videos subcategories. These subcategories allow you to quickly return a list of all pictures or all videos in folders that Windows Photo Gallery can use.

Figure 9-3. The Navigation Pane

Recently Imported

Shows a list of pictures and videos recently imported from a digital camera or other media source.

Tags

Under the Tags category, you'll find a list of all the tags you've used with pictures and videos. Tags are keywords that aid in searching and organizing your media. Clicking "Create a New Tag" allows you to create a new tag to be used as a keyword. Clicking "Not Tagged" displays all pictures and videos that you haven't tagged. You can drag pictures or videos from the Not Tagged category to a named tag category to add the tag to those items.

Date Taken

Use Date Taken to navigate through pictures and videos according to the year, month, and date they were created.

Ratings

Use Ratings to navigate through pictures and videos according to the star rating you've assigned to them. Assign a low star rating to your least favorite pictures and a high star rating to your favorite pictures. Clicking "Not Rated" displays all pictures and videos that you haven't rated. You can drag pictures or videos from the Not Rated category to a rating category to assign the rating to those items.

Folders

Use Folders to determine which folders are associated with Windows Photo Gallery and to navigate through pictures and videos using views of these folders.

 The Navigation Pane lists the total number of items in Windows Photo Gallery as well as the total number of items you've selected. By default, Windows Photo Gallery uses only your personal Pictures folder and the Public Pictures folders. See the "Building Your Photo and Video Gallery" section, later in this chapter, for details on adding pictures and videos to your library.

Like many other Windows programs, Windows Photo Gallery has a Search box. You can use the Search box to quickly search for pictures and videos. The Search feature matches complete or partial words in the media information associated with pictures and videos. This allows you to search on filename, tags, and other information associated with pictures and videos.

You can search your media by completing the following steps:

1. Click in the Search box.
2. Type your search text.

Windows Photo Gallery returns matches as you type. Click the Clear button to clear the search results.

Organizing Your Gallery

Microsoft designed Windows Photo Gallery to help you create and organize a picture and video gallery. Your gallery automatically contains pictures in your personal Pictures folder, videos in your personal Videos folder, shared pictures in your computer's Public Pictures folder, and shared videos in your computer's Public Videos folder. Your gallery can also include other folders that you've added as well as pictures and videos from cameras. Within your gallery, your pictures and videos are grouped and sorted automatically so that you can browse them by tags, date taken, ratings, folders, and more.

Grouping and Sorting Your Gallery

The work area of Windows Photo Gallery includes the Choose a Thumbnail View button. You can use the Choose a Thumbnail View button to display the view and grouping options shown in Figure 9-4. You also have a number of Group By and Sort By options.

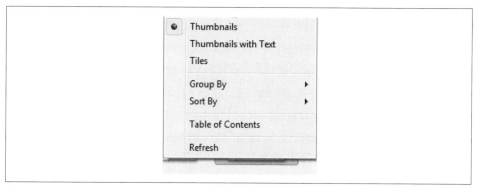

Figure 9-4. Options for viewing and grouping thumbnails

Group By options, shown in Figure 9-5, control how Windows Photo Gallery groups related sets of pictures and videos in the All Pictures, All Pictures → Pictures, All Pictures → Videos, and any other views you select. By default, pictures and videos are automatically grouped, which typically means they're grouped by month and year taken if your gallery includes media taken over several years, or day and month taken if your gallery includes media taken only in a particular year. The grouping options are similar to those you can select by browsing the Navigation Pane. You can group pictures and videos by date taken, month taken, year taken, rating, tag, and folder. Additional options not in the Navigation Pane include file size, image size, and camera.

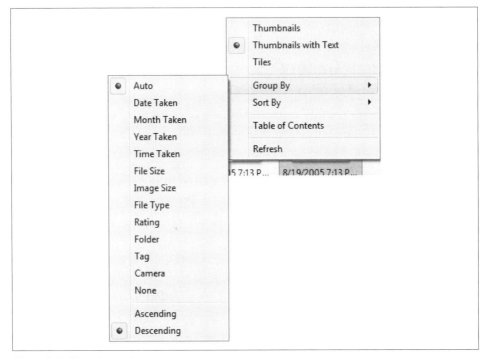

Figure 9-5. Grouping options

If you select Group By → None, you'll get one long list of pictures and videos, which by default is sorted by date taken. By default, groups are organized in ascending order, which means that with time-related groupings the newest groups are listed first. You can also organize groups in descending order, which means that with time-related groupings the oldest groups are listed first.

Sort By options, shown in Figure 9-6, control how Windows Photo Gallery sorts pictures and videos within grouped sets. By default, pictures and videos are sorted in ascending order according to the date taken. You can also sort within groups by date modified, file size, image size, rating, caption, and filename.

Figure 9-6. Sorting options

A handy way to see how many pictures and videos you have in each grouping is to click the Choose a Thumbnail View button and then select Table of Contents. This turns on the Table of Contents Pane. As shown in Figure 9-7, when you group by year taken you can easily see the relative number of pictures and videos you've taken each year.

Other handy groupings to use with the Table of Contents Pane are:

Month taken
> If you group by month taken, you can see the relative number of pictures you took in each month over time. Click a month in the table of contents to view the pictures and videos taken that month.

File size
> If you group by file size, you can see a comparison of the smallest to largest file sizes in the table of contents. Click a file size, such as Largest, in the table of contents to view the pictures and videos with that relative size rating.

Image size
> If you group by image size, you can see a comparison of the smallest to largest image sizes in the table of contents. Click an image size, such as Smallest, in the table of contents to view the pictures and videos with that relative size rating.

File type
> If you group by file type, you can see the relative number of each type of picture and video file in the table of contents. Click a file type, such as Bitmap, in the table of contents to view the pictures or videos with that file type.

Camera
> If you group by camera, you can see the relative number of pictures and videos you've taken with each of your digital cameras. Click a camera type, such as Sony Cybershot, in the table of contents to view the pictures or videos taken with it.

Figure 9-7. Using the Table of Contents Pane to see how many pictures and videos you have in each grouping

Viewing and Managing Ratings, Tags, and Captions

To get more details about pictures and videos, click the Choose a Thumbnail View button and then select Tiles. As Figure 9-8 shows, you'll see the following:

- Filename and file extension
- Date taken or created
- File size
- Image size or video runtime
- Rating
- Caption

With the Tiles view, you can add ratings and captions to individual pictures and videos. To add a rating, click the picture or video to select it, move the pointer over the star rating until the desired rating is highlighted, and then click. To add or edit a caption, click Add Caption or click the existing caption, type the desired caption, and then press Enter or click another area of the window.

Another way to get more detailed information about pictures and videos is to turn on the Info Pane by clicking the Info button on the toolbar. The Info Pane is also shown in Figure 9-8.

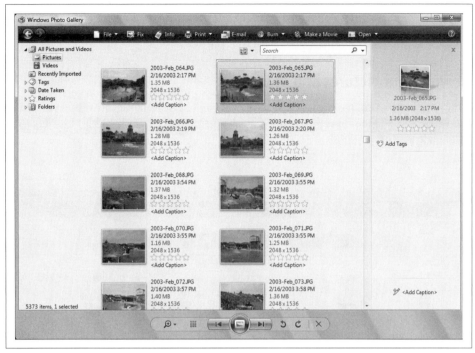

Figure 9-8. Getting more detailed information about pictures and videos

With the Info Pane, you can do things that you can't do with the Tiles view. You can:

- Add the same rating to multiple items by clicking the pictures and videos you want to rate, moving the pointer over the star rating in the Info Pane until the desired rating is highlighted, and then clicking.

- Add or edit the captions for multiple items by clicking the pictures and videos you want to work with, clicking the Click to Edit Caption text in the Info Pane, typing the desired caption, and then pressing Enter or clicking another area of the window.

- Add the same tag to multiple items by clicking the pictures and videos you want to work with, clicking the Add Tags text, typing the desired tag, and then pressing Enter.

- Remove a tag from multiple items by clicking the pictures and videos you want to work with, right-clicking the tag to remove, and then selecting Remove Tag.

- Assign a tag that is used with some selected pictures of videos by right-clicking the tag to assign and then selecting Assign to All.

All these techniques help you provide additional information for your pictures and videos. You can also use tags and ratings to help you view and organize your pictures and videos in different ways. Once you've assigned tags, you can click the Tags node in the Navigation Pane to see a list of all the tags you've assigned. Then, by clicking a tag, you can view all the pictures and videos with that tag.

Once you've assigned ratings, you can also click the Rating node in the Navigation Pane to see a list of all the ratings you've assigned. Then, by clicking a rating, you can view all the pictures and videos with that rating.

Viewing Your Pictures and Videos

Windows Photo Gallery provides several ways to view your pictures and videos. If you move the pointer over a picture for several seconds, you'll see a close-up preview such as the one shown in Figure 9-9. With videos, you'll see a preview of the first frame of the video.

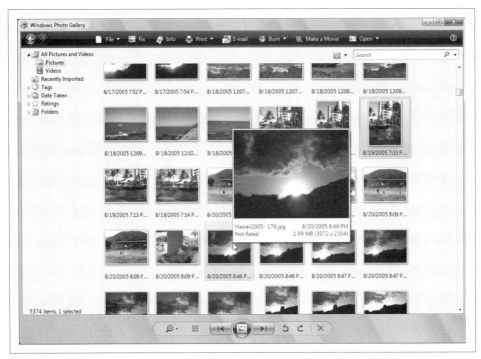

Figure 9-9. Previewing a picture by hovering over it

You can open a picture for viewing or play a video by double-clicking it. The picture or video will then fill the work area. If the Info Pane is displayed, you can close it by clicking the Close button. This will give you more area for viewing pictures and videos.

When viewing pictures, the Controls toolbar is displayed in the lower portion of the main window, as shown in Figure 9-10.

Figure 9-10. Controls for pictures

From left to right, the controls on the toolbar are:

Magnify
> Increases or decreases magnification by zooming in or out.

Actual Size
> Lets you view the picture at its actual size. You can also press Ctrl-Alt-0 to switch between actual size and current preview size.

Previous
> Moves to the previous picture or video. You can also view the previous picture by pressing the left arrow key on your keyboard.

Play Slide Show
> Plays a slide show of the currently listed pictures. You can also play a slide show by pressing F11. To stop the slide show, press the Esc key.

> Picture slide shows start with the picture you are viewing and continue through all pictures in the currently select node in the Navigation Pane. With this in mind, you can play slide shows of all pictures taken during a specific year, month, or date by clicking the related Date Taken node, double-clicking the first picture, and then starting a slide show by clicking the Play Slide Show button. You can play slide shows of all pictures with a particular tag or rating by selecting the tag or rating, double-clicking the first picture, and then starting the slide show by clicking the Play Slide Show button.

Next
> Moves to the next picture or video. You can also view the next picture by pressing the right arrow key on your keyboard.

Rotate Counterclockwise
> Rotates the selected picture counterclockwise. You can also rotate a picture counterclockwise by pressing the Ctrl key and the comma (,) key.

Rotate Clockwise
> Rotate the selected picture clockwise. You can also rotate a picture clockwise by pressing the Ctrl key and the period (.) key.

Delete
> Deletes the selected picture. You can also delete a picture by pressing the Delete key. Deleting a picture will remove it from the gallery and your computer.

When viewing videos, Windows Photo Gallery displays the Controls toolbar in the lower portion of the main window, as shown in Figure 9-11.

Figure 9-11. Controls for videos

From left to right, the controls on the toolbar are:

Timeline
  Tracks the video timeline and the current frame position within the video. If you click and drag the Current Frame button on the end of the timeline slider, you can fast-forward or rewind through a video. If you click a specific part of the timeline, you can go to that time in the video.

Play
  Plays the video. You can also play the video by pressing the H key.

Stop
  Stops the video. You can also stop the video by pressing the Home key.

Previous
  Moves to the previous video or picture. You can also view the previous video or picture by pressing the left arrow key on your keyboard.

Play Slide Show
  Plays a slide show of pictures. If you click this button when viewing videos, you'll see a warning dialog box specifying that you can play only picture slide shows.

Next
  Moves to the next picture or video. You can also view the next picture by pressing the right arrow key on your keyboard.

Delete
  Deletes the selected video. You can also delete a video by pressing the Delete key. Deleting a video will remove it from the gallery and your computer.

Building Your Photo and Video Gallery

As you've seen, Windows Photo Gallery handles most of the important organization tasks for you, and this makes adding to your gallery easy. All you need to do is add picture and video folders to monitor, or copy pictures and videos to folders that Windows Photo Gallery already monitors. You can also get pictures and videos from cameras. Using the built-in print, email, and burn features, getting your media out of your gallery is just as easy. You can print copies of your pictures and videos, save copies of your media to data CDs and DVDs, and email pictures and videos to friends.

Adding or Removing Media Folders

Whenever you start Windows Photo Gallery, it checks your Pictures and Videos folders for any picture or video files you've added and then updates your gallery to reflect these changes automatically. Because of this, the easiest way to add media to your gallery is simply to move the media files to the appropriate personal folder. To add digital pictures to your library, simply copy or move the digital pictures to your Pictures folder. To add videos to your library, simply copy or move the videos to your Videos folder.

Windows Photo Gallery also monitors the Public Pictures and Public Videos folders. Therefore, if you have pictures or videos that you'd like to share with others who use your computer, you can put the shared pictures and videos in these folders.

You can have Windows Photo Gallery add media from and monitor other folders in exactly the same way by completing the following steps:

1. Right-click the Folders category in the Navigation Pane, and then select Add Folder to Gallery. This displays the Add Folder to Gallery dialog box.

2. In the Add Folder to Gallery dialog box, select the folder containing pictures, videos, or both that you'd like to add, and then click OK.

As long as you have appropriate permissions to access the folder, Windows Photo Gallery will then begin adding pictures and videos from the folder to your gallery. How long this takes depends on how many pictures and videos you are adding.

You can remove a folder that you added if you no longer want to include a folder's items in your gallery. To do this, right-click the folder and then select Remove from Gallery. When prompted, confirm that you want to remove the folder from the gallery by clicking Yes. Removing the folder from the gallery tells Windows Photo Gallery to stop monitoring the folder. It doesn't delete the folder or its contents from your computer.

Getting Your Digital Pictures

One way of using a digital picture camera with your computer is to connect the camera directly. After you run your digital camera's Setup program, you can connect most digital cameras directly to your computer using a Universal Serial Bus (USB) or FireWire cable. With your camera turned on, you then access the digital pictures on it as you would any other device with removable storage. In Windows Photo Gallery, you can also select the Import from Camera or Scanner option on the File menu to import digital pictures directly.

Rather than connecting your camera directly, you can purchase a memory-card reader that plugs into a USB slot on your computer. Once you've connected the card reader to your computer, you simply insert the memory card. As with a direct camera connection, you then access your digital pictures as you would any other device with removable storage. Because most digital cameras use memory sticks, computers and monitors increasingly are being shipped with built-in memory card slots. You simply insert your memory card into the slot that works with the type of memory card you have.

Table 9-1 provides an overview of the picture formats Windows Photo Gallery supports. Windows Photo Gallery is meant to be used with digital cameras and scanners and not with web images. Because of this, it does not support some older file formats, such as GIF.

Table 9-1. Picture formats supported by Windows Photo Gallery

File type	File extensions
Bitmap image	*.bmp*
JPEG image	*.jpg, .jpeg, .jfif*
PNG image	*.png*
TIFF image	*.tif, .tiff*
Word Perfect image	*.wpg*

You'll find that viewing pictures in Windows Photo Gallery is similar to viewing pictures in Windows Media Player. The two applications do in fact share subcomponents. However, Windows Media Player provides only basic features for viewing pictures and playing slide shows. Windows Photo Gallery, on the other hand, has extended viewing, editing, and slide show features.

Getting Your Videos

When it comes to video cameras, getting videos to your computer requires a mixed bag of tricks. This is because, unlike digital picture cameras, you can capture video from both analog video cameras and digital video cameras.

Capturing video from analog video cameras

Analog video cameras have tapes, which come in a variety of types and sizes. You'll need to install the video capture program that came with your camera before capturing video. If your computer's video card has video capture or input features, you can connect your video camera to your computer using an audio/video (A/V) cable.

An A/V cable for an older video camera will have a connection jack on one end that plugs into your video camera and mono audio and video connectors on the other end of the plug. You plug the audio and video connectors into the audio and video jacks on your video card. If your video card has stereo inputs, you'll need a Y connector cable that passes the mono audio into left and right stereo channels.

An A/V cable for a newer video camera will have a connection jack on one end that plugs into your video camera and stereo audio and video connectors on the other end of the plug. You plug the audio and video connectors into the left audio, right audio, and video jacks on your video card. If your video card has mono input for audio, you'll need a Y connector cable that passes the left and right stereo channels into the mono input channel.

To capture video, you'll need to turn your camera on and then start the video capture program. After you rewind the tape to the beginning or position the tape at the desired start point, press Play on the video camera and then begin to capture the video. When you are finished capturing, you'll need to save the video using a format that Windows Photo Gallery supports.

Getting video from digital video cameras

Digital video cameras store data digitally on a data disc, memory card, or hard disk drive. Table 9-2 provides an overview of the digital video formats Windows Photo Gallery supports.

Table 9-2. Video formats supported by Windows Photo Gallery

Video formats	File extensions
DVD video	.mpa, .m1v, .m2v, .mp2, .mp2v, .mpv2
MPEG 1 and MPEG 2 video	.mpe, .mpeg, .mpg
Windows Media Audio/Video Professional	.asf, .wm, .wmv

As with digital picture cameras, one way of using a digital video camera with your computer is to connect the camera directly. After you run your digital camera's Setup program, you can connect most digital video cameras directly to your computer using a USB or FireWire cable. With the camera turned on, you then access the digital media on your camera as you would any other device with removable storage or a CD/DVD drive. Most digital video cameras can take digital pictures as well as digital videos.

If your digital video camera uses data discs in a size and format that your computer's CD/DVD drive can read, you have it easy. All you need to do is insert the data disc into the CD/DVD drive and then you can work with your media as you would any other data disc. In Windows Photo Gallery, you can also select the Import from Camera or Scanner option on the File menu to import digital videos and pictures directly.

If your digital video camera uses memory sticks, you can purchase a memory card reader that plugs into a USB slot on your computer. Once you've connected the card reader to your computer, you simply insert the memory card and access your digital media as you would any other device with removable storage. Because most digital cameras use memory sticks, computers and monitors increasingly are being shipped with built-in memory card slots. You simply insert the memory card into the slot that works with the type of memory card you have.

Importing Digital Pictures from Cameras, Scanners, CDs, and DVDs

You can import digital pictures into your gallery and automatically name your imported items by completing the following steps:

1. Connect your camera or scanner to your computer, insert a data CD or DVD containing pictures into your CD/DVD drive, or connect your memory card reader to your computer with a memory stick inserted.

2. You'll usually see an AutoPlay dialog box similar to the one shown in Figure 9-12. In the AutoPlay dialog box, you'll want to click "Import pictures" to begin the import process. If you don't see the AutoPlay dialog box and the default option doesn't begin a picture import, you can reset the AutoPlay options as discussed in the "Changing the Default AutoPlay Settings" section, later in this chapter.

 If you always want to import pictures when you connect this camera or insert this type of memory card, select the "Always do this for pictures" checkbox and click "Import pictures." Then, the next time you import pictures, you'll bypass the AutoPlay dialog box and go straight to the Import Pictures and Videos dialog box.

Figure 9-12. Selecting an AutoPlay option

3. After the Import Pictures Wizard determines how many pictures are available for importing, you'll see the Importing Pictures and Videos dialog box, shown in Figure 9-13. If you don't see the Importing Pictures and Videos dialog box, it's because you've turned off prompting for a tag on import. You can reenable prompting, as discussed in the "Configuring Import Settings" section, later in this chapter.

Figure 9-13. Setting the tag for your pictures

4. In the "Tag these pictures" text box, enter a tag for the pictures you are importing. The tag is also used to set the filename of the pictures. Files named after a tag are numbered sequentially.

5. Click Import to import the pictures into a subfolder of your default pictures. The subfolder is named with the date imported and the tag you specified previously.

Importing Digital Videos from Cameras, CDs, and DVDs

You can import digital videos into your gallery and automatically name your imported items by completing the following steps:

1. Connect your camera to your computer or insert a data CD or DVD containing pictures into your CD/DVD drive.

2. You'll usually see an AutoPlay dialog box similar to the one shown in Figure 9-12. In the AutoPlay dialog box, you'll want to click "Import videos" to begin the import process. If you don't see the AutoPlay dialog box and the default option doesn't begin a video import, you can reset the AutoPlay options as discussed in the "Changing the Default AutoPlay Settings" section of this chapter.

 If you always want to import videos when you connect this camera or insert this type of memory card, select the "Always do this for videos" checkbox and then click "Import videos." The next time you import videos, you'll bypass the AutoPlay dialog box and go straight to the Import Pictures and Videos dialog box.

3. After the Import Videos Wizard determines how many videos are available for importing, you'll see the Importing Pictures and Videos dialog box, shown in Figure 9-13. If you don't see the dialog box, it's because you've turned off prompting for a tag on import. You can reenable prompting, as discussed in the "Configuring Import Settings" section of this chapter.

4. In the "Tag these videos" text box, enter a tag for the videos you are importing. The tag is also used to set the filename of the videos. Filenames include the tag and a sequential numeric suffix, such as *Halloween 001.jpg*, *Halloween 002.jpg*, and so on.

5. Click Import to import the videos into a subfolder of your default videos folder. The subfolder is named with the date imported and the tag you specified previously.

Changing the Default AutoPlay Settings

AutoPlay settings are designed to make your life easier by remembering your preferred choices for various types of media and then performing related actions for you automatically. Sometimes, though, the AutoPlay settings won't perform the desired action and you'll want to reset them so that the AutoPlay dialog box is displayed.

You can reset the AutoPlay settings by completing the following steps:

1. In the Windows Photo Gallery main view, click File and then select Options. This displays the Windows Photo Gallery Options dialog box.

 If the File menu doesn't have an Options item, it's because you aren't in the main view. Click the Back to Gallery button and then repeat this step.

2. On the Import tab, click the "Change default AutoPlay options" link. This displays the AutoPlay page in the Control Panel, as shown in Figure 9-14.

3. Make sure the "Use AutoPlay for all media and devices" checkbox is selected.

4. To ensure that the AutoPlay dialog box is displayed, set the AutoPlay options for Pictures and Video Files to "Ask me every time."

5. Click Save to save your settings.

Configuring Import Settings

The import settings in Windows Photo Gallery control how digital pictures and digital videos are imported. You can set separate default settings for cameras, CDs and DVDs, and scanners by completing the following steps:

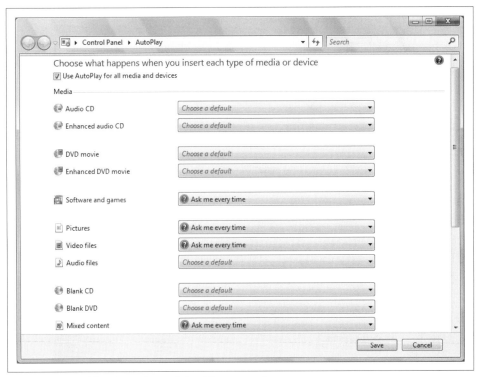

Figure 9-14. Enabling AutoPlay and AutoPlay prompting

1. In the Windows Photo Gallery main view, click File and then select Options.

    If the File menu doesn't have an Options item, it's because you aren't in the main view. Click the Back to Gallery button and then repeat this step.

2. In the Windows Photo Gallery Options dialog box, click the Import tab, as shown in Figure 9-15.

3. On the "Settings for" list, select Cameras, CD and DVDs, or Scanners as appropriate.

4. The "Import to" list shows the default import location. If you want to set a different default import location, click Browse and then use the Browse for Folder dialog box to select the folder to use. This folder should be one that is monitored by Windows Photo Gallery or a subfolder of a monitored folder.

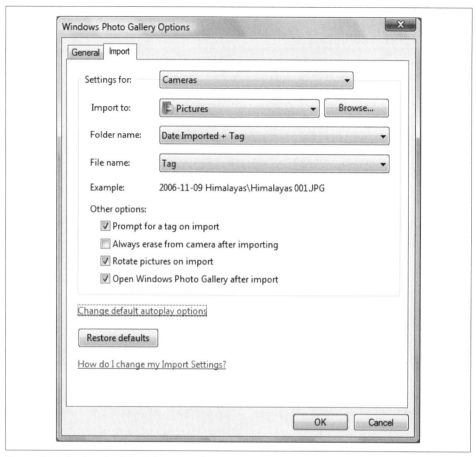

Figure 9-15. Setting the default import options

5. Use the Folder Name list options to specify the naming scheme of the folder created for storing the imported items. You can set this to:

   - Date Imported + Tag
   - Date Taken + Tag
   - Tag + Date Imported
   - Tag + Date Taken
   - Tag + Date Taken Range
   - Tag

6. Use the "File name" list options to specify the default naming scheme for imported pictures and videos. You can select "Tag," "Original file name," or "Original file name (preserve folders)." With tags, filenames include the tag and a sequential numeric suffix, such as *Halloween 001.jpg, Halloween 002.jpg*, and so on.

7. If you are using the original filenames, you probably don't need to prompt for a tag on import. Clear the "Prompt for a tag on import" checkbox to bypass the Importing Pictures and Videos dialog box and begin importing automatically. Otherwise, select the "Prompt for a tag on import" checkbox to ensure that the Importing Pictures and Videos dialog box is displayed.

8. If you don't want to keep the pictures or videos on your camera or memory stick after importing, select the "Always erase from camera after import" checkbox. Because pictures or videos are erased only when the import completes successfully, you don't have to worry about accidentally deleting pictures that didn't get imported.

9. If your camera has a sensor that can detect whether you took a picture horizontally or vertically, Windows Photo Gallery can use the related information to automatically rotate pictures that would otherwise appear to be sideways on your computer. To enable automatic rotation, select the "Rotate pictures on import" checkbox.

10. To ensure that pictures are opened in Windows Photo Gallery after importing, select the "Open Windows Photo Gallery after import" checkbox.

11. Click OK to save your settings.

Fixing Your Pictures

Windows Photo Gallery has built-in features for fixing pictures. In any picture-related view, you can click the Rotate Clockwise or Rotate Counterclockwise button on the Controls toolbar to rotate pictures to the proper orientation. If you select multiple pictures with the same orientation problem, you can rotate them all to the proper orientation at the same time by clicking the Rotate Clockwise or Rotate Counterclockwise button.

Editing picture color, brightness, and contrast

You can perform additional editing of individual pictures by completing these steps:

1. In Windows Photo Gallery, click the picture you want to edit and then click the Fix button on the toolbar.

2. As Figure 9-16 shows, the picture is then displayed in view mode with the Fix Pane.

3. If the color, brightness, or contrast setting in your picture doesn't look right, you can correct or enhance it automatically by clicking Auto Adjust.

4. If the brightness and contrast still don't look right, you can adjust them independently by clicking Adjust Exposure and then using the Brightness and Contrast sliders to achieve the desired results.

Figure 9-16. Editing the picture using the Fix Pane options

5. If the colors still don't look right, you can adjust them by clicking Adjust Color. You can then use these color settings to adjust the color:

Color Temperature
> Use this slider to adjust the overall tone of the picture. Move the slider to the left to make the colors appear cooler (bluer). Move the slider to the right to make the colors appear warmer (redder).

Tint
> Use this slider to adjust the predominant color in the picture by adding or removing green. Move the slider to the left to remove green. Move the slider to the right to add green.

Saturation
> Use this slider to make the colors in the picture more or less vivid. Move the slider to the left to make the colors less vivid. Move the slider to the right to make the colors more vivid.

6. Click the Back to Gallery button to save the changes to the picture automatically.

Using undo and redo while fixing pictures

While you are fixing your picture, you can use the Undo button to undo any changes you don't like and the Redo button to redo changes you previously undid. Multiple undo and redo changes are saved, allowing you to step backward and forward through changes. You can also undo and redo specific changes.

To undo a specific change or changes, follow these steps:

1. Click the option button to the right of the Undo button. This displays a short-cut menu with a list of Undo changes, as shown in Figure 9-17.

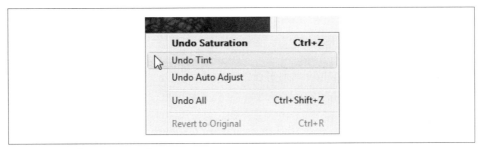

Figure 9-17. Choosing an undo option

2. The most recent change is listed first and in bold. To undo this change, click it or press Ctrl-Z.
3. To undo a specific change, click the change you want to undo in the list.
4. To undo all changes, click Undo All or press Ctrl-Shift-Z.

To redo a specific change or changes, follow these steps:

1. Click the option button to the right of the Redo button. This displays a shortcut menu with a list of Redo changes, as shown in Figure 9-18.

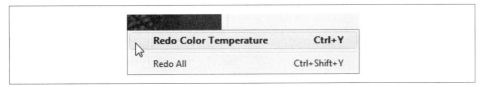

Figure 9-18. Choosing a redo option

2. The most recent change is listed first and in bold. To redo this change, click it or press Ctrl-Y.
3. To redo a specific change, click the change you want to redo in the list.
4. To redo all changes, click Redo All or press Ctrl-Shift-Y.

Restoring the original version of a picture

Whenever you edit a picture using the Fix Pane, Windows Photo Gallery automatically saves a copy of the original picture. If you're unhappy with the results, follow these steps to restore the original picture at any time (prior to automated deletion of the original):

1. In Windows Photo Gallery, click the picture you want to restore and then click the Fix button on the toolbar.

2. The Undo button is changed to a Revert button. To revert to the original version of the picture, click the Revert button.

3. Confirm the action when prompted by clicking Revert again.

4. Click the Back to Gallery button.

Controlling when the original versions of pictures are deleted

When you fix a picture in Windows Photo Gallery, Windows saves a copy of the original in case you later want to undo the changes. By default, these copies are never erased, but over time, you may find that they are using up space on your disk drive. To free up this space, you can have Windows automatically delete originals after a specified period. To do this, complete the following steps:

1. In the Windows Photo Gallery main view, click File and then select Options. This displays the Windows Photo Gallery Options dialog box, as shown in Figure 9-19.

2. On the General tab, use the "Move originals to Recycle Bin after" list to specify whether and when originals are moved to the Recycle Bin. To save originals indefinitely, select Never. To save originals for a specific amount of time and then delete them, select the desired retention time, such as "One week" or "One month."

3. Click OK to save your settings.

Sharing Your Photo and Video Gallery

Using the built-in print, email, and burn features, getting your media out of your gallery is just as easy as getting it into your gallery. You can print copies of your pictures and videos, save copies of your media to data CDs and DVDs, and email pictures and videos to friends.

Printing Your Pictures

Windows Photo Gallery features a smart printing feature that allows you to print enhanced, high-quality pictures. You can print multiple pictures at a time by selecting them before you start printing. You can then print pictures at full-page size, or you can combine pictures and print them at these smaller sizes:

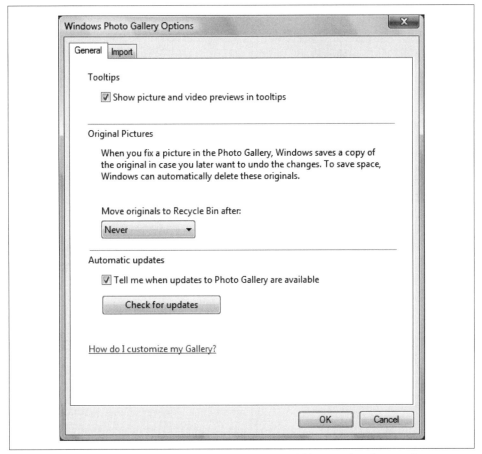

Figure 9-19. Specifying when, if ever, copies of originals should be moved to the Recycle Bin

- 4×6 with two pictures per page
- 5×7 with two pictures per page
- 8×10 with one picture per page
- 3.5×5 with four pictures per page
- Wallet size with nine pictures per page
- Contact sheet with 35 pictures per page

When you're printing pictures, keep the following in mind:

- If you're printing at a size larger than the original picture size, you may get a blurry picture. For the best results, print pictures using a size equal to or smaller than the original picture size.
- If you're printing to regular paper or paper not designed for photos, you won't get the best results. For the best quality, print pictures on premium photo paper. With premium glossy or matte paper, you'll usually want to print to the shiniest side.

In Windows Photo Gallery, you can print pictures by completing the following steps:

1. Select the pictures you want to print.

2. Click the Print button on the toolbar and then select Print.

3. In the Print Pictures dialog box, shown in Figure 9-20, use the Printer list to select the printer you want to use.

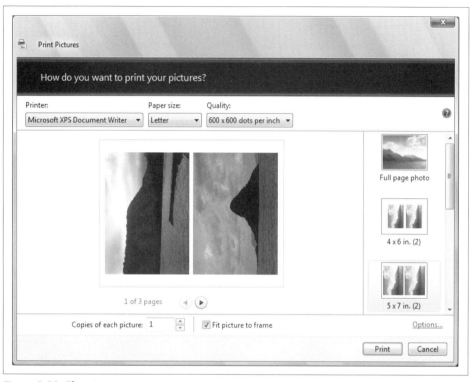

Figure 9-20. Choosing your printing options

4. Use the "Paper size" list to select the paper size you want to use, such as Letter or Legal. To use a size not listed, choose More and then click the size you want to use, or click "User defined size" at the bottom of the list.

5. Use the Quality list to select the print quality, such as 600×600 dots per inch (dpi). In most cases, you'll want to print using the highest dpi setting that the printer supports.

6. In the left pane, select the picture size, such as 4×6 in.

7. Select the "Fit picture to frame" checkbox to have Windows enlarge the picture to fit the exact size you've selected. If you want the picture to print at its original proportions, clear this checkbox, but keep in mind that you may have gaps because the digital picture isn't proportioned exactly to the dimensions you selected.

8. Use the "Preview next print page" and "Preview previous print page" buttons to review how the pictures will print.

 By default, the pictures are enhanced and sharpened before printing and the Print Pictures dialog box hides options that may not be compatible with your printer. To change these print settings, click the Options link.

9. Click Print to print your pictures.

Emailing Your Pictures and Videos

Windows Photo Gallery makes it easy to send copies of pictures and videos to your friends as attachments to an email message. With pictures, it'll even show you the estimated size of the attached pictures and let you resize pictures automatically so that they have smaller file sizes.

Emailing pictures

In Windows Photo Gallery, you can email pictures to your friends by completing the following steps:

1. Select the pictures you want to email and then click the Email button.

2. In the Attach Files dialog box, shown in Figure 9-21, the total estimated size of the attached pictures is listed. To reduce the size of the attachments, use the "Picture size" list to select a new size. Windows will then resize the pictures if you've changed the picture size.

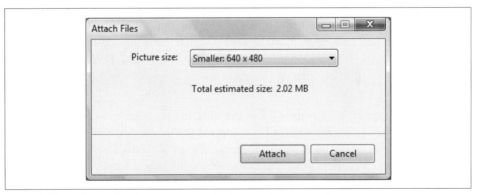

Figure 9-21. Reducing the picture size to make the attachments smaller

3. When you click Attach, Windows will open a new email message in your default mail program and attach the pictures to this message.

4. After you complete the To, Cc, Subject, and message body fields as appropriate, you can send the message with your pictures attached by clicking Send.

Emailing videos

In Windows Photo Gallery, you can email videos to your friends by completing the following steps:

1. Select the videos you want to email and then click the Email button.

2. Windows opens a new email message in your default mail program and attaches the videos to this message.

3. After you complete the To, Cc, Subject, and message body fields as appropriate, you can send the message with your videos attached by clicking Send.

Burning Data CDs and DVDs

Windows Photo Gallery has built-in CD and DVD burning features. You can use these features to create archive copies and to share pictures and videos with others. Before you burn data CDs and DVDs, you should familiarize yourself with the disc types and disc filesystem options that are available.

You don't necessarily have to use Windows Photo Gallery to burn data CDs and DVDs. Anytime you insert a blank CD or DVD, Windows Vista shows a Burn button on the Windows Explorer toolbar. Clicking this button starts the Burn a Disc Wizard, and you can burn discs in much the same way as discussed in this section.

Navigating the available types of data discs

With data CDs and DVDs, you can burn any files in your gallery to create a data disc. As discussed in Chapter 8, if you create a data DVD with pictures in JPEG format, any newer DVD player that supports this format can read and play the disc as a slide show. An alternative to this is to make a movie as a DVD-Video using your pictures. You will then be able to play the DVD in just about any DVD player, providing that you use a standard type of DVD disc. Since data DVDs can hold an enormous number of JPEG images, you can create photo-album slide shows that run for hours.

When you are working with data CDs and DVDs, you need to keep in mind that computer and home or car CD and DVD players are different. Your computer DVD player typically is designed to read commercially produced CD-ROMs and DVD-ROMs as well as computer-burned CDs and DVDs in specific formats. To make matters worse, different Windows programs may have varying support for different disc types. Case in point: Windows Photo Gallery supports a similar but different set of disc types than Windows Media Player 11.

While Windows Photo Gallery won't burn audio CDs, it does give you more burning options for data discs than Windows Media Player does. Windows Photo Gallery supports burning data CDs to CD-R, CD+R, and CD-RW. Windows Photo

Gallery supports burning data DVDs to DVD-R, DVD-RW, DVD+R, DVD+RW, and DVD-RAM. DVDs can be either single-sided and single-layered or single-sided and dual-layered. While DVD-Audio and DVD-Video aren't supported for data disc burns, you can make a movie as a DVD-Video, as discussed in Chapter 10.

Many CD/DVD burners support multiple disc types. Of the many types of writable discs, not all discs can be formatted with a filesystem and used in the same way. To help you choose the right disc for the task, Table 9-3 provides some tips and advice.

Table 9-3. Navigating CD and DVD options

Disc type	How used	Compatible with
CD-R, CD+R, DVD-R, DVD+R	These disc types are recordable. Data cannot be deleted once recorded.	Compatible with many computers and newer CD/DVD players
CD-RW, DVD-RW, DVD+RW	These disc types are re-recordable. Data can be deleted after it is recorded, and you can write data to the disc many times.	Compatible with many computers and newer CD/DVD players
DVD-RAM	These disc types are re-recordable. Data can be deleted after it is recorded, and you can write data to the disc many times.	Compatible with fewer computers and CD/DVD players

Navigating data disc filesystem options

Most Windows programs create data discs using a mastered approach and discs are written in the appropriate filesystem format automatically. With a mastered approach, you select a collection of files that you want to copy to a disc and then burn all the files at once. When you are burning large collections of files, this is a convenient approach with the added bonus of compatibility with any computer or device that supports the type of data disc you are using.

When you burn files to data discs using mastering, you burn files in a session. In many CD/DVD burning programs, you have the option of leaving a session open to allow you to add files later, and then you close the session when you are done adding files. By closing the session, you finalize the disc and allow it to be read on other computers and devices. Otherwise, while a session is open, the disc can be read only on your computer. Windows Photo Gallery uses the built-in CD/DVD burn feature of Windows Vista. Instead of opening a session, Windows Vista creates a burn list and copies files you want to burn to a temporary folder. Once you've collected all the files you want to burn, you can open a burn session, write the files, and then close the burn session. Once the burn session is closed, you can no longer add to the disc.

With Windows Photo Gallery, you can create data discs with what Windows Vista calls a "live filesystem." A data disc with a live filesystem works like any other type of removable storage, such as a USB flash key or a removable disc drive. You can copy files to the disc immediately without having to burn them, simply by copying and pasting files or by dragging and dropping files. If the disc is re-recordable, you can remove files simply by selecting them and deleting them. If you eject the disc, you can insert it into your CD/DVD drive later and continue to use it like removable storage. The major drawback, however, is that home and car CD/DVD players cannot read data discs with a live filesystem—only computers can.

Technically, data discs with a live filesystem are formatted using the Universal Disc Format (UDF) rather than the standard CD File System (CDFS). Although UDF has been around for a long time, you might not have heard of it before, because although Windows has supported UDF since Windows 98, you needed to purchase a separate CD/DVD burner program to actually create and use UDF. That is no longer the case with Windows Vista.

At the time I wrote this book, Windows Vista supported burning data discs in these UDF versions:

UDF 1.5

This format is compatible with Windows 2000 and later versions of Windows. It might not be compatible with Windows 98 or Apple computers.

UDF 2.0

This format is compatible with Windows XP and later versions of Windows. It might not be compatible with Windows 98, Windows 2000, or Apple computers.

UDF 2.01

This is the default format, and it includes a major bug fix that you'll want to take advantage of in most cases. This format is compatible with Windows XP and later versions of Windows. It might not be compatible with Windows 98, Windows 2000, or Apple computers.

UDF 2.5

This format is optimized for Windows Vista. It might not be compatible with earlier versions of Windows or Apple computers.

Burning data disc masters

You can burn a mastered disc by completing the following steps:

1. Insert a blank disc into your CD/DVD burner. If the AutoPlay dialog box is displayed, close it by clicking the Close button (the button with the red *X*).

2. In Windows Photo Gallery, select one or more of the pictures and videos you want to burn to disc.

3. Click the Burn tab and then click Data Disc.

4. In the Burn a Disc Wizard, type a disc title, click the "Show formatting options" button, and then select Mastered, as shown in Figure 9-22.

5. When you click Next, the data disc is opened in Windows Explorer, as shown in Figure 9-23. The "Files Ready to Be Written to the Disc" Pane shows the pictures and videos you've selected. This is your burn list. Don't close this window.

Figure 9-22. Creating a mastered data disc

Files on the burn list are copied from their original location and written as temporary files to a temporary folder. This temporary folder is created in your personal profile. Copies of these files are created to be sure that all the files are in one place and that you have appropriate permissions to access the files before trying to burn the disc.

6. To add more pictures and videos, select them in Windows Photo Gallery, click Burn, and then select Data Disc. If you try to add any pictures or videos that are already added to the burn list, you'll see the Copy File dialog box shown in Figure 9-24. Before you click "Copy and Replace," "Don't Copy," or "Copy, but keep both files" as appropriate, you might want to select the "Do this for the next... conflicts" checkbox to perform the same action for all duplicate copies.

7. To add files that are on your computer but are not in your gallery, drag the files to the burn list in Windows Explorer. You can add any type of file using this technique; not just pictures or videos.

8. If you want to remove a picture or video from the burn list, click it and then click "Delete temporary files." When prompted to confirm the action, click Yes. The related temporary file is then moved from the burn list to the Recycle Bin. The original version of the picture or video will still exist in its original location.

9. Once you've added all the files you want to burn, access the burn list in Windows Explorer. Click an open area within the burn list and then press Ctrl-A. Note the total size of all selected files, and remove files as necessary so that all the files fit on one disc. Unlike Windows Media Player, the Burn to Disc Wizard will not burn files to multiple discs.

Figure 9-23. Adding files to the burn list

 If you are unsure of the total capacity of a disc, simply look at another disc of the same type. The capacity is written on the disc. Most data CDs can hold up to 700 MB of data. Most single-sided single-layered DVDs can hold up to 4.7 GB of data.

10. When you are ready to continue, click Burn to Disc. In the Burn to Disc Wizard, the disc title is set using the title you provided previously, and the recording speed is set to the maximum speed supported by the CD/DVD drive.

11. When you click Next, Windows Vista will add the files you selected to a disc image and then write the files to your data disc. When finished burning the disc, Windows Vista will automatically eject the disc. By default, the temporary files are deleted and you can click Finish to exit the Burn to Disc dialog box. If you want to burn the same files to another disc, select the "Yes, burn these files to another disc" checkbox before clicking Finish.

Figure 9-24. Resolving conflicts by selecting an appropriate option

Keep the following in mind when working with the Burn to Disc Wizard:

- If you miscalculated the capacity of your data disc, you'll see an error and will have to click Cancel or Finish. Both actions exit the Burn to Disc Wizard. Don't worry; you don't have to start over. Simply click Start and then click Computer. In the Computer window, double-click the CD/DVD drive you were working with under Devices with Removable Storage.

 Rather than deleting items, you can change the type of disc you're working with. If you inserted a CD but want to use a DVD instead, simply eject the CD and insert a DVD. You'll then see the Burn to Disc Wizard.

- If an error occurs while burning, you'll see an error message. As shown in Figure 9-25, you'll have the option of trying again with a different disc, deleting the temporary files that have not burned, or saving all the temporary files and trying to burn them later. If you try again, make sure you select a slower burn speed. Although your CD/DVD drive may be able to burn at a high speed, the disc itself may not be rated for burning at the speed you've selected.

Generally, if you see a burn error, only a portion of your files will be written to the disc. If the burn session is still open, you can try to burn to the disc again. However, in some cases, you may find that you have to use a new blank disc.

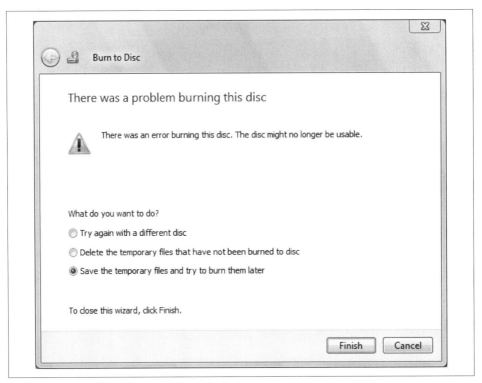

Figure 9-25. Specifying what you want to do if a burn error occurs

Burning a data disc with a live filesystem

You can burn a data disc with a live filesystem by completing the following steps:

1. Insert a blank disc into your CD/DVD burner. If the AutoPlay dialog box is displayed, close it by clicking the Close button (the button with the red X).

2. In Windows Photo Gallery, select one or more of the pictures and videos you want to burn to disc.

3. Click the Burn tab and then click Data Disc.

4. In the Burn a Disc Wizard, type a disc title, click the "Show formatting options" button, and then select Live File System, as shown in Figure 9-26.

Figure 9-26. Creating a live data disc

5. By default, Windows Vista burns live discs using UDF Version 2.01. If you want to change the UDF version used, click the "Change version" link, select the UDF version to use, and then click OK.

6. When you click Next, Windows Vista formats the data disc and then copies the selected pictures and videos to the disc. The data disc is opened in Windows Explorer, as shown in Figure 9-27.

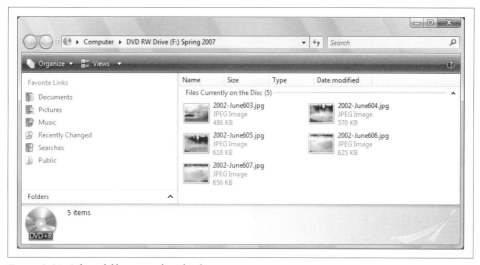

Figure 9-27. Selected files, copied to the disc

7. Because you are working with a live disc, there is no burn list. You can now work with the disc as follows:

- To add files that are on your computer but not in your gallery, drag the files to the burn list in Windows Explorer. You can add any type of file using this technique; not just pictures or videos.

- To add pictures and videos in your gallery, select the pictures and videos in Windows Photo Gallery, click Burn, and then click Data Disc. The files will be copied to the live data disc.

- To remove a picture or video from the disc, click it and then press Delete, or right-click it and then select Delete. With re-recordable discs, the file is removed and the space is freed for other files. With recordable discs, the file is marked as deleted but actually still exists on the disc. Because of this, the space used by the deleted file is still allocated and cannot be used by other files.

While the disc is inserted, Windows Vista will maintain an open burn session for the disc. If you eject the live data disc, Windows Vista will close the burn session so that you can use the disc with other computers. From then on, whenever you insert the disc, you'll be able to add or remove files using Windows Explorer, Windows Photo Gallery, and other Windows programs. Windows Vista will open another burn session only if you modify the disc's contents. As before, you can close the session by ejecting the disc.

 You can also close a burn session by right-clicking the CD/DVD drive in the Computer window and selecting "Close session."

CHAPTER 10

Making Video DVDs and Movies

Windows Vista is the first version of Windows with built-in support for burning DVDs. As you've seen in earlier chapters, you can use these features to create data DVDs in Windows Media Player and Windows Photo Gallery. If you are running the Windows Vista Home Premium or Ultimate edition, you can also use these features to create video and movie DVDs using Windows DVD Maker and Windows Movie Maker.

The differences between Windows DVD Maker and Windows Movie Maker mostly have to do with your level of involvement and the level of customization you want. With Windows DVD Maker, your video DVDs can have digital-picture slide shows with soundtracks, and digital videos that include their own soundtracks. When you add pictures and videos, Windows DVD Maker handles most of the background tasks for you so that you can produce video DVDs with minimal fuss. In fact, you can design a full-featured video DVD complete with title, menu, soundtrack, pan and zoom motion for your picture slide shows, and notes, all in just a few minutes.

If you want more than the essentials, you will need to use Windows Movie Maker. With Windows Movie Maker, you have full control over every aspect of movie production. You can create movies using digital pictures and videos. To create professional-looking movies, you can add titles, effects, transitions, and credits. Your movies can also have soundtracks that combine narration, music, and other types of audio. A finished movie, however, is not a finished DVD production. Therefore, after you produce your movie, you'll have to use Windows DVD Maker to create a finished DVD production.

So there you have it—two ways to create video DVDs with two different approaches. One allows you to produce finished DVDs. The other is a movie maker with enough added production capabilities to please even the most ardent recreational video producer.

Creating Video DVDs with Windows DVD Maker

Windows DVD Maker helps you create videos and complete DVDs with minimal fuss. That's why it's my favorite of the two video makers included with the Windows Vista Home Premium and Ultimate editions.

Getting Started with Windows DVD Maker

You can start and use Windows DVD Maker in several ways. When you are working with Windows Photo Gallery, you can select the initial pictures and videos you want to work with and then click Burn → Video DVD to open Windows DVD Maker with these items selected. Otherwise, you can start Windows DVD Maker by clicking Start → All Programs → Windows DVD Maker.

As Table 10-1 shows, Windows DVD Maker works with a wide variety of image, sound, and video formats. This list is different from the formats supported by Windows Photo Gallery and Windows Media Maker. The most notable changes are that Windows DVD Maker supports GIF images but does not support the AIFF or AU sound format. Also of note is that Windows DVD Maker supports the Microsoft Digital Video Recorder format, allowing you to create video DVDs with recorded TV.

Table 10-1. File formats supported by Windows DVD Maker

File format/type	File extensions
Bitmap image	.bmp
DIB image	.dib
GIF image	.gif
JPEG image	.jpg, .jpe, .jpeg, .jfif
PNG image	.png
TIFF image	.tif, .tiff
Word Perfect image	.wdp
Windows Meta File	.wmf, .emf
Sound formats	
MP3 audio	.mp3, .m3u
WAV audio	.wav
Windows Media Audio	.wma
Video formats	
AVI video	.avi
DVD video	.mpa, .m1v, .m2v, .mp2, .mp2v, .mpv2, .mp2v
MPEG 1 and MPEG 2 video	.mpe, .mpeg, .mpg

Table 10-1. File formats supported by Windows DVD Maker (continued)

File format/type	File extensions
Audio/Video format	
Windows Media Audio/Video Professional	*.asf, .wm, .wmv*
Recorded TV format	
Microsoft Digital Video Recorder	*.dvr-ms*

When working with digital pictures, digital videos, and sounds, it is also important to note that Windows DVD Maker works with files that are already in the proper formats, and doesn't include features for converting formats. Additionally, all the files you want to use must be on your computer's disk drive, on a data disc you've inserted into your CD/DVD drive, or on a device with removable storage connected to your computer. Although Windows DVD Maker can read music and other sound files from a data disc, it doesn't include features for ripping raw CD audio files from audio discs.

When you start working with Windows DVD Maker, you may notice that the program works more like an extended wizard than a standalone program, and that's because it's designed to help you through the steps involved in video production. The first time you start Windows DVD Maker, you'll see the page shown in Figure 10-1. This page introduces Windows DVD Maker. Once you click "Choose Photos and Videos" to continue, you won't see this page again unless you are using a new user account.

Windows DVD Maker has two main pages. The first page you see in Windows DVD Maker is the "Add pictures and video to the DVD" page shown in Figure 10-2. You'll use this page to add items, set the play order, and configure the DVD burning and playback options.

When you click Next, you'll see the "Ready to burn disc" page, which is shown in Figure 10-3. On this page, you can customize the DVD menu style and text, as well as set up your picture slide show and add an audio soundtrack. You can also preview and burn your video from this page.

Using the options provided on these two pages, you create video DVDs by following a series of prescribed steps. The basic steps are as follows:

1. Add your pictures and videos, and then set the play order.
2. Set the DVD burning and playback options.
3. Customize the DVD menu style and text.
4. Set up your picture slide show and add an audio soundtrack.
5. Preview and save your video project.
6. Burn your video.

I discuss tasks related to each step in the sections that follow.

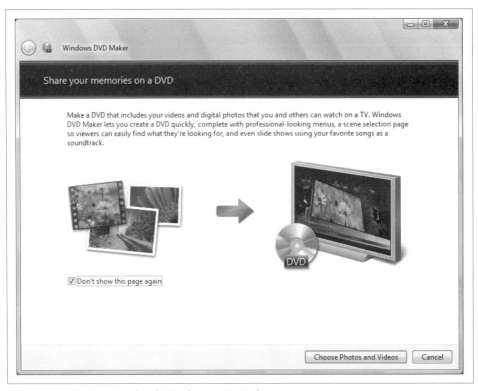

Figure 10-1. Getting started with Windows DVD Maker

Figure 10-2. The "Add pictures and video to the DVD page"

Figure 10-3. The "Ready to burn disc page"

Adding Your Pictures and Videos, and Setting the Play Order

With Windows DVD Maker, you can create video DVDs that include and combine pictures, videos, and recorded TV. Windows DVD Maker works with these different media types in different ways. Digital videos and recorded TV shows you select are added as individual items on the burn list. Pictures you select are added to a "Slide show" folder. Each video can have up to 998 videos or recorded TV shows but only one "Slide show" folder. The "Slide show" folder is handled as a media item separate from videos and recorded TV, and can itself hold up to 999 pictures.

Selecting pictures and videos for your DVD

Windows DVD Maker gives you several ways to select the pictures and videos to include in your video. My favorite way is to select all the pictures and videos I want to use in Windows Photo Gallery first and then add the selected items automatically to Windows DVD Maker. One way to do this is to click the first picture or video to add, hold the Ctrl key, and then select each additional picture or video to add individually. When you are done selecting items, you release the Ctrl key, and then click Burn → Video DVD in Windows Photo Gallery. Unfortunately, once you've selected an initial list in Windows Photo Gallery and accessed Windows DVD Maker, you can't go back to Windows Photo Gallery and select an additional set of pictures and videos to add. This means you'll have to select all the pictures and videos first to make the most out of this shortcut.

Sometimes, though, you want to add hundreds of items to a video, and it isn't always practical to select each item individually in Windows Photo Gallery before starting Windows DVD Maker. Here's one handy workaround I've come up with:

1. In Windows Photo Gallery, turn on the Info Pane by clicking the Info button.

 Only one instance of Windows DVD Maker can be open at a time. Because of this, you must start Windows Photo Gallery and then click Burn → Video DVD to open Windows DVD Maker.

2. Select one or more items that you want to add to the video DVD.

3. In the Info Pane, click Add Tags, type a unique name that identifies the video you are creating, such as Stanek Family DVD Volume 1, and then press Enter (see Figure 10-4).

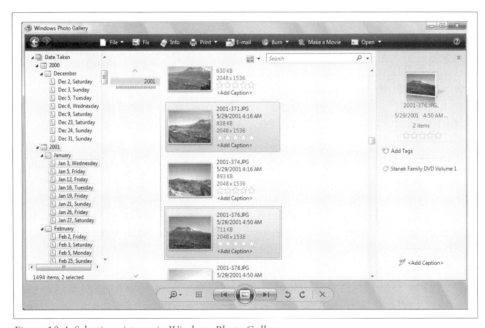

Figure 10-4. Selecting pictures in Windows Photo Gallery

4. Repeat steps 2 and 3 until you've added this tag to all the pictures and videos for the video DVD. You don't have to type the tag each time, however. Instead, when you click Add Tags, select the tag in the list provided, and then press Enter.

5. In the Navigation Pane, double-click Tags to expand the list of tags associated with your pictures and videos, and then click the tag you're using for the video.

6. In the work area, select all the items for the video by clicking the first item in the list, holding the Shift key, and then clicking the last item in the list. Alternatively, you can press Ctrl-A.

7. Click Burn and then click Video DVD to open Windows DVD Maker with these items selected.

I often find myself creating video DVDs related to specific dates on which I took pictures and videos. With that in mind, here's another handy workaround I've come up with:

1. In Windows Photo Gallery, right-click Date Taken and then select Expand All.

2. In the Navigation Pane, click the node for the first year, month, or date to include in the video.

3. While holding the Ctrl key, click the next node to include in the video and repeat this step until you've selected all the pictures and videos for the video.

4. Release the Ctrl key.

5. In the work area, select all the related items by clicking the first item in the list, holding the Shift key, and then clicking the last item in the list. Alternatively, you can press Ctrl-A.

6. Click Burn and then click Video DVD to open Windows DVD Maker with these items selected.

7. In Windows DVD Maker, the total runtime of all selected items is shown in the lower-left corner of the main window.

In Windows DVD Maker, you can select the items to add to your video by completing the following steps:

1. On the "Add pictures and video to the DVD" page, click the "Add items" button on the toolbar.

2. As shown in Figure 10-5, use the Add Items to DVD dialog box to browse to a folder containing pictures or videos you want to add.

3. Select the items to add using one of the following techniques:

   • Select an individual item by clicking it.

   • Select a series of items by clicking the first item, pressing and holding the Shift key, clicking the last item, and then releasing Shift.

   • Select multiple items individually by clicking the first item, pressing and holding the Ctrl key, clicking each additional item in turn, and then releasing Ctrl.

4. Click Add.

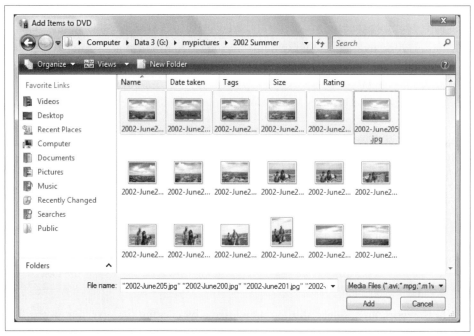

Figure 10-5. Selecting items to add

As Figure 10-6 shows, Windows DVD Maker lists the runtime of all selected items as a portion of the total running time possible in the lower-left corner of the main window. This runtime may change if you modify the slide show properties. Most single-sided DVDs can have a total running time of up to 150 minutes. Most single-sided double-layered DVDs can have a total running time of up to 300 minutes.

If you want your video to play on home DVD players, you'll want to ensure wide compatibility for your video by using a single-sided single-layered DVD rather than a single-sided double-layered DVD. In addition, if your DVD burner supports multiple formats, the type of disc you use will determine the format. DVD-R and DVD+R have the widest support, with DVD-RW and DVD+RW close behind in terms of support.

When trying to find pictures and videos to include, don't overlook the value of the Favorite Links panel in the Add Items to DVD dialog. The related options allow you to navigate quickly to various locations on your computer. The Recently Changed link can also come in handy. If you've forgotten pictures or videos in your original list, you can go back to Windows Photo Gallery and add a tag to these items. By adding a tag to these items, you give these items a new modification date. In Windows DVD Maker, you can then quickly include these items by completing these steps:

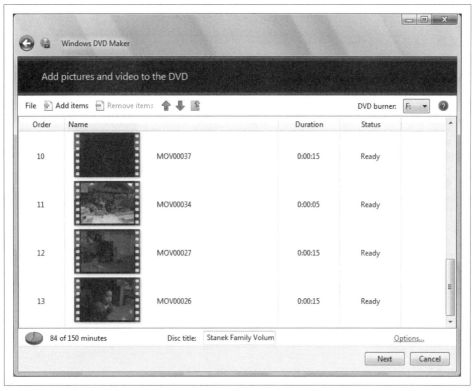

Figure 10-6. Checking the video runtime

1. On the Add Pictures and Video to the DVD page, click Add Items to display the Add Items to DVD dialog box.

2. Click the Recently Changed link under the Favorite links to access the Recently Changed view, as shown in Figure 10-7.

3. Click the Date Modified heading to sort the items according to most recently changed. The items you just tagged will now be listed at the top of the Recently Changed list.

4. Select the items to add using one of the techniques discussed previously, and then click Add.

Setting the play order

In Windows DVD Maker, the listing order sets the order in which items are played (see Figure 10-8). The first item on the list plays first, the second item plays second, and so on. You can control an item's play order using the Move Up and Move Down buttons. Click an item you want to move and then click the Move Up or Move Down button until the item is in the desired position on the playlist. When setting the play order, note the duration and status of each item.

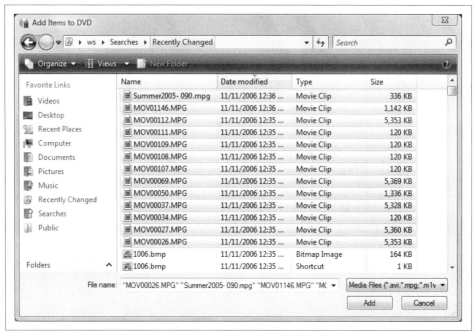

Figure 10-7. Adding pictures and videos to your DVD

On video DVDs that include both digital pictures and digital videos, I've found that it's often best to have the picture slide show first. One of the reasons for this is that you can sync the slide show to a music soundtrack, and this helps to keep the audience engaged. Additionally, if you show the live video first, it seems anticlimactic for you then to start showing a slide show—even if that slide show does have a cool soundtrack. After all, it is hard for digital pictures to compete with live action.

Pictures in the "Slide show" folder also have a play order. If you double-click the "Slide show" folder, you can then view and set the play order for pictures, as shown in Figure 10-9. You can control the play order of pictures in the slide show using the Move Up and Move Down buttons. Click a picture you want to move and then click the Move Up or Move Down button until the picture is in the desired position on the playlist. When you are done working with pictures, you can click the parent folder button to go back to the main burn list. This button shows a folder icon and an up arrow.

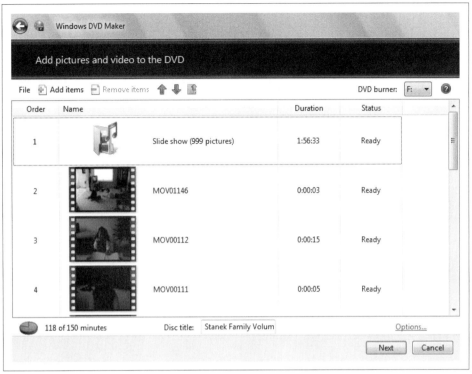

Figure 10-8. Setting the play order of your picture slide show and videos

If your pictures span a period of months or years rather than hours or days you may want to ensure that the pictures are viewed in the order that they were taken. This seems to be one of the best approaches. But there's one interesting effect when you're doing a tribute to an individual, and that is to work from the present to the past, especially if you have pictures that go through the person's life from the present to when he was a child. Alternatively, you can go from a person's childhood to the present, but it is sort of fun to slip back slowly into past memories.

By default, each picture in the slide show is displayed for seven seconds. You'll be able to change this setting and sync the slide show length with your soundtrack later. See the "Customizing Your Picture Slide Show and Adding an Audio Soundtrack" section, later in this chapter, for details.

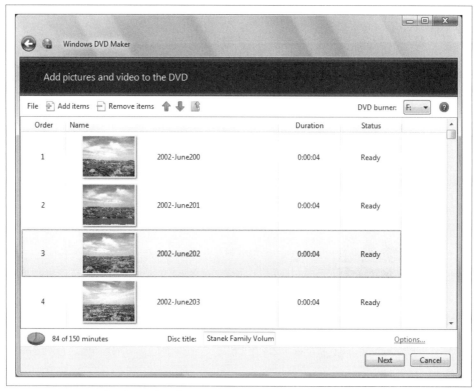

Figure 10-9. Setting the play order of pictures

Setting the DVD Burning and Playback Options

Windows DVD Maker allows you to add a DVD menu to your videos, to encode your videos using an aspect ratio for widescreen or standard screen, and to format your videos using either NTSC or PAL video format. In Windows DVD Maker, you can set these and other options by completing the following steps:

1. On the "Add pictures and video to the DVD" page, the "DVD burner" list shows which drive will be used for burning the DVD. If your computer has multiple DVD burners, select the disc you want to use.

2. Use the "Disc title" text box to set the working title for the DVD.

3. The Options link is in the lower-right corner. Click this link to display the Options dialog box shown in Figure 10-10.

Figure 10-10. Setting the DVD options

4. Under "Choose DVD playback settings," choose how you want the DVD to play by selecting one of the following options:

- If you want the DVD menu to display when the disc is inserted in a DVD player, click Start with DVD Menu.

- If you want the video to play immediately when the disc is inserted in a DVD player and show the menu at the end, click "Play video and end with DVD menu."

5. If you want the video to play automatically and loop continuously, click "Play video in a continuous loop." With this setting, you will see the menu only if you choose the Menu option using the remote control for your DVD player.

6. Under "DVD aspect ratio," choose the DVD aspect ratio. The aspect ratio is expressed as the relation of the video width to the video height. For widescreen, choose 16:9 as the aspect ratio. For standard (full) screen, choose 4:3 as the aspect ratio.

When deciding which aspect ratio to choose, consider who will be playing your video and the type of screen she has. Although all monitors and TVs can play videos recorded in either aspect ratio, your video will look best when using the native format supported by the monitor or TV. A widescreen video will look best on a widescreen monitor or TV. A standard video will look best on a standard monitor or TV.

7. Under "Video format," select either NTSC or PAL. If you are unsure which format to use, don't change the default format because this is set based on the Regional and Language Options in the Control Panel. You will need to change the format only when you plan to share your video DVD with a friend who lives in another country or region.

Video signals are broadcast using a standard format. NTSC is the standard format in North America and Japan. PAL is the standard format for most of Europe. While there are other broadcast standards, such as SECAM used in France and variations of PAL used in some European countries, NTSC and PAL are the standard formats in widest use.

8. The "DVD burner speed" list is set by default to Fastest, allowing you to encode the DVD at the fastest speed your DVD burner supports. The rated speed of the DVDs you are using will largely determine your success when burning at faster speeds. If you experience problems when burning DVDs at the fastest speed supported, try using a slower setting or discs rated for a higher burn speed. On some DVDs, the top-rated burn speed is imprinted clearly as part of the label. On other DVDs, you may have to look closely at the packaging or the small-print lettering on the DVD itself.

9. By default, Windows DVD Maker creates a working version of the DVD in a temporary folder within your profile. Because your profile is stored on the system drive, which is typically the C: drive, this drive must have at least 5 GB of available disk space when you are creating a single-sided single-layered DVD, and 10 GB of available disk space when you are creating a single-sided double-layered DVD. If you want to choose a folder on another drive for the temporary files, click Browse and then use the Browse for Folder dialog box to select the new folder to use.

10. Click OK to save your settings.

Customizing the DVD Menu

Video DVDs can include a menu that is displayed either at the start of the video or at the end of the video. The primary options on this menu are as follows:

Play
> Plays the video from the start

Scenes
> Displays a scenes selection page, allowing you to navigate to a particular part of the video

Notes
> Displays a notes page if you've added notes to the video

You can customize the menu and the related menu pages on the "Ready to burn disc" page. From the "Add pictures and video to the DVD" page, you can display the "Ready to burn disc page," which is shown in Figure 10-11, by clicking Next.

Figure 10-11. Choosing the menu style

On the "Ready to burn disc" page, you can use the options on the Menu Styles list to choose a menu style, such as Highlights or Video Wall. When you select a style, Windows DVD Maker displays a large preview of that style in the main work area.

After you've selected a menu style, you can customize the menu text by completing the following steps:

1. Click the "Menu text" button on the toolbar. This displays the "Change the DVD menu text page," shown in Figure 10-12.

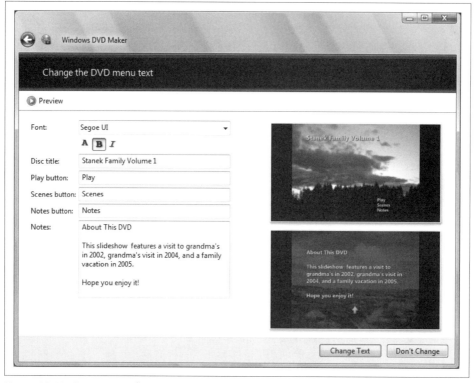

Figure 10-12. Customizing the DVD menu text

2. Each menu has default font settings. If you want to change the font used for menu text, click the Font list and select the font you want to use.

3. To change the font color, click the Font Color button (it shows the letter A), choose a color in the Color dialog box, and then click OK.

4. Most menu text is displayed in bold but not italics by default. To toggle bold and italics on and off, click the related buttons.

5. If you didn't already set the disc title, type in the text box provided.

6. By default, the text for the Play, Scenes, and Notes buttons says Play, Scenes, and Notes, respectively. If you want to make this text more descriptive, enter the text you'd like to use in the fields provided. For example, you may want to use Play Video, View Scenes, and Display Notes instead of the default text.

7. The Notes button is displayed only when you type notes for the DVD. If you want to add notes to the DVD, enter the notes in the text box provided. As shown in the example, you may want to preface your notes with a heading, such as the one shown, leave a blank space, and then type the main text of your note.

8. When you are finished customizing the menu text, click Change Text to save your changes and return to the "Ready to burn" page.

After you've customized the menu text, you can customize the menu style by completing the following steps:

1. Click the "Customize menu" button on the toolbar. This displays the "Customize the disc menu style" page, shown in Figure 10-13.

Figure 10-13. Customizing the DVD menu style

2. The Font options on this page are the same as those on the "Change the DVD menu text" page. If you've already set the font options, you don't need to again.

3. Each menu style has two key characteristics: a background and one or more cut frames in the foreground. With some menu styles, you can specify a picture or video to display in the background and a picture or video to display in the cut frames. Click the Browse button to the right of the "Background video" text box to set the background video. Click the Browse button to the right of the "Fore-ground video" text box to set the foreground video for the cut frames.

4. To play an audio file whenever the DVD menu is accessed, click the Browse button to the right of the "Menu audio" text box. Use the "Add audio to the menu" dialog box to select the audio file to play, and then click Add. When choosing an audio file, keep in mind that only a 5–10-second clip of the selected audio file is played, and this clip comes from the beginning of the audio file.

5. On the scenes page in the finished DVD, scene buttons show a preview of scenes to which you can navigate in the video. Each menu style has a default button style, but you can choose your own button style using the options on the "Scenes button styles" list.

6. When you are finished customizing the menu style, click Change Style to save your changes and return to the "Ready to burn" page.

Customizing Your Picture Slide Show and Adding an Audio Soundtrack

After you configure the DVD menu for the video, the next step is to customize the slide show and add an audio soundtrack by completing these steps:

1. Only video DVDs that have digital pictures have slide shows. If your DVD has pictures, click the "Slide show" button on the "Ready to burn" page. This displays the "Change your slide show settings" page shown in Figure 10-14.

2. By default, each picture is set to display for seven seconds. Use the "Picture length" list to select the desired display time, such as five seconds. When you make changes to the picture length, note the corresponding change in the running time for the slide show.

3. Use the Transition list to specify whether and how transitions are used to move from one picture to the next in the slide show. After you select a transition, click Preview and then play the video to see what the transition will look like.

4. To give your pictures the effect of live motion, select the "Use pan and zoom effects for pictures" checkbox. Some of the transitions work best when panning and zooming is turned off. Others work best when panning and zooming is turned on. As an example, cross-fade works well with pan and zoom turned on, while inset works best with pan and zoom turned off.

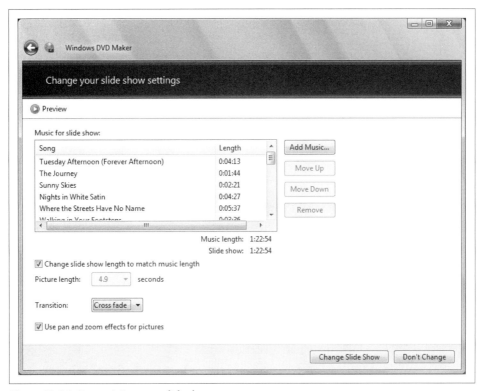

Figure 10-14. Customizing your slide show

5. If you want your slide show to have a soundtrack, click Add Music. This displays the Add Music to Slide Show dialog box shown in Figure 10-15.

6. Because your Music folder is the default location for your music, the Add Music to Slide Show dialog box accesses this folder by default. In your Music folder or any other default folder for music, you'll see your music organized by artist. If you double-click the folder for an artist, you'll find either the related album or subfolders for each album when multiple albums by one artist are stored on your computer.

7. Once you've worked your way through the folders and subfolders for artists and albums, you'll see a list of songs. You can select songs to add to the DVD using any of the following techniques:

   • Select an individual song by clicking it.

   • Select a series of songs by clicking the first song, pressing and holding the Shift key, clicking the last song, and then releasing Shift.

   • Select multiple songs individually by clicking the first song, pressing and holding the Ctrl key, clicking each additional song in turn, and then releasing Ctrl.

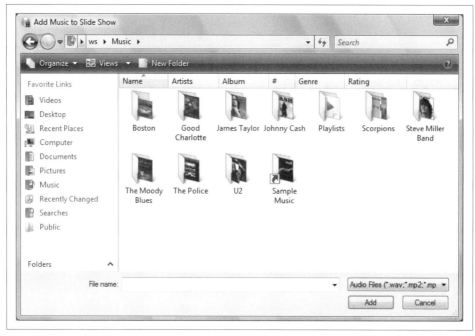

Figure 10-15. Adding your music

8. Click Add to close the Add Music to Slide Show dialog box and add your selected songs to the "Music for slide show" list. You can repeat steps 2–5 to add songs by other artists or from other albums. Each time you add songs, note the music length and the slide show running time. When the music length is within a few minutes of the slide show running time, you can select the "Change slide show length to match music length" checkbox to sync the soundtrack and the slide show running times.

9. When you are finished customizing the slide show, click Change Slide Show to save your changes and return to the "Ready to burn" page.

Previewing and Finishing Your Video Project

After you've customized the DVD menu and slide show, you can click Preview to get a preview of what the finished DVD will look like (see Figure 10-16). You can always choose a different menu style and different customization options if you aren't pleased with the results. Keep in mind, however, that the way the DVD looks on your screen probably won't match what the DVD will look like when it's finished. This is because processing and fully encoding a DVD requires a great deal of processing power, and Windows DVD Maker doesn't fully process or encode the DVD to generate the preview.

Figure 10-16. Previewing your DVD

When you are ready to continue, you can save your video as a Windows DVD Maker Project. Project files are saved with the file extension *.msdvd*. Unlike your video, which may be multiple gigabytes in size, project files are relatively small. They contain the settings for the DVD menu, menu text, and slide show. They also contain a file manifest that has the file paths to all the items included in the video.

You can save as a project file and then burn your DVD by following these steps:

1. Click File and then select Save As.

2. In the Save Project dialog box, shown in Figure 10-17, type a descriptive name for your video and then click Save.

 By default, your project is saved in your personal Videos folder. If you don't want to use this folder, click the Browse for Folders button to expand the dialog box and include additional folder browsing features. You can then select a folder in which to save your project.

3. If you haven't already done so, insert a blank disc into your DVD player. If the AutoPlay dialog box is displayed when you insert the DVD, click the Close button.

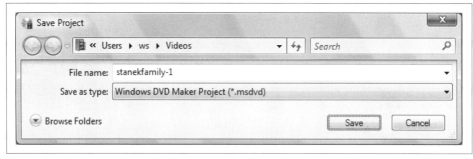

Figure 10-17. Saving your video project

4. When you click the Burn button, Windows DVD Maker will begin to encode your DVD. As shown in Figure 10-18, you'll see a Burning dialog box that tracks the progress of the encoding process. Encoding and burning your DVD can take several hours. During this time, you shouldn't perform other tasks on the computer that might cause burn problems, such as trying to rip or play a CD or DVD on a different drive.

 The total time required to burn a DVD will depend on the speed of your DVD burner as well as the speed of your computer's CPU and the amount of RAM on your computer. If you haven't already used ReadyBoost with a USB flash device, as discussed in Chapter 3, this may be a good time to do so because it may give your computer a needed boost. On a computer with a 1 GHz processor, 1 GB of RAM, and a 4× DVD burner, I found that burning a DVD took about one hour per gigabyte of data.

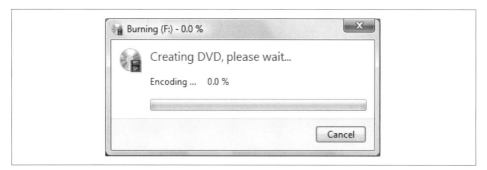

Figure 10-18. Creating your DVD video

5. When encoding is complete, Windows DVD Maker will eject the DVD and display the "Your disc is ready" message, as shown in Figure 10-19. To make another copy, insert a blank DVD and then click "Make another copy of this disc." Otherwise, click Close to return to the Windows DVD Maker main window.

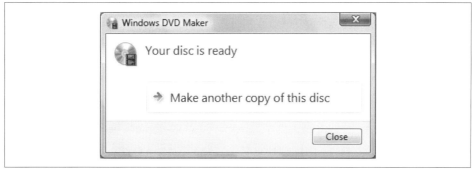

Figure 10-19. The message that Windows DVD Maker displays when the disc is ready

Opening and Burning Saved Projects

You can open saved projects using the Search box on the Start menu. Click Start and then type **video** into the Search box to see a list of all videos and related video project files. Double-click the *.msdvd* project file you want to open. Windows Vista will then start Windows DVD Maker and open the selected project file for editing.

In Windows DVD Maker, you can open saved projects by completing the following steps:

1. On the "Add pictures and video to the DVD" page, click File and then click Open Project File. This displays the Open Project dialog box.

2. In the Open Project dialog box, the last folder location you used for saving project files is opened by default. If this isn't the folder you want to use, browse to the folder containing the saved project file.

3. Click the project file and click Open. Windows DVD Maker will then read the project file and begin adding the items it references. As shown in Figure 10-20, the progress of this import process is tracked in the Add Items dialog box.

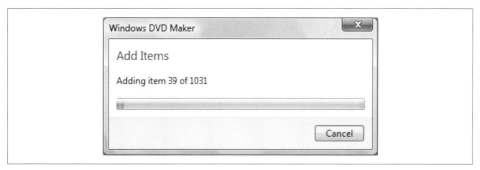

Figure 10-20. Opening a saved project

4. When Windows DVD Maker finishes adding items, review the order of videos and pictures, check to make sure the DVD burner you want to use is selected, and then click Next.

5. On the "Ready to burn" page, you'll see a preview of the DVD menu. You can make any necessary changes and then click Burn to start burning the DVD.

6. If you haven't already inserted a DVD, you'll be prompted to insert one. As before, the DVD burning process may take several hours.

Creating Movies with Windows Movie Maker

After you've created a few video DVDs in Windows DVD Maker, you may want to do a bit more in terms of production. This is where Windows Movie Maker comes into the picture. With Windows Movie Maker, you produce the video every step of the way, from beginning title to end credits.

Getting Started with Windows Movie Maker

You can start and use Windows Movie Maker in several ways. When you are working with Windows Photo Gallery, you can select the initial pictures and videos you want to work with and then click Make a Movie to open Windows Movie Maker with these items selected. Otherwise, you can start Windows Movie Maker by clicking Start → All Programs → Windows Movie Maker.

As Table 10-2 shows, Windows Movie Maker works with a wide variety of image, sound, and video formats. This list is different from the formats supported by Windows DVD Maker. The key change is that Windows Movie Maker supports AIFF and AU sound formats, and Windows DVD Maker does not.

Table 10-2. File formats supported by Windows Movie Maker

File format/type	File extensions
Bitmap image	.bmp
DIB image	.dib
GIF image	.gif
JPEG image	.jpg, .jpe, .jpeg, .jfif
PNG image	.png
TIFF image	.tif, .tiff
Word Perfect image	.wdp
Windows Meta File	.wmf, .emf

Table 10-2. File formats supported by Windows Movie Maker (continued)

File format/type	File extensions
Sound formats	
AIFF sound	.aif, .aifc, .aiff
AU sound	.au, .snd
MP3 audio	.mp3, .m3u
WAV audio	.wav
Windows Media Audio	.wma
Video formats	
AVI video	.avi
DVD video	.mpa, .m1v, .m2v, .mp2, .mp2v, .mpv2, .mp2v
MPEG 1 and MPEG 2 video	.mpe, .mpeg, .mpg
Audio/Video format	
Windows Media Audio/Video Professional	.asf, .wm, .wmv
Recorded TV format	
Microsoft Digital Video Recorder	.dvr-ms

As with Windows DVD Maker, Windows Movie Maker works with files that are already in the proper formats and doesn't include features for converting formats. Unlike Windows DVD Maker, however, Windows Movie Maker includes features for importing video and audio from digital video cameras. Windows Movie Maker doesn't include features for ripping raw CD audio files from audio discs. However, you can use any existing audio, video, or pictures on your computer's disk drive, a data disc you've inserted into your CD/DVD drive, or a device with removable storage connected to your computer. You can also add narration using a microphone. The same narration features allow you to record input from other sources as well.

When you start working with Windows Movie Maker, shown in Figure 10-21, you'll see that it has these key features:

A Tasks Pane
Lists the common tasks that you may need to perform when making a movie

A Collection Pane
Provides options for listing effects and transitions as well as collection folders for media you've imported into Windows Movie Maker

A Preview Pane
Allows you to preview the video

A work area
Allows you to manage the media items you've added to the video

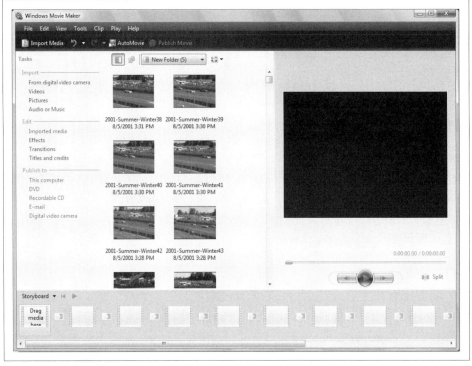

Figure 10-21. Getting started with Windows Movie Maker

Using the options provided in the main window, you create movies by following a series of prescribed steps. The basic steps are as follows:

1. Create your storyboard.
2. Edit the storyboard.
3. Add effects and transitions.
4. Add narration, music, and other audio.
5. Add titles, credits, and overlays.
6. Set the video options.
7. Preview and save your video project.
8. Publish your movie.

I discuss tasks related to each step in the sections that follow.

Creating Your Storyboard

In Windows Movie Maker, each video you are producing is created as a video project with a storyboard. The storyboard provides a representation of each media item you've added to the video in the order the items are played. In this way, the storyboard not only serves as an outline for the presentation, but it also lets you visualize the project in a way you otherwise would not be able to. At a glance, you can see the work from start to finish, and this is extremely important in the way you conceptualize the project.

As you add media items to your video, you build the storyboard and set the play order for each item you are including. To your storyboard, you can add titles, credits, effects, and transitions. Unlike Windows DVD Maker, Windows Movie Maker doesn't put pictures into a separate folder. Instead, all media items are added to the same storyboard, and that storyboard can have many thousands of media items.

As with Windows DVD Maker, you can select all the pictures and videos you want to use in Windows Photo Gallery first, and then add the selected items automatically to Windows Movie Maker. After you use the same tricks discussed previously, click Make a Movie to open Windows Movie Maker with these media items. Windows Movie Maker will then analyze the media items and create a movie for you automatically using these media items (see Figure 10-22). Your AutoMovie will have a title frame, automatic fade settings for each media item, automatic transition settings between media items, and an end credits frame. This will save you considerable time in terms of finalizing your movie.

Figure 10-22. Creating an AutoMovie

In Windows Movie Maker, you can select the items to add to your video by completing the following steps:

1. On the Task Pane, click the appropriate Import option.

2. As shown in Figure 10-23, use the Import Media Items dialog box to browse to a folder containing pictures or videos you want to add.

3. Select the items to add using one of the following techniques:

   • Select an individual item by clicking it.

   • Select a series of items by clicking the first item, pressing and holding the Shift key, clicking the last item, and then releasing Shift.

   • Select multiple items individually by clicking the first item, pressing and holding the Ctrl key, clicking each additional item in turn, and then releasing Ctrl.

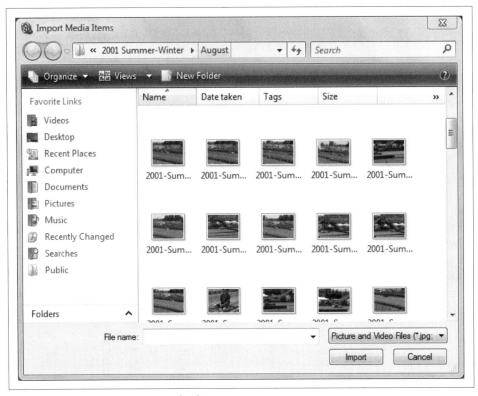

Figure 10-23. Importing pictures and videos

4. When you click Import, Windows Movie Maker adds the items to a Collections folder and then displays the items in this folder in the Collections Pane. As shown in Figure 10-24, any item you select in the Collections Pane is displayed in the Preview Pane.

5. At this point, the items are not added to the storyboard. You can add items to the storyboard using these techniques:

   • To arrange items in a specific order before selecting them, right-click in the Collections Pane, point to Arrange Icons By, and then select the desired arrangement, such as Date Taken, File Name, or Name and Date.

   • To add an item to the storyboard, click it and drag it to the desired location in the storyboard. When you drag the item to the storyboard, you'll see a position pointer that indicates where the item will be added.

   • To place an item on a part of the storyboard not displayed, click and drag the item to the left or right edge of the storyboard.

Figure 10-24. Selecting pictures or videos to preview them

- To select multiple items, use the previously discussed Shift and Ctrl techniques and then drag those items to a desired location in the storyboard.
- To select and then add all items to the end of the storyboard, right-click in the Collections Pane and then click Select All. Right-click again and then select Add to Storyboard. Alternatively, press Ctrl-A and then press Ctrl-D.

Editing Your Storyboard

As you add media items to the storyboard, Windows Movie Maker lists the runtime of the video as the second time entry in the preview area. This runtime may change if you modify the transitions and effects applied. Most single-sided DVDs can have a total running time of up to 150 minutes. Most single-sided double-layered DVDs can have a total running time of up to 300 minutes.

After you add items, you can fine-tune the play order. To change the play order of an item or a group of items, select the item or items and then drag left or right until you reach the desired position. To remove an item, right-click it and then select Remove. Removing an item removes it from the storyboard but does not delete it from your computer.

While you are optimizing the play order, you may want to preview the video. As Figure 10-25 shows, the Preview Pane provides the following button controls:

Play/Pause
> If you click the Play button, the video plays from the current position in the storyboard. Clicking the Play button again pauses playback.

Previous Frame
> Rewinds to the previous frame of the video.

Next Frame
> Advances to the next frame of the video.

Split
> Splits a video clip you are playing into two clips at the current position.

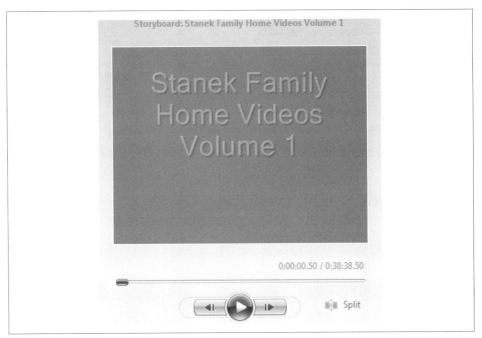

Figure 10-25. Using the Preview controls to manage playback

Above the button controls, you'll find a Timeline slider for previewing your video and managing playback. If you click and drag the Current Frame button on the end of the Timeline slider, you can fast-forward or rewind through a video. If you click a specific part of the timeline, you can go to that time in the video.

 On the left side of the Storyboard Pane, you'll find Play/Pause buttons as well as a Rewind Storyboard button. Clicking the Rewind Storyboard button moves to and selects the first storyboard in your video.

Anytime you are working with video clips, you have several editing options. When you are playing video clips, you can:

- Click the Split button to split the video into two clips at the current position.
- Trim the video so that it only includes footage from the current position to the end of the clip by clicking Clip → Clip Trim Beginning, or by pressing I.
- Trim the video so that it only includes footage from the current position to the beginning of the clip by clicking Clip → Clip Trim End, or by pressing O.
- Clear trim points to restore the original video clip by clicking Clip → Clear Trim Points.
- Combine video clips you previously split by selecting the videos and then clicking Clip → Combine, or by pressing N.

While you are fixing your storyboard, you can use the Undo button to undo any changes you don't like, or the redo button to redo changes you previously undid. Multiple undo and redo changes are saved, allowing you to step backward and forward through changes. You can also undo and redo specific changes.

To undo a specific change or changes, follow these steps:

1. Click the option button to the right of the Undo button. This displays a shortcut menu with a list of Undo changes, as shown in Figure 10-26.
2. The most recent change is listed first. To undo this change, click it.
3. You can also undo multiple actions, but only in the exact order in which they were performed. To undo multiple actions, drag down until all the actions you want to undo are selected, and then click the shortcut menu.

Figure 10-26. Selecting the changes to undo

To redo a specific change or changes, follow these steps:

1. Click the option button to the right of the Redo button. This displays a shortcut menu with a list of Redo changes, as shown in Figure 10-27.
2. The most recent change is listed first. To redo this change, click it.
3. You can also redo multiple actions, but only in the exact order in which they were performed. To redo multiple actions, drag down until all the actions you want to redo are selected, and then click the shortcut menu.

Figure 10-27. Selecting the changes to redo

By default, each picture in the slide show is displayed for 5 seconds, and transitions last 1.25 seconds. You'll be able to change this setting later. See "Setting Video Options," later in this chapter, for details.

Creating an AutoMovie

After you finish creating and editing your storyboard, you are ready to move on to the next phase of video production, which involves adding effects, transitions, titles, credits, and a soundtrack. While you can perform each of these tasks manually, you can also have Windows Movie Maker perform them for you automatically using the AutoMovie feature. Not only is this a great timesaver, but it also allows you to see firsthand how various approaches to video production work.

To create an AutoMovie, complete the following steps:

1. In Windows Movie Maker, click the AutoMovie button on the toolbar.
2. As shown in Figure 10-28, you can now select one of the following AutoMovie editing styles:

   Fade and Reveal
   > Applies fade and reveal transitions throughout the video.

   Flip and Slide
   > Applies flip, slide, reveal, and page curl transitions throughout the video.

   Highlights Movie
   > Adds cut and fade transitions throughout the video, and inserts title and credit frames.

   Music Video
   > Attempts to sync the video to music you select. This works best if the selected music is as long in duration as the video.

   Old Movie
   > Applies the film age effect to media items.

   Sports Highlights
   > Selects video clips showing action, and inserts title and credit frames.

3. Click the "Enter a title for the movie" link and then type the title text, as shown in Figure 10-29.

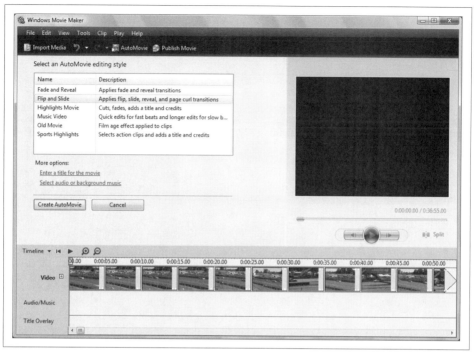

Figure 10-28. Selecting the editing style

4. Click the "Select audio or background music" link to display the "Add audio or background music" page shown in Figure 10-30.

5. To select audio or music files to play with the video, click the Browse link. In the Open dialog box, select the first audio file you want to use in the video and then click Open. Repeat this process to select each additional audio file to include.

 The total running time of all the audio files you select should be at least as much as or more than the total running time of the video. If it isn't, Windows Movie Maker will fill in the tracks from last to first, starting at the end of the video, and there will be a gap at the beginning of the video with no soundtrack.

6. Use the "Audio levels" slider to control whether the audio from the video or the audio/music you've added should have precedence. To play your audio/music without hearing the audio from the video, move the slider all the way to the right. To mix the audio from the video back in, move the slider to the left. The more you move the slider to the left, the more prevalent the audio from the video will be.

7. Click Create AutoMovie to have Windows Movie Maker create the movie for you. If you don't like the results, you can always fine-tune the movie before finalizing it.

Figure 10-29. Setting the movie title

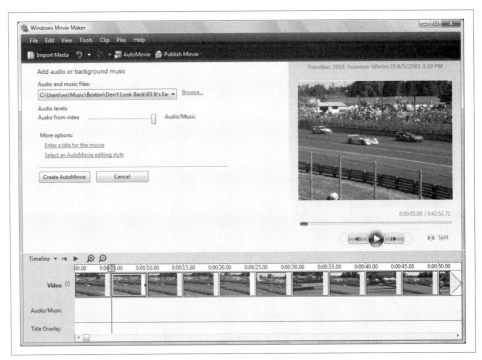

Figure 10-30. Setting the audio options

Adding Effects to Your Video

Your videos can have effects that are used when a media item is first displayed. You can add the same effect to multiple items, and a single item can have multiple effects as well. In the lower-left corner of the item's storyboard is an Effects button. The appearance of this button tells you whether an item has effects associated with it.

An item with no effects has an Effects button as shown in Figure 10-31.

Figure 10-31. The Effects button for an item with no effects

An item with one associated effect has an Effects button as shown in Figure 10-32.

Figure 10-32. The Effects button for an item with an associated effect

An item with multiple associated effects has an Effects button as shown in Figure 10-33.

Figure 10-33. The Effects button for an item with multiple associated effects

You can add effects to media items by completing the following steps:

1. In Windows Movie Maker, click Effects in the Tasks Pane to display the available effects in the Collections Pane, as shown in Figure 10-34.

2. To see how an effect works, click it and press the Play button in the Preview Pane.

3. To use an effect, click it and then drag it to the item to which the effect should be added. Alternatively, click the effect, press Ctrl-C, click the item to which the effect should be added, and then press Ctrl-V.

4. Repeat this process to add multiple effects to the same item

Another way to manage multiple effects applied to the same item is to follow these steps:

1. Right-click the item's Effects button in the storyboard and then select Effects.

2. Use the Add or Remove Effects dialog box, shown in Figure 10-35, to manage the effects associated with the selected item:

- To add an effect, select it in the "Available effects" list and then click Add.
- To remove an effect, select it in the "Displayed effects" list and then click Remove.
- To change the order of displayed effects, click an effect and then use the Move Up or Move Down button to position it.

3. Click OK.

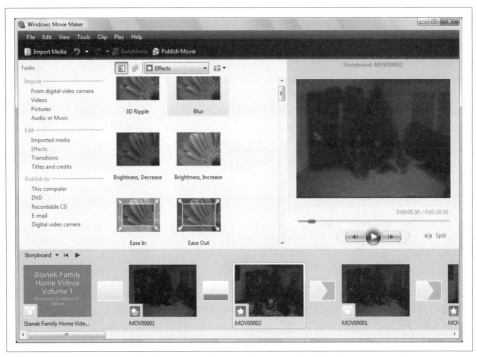

Figure 10-34. Viewing and selecting effects

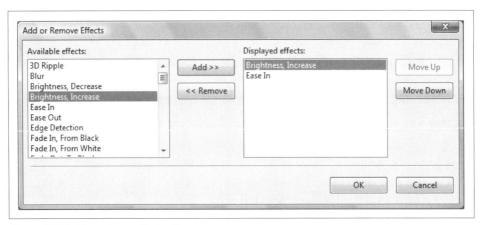

Figure 10-35. Managing multiple effects

To add the same effect to multiple items, follow these steps:

1. On the storyboard, select all the items that you want to use the same effect.
2. Right-click the effect to apply and then select Add to Storyboard.
3. Repeat this process to add multiple effects to multiple items.

To remove all effects from a media item, right-click the Effects button and then select Remove Effects.

Adding Transitions to Your Video

Your videos can have transitions that are used when moving between media items. You can use only one transition between media items. For example, you can transition by slowly revealing the new media item or by sweeping in, but not by using both techniques.

As shown in Figure 10-36, you'll find a transition board to the right of each media item. If a current transition is applied, the transition board will show a summary graphic. If no current transition is applied, the transition board will be dimmed.

Figure 10-36. Using transitions

You can add transitions to media items by completing the following steps:

1. In Windows Movie Maker, click Transitions in the Tasks Pane to display the available transitions in the Collections Pane, as shown in Figure 10-37.
2. To see how a transition works, click it and then press Play in the Preview Pane.
3. To use a transition, click it and then drag it to the item to which the transition should be added. Alternatively, click the transition, press Ctrl-C, click the item to which the transition should be added, and then press Ctrl-V.

To add the same transition to multiple transition boards, follow these steps:

1. On the storyboard, select all the transition boards that you want to use the same transition.
2. Right-click the transition to apply and then select Add to Storyboard.

To remove a transition from a transition board, right-click the transition board and then select Remove.

Figure 10-37. Viewing and selecting transitions

Adding Narration, Music, and Other Audio

You can add narration, music, and other audio to your videos. To add narration, you will need a sound card with a microphone jack and a microphone. You will then need to connect the microphone to the microphone jack on your computer. Once you do this, you can narrate the video by completing these steps:

1. In Windows Movie Maker, display the timeline instead of the storyboard by clicking View and then selecting Timeline. Alternatively, you can press Ctrl-T to toggle between the storyboard and the timeline.

2. Click Tools → Narrate Timeline to display the Narrate Timeline Pane, as shown in Figure 10-38.

3. Click the "Show options" link to display the additional options for narration.

4. To mute your computer's speakers, click the "Mute speakers" checkbox.

5. On the "Audio device" list, select the microphone or audio source you are using as the audio input device.

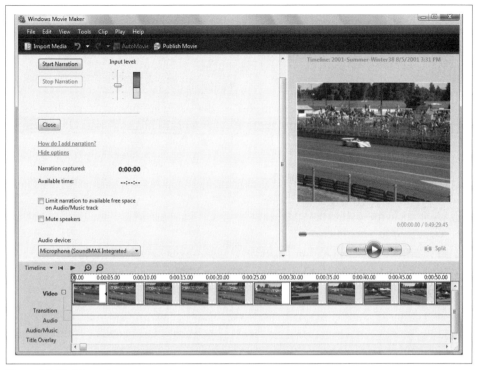

Figure 10-38. Narrating your movie

6. On the timeline, click a media item to set the start position of the narration. If you want to insert the narration starting at the beginning of the video, click the first media item.

7. Click Start Narration to begin recording and then speak into your microphone. As you narrate, the timeline moves to show you the current position in the video. Note also that the "Narration captured" value shows you the total length of your narration.

8. Click Stop Narration to stop recording your narration.

9. You can then play back the video to see and hear the results.

You can record input from other audio sources using the Line In jack on your computer's audio card. After you connect an audio cable from the alternate audio source to your computer's Line In jack, select Line In as the audio source in the "Audio device" list. When you start playback on the alternate audio source and then click the Start Narration button, the audio from the alternate source is recorded and inserted into your movie. To stop recording audio from the alternate source, click the Stop Narration button.

To add music or other audio to your video, complete the following steps:

1. In Windows Movie Maker, display the timeline instead of the storyboard by clicking View and then selecting Timeline. Alternatively, you can press Ctrl-T to toggle between the storyboard and the timeline.

2. If the Collections Pane isn't displayed, display it by clicking View → Collections.

3. On the standard toolbar, click Import Media. Use the Import Media Items dialog box to select one or more audio files to work with, and then click Import. The audio files will be added to the Collections Pane.

4. On the timeline, click a media item to set the start position for the music you are adding. If you want to insert the music starting at the beginning of the video, click the first media item.

5. Right-click the audio file you want to insert at the current position, and then select Add to Timeline.

6. In the timeline, scroll left and right to check the placement of the audio file. You can also click Play to play the video from the current position.

7. Repeat steps 4–6 to add other audio files to the video.

You can manage audio files you inserted into the timeline using the following techniques:

- To trim the beginning of the audio file, position the pointer over the beginning of the audio clip, click, and then drag to the right.

- To trim the ending of the audio file, position the pointer over the end of the audio clip, click, and then drag to the left.

- To move an audio clip to a different position in the timeline, move the pointer left or right over the audio clip until the selection pointer is displayed. Click and then drag the audio file to the desired position in the timeline.

If the playback volume of the audio is too soft or too loud, you should right-click the entry for the audio in the timeline and then select Volume. In the Adjust Clip Volume dialog box, shown in Figure 10-39, use the "Adjust volume level" slider to adjust the volume of the audio clip, and then click OK.

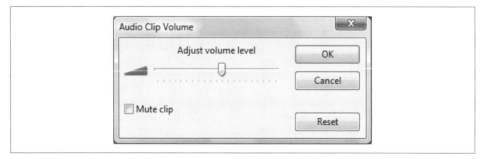

Figure 10-39. Adjusting the volume level of an audio clip

While you are editing the video, you may sometimes want to mute an audio track temporarily. In the Adjust Clip Volume dialog box, you can mute the audio volume completely by selecting the "Mute clip" checkbox.

By default, the audio levels are set to mix the audio from the video clip and the audio/music you've added at equal levels of volume. You can control whether the audio from video clips or the audio/music you've added should have precedence by clicking Tools and then clicking Audio Levels. This displays the Audio Levels dialog box shown in Figure 10-40.

Figure 10-40. Setting the balance between audio from video and audio/music

To play your audio/music without hearing the audio from the video, move the slider all the way to the right. To mix the audio from the video back in, move the slider to the left. The more you move the slider to the left, the more prevalent the audio from the video will be. When you are finished setting the volume levels, click the Close button in the Audio Levels dialog box.

Adding Titles, Credits, and Overlays

Your videos can have title frames, credits, and title overlays. You can add title frames at the beginning of the video or before a selected clip. You can add credits to the end of the video. Title overlays are title frames displayed over the top of a selected media item.

You can add titles to your video by completing these steps:

1. In Windows Movie Maker, click Tools and then click Titles and Credits.
2. In the Titles Pane, click one of the following links:
   • Title at the Beginning
   • Title Before the Selected Clip
   • Title on the Selected Clip
3. If you are inserting a title before or on a clip, select the clip to use in the timeline.
4. As shown in Figure 10-41, enter the primary title in the first text box provided and any subtitle in the second text box provided.

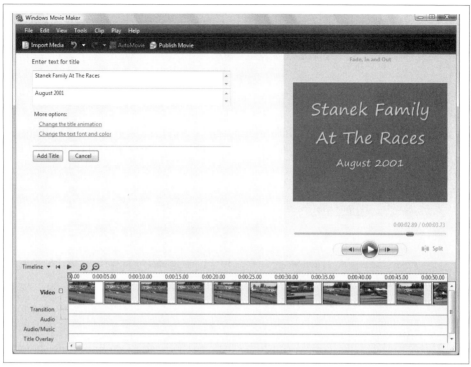

Figure 10-41. Adding a title to the movie

5. Click the Change the "Title animation" link.

6. Choose the title animation. Different animations are provided for one-line titles and two-line titles. Use a two-line title animation if you entered a subtitle.

7. Click the "Change the text font and color" link.

8. Use the options provided to set the title font and color.

9. Click Add Title to add the title to a new frame at the beginning of the video.

You can add credits to the end of the video by completing these steps:

1. In Windows Movie Maker, click Tools and then click Titles and Credits.

2. In the Titles Pane, click the "Credits at the End" link.

3. As shown in Figure 10-42, enter the primary end credit or video title in the first text box provided.

4. In the subsequent rows, you can enter video credits by role/title and name. Enter a role/title in the first column and the associated name in the second column.

5. Click the "Change the title animation" link.

6. Choose the credits animation. Different animations are provided for credits than for titles.

7. Click the "Change the text font and color" link.

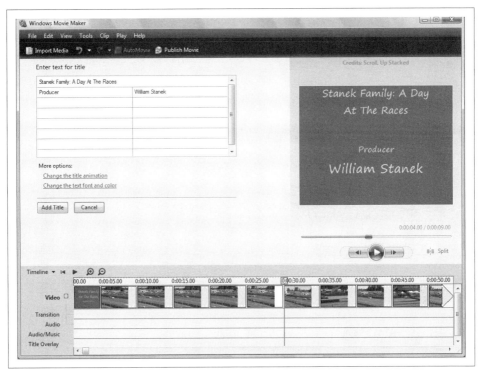

Figure 10-42. Adding credits to the movie

8. Use the options provided to set the title font and color.

9. Click Add Title to add the credits to a new frame at the end of the video.

Setting Video Options

Windows Movie Maker allows you to encode your video using an aspect ratio for widescreen or standard screen, and to format your video using either NTSC or PAL video format. In Windows Movie Maker, you can set these and other options by completing the following steps:

1. Click Tools and then click Options to display the Options dialog box shown in Figure 10-43.

2. By default, Windows Movie Maker creates a working version of the DVD in a temporary folder within your profile. Because your profile is stored on the system drive, which typically is the C: drive, this drive must have at least 5 GB of available disk space when you are creating a single-sided single-layered DVD, and 10 GB of available disk space when you are creating a single-sided double-layered DVD. If you want to choose a folder on another drive for the temporary files, click Browse and then use the Browse for Folder dialog box to select the new folder to use.

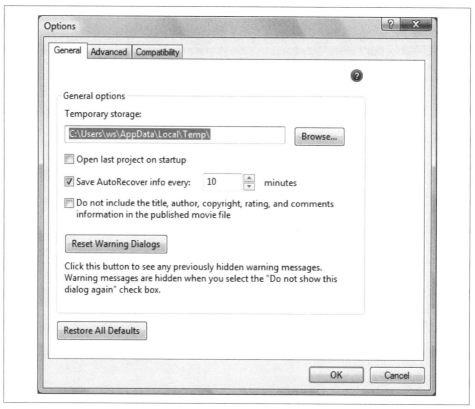

Figure 10-43. Setting the save and recovery options

3. By default, AutoRecover data for your video project is saved every 10 minutes. Similar to Microsoft Office applications, such as Word, this allows you to recover to the last saved position should something unexpected happen while you are making your movie. If Windows Movie Maker freezes or the power goes out, the last saved position will be loaded automatically the next time you restart Windows Movie Maker. If you want to use a different AutoRecover interval, enter the desired interval in the text box provided, such as five minutes.

4. Click the Advanced tab, as shown in Figure 10-44.

5. By default, pictures are displayed for 5 seconds and transitions are displayed for 1.25 seconds. You can change the display time for pictures by entering a new display time in the "Picture duration" text box. You can change the display time for transitions by entering a new display time in the "Transition duration" text box.

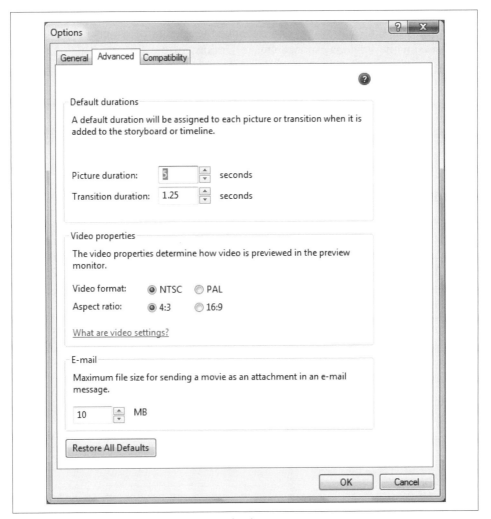

Figure 10-44. Configuring the default options for the movie

When deciding on the duration of pictures and transitions, keep in mind the prospective audience and the tempo of your music. If your music has a relatively fast beat, you may want to use a shorter display duration. If your music has a slower beat, you might want to use a longer display duration. In most cases, you'll want pictures to be displayed for between four and eight seconds, with transitions of one to one and a half seconds.

6. Under "Video format," select either NTSC or PAL as the video format. If you are unsure which format to use, don't change the default format because this is set based on the Regional and Language Options in the Control Panel. You will need to change the format only when you plan to share your video with a friend who lives in another country or region.

7. Under "Aspect ratio," choose the aspect ratio. The aspect ratio is expressed as the relation of the video width to the video height. For widescreen, choose 16:9 as the aspect ratio. For standard (full) screen, choose 4:3 as the aspect ratio.

8. Click OK to save your settings.

Previewing and Finishing Your Movie Project

When you are finished fine-tuning your movie, you'll want to preview it to ensure that the movie is exactly as you want it to be. You can preview the movie at full-screen size by clicking View and then selecting Full Screen. Alternatively, press Alt-Enter. To exit full-screen preview mode, press the Esc key. You can also preview at alternative display sizes by clicking View, pointing to Preview Monitor Size, and then selecting the desired display size.

When you are ready to continue, you can save your video as a Windows Movie Maker Project. Project files are saved with the file extension *.mswmm*. Although Windows Movie Maker Project files can run multiple megabytes in size, they are still considerably smaller than your final movie file.

You can save as a project file by completing the following steps:

1. Click File and then select Save As.

2. In the Save Project As dialog box, shown in Figure 10-45, type a descriptive name for your video and then click Save.

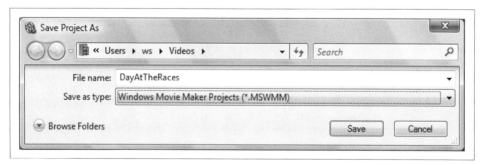

Figure 10-45. Saving your movie project

Although you can use spaces in the video name, I've chosen not to use spaces in the example to make it easier to work with the file. With this project name, if you were to click Start and then type **dayat** into the Search box, you'd see this project file in the Files list and could then double-click the filename to open the movie in Windows Movie Maker. Of course, you could also click Start and then type `movie` into the Search box to see a list of all movies and related movie project files.

By default, your project is saved in your personal Videos folder. If you don't want to use this folder, click the Browse for Folders button to expand the dialog box and include additional folder browsing features. You can then select a folder in which to save your project.

After you save your project, you can publish your movie. Publishing your movie creates the finished video file. In most cases, you'll want to publish the movie to your computer or to a DVD. If you publish the movie to your computer, you'll select the encoding settings as shown in Table 10-3.

Table 10-3. Movie encoding settings for Windows Movie Maker

File type	File extension	Aspect ratio	Bit rate	Display size	Frames per second
DV-Video	.avi	4:3	28.6 Mbps	720 × 480	30
Windows Media Portable Device	.wmv	4:3	1.0 Mbps	640 × 480	30
Windows Media DVD Quality	.wmv	4:3	3.0 Mbps	720 × 480	30
Windows Media DVD Widescreen Quality	.wmv	16:9	3.0 Mbps	720 × 480	30
Windows Media HD 720p	.wmv	16:9	5.9 Mbps	1,280 × 720	30
Windows Media HD for Xbox 360	.wmv	16:9	6.9 Mbps	1,280 × 720	30
Windows Media HD 1080p	.wmv	16:9	7.8 Mbps	1,440 × 1,080	30
Windows Media Low Bandwidth	.wmv	4:3	117 Kbps	320 × 240	15
Windows Media VHS Quality	.wmv	4:3	1.0 Mbps	640 × 480	30

To publish your movie to a video file on your computer, complete the following steps:

1. Click Publish Movie on the toolbar. This starts the Publish Movie Wizard.

2. On the "Where do you want to publish your movie?" page, click "This computer" and then click Next.

3. On the "Name the movie you are publishing" page, type a name for the movie file. A default name is set for you based on the name of your project.

4. Using the "Publish to" list, select Videos to publish the movie to your personal Videos folder, or Public Videos to publish the movie to the shared Public Videos folder. Alternatively, click Browse to display the Browse for Folder dialog box and select a different folder.

5. Click Next. On the "Choose the settings for your movie" page, shown in Figure 10-46, choose "More settings" and then choose the desired movie setting. Note the estimated space required and ensure that you have enough free space for this setting.

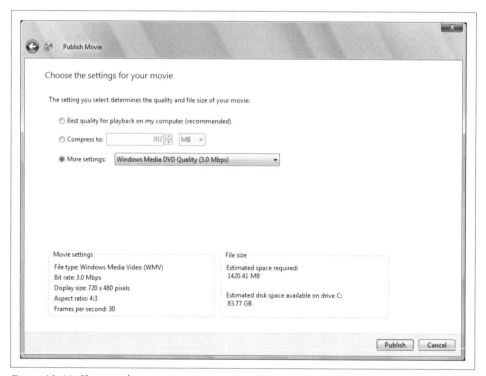

Figure 10-46. Choosing the movie settings

When choosing a format, keep in mind the quality and resolution of the original media items. Windows Movie Maker will let you create a full-length video in DV-AVI for a whopping 60 GB of space, but if your original media isn't high-quality, you'll be wasting a lot of disk space.

6. Click Publish to publish the movie to the previously selected folder. As shown in Figure 10-47, you can track the progress of the publish process by minutes remaining and percent complete. The bit rate of the movie setting you choose will largely determine how long it takes to publish the movie.

7. When Windows Movie Maker finishes publishing the movie, click Next and then click Finish.

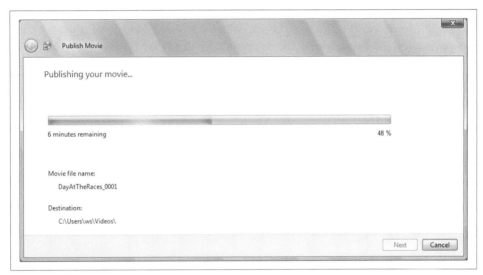

Figure 10-47. Reviewing the publish progress

To create a finished DVD with your movie, complete the following steps:

1. Click Publish Movie on the toolbar. This starts the Publish Movie Wizard.

2. On the "Where do you want to publish your movie" page, click DVD and then click Next.

3. Windows Vista will save and close your project and then open Windows DVD Maker. At the warning prompt, click OK to continue.

4. In Windows DVD Maker, you can produce the finished DVD just as I discussed previously.

Opening and Producing Saved Projects

You can open saved projects using the Search box on the Start menu. Click Start and then type **movie** into the Search box to see a list of all movies and related movie project files. Double-click the *.mswmm* project file you want to open. Windows Vista will then start Windows Movie Maker and open the selected project file for editing.

Alternatively, in Windows Movie Maker, you can open saved projects by completing the following steps:

1. Click File and then click Open Project file. This displays the Open Project dialog box.

2. In the Open Project dialog box, the last folder location you used for saving project files is opened by default. If this isn't the folder you want to use, browse to the folder containing the saved project file.

3. Click the project file and click Open. Windows Movie Maker will then read the project file and begin adding the items it references.

4. When Windows Movie Maker finishes adding items, review the movie storyboard and timeline.

5. After you make any necessary changes, click Publish Movie to start the Publish Movie Wizard and produce your movie.

CHAPTER 11

Securing and Sharing Your Data

As discussed in earlier chapters, User Account Control (UAC) is part of Windows Vista's massive top-to-bottom security shield reconstruction, and it is meant to help protect your computer from malicious software and network-based attacks. In upcoming chapters, you'll learn about built-in security programs, such as Windows Defender and Windows Firewall, which are also designed to protect your computer from malicious software and network-based attacks. While these security features work wonderfully and do their job if configured properly, they don't protect you from insiders whose computers are connected to the same local network as your computer, or from those who have a user account on your computer.

Without some additional protections for your files and data, your roommate, co-worker, teenager, or anyone else with local access to your computer will be able to read your email messages and go through your files and records. Just think what might happen if one of these people finds that picture of you—you know the one, the one you thought you deleted but didn't—and then prints or sends it out to a few dozen of your closest friends. This is where file access and sharing permissions come into the picture.

File access permissions control who can access your files and other data. *Sharing permissions* control who can access files and other data that you want to share selectively. If your computer doesn't have properly configured file access and sharing permissions, you don't have any private files or data. You might as well print out the photos, letters, or whatever other private files are on your computer and hand out copies to everyone at the office or at home. Because you don't want to do that and because you *do* want to keep your private files private, you should take the time to properly configure file access and sharing permissions. Best of all, thanks to a feature called *inheritance*, which ensures that any permissions you apply to the root folder of a disk drive or any other folder are also applied to the new files created in that folder, you will rarely have to change permissions once you configure them appropriately.

Securing Your Data

Disk drives and devices with removable storage are formatted with a filesystem. The filesystem allows you to create and manage files. The format of the disk that you are working with determines the file security options that are available. You can format disks by using either File Allocation Table (FAT) or NT File System (NTFS). As discussed in the sections that follow, FAT and NTFS are a bit different in the way they work.

FAT Versus NTFS

Both FAT and NTFS come in several different variations, and in some cases, the type of device you are working with determines which variation is used. With FAT, the number of bits used with the allocation table determines the variant you are working with and the maximum volume size. You'll find that USB flash devices and MP3 players with 4 GB or less of storage are formatted with the 16-bit version of FAT. FAT16, also known simply as FAT, defines its file allocation tables using 16 bits. FAT16 is used because it is the most efficient version of FAT for volume sizes of up to 4 GB.

If you use devices with removable storage that have file sizes larger than 4 GB, such as a removable hard disk, the device will in most cases use the 32-bit version of FAT, known as FAT32. FAT32 defines its file allocation tables using 32 bits, which allows you to have volumes larger than 32 GB. Devices with removable storage use FAT because it has no security controls, allowing you to access your data on multiple computers simply by connecting your device to those computers.

On the other hand, NTFS allows you to control access to files and folders by assigning permissions. At home, your computer will typically have file access permissions only for accounts configured on the local computer. At the office, your computer will typically have file access permissions for accounts configured on the local computer as well as accounts configured for your network. While NTFS supports just about any volume size you'll want to work with, you can't necessarily move devices formatted with NTFS from one computer to another and gain access to all the data on these devices. You may not be able to do this because NTFS access permissions are set using accounts that are specific to a single computer, to a network, or to both.

File Attributes

All files and folders, whether on FAT- or NTFS-formatted disks, can be marked with attributes that give you limited control over how a file or folder is used. The file attributes you can use are:

Read-only
   Specifies that the file or folder is read-only and cannot be modified

Hidden
   Specifies that the file or folder is hidden and can be viewed only if the folder
   option "Show hidden files and folders" is enabled

System
   Identifies a system file or folder that can be viewed only if the folder option
   "Hide protected operating system files" is disabled

You can view or change the Read-Only and Hidden attributes on a file or folder by
completing the following steps:

1. In Windows Explorer, right-click the file or folder to display its Properties dialog box.

2. On the General tab, shown in Figure 11-1, select the Read-only checkbox to
   make a file or folder read-only. Clear the Read-only checkbox to allow a file or
   folder to be read and modified.

3. To hide a file or folder so that it can be viewed only if the folder option "Show
   hidden files and folders" is enabled, select the Hidden checkbox. Otherwise,
   clear this checkbox to allow a file or folder to be viewed normally.

4. Click OK to save your changes.

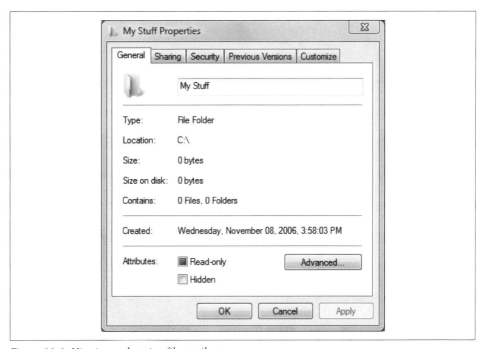

Figure 11-1. Viewing and setting file attributes

Generally, Windows Vista manages the system attribute. Windows Vista marks files and folders that you shouldn't modify as being system files. You can view files and folders marked with the hidden and system attributes by completing the following steps:

1. In Windows Explorer, click Organize on the toolbar and then select Folder and Search Options.

2. On the View tab, shown in Figure 11-2, select "Show hidden files and folders" to show hidden files and folders.

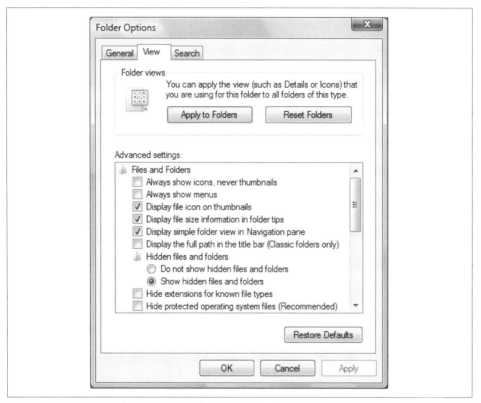

Figure 11-2. Showing hidden files and folders

3. To show system files and folders, clear the "Hide protected operating system files" checkbox.

4. Click OK to save your settings.

Although these attributes can be set on files and folders, anyone with access to a disk or device can override or change these settings. This means there are no safeguards for file access or deletion that someone can't override easily.

NTFS Permissions

While access flags are your only choice for controlling how files or folders are used with FAT, NTFS allows you to control the way files are used with both access flags and NTFS permissions. NTFS permissions provide granular control over the way files and folders are used. When you strip away all the needless stuff you really shouldn't worry about, NTFS permissions boil down to these five things:

Basic permissions
> Top-level permissions that you can assign to user and group accounts

Special permissions
> Low-level permissions that you can assign to user and group accounts

Ownership permissions
> Permissions that identify a file or folder's highest permission holder

Inherited permissions
> Permissions that are inherited from the folder in which a file or folder is stored

Effective permissions
> Permissions in effect for a particular user or group based on the combination of all permissions assigned to that user or group

You assign basic permissions and other permissions to the various user and group accounts available on your computer or on your network. Accounts on your computer include those accounts created by the operating system as well as accounts you've created. Local accounts on your computer are named using the following syntax:

    ComputerName\AccountName

This means that if your computer is named DadsComputer and your user account is Dad, you'll see the account referenced as *DadsComputer\Dad*.

Network accounts are named using the following syntax:

    DomainName\AccountName

This means that if your workplace domain is TheOffice and your user account is WilliamS, you'll see the account referenced as *TheOffice\WilliamS*.

If you want to manage permissions for multiple users, you will typically do this using group accounts. Your computer has several standard group accounts, including Administrators and Users. Any user that is a member of your computer's Administrators group has administrator access permissions on your computer. Any user that is a member of your computer's Users group has user access permissions on your computer. At the office, your network has Administrators and Users groups that apply to the entire network as well.

Controlling Access to Your Data

When your disk drive or storage device is formatted using NTFS, you can use NTFS permissions to control access to your data. As mentioned earlier, NTFS permissions can be broken down into five broad categories: basic permissions, special permissions, ownership permissions, inherited permissions, and effective permissions. The sections that follow discuss how to use each type of permission.

Basic Permissions

With NTFS, permissions are stored in the filesystem as part of the access control list (ACL) assigned to a file or a folder. As described in Table 11-1, files and folders have a slightly different set of basic permissions.

 When working with permissions, keep in mind that some permissions are inherited based on the permissions of a parent folder. Inherited permissions are applied automatically, and you cannot edit inherited permissions without first overriding them.

Table 11-1. Basic permissions for files and folders

Permission	How it's used	Used with...
Full Control	Grants full control over the selected file or folder. Permits reading, writing, changing, and deleting files and subfolders. Also permits changing permissions, deleting files in the folder regardless of their permissions, and taking ownership of a folder or a file. Selecting this permission selects all the other permissions as well.	Files and folders
Modify	Permits reading, writing, changing, and deleting a file or folder. With folders, permits creating files and subfolders, but does not allow taking ownership of a file or folder. Selecting this permission selects all the permissions below it.	Files and folders
Read & Execute	Permits executing files. With folders, permits viewing and listing files and subfolders as well as executing files. If applied to a folder, this permission is inherited by all files and subfolders within the folder. Selecting this permission selects the List Folder Contents and Read permissions as well.	Files and folders
List Folder Contents	Permits viewing and listing files and subfolders as well as executing files. Inherited only by subfolders and not by files within the folder or its subfolders.	Folders only
Read	Permits viewing and listing the contents of a file or folder. Permits viewing file attributes, reading permissions, and synchronizing files. Read is the only permission needed to run scripts. Read access is required to access a shortcut and its target.	Files and folders
Write	Permits creating new files in folders and writing data to existing files. Permits viewing file attributes, reading permissions, and synchronizing files. Doesn't prevent deleting a folder or file's contents.	Files and folders

Viewing and modifying existing basic permissions

You can view or modify a file or folder's existing basic permissions by completing the following steps:

1. In Windows Explorer, right-click the file or folder you want to work with and then select Properties.

2. In the Properties dialog box, select the Security tab. As shown in Figure 11-3, the "Group or user names" list shows all users and groups with basic permissions for the selected file or folder. If you select a user or a group in this list, the assigned permissions are displayed in the "Permissions for" list.

 If permissions are shaded (unavailable), it means they have been inherited from a parent folder. I cover inheritance in detail in the "Inherited Permissions" section, later in this chapter.

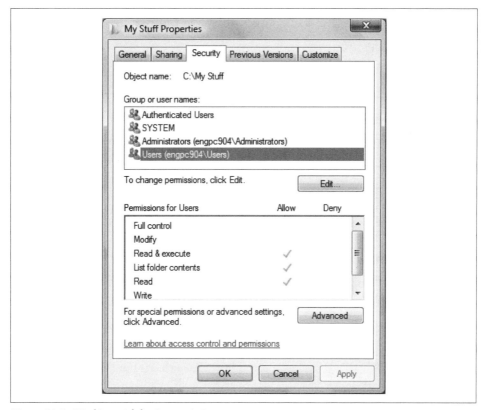

Figure 11-3. *Working with basic permissions*

3. Before you can change or remove permissions, you'll need to click Edit. This opens an editable view of the Security tab in a new dialog box.

4. Click the existing user or group whose permissions you want to modify.

5. To modify existing permissions, use the Allow and Deny columns in the "Permissions for" list. Select checkboxes in the Allow column to add permissions, and clear checkboxes to remove permissions.

6. To prevent a user or a group from using a permission, select the appropriate checkbox in the Deny column. Denied permissions have precedence over other permissions.

7. Click OK to save your changes.

Adding new basic permissions

You can add new basic permissions to a file or folder by completing the following steps:

1. In Windows Explorer, right-click the file or folder you want to work with and then select Properties.

2. In the Properties dialog box, select the Security tab. The "Group or user names" list shows all users and groups with basic permissions for the selected file or folder.

3. If a user or group whose permissions you want to assign isn't already listed, click Edit. This opens an editable view of the Security tab in a new dialog box.

4. Click Add to display the Select Users or Groups dialog box, shown in Figure 11-4.

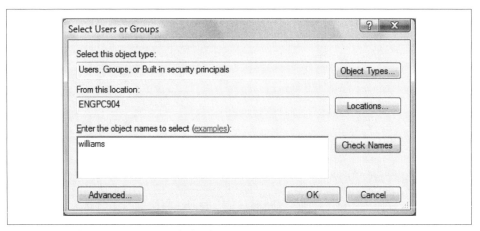

Figure 11-4. Select Users or Groups dialog box

5. Type the name of a user or a group account. Click Check Names and then do one of the following:

- If a single match is found for each entry, the dialog box is automatically updated as appropriate and the entry is underlined.

- If multiple matches are found, you'll see an additional dialog box that allows you to select the name or names you want to use, and then click OK.

- If no matches are found, you've probably entered an incorrect name. Modify the name in the Name Not Found dialog box and then click Check Names again.

6. Configure permissions for each user and group you added by selecting an account name and then allowing or denying access permissions as appropriate.

7. Click OK to save your settings.

Removing basic permissions

You can remove a user or group's basic permissions by following these steps:

1. In Windows Explorer, right-click the file or folder you want to work with and then select Properties.

2. In the Properties dialog box, select the Security tab. The "Group or user names" list shows all users and groups with basic permissions for the selected file or folder.

3. Click Edit to open an editable view of the Security tab in a new dialog box.

4. Click the existing user or group whose permissions you want to remove, and then click Remove.

5. Click OK to save your changes.

Special Permissions

Each basic permission is actually a set of special permissions. Because of this, whenever you allow or deny a basic permission, Windows Vista works behind the scenes to manage the related special permissions for you. Table 11-2 lists the special permissions related to each basic permission.

Table 11-2. Basic permissions and the related special permissions

Basic permission	Related special permissions
Read	List Folder/Read Data
	Read Attributes
	Read Extended Attributes
	Read Permissions

Table 11-2. Basic permissions and the related special permissions (continued)

Basic permission	Related special permissions
Read & Execute or List Folder Contents	All special permissions for Read listed previously
	Traverse Folder/Execute File
Write	Create Files/Write Data
	Create Folders/Append Data
	Write Attributes
	Write Extended Attributes
Modify	All special permissions for Read listed previously
	All special permissions for Write listed previously
	Delete
Full Control	All special permissions listed previously
	Delete Subfolders and Files
	Change Permissions
	Take Ownership

Viewing and modifying existing special permissions

You can view and set special permissions for a file or a folder by completing the following steps:

1. In Windows Explorer, right-click the file or folder you want to work with and then select Properties.

2. In the Properties dialog box, select the Security tab and then click Advanced. In the "Advanced Security Settings for" dialog box, shown in Figure 11-5, the permissions are presented much as they are on the Security tab. The key difference is that you now have additional advanced options.

3. On the Permissions tab, click Edit. This opens an editable view of the Permissions tab in a new dialog box.

4. Click the existing user or group whose permissions you want to modify, and then click Edit. This displays an editable "Permission Entry for" dialog box (see Figure 11-6). If any permissions are shaded (unavailable), they are being inherited from a parent folder. You can override the inherited permission, if necessary, by selecting the opposite permission, such as Deny rather than Allow.

5. To modify existing permissions, use the Allow and Deny columns in the Permissions For list. Select checkboxes in the Allow column to add permissions, and clear checkboxes to remove permissions.

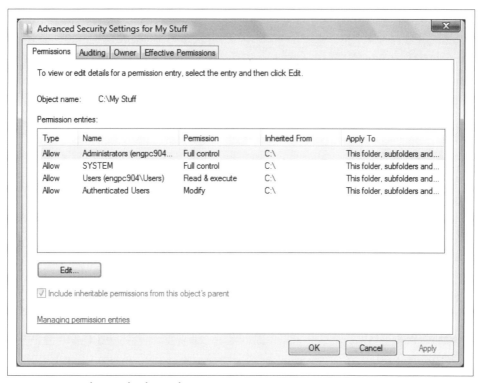

Figure 11-5. *Working with advanced permissions*

6. To prevent a user or a group from using a permission, select the appropriate checkbox in the Deny column. Denied permissions have precedence over other permissions.

7. Click OK to save your changes.

Adding new special permissions

You can add new special permissions to a file or folder by completing the following steps:

1. In Windows Explorer, right-click the file or folder you want to work with and then select Properties.

2. In the Properties dialog box, select the Security tab and then click Advanced. This opens the "Advanced Security Settings for" dialog box.

3. On the Permissions tab, click Edit. This opens an editable view of the Permissions tab in a new dialog box.

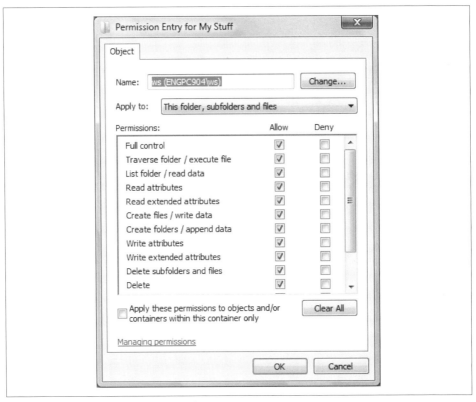

Figure 11-6. Setting individual advanced permissions

4. If a user or group whose permissions you want to assign isn't already listed, click Add to display the Select User or Group dialog box.

5. Type the name of a user or a group account. Click Check Names and then do one of the following:

   • If a single match is found for each entry, the dialog box is automatically updated as appropriate and the entry is underlined.

   • If multiple matches are found, you'll see an additional dialog box that allows you to select the name you want to use, and then click OK.

   • If no matches are found, you've probably entered an incorrect name. Modify the name in the Name Not Found dialog box and then click Check Names again.

6. In the "Permissions Entry for" dialog box, configure permissions for the user or group you added by allowing or denying access permissions as appropriate.

7. Click OK to save your settings.

Removing new special permissions

You can add new special permissions to a file or folder by following these steps:

1. In Windows Explorer, right-click the file or folder you want to work with and then select Properties.

2. In the Properties dialog box, select the Security tab and then click Advanced. This opens the "Advanced Security Settings for" dialog box.

3. On the Permissions tab, click Edit. This opens an editable view of the Permissions tab in a new dialog box.

4. Click the existing user or group whose permissions you want to remove, and then click Remove.

5. Click OK to save your changes.

Ownership Permissions

The owner of a file or a folder is the highest permission holder. Regardless of whether the permissions on the file or folder allow the owner to open the file or folder, the owner can always reset the permissions via the file or folder's Properties dialog box. The default owner of a file or a folder is the person who created the resource.

You can assign or take ownership if you have the required permissions or privileges. Individuals with the required permissions include the owner and anyone with an administrator account.

If you are an administrator or the current owner of a file, you can assign ownership of a file or a folder to another user or group by completing these steps:

1. In Windows Explorer, right-click the file or folder you want to work with and then select Properties.

2. In the Properties dialog box, select the Security tab and then click Advanced. This opens the "Advanced Security Settings for" dialog box.

3. On the Owner tab, click Edit. This opens an editable view of the Owner tab in a new dialog box (see Figure 11-7).

4. Click "Other users or groups" to display the Select User or Group dialog box.

5. Type the name of a user or a group account. Click Check Names and then do one of the following:

   - If a single match is found for each entry, the dialog box is automatically updated as appropriate and the entry is underlined.

   - If multiple matches are found, you'll see an additional dialog box that allows you to select the name you want to use, and then click OK.

   - If no matches are found, you've probably entered an incorrect name. Modify the name in the Name Not Found dialog box and then click Check Names again.

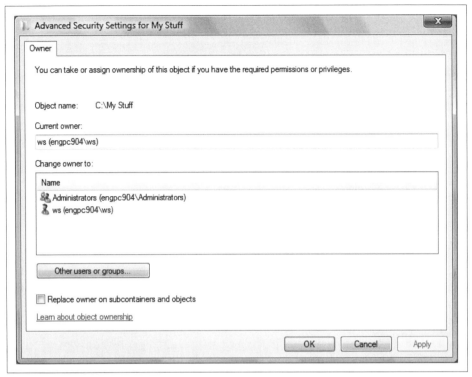

Figure 11-7. Assigning ownership permission

6. In the "Change owner to" listbox, select the new owner. If you're taking ownership of a folder, you can take ownership of all subfolders and files within the folder by selecting the "Replace owner on subcontainers and objects" checkbox.

7. Click OK twice to save your settings.

If you are an administrator, you can take ownership of a file or a folder by completing the following steps:

1. In Windows Explorer, right-click the file or folder you want to work with and then select Properties.

2. In the Properties dialog box, select the Security tab and then click Advanced. This opens the "Advanced Security Settings for" dialog box.

3. On the Owner tab, click Edit. This opens an editable view of the Owner tab in a new dialog box.

4. In the "Change owner to" listbox, select the new owner. If you're taking ownership of a folder, you can take ownership of all subfolders and files within the folder by selecting the "Replace owner on subcontainers and objects" checkbox.

5. Click OK twice to save your settings.

Inherited Permissions

By default, all files and folders contained in a folder inherit the permissions assigned during installation or assigned by you when you modify folder permissions. For a disk or other storage device, the top-level folder for inherited permissions is the root folder. For example, the top-level folder for the *C:* drive is the *C:* folder. Any permissions assigned to this folder are inherited by all other folders on the *C:* drive automatically. The same is true when you assign permissions to folders at any other level of the folder hierarchy. For example, if you change the permissions for the *C:\Data* folder, all files and folders contained in the *C:\Data* folder inherit these permissions by default.

When you are working with permissions, you can easily determine whether a permission is inherited. Inherited permissions are shaded (unavailable) and directly assigned permissions are not shaded. If you don't want a file or a folder to have the same permissions as a parent folder, you have several choices. You can:

- Access the parent folder and configure the permissions you want all included files and folders to have.
- Try to override an inherited permission by selecting the opposite permission. In most cases, Deny overrides Allow.
- Stop inheriting permissions from the parent folder and then copy or remove existing permissions as appropriate.

If you want a file or a folder to stop inheriting permissions from a parent folder, follow these steps:

1. In Windows Explorer, right-click the file or folder you want to work with and then select Properties.
2. In the Properties dialog box, select the Security tab and then click Advanced. This opens the "Advanced Security Settings for" dialog box.
3. On the Permissions tab, click Edit. This opens an editable view of the Permissions tab in a new dialog box.
4. Clear the "Include inheritable permissions from this object's parent" checkbox.
5. In the Windows Security dialog box, shown in Figure 11-8, click Copy to copy over the permissions that were applied previously through inheritance, or click Remove to remove the inherited permissions and apply only the permissions that you explicitly set on the folder or file.
6. After you modify or remove additional permissions as necessary, click OK to save your settings.

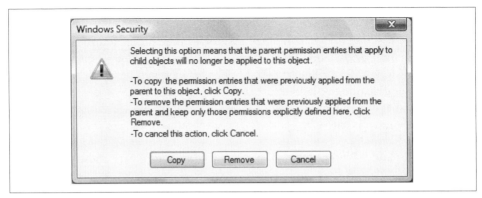

Figure 11-8. Copying or removing permissions

Effective Permissions

Because anyone with a user account can belong to multiple groups and those groups can all have different permissions with regard to a file or folder, it is sometimes difficult to figure out exactly what permission you or someone else has with regard to a file or folder. To remove the guesswork involved, Windows Vista lets you view the exact set of effective permissions for a particular user or group by completing just a few steps.

If you want to view effective permissions, follow these steps:

1. In Windows Explorer, right-click the file or folder you want to work with and then select Properties.

2. In the Properties dialog box, select the Security tab and then click Advanced. This opens the "Advanced Security Settings for" dialog box.

3. On the Effective Permissions tab, click Select to display the Select User or Group dialog box.

4. Type the name of a user or a group account. Click Check Names and then do one of the following:

   • If a single match is found for each entry, the dialog box is automatically updated as appropriate and the entry is underlined.

   • If multiple matches are found, you'll see an additional dialog box that allows you to select the name you want to use, and then click OK.

   • If no matches are found, you've probably entered an incorrect name. Modify the name in the Name Not Found dialog box and then click Check Names again.

The complete set of special permissions for the selected user or group is listed as shown in Figure 11-9.

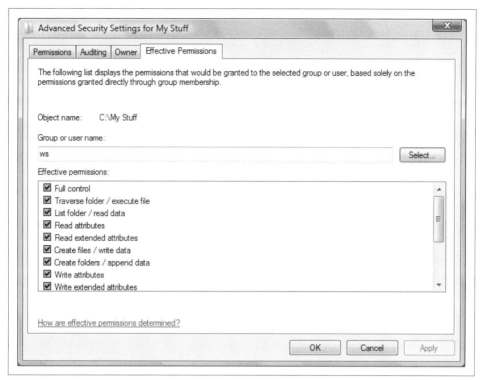

Figure 11-9. Viewing effective permissions

Sharing Your Data

You'll often find that you want to share your documents, pictures, videos, and other types of files with someone else. One of the most basic ways to share your files is to send a file to someone by attaching it to an email message. Most instant messaging programs will allow you to share files with other people while you are chatting with them as well. Other ways to share files include copying the files to a data disk or a device with removable storage, such as a USB flash device. Windows Vista offers other ways to share your data beyond these basic techniques, and these built-in sharing features are the subject of this section.

Enabling Sharing

Windows Vista supports two file-sharing models: standard file sharing and public file sharing. With standard file sharing, you can share files from any folder on your computer. Because you don't need to move files from their current location, standard file sharing is also referred to as *in-place file sharing*. Unlike earlier versions of Windows, Windows Vista allows you to share individual files as well as folders.

You can enable standard file sharing only on disks formatted with NTFS. Two sets of permissions determine precisely who has access to shared files: NTFS permissions and share permissions. Together, these permissions enable you to control who has access to shared files and the level of access assigned. You do not need to move the files you are sharing.

With public file sharing, you share files from a computer's Public folder simply by copying or moving files to the Public folder. Public files are available to anyone who logs on to your computer locally regardless of whether he has a standard user account or an administrator user account on the computer. You can also grant network access to the Public folder. If you do this, however, there are no access restrictions. The public folder and its contents are open to everyone who can access your computer over the local network.

Another type of sharing is printer sharing. Windows Vista allows you to share printers attached to your computer. Windows Vista also allows you to share media in your Windows Media Player library. When you share your media, you can play media from another computer or from an Xbox 360 or other networked digital media player, and let others who can log on to your computer over the network play media from your computer.

If you aren't careful when configuring your network settings, as discussed in Chapter 14, you could suddenly find that the wrong people can access your public files. To prevent this, you can restrict access by turning on password-protected sharing. When password-protected sharing is turned on, only people with a user account and password on your computer can access shared files, shared printers, and the Public folder.

You can manage the various file-sharing features by completing the following steps:

1. Click Start and then click Network. On the Explorer toolbar, click Network and Sharing Center.

2. In the Network and Sharing Center, you control sharing using the options under Sharing and Discovery. Separate options are provided for file sharing, Public folder sharing, printer sharing, password-protected sharing, and media sharing. The status of each sharing option is listed as On or Off, as shown in Figure 11-10.

3. File-sharing options control standard file sharing. To configure file sharing, expand the File Sharing Panel by clicking the related Expand button (see Figure 11-11). To enable file sharing, select "Turn on file sharing." To disable file sharing, select "Turn off file sharing." Click Apply.

4. Public folder sharing options control Public folder sharing on your computer. To configure Public folder sharing, expand the Public Folder Sharing Panel by clicking the related Expand button (see Figure 11-12). Choose one of the following options and then click Apply:

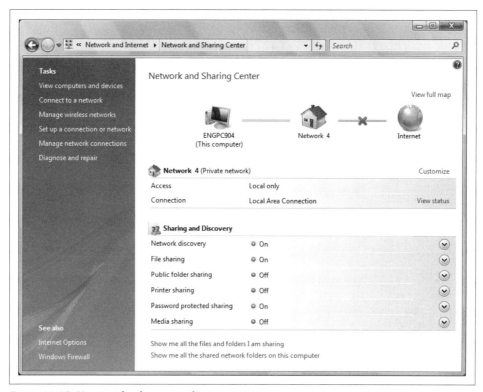

Figure 11-10. Viewing the sharing configuration

Figure 11-11. Configuring file sharing

Turn on sharing so anyone with network access can open files
> Enables Public folder sharing so that anyone with local network access can open files in the Public folder.

Turn on sharing so anyone with network access can open, change, and create files
> Enables Public folder sharing so that anyone with local network access can open, change, and create files in the Public folder.

Turn off sharing
> Disables Public folder sharing, preventing local network access to the Public folder. Anyone who logs on locally to your computer can still access the Public folder and its files.

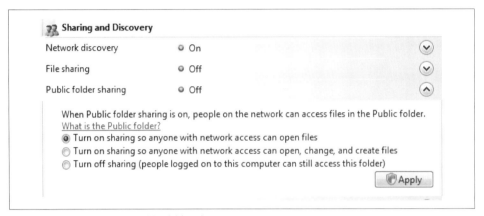

Figure 11-12. Configuring public folder sharing

5. Printer sharing allows you to share printers attached to your computer. To configure printer sharing, expand the Printer Sharing Panel by clicking the related Expand button (see Figure 11-13). To enable printer sharing, select "Turn on printer sharing." To disable printer sharing, select "Turn off printer sharing." Click Apply.

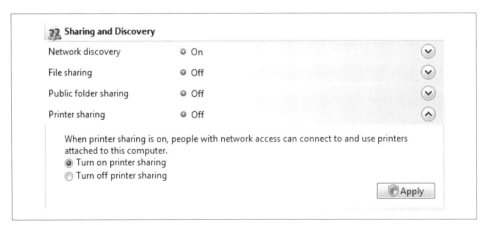

Figure 11-13. Configuring printer sharing

6. Password-protected sharing allows you to restrict access so that only people with a user account and password on your computer can access shared files, shared printers, and the Public folder. To configure password-protected sharing, expand the Password Protected Sharing Panel by clicking the related Expand button (see Figure 11-14). To enable password-protected sharing, select "Turn on password protected sharing." To disable password-protected sharing, select "Turn off password protected sharing." Click Apply.

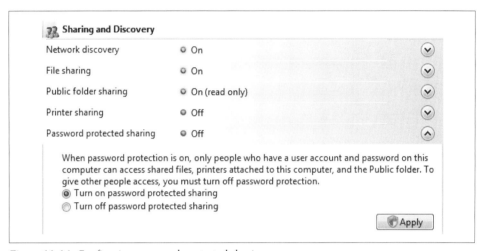

Figure 11-14. Configuring password-protected sharing

7. Media sharing allows you to share your Windows Media Player library. To configure media sharing, expand the Media Sharing Panel by clicking the related Expand button and then click Change. This displays the Media Sharing dialog box shown in Figure 11-15. To enable media sharing, select the "Share my media" checkbox. To disable media sharing, clear the "Share my media" checkbox. Click OK.

For Public folder sharing, printer sharing, and media sharing, turning on sharing is all you need to do. For file sharing, however, you have more work to do. You must specify files and folders to share, and configure sharing permissions.

Configuring Standard File Sharing

With standard file sharing, two levels of permissions are used: share permissions and NTFS permissions. Share permissions define the maximum level of access, and no one can ever have more permissions than those granted by the share. NTFS permissions set on files and folders further restrict the permitted actions. Table 11-3 lists the share permissions you can assign.

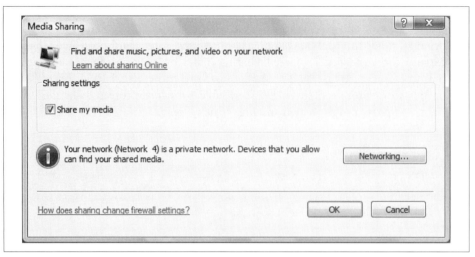

Figure 11-15. Configuring media sharing

Table 11-3. Share permissions

Permission	How it's used
Owner/Co-owner	Grants full access to the shared file or folder. People with this permission can read files, change files, change file and folder permissions, and take ownership of files and folders.
Contributor	Grants permission to read files, create files and subfolders, modify files, change attributes on files and subfolders, and delete files and subfolders.
Reader	Grants permission to view file and subfolder names, read files and file attributes, access the subfolders of the share, and run program files.

As with NTFS permissions, you can assign share permissions to both users and groups. If you've granted share permissions to a group and a user is a member of that group, the user also has those permissions. If a user is a member of multiple groups, the user's effective share permissions are the highest level assigned. For example, if someone is a member of Group A, to which you've assigned Reader permission, and Group B, to which you've assigned Owner/Co-owner permission, this person's effective permissions are those of Owner/Co-owner.

You can override this behavior by specifically denying an access permission. Denying permission takes precedence and overrides permissions that you've granted to groups. If you don't want a user or a group to have a permission, configure the share permissions so that the user or the group is denied that permission. For example, if you don't want the user to have Owner/Co-owner permission, deny this permission to the user's account.

You can share a file or folder and set the share permissions by completing the following steps:

1. In Windows Explorer, right-click the file or folder you want to share and then select Properties.

2. In the Properties dialog box, select the Sharing tab. As shown in Figure 11-16, the details on this tab indicate whether the file or folder is shared already.

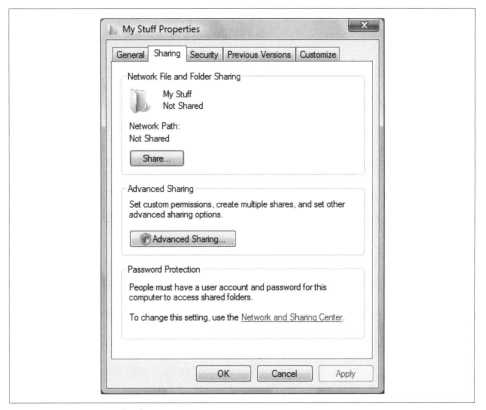

Figure 11-16. Viewing the sharing status

3. If a file or folder is shared already, note the share path. This is the path you and others can use to access the folder over the network.

4. If a file or folder is not yet shared, you can share it. Click Share. In the File Sharing dialog box, shown in Figure 11-17, click the selection button (the down arrow) to the right of the text entry field provided to display a list of accounts and options.

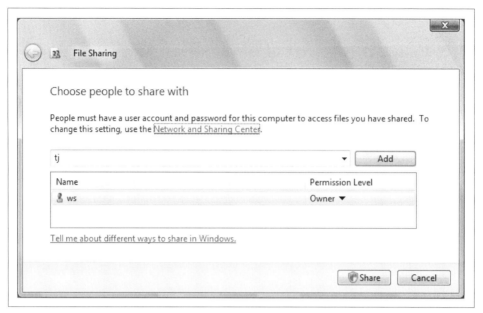

Figure 11-17. Configuring file sharing

5. At home, you can do the following:

   - If you've turned on password-protected file sharing, you'll see a list of user accounts on your computer. Select a user account and then click Add.

   - If you've turned off password-protected file sharing, you'll see a list of user and group accounts on your computer. Select a user or group account and then click Add.

6. At the office, you have the additional option of clicking Find to open the Select Users or Groups dialog box. You can then use this dialog box to select network users and groups as well as users and groups on your computer.

7. Users and groups are added to the Name list. You can configure permissions for each user and group added by clicking an account name to display the Permission Level options, and then choosing the appropriate permission level. The options for permission levels are Reader, Contributor, and Co-owner.

8. Click Share to create the share. On the "Your folder is shared" page, shown in Figure 11-18, you'll see the share name. To email someone a link to the shared resource, click E-mail. To copy to the Windows clipboard a link to the shared resource, click Copy.

9. Click Done when you are finished.

As shown in Figure 11-19, the icon associated with shared files and folders shows a smaller icon of two people to indicate that the file or folder is shared.

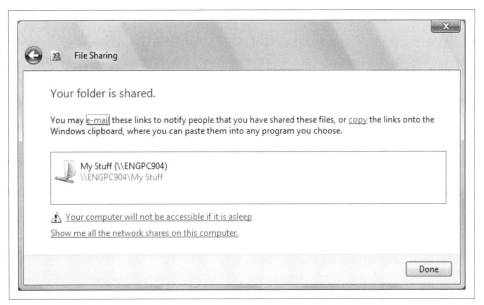

Figure 11-18. Noting the sharing path

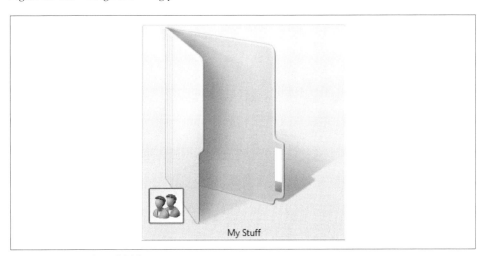

Figure 11-19. A shared folder

If you right-click a file or folder that is shared and select Share, you'll see a different view of the File Sharing dialog box. You can:

- Click "Change sharing permissions" to display the original view of the File Sharing dialog box. You can then add people, remove people, and change permissions.

- Click "Stop sharing" to remove sharing from the file or folder. After Windows Vista removes sharing, click Done to close the File Sharing dialog box.

Accessing Shared Data

Once you share your data, other people can connect to it as a network resource or map to it by using a driver letter on their computer. Once a network drive is mapped, other people can access it just as they would a local drive on their computer.

You can map a network drive to a shared file or folder by following these steps:

1. Click Start and then click Computer. In Windows Explorer, select Map Network Drive from the Tools menu. This displays the Map Network Drive dialog box, shown in Figure 11-20.

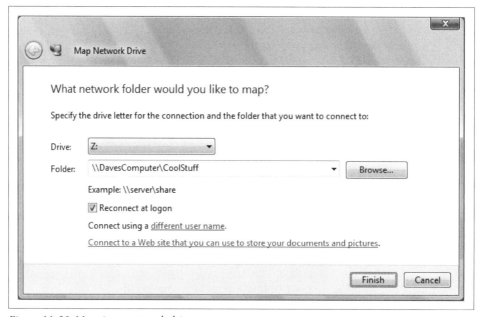

Figure 11-20. Mapping a network drive

2. Use the Drive field to select a free drive letter to use.

3. Click the Browse button to the right of the Folder field. In the Browse for Folder dialog box, expand the Network folders until you can select the name of the workgroup or the domain with which you want to work.

4. When you expand the name of a computer in a workgroup or a domain, you'll see a list of shared folders. Select the shared folder you want to work with and click OK.

5. Select "Reconnect at logon" if you want Windows Vista to connect to the shared folder automatically at the start of each session.

6. If your current logon doesn't have appropriate access permissions for the share, click the "Different user name" link. In the Connect As dialog box, enter the username and password of the account with which you want to connect to the shared folder, and then click OK.

7. Click Finish.

You can stop mapping a network drive to a shared file or folder by completing the following steps:

1. Click Start and then click Computer.

2. In Windows Explorer, under Network Location, right-click the network drive icon and choose Disconnect.

Accessing Shared Folders Offline

An offline folder is a shared folder designated for use offline. Offline folders provide an easy way for you to use files on shared folders regardless of where you are. You use offline folders as follows:

1. When you are using a laptop computer to access a shared folder over the network, you might want to make the shared folder available for offline use.

2. You then designate the files that your computer should store so that you can use them while disconnected from the network.

3. When you later connect to the network, your computer automatically synchronizes any changes you make back to the shared folder.

As with just about every feature discussed in this book, it is important to remember that your office administrators can enable and disable offline folders. If they have disabled this or another feature, they probably did so for a good reason. Offline folders are sometimes disabled to prevent problems with multiple users changing the same documents, or to protect potentially sensitive documents.

You can configure a shared folder so that it is available for offline use by completing the following steps:

1. In Windows Explorer, right-click the folder you want to use offline and then select Properties.

2. In the Properties dialog box, select the Sharing tab. The details on this tab indicate whether the folder is shared already. The folder must be shared to configure it for offline use.

3. Click Advanced Sharing.

4. In the Advanced Sharing dialog box, click Caching.

5. In the Offline Settings dialog box, shown in Figure 11-21, select one of the following options:

Only the files and programs that users specify will be available offline
   With this option, only files you specifically designated will be available for offline use.

All files and programs that users open from the share will be automatically available offline
   With this option, all files in the selected folder will be available for offline use.

6. Click OK twice.

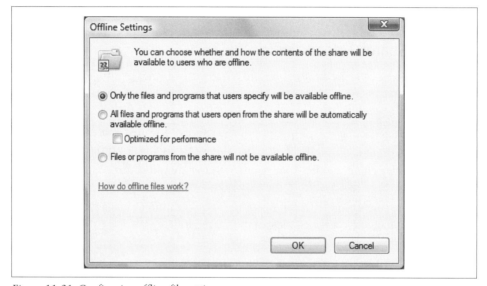

Figure 11-21. Configuring offline file settings

Once you've ensured that a folder is available for offline use, you can specify the files and folders to use offline. To copy the entire contents of a shared folder to your computer and make it available for offline use, complete the following steps:

1. Click Start and then click Computer. This opens the Computer console.
2. Under Network Location, right-click the shared location and then select Always Available Offline.

To copy only certain files to your computer and make them available offline, complete the following steps:

1. Click Start and then click Computer. This opens the Computer console.
2. Under Network Location, double-click the shared location to open it.
3. Right-click a file you want to make available offline and then select Always Available Offline.

Working Offline and Syncing

Whenever your computer is not connected to the local area network (LAN), you are considered to be working offline. When you are working offline, you can access only network folders that are cached on your computer for offline use. When you reconnect to the network, Windows Vista automatically will synchronize any changes you've made to the files while offline. Sometimes there may be conflicts between changes you've made to files and changes other people have made to files. You can manage conflicts and the synchronization process in the Sync Center, shown in Figure 11-22.

Figure 11-22. Checking the sync status

In the Sync Center, you'll see a sync partnership for every shared folder that has locally cached contents. You can work with the Sync Center by following these steps:

1. Click Start → Control Panel. In the Control Panel, click Network and Internet.

2. On the Network and Internet page, click Sync Center.

3. In the Sync Center, currently defined sync partnerships are listed according to name, status, progress, conflict count, error count, and category. You can now manage syncing using the following techniques:

   - To manually sync all offline files and folders, click Sync All. Sync All is available only when no individual sync partnerships are selected.

   - To manually sync a specific network share, click the sync partnership that you want to work with and then click Sync.

   - To check for errors, click "View sync results" under Tasks. You can use the sync details to determine when syncing was started, stopped, or completed, and to determine whether there are problems with the synchronization configuration.

Synchronization conflicts can occur if you make changes to a file offline that is updated online by someone else. You can view and resolve synchronization conflicts by following these steps:

1. In the Sync Center, click "View sync conflicts" under Tasks.

2. Any existing conflicts are listed in the main pane. Double-click a conflict you want to resolve.

3. You can now:

   • Click the version you want to keep. To keep the local version and overwrite the network version, click the version listed as On This Computer. To keep the network version and overwrite the local version, click the version listed as being on the shared network location.

   • Click Keep Both Versions to write the local version to the shared network location with a new filename. The new filename will be the same as the old filename, but with a numeric suffix, indicating the version increment.

Devices you've used with Windows Media Player can have sync partnerships with your computer as well. You can view and manage these sync partnerships by completing the following steps:

1. Connect the device to your computer.

2. In the Sync Center, click "Set up new sync partnerships" under Tasks. As Figure 11-23 shows, you'll see a list of devices with sync partnerships.

3. When you right-click the device and then select Set Up, Windows Vista opens Windows Media Player with the device selected and displays the device's Windows Media Player – Device Setup dialog box.

4. Complete the setup of the device, as discussed in the "Syncing Your Media to MP3 Players and Other Devices" section in Chapter 8.

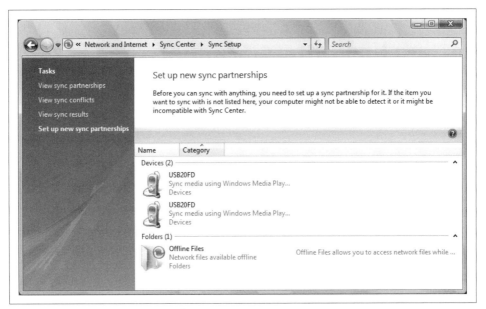

Figure 11-23. Viewing sync partnerships

CHAPTER 12

Setting Up Printers, Scanners, and Fax Machines

Not unlike many offices, scattered about my office is a jumbled assortment of printers, scanners, and fax machines. Getting these devices—some of them more than a few years old—to work with Windows Vista wasn't a picnic. Here are some of the problems I encountered along the way:

- A software installation disk would not install the device because Windows Vista wasn't a supported operating system.
- A setup program used a Java Runtime Environment (JRE) that was incompatible with my computer's configuration.
- A setup program worked correctly but configured the device incorrectly.

Because of problems such as these, you might find that getting your printers, scanners, and fax machines to work with Windows Vista is a frustrating experience, and this is why in this chapter I'll give you a quick and easy workaround for each of these problems, and more. In addition, I have to let Windows Vista off the hook on this one. The underlying problems I encountered weren't Windows Vista's fault. The problems were the fault of setup programs and drivers that weren't designed for Windows Vista—not unlike many of the setup programs and drivers you'll probably use with your printers, scanners, and fax machines as well.

Installing Printers, Scanners, and Fax Machines

To Windows Vista, printers, scanners, and fax machines are all pretty much the same thing. Windows Vista prints to and accepts input from any of these devices in similar ways. What sets these devices apart, however, is the way they are connected.

Printers, scanners, and fax machines can be either physically attached or network-attached. A physically attached device is connected directly to your computer with a serial, parallel, or USB cable. A network-attached device is connected directly to your network and accessed remotely rather than directly.

Both physically attached and network-attached devices can be shared as well. The computer sharing these devices for other computers on the network is referred to as a *print server*, regardless of whether the computer is actually running a server version of Windows. The print server also handles sending the formatted document and receiving an incoming document. For ease of reference, I'll refer to both processes as *spooling*. A key advantage of using a computer as a print server is that your printers, scanners, and fax machines will have a central queue that you can manage.

At home or at the office, you don't have to share printers, scanners, or fax machines from your computer, or any computer, for that matter. Instead, you can have everyone connect directly to a network-attached device. When you do this, the network device is handled much like a local device attached directly to a computer. However, everyone who uses a network-attached device will then have separate queues, which can make tracking down problems extremely difficult.

Installing Physically Attached Printers, Scanners, and Fax Machines

Physically attached printers, scanners, and fax machines are connected directly to your computer through a serial, parallel, or USB cable and you can install them by completing the following steps:

1. Run the setup program for the printer, scanner, or fax machine.
2. Connect the printer, scanner, or fax machine to your computer using the appropriate serial, parallel, or USB cable, and then turn on the device.
3. Let Windows Vista automatically detect and install the device.

However, not all printers, scanners, and fax machines have or need setup programs. With my HP All-In-One Printer/Scanner/Fax/Copier machine, all I needed to do was to connect a USB cable between my computer and the device, and then turn it on.

If Windows Vista detects but isn't able to install the printer, scanner, or fax machine automatically, it starts the Found New Hardware Wizard. You can use this wizard to complete the installation by following these steps:

1. In the Found New Hardware Wizard, click "Locate and install driver software (recommended)" to continue with the installation (see Figure 12-1).
2. The Driver Software Installation component will then search for preconfigured drivers according to your Windows Update Driver Settings (see Figure 12-2). As discussed in Chapter 5, your computer will search its driver cache and may search the Windows Update site.
3. If the automated process fails, you'll be prompted to insert the setup disk that came with your computer, as shown in Figure 12-3. If you have an installation disk for the device, insert the disk, follow the prompts to complete the installation, and skip the remaining steps.

Figure 12-1. Locating and installing the driver

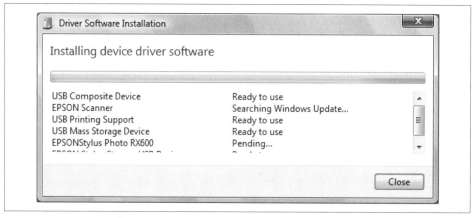

Figure 12-2. Beginning the automated install

4. If you don't have an installation disk, click "I don't have the disk. Show me other options." Then follow the remaining steps in this procedure.

5. Click "Browse my computer for driver software" and then click Browse to select a search location.

6. Use the Browse for Folder dialog box to select the start folder for the search, and then click OK. All subfolders of the selected folder are searched automatically.

7. When you click Next, the wizard will search for and install any appropriate driver. If the wizard can't find an appropriate driver, you'll need to obtain one and then manually install the device driver.

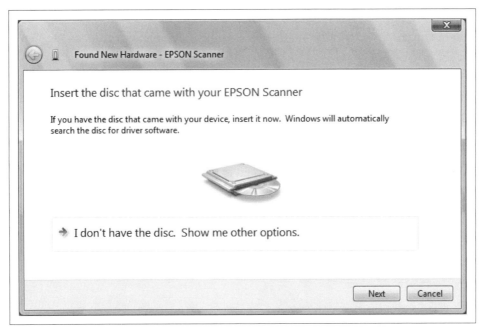

Figure 12-3. Continuing the install manually because a problem has occurred

As discussed previously, I encountered a number of problems with the setup programs for printers, scanners, and fax machines. One setup program displayed a warning stating the device would not be installed because I wasn't using a supported operating system. Worse yet, the setup program caused the computer to become unresponsive. I couldn't exit the setup program or clear the window. To resolve this problem with minimal fuss, I simply logged off and then logged back on. Afterward, I visited the support area of the manufacturer's web site and searched for the drivers for the device. Each driver I found had a specific set of supported operating systems. While there wasn't a driver for Windows Vista, I did find a driver that supported Windows 2000 and Windows XP. I downloaded and installed that driver to get the device to work. Generally, Windows 2000 and Windows XP drivers will work with Windows Vista. Most older drivers won't, however.

I also encountered a problem with a setup program that used a JRE. Although some earlier versions of Windows include a JRE, Windows Vista does not. If you want to use Java with Windows Vista, this is something you have to install separately. In theory, the JRE shouldn't have had a problem running because the setup program was designed as a standalone program rather than an applet that runs within a browser window. I solved this problem using the old-school method of doing a manual printer install and selection. You can use a manual install and selection as well if you encounter problems with a printer, scanner, or fax machine.

Installing a printer or fax machine manually

You can install a printer or fax machine manually by completing the following steps:

1. Click Start and then click Control Panel.

2. In the Control Panel, click Hardware and Sound and then click the "Add a printer" link under the Printers heading. This starts the Add Printer Wizard.

3. In the Add Printer Wizard, click "Add a local printer."

4. On the "Choose a printer port" page, shown in Figure 12-4, click the "Use an existing port" list to display a list of ports on your computer. Choose the appropriate LPT, COM, IR, or USB port, and then click Next.

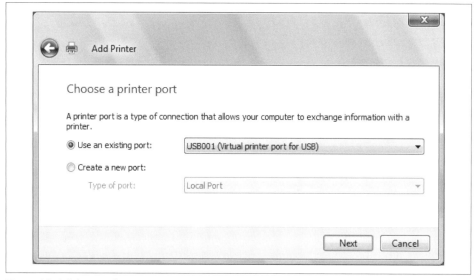

Figure 12-4. Selecting the port to use

5. As shown in Figure 12-5, you must now specify the device manufacturer and model. This allows Windows Vista to assign a driver to the device. If the device manufacturer and model you are using are displayed, choose a manufacturer and a model, and then skip steps 6–8.

6. If the device manufacturer and model you're using aren't displayed in the list, download the driver from the manufacturer's web site and then extract the driver files.

7. Click Have Disk. In the Install From Disk dialog box, click Browse.

8. In the Locate File dialog box, locate the *.inf* driver file for the device and then click Open.

9. Click Next. On the "Type a printer name" page, shown in Figure 12-6, type a name for the device or accept the default name. You'll see this name on the Printers page in the Control Panel.

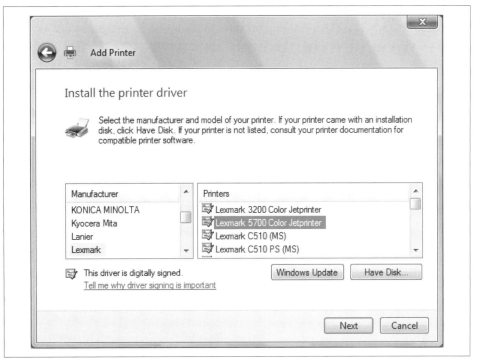

Figure 12-5. Selecting the manufacturer and printer type

Figure 12-6. Setting the printer options

10. The device is set automatically as the local default. If you don't want the device to be the default, clear the "Set as the default printer" checkbox.

11. When you click Next, the Add Printer Wizard will install the printer and print a test page. If the wizard encounters a problem when printing the test page, you'll

see a prompt detailing the problem found (see Figure 12-7). Once you resolve the problem, click Continue to continue printing the test page, or click Cancel Printing to cancel printing the test page. Click Finish.

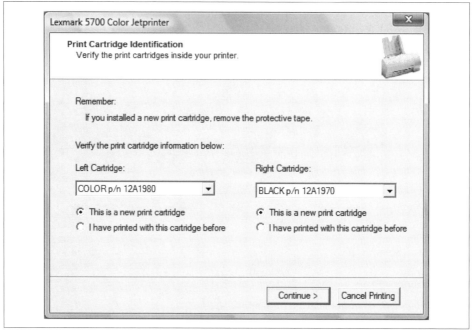

Figure 12-7. Prompt detailing the problem found

12. The Printers page in the Control Panel will have an additional icon with the name set the way you specified. You can change the printer or fax properties and check printer or fax status at any time.

Installing a scanner manually

You can install a scanner manually by completing the following steps:

1. Click Start and then click Control Panel.

2. In the Control Panel, click Hardware and Sound and then click Scanners and Cameras.

3. In the Scanners and Cameras window, click Add Device. This starts the Scanner and Camera Installation Wizard.

4. Click Next.

5. You must now specify the device manufacturer and model. This allows Windows Vista to assign a driver to the device. If the device manufacturer and model you are using are displayed, choose a manufacturer and a model, and then skip steps 6–8.

6. If the device manufacturer and model you're using aren't displayed in the list, download the driver from the manufacturer's web site and then extract the driver files.

7. Click Have Disk. In the Install from Disk dialog box, click Browse.

8. In the Locate File dialog box, locate the *.inf* driver file for the device and then click Open.

9. Click Next. On the "What is the name of your device" page, type a name for the scanner or accept the default name. You'll see this name in the Scanners and Cameras window.

10. Click Next and then click Finish.

11. The Scanners and Cameras window will have an additional icon with the name set the way you specified. You can change the scanner properties and check scanner status at any time.

Installing Network-Attached Printers, Scanners, and Fax Machines

A network-attached printer, scanner, or fax machine is a device that's attached directly to the network using a wireless connection or a network cable. Network-attached printers, scanners, and fax machines are configured so that they're accessible to network users as shared devices. Remember that the server on which you configure the print device becomes the print server for the device you're configuring.

You can install a network-attached printer or fax machine by completing these steps:

1. Click Start and then click Control Panel. In the Control Panel, click Hardware and Sound and then click Printers.

2. In the Printers window, click Add a Printer on the toolbar. This starts the Add Printer Wizard.

3. In the Add Printer Wizard, click "Add a network, wireless, or Bluetooth printer." As shown in Figure 12-8, the Add Printer Wizard will then begin searching for available devices.

4. If the wizard finds the device you want to use, click it in the list of devices found. Click Next and then click Finish. Skip the remaining steps.

5. If the wizard doesn't find the device you want to use, click "The printer that I want isn't listed."

6. On the "Find a printer by name or TCP/IP address" page, select "Add a printer using a TCP/IP address or hostname," and then click Next.

7. On the "Type a printer hostname or IP address" page, shown in Figure 12-9, use the "Device type" list to select the type of device. If you don't know the type of device, choose Autodetect.

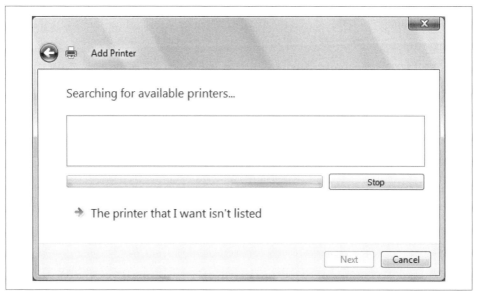

Figure 12-8. Searching for available printers

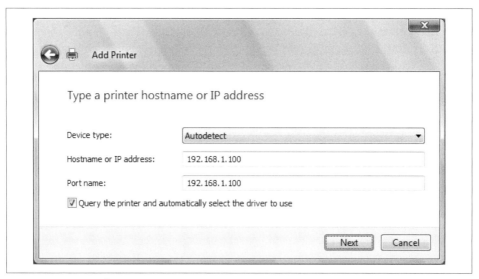

Figure 12-9. Setting the printer options

8. In the "Hostname or IP address" text box, type the hostname or Internet Protocol (IP) address of the device. If you are unsure, use the device's control menu to print a configuration page.

9. The port name is set for you based on the hostname or IP address entry. The port name doesn't matter as long as it's unique for your computer.

10. When you click Next, the wizard attempts to contact the device. If the wizard is unable to detect the print device, make sure that the print device is turned on and connected to the network. Also, ensure that you typed the correct IP address or printer name in the previous page. If you entered incorrect information, click the Back arrow and then retype this information.

11. If the information is correct, you'll need to identify the device further on the Additional Port Information Required page shown in Figure 12-10. In the Device Type area, click Standard, and then select the printer or network adapter used by the printer. Alternatively, click Custom and then click Settings to define custom settings for the printer, such as protocol and Simple Network Management Protocol (SNMP) status.

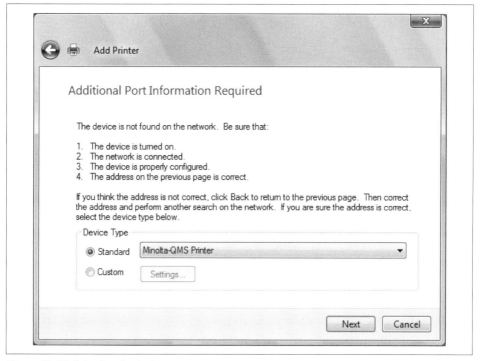

Figure 12-10. Selecting the device type

12. When you click Next, the wizard will attempt to detect the device model. If auto-detection is successful, follow steps 9–12 in the "Installing a printer or fax machine manually" section, earlier in this chapter, to complete the installation. If auto-detection fails, follow steps 5–12 in the "Installing a printer or fax machine manually" section to complete the installation.

Xerox makes a network-attached scanner called the Xerox WorkCentre Pro Scanner. This device installs in the same way as a directly attached scanner. When you complete the installation, the scanner should be configured automatically. If it isn't, follow these steps to set the IP address for the scanner:

1. Click Start and then click Control Panel.

2. In the Control Panel, click Hardware and Sound and then click Scanners and Cameras.

3. In the Scanners and Cameras window, click the scanner and then click Properties.

4. On the Device Settings tab, type the hostname or IP address of the scanner and then click OK.

Sharing Printers, Scanners, and Fax Machines

After you install printers, scanners, and fax machines, you can use the devices with your computer. When you are printing, scanning, or faxing, all you need to do is select the device in your application. If you want other people on your network to be able to use printers, scanners, and fax machines you've installed, you can do this too.

Sharing Printers and Fax Machines

After you install a physically attached or network-attached printer or fax machine, you can allow anyone else on your network to connect to it by sharing it. Friends and coworkers on your network can then connect to the shared printer or fax machine.

You can share a printer or fax machine by following these steps:

1. Enable printer sharing on your computer, as discussed in the "Enabling Sharing" section of Chapter 11.

2. Click Start and then click Control Panel. In the Control Panel, click Hardware and Sound and then click Printers.

3. In the Printers window, right-click the printer you want to configure and then select Sharing.

4. On the Sharing tab, you'll see any current sharing options. If there are no current sharing options, all sharing options are dimmed, as shown in Figure 12-11.

 Some types of fax machines cannot be shared. If this is the case with your fax machine, this will be stated on the Sharing tab.

5. To change the sharing options, click "Change sharing options." This opens an editable version of the Sharing tab.

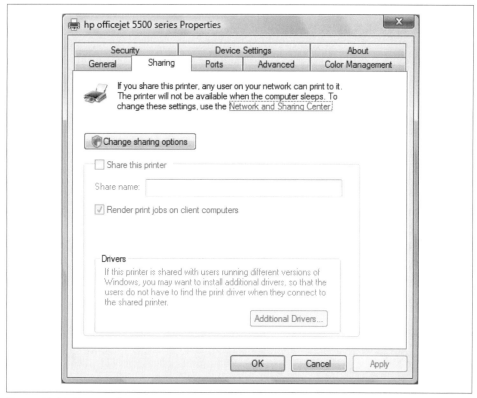

Figure 12-11. Viewing the sharing status

6. When you select the "Share this printer" checkbox, Windows Vista fills in a share name for you. You can change the default name as necessary.

7. By default, print jobs are generated on the computer of the person printing a document. This is usually the desired setting. If you want to generate the print file on your computer, clear the "Render print jobs on client computers" checkbox.

8. Click Additional Drivers. In the Additional Drivers dialog box, select the types of processors other people on the network are using to ensure that your computer provides the appropriate drivers during setup.

9. Click OK.

Connecting to Shared Printers and Fax Machines

When you are sharing printers and fax machines, you need to keep in mind that other people on your network might not be running Windows Vista. Don't worry, though; connecting to a shared printer with Windows 2000 or later is easy. Why? Because computers running Windows 2000 or later can install the printer drivers automatically once a printer is shared. The trick, of course, is to ensure that your computer provides the necessary drivers when someone tries to connect to your printer or fax machine. When you were sharing your printer or fax machine, you selected drivers for other computers as part of the sharing configuration. If you need to, you can add drivers for other types of computers by completing the following steps:

1. Click Start and then click Control Panel. In the Control Panel, click Hardware and Sound and then click Printers.

2. In the Printers window, right-click the printer you want to configure and then select Sharing.

3. On the Sharing tab, you'll see any current sharing options. Click "Change sharing options."

4. Click Additional Drivers.

5. In the Additional Drivers dialog box, select the types of processors other people on the network are using to ensure that your computer provides the appropriate drivers during setup.

6. Click OK.

Once you've shared the printer and ensured that the drivers are available, anyone running Windows 2000 or Windows XP can connect to and use the printer by following these steps:

1. In Windows Explorer, click the Folders button on the toolbar to display the Folders Pane.

2. Expand My Computer, expand the Control Panel, and then select Printers and Faxes.

3. In the Folders Pane, expand My Network Places and then navigate My Network Places to the computer sharing the printer.

4. When you select the Printers and Faxes node on this computer, you'll see the shared printers and fax machines (see Figure 12-12).

5. Click the printer or fax machine and drag it to My Computer → Control Panel → Printers and Faxes.

Anyone running Windows Vista or later can connect to and use the printer by following these steps:

1. Click Start and then click Control Panel. In the Control Panel, click Hardware and Sound and then click Printers.

2. Open a second window by clicking Start and then clicking Network.

Figure 12-12. Selecting the printer to use

3. In the Network window, double-click the computer sharing the printer.

4. In the Network window, click the printer or fax machine and drag it to the Printers window.

Sharing and Connecting to Scanners

Physically attached and network-attached scanners cannot be shared in the same way as printers and fax machines can. Physically attached scanners must be connected directly to the computer of the person who wants to use the scanner. Although network-attached scanners are technically shared, they don't have sharing settings you need to configure through your computer. You connect to and use a network-attached scanner by performing an install, as discussed previously.

Configuring Printer, Scanner, and Fax Machine Properties

Like any other device, printers, scanners, and fax machines have properties that you can configure. This section looks at the properties you'll work with most.

Changing Ports for Printers, Scanners, and Fax Machines

If a setup program works correctly but configures the device incorrectly, the likely problem is the associated port. Each printer, scanner, and fax machine you use with your computer is configured to work with a specific port. USB printers, fax machines, and scanners use virtual USB ports. Parallel and serial printers use LPT and COM ports. Network-attached printers use standard Transmission Control Protocol/Internet Protocol (TCP/IP) ports. A problem you may encounter is the case of a printer being configured to print using the FILE port instead of the correct port. Because the FILE port prints documents to a raw printer file, your computer won't spool to the device.

You can view and set the ports for a printer or fax machine by following these steps:

1. Click Start and then click Control Panel. In the Control Panel, click Hardware and Sound and then click Printers.

2. In the Printers window, right-click the printer you want to configure and then select Properties.

3. In the Properties dialog box, select the Ports tab, as shown in Figure 12-13.

4. In the Port column, clear the checkbox for the incorrect port and then select the checkbox for the correct port.

5. Click OK.

If you are experiencing problems with a TCP/IP port, ensure that the IP address associated with the port is correct. The IP address typically is listed as part of the name of the port. If the IP address isn't correct and no port is available for the correct IP address, follow these steps to resolve the problem:

1. On the Ports tab, click Add Port.

2. In the Printer Ports dialog box, click Standard TCP/IP Port and then click New Port.

3. In the Add Standard TCP/IP Printer Port Wizard, click Next.

4. Type the IP address of the printer or fax machine and then click Next.

5. When you click Next, the wizard attempts to contact the device. If the wizard is unable to detect the print device, make sure that the print device is turned on and is connected to the network. Also ensure that you typed the correct IP

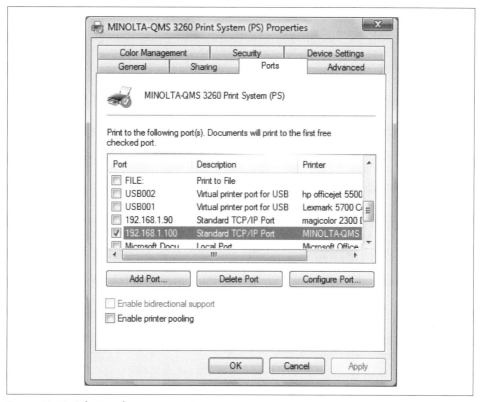

Figure 12-13. Selecting the correct printer port

address or printer name in the previous page. If you entered the incorrect information, click the Back arrow and then retype this information.

6. If the information is correct, you'll need to identify the device further on the Additional Port Information Required page. In the "Device type" area, click Standard, and then select the printer or network adapter the printer uses. Alternatively, click Custom and then click Settings to define custom settings for the printer, such as protocol and SNMP status.

7. When you click Next, the wizard will attempt to detect the device model. If auto-detection is successful, follow steps 9–12 in the "Installing a printer or fax machine manually" section to complete the installation. If auto-detection fails, follow steps 5–12 in the "Installing a printer or fax machine manually" section to complete the installation.

To resolve a problem with a network-attached scanner, follow these steps:

1. Click Start and then click Control Panel.

2. In the Control Panel, click Hardware and Sound and then click Scanners and Cameras.

3. In the Scanners and Cameras window, click the scanner and then click Properties.

4. On the Device Settings tab, the current hostname or IP address is listed. If this information isn't correct, enter the correct hostname or IP address of the scanner, and then click OK.

Changing Printer, Scanner, and Fax Machine Drivers

You can manage drivers for printers, scanners, and fax machines just like you can any other drivers. To change the drivers for a printer or fax machine, follow these steps:

1. Click Start and then click Control Panel. In the Control Panel, click Hardware and Sound and then click Printers.

2. In the Printers window, right-click the printer you want to configure, point to "Run as administrator," and then select Properties.

3. On the Advanced tab, click New Driver.

4. Use the Add Printer Driver Wizard to select and install the new driver.

To change the drivers for a scanner, follow these steps:

1. Click Start and then click Control Panel.

2. In the Control Panel, click Hardware and Sound and then click Scanners and Cameras.

3. In the Scanners and Cameras window, click the scanner and then click Properties.

4. On the Device Settings tab, click New Driver.

Setting Printer Scheduling, Prioritization, and Other Options

The Advanced tab of the Printer properties dialog box provides most of the options you'll want to configure. You can use these options to configure your printer by completing the following steps:

1. Click Start and then click Control Panel. In the Control Panel, click Hardware and Sound and then click Printers.

2. In the Printers window, right-click the printer you want to configure and then select Properties.

3. In the Properties dialog box, select the Advanced tab, as shown in Figure 12-14.

4. Use the following options to optimize the printer configuration:

   Always available and available from
   Printers are either always available or available only during the hours specified. Select "Always available" to make the printer available at all times or select "Available from" to set specific hours of operation. Print jobs sent outside the designated hours are held in the printer's queue until the scheduled use time.

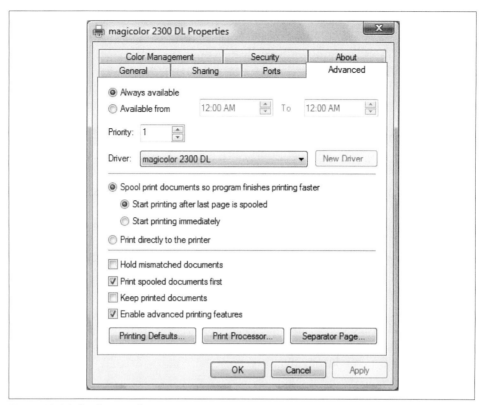

Figure 12-14. Configuring the printer as necessary

Priority

Print jobs always print in order of priority. Jobs with higher priority print before jobs with lower priority. Use the Priority box to set the default priority.

Driver

Shows the current driver being used for the printer. If you click the Driver list, you'll see a list of all printer drivers being used on your computer. See "Changing Printer, Scanner, and Fax Machine Drivers," earlier in this chapter, for more information.

Spooling options

The spooling options control whether and how a document is spooled to a hard disk before being sent to the printer. Spooling a document before printing allows applications to finish printing faster. To enable spooling, select "Spool print documents so program finishes printing faster." To disable spooling, select "Print directly to the printer." With spooling, select "Start printing after last page is spooled" if you want to ensure that the entire document makes it into the print queue before printing. Otherwise, select "Start printing immediately" if you want printing to begin immediately when the print device isn't already in use.

Hold mismatched documents

A mismatch can occur if a document tries to use a form or type of paper not currently available in a printer tray. Typically, printers will stop all printing and wait for the mismatch to be resolved. If you want the printer to hold mismatched documents rather than try to prevent them, select this option.

Print spooled documents first

Select this option to allow the printer to print jobs that have completed spooling before jobs in the process of spooling, regardless of whether the spooling jobs have higher priority. This helps to maximize printer efficiency by ensuring that documents that have started printing can finish printing without interruption.

Keep printed documents

Select this option to keep a copy of documents in the printer queue on the print server. If you're printing files that can't easily be re-created, you might want to use this option so that you can easily reprint a document without having to re-create it.

Enable advanced printing features

Select this option to allow the use of advanced printing options, if available, such as "Page order" and "Pages per sheet." If you encounter compatibility problems when using advanced options, you can disable the advanced printing features by clearing this checkbox.

Printing Defaults

Clicking this button displays the Printing Defaults dialog box, which you can use to specify defaults for paper sources, document sizes, color matching, print resolution, and more.

Print Processor

Clicking this button displays the Print Processor dialog box, which you can use to set the print processor and default data type for a printer. The print processor is the software component that tells your computer how to render the raw printer data. About the only time you may need to configure print processor options is when you are working with an older Unix printer.

Separator Page

At the office, separator pages may be a requirement. To select a separator page to print before each document, click the Separator Page button. In the Separator Page dialog box, click Browse, scroll down, and then click Sysprint.sep if you have a PostScript printer or Pcl.sep if you have a PCL printer. Click Open and then click OK.

Managing Print, Fax, and Scan Jobs

Documents you print can be either spooled or sent directly to the printer. When you use spooling with printing rather than direct-to-printer printing, documents that are waiting to print or are in the process of printing are stored on the print server as a print job. If you encounter problems while printing, you may want to check the status of print jobs and pause or cancel a print job as necessary. Because fax machines and scanners typically can be used to both send and receive documents, they typically have incoming jobs and outgoing jobs that you can manage.

Working with Print Jobs

You manage the print jobs associated with a printer using the print management window. If the printer is configured on your computer, you can access the print management window by completing the following steps:

1. Click Start and then click Control Panel. In the Control Panel, click Hardware and Sound and then click Printers.
2. In the Printers window, double-click the printer you want to work with.

If the printer isn't configured on your computer, you can manage the printer remotely by completing these steps:

1. Click Start and then click Network.
2. Double-click the computer sharing the printer.
3. Double-click the printer.

You can now manage print jobs for the selected printer using the print management window shown in Figure 12-15. The print management window provides details about documents being printed or waiting to print on the selected printer. These details include:

Document Name
Shows the name of the application that printed the document, and the document name.

Status
The status of the print job. Document status entries you'll see include Printing and Error – Printing.

Owner
The person who printed the document.

Pages
The number of pages in the document.

Size
> The document size in kilobytes or megabytes.

Submitted
> The time and date the print job was submitted.

Port
> The port used for printing.

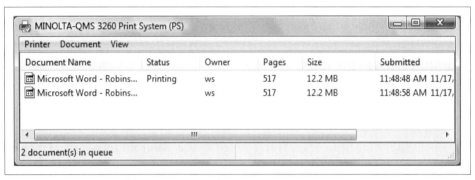

Figure 12-15. Viewing and managing print jobs

You can set the status of individual documents using the Document menu in the print management window. To cancel printing or change the status of a document, follow these steps:

1. Select the document in the print management window.

2. On the Document menu, use one of the following options to change the status of the print job:

   Cancel
   > Cancels printing of the document and removes the print job.

   Pause
   > Puts the document on hold and lets other documents print.

   Resume
   > Resumes printing of a paused document. Printing resumes from where it left off.

   Restart
   > Starts printing the document again from the beginning.

 Sometimes when you cancel a print job that's currently printing, the printer might continue to print part of the document or all of it. This can occur because most printers cache documents in an internal buffer and may print the contents of this cache before checking for updates.

Working with Printers

The title bar in the print management window provides details on the status of the printer itself. If printing is paused or the printer is offline, you'll see related status details on the title bar, as shown in Figure 12-16.

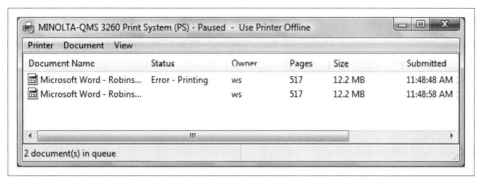

Figure 12-16. Checking the status of the printer as well as print jobs

Before you try to repair or resolve a problem with a printer used by multiple people, you may want to pause printing. Using the print management window, you do this by selecting the Pause Printing option from the Printer menu. A checkmark indicates that the option is selected. When you pause printing, the printer completes the current job and then puts all other print jobs on hold. When printing is paused, the printer accepts but does not print new print jobs. To resume printing, select the Pause Printing option a second time. This should remove the checkmark next to the option.

When you have problems with a printer, you may find that many of the print jobs currently waiting to print are simply reprints of the same document or of documents that are no longer needed. In this case, you can use the print management window to empty the print queue and delete all its contents. To do this, select the "Cancel all documents" option from the Printer menu.

In addition to pausing a printer, you can also designate a printer as being offline. Using the print management window, you specify that a printer is offline by selecting the "Use printer offline" option from the Printer menu. A check mark indicates that the option is selected. When the printer is offline, the printer does not accept new print jobs but will print existing jobs waiting to print as long as printing is not paused. To designate that a printer is back online, select the "Use printer offline" option a second time. This should remove the checkmark next to the option.

 If a printer is designated as being both offline and paused, you must clear both to restore normal printing operations.

Working with Scanners and Fax Machines

Unlike printers, scanners and fax machines use helper applications when receiving and sending documents. The default helper application is Windows Fax and Scan.

Scanning images

Most scanners have a menu option that allows you to scan images to your computer, to a memory card, or to an email message. With this in mind, you can scan an image by completing the following steps:

1. Put the image you want to scan on the scanner bed.
2. Click the Scan button on the scanner. This should display a Scan menu.
3. On the Scan menu, select the appropriate scanning option, such as Scan to PC, and then press the OK or Start button.

Managing scanned documents

You can access a scanner management window for your scanner by completing these steps:

1. Click Start and then click Control Panel. In the Control Panel, click Hardware and Sound and then click Printers.
2. In the Printers window, double-click the scanner you want to work with.
3. To view scans sent to the computer, click Scan in the Navigation Pane. As shown in Figure 12-17, scans are listed by date, filename, file type, size, and source.
4. You can preview a scan by selecting it in the Documents list.
5. Use the following options on the toolbar to manage the scan:

    Delete
    > Deletes the scan from the computer

    Forward as Fax
    > Forwards the scan as a fax file

    Forward as E-mail
    > Forwards the scan as an attachment to an email message

    Save as
    > Saves the scan to a file on your computer

    Print
    > Prints the scanned document to a printer

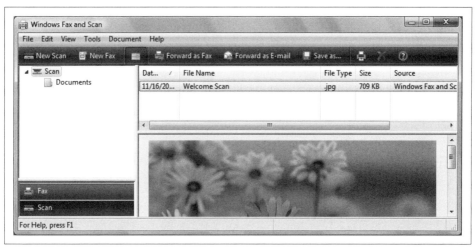

Figure 12-17. Viewing scans sent to the computer

Managing faxed documents

You can access a fax management window for your fax machine by completing these steps:

1. Click Start and then click Control Panel. In the Control Panel, click Hardware and Sound and then click Printers.

2. In the Printers window, double-click the fax machine you want to work with.

3. To view faxes sent or received by the computer, click Fax in the Navigation Pane, as shown in Figure 12-18.

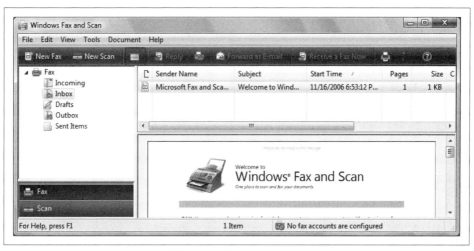

Figure 12-18. Viewing incoming and outgoing faxes

4. In the Navigation Pane, select one of the following to view related options:

   Incoming
   > Shows incoming faxes that are in the process of being received

   Inbox
   > Shows incoming faxes that have been received and are waiting for your attention

   Drafts
   > Shows drafts of faxes that have not been sent

   Outbox
   > Shows outgoing faxes that are in the process of being sent

   Sent Items
   > Shows outgoing faxes that have been sent

5. Use the following options on the toolbar to manage faxes:

   Delete
   > Deletes the fax from the computer

   Forward as Fax
   > Forwards the fax to another fax machine

   Forward as E-Mail
   > Forwards the fax as an attachment to an email message

   Print
   > Prints the faxed document to a printer

You can save a fax as a TIF image file on your computer by following these steps:

1. In Windows Fax and Scan, select the fax you want to save.
2. Click "Save as" on the File menu.
3. In the "Save as" dialog box, select a save location, type a name for the file, and then click Save.

Receiving faxes

Most fax machines will receive faxes automatically if they are connected to a telephone line. If your computer has a fax card or your fax machine can send you faxes directly, the fax should be received automatically into the Inbox of Windows Fax and Scan. In some cases, you may need to tell your computer to receive the fax. In Windows Fax and Scan, you can answer an incoming phone call and receive a fax by clicking the "Receive a Fax Now" button on the toolbar.

CHAPTER 13

Making the Most of Your Computer's Accessories

If you haven't already noticed, let me be the first to tell you that Windows Vista has more accessories than you'll probably ever use. Hidden among all those accessories are some true gems, including the Snipping Tool, a handy utility that you can use to capture screens and windows, and Windows Speech Recognition, a program you can use to dictate documents and control programs using your voice and a microphone. You'll find plenty of extras for both laptops and Tablet PCs too, including the Mobility Center, Pen Flicks, Sticky Notes, Input Panel, and Windows Journal. You'll also find accessories for making your computer more accessible to the handicapped, including the Ease of Access Center, Magnifier, Narrator, and On-Screen Keyboard.

Capturing Screens and Windows with the Snipping Tool

One of my favorite accessories in Windows Vista is the Snipping Tool. The Snipping Tool captures any screen elements that you select, including text and images. A captured element is referred to as a *snip*, and you can insert snips easily into documents and email messages.

Creating Snips

You can open the Snipping Tool by clicking Start, clicking All Programs, clicking Accessories, and then selecting Snipping Tool. The Snipping Tool starts in New Snip mode, which is the mode for capturing snips. The Snipping Tool has four capture modes:

Free-form Snip
> In Free-form Snip mode, you outline the area that you want to snip by drawing freehand around it. You capture a snip in this mode by clicking and then dragging to outline the area you want to capture.

Rectangular Snip
> In Rectangular Snip mode, you outline the area that you want to snip by drawing a rectangle around it. You capture a snip in this mode by clicking and then dragging around the area that you want to capture.

Window Snip

In Window Snip mode, you capture an entire window as a snip. You capture a snip in this mode by moving the mouse pointer over the window that you want to capture, and then clicking.

Full-screen Snip

In Full-screen Snip mode, you capture the full screen as a snip. When you select this mode, the full screen is captured automatically.

Figure 13-1 shows the Snipping Tool in New Snip mode. From left to right, the buttons on the toolbar are used as follows:

New

The New button starts a new capture using the default mode or the last capture mode you used.

Capture Options

The Capture Options button to the right of the New button sets the capture mode.

Cancel

The Cancel button cancels the current capture.

Options

The Options button sets capture options.

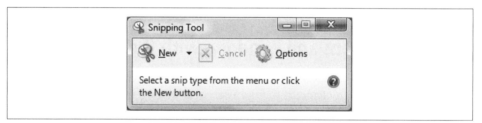

Figure 13-1. Using the Snipping Tool to capture windows and screens

You can capture a snip by following these steps:

1. Click Start, click All Programs, click Accessories, and then select Snipping Tool. The Snipping Tool is displayed in the foreground, and the rest of the screen is brightened automatically to make it easier to distinguish the Snipping Tool interface elements from the background elements you are capturing.

2. Click the Capture Options button and select the capture mode you want to use.

3. Capture your snip. As Figure 13-2 shows, you capture a rectangular snip by clicking and then dragging around the area that you want to capture.

4. When you release the mouse button, the Snipping Tool captures the snip and shows the editing view. You can then use the editing view to edit the snip, as discussed in the next section, "Editing and Saving Your Snips."

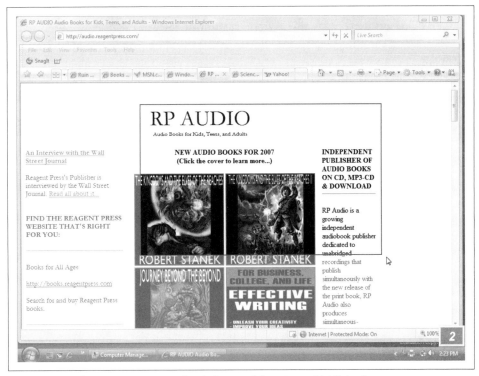

Figure 13-2. Selecting your snip area by clicking and dragging to highlight the area to copy

Editing and Saving Your Snips

After you've captured a snip, the Snipping Tool window changes to Edit Mode. In this mode, you can mark up a snip by using the pen, highlighter, or eraser tool. By default, snips are captured using a single-file Hypertext Markup Language (HTML) format that can recognize separate text and image components. You can also save snips as JPEG, PNG, or GIF image files so that the entire snip is handled as a single picture.

Figure 13-3 shows the Snipping Tool in Edit Mode. From left to right, the buttons on the toolbar are used as follows:

New Snip
> The New Snip button switches to New Snip Mode and discards the current snip. If you click New Snip before saving a snip, the current snip is lost.

Save As
> The Save As button allows you to save the current snip as a single-file HTML document or as a JPEG, PNG, or GIF image.

Copy

The Copy button copies the current version of the snip to the Windows clipboard. You can then paste it into documents or email messages using Ctrl-V.

Send Snip

The Send Snip button allows you to send the snip to someone in an email message. Click the Send Snip Options button to see additional send options, such as "Send to e-mail recipient (as attachment)."

Pen

Clicking the Pen button selects the pen so that you can use it to add notes to the snip. Obviously, this feature works best when you have a pen input device. If you click the Pen Options button, you can set the pen color. The default pen color is blue. To change the ink thickness, change the pen tip type. To select a custom color, click the Customize option.

Highlighter

Clicking the Highlighter button selects the highlighter so that you can use it to highlight areas of the snip.

Eraser

Clicking the Eraser button allows you to erase pen ink and highlights by clicking on them.

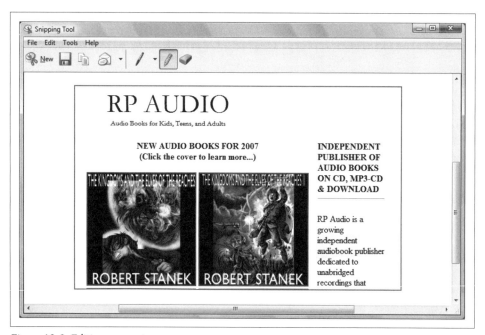

Figure 13-3. Editing your snip

After you edit your snip, you can copy it to the clipboard by clicking Copy and then paste it into a document or email message by accessing the document or message and then pressing Ctrl-V. To save your snip to a file, click Save As. In the Save As dialog box, type a filename for the snip, use the "Save as type" list to select the file type, such as JPEG or PNG, and then click Save.

Setting Snipping Options

By default, any snips you capture have a thick red selection line around them. The selection line is meant to help you distinguish snips from other content if you later add the snips to other documents. You can change the color of the line or stop using the selection line by following these steps:

1. In the Snipping Tool, click Tools and then click Options. This opens the Snipping Tool Options dialog box shown in Figure 13-4.

2. To set the ink color for the selection line, click the "Ink color" list and then choose the color to use.

3. To stop using the selection line, clear the "Show selection ink after snips are captured" checkbox.

4. Click OK.

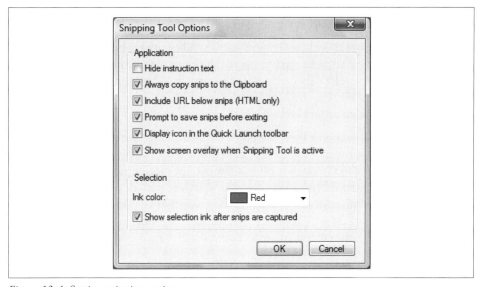

Figure 13-4. Setting snipping options

Getting Your Computer to Listen

If you hear someone talking to his computer, odds are he's not going crazy—he's using Windows Vista's built-in speech recognition software to take his computing experience to the next level. Speech recognition software allows you to dictate documents and email messages. It also allows you to browse the Web and navigate program menus using voice controls. Not only does this allow you to create documents quickly and perform common tasks, but it can also reduce the risk of repetitive stress injuries.

Getting Started with Speech Recognition

You can access Windows Vista's speech recognition software by clicking Start → All Programs → Accessories → Ease of Access, and then selecting Windows Speech Recognition. However, before you do this, you should take a moment to learn more about this powerful feature.

Speech recognition allows you to control your computer by speaking into a microphone. When you talk, the software uses context-sensitive controls to determine whether to convert your words to text, as with dictation, or to navigate program menus, as with control commands. Generally, when you use speech recognition, Windows Vista enters your dictation text into the current active document and your control commands are used to navigate the current active program's menus.

Speech recognition works best when you use a quality microphone, such as a USB headset microphone or an array microphone. The environment in which you use the microphone should be relatively quiet. If it isn't, you may find that background noise is interpreted as spoken speech. A microphone with noise cancellation technology may resolve this problem.

Having started with speech recognition software in the early days of Dragon Dictate, I found the built-in software easy to use and surprisingly reliable. The software provides enhanced user interfaces that offer a simple yet more efficient way to dictate text, make changes, and correct mistakes. The software includes an interactive tutorial that teaches you while you are training the computer to understand your voice. The software also improves in accuracy over time by learning as you use it, and by prompting for clarification when you give a command that can be interpreted in multiple ways.

Windows Speech Recognition isn't designed to handle every type of writing or to work with every type of application. Rather, it is intended for those who frequently use word processing applications, email applications, and web browsers. By using speech recognition with these programs, you can use your voice to enter text and perform commands, thereby significantly reducing the use of the keyboard and mouse.

Speech recognition dictation works only in applications that support the Microsoft Text Services Framework. Applications that support this framework include:

- Microsoft Office Word
- Microsoft Office Outlook
- Microsoft Internet Explorer
- Nearly all applications included with Windows Vista

Speech recognition won't work with applications that don't support the Text Services Framework, such as Microsoft Office PowerPoint, Microsoft Office Excel, and Corel WordPerfect.

Configuring Speech Recognition for First Use

Before you can use Windows Speech Recognition, you must ensure that your computer has a sound card and that the sound card is properly configured. You must then connect a microphone to the sound card's microphone jack. Speaking into the microphone is what triggers the software.

Once you've connected your microphone, you can configure Windows Speech Recognition for first use. However, you won't be able to complete the setup of the software until you've adjusted the microphone volume to a proper level. To adjust the input levels for your microphone, follow these steps:

1. Click Start, and then click Control Panel.
2. In the Control Panel, click Hardware and Sound and then click Sound.
3. In the Sound dialog box, double-click Microphone on the Recording tab.
4. On the Levels tab, use the Microphone slider to adjust the input level for the microphone, as shown in Figure 13-5.
5. On the Custom tab, select the MIC Boost checkbox if you need to boost the input levels for your microphone.
6. Click OK.

Figure 13-5. Setting the audio input levels for your microphone

To set up the speech software for first use, complete the following steps:

1. Click Start, click All Programs, and then click Accessories.

2. Click Ease of Access, and then click Speech Recognition. This starts the Set up Speech Recognition Wizard.

3. On the Welcome to Speech Recognition page, read the introductory text and then click Next.

4. On the Select the "Type of microphone you would like to use" page, shown in Figure 13-6, select the type of microphone you are using.

Figure 13-6. Selecting the type of microphone you are using

5. On the "Set up your microphone" page, follow the instructions for setting up and positioning your microphone. Different directions are provided for each type of microphone. Click Next.

6. On the "Adjust the microphone volume" page, shown in Figure 13-7, read the sample text aloud into your microphone. Adjust the microphone volume if the levels are too low or too high.

7. Click Next twice. On the "Improve speech recognition accuracy" page, specify whether the speech recognition software should scan your documents and email messages to learn the words and phrases you use. If you want to enable this feature, click "Enable document review." Otherwise, click "Disable document review" to turn off this feature. Click Next.

8. On the "Print the speech reference card" page, click "View reference sheet." In Windows Help and Support, click Print to print out the reference sheet.

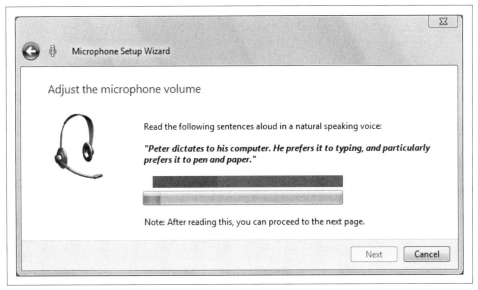

Figure 13-7. Reading the sample to check the input levels

9. In the Set up Speech Recognition Wizard, click Next twice and then click Start Tutorial.

10. Follow the prompts and work your way through the tutorial. While you are learning about speech recognition, Windows Speech Recognition will also train the computer to recognize your voice.

Using Speech Recognition for Dictation

The most common way you'll use speech recognition is for dictating documents. You dictate documents by following these general steps:

1. Start your word processing application.

2. Create a new document or open an existing document.

3. Dictate the document.

4. Save the document.

In Microsoft Office Word or WordPad, you can use speech recognition to perform these tasks by following these steps:

1. If speech recognition is not running, start it. Click Start, click All Programs, and then click Accessories. Click Ease of Access, and then click Speech Recognition.

2. Say "start listening."

3. Say "open Word" to open Microsoft Office Word or "open WordPad" to open WordPad.

4. Start dictating. Use the spoken-word commands for punctuation marks and special characters as necessary. For example, to insert a comma, you say "comma." To end a sentence with a period, you say "period."

5. To correct mistakes, say "correct" and the word that the computer typed by mistake. Select the correct word from the list offered, or say the correct word again. For example, if the computer misrecognized days as daze, say "correct daze," and then select the right word from the list or say the word "days" again.

6. To save the document, say "file," say "save as," and then say the name of the document, such as "My Shopping List." Finish by saying "save."

Using Laptop and Tablet PC Extras

All laptop computers include the Mobility Center for optimizing laptop settings. When you are working with laptops, you may also need to connect to a network project, and there's an option for this, too. When you are working with Tablet PCs, you'll find even more accessories, including tools for configuring Tablet PC pens, Input Panel for entering text using a pen, Sticky Notes for taking notes using a pen, and Windows Journal for creating journal entries using a pen.

 Tablet PC extras are provided as Windows features that you can turn on and off. Click Start → Control Panel. In the Control Panel, click Programs. Click "Turn on or off Windows features." This displays the Windows Features dialog box. Select or clear Tablet PC Optional Components as appropriate, and then click OK.

Navigating the Windows Mobility Center

The Windows Mobility Center provides a central console for accessing the most commonly used mobile PC settings. On a laptop or Tablet PC, you can access the Mobility Center by right-clicking the Power icon in the taskbar's notification area and then selecting Mobility Center. However, if you've disabled the display of the Power icon, you won't be able to access it on the taskbar. Instead, click Start and then click Control Panel. In the Control Panel, click Additional Options or Mobile PC as appropriate for your computer, and then click Mobility Center.

As Figure 13-8 shows, each configurable mobile PC setting is managed through a separate control tile. Generally, control tiles allow you to make direct adjustments to your mobile PC settings by using available options such as a toggle button to turn presentation settings on and off, or a slider to adjust the brightness of the screen.

The control tiles available depend on the type of mobile PC and the mobile PC manufacturer. Typically, laptops have seven standard control tiles and Tablet PCs have either seven or eight standard control tiles. The most common control tiles are:

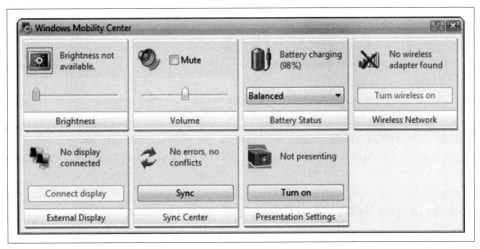

Figure 13-8. Managing laptop settings

Brightness

Displays the current brightness setting. If brightness is configurable on your computer, you can use the slider provided to adjust the brightness of the display.

Volume

Displays the current volume setting. If volume is configurable on your computer, you can use the slider provided to adjust the volume.

Battery Status

Displays the status of the computer's battery. You can use the selection list provided to change quickly from one power plan to another. If you've created custom power plans, these are available as well.

Wireless Network

Displays the status of your wireless network connection. Click "Turn wireless on" to enable your wireless connection for use.

External Display

Provides options for connecting a secondary display to give a presentation. If a secondary display is available and you've connected the cables, you can click "Connect display" to connect to the display.

Sync Center

Displays the status of file synchronization. Click Sync to start a new sync using Sync Center.

Presentation Settings

Displays whether you are in presentation mode. In presentation mode, the display and hard disk do not go into sleep mode due to inactivity. Click "Turn on" to enter presentation mode.

Tablet Display

Displays the current display orientation. Click "Change orientation" to change from landscape to portrait display or vice versa.

If your mobile PC includes other control tiles, these were probably provided by the PC manufacturer. You can learn more about these control tiles from the documentation that came with your mobile PC, or by visiting the manufacturer's web site.

Connecting to Networked Projectors

At the office, you may find that your meeting rooms and conference centers have networked projectors set up for use during presentations. To use this type of projector, you must connect your laptop or Tablet PC to the local area network (LAN) and then connect to the project over the network. In most cases, connecting your computer to the network is as simple as plugging in an Ethernet cable or ensuring that you are using the correct wireless network connection.

Once you are connected to the network in the conference or meeting room you are using, you can connect to the networked projector by completing the following steps:

1. Click Start, click All Programs, click Accessories, and then click Connect to a Network Projector.

2. The first time you use a network projector with your laptop, you'll see a warning prompt about Windows Firewall, as shown in Figure 13-9. To use the projector, you must allow Windows Vista to communicate through Windows Firewall, so click Yes.

3. Next, specify how you want to connect to the projector, as shown in Figure 13-10.

4. If you want to select from projectors found on the local network, click "Search for a projector." The wizard searches for projectors on the network and returns its results along with a list of any projectors you've used recently. Click the projector you want to use, provide the access password for the projector if necessary, and then click Connect.

5. If you know the network address of the projector, click Enter the "Projector address." On the "Enter the network address of a projector" page, shown in Figure 13-11, type the network address of the projector, such as *http://intranet.theoffice.local/projectors/projector4*. Enter any required access password, and then click Connect.

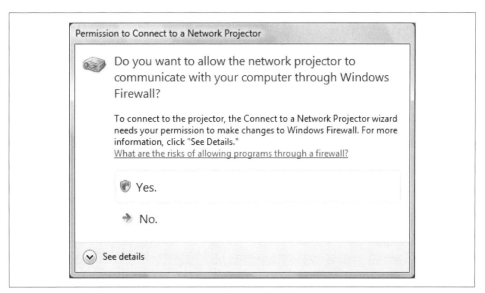

Figure 13-9. Allowing your computer to communicate with the projector

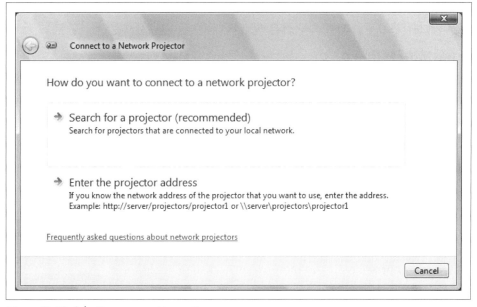

Figure 13-10. Selecting a connection option

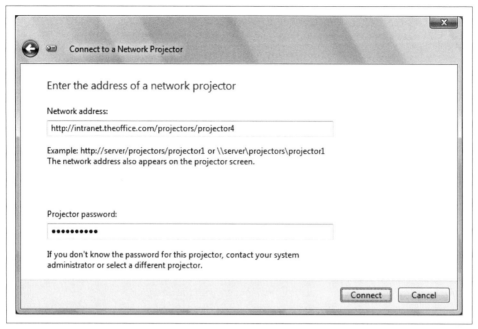

Figure 13-11. Entering the projector address and password

Using Your Tablet PC Pen

Tablet PCs use pens as input devices. You can use pens for writing as well as for interacting with items on the screen by tapping and flicking. To ensure that your Tablet PC recognizes your tapping and flicking actions, you should take a few minutes to configure the related options.

Tapping your pen

Pen taps allow you to perform actions equivalent to using a mouse. You can perform the following actions:

- Double-tapping the pen on the screen is equivalent to a double-click mouse action.
- Pressing and holding the pen to the screen is equivalent to a right-click mouse action, or pressing the pen button to perform a right-click.
- On some Tablet PC pens, you can grip the top of the pen to erase ink from the screen.

You can set pen tap options by following these steps:

1. Click Start, and then click Control Panel.
2. In the Control Panel, click Hardware and Sound, scroll down, and then click Pen and Input Devices. This displays the Pen and Input Devices dialog box with the Pen Options tab selected, as shown in Figure 13-12.

Figure 13-12. Setting Tablet PC pen options

3. To configure double-tapping, click "Double-tap" in the "Pen action" section and then click Settings. As Figure 13-13 shows, you can then adjust how quickly you can tap the screen and the distance the pointer can move between tapping. Use the test area provided to test your settings. Fine-tune your settings as necessary and then click OK.

4. To configure pressing and holding, click "Press and hold" in the "Pen action" section and then click Settings. As Figure 13-13 shows, you can then change the amount of time you must press and hold the pen to the screen to perform the equivalent of a right-click, and the amount of time to perform the right-click action. Use the test area provided to test your settings. Fine-tune your settings as necessary and then click OK.

5. To open Input Panel automatically when you move the pen quickly from side to side while it is positioned slightly above the screen, click Start Tablet PC Input Panel in the "Pen action" section and then click Settings. Select the "Enable start input panel gesture" checkbox. Use the slider to specify the relative distance you must move the pen from side to side, and then click OK.

6. To allow clicking the pen button to be used as a right-click equivalent, select the "Use the pen button as a right-click equivalent" checkbox.

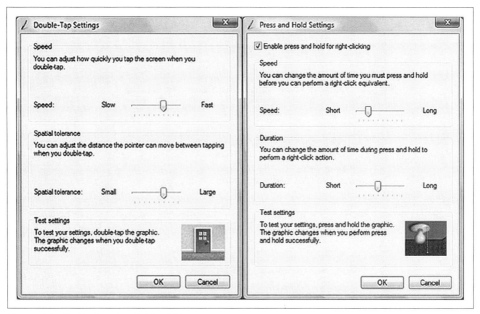

Figure 13-13. Configuring Tablet PC pen settings

7. To allow erasing ink by gripping the top of the pen (if supported) select the "Use the top of the pen to erase ink" checkbox.

8. Click OK to save the settings.

Each tapping action of the pen is accompanied by some type of visual feedback. To view or change visual feedback options, follow these steps:

1. Click Start, and then click Control Panel.

2. In the Control Panel, click Hardware and Sound, scroll down, and then click Pen and Input Devices.

3. In the Pen and Input Devices dialog box, click the Pointer Options tab, as shown in Figure 13-14.

4. A different type of visual feedback is provided for each pen tap action. If you don't want to see visual feedback for a tap action, clear the related checkbox.

5. If you don't want pen cursors to be shown instead of mouse cursors when you use the pen, clear the "Show pen cursors instead of mouse cursors when I use my pen" checkbox.

6. Click OK to save the settings.

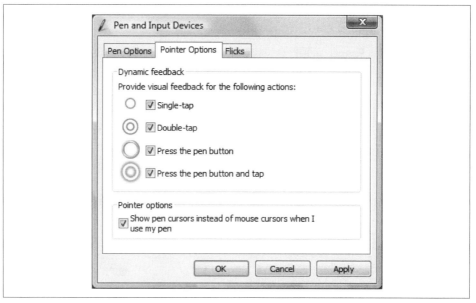

Figure 13-14. Configuring visual feedback

Flicking your pen

Pen flicks allow you to perform navigation and editing actions by flicking the pen in a specific direction. Only navigational flicks are enabled by default.

The navigational flicks are as follows:

- Flick left to go back—equivalent to clicking the Back button in Windows Explorer or Internet Explorer.
- Flick right to go forward—equivalent to clicking the Forward button in Windows Explorer or Internet Explorer.
- Flick up to drag up—equivalent to dragging a selected item up or to using a scroll bar to scroll up the page in an extended document or the browser window.
- Flick down to drag down—equivalent to dragging a selected item down or to using a scroll bar to scroll down the page in an extended document or the browse window.

The editing flicks you can enable are as follows:

- Flick up and to the right to copy a selected item to the clipboard.
- Flick down and to the right to paste a previously selected item into a document or email message.
- Flick up and to the left to delete a selected item.
- Flick down and to the left to undo a previous action.

You can set pen flick options by following these steps:

1. Click Start, and then click Control Panel.

2. In the Control Panel, click Hardware and Sound, scroll down, and then click Pen and Input Devices.

3. In the Pen and Input Devices dialog box, select the Flicks tab, as shown in Figure 13-15.

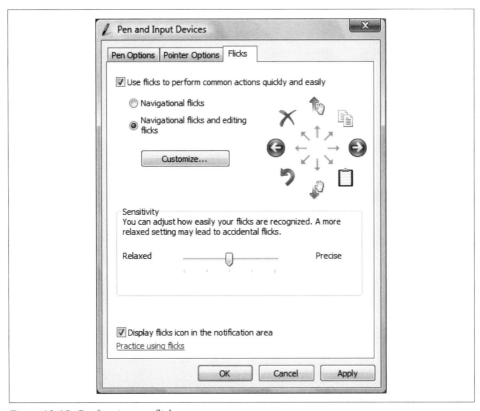

Figure 13-15. Configuring pen flicks

4. To enable flicks, select the "Use flicks to perform common actions quickly and easily" checkbox. Clear this checkbox to disable flicks.

5. When flicks are enabled, use the options provided to enable only navigational flicks or both navigational and editing flicks.

6. If you've enabled both navigational and editing flicks, you can click Customize to define alternative actions for each possible pen flick. Any alternative actions override the default actions.

7. Use the Sensitivity slider to adjust how easily pen flicks are recognized. In most cases, you'll want the sensitivity to be midway between Relaxed and Precise. However, if you are having issues with accidental flicks, you may want to use a more precise setting.

8. Click OK to save the settings.

Writing with your Tablet PC pen

When you are using a Tablet PC, you can enter text using the Tablet PC pen and a utility program called Input Panel. Input Panel converts to typed text any handwriting you enter using the pen, and it supports AutoComplete, Back-of-Pen erase, and scratch-out gestures.

On a Tablet PC, the Input Panel icon is displayed next to text entry areas in programs that accept handwriting input from a Tablet PC pen. With Microsoft Office Word, Windows Mail, and other Windows programs, this allows you to display Input Panel by tapping the icon. You can then use the pen to write and insert the converted text by clicking the Insert button. In Input Panel, the Insert button is displayed below and to the right of your converted text. You can also start Input Panel by selecting Start → All Programs → Accessories → Tablet PC, and then selecting Tablet PC Input Panel.

Input Panel has changed in several ways since it was introduced with Microsoft Windows XP Tablet PC Edition. When you run Input Panel, it appears as a tab on the left side of the screen. To open Input Panel, move the mouse pointer over the tab and then click to slide Input Panel out from the edge of the screen. Clicking the Close button hides Input Panel.

By default, Input Panel floats in a separate window. You can move Input Panel by dragging it to a desired position or by docking it at the top or bottom of the screen. If you then hide Input Panel, it will slide out from the same location the next time you open it. The Input Panel tab on the side of your screen remains available even if the program you are using is running in full-screen mode.

Input Panel has three input modes:

Writing Pad Mode
> Use Writing Pad Mode, shown in Figure 13-16, when you want to write continuously with the pen as though you are writing on a lined sheet of paper. Each word you write is converted to text separately and then displayed. If you click the word, you can correct letter case, change punctuation around the word, modify the letters, or delete letters. The buttons on the right provide quick access to common functions. Click Num to display the number pad, which contains the digits 0 through 9 and arithmetic symbols. Click Sym to display the symbols pad, which contains options for the most commonly used characters. Click Web to display the web pad, which contains character shortcut options for entering URLs.

Figure 13-16. The writing pad

Character Pad Mode

Use Character Pad Mode, shown in Figure 13-17, to enter single letters, digits, and symbols. Each character you write is converted to text separately. Clicking below a character displays an options menu with a list of related characters, such as those that are alternatives to the character you've entered or are frequently confused with the character you've entered. The buttons on the right provide quick access to common functions, as discussed previously.

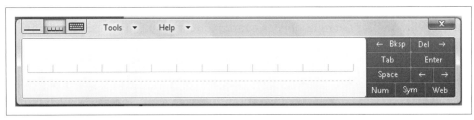

Figure 13-17. The character pad

On-Screen Keyboard Mode

Use On-Screen Keyboard Mode, shown in Figure 13-18, to display an on-screen keyboard that allows you to use pen taps to select characters, press function keys, or click a special-purpose key, such as Home, Page Up, or Insert. To use the function keys, you must first tap the Func key. Also, note that the Ctrl, Windows, and Alt keys are provided, allowing you to enter keystroke combinations, such as Ctrl-Alt-Delete, by tapping each required key. Between the right Alt key and the right Ctrl key, you'll find a properties button. Clicking this button is the equivalent of right-clicking and selecting Properties in the active window.

Figure 13-18. The on-screen keyboard

With Input Panel, AutoComplete works much like AutoComplete in other Microsoft programs. As you enter text, AutoComplete lists possible matches based on items that you've entered before. If an item in the list matches the text that you want to enter, simply tap the suggestion to enter it in the text entry area.

You can enable and disable AutoComplete and other Input Panel options by following these steps:

1. In Input Panel, click Tools, and then click Options. This opens the Options dialog box shown in Figure 13-19.

2. On the Settings tab, clear the "Suggest matches in Input Panel when possible…" checkbox.

3. Optionally configure where the Insert button appears and how it works.

4. Click OK.

Figure 13-19. Configuring Input Panel options

Back-of-Pen Erase allows Input Panel to support Tablet PC pens that have erasers. If the Tablet PC pen has an erase function, you can use the eraser to delete entries from Input Panel. Another way to delete entries is to use scratch-out gestures. As in Windows XP, the Windows Vista Input Panel supports the Z-shaped scratch-out gesture. If you draw a Z over an entry or a series of entries, the entry or entries are deleted.

Windows Vista supports these scratch-out gestures as well:

Strikethrough scratch-out
> Delete entries by drawing a horizontal line across an entry or a series of entries. You can draw the horizontal line from right to left or left to right.

Angled scratch-out
> Delete entries by drawing a line at an angle across an entry or a series of entries. You can draw the line at an angle from the upper right to the lower left or from the upper left to the lower right.

Vertical scratch-out
> Delete entries by drawing an *M* or a *W* over an entry or a series of entries. The *M* or *W* should be larger than the entries you are deleting.

Circular scratch-out
> Delete entries by drawing a circle over an entry or a series of entries. You can draw the circle around or within the entries.

If you'd rather use only the Z-shaped scratch-out, you can disable the other types of scratch-out gestures. Follow these steps to configure gestures that you can use:

1. In Input Panel, click Tools, and then click Options.

2. In the Options dialog box, select the Gestures tab shown in Figure 13-20.

3. Configure the way gestures are used by doing one of the following:

   - To allow all scratch-out gestures, select "All scratch-out and strikethrough gestures."

   - To allow only Z-shaped gestures, select "Only the Z-shaped scratch-out gesture...."

   - To disable all scratch-out gestures, select "No scratch-out or strikethrough gestures."

4. Click OK.

Creating Sticky Notes

Love the Notes gadget for Windows Sidebar, but wish it could do more? Well, Sticky Notes might be exactly what you are looking for. Sticky Notes provides a scratch pad in which you can record both written and voice memos. Because any sticky notes you create remain in the stack of sticky notes until you delete them, you don't have to worry about losing notes when you log off or shut down your computer.

You can start Sticky Notes by clicking Start → All Programs → Accessories → Tablet PC, and then selecting Sticky Notes. As shown in Figure 13-21, Sticky Notes gives you a scratch pad on which you can write notes using the pen. You can create a new note by clicking the New Note button. To add to the current scratch pad, simply use the pen to write the text of the note.

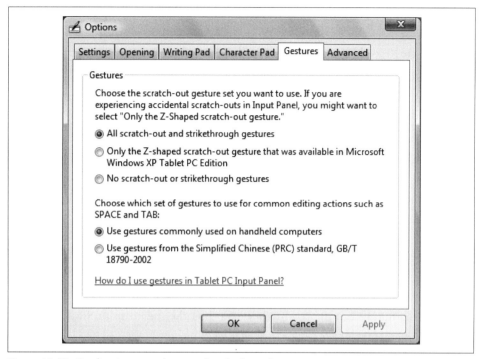

Figure 13-20. Configuring scratch-out and strikethrough gestures

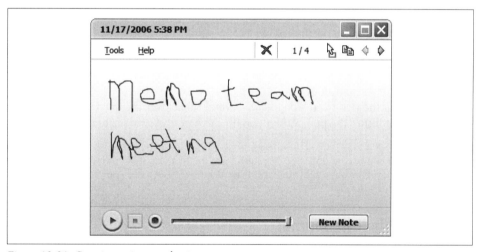

Figure 13-21. Creating written and voice memos

If you've connected a microphone to your computer, you can dictate and work with voice memos by following these steps:

1. Click the Record button to start recording your voice note.
2. Dictate your memo into your microphone.
3. Click Stop to stop recording.
4. Click Play to play back your voice memo.

With a recorded voice memo, you can also:

- Click and drag the Locate slider to move forward or backward through your memo, and then press Play to resume playback.
- Play back your voice memo from the beginning by clicking Stop and then clicking Play.

As you add notes, your stack of sticky notes grows. You can navigate the stack by using the Previous Note and Next Note buttons on the toolbar. You can drag a written note from the notepad and insert it into a document as an image by following these steps:

1. Click the Drag and Drop button on the toolbar.
2. Hold the mouse button down while you drag the memo from Sticky Notes to your document.
3. Release the mouse button when the pointer is at the appropriate location in your document.

An alternative to using drag and drop is to copy a written note to the clipboard by clicking the Copy button on the toolbar. In an application, such as Microsoft Office Word, you can then use the paste function to insert the note as an image.

If you no longer want a sticky note, click the Delete button (the red *X*) on the toolbar, and then confirm the action by clicking Yes. Rather than deleting notes, you can erase notes by moving the pen from side to side several times over the entries that you want to erase without lifting the pen. When you lift the pen, the entries are removed.

 If you use Sticky Notes regularly, you might want Sticky Notes to run automatically each time you start Windows Vista and log on. To do this, click Tools, click Options, and then select Open at Startup.

Creating a Windows Journal

Another Tablet PC extra is Windows Journal. Windows Journal gives you a virtual journal that you can use with the Tablet PC pen in much the same way you would use a stationery pad and an ink pen. You may prefer Windows Journal to Sticky Notes when you are writing longer notes and memos with the Tablet PC pen.

You can open Windows Journal by clicking Start → All Programs → Accessories → Tablet PC, and then selecting Windows Journal. The first time you start Windows

Journal you'll be prompted to install the Journal Note Writer print driver. When prompted, click Install to allow Windows Vista to install the driver. When Windows Vista finishes installing the driver, click Close. By installing the driver, you ensure that you can navigate, print, annotate, and share your journal.

As shown in Figure 13-22, the Windows Journal main window looks like a notepad with lined paper, and you can use the Tablet PC pen to write your notes directly on the paper. Using Windows Journal is similar to using Sticky Notes. Your journal can have a stack of pages just like a real journal. When a journal has multiple pages, you can navigate pages by clicking and dragging the scroll bar down and up. Beneath the scroll bar are several buttons:

Previous
Displays the previous page. You can also display the previous page by pressing Page Up on the keyboard. If you're on the first page of the journal, this button is dimmed.

Next
Displays the next page. You can also display the next page by pressing Page Down on the keyboard. If you're on the last page of the journal, this button is replaced by the New Page button.

New Page
Creates a new page. This button works only if you're on the last page of the journal and you've written on the page.

Using the pen, you can convert handwriting to text, edit converted text, and copy converted text to the clipboard. This allows you to use handwriting entered into Windows Journal as text in other programs. To copy handwriting as text and edit it, follow these steps:

1. Click the Selection Tool button on the toolbar or choose Selection Tool on the Edit menu.
2. Press and hold the pen to the screen.
3. Drag the pen around the handwriting you want to select.
4. Right-click the selection and then choose Copy as Text. Windows Journal converts the handwriting to text automatically and then displays the Copy as Text dialog box, as shown in Figure 13-23.
5. In the Copy as Text dialog box, tap a word or character that you want to correct and then choose a replacement from the Alternative list as necessary.
6. Click Copy to copy the text to the clipboard.

When working with Windows Journal, you might also want to insert a page before the current page. To insert a page before the current page, click New Page on the Insert menu. The Insert menu also has options for inserting text boxes, flags, and pictures. You use a text box to insert typed text. You use a flag to mark a part of the journal with a flag icon. To insert a picture, follow these steps:

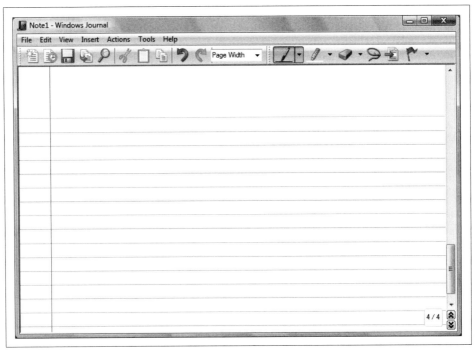

Figure 13-22. Creating a journal to take notes

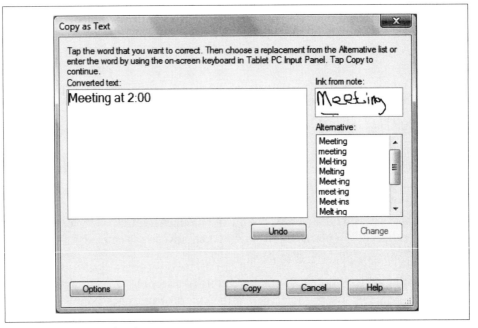

Figure 13-23. Copying handwriting as text

1. In Windows Journal, click Insert and then click Picture.

2. In the Insert Picture dialog box, select the picture to insert and then click Insert. Pictures can be in JPEG, GIF, PNG, WMF, EMF, or BMP format.

3. The selected picture is inserted into the journal and selected so that you can click it and drag it within the journal.

4. After you drag the picture to the desired location, you can drop the picture in that location by clicking another part of the journal.

5. If you later want to move the picture, choose the Selection Tool option on the Edit menu and then click the picture to select it. You can then drag and drop the picture in a new location.

Windows Journal uses a college-ruled notepad as the default stationery style. You can change to other stationery as well. To do this, follow these steps:

1. In Windows Journal, click Options on the Tools menu.

2. On the Stationery panel, make sure that the Stationery option is selected, and then click Default Page Setup.

3. In the Default Page Setup dialog box, click the Style tab, as shown in Figure 13-24.

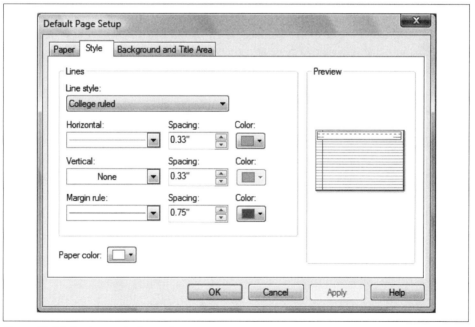

Figure 13-24. Setting up the journal pages

4. Use the "Line style" list to choose the style to use. Options include Standard ruled, Narrow ruled, Wide ruled, Large grid, Small grid, and Blank.

5. Use the Horizontal list to select the style for horizontal lines on the paper and the related Color list to select a line color.

6. Use the Vertical list to select the style for vertical lines on the paper and the related Color list to select a line color.

7. Use the "Margin rule" list to select the style for margin rule lines on the paper and the related Color list to select a line color.

8. Use the "Paper color" list to select a background color for the paper.

9. Click OK twice.

Making Your Computer More Accessible

Windows Vista's accessibility tools are designed mainly to help users who have some form of visual or motor impairment. Still, users without such impairments can sometimes benefit from using them as well.

Using the Ease of Access Center

In Windows Vista, all accessibility tools are accessible from the Ease of Access page in the Control Panel. To display this page, as shown in Figure 13-25, click Start, click Control Panel, click Ease of Access, and then click Ease of Access Center. The Ease of Access page has three main areas:

Quick access to common tools
> Use these options to turn common accessibility features on and off. These features include High Contrast, Narrator, Magnifier, and On-Screen Keyboard utilities. By default, Windows Vista uses the Narrator feature to read these options aloud and automatically highlights each option in turn. When an option is highlighted, you can press the Space bar to select it.

Get recommendations…
> When you click the "Get recommendations…" link, Windows Vista starts a Recommendation Wizard that is similar to, but more intuitive than, the Accessibility Wizard in Windows XP. The five questions in this Recommendation Wizard are designed to help Windows Vista determine and suggest the best accessibility options for you to use.

Explore all settings
> If you don't want to use the Recommendation Wizard, you can use the additional options provided to find related settings that might improve accessibility. You can optimize the computer for the blind, optimize the visual display to make it easier to see, set up alternative input devices, adjust settings for the mouse and keyboard, use text or visual alternatives to sounds, and adjust settings for easier reading and typing.

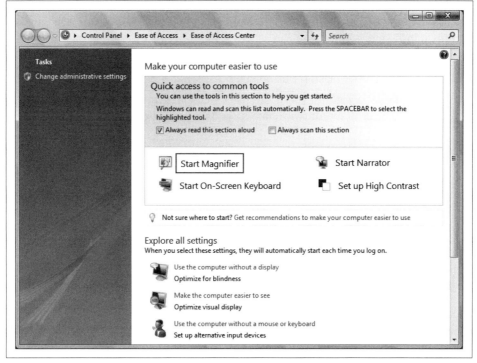

Figure 13-25. Configuring accessibility options for your computer

Using the Magnifier

The Magnifier enlarges part of the screen in a separate window to make it easier for those with limited vision to work with a computer. By default, the Magnifier window is docked at the top of the screen and displays the area around the cursor, the text you are editing, or the focus of the keyboard. You can resize the Magnifier window by moving the mouse pointer over the edge of the window and then dragging the window border. If you move the mouse pointer over the Magnifier window, you can click and drag the window to make it float.

You can turn on and use the Magnifier by completing these steps:

1. Click Start, and then click Control Panel.
2. In the Control Panel, click Ease of Access and then click Ease of Access Center.
3. Click Start Magnifier. As you move the mouse pointer to a desired area of the screen, the current position is shown magnified.

To exit the Magnifier and prevent it from starting automatically, follow these steps:

1. Click the Magnifier taskbar button. This displays a Properties dialog box.
2. Click File and then click Exit. Alternatively, click the Magnifier window and then press Alt-X.

While the Magnifier is running, you can increase magnification by pressing the Ctrl key and the equals sign (=) key, or decrease magnification by pressing the Ctrl key and the minus sign (–) key. You can set Magnifier options by completing the following steps:

1. Click the Magnifier taskbar button. This displays a Properties dialog box.
2. Use the "Scale factor" list to set the magnification level of the Magnifier window. The default scale is 2×, or twice normal, and you can select a value as high as 16×.
3. To reverse the colors on the screen, select the "Invert colors" checkbox.
4. By default, the Magnifier is docked at the top of the screen. Using the "Dock position" list, you can set the dock position as Top, Bottom, Left, or Right. If you want the Magnifier window to float rather than be docked, clear the Docked checkbox.
5. When you have finished configuring your settings, click Hide to close the Properties dialog box. Your preferences are remembered each time you start and use the Magnifier.

Using the On-Screen Keyboard

The On-Screen Keyboard is designed to make it easier to use a mouse or an alternative input device for typing. Similar to Input Panel, characters typed on the On-Screen Keyboard are inserted into the current application.

You can turn on the On-Screen Keyboard by completing these steps:

1. Click Start, and then click Control Panel.
2. In the Control Panel, click Ease of Access and then click Ease of Access Center.
3. Click Start On-Screen Keyboard.

To exit the On-Screen Keyboard and prevent it from starting automatically, click File and then click Exit.

When the keyboard is on, as shown in Figure 13-26, use the mouse, pen, or other input device to select characters, press function keys, or click a special-purpose key, such as Home, Page Up, or Insert. Ctrl, Windows, and Alt keys are provided, allowing you to enter keystroke combinations, such as Ctrl-Alt-Delete, by clicking each required key. Between the right Windows logo key and the right Ctrl key, you'll find a Properties button. Clicking this button is the equivalent of right-clicking and selecting Properties in the active window.

By default, the keyboard is configured to type characters when you click the keys. You can also configure the keyboard to use hovering to select characters or to accept input from a joystick. With hovering, you move the pointer over a character for a specified period, such as 1 second, to select that character. With a joystick, you move the joystick and then click the joystick button when over a character to select that character.

Figure 13-26. Using the On-Screen Keyboard to input text, and pressing keys using a mouse, joystick, or Tablet PC pen

You can configure the way characters are selected by completing the following steps:

1. In the On-Screen Keyboard, select Typing Mode on the Settings menu.

2. In the Typing Mode dialog box, shown in Figure 13-27, choose an appropriate typing mode.

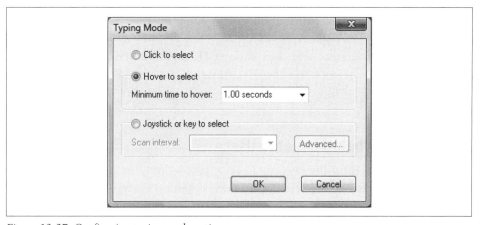

Figure 13-27. Configuring typing mode options

3. To click to select a key, choose "Click to select."

4. To hover to select a key, choose "Hover to select" and then set the minimum hover time, such as 1.00 seconds.

5. To use a joystick to select a key, choose "Joystick or key to select" and then set the interval at which Windows Vista scans for button presses on the joystick, such as 0.50 seconds.

6. Click OK to save your settings. Your preferences are remembered each time you start and use the On-Screen Keyboard.

Using Narrator

Narrator is a text-to-speech program that reads aloud what is displayed on the screen as you navigate the keyboard. You can use the program to read aloud users' keystrokes, system messages, menu commands, and dialog box options.

You can turn on Narrator by completing these steps:

1. Click Start, and then click Control Panel.
2. In the Control Panel, click Ease of Access and then click Ease of Access Center.
3. Click Start Narrator.

To exit Narrator and prevent it from starting automatically, click File and then click Exit.

Narrator's default voice is Microsoft Anna. You can configure Narrator using the following techniques:

- By clicking the Voice Settings button in the Microsoft Narrator window, you can modify the speed, volume, and pitch of the default voice.

- By default, Narrator echoes user keystrokes, announces both system messages and scroll notifications, and automatically monitors screen elements. You can use the Preferences menu options to toggle these options on and off.

- By selecting Preferences and then clicking "Background message settings," you can configure whether and when background messages are discarded if they have not been presented to the user. By default, messages are discarded after 30 seconds.

Making the Keyboard Easier to Use

For those who have difficulty pressing keys on keyboards or reading on-screen text, Windows Vista includes several other useful accessibility features to make the keyboard easier to use. To access and turn on these features, complete the following steps:

1. Click Start, and then click Control Panel.
2. In the Control Panel, click Ease of Access and then click Ease of Access Center.
3. In the Ease of Access Center, under Explore All Settings, click "Make the keyboard easier to use." This displays the "Make the keyboard easier to use" page, shown in Figure 13-28.
4. The Mouse Keys feature lets you move the mouse around the screen using the left, right, up, and down arrows on the numeric keypad. To enable Mouse Keys, select the "Turn on Mouse Keys" checkbox.

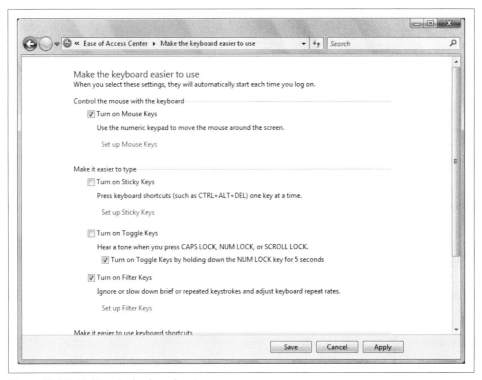

Figure 13-28. Making the keyboard easier to use

5. The Sticky Keys feature lets you press key combinations, such as Ctrl-Alt-Delete, one key at a time. Modifier keys are locked and selected automatically if you press them twice in a row. To enable Sticky Keys, select the "Turn on Sticky Keys" checkbox.

6. The Toggle Keys feature plays a warning tone whenever you press the Caps Lock, Num Lock, or Scroll Lock key. To enable Toggle Keys, select the "Turn on Toggle Keys" checkbox.

7. The Filter Keys feature lets you automatically filter unintentional keystrokes. When this feature is enabled, you must press and hold a key for a specific length of time before it is accepted or repeated. To turn on Filter Keys, select the "Turn on Filter Keys" checkbox.

8. Click Save to save and apply your settings.

PART III

Connecting and Networking

CHAPTER 14

Setting Up Your Network

One of the best features of today's computers is their capability to connect to and communicate with one another over networks. Whether you are working at home, at the office, or away from home, you might want to set up a network, too. Setting up a network allows you to connect your computer to other computers so that you can easily share files, media, and devices. You might also want to set up a network to connect your computer to your Xbox, TiVo, and other devices, such as a network printer.

For Windows Vista, Microsoft has introduced new networking tools that replace the tools used in earlier releases of Windows. While there are many changes, the earlier functionality has remained, and new features have been added. Before diving into the specifics of the new networking features, I'll discuss the essentials of setting up a home or small-business network for use with wired and wireless networks. If you run into problems setting up your networking, see the troubleshooting tips at the end of this chapter.

Understanding Home and Small-Business Networks

With a small investment in time and resources, you can set up a home or small-business network to connect multiple computers and devices together to share files, media, and resources. Unlike a network at a larger organization that uses Active Directory domains, your network will use peer-to-peer networking, with each computer configured as part of the same workgroup or separate workgroups. In a workgroup configuration, member computers can connect to and communicate with one another and with other devices on the network. When you want to access resources on remote computers over the network, you'll need to have a logon account on that computer or other appropriate logon credentials. If other people want to connect to your computer, they'll need a logon account on your computer or other appropriate logon credentials as well.

Requirements for Building a Small Network

Every computer you want to connect to your network requires a network interface card (NIC), also called a *network adapter*. Some motherboard manufacturers include a network adapter on the board, making connecting to a network very easy. You can purchase additional network adapters at any office supply store or computer hardware supplier. Ethernet is the single most common network standard in the world, and integrated network adapters always fall into this category. Additional network standards exist, and they work very well with Windows Vista, but Ethernet has the most use. This chapter only discusses its use as a network medium for shared network resources.

Networking machines together requires several different items to allow the functionality you desire. Table 14-1 lists the different requirements and functionality of the components available.

Table 14-1. Small-network functionality requirements

Hardware	Internal network	Internet connectivity	Internal network with Internet	Internal network with secure Internet
Network cables	X	X	X	X
Network cards	X	X	X	X
Cable/DSL modem		X	X	X
Ethernet router	X		X	X
Firewall				X

As the table shows, you can set up an isolated internal network using network cables, network cards, and an Ethernet router. I recommend an Ethernet router over a hub or switch to allow you to connect your network to the Internet later, without having to purchase an Ethernet router. As an example, the D-Link Ethernet Broadband router has four Ethernet ports for connecting your computers and network devices, and an additional port for connecting to the Internet. The LinkSys Wireless G Broadband router has four Ethernet ports for connecting your computers and network devices, wireless connection capability, and an additional port for connecting to the Internet.

You can create a simple network to connect your computer to the Internet using a network card, two network cables, and a cable/DSL modem. Typically, your ISP will supply the necessary cable/DSL modem.

By merging the components required for an internal network with those that are required for connecting to the Internet, you could create an internal network with Internet connectivity. This type of network would allow multiple computers to share resources and to connect to the Internet through your ISP's cable/DSL modem. While most ISPs will allow you to connect multiple computers to the Internet through their cable/DSL service, some won't, and you might need to purchase a service upgrade to allow this type of connectivity.

For secure connectivity to the Internet, you'll need a firewall. While Windows Vista includes Windows Firewall, this software firewall protects only your computer. It doesn't protect the other computers or devices on your network. Both of the broadband Ethernet routers mentioned previously include a hardware firewall, which will fully protect your network.

 On a home or small-business network, you shouldn't stop using Windows Firewall just because your network has a firewall. In most cases, your computer still needs the protection Windows Firewall offers.

You can expand your home or small-business network beyond the ports on your Ethernet router by connecting network hubs or switches to the router instead of individual computers or devices. Hubs and switches work in a similar manner, allowing computers or devices to connect to a network. While each allows a central point of connectivity, hubs and switches work in different ways.

Hubs send all packets transmitted on the network to each host, making connectivity very simple. The downside of hubs falls directly on their inability to send packets to only a single host, which forces shared connectivity to each host connected to the hub. This drastically decreases the amount of available bandwidth to transmit data. If you have a 100 Mbps hub with 10 hosts connected, each host has approximately 10 Mbps of network bandwidth available to transmit data. The transmission of data happens only in a half-duplex manner, greatly reducing network throughput. The upside of a hub lies in its capability to transmit data to all ports at the same time. When you have network difficulties and you want to mirror the data on the network for monitoring purposes, hubs offer this functionality by default.

Switches differ from hubs with their inherent capability to transmit data from a single host to another single host, without sending the packets to all the hosts on the switch. This functionality allows for greater data throughput. If you have a 100 Mbps switch, each host on the switch may transfer data at 100 Mbps. A switch stores a routing table to keep track of the hosts connected. The routing table holds the machine (MAC) address of the network adapter for each computer or device, and the switch uses this table to determine to which host to send the data.

Installing Network Adapters in Your Computers

Installing network adapters in your computers requires you to open the case of the computer and install a card. If you do not feel comfortable completing this task, contact a computer repair or service company to install the network card. If installing cards falls into the "old hat" routine, then power down, unplug the computer, open the case, find the first available slot in your machine, insert the card with the gold leads down into the slot, and press firmly to insert the card. Once you have completed this task, screw in the top of the card to connect it to your chassis. This alleviates "wiggle" in the card, which could create shorts or cause intermittent connectivity problems.

On the other hand, if you are using an integrated network card in your machine that has not been enabled, reboot the system into the Basic Input Output System (BIOS). Most OEMs use the Delete key. Press the Delete key every second or so after the reboot to enter the main BIOS section. Usually, you can find the network card settings under Integrated Devices. Once you have found the network card settings in your BIOS, select the desired device and enable it. If you need two network cards and the board has two network cards, enable each one. Very rarely will you need this type of configuration on a standard home system. Once you have enabled the device(s) on your system, save the changes in the BIOS and reboot the system into the operating system.

After installing or enabling the network card physically or logically, allow the system to boot into the operating system. When you have completed this task, click the Start button, right-click on the computer icon, and select Manage. This opens the Computer Management window, which allows you greater flexibility in managing the different aspects of your system. Once Computer Management starts, click the Device Manager node in the left pane. In the main pane, expand the Network Adapters node by clicking on the "+" icon to view the network adapters installed in your machine. Right-click on the adapter you previously installed or enabled, and select Properties. On the Driver tab, verify the Driver Provider details. As necessary, install the device driver as discussed in Chapter 5.

 If you do not see a network adapter listed in the Device Manager screen under Network Adapters, you should verify that the device does not show up under Other Devices as a network controller. If this happens, don't worry. Simply install the device driver as discussed in Chapter 5.

Installing Ethernet Routers, Hubs, and Switches

Installing an Ethernet router, hub, or switch requires you to remove the device from the packaging and plug it into a power source using the power cable provided by the manufacturer. After you plug in the device, you should see it begin to flash green and amber-colored lights. The network device will accept connections and begin transmitting data when the initialization process completes. You can tell that the initialization process has completed when the lights on the unit quit flashing.

After the initialization process completes, you need to connect the network cables to the Ethernet router to provide connectivity to the computers and devices that you want to network together. To establish an Internet connection, connect a network cable between your cable/DSL modem and the Ethernet router's Internet port. Cable modems should automatically assign an IP address to your router for external connectivity to the Internet. DSL modems usually require a client username and password. You should have received this information when you signed up for Internet connectivity, or you can contact support and receive this information from your ISP.

When you have added the first connection to the Ethernet router, you must then connect the cables to the network cards on your computers and devices. When you have completed this task, you should see a green LED light up on each network card and possibly see the amber activity light. If you see both of these signs, you have successfully completed the physical connectivity portion of the networking process. If you do not see both of these lights, it does not mean you have failed, as there may be no data transmission on the line while you are connecting the cables.

 If you want to connect more computers or devices than the ports on the Ethernet router allow, you'll need a hub or switch. With a hub or switch, you connect a network cable between the hub/switch and the Ethernet router. Then, instead of connecting the cables for computers or devices directly to the Ethernet router, you connect the cables to the hub or switch.

To finalize the router setup, you need to configure the network services available on your router. Using the Dynamic Host Configuration Protocol (DHCP), you can assign IP addresses to the computers and devices connected to your router. With the help of your user manual, log on to the router and select the screen to configure DHCP. You need to assign a network IP range for use on your network. If you have only a small group of users, use the 192.168.0.1 range for use on your network, or a similar network ID. Most routers have the functionality turned on automatically. You may also need to input the DNS addresses of your ISP or the MAC address of a network card.

To complete connectivity to the network, you must configure the network cards on your computers and devices. See the "Configuring the IPv4 and IPv6 Protocols" section, later in this chapter, for details.

Mapping Your Networking Infrastructure

Windows Vista provides a whole new way to navigate and manage the networking features of your computer. For mapping your networking infrastructure, Windows Vista provides the Network and Sharing Center, Network Map, Network Connections, and People Near Me. You can access and work with these utilities as discussed in the sections that follow.

Using the Network and Sharing Center

The Network and Sharing Center is a central console for managing your networking experience. You can access the Network and Sharing Center by following these steps:

1. Click Start, and then click Control Panel.
2. In the Control Panel, click Network and Internet and then click Network and Sharing Center.

Once you've accessed the Network and Sharing Center, shown in Figure 14-1, you can use it to manage your general network settings and network status. When you are connected to a network, the Network and Sharing Center provides an overview of your networking configuration. The three main areas in the Network and Sharing Center are:

Network overview

> Provides a visual overview of your network infrastructure, including whether you are connected to a network and whether you can access the Internet from that network. If your computer has multiple active network connections, the network overview states that you are connected to multiple networks. Clicking "View full map" opens the Network Map window. See "Viewing the Network Map," later in this chapter, for more information.

Network details

> Provides details about the network(s) to which the computer is connected and the types of access for those networks. A connection to a LAN is shown as "Local only." A connection to a LAN that in turn connects to the Internet is shown as Local and Internet. Clicking "View status" allows you to manage the related network connection. See "Viewing and Managing Your Network Connections," later in this chapter, for more information.

Sharing and Discovery details

> Shows the status of different aspects of network discovery and sharing. You will see On or Off listed as a status. Clicking the Expand button for a feature allows you to manage the aspects of that feature. Clicking the Shrink button minimizes the management section. Network discovery must be on to discover information about your network. When you are connected to a private network or a domain, network discovery is turned on automatically to allow you to discover computers and devices. When you are connected to a public network, network discovery is turned off to prevent other people from discovering and then trying to access your computer. To enable network discovery if it isn't already enabled, click the Expand button to the right of Network Discovery. On the management panel, click "Turn on Network Discovery" and then click Apply.

In the Network and Sharing Center, you'll see several links at the bottom of the main pane. You can click the "Show me all the files and folders I am sharing" link to view the files and folder you've shared on your network. You can also click the "Show me all the shared network folders on this computer" link to view all of the shared folders available on your computer. These settings make it easier to view all of the shared content without having to go through so many different windows or searches to find this information. This aspect alone is superior to what is available in Windows XP, and it allows you greater flexibility and control over your shared content.

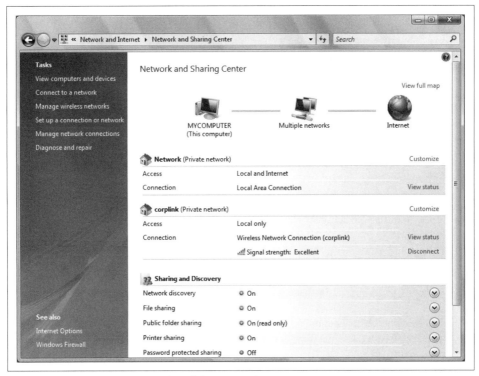

Figure 14-1. Viewing your network and sharing configuration

In the left pane of the Network and Sharing Center screen, you'll find options that offer you the ability to view computers and devices, connect to a network, manage wireless networks, set up a connection or network, manage network connections, and diagnose and repair network connections.

Clicking "View computers and devices" opens the Network List window shown in Figure 14-2. In the Network List window, you have the ability to view the different network resources associated with each machine discovered on your network. You can isolate the resources by Documents, Pictures, Music, or Recently Changed, or you can search for individual resources.

Clicking "Connect to a network" allows you to connect to a known network using the window shown in Figure 14-3. This includes wired connections to known networks discovered, as well as wireless connections Windows Vista discovered during the browsing process while opening the window. If you see the desired network you want to connect to, click Connect, and Windows Vista will automatically try to connect you to the network. You can also disconnect from a network by clicking the network and then clicking Disconnect.

Clicking "Manage wireless connections" allows you to see wireless connections already configured or available for your use, as shown in Figure 14-4. You may also:

Figure 14-2. Accessing the network list of computers and devices

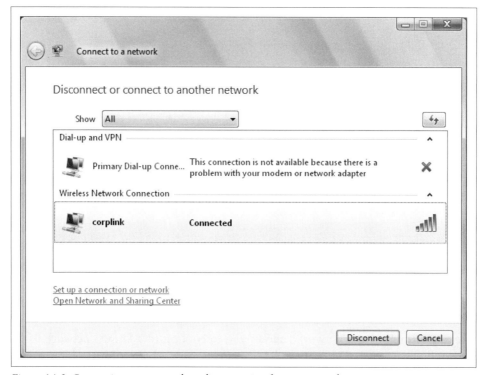

Figure 14-3. Connecting to a network or disconnecting from a network

- Add a wireless connection by selecting the Add button. When you select that option, you are presented with a window asking you for specific information about how you want to add a network. You can add a network that is in range of the computer, manually create a network profile, or create an ad hoc network. If you have already enabled a wireless connection, select the first option, which allows you to connect to the wireless network and saves a configuration profile for future use. If you would like to create a new wireless profile, you need to know the network name or Shared System Identification (SSID) and security key, if enabled. This option also creates a configuration profile for the wireless network for future use. The last option allows you to create an ad hoc network connection. An ad hoc network is a temporary network for the transmission of files among machines not connected via a wireless access point. This option works well if you need to transfer data with someone else and you both have a wireless card in your computer.

- View the properties of a selected wireless adapter by clicking the "Adapter properties" button. You will see a window that allows you to manipulate the different protocols associated with the wireless adapter, including TCP/IP properties, file and printer sharing, and the Microsoft network client protocol. These settings reside on the Networking tab; the Sharing tab allows you to manage sharing of the network resources associated with the wireless network adapter. Selecting the Configure button on the Networking tab allows you to view and manage additional features of your wireless adapter.

- View the profile of a selected connection by clicking the Profile button. The default setting in Windows Vista is "Use all-user profiles only." This setting allows users on the network to access resources on your computer if they have a user account associated with your computer and sharing is configured appropriately. Selecting the "Use all-user and per-user profiles" allows remote users to create connections accessible only to them, which can cause a loss of network connectivity if you log off or switch users on the local system. Microsoft recommends that you use the "Use all-user profiles only" option, which allows greater flexibility and lessens the chance of lost network connectivity.

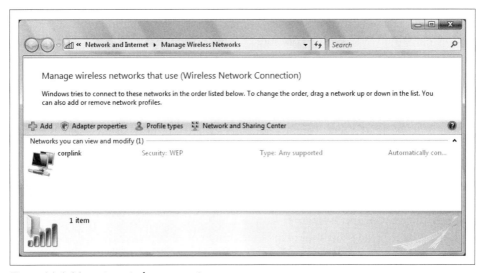

Figure 14-4. Managing wireless connections

Clicking "Set up a connection or network" allows you to manage the different types of network connections available to you. As shown in Figure 14-5, you may connect to the Internet, set up a wireless router or access point, manually connect to a wireless network, set up a wireless ad hoc (computer-to-computer) network, set up a dial-up connection, or connect to a workplace. If you need to set up a wireless router or access point on your network, select the "Set up a wireless router or access point" selection from the list and click Next. The wizard allows you to configure a wireless router or access point, set up the properties for file and printer sharing, save the network configuration for future use, and make the network a private network. If you have all of the required information to set up your wireless network, click the Next button and follow the steps provided by the wizard. Keep the following in mind:

- The wizard starts by detecting network hardware and settings. If you have an access point, Windows Vista discovers it, and if the device allows automatic configuration, it will connect to the device. If your device does not allow automatic configuration, you have the option to "Configure this device manually," or "Create wireless network settings and save to USB flash drive." Selecting the first choice opens an authentication dialog window for connecting to your device. This allows you to configure the access point or router, manually following the information in the user's manual associated with the network device.

- The latter choice allows you to copy network settings and transfer the settings to multiple computers. This feature also allows you to share the settings across the network after configuration of the central connection for hosts associated with the network. You must input the Network Name (SSID) and click the Next button. You must then enter the pass phrase for network connections and click the Next button. Next, select the file and printer sharing options, which consist of "Do not allow file and printer sharing," "Allow sharing with anyone with a user account and password for this computer," and "Allow sharing with anyone on the same network as this computer." After selecting the properties of file and printer sharing, click the Next button and identify the USB key or path where you want to save the network settings for future use.

Clicking "Manage network connections" allows you to view and change the properties of your computer's network adapters. As shown in Figure 14-6, this includes standard network adapters, wireless adapters, Microsoft VPN connections, and any other software or hardware adapter allowing you network connectivity.

Clicking "Diagnose and repair" starts Network Diagnostics, a tool that allows you to have Windows Vista automatically try to detect problems with your network connectivity. Network Diagnostics can help to identify different problems related to an inability to connect to the Internet, connect to network resources, or find resources on the network. While this tool helps to identify network problems, it does not substitute for the tools available to find and diagnose low-level problems, such as the

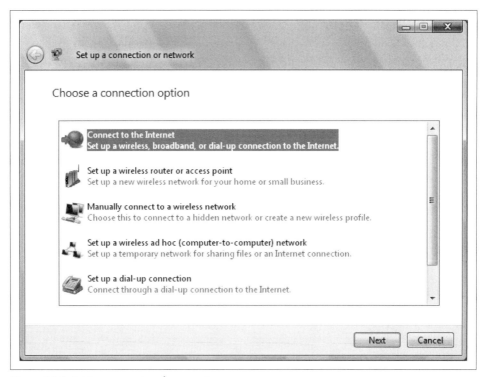

Figure 14-5. Setting up a network connection

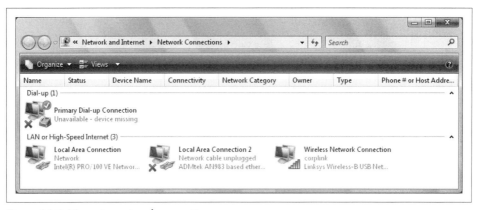

Figure 14-6. Managing network connections

Event Viewer and command-line tools like Ping and Tracert. This tool will enable and disable your network adapter, check for a new IP address from the DHCP server, and check for connectivity. If you have recently set up a network connection and you find that it does not work, this tool will help to identify these simple problems.

Viewing the Network Map

When network discovery is enabled, you can use the Network Map to display an expanded view of your network. As Figure 14-7 shows, the expanded Network Map view includes your computer, the computers near your computer, and the devices near your computer. You can access the Network Map by following these steps:

1. Click Start, and then click Control Panel.

2. In the Control Panel, click Network and Internet and then click Network and Sharing Center.

3. In the Network and Sharing Center, under Network Map, click "View full map."

4. If your computer has more than one network connection, use the "Network map of" list to select the network connection for which the map should be created.

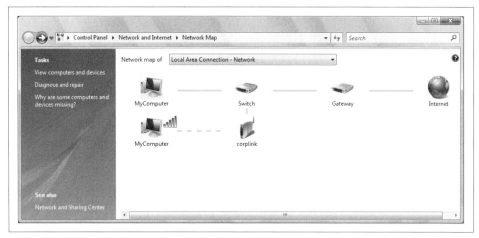

Figure 14-7. Viewing a Network Map

On the Network Map, you'll see solid lines connecting the selected network connection to your network devices. You may also see dashed lines to other devices for alternative connections. If there's a problem with a particular segment of your connection, you'll see a red *X* on the connecting line. Clicking the red *X* works the same as when you click the "Diagnose and repair" option in the Network and Sharing Center.

Viewing and Managing Your Network Connections

Network connections contain the configuration properties that allow your computer to connect to a network. Windows Vista automatically creates a local area connection for each network adapter you've configured. As you configure dial-up, broadband, or wireless, Windows Vista will create related connections as well.

You can quickly obtain a list of network connections for your computer by completing the following steps:

1. Click Start, and then click Control Panel.
2. In the Control Panel, click Network and Internet and then click Network and Sharing Center.
3. In the Network and Sharing Center, click "Manage network connections" under Tasks. This opens the Network Connections window, shown in Figure 14-8.

Figure 14-8. Viewing network connections

The Network Connections window has several different views. You can access these views by clicking the Views button and then selecting the desired view. The view you'll use most often is the Details view. This view shows you:

Name
    The name of your computer's connections, organized by connection type, such as LAN or High-Speed Internet

Status
    The name of the network to which a connection is connected, or the error status, such as "Unavailable – device missing or network cable unplugged"

Device Name
    The manufacturer and type of network adapter

Connectivity
    The type of connectivity for active connections, such as "Access to Local only" or "Access to Local and Internet"

Network Category
    The network category, which can be Private, Public, or Domain

Owner
    The owner of the connection, such as the System account

Type
    The type of connection, such as Dial-up

Phone # or Host Address
    The phone number associated with a dial-up connection, or the host address associated with a remote access connection

When you select a connection in the Network Connection window, the toolbar options allow you to work with the connection in several different ways. The option buttons are used as follows:

Diagnose This Connection
    Opens Network Diagnostics for troubleshooting the connection

View Status of This Connection
    Displays the connection's Status dialog box, which you can use to get details about and manage the TCP/IP configuration

Change Settings of This Connection
    Displays the connection's Properties dialog box, which you can use to manage the TCP/IP configuration

Disable This Network Device
    Allows you to disable the network device so that your computer doesn't try to use it

Rename This Connection
    Allows you to change the name of a selected connection by clicking this button, typing the new name for the connection, and then pressing Enter

Using People Near Me

The People Near Me feature truly adds some needed functionality to Windows Vista. With this feature, you are able to manage a profile of yourself for others to see, add a picture of yourself, and approximate where a person resides in proximity to you. When you use it in conjunction with other applications such as Microsoft Streets and Trips or Microsoft MapPoint, you can actually find people close to you with whom to chat.

Suppose you are sitting in an Internet café and you wonder whether someone around you has a connection open; with People Near Me, you can check the map to find people in your proximity. Once you find someone, you can read her profile, check out her picture to verify that she is who she says she is, and then begin to chat or share files. People Near Me shares the picture that appears on the Welcome screen and Start menu.

 This feature actually installs a virtual network adapter in the computer to give itself the desired functionality, and it uses this device for its communications. Please remember that any application allowed network connectivity has the potential to allow other people to see and manipulate your data.

You can configure People Near Me by completing these steps:

1. Click Start, and then click Control Panel.

2. In the Control Panel, click Network and Internet and then click People Near Me. This opens the People Near Me dialog box shown in Figure 14-9.

Figure 14-9. Configuring People Near Me

3. In the text box provided, enter the name you want other people to see.

4. If you want to select a picture for your account or make your account picture viewable, click the "Make my picture available" checkbox and then click the "Change picture" button. Use the "Change your picture" page in the Control Panel to select a picture to use with your account.

5. Use the "Allow invitations from" list to select from whom you want to allow invitations. Choices are Anyone, Trusted Contacts, and No One.

6. To allow display notifications when someone wants to talk to you, select the "Display a notification when an invitation is received" checkbox.

7. To sign in automatically when Windows Vista starts, select the "Sign me in automatically when windows starts" checkbox.

You can manually sign in to the People Near Me service by following these steps:

1. Click Start, and then click Control Panel.
2. In the Control Panel, click Network and Internet and then click "Sign in or out of People Near Me." This opens the People Near Me dialog box to the Sign in tab, as shown in Figure 14-10.

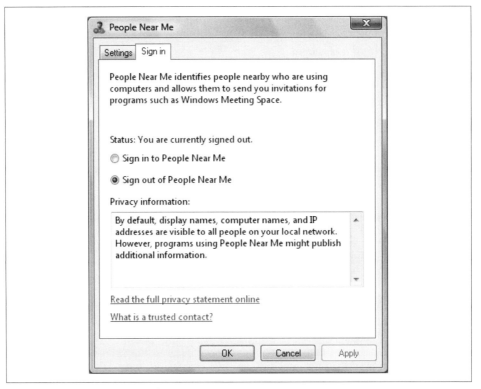

Figure 14-10. Signing in to People Near Me

3. To sign in to the service, select "Sign in to People Near Me" and then click the OK button.
4. When prompted, you'll need to verify your display name and settings before you can sign on. If you agree with all of the criteria, click OK again. People Near Me makes changes to Windows Firewall to allow access and displays a notification icon in the task tray.

To change your preferences, right-click the icon in the task tray and then select Properties. This feature also allows you to disconnect from the service by signing out or exiting the program.

Networking with TCP/IP

While Windows Vista has the capability of using several networking protocols, the primary protocols used are TCP and IP. Windows Vista uses the TCP/IP protocol for networking among peer-to-peer networks, domain-controlled networks, and the Internet. TCP/IP is a vital protocol set for using your operating system fully.

Windows Vista contains a new TCP/IP stack, referred to as a dual stack, that works with IP Version 4 (IPv4) and IP Version 6 (IPv6). IPv4 uses a limited 32-bit address space, defined by four octets and a subnet mask composed of four octets. IPv6 uses a 128-bit addressing scheme, allowing for the needed IP growth of the Internet.

Understanding IPv4

IP addresses used with IPv4 can be divided into two parts: the network ID and the host ID. The network ID identifies the network on which a computer or device is located and the host ID identifies the computer or device.

An example of an IPv4 address is 192.168.1.1, which shows the four distinct sets of numbers divided by a period, or dot. Each section separated by a dot is referred to as an *octet*, which correlates to an eight-bit number in binary form.

The second set of numbers associated with an IPv4 address is the subnet mask. The subnet mask identifies which parts of the IP address belong to the network ID and which parts belong to the host ID.

Subnet masks use four distinct octets separated by a period, or dot, just like the IP address. Subnet masking correlates to the network ID and the actual host ID of the computer by giving binary values of either a 1, for a bit that belongs to the network ID, or 0, for a bit that belongs to the host ID. An example of a subnet mask is 255.0.0.0, which is read in binary as 11111111.00000000.00000000.00000000. Thus, the first 8 bits of the IP address belong to the network ID and the final 24 bits belong to the host ID.

When you use standard subnet masks, you are said to be using a *classful network*. Classful networks are defined in three different classes: Class A, Class B, and Class C. Table 14-2 shows examples of the different classful networks. Table 14-3 shows network ID examples, and Table 14-4 gives some examples of subnet forms translated into binary to help you understand the differences in their formats and to differentiate the network ID portion of the subnet from the host ID portion of the subnet.

Table 14-2. IPv4 subnet example

Subnet class	Example	Maximum nodes
Class A	255.0.0.0	16,777,214
Class B	255.255.0.0	65,534
Class C	255.255.255.0	254

Table 14-3. IPv4 network example

Network ID	Subnet mask	Host IP range	Broadcast address
10.0.0.0	255.0.0.0	10.0.0.1–10.255.255.254	10.255.255.255
169.254.0.0	255.255.0.0	169.254.0.1–169.254.255.254	169.254.255.255
192.168.1.0	255.255.255.0	192.168.1.1–192.168.1.254	192.168.1.255

Table 14-4. IPv4 subnet to binary form example

Decimal subnet form	Binary subnet form
255.0.0.0	11111111.00000000.00000000.00000000
255.255.0.0	11111111.11111111.00000000.00000000
255.255.255.0	11111111.11111111.11111111.00000000

For every network, two host addresses are reserved: the network address and the broadcast address. The network address is used to identify the unique network. The broadcast address is used to broadcast a message to all hosts on a network. On a classful network, address 0 is reserved to indicate the network number, and address 255 is reserved for the broadcast address.

Class A networks use the first octet in the range of 1–126. The remaining three octets define unique host IDs. Each Class A network may contain up to 16,777,214 nodes.

Class B networks use the first two octets in the range of 128–191. The remaining two octets define the unique host IDs. Each Class B network may contain up to 65,532 nodes.

Class C networks use the first three octets in the range of 192–223. The remaining octet is for unique host IDs. Each Class C network may contain up to 254 hosts.

 Out of these IP address ranges, you may note that some ranges are missing. The 127 network is reserved for local loopback. Your computer typically uses the address 127.0.0.1 to send messages to itself. The network addresses from 224 to 239 are used for multicast IPv4 addresses.

When you are working with IPv4, data is sent in discreet packets of information with a header and a payload. IPv4 headers are variable in size, between 20 and 60 bytes, in 4-byte increments. Each bit range is broken into different sections, which correspond to the range of a related field in a packet. Bit ranges consist of 0–3, 4–7, 8–15, 16–18, and 15–31. These correspond to the values 0, 32, 64, 96, 128, 160, and 160/152+ for data. See Table 14-5 for examples of the ranges and their use. The IP payload is of variable size as well, ranging from 8 bytes to 65,515 bytes. Although most people will never use this information on a regular basis, it is very useful for understanding how to troubleshoot network problems.

Table 14-5. IPv4 packet information

+	Bits 0–3	4–7	8–15	16–18	15–31
0	Version	Header length	Type of service	Total length	
32	Identification			Flags	Fragment offset
64	Time to Live (TTL)	Protocol		Header checksum	
96	Source address information				
128	Destination address information				
160	Optional information				
160/152+	Data transmitted				

Using Private IPv4 Addresses and Networking Protocols

Some IP addresses designated for Class A, B, and C networks are defined as public and others are defined as private. Public IP addresses are assigned by ISPs. ISPs obtain their IP addresses from a local or national Internet registry. When you connect directly to the Internet through dial-up or by connecting an ISP's cable/DSL modem directly to your computer, your computer uses a public IP address assigned by your ISP. Not every computer that connects to the Internet needs its own IP address, however. If it did, the IPv4 addressing scheme would have run out of new addresses a long time ago. This is where private IP addresses come into the picture.

When you set up a network, you assign the computers on the network private IP addresses. Private IP addresses are defined as follows:

- Class A private IP addresses include the addresses from 10.0.0.0 through 10.255. 255.255.

- Class B private IP addresses include the addresses from 172.16.0.0 through 172.31.255.255.

- Class C private IP addresses include the addresses from 192.168.0.0 through 192.168.255.255.

Since private IP addresses are not routable to the Internet, your network can use the same private IP addresses that other people are using with their networks. When a computer is connected to a network that in turn connects to an ISP, your Ethernet router is the device that is assigned a public IP address. Generally speaking, the router's public IP address is the address by which all the computers on your network will be identified when they are accessing resources on the Internet.

On a network, private IP addresses are assigned in one of three ways:

Static IP address
    A fixed IP address that you manually assign to a computer or device

Dynamic IP address
    An IP address automatically assigned to a computer or device by DHCP

Automatic private IP address
    An IP address automatically assigned to a computer by the operating system when a DHCP server cannot be contacted

On a home or small-office network, you can use the DHCP service capability of your Ethernet router to assign IP addresses. Refer to the user manual of your router to find the correct procedure to configure the DHCP service to assign IP addresses automatically to computers and devices connecting to your network. Once you've configured the DHCP service, you must configure the network adapters of computers and devices to use DHCP, which is typically the default IP addressing scheme.

Understanding IPv6

Although IPv4 allows for more than four billion networked computers and devices, the world is running out of available IPv4 addresses. Rather than allow there to be a shortage of available addresses, organizations have worked together to create several solutions to the problem. One of these solutions is IPv6. Unlike IPv4, which uses 32-bit addresses, IPv6 uses 128-bit addresses, which offer literally enough IP addresses so that there's one IP address for each square yard of the Earth's surface. Or put another way, there are about 340,282,237,000,000,000,000,000,000,000,000,000,000 available addresses—give or take a few hundred million quadrillion.

To make it easier to track all those IP addresses, IPv6 uses hexadecimal numbers rather than decimal numbers to define the address space. This means that instead of allowing only the numbers 0 through 9 for each position in the IP address, IPv6 allows the values 0 through 9 and A through F, with A representing 10, B representing 11, and so on, up to F representing 15. Thus, the values 0 through 15 can be represented using the values 0 through F.

IPv6's 128-bit addresses are divided into eight 16-bit blocks delimited by colons. With standard IPv6 addresses, the first 64 bits represent the network ID and the last 64 bits represent the network interface being used. Since many IPv6 address blocks are set to 0, a contiguous set of 0 blocks can be expressed as ::, a notation referred to as the double-colon notation. Table 14-6 shows an example of an IPv6 IP address and an abbreviated IP address.

Table 14-6. IPv6 address example

IPv6 address	Truncated IPv6 address
FE80:0:0:033C:FB:B335:FE4F:752B	FE80::033C:FB:B335:FE4F:752B

Just as there are different types of IPv4 addresses, there are different types of IPv6 addresses. As Table 14-7 shows, the type of an IPv6 address is identified by the high-order bits of the address. The IPv6 address 0:0:0:0:0:0:0:1 is used for local loopback. IPv6 addresses beginning with FF00 are used for multicast transmissions. IPv6 addresses beginning with FE80 are used for link-local unicast transmissions. Link-local unicast IPv6 addresses are the equivalent of IPv4 private addresses because they are not globally reachable on the Internet. Global unicast IPv6 addresses are the equivalent of IPv4 public addresses because they are globally reachable on the Internet and must be assigned by an IP address authority.

Table 14-7. IPv6 subnet prefix example

IPv6 subnet prefix length	Associated network addresses
2001:1234:5678::/48	2001:1234:5678:: through address 2001:1234:5678::FFFF:FFFF:FFFF:FFFF

IPv6 doesn't use subnet masks to identify which bits belong to the network ID and which bits belong to the host ID. Instead, each IPv6 address is assigned a subnet prefix length that specifies how the bits in the network ID are used. The subnet prefix length is represented in decimal form. For example, if 48 bits in the network ID are used the subnet prefix length is written as /48. Table 14-8 shows an example of the subnet prefix length and the associated network range.

Table 14-8. IPv6 address types

Address type	Binary prefix	IPv6 notation
Unspecified	000000	::/128
Loopback	000001	::1/128
Multicast	11111111	FF00::/8
Link-Local unicast	1111111010	FE80::/10
Global unicast	All other addresses	

IPv6 allows for a greater than 64 KB payload in an IPv4 packet, which designers refer to as a *jumbogram*. These jumbograms greatly increase the throughput of high-performance networks. IPv4 does not support this type of transmission, and it has a 64 KB payload limit.

IPv6 packets are composed of two parts: a header and a payload section. The first 40 octets of an IPv6 packet contain the header, composed of the source and destination addresses, including an IPv4 version where necessary, traffic class section, flow label (for packet priority information), payload length, next header addressing section, and hop limit. The payload section consists of the actual data sent during transmission. The payload section can contain either 64 KB of information, like the IPv4 standard, or a jumbogram for true IPv6 "high-throughput" networking architectures. Table 14-9 shows an example of an IPv6 packet.

Table 14-9. IPv6 packet example

Bit 0	4	8	12	16	20	24	28	32
	Version	Traffic class		Flow label				
	Source address information							
	Destination address information							

 IPv6 developers also implemented IP Security (IPSec) into the protocol. IPSec lies within the IP network layer, and encrypts and authenticates as an integrated part of the protocol by default. This eliminates additional overhead in encoding and decoding packets using IPSec functionality.

Configuring the IPv4 and IPv6 Protocols

Each network adapter configured on your computer has a separate IP addressing configuration, which you can manage through the associated network connection. The network connection for the first network adapter on the computer is named Local Area Connection; the second network adapter is named Local Area Connection 2, and so on. Connections for wireless, dial-up, or broadband have the name you assigned when you created the connection.

During installation of the operating system, the Setup program automatically installed the necessary networking components for your computer if a network adapter was detected. In addition to TCP/IPv4 and TCP/IPv6, Windows Vista uses the following networking components:

Client for Microsoft Networks
> Allows you to connect to Microsoft-based networking services. If you are connecting to a Windows domain, you are required to use this protocol.

QoS Packet Scheduler
> Offers the capability to define which protocols and applications have precedence in a situation where multiple applications or protocols request access to the same network resources. This protocol gives you the ability to raise or lower the priority of the requests made. Basically, the Quality of Service (QoS) Packet Scheduler works as a traffic cop by allowing you to control the rate of flow and prioritization of services available.

File and Printer Sharing for Microsoft Networks
> Allows other computers to connect to and access resources on your computer when using Microsoft networking protocols. This feature also allows you to access resources on remote machines connected to your network and on the Internet.

Link-Layer Topology Discovery Mapper I/O Driver
    Allows your computer to discover and locate other computers and devices on the network. Also used to determine the available network bandwidth.

Link-Layer Topology Discovery Responder
    Allows your computer to be discovered and located by other computers and devices on the network.

Although you will probably use only IPv4 on your home or small-office network, you should understand how IPv6 works and be able to configure the protocol. You can manually assign IPv4 and IPv6 addresses using static IP addresses, or automatically assign them using dynamic IP addresses. You configure the IPv4 and IPv6 protocols in exactly the same way, with the following exceptions:

- IPv4 uses subnet masks, and IPv6 uses subnet prefix lengths.
- IPv4 uses both DNS and WINS for locating computers and devices on the network, and IPv6 uses only DNS.
- IPv4 allows for automatic private IP addressing if a DHCP server cannot be located, and IPv6 simply assigns the computer a local–local unicast (private) IP address based on the MAC address of the network adapter.

On a per-network-connection basis, you can configure the networking protocols used by completing the following steps:

1. Click Start, and then click Control Panel.
2. In the Control Panel, click Network and Internet and then click Network and Sharing Center.
3. In the Network and Sharing Center, click "Manage network connections" under Tasks. This opens the Network Connections window.
4. Right-click the network connection you want to configure and then select Properties. This displays a Properties dialog box, as shown in Figure 14-11.
5. On the Networking tab, you can use the checkboxes provided to manipulate the different protocols associated with the network adapter. You can turn the different protocols on and off by clicking the checkbox associated with each protocol:
    - If you are using file and printer sharing on your network, you must enable both Client for Microsoft Networks, and File and Printer Sharing for Microsoft Networks. The QoS protocol offers greater flexibility in the flow of data by prioritizing the different requests made by the client.
    - If you are using the IPv6 protocol for connectivity, you also must use the QoS Packet Scheduler, which Windows selects by default. If you are not using this protocol, you should disable it by unchecking the box associated with this protocol.
    - If you are using the IPv4 protocol for connectivity, you must leave the Internet Protocol Version 4 (TCP/IPv4) box checked.

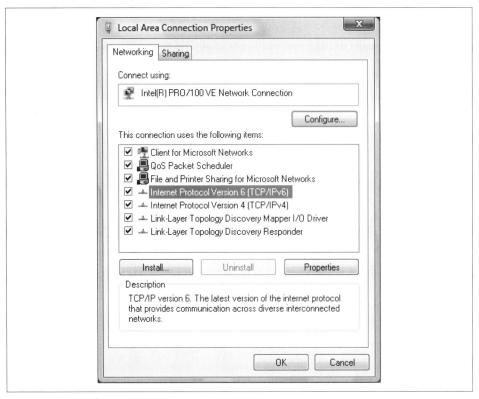

Figure 14-11. Configuring connection properties

- If you are using the IPv6 protocol for connectivity, you must leave the Internet Protocol Version 6 (TCP/IPv6) box checked.

- If you want to be able to use the network connection to discover and locate other computers and devices, you must leave the Link-Layer Topology Discovery Mapper I/O Driver box checked.

- If you want other people to be able to discover your computer through the network connection, you must leave the Link-Layer Topology Discovery Responder box checked.

 While the discovery protocols add some overhead to your computer, they offer some real value to the capabilities of networking in Windows Vista. Most of the time, you should leave these protocols enabled, unless you are leery of security issues associated with other people discovering your computer. If you are concerned about the security aspects, verify that you have Windows Firewall enabled on your computer and make sure the hardware firewall on your Ethernet router is properly configured. While firewalls will not eliminate all problems associated with security, they will drastically decrease the potential to have data stolen.

6. To configure IPv4 or IPv6, double-click Internet Protocol Version 4 (TCP/IPv4) or Internet Protocol Version 6 (TCP/IPv6) as appropriate. As Figure 14-12 shows, the options available are nearly identical whether you are working with IPv4 or IPv6. Repeat this as necessary to configure both IPv4 and IPv6.

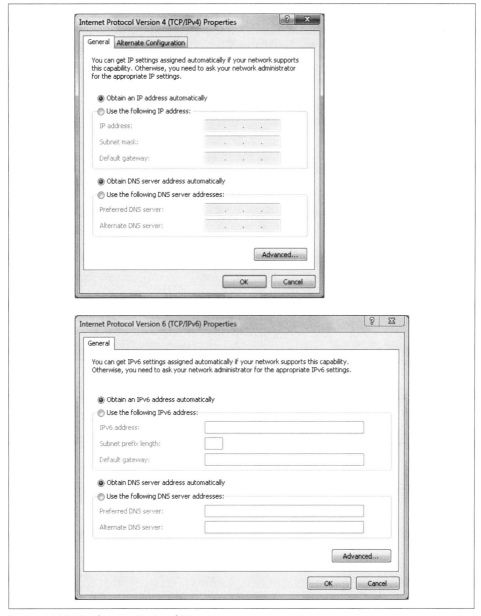

Figure 14-12. Configuring IPv4 and IPv6

7. The General tab allows you to select either Obtain an IP Address Automatically or "Use the following IP address." If you have enabled DHCP on a network device such as a router, you should choose the first option. This allows DHCP to configure the options of the protocol for IP addressing and the default gateway for accessing the network. You should also choose "Obtain DNS server addresses automatically" to ensure that your computer gets the correct DNS servers for name lookups. Windows Vista defaults to the automatic configuration, as you'll typically have a device providing your IP addressing dynamically.

8. To configure the network adapter to use a manually assigned IP address, do the following:

    a. Select the "Use the following IP address" option. For IPv4 addressing, enter the IP address you want to associate with the network adapter in the "IP address" text box and then enter the subnet mask in the "Subnet mask" text box. For IPv6 addressing, enter the IP address in the IP address text box and then enter the subnet prefix in the "Subnet prefix length" text box.

    b. Select the "Use the following DNS server addresses" options. Enter the DNS server address of either your local DNS server or your ISP into the "Preferred DNS server" text box. If you have additional DNS server information to provide, enter the address into the "Alternate DNS server" text box.

9. Click OK to save your settings.

 If you are manually configuring your IP address, you must have an IP address, subnet mask or subnet prefix, and IP addresses for DNS servers. If you have a computer that connects to a network router that in turn connects to your ISP's cable/DSL modem, you should carefully weigh the options available with TCP/IP. When enabling network connectivity without a hardware firewall, you should verify that Windows Firewall is on. You should also carefully consider whether you need file and printer sharing. Enabling file and printer sharing without a firewall may make your computer accessible to other people.

Regardless of how you connect to a network, you are required to add your computer to either a workgroup, also know as a peer-to-peer network, or a domain. *Workgroups* are small groups of computers with individual user rights assigned by the computer. *Domains* are groups of computers with a centralized authentication mechanism. Each works to its own benefit and small networks seldom use domains, unless you are willing to put the capital out to purchase a server operating system. To add your computer to an existing workgroup or connect to a domain, use the techniques discussed in the "Configuring the Computer Name" section in Chapter 20.

Advanced Networking Concepts

Windows Vista includes support for advanced network features, which include IPSec and VPN. These protocols have existed for some time, but they are more readily available and usable in Windows Vista than they were in earlier releases of Windows.

Understanding the OSI Model

The Open Systems Interconnection (OSI) model defines the ways protocols operate by breaking the different aspects of protocols into layers. The OSI model uses seven layers with different purposes to define how protocols function. Each layer may use the functionality of the first layer below it and export functionality to the next layer above it. See Table 14-10 for a detailed listing of the OSI model's layers.

Table 14-10. OSI layer reference

Layer level	Layer name
Layer 1	Physical
Layer 2	Data Link
Layer 3	Network
Layer 4	Transport
Layer 5	Session
Layer 6	Presentation
Layer 7	Application

OSI layer 1 covers all of the physical connectivity specifications of devices. This includes any electrical voltage, pin-outs, connectors, cables, and hubs. Layer 1 defines all network adapters, network devices that do not work in layer 2, and host bus adapters used in storage area networks (SANs). The main purpose of layer 1 includes establishing a connection or disconnection from a network medium. Layer 1 also covers modulation and flow control over the network medium.

OSI layer 2 controls the means of controlling data transfer among network entities. Layer 2 also handles the control mechanism of data transferred among network entities. Bridges and switches both work within layer 2. Although there are layer 3 switches, they work on layer 2 without the use of a router.

OSI layer 3 controls the functional means of transferring data among network entities. Layer 3 handles the variable length sequences to and from destinations among networks. It also handles QoS for the transport layer. Routing also occurs at layer 3 (in fact, routing is the most common use of layer 3).

OSI layer 4 controls the transfer of data among users, and provides reliable data transfer to the layers above itself. Layer 4 controls flow as well as errors. This layer controls the retransmit of packets lost in transport among users. TCP uses this layer as the control portion of the protocol. Layer 4 also converts data into the User Datagram Protocol (UDP) and Stream Control Transmission Protocol (SCTP) formats.

OSI layer 5 controls the networked communications between computers. This includes managing and terminating connections among machines. Layer 5 controls duplex modes on network traffic, which includes full- and half-duplex operations. TCP uses layer 5 to control the flow of data and to terminate connections.

OSI layer 6 provides a standard interface to transform data into the correct format for the application layer. Standard uses of layer 6 include data encryption, compression, and specific types of encoding, including Multipurpose Internet Mail Extension (MIME) encoding. Layer 6 also allows for the transformation into and out of the eXtensible Markup Language (XML) format.

OSI layer 7 controls the means a user needs to access network resources through an application. Programs that use layer 7 include Simple Mail Transfer Protocol (SMTP), HTTP, FTP, Telnet, IPSec, IM, and other applications.

Each layer of the OSI model handles different portions of the networking process and helps to define the process of finding errors, or just understanding how the complex process of networking actually works. Armed with the information from the OSI model, we can begin to truly understand, create, and even fix networks as well as the protocols used to transmit data across networks.

Introducing IPSec

IPSec offers the ability to encrypt network transmissions at the adapter level. IPSec varies from Secure Sockets Layer (SSL) in terms of the OSI layer it encrypts. SSL typically encrypts at the application/protocol layer (OSI layer 7), and IPSec encrypts data at the transport layer (OSI layers 4–7). Since SSL works only at the application protocol layer, if you transmit data over any other port or use any application other than the one bound to the SSL protocol, that data is not encrypted. IPSec, however, encrypts all of the data transmitted from the network adapter at the transport layer.

IPSec includes two encryption mechanisms: transport and tunneling. Most implementations use the tunneling version, which encapsulates the entire packet. This feature allows for routable information to other hosts to be unencrypted while the internal header and the rest of the data stay encrypted. This makes it possible to use Network Address Translation (NAT), which lets you use a single device to allow traffic into and out of the network using internal IP addressing—something your Ethernet router does for you automatically.

The transcript mechanism usually consists of one-to-one communication among computers on the same network. Transport encrypts the data, not the header, and creates a hash of the packet. Using the transport method does not allow you to use NAT, thereby making external communications difficult. The reason lies in the method: transport creates a hash of the packet; when it hashes the packet, it rewrites part of the header, making the header value mismatch the rest of the packet, thereby rendering the packet invalid.

You may ask yourself, "How does it encrypt the data?" That is a very good question. First, the adapters create a trusted relationship by importing a digital certificate into each network adapter. When the adapter connects to the network, possibly via a VPN tunneling server or Active Directory domain controller, it verifies the digital certificate, trades private and public keys that are associated with the certificate, and verifies the machine (MAC) address of the network adapter. The adapter creates a hash value for each packet transmitted to the adapter, including a timestamp, alleviating replay attacks against the adapter.

Introducing VPN

If you are a traveler and you work in a corporate environment, you have probably used a VPN connection to connect to your corporate network on the road, in order to check your email, or possibly to update sales orders and the like. VPN makes connecting to remote networks secure and easy.

VPN allows remote users to connect to a network confidentially over a public network. VPN uses standard protocols (TCP/IP, SSL) to traverse the public network, making it very easy to use. VPN consists of two types: Secure VPN and Trusted VPN. Each type uses different processes to gain connectivity to a remote network.

Secure VPN uses cryptographic tunneling protocols to gain private access to the remote network. Secure VPN can use IPSec to encrypt the data traversing the VPN connection. Secure VPN also supports SSL to encrypt the data, essentially creating a web proxy, not really a VPN connection. Point-to-Point Tunneling Protocol (PPTP), the original VPN protocol, has aged and does not secure data as well as Layer 2 Tunneling Protocol (L2TP). In addition, Layer 2 Tunneling Protocol Version 3 (L2TPv3) also works in Windows Vista.

Trusted VPN does not use a cryptographic set to allow tunneling. Instead, it uses the provider's network to encrypt data. Usually, Multi-Protocol Label Switching (MPLS) makes up the trusted VPN tunnel, but this type of VPN also supports use of the Layer 2 Forwarding (L2F) protocol.

Most networks supporting VPN give you access to a VPN client, which you install. If you use Routing and Remote Access Service (RRAS) on your network, you can use the Connect to a Workplace option in the Connect to a Network window. You have the choice of connecting directly to your workplace or using your Internet connection. Direct connection requires a phone line and does not use the Internet. Of course, the other choice requires you to have a connection to the Internet. Click your desired option and enter the name of the server, or IP address. Give the destination a meaningful name; select the security properties, which consist of Smart Cards, Sharing, and Just Set Up; and then click the Next button. Enter your username, password, and optional domain information and then click the Create button. To connect, click the Connect Now button and you should connect to the VPN server.

Troubleshooting Common Problems on Small Networks

As with any type of technology, sometimes things just don't work out the way you want them to. This truth brings us to the troubleshooting portion of this chapter. Learning about the different tools available to help identify and solve problems with networking is paramount to successfully sharing resources locally or across the globe.

The first step to learning about troubleshooting falls into the theoretical arena with the OSI model. See Table 14-10 for a list of the OSI model layers and their names. The OSI model helps us break networks into different layers in terms of how they correspond to the different applications and protocols we use to transmit data. Each protocol works in different ways, and the OSI model helps us understand how they function and what they do.

Using the Network Diagnostics and Repair Option

Windows Vista offers the ability to self-diagnose network connectivity problems using Windows Network Diagnostics. This feature can help to identify problems with network adapters and TCP/IP issues. If you do not have a cable properly connecting the adapter to the network, it will also notify you of this problem. The wizard goes through a simple set of tests to determine the problem, alleviating the need to complete these tasks manually. However, if the wizard cannot fix the problem, you must determine the problem yourself, as discussed in the other troubleshooting sections of this chapter.

You can diagnose and repair network problems by completing these steps:

1. Click Start, and then click Control Panel.
2. In the Control Panel, click Network and Internet and then click Network and Sharing Center.
3. In the left pane, under Tasks, click "Diagnose and repair."
4. When Windows Network Diagnostics finishes testing your network configuration, you'll see a list of possible solutions, as shown in Figure 14-13. Follow the instructions provided to try to correct the problem, or click a solution to have Windows Network Diagnostics perform a troubleshooting task for you.

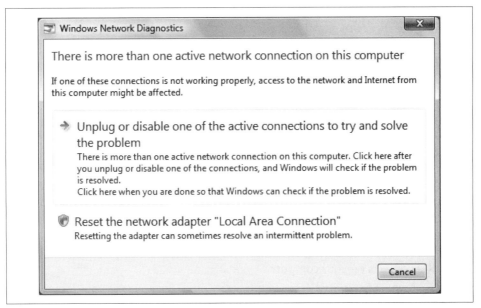

Figure 14-13. *Diagnosing your networking problem*

Checking Physical Connectivity

Using the functionality of the OSI model, you can identify where protocols function to aid in troubleshooting network problems. If you are unable to connect to a network, you should begin at the layer 1 level. This layer tells you to look specifically at the physical connectivity of your computer to the network. Identifying whether your cabling works correctly should be the first step of network troubleshooting. You can usually verify that you have physical connectivity by making sure that the link light is lit on the network adapter. Usually if your link light is lit and the activity light is showing activity by flashing, you can assume physical connectivity. If you complete the troubleshooting steps in the section but you still have issues connecting to the network properly, replace the network cable. If you have doubts as to whether you have connectivity, take a few minutes to replace the network cable, as it is easy and inexpensive to replace this piece of equipment. Telltale signs that you need to replace your cable include no link light when connected to a powered-on network device, and the fact that you can either only send or only receive data.

If you have verified that you have physical connectivity, you must determine whether the network adapter exists within Device Manager on your computer. If your computer sees the network adapter, verify that you have the latest driver installed. Sometimes you can have problems with network functionality due to an old device driver associated with the network adapter. This scenario can happen after a software update to the operating system and when a third-party application makes changes to a shared control file, or to a file the driver relies upon for quality communications. If your network adapters are integrated into the motherboard, you must flash the BIOS to update the firmware associated with the adapters and update the driver for the operating system.

If you still cannot connect to the network, check your TCP/IP configuration settings, as discussed previously in the "Configuring the IPv4 and IPv6 Protocols" section of this chapter. You can also use the techniques discussed in the upcoming "Using the Command Line to Diagnose Network Problems and "Fixing Network Problems" sections to help you with troubleshooting configuration issues. If none of these efforts resolves the problem, try replacing the network adapter with a second network adapter. This should verify connectivity problems or resolve the issue. If the problem follows the adapter, you can assume the adapter has a problem. If you still cannot connect to the network with a new adapter, verify that the slot in the motherboard works correctly. If your network adapters are integrated into the motherboard, you can still add a different physical network adapter into a slot on the motherboard. You may then want to disable the integrated adapters in the BIOS to avoid IRQ conflicts on your computer.

To check the functionality of the slot in the motherboard, install the network adapter into a different slot on the motherboard. If you still cannot connect to the network or see an adapter, you should update the BIOS on your motherboard or contact the manufacturer's technical support to either identify the problem with the board or get a replacement board, assuming you have warranty support on the board in question. Once you have the replacement board, you can connect the network adapter to verify connectivity.

Using the Command Line to Diagnose Network Problems

Microsoft offers many different tools to help diagnose network problems. The best tools for testing your network are those available at the command line. For troubleshooting, be sure to start the command line with elevated privileges by completing the following steps:

1. Click Start, click All Programs, and then click Accessories.
2. Right-click Command Prompt and then select "Run as administrator."
3. This opens an administrator command prompt that you can use to perform any necessary troubleshooting procedures.

To begin troubleshooting, you should first determine the IP configuration for all network adapters on your computer. To accomplish this task, type **IPconfig /all** at the command prompt you opened previously. You will see the output of the TCP/IP stack concerning the characteristics of your local machine, similar to Example 14-1, which gives you a great view of the properties controlling access to your network and its resources. You can see immediately the name of the host, type of connection, routing capability, DNS name, MAC address, IP address, DHCP server IP address, subnet, default gateway, and IP address for each adapter connected to the computer.

Example 14-1. IPConfig /all output

```
C:\>IPconfig /all
Windows IP Configuration
    Host Name . . . . . . . . . . . . : RC1-5600
    Primary Dns Suffix  . . . . . . . :
    Node Type . . . . . . . . . . . . : Hybrid
    IP Routing Enabled. . . . . . . . : No
    WINS Proxy Enabled. . . . . . . . : No
    DNS Suffix Search List. . . . . . : globalsuite.net

Wireless LAN adapter Wireless Network Connection:
    Media State . . . . . . . . . . . : Media disconnected
    Connection-specific DNS Suffix  . : ok.cox.net
    Description . . . . . . . . . . . : Broadcom 802.11g Network Adapter
    Physical Address. . . . . . . . . : 00-14-A5-A0-15-F1
    DHCP Enabled. . . . . . . . . . . : Yes
    Autoconfiguration Enabled . . . . : Yes

Ethernet adapter Local Area Connection:
    Connection-specific DNS Suffix  . : globalsuite.net
    Description . . . . . . . . . . . : Realtek RTL8139/810x Fast Ethernet NIC
    Physical Address. . . . . . . . . : 00-16-36-46-FF-15
    DHCP Enabled. . . . . . . . . . . : Yes
    Autoconfiguration Enabled . . . . : Yes
    Link-local IPv6 Address . . . . . : fe80::2da2:3d:9f2e:297c%10(Preferred)
    IPv4 Address. . . . . . . . . . . : 158.18.184.133(Preferred)
    Subnet Mask . . . . . . . . . . . : 255.255.0.0
    Lease Obtained. . . . . . . . . . : Tuesday, September 12, 2006 5:07:01 PM
    Lease Expires . . . . . . . . . . : Wednesday, September 13, 2006 5:37:00 PM
    Default Gateway . . . . . . . . . : 158.18.0.1
    DHCP Server . . . . . . . . . . . : 158.18.0.1
    DHCPv6 IAID . . . . . . . . . . . : 234886710
    DNS Servers . . . . . . . . . . . : 4.2.2.1
    NetBIOS over Tcpip. . . . . . . . : Enabled
```

The first setting you need to verify is the IP address of the computer. If you are using DHCP on a network device, make sure you see DHCP Enabled. . . . . : Yes in the output of the IPCONFIG /ALL command. If you see this setting, verify that you have received an IP address. If you do not have an IP address, check whether you can see an address for the DHCP server. When identifying the IP address, if you see either 0.0.0.0 or 169.265.X.X as an IP address, you did not connect to the DHCP server. You can try to reapply for an IP address by typing the **Ipconfig /renew** command at the command line. If this fails to give you an IP address, try inputting a static IP address within the subnet of the DHCP server to see if you can gain access to the network. If you can, make sure the DHCP server is running correctly. Alternatively, simply unplug and then plug in the device to force it to reset itself.

Windows offers a host of commands for testing your network, but by far the king of all commands is ping. Pinging allows you to direct specific-size packets at a computer to verify connectivity. Ping actually echoes back with information on the connectivity to another computer. If you wanted to verify your ability to send packets, you should first ping your computer on the local loopback address, 127.0.0.1. The loopback address provides a simple mechanism for testing your network adapter. If you can receive packets at this address, you should proceed to verify that name resolution is working correctly. You can accomplish this task by pinging the name of another computer, such as a web site on the Internet. If you are unable to ping the loopback adapter, check the TCP/IP settings of the network adapter to verify that you have enabled the TCP/IP protocol. See Example 14-2 for examples of how to ping different network hosts by name or IP address.

Example 14-2. Ping command

```
C:\>ping 127.0.0.1

Pinging 127.0.0.1 with 32 bytes of data:

Reply from 127.0.0.1: bytes=32 time<1ms TTL=128
Reply from 127.0.0.1: bytes=32 time<1ms TTL=128
Reply from 127.0.0.1: bytes=32 time<1ms TTL=128
Reply from 127.0.0.1: bytes=32 time<1ms TTL=128

Ping statistics for 127.0.0.1:
    Packets: Sent = 4, Received = 4, Lost = 0 (0% loss),
Approximate round trip times in milliseconds:
    Minimum = 0ms, Maximum = 0ms, Average = 0ms

C:\>ping google.com

Pinging google.com [72.14.207.99] with 32 bytes of data:

Reply from 72.14.207.99: bytes=32 time=52ms TTL=235
Reply from 72.14.207.99: bytes=32 time=75ms TTL=235
Reply from 72.14.207.99: bytes=32 time=51ms TTL=235
Reply from 72.14.207.99: bytes=32 time=52ms TTL=235

Ping statistics for 72.14.207.99:
    Packets: Sent = 4, Received = 4, Lost = 0 (0% loss),
Approximate round trip times in milliseconds:
    Minimum = 51ms, Maximum = 75ms, Average = 57ms
```

If you cannot receive packets by pinging another computer, you should proceed to ping the IP address of your default gateway. You can find the IP address of your default gateway in the output of the IPconfig /all command.

If you are unable to ping your default gateway, either contact your network administrator or check the gateway. In most instances, your gateway consists of an Ethernet router or similar device, and you should check the device for proper functionality. You can identify errors with packets on the device by looking for orange lights identifying packet collisions or another error. Try resetting the device by unplugging it, waiting a few seconds, and powering it on again. Alternatively, if the device has a

Reset button, you can press this button as well. If this process does not work, you may need to replace the network device. If your default gateway consists of a cable modem or DSL router, contact your service provider for steps to alleviate your problem.

If you can ping your default gateway but are unable to connect to the Internet and you are using a network router or other personally managed network device for a gateway, check the cable going to your outside provider. You should also try to ping outside your internal network to test for outside connectivity. If you can successfully ping an external IP address your gateway should be in good shape. If you can ping by IP address externally but not to a name, such as *Google.com*, you need to verify that you have input the IP address, of your DNS server properly in the TCP/IP configuration. With DHCP, the network device usually provides the DNS server address, so you would need to check the configuration of the device. If you verify these settings but still cannot connect to the Internet, use the NSLookup command to check for DNS resolution. See Example 14-3 for an example of how to use the NSLookup command.

Example 14-3. NSLookup output

```
C:\>nslookup
Default Server: ns1.securestream.net
Address:  69.150.220.8

> securestream.net
Server:  ns1.securestream.net
Address:  69.150.220.8

Name:    securestream.net
Address:  69.150.220.9
```

To verify DNS resolution for connectivity to the Internet or possibly your Active Directory domain, type **NSLookup** at the command line. You should receive a > prompt. Type the name of the domain to which you want to connect and press the Enter key. If you receive output showing the IP addresses of the domain, your resolution works correctly. If you receive output that says something like "Non-Existent" domain, you should try another DNS server for output or contact your ISP to find out why its DNS server fails queries.

If you can query the DNS name correctly but are still having problems with Internet connectivity, use the TRACERT command to check the routing device hops between yourself and the desired location. At the command line, you can accomplish this task by typing:

```
TRACERT <Destination IP or Name>
```

You will see a maximum of 30 hops to the destination, including an IP address, and possibly the name of the device. If you see expirations or "Device not found," there are problems outside of your control. You should contact your service provider to determine whether it is aware of these problems and is working to correct them.

Fixing Network Problems

TCP/IP networking has many different facets, and additional protocols that ride on top of it. While it is the single most prolific technology in use today, there are inherent problems with some implementations. Use Table 14-11 to help diagnose common problems with network connectivity or protocol issues.

Table 14-11. Troubleshooting matrix

Problem	Resolution
No IP Address	Check DHCP scope on the router or server.
	Input a static IP address.
Cannot Ping Machine	Ping 127.0.0.1.
	Ping *<Host Name>*.
	Ping *<Default Gateway>*.
Cannot Ping 127.0.0.1	Verify that the TCP/IP protocols are enabled on the adapter.
	Verify that the adapter is enabled in Device Manager.
Cannot Ping Default Gateway	Verify that the gateway has network connectivity.
	Check the cables connecting your computer to the network device.
	Reset the network device by powering it off and then powering it on.
	Contact your ISP.
	Replace the network device.
Cannot Reach Internet	Check gateway connectivity using TRACERT *<IP Destination>*.
	Verify DNS resolution using NSLookup.
	Input DNS server addresses as part of the network device DHCP configuration.
	Input DNS server addresses in the TCP/IP properties of the network adapter.
No Network Connectivity	Check the cable connecting the network adapter to the network.
	Check Link/Act status on the adapter.
	Update the network adapter driver.
	Flash BIOS on motherboard (integrated adapters only).
	Move the network adapter to a different slot on the motherboard.
	Replace the network adapter.
Only Send or Receive Packets	Reseat the network cable.
	Replace the network cable.

CHAPTER 15

Protecting Your Computer with Windows Defender and Windows Firewall

Hackers and malicious individuals enjoy nothing more than creating nasty programs that destroy your data or cause your computer to crash. Your computer is at risk every time you connect to the Internet, browse the Web, or work with files from another computer. To protect your computer and your data, you need to secure your computer with protection software.

Microsoft has taken a firm stance with security in Windows Vista. It has added many new security features in this release, alleviating some of the most common security threats used against Windows users. Some of the features in Windows Vista are updated versions of security enhancements to Windows XP, and some are newcomers to the scene. This chapter discusses the nature of many common security threats, and the applications Microsoft offers to eliminate them. We will discuss malware, viruses, spyware, and the tools available to eliminate these threats from your Windows Vista installation. We will also discuss Windows Defender and the updated version of Windows Firewall.

Please take the time to read this chapter and understand how to use the products Windows Vista offers to help you retain the data on your computer, reduce security problems, and eliminate programs that may try to leech computer resources or exploit your personal data. Malware, viruses, and spyware are serious problems, and protecting against them is vital to the use of a computer housing any type of confidential or private information.

Navigating the Computer Security Maze

It seems like every time Microsoft or other software providers find a better way to protect your computer, hackers and malicious individuals find new ways to exploit computer vulnerabilities. In this section, we'll introduce the various techniques being used to attack computers and discuss the software programs used to prevent these types of attacks.

Introducing Malware

Many people spend a lot of time on the Internet browsing web sites, downloading data, and never thinking of the potential problems of malicious software creeping onto their computers. Some software simply reports your surfing habits, and other software tries to take control of your computer. Malware consists of programs that are suspicious in nature and have the malicious intent of infiltrating your computer without your consent. The industry also defines malware as software with a legitimate purpose that contains harmful bugs that ravage a computer.

Before the proliferation of broadband Internet connections, most malware was kept in check by the limited bandwidth of dial-up Internet connections. When you dialed into your service provider you were usually given a protected, dynamically assigned address, which kept you secure because it wasn't directly connected to the Internet and didn't really have the bandwidth to allow your computer to be compromised without your knowledge. If you felt you had a security issue, you simply disconnected from the Internet. Then when you reconnected, your computer had a new IP address and you had a fresh start on security. At that time, most computers were not left online all the time and were not available for people to try to connect to and harm.

Because broadband connections are readily available, many people today simply leave their computers connected to the Internet all the time. This works against the computer owner, especially if she connects directly to a cable or DSL modem. With a direct connection to the Internet, you have left your computer open to numerous attacks by potentially harmful users of your computer. This is where malware comes into play. Malicious individuals have the opportunity to footprint your computer in an attempt to find vulnerabilities, and eventually your computer succumbs to an attack, which allows someone to load software on your computer without your consent.

Another way for malicious software to get onto your computer is via the Internet. You may recall a time when you visited a web site and were faced with numerous pop ups asking you to vote for a web site or install specific add-ons in order to see the content of a web site. More than likely, you either purposefully clicked, allowing the malicious program to load, or you were misled into clicking the wrong button and the software loaded by itself. Many of these web sites load harmful software to take advantage of your computer without your consent. Some even load dialers onto your computer to use your modem to make phone calls that are then charged to you.

Other malicious programs get loaded onto a computer without the owner knowing they are there because they are able to mask their running processes. The industry calls this particularly heinous type of software a *rootkit*. Rootkits conceal their running processes and files, and sometimes they even morph process names and files to conceal their true nature. Most of the time rootkits disguise themselves as drivers, parts of the operating system, or kernel modules.

Kernel-level rootkits replace portions of code programmed into the computer kernel. The modified code added by the rootkit usually hides an additional program, allowing remote users to use the infected computer. Usually kernel-level rootkits replace a computer driver, device driver, or additional module to accomplish their goal. If the rootkit has bugs in the code, it may compromise the integrity of the computer from a stability standpoint, in addition to introducing the security implications of infection. These types of rootkits are extremely difficult to identify and clean, which makes them extremely dangerous.

Other common types of rootkits include library-level kits and application-level rootkits. A library-level kit will replace a computer call with modified code to mask the information about the hijacked module. Application-level rootkits replace common applications with modified code or a Trojan. These applications mimic the behavior of the previous application and mask their modification of the computer. Sometimes application-level rootkits replace patches loaded onto a computer for security purposes.

Virtualized rootkits modify the boot sequence of a computer to load their content instead of the intended operating system. Once they have introduced their payload, they load the operating system as a virtual computer, which enables them to gain control of all calls to the hardware by the guest operating system. While none of these rootkits exists in the wild, they do exist in controlled environments. For example, Microsoft and the University of Michigan jointly developed a virtual rootkit, which they termed Virtual Machine Based Rootkit, or VMBR.

Rootkits also serve as a tool to abuse an infected computer using a program called a *backdoor*. Backdoors also fall into the category of malware. Backdoors are programs that allow attackers to use a computer for their personal use or profit. Backdoors allow the attacker to manipulate the compromised computer to perform single or even strategic attacks against other people's computers. In addition to allowing remote connectivity to the computer, backdoors may also allow an attacker to run software at an elevated level usually reserved for administrators of the compromised computer.

Additional malware programs include key loggers and denial-of-service attack tools. Key loggers usually log or directly send keystrokes from the compromised computer to another user on a remote computer. Denial-of-service attack tools are loaded by an attacker or rootkit and allow the compromised computer to be used against web servers, denying users the ability to connect to the web server.

Denial-of-service tools accomplish their task by overloading the server with requests until the computer under attack runs out of available resources to honor the overwhelming number of synchronization packets sent requesting an acknowledgment. Single-user computers are used in these types of attacks. While a standard denial-of-service attack uses a single computer to try to accomplish this goal, a distributed denial-of-service attack uses any number of compromised computers, making it even more difficult to stop the attack by blocking requests from a single IP address.

Whatever the flavor of malware, most of it provides no value to the computer on which it exists. Malware has many impractical purposes, including malicious use of the infected computer. It may also allow the use of personal information housed on the infected computer for profiteering, or identity theft. Malware makes up a very large portion of the problems inherent to the Internet in its current state, and it poses a great threat to private information housed on private networks. The worst part of malware seems to be computer users' lack of knowledge of how to remove and prevent these types of programs from infecting their computers. This includes home users and corporate IT professionals alike. Malware may arguably be the worst threat against computers to date.

Understanding Antimalware Programs

Recently more companies have realized the potential harm of malware programs, and they have tried to take steps to begin removing malware from their environments. With the onset of the Sarbanes-Oxley and HIPAA acts, compliance is on the rise and many people have started to realize how vulnerable their private data has become to outside entities. Armed with this knowledge, security practices have become increasingly important for many organizations, and everyone feels the pain as we struggle to maintain a balance between user-friendly computing and secure computing. To combat the problem with malware, many vendors now offer tools that will remove even the toughest malware out there. The industry refers to these programs as *antimalware tools*.

Antimalware tools scan and remove malware from infected computers. If you type "antimalware" in a search engine, you will discover some of the more than 13 million web pages on the topic. The reason for this relates directly to the inexhaustible amount of malware floating around on the Internet. As discussed previously, most users have become aware of the problem with this type of software only in the last few years. Some people were aware of the problem early and tried to explain to others how difficult it may become, especially in the corporate world, but mostly it was ignored. Now antimalware has taken the lead in the battle for securing your data.

Antimalware programs work similarly to antivirus scanners—identifying malicious programs on the suspect computer, whether in RAM, on the hard drive, or on network shares connected to the computer. Once the antimalware program has identified the threat, it will either alert the user for further instructions on how to handle the problem, or it will delete the program and eliminate any registry entries associated with the rogue program.

As with antivirus engines, multiple malware scanners are your best bet for eliminating malware programs from suspect computers. You can find these types of programs online, and using them will eliminate the vast majority of malware on an infected computer. For the purposes of malware removal, Windows Vista offers Windows Defender, arguably the largest and most powerful antimalware engine available.

In addition to Windows Defender, two other powerful antimalware engines are Ad-Aware from Lavasoft and Search & Destroy from Spybot. You should take the time to run different malware engines on your computer. Each program provides different capabilities, including the prevention of registry edits without your approval, and dictionary scans to identify the malware on the computer.

Antimalware programs can identify and remove many of the unwanted programs on your computer, including unwanted browser help objects, startup programs, registry settings, toolbar buttons, Winsock hijackers, Internet Explorer plug-ins, ActiveX controls, DNS hacks, and anonymous proxy rerouters. Each type of unwanted program relates to methods that malware writers employ to get their malicious code onto your computer. Some of the methods employ deceptive tactics to make you believe you are loading a beneficial program onto your computer while manipulating data on your computer so that it can be accessed on remote servers. These programs leave you vulnerable to the less than savory strategy of the malware writer.

Currently many antivirus companies are beginning to enter the world of malware removal by either using third-party applications or purchasing the engines of antimalware programs and integrating them into their own products for malware identification and removal. While malware may seem similar to a virus, it is indeed a separate category of malicious code. Viruses replicate themselves from computer to computer; malware is a silent threat that users usually unknowingly install.

Also, note that you may have to hand-edit the registry to remove some types of malware. If you require this type of intervention, take great care when editing your computer's registry. Editing the registry can render a computer unusable and require the intervention of a recovery service or large amounts of time to correct. If you are not comfortable editing the registry, consult a computer service or repair shop to remove these types of malicious programs. Most computer service companies can remove these programs within a short period and require only a small fee to clean your computer. This can help immensely when the programs are embedded into the computer or have metamorphic qualities.

Understanding Computer Viruses

The industry defines a computer *virus* as a program that spreads by inserting itself into executable code, documents, or programs, and then self-replicates to other computers using the compromised file. We refer to a computer with a virus as *infected*, and we try to inoculate the computer against future infections. Viruses fall into the broad category of malware, to the extent that they are usually malicious and sometimes harbor backdoors or Trojans.

Viruses were extremely common in the earlier days of computing and they had a devastating effect on computers. Viruses come in all shapes and sizes, as well as varying strengths of maliciousness. Some of the methods viruses used to execute included time bombs that would go off at a predetermined time, and logic bombs that a user triggered by completing some predefined action on the computer.

Another very nasty virus included the stealth boot virus, which attacked the boot sector of the host computer or floppy disk. This virus would not allow the computer to boot, and it required considerable work to remove. This type of virus was more common due to the lack of networks available. Most files were moved from computer to computer via floppy disks. Once the infected floppy was inserted into the receiving computer, the virus code executed, infecting the new computer.

Viruses are terrible in the sense that they can replicate themselves at an inexhaustible rate. Luckily, we do not see as many traditional disk viruses as before. However, now that we have the ability to transmit data at gigabit speeds and process data in the gigahertz range, viruses pose an even greater threat than previously known. This brings us to the subject of worms.

Computer worms have taken on the traditional role of the computer virus. A *worm* is defined as a piece of software using a computer network to copy itself and generate new hosts by compromising security flaws in applications or the host operating system. Once a worm makes it onto a network, it begins to scan for other computers with a similar or identical flaw used to infect the first host. The more hosts the worm can find to replicate itself, the greater the impact it has on the host computer and network. Some worms have generated so much traffic that they have literally brought the Internet to its knees.

The first worm was created at the Xerox PARC laboratory in Palo Alto, California. One of the computer scientists at the lab created a worm to use on the different host computers in the facility to process data for a centralized program. This was in the early days of the PC. Before this, all users connected to a CPU. To garner the processing power of the individual PCs in the facility as a single unit, the scientist broke his data into chunks for each PC to process. Once the PCs finished their work, they transmitted the results back to the controlling node. At one point, the worm began using more and more resources of the host's computers, until it failed to give the user computer availability. This required the creator to find a way to disarm the worm, which in turn gave the user use of the infected computer and the network it flooded with traffic. Although this worm had no malicious intent against the host computer, some of the more recent incarnations of this type of program have caused considerable damage to entire networks. Some worms have rendered entire networks unusable for days, weeks, and even months, due to their inherent capability to replicate themselves.

The most recent embodiment in the computer virus family comes in the form of email viruses. Recent years have given us some particularly nasty specimens, including (but not limited to) the ILOVEYOU, MELISSA, and, of course, Mydoom viruses. Each of these email viruses had a devastating effect on computers, causing many providers to turn off their email computers to prevent the virus from taking over and spreading. Most email viruses use the address book of the user executing an email program to spread themselves to other users, who in turn execute the program, allowing their address books to be manipulated by the virus and spread even farther.

Almost all viruses execute with the use of another program, replicate themselves, and continue their path of destruction. Some replace executable files on the computer they infect, which the operating system executes, releasing the virus to spread to other computers. All types of computers are susceptible to viruses. Additionally, all operating systems have vulnerabilities allowing the execution of virus-ridden code, so no one vendor offers a completely safe product.

While some viruses try to inundate a network to eliminate its use, others are malicious and want to destroy data on a computer. Viruses can be embedded in all types of files, including video, audio, document, and image files. Some of the newer viruses are embedded into JPEG images for execution. This is especially dangerous because the browser has the intrinsic capability to execute and display images. Browsers make up the largest group of applications in use on computers today. With this fact evident, the propagation of viruses could become even greater in the future than in the past.

As with malware, viruses that take the place of programs used by the operating system may cause instability of the host computer. This can cause crashes, hangs, and intermittent lock-ups. Trojans fall into this category as well, but they work slightly differently than viruses. Trojans follow true to their name. Trojans are also referred to as Trojan horses, relating to the famous story told by Homer in *The Iliad* of the great battle between the Greeks and the Trojans over Princess Helen. To get a Trojan on your computer, you must invite the program onto your computer. Usually you do this by loading a utility or other program that has a valid use on the computer. Unbeknownst to you, the program includes a Trojan, which gives an external user the ability to use the computer remotely. The remote user can then cause great harm to the data on the computer or expose its use for personal gain.

The Trojan may lie dormant on the computer until you open the program, and then it may require the use of a specific program to open a predefined network port. Once you meet the criteria for the Trojan to work, it allows a remote user to manipulate the infected computer for his purposes. These purposes usually fall in line with malicious uses including profiteering, denial-of-service attacks, distributed denial-of-service attacks, key logging, and identity theft.

As you can see, the lines between malware and viruses are very blurry in terms of the devastation they can wreak on a computer. The difference lies in the way the program comes to reside on the infected host computer. Malware makes its way onto the computer without your knowledge and allows remote control of the computer. Malware does not replicate itself to gain the use of other computers. Viruses always replicate themselves. Sometimes viruses employ the same method of installation on the infected host computer, but they always replicate themselves to other computers. They act in very much the same way as a virus acts in the human body, which is how they received their name. The good news is that since the popularity of the Internet, many viruses have been permanently eradicated from the industry, due to the capability to transfer code to eliminate the viruses from infected computers.

Introducing Antivirus Programs

The intent of an antivirus program is to identify, inoculate, disinfect, or clean a virus or other malware program from a computer. Antivirus programs usually work in two different ways. Most scan a computer in its entirety, looking for known viruses based on their databases of virus listings, and then they delete, inoculate, remove, or quarantine the infected file. Other antivirus programs watch file behavior on the computer. If the program detects unusual behavior, it will usually capture the file, scan it, and then either ask the user for input on how to handle the issue or quarantine the file for further inspection and possible deletion.

Most current commercial antivirus programs use both of these methods to detect and eradicate viruses from infected computers. This helps eliminate the threat of infection by watching the most consistent way viruses try to infiltrate computers. The most common elements of virus removal involve repair of the file itself. This consists of the antivirus program trying to remove the offending code from the infected file. If the removal process does not work, the antivirus program usually will quarantine the file discovered and prompt you for further instructions on how to handle the problem with the infected file. When you log on to the computer after the quarantine process, you must decide whether to try to repair the file again or delete the infected file.

It should be noted that you should always attempt to use multiple antivirus programs to repair either files of a sensitive nature or those used by the operating system before deleting the files. If you have a virus in a file you want to keep, you should try to use multiple antivirus engines to repair the file. This also holds true for operating system files. Operating system files infected with viruses may render the infected computer incapable of operating correctly, sometimes to the point where the infected computer will not boot into the operating system. Infections of this type require a boot disk with an antivirus program to remove the virus from the computer. McAfee Stinger is one example of this type of antivirus program.

Antivirus programs detect viruses via dictionary scans, behavior analysis, and other methods. Each detection technique follows a specific type of logic in order to find, repair, remove, or delete an infected file. Each approach is unique. Most antivirus engines employ at least two of these types of analysis in order to identify viruses. The third category is usually used only when specific types of viruses are encountered. Each approach helps us to identify the methods virus writers employ to launch their code so that we can begin the process of eradicating viruses from our environment.

Dictionary scanning uses a database of known antivirus types. When the antivirus program scans the computer in question, it looks for specific code listed in the files it scans. If it discovers suspect code, it will try to identify the virus strain, report the infection, and complete whatever predefined options the user has defined in case of corruption. Usually a dictionary-based antivirus program scans the files when the operating system opens the files for use. This includes files, programs, email, and other known methods of attack.

Not all virus writers allow their code to remain static. That means the code may be able to change or "morph" into something different to eliminate the effectiveness of dictionary scanning. These types of viruses fall into the *polymorphic* and *metamorphic* categories. They modify themselves to prevent detection, and even employ encryption to help hide portions of themselves from antivirus programs.

Polymorphic code changes into different forms while keeping the original algorithm intact, allowing the same action to occur when executed but letting the code slip past dictionary analysis. This helps the code hide its presence from antivirus programs trying to detect and rid infected computers of viruses. Malicious-virus programmers use this type of mechanism to keep their code "in the wild," allowing the virus to propagate freely without detection.

Metamorphic code literally reprograms itself by translating itself into a similar representation, and then back into the original form. Metamorphic code can also use different operating systems affected by the virus. That means a single virus could employ different methods of infecting Windows, Linux, and BSD in the same code. This method allows the virus to slip through detection of dictionary analysis by antivirus programs. Programmers go to great lengths to see that their viruses do maximum damage by eliminating the simplest of detection efforts by the public.

Suspicious behavior uses a different approach to virus identification. This approach does not employ dictionary databases to find and eradicate viruses. Instead, it monitors a program's behavior on the computer. When the antivirus program sees a program attempt to write data into an executable program, the antivirus program will identify the behavior, flag it as a potential problem, and ask the user what to do with the offending file.

Metamorphic viruses that reprogram themselves create brand-new types of viruses. Since the new virus does not have a signature to match in a database, the behavior analysis method allows the antivirus program to capture and begin to identify the new offending virus. However, if the user accepts the behavior of the offending virus, this allows the virus to propagate, eliminating the effectiveness of the antivirus program. This type of analysis also lends itself to lots of false positives, making it a less effective technique than other methods of virus identification and eradication.

Other approaches to identify, capture, and eliminate viruses include *heuristic analysis* and *sandboxes*. Each method employs different processes to identify and capture viruses in an effort to eradicate their capability to propagate. Heuristic analysis may emulate the beginning lines of code executed by a program to identify the program's behavior as self-modifying, or it may use a similar technique to discover that a program is looking for other executable files. In either case, the antivirus program may flag the file as a virus. Heuristic filters employ replicable methods to study, ascertain, or identify viruses through their perceived behavior.

Sandboxes emulate an operating system and allow code to run in a simulated environment. When the code runs, the antivirus program analyzes the emulated operating system for changes that are perceived as a virus. These types of analysis require sophisticated programs and use large amounts of computer resources to run. These features lend themselves to finding new viruses and keeping them out of the user environment, but they do not lend themselves to real-time analysis, requiring the antivirus program to run either as a managed background process or during off-peak usage times.

Each process lends itself to different types of virus identification and removal processes. Not all antivirus programs use the same methods of identification; therefore, it is often a good idea to use multiple antivirus solutions to identify viruses on your computer. No one antivirus program can identify and eliminate all viruses. Take the time to research the different antivirus programs available, including free scanners online, to help identify and eliminate viral code from your computer.

Understanding Spyware

Spyware falls into a broad category of software designed to gain control of a computer without the user's consent. As the name suggests, the program loaded onto the computer spies on the user, and the industry has come to realize that spyware also allows a remote user to control how the computer operates. Sometimes spyware only offers the data housed on the computer for use in spying on a user's habits. Some companies use this data for targeted advertising or to manipulate content based on the user's browsing habits.

Spyware watches what you do on your computer and sends the data over the Internet to a collection point for future use. Sometimes these collection points are data warehouse computers that let marketing groups purchase browsing habits to begin an advertising campaign based on the way you and other people browse the Web, thereby allowing them greater financial gain. Some types of spyware will attempt to record your keystrokes in the hopes of getting personal information for monetary gain. These programs try to intercept any usernames, passwords, or credit card information you use while online, and they are the most dangerous type of spyware.

Other spyware programs monitor the use of web sites on the compromised computer. They then attack you with a barrage of pop-up windows. Some simply begin popping up advertisements of competitor web sites in the hopes of gaining advertising dollars through your clicking on the advertisements. Most of these types of programs fall into a category called *adware*. Not all pop-up windows are associated with programs loaded on the computer; some simply are generated by the code on a web site. With this in mind, if you see pop ups on a regular basis whenever you use your browser, you probably need to look into cleaning spyware off your computer. If you visit a web site and get the same pop up or a similar pop up every time, it is probably due to the code on the web site. For example, the Barnes & Noble web site (*http://www.bn.com*) has for many years displayed a pop up with the latest advertisement whenever you visit the home page. This type of pop up is not the result of adware or spyware. However, if you visit the Barnes & Noble web site and get pop ups for competing or unrelated sites, this is probably the result of adware or spyware.

Most spyware capitalizes on the integration of the Internet Explorer browser into the Windows operating system. This integration allowed individuals to write code to get information from the browser and the operating system, and it allows companies to pull information from unsuspecting users when they visit a web site using ActiveX controls and other applications loaded onto your computer.

An example of a program that integrates the Internet Explorer browser into the Windows operating system is the Alexa toolbar. The Alexa toolbar is an application defined as a browser help object that includes some useful tools, such as a pop-up blocker, a search engine, and a link to Alexa.com and Amazon.com. The toolbar also reports the web site usage of the local computer to a collection point at Alexa. Some dispute the Alexa toolbar spyware classification, because the user has to agree to an end user license agreement (EULA), but its preferred method of installation leaves some room for argument.

One of the most prolific spyware programs was Gator. This program offered to house your personal passwords for applications and web sites. While the program held on to your personal data, it also spied on the browsing habits of users and sent the information back to Claria Corporation. This same company also popularized its Bargain Buddy program, which loaded onto the computer in a not-so-above-the-board manner. Claria then paid the installing web site money for loading the software, and the program began popping up advertisements to the user.

Some of the more recent applications of spyware include software advertised as a spyware removal tool. While these tools advertise removal of spyware on infected computers, they actually cause damage to the computer on which they are installed. Some argue against the use of the term *spyware* for these programs because they actually require the user to install them on the computer, and some include a EULA, which flies in the initial definition of spyware.

Another prolific installation path for spyware programs includes the offer of a usable program for peer-to-peer file transfers or other uses that then piggyback the spyware onto the computer when the user installs the program. Kazaa worked in this manner by tricking the user into installing the program, and then allowing the spyware to work in the background without the user's knowledge. After its prolific use on the Internet, someone noticed the problem with the application and made it publicly known that the software was pilfering data from the computer on which it was installed. Kazaa then proceeded to create a new, "lite" version of the product without the spyware attached. Of course, most of these programs have fallen under attack by the Recording Industry Association of America (RIAA) in the battle against music theft and user rights, and they do not have the same user base as they once did.

Not all spyware comes packaged in the cloak-and-dagger style. Another prolific spyware program, named Bonsai Buddy, advertised itself as a companion for children while they surf the Web. It even claimed to allow product price comparisons for the user. What the user did not understand when he loaded the program was that it was spying on his very usage of the computer. It goes to show that you need to take the time to research the programs asking for your approval before you install them on your computer.

You are the main line of defense against spyware and other malicious programs targeting your computer. Take the time to consider what you are installing, and block your children's ability to install programs onto computers. Some spyware applications come packed with freeware utilities or even games. This makes children a prime target for the installation of programs that may undermine the stability of the computer or that may allow someone to steal your private data.

Introducing Antispyware Programs

Antispyware falls into the same category as antimalware does. Before the proliferation of this type of code across the Internet, a distinction was made between the two types of programs. However, in recent years, these antispyware and antimalware programs have morphed into the same program. Usually you can eliminate spyware using freeware antimalware tools or antivirus scanners. Some specialty tools list themselves as spyware removal tools, but they also help eradicate malware.

It may be more accurate to call spyware *adware* or *nuisance software*. While some of these offending programs do actually send user data across the Web, they usually do not have a malicious intent against the user. They typically use the data to advertise goods or services to the user by scanning the user's computer for patterns of behavior on browser use. Windows Defender, which is included with Windows Vista, will find most types of spyware programs on your computer.

For many in the industry, spyware programs were both a wake-up call and the proverbial straw that broke the camel's back. Many companies in the security business underestimated the threat posed by spyware and were not ready to combat the unique problems it created. This left many people running McAfee, Norton, and other security products without real protection against spyware, until recently. Not only did this leave many longtime users of these security products outraged, but it also created a backlash that was heard throughout the security industry. Why did this occur? Well, most of the security products—even those sold as total security shields—protected your computer from viruses, hackers, abuse, and sometimes even spam, but they did not protect your computer from spyware. In fact, only the latest 2007 editions of the McAfee and Norton security products truly protect you from spyware as well as all the other bad things out there on the Internet.

The backlash created by consumer outrage did have some positive effects, though. As ISPs noticed that people were increasingly canceling their memberships because their computers simply could not be made safe on the Internet, many began offering free security solutions. At the time of this writing, two of the largest ISPs in the United States—Comcast and AOL—provide McAfee security products free to subscribers. Comcast subscribers get a free subscription to McAfee VirusScan, Personal Firewall Plus, Privacy Service, and SpamKiller. AOL included McAfee VirusScan and Personal Firewall Plus in the AOL Safety and Security Center, and it offers spyware protection, phishing protection, and spam protection.

You should note that not all antispyware programs work as advertised. Some of these programs disguise themselves as removal tools, but in fact they install and advertise themselves for use to remote users for malicious intent, or they install advertisement programs onto the computers themselves. Take the time to research any product before you install it on your computer. All reputable programs have web sites explaining the use and purpose of their programs.

Most of the tools available require you to go online to update their databases of known spyware to aid in the removal of these programs. As with any tool you use to remove unwanted programs, take the time to either update it regularly or allow it to connect and retrieve its updates automatically. Most of these programs have a mechanism built in to allow this type of automation and allow the user to go on without the effort to check them as frequently. This does not mean you should set it and forget it. You still need to take the time to verify that they are updating correctly, because from time to time they may not work as advertised.

As with malware, you may occasionally have to hand-edit the registry to remove some types of spyware. If you require this type of intervention, please take great care when editing your computer's registry. Editing the registry can render a computer unusable and require the intervention of a recovery service or large amounts of time to correct. If you are not comfortable editing the registry, consult a computer service or repair shop to remove these types of malicious programs. Most computer service companies can remove such programs within a short period and require only a small fee to clean your computer. This can help immensely when the programs are embedded into the computer or have metamorphic qualities.

Introducing the Windows Security Center

Microsoft introduced the Security Center in Windows XP. Windows Vista follows suit, and its Security Center offers greater flexibility than the previous offerings of the product. Here you are presented with a console to manage the most common security tasks and elements associated with your computer. Microsoft has made it very simple and effective to use, and continues with the standard "lighting" scheme of red, yellow, and green for ease of use. Figure 15-1 shows an example of the Security Center management window and its available features.

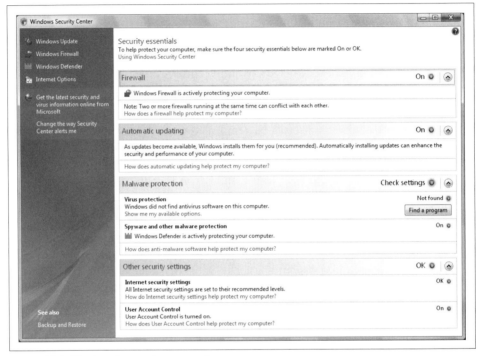

Figure 15-1. Viewing the security status of your computer

The Security Center offers you the ability to manage security operations on the computer from a single interface. You can find the Security Center in the Control Panel within Windows Vista. To open the Windows Security Center, follow these steps:

1. Click Start and then click Control Panel.

2. In the Control Panel, click Security and then click Security Center.

 When working in a workgroup configuration, you'll find options for turning the various security features on and off. These features are not available when your computer is a member of a domain. Further, in a domain configuration, it's unlikely that you'll be able to change security-related settings, because they're usually managed through Group Policy.

Using the Security Center, you can easily identify common security features and the tasks associated with securing your operating system. With the Security Center you can manage Windows Firewall, Windows Update, Windows Defender, and Internet Options. You are presented with a checklist on the right side of the main window that lists the various security features inherent to the operating system and their status on the computer. The Security Center also lists virus protection and options available if you have not already installed an antivirus solution on the computer.

Using Windows Defender

With the advent of so much suspicious software on the Internet freely working its way onto individual computers, a solution was bound to surface. Microsoft has introduced Windows Defender to champion the removal of spyware and other unwanted software from your computer. Windows Vista uses Windows Defender by default to aid in the identification and removal of spyware and malicious programs from your computer. You may remember Microsoft AntiSpyware as a software program for removing and quarantining spyware on earlier releases of Windows. Microsoft has greatly enhanced this program with the introduction of Windows Vista and renamed it Windows Defender.

Working with Windows Defender

Microsoft purchased an antispyware tool originally created by GIANT Company Software, called GIANT AntiSpyware. This product originally aided in the fight against spyware on Windows 95 and Windows 98. When Microsoft purchased the product, it did not keep support for these older versions of Windows. However, Sunbelt Software offers a compatible version of the GIANT product that supports these older computers.

Microsoft announced the release of Windows Defender (then called Microsoft Anti-Spyware) at the 2005 RSA security conference. With the announcement, it stated that the product was freely available to all valid licensed users of the Windows 2000, XP, and Server 2003 products. It championed Microsoft AntiSpyware as a product to help users worldwide in the fight against spyware and malware. Windows Defender offers even greater capability than the older versions, helping to ward off infection by employing several real-time security agents monitoring well-known areas of Windows that spyware and malware change regularly.

Microsoft has also integrated support for Microsoft SpyNet into the Windows Defender product. This support allows users to report spyware and malware to Microsoft in an effort to help update a centralized database that Microsoft houses to thwart the spread of spyware and malware. Microsoft uses these reports to determine the validity of the code submitted. This helps all computer users fight the spread of malicious programs across the Internet.

Microsoft has significantly redesigned its antispyware product in the release of Windows Defender. It has rewritten the core engine in C++, replacing the original GIANT engine written in Visual Basic. This change alone allows for considerably greater performance because it is now compiled code. Windows Defender also offers an easier user interface, and now runs as a service under the Windows Vista operating system, giving you greater protection because it runs all the time, not just when you log on and use your computer. To ensure that you have a valid license for the operating system, Windows Defender uses the Windows Genuine Advantage validation routine when updating content.

Windows Defender is the first iteration of a code rewrite since Microsoft purchased the original GIANT product. Previous releases were rebrandings of the original GIANT product, with some added functionality. Microsoft has also introduced more points of entry into the Windows Defender program than previously available in the rebranded product releases, making it easier to find and manage the product in Windows Vista. In addition, Microsoft has added additional advanced features to Windows Defender. Table 15-1 lists the advanced features available in Windows Defender.

Table 15-1. Advanced features in Windows Defender

Feature	Description
Computer Configuration	Monitors settings used for security in Windows
Internet Explorer Add-ons	Monitors programs running at startup of Internet Explorer
Internet Explorer Downloads	Monitors files designed for use with Internet Explorer for malicious activity
Internet Explorer Settings	Monitors Internet Explorer security settings for tampering
Auto Start	Monitors programs allowed to start automatically when you start your computer
Windows Add-ons	Monitors utilities installed under the operating system
Application Execution	Monitors programs during their startup procedure, and during their continued operation on the computer
Application Registration	Monitors files in the operating system that allow programs to register for execution
Services and Drivers	Monitors services and drivers and their subsequent interaction with the operating system and programs installed on the computer

Microsoft offers some improvements in this latest release of the tool. Most offer greater flexibility through improved controls. This release also offers support for additional platforms previously unable to use the tool. Microsoft has also improved the usability of the product for physically disabled individuals or others with additional impairments. The improvements in Windows Defender include the following:

- A new scanning engine
- A streamlined user interface
- Improved software control with Software Explorer

- Multiple-language support
- Protection technologies for all users, including administrators
- Assistive technology for impaired individuals
- Support for Windows XP Professional x64 Edition
- Automated cleaning settings

Microsoft integrated Windows Defender into the Internet Explorer browser engine to offer protection from files downloaded during your browser session. Windows Defender scans programs in real time. This feature allows greater flexibility in the fight against malicious code on your computer. It also helps in identifying and removing accidental download of malicious code without your knowledge. Windows Defender also allows you to schedule scanning and removal of unwanted programs. This gives you the option of choosing a specific time that works better with your usage of the computer.

To keep the detection database up-to-date, you have the option of allowing Windows Defender to complete automatic updates. This lets you continue working without having to update your antispyware definitions manually. However, you should still check the program periodically to verify that it has updated itself correctly.

Configuring Windows Defender

Microsoft offers a new interface for Windows Defender compared to previous versions of the product. There are several points of entry into the product, making it easier to find and manage. Using the menu, you can start Windows Defender by clicking Start → All Programs → Windows Defender. In the Security Center, you can start Windows Defender by clicking the Windows Defender option in the left pane. Figure 15-2 shows an example of the Windows Defender management window.

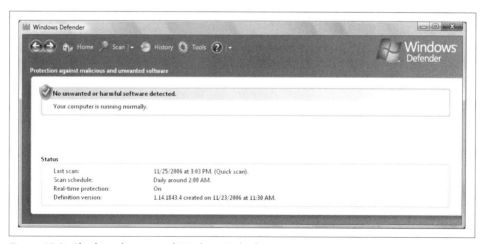

Figure 15-2. Checking the status of Windows Defender

You can always access the Windows Defender main page by clicking the Home button on the toolbar. In the main window, you will see the status of protection against malicious and unwanted software. In the lower portion of the window, you will see the status of the product, including the last scan date, scan type, scan schedule, real-time protection status, and definition version. Windows Defender offers you several default options on how to handle potential spyware. These default options are based on definitions.

Windows Defender has five different alert levels, each associated with an action. Windows Defender follows actions dictated by alert levels. Table 15-2 provides an overview of the different alert levels, their associated descriptions, and the actions Windows Defender takes in the default configuration state.

Table 15-2. Windows Defender alert levels

Alert level	Associated with...	Action taken
Severe	Widespread or exceptionally malicious programs, similar to viruses or worms, which negatively affect your privacy and the security of your computer, and can damage your computer.	Windows Defender removes this type of software immediately.
High	Programs that might collect your personal information and negatively affect your privacy or damage your computer—for example, by collecting information or changing settings, typically without your knowledge or consent.	Windows Defender removes this type of software immediately.
Medium	Programs that might affect your privacy or make changes to your computer that could negatively impact your computing experience—for example, by collecting personal information or changing settings.	Windows Defender alerts you. Review the alert details to see why the software was detected. If you do not like how the software operates or if you do not recognize and trust the publisher, consider blocking or removing the software.
Low	Potentially unwanted software that might collect information about you or your computer or change how your computer works, but is operating in agreement with licensing terms displayed when you installed the software.	Windows Defender alerts you. Review the alert. This software typically is benign when it runs on your computer, unless it was installed without your knowledge. If you are not sure whether to allow the program to run, review the alert details or see if you recognize and trust the publisher of the software.
Not Yet Classified	Programs that typically are benign unless they are installed on your computer without your knowledge.	Windows Defender alerts you. Review the alert. If you recognize and trust the software, allow it to run. If you do not recognize the software or the publisher, review the alert details to decide how to take action. If you are a SpyNet community member, check the community ratings to see if other users trust the software.

If you click the Tools button on the toolbar and then click Options on the Tools and Settings page, you'll be able to change the default configuration settings to meet your needs. The options are divided into five broad categories:

- Automatic scanning
- Default actions
- Real-time protection options
- Advanced options
- Administrator options

The "Automatic scanning" settings, shown in Figure 15-3, allow you to change how the automatic scanning of your computer works. You have the following options:

- To enable or disable automatic scanning, select or clear the "Automatically scan my computer" checkbox as appropriate.
- Use the Frequency list to control the frequency at which Windows Defender scans the computer. You can choose Daily to scan daily, or you can choose to scan on a specific day of the week, such as Sunday.
- Use the "Approximate time" list to choose the approximate time at which Windows Defender will scan the computer. The actual time of the scan will depend on whether the computer is started and the current activity level. If your computer is off during a scheduled scan time, Windows Defender will try to scan your computer the next time you turn it on.
- Use the Type list to choose the type of scan you desire. You can perform a quick (partial) scan or a full computer scan.
- To enable or disable automatic updating before scanning, select or clear the "Check for updated definitions before scanning" checkbox as appropriate.
- To enable or disable automatic handling of potential spyware, select or clear the "Apply default actions to items detected during a scan" checkbox as appropriate.

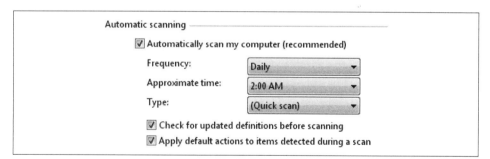

Figure 15-3. Configuring automatic scanning options

The "Default actions" settings, shown in Figure 15-4, allow you to customize the default actions to take when Windows Defender detects potential spyware. The default action is based on the settings in the spyware definition file. You can configure high alert, medium alert, and low alert items separately so that the items are either ignored or removed.

Default actions
Choose the action that you want Windows Defender to display (or apply, if you selected this option in automatic scanning) when items with these alert levels are detected. Understanding Windows Defender alert levels
High alert items:
Default action (definition-bas
Medium alert items:
Default action (definition-bas
Low alert items:
Default action (definition-bas

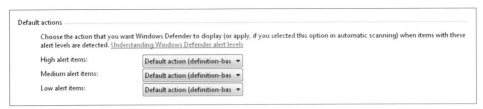

Figure 15-4. Configuring default actions

The "Real-time protection options," shown in Figure 15-5, allow you to customize the way in which real-time protection works. First, you can turn this feature either on or off. Second, you have the ability to customize the security agents that are run as part of real-time protection.

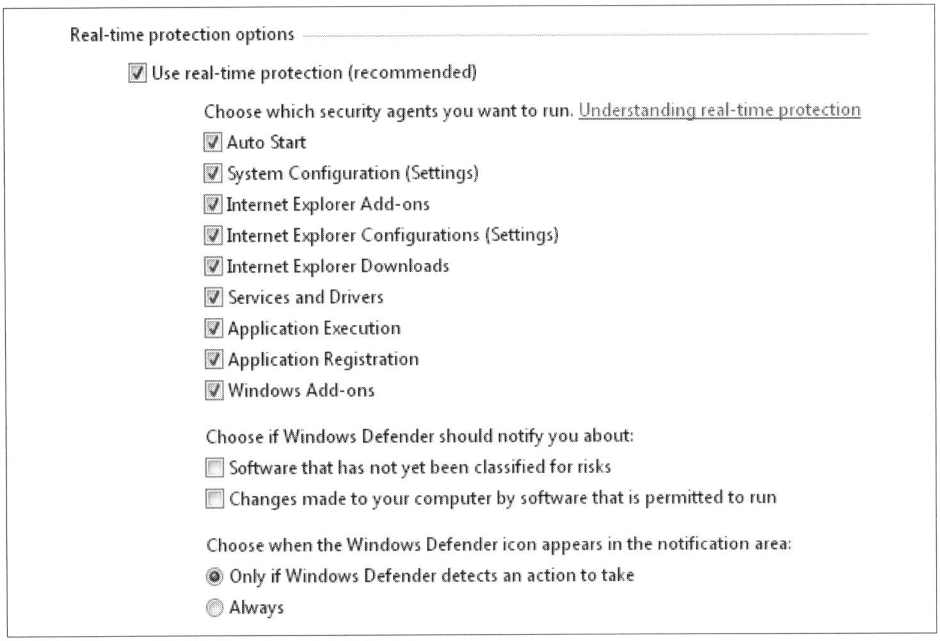

Real-time protection options
Use real-time protection (recommended)
Choose which security agents you want to run. Understanding real-time protection
Auto Start
System Configuration (Settings)
Internet Explorer Add-ons
Internet Explorer Configurations (Settings)
Internet Explorer Downloads
Services and Drivers
Application Execution
Application Registration
Windows Add-ons
Choose if Windows Defender should notify you about:
Software that has not yet been classified for risks
Changes made to your computer by software that is permitted to run
Choose when the Windows Defender icon appears in the notification area:
Only if Windows Defender detects an action to take
Always

Figure 15-5. Configuring real-time protection options

The available security agents are:

Auto Start
: Monitors programs that run during operating system startup. Turning on this option allows you to control the behavior of these programs, and removes their capability to spy on you without your knowledge.

System Configuration (Settings)
: Monitors the security settings in Windows Vista. Some malware programs will try to change the security settings to allow themselves access to privileged computer and user information. This option disallows programs from using these features without your express consent.

Internet Explorer Add-ons

Monitors Internet Explorer add-ons to help maintain the integrity of the browser by blocking potentially malicious browser add-ons from installing and running. These features help maintain a first line of defense against malware or malicious content coming through the browser.

Internet Explorer Configurations (Settings)

Monitors Internet Explorer configuration to help maintain the integrity of the browser by watching security settings for changes by browser objects.

Internet Explorer Downloads

Monitors Internet Explorer downloads to help maintain the integrity of the computer by blocking, or alerting you, about potentially dangerous types of downloads.

Services and Drivers

Monitors the services and drivers on the computer. This feature allows Windows Defender to watch how these items interact with the operating system. Sometimes spyware and malware use computer services and drivers to collect information about the computer on which they reside. They may also use these items to run undetected on the computer. Using this feature allows you to eliminate this type of covert processing on your computer.

Application Execution

Monitors how programs react when started and while running on the computer. Windows Defender has the capability to maintain a record of actions by programs processing on the computer and to stop a program if suspicious behavior begins. This helps eliminate unwanted background processing on the computer.

Application Registration

Monitors the operating system where files can register for execution on the computer. Unwanted programs may try to register to run on the computer, and Windows Defender can stop them from registering before they can fully start. This prevents unwanted programs from gaining access to important information on the computer or opening additional vulnerabilities on the computer.

Windows Add-ons

Monitors add-on programs, usually considered utilities, on the computer. This prevents unwanted programs from automatically gaining access to install additional programs onto the computer. Sometimes these utilities will try to add programs that give remote users access to privileged information on the computer. Windows Defender has the capability to stop this type of behavior, protecting the computer from malicious content unknown to the user.

Each real-time protection option works in conjunction with the alerts defined within Windows Defender. This allows Windows Defender to operate behind the scenes to protect the computer in real time. These options happen automatically without the need for user intervention to handle mundane tasks associated with elimination of threats to the computer. You can also control whether Windows Defender should notify you about software that hasn't been classified for risks and changes to your computer by software that is permitted to run. By selecting these actions, you can help Windows Defender detect new types of malware and malware that is embedded in otherwise benign software.

The "Advanced options," shown in Figure 15-6, allow you to control the way scanning works. By default, all advanced options are selected, and this is generally the configuration you'll want to use. By allowing Windows Defender to scan archived files and folders, you ensure that archived files and folders, such as those that are stored in a *.zip* file, are scanned. Because some malware programs will try to hide in archived files and folders, scanning archives is a good idea. It is also a good idea to allow Windows Defender to use heuristics to detect new types of malware and to ensure that a restore point is created before applying actions to detected items.

Advanced options

☑ Scan the contents of archived files and folders for potential threats
☑ Use heuristics to detect potentially harmful or unwanted behavior by software that hasn't been analyzed for risks
☑ Create a restore point before applying actions to detected items

Do not scan these files or locations:

[Add...]

[Remove]

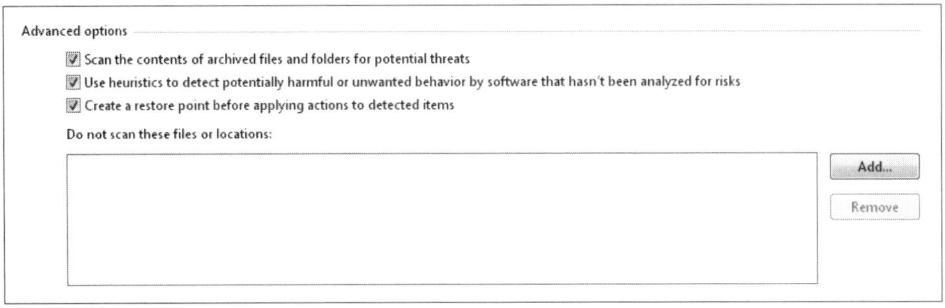

Figure 15-6. Configuring advanced options

The "Administrator options," shown in Figure 15-7, control whether Windows Defender is enabled and who can use it. By default, Windows Defender is turned on and anyone who logs on locally to the computer can use it. This is the configuration you should use to ensure that your computer is protected from malware.

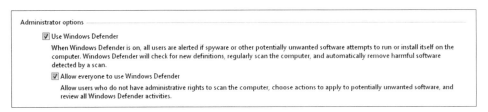

Administrator options

☑ Use Windows Defender
When Windows Defender is on, all users are alerted if spyware or other potentially unwanted software attempts to run or install itself on the computer. Windows Defender will check for new definitions, regularly scan the computer, and automatically remove harmful software detected by a scan.
☑ Allow everyone to use Windows Defender
Allow users who do not have administrative rights to scan the computer, choose actions to apply to potentially unwanted software, and review all Windows Defender activities.

Figure 15-7. Configuring administrator options

When you have finished changing your settings, click the Save button. This ensures that your configuration settings are saved for future use. This also keeps you from having to change the options again.

Which options you select in Windows Defender depends on how you use your computer. Take the time to consider the implications of turning these options on or off. If you want to turn off a setting that is normally turned on, realize the gap in protection you are opening on your computer, and take related action to protect your computer in another manner, if possible.

You are the first and last lines of defense against malicious programs on your computer. Pay close attention to the content you access with your browser. Also, take the time to scan your computer regularly for spyware content to help Windows Defender protect your computer. As with antivirus programs, you should employ different dictionaries and programs to defend your computer against malware and spyware.

Scanning Your Computer for Spyware and Malware

In Windows Defender, you can run a quick scan of your computer by clicking the Scan button on the toolbar. A quick scan checks the most common areas of the computer affected by spyware, including the computer's memory and the program executable files and registry settings currently in use. Figure 15-8 shows an example of a quick scan being performed.

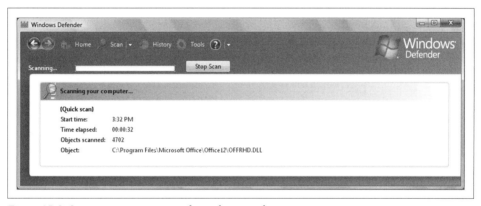

Figure 15-8. Scanning your computer for malware and spyware

Using the Scan Options button on the toolbar, you have the option of performing a full scan or a custom scan, in addition to a quick scan. A full scan scans the entire operating system and every file on the hard drive. A custom scan allows you to define the specific areas you want to scan for spyware or malware on the computer.

Regardless of which type of scan you choose, you'll see a results window, similar to the one shown in Figure 15-9, when the scan completes. The scan statistics show you the start time of the scan, the total elapsed time of the scan, and the number of items scanned. The scan status shows the last scan date and time, scan type, scan schedule, real-time protection status, and a definition version of the product.

Using Windows Defender Tools

In Windows Defender, you can access the Tools and Settings page, shown in Figure 15-10, by clicking the Tools button on the toolbar. As the previous section discussed how to configure general and administrative options, let's now look at the other selections available on this page.

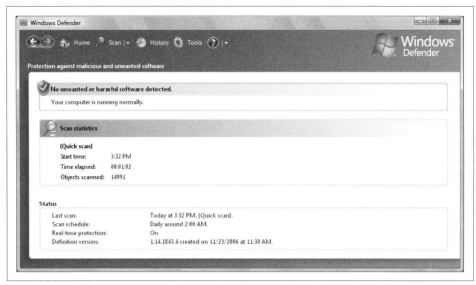

Figure 15-9. Viewing the scan results

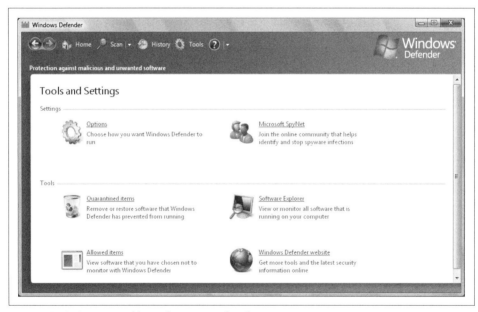

Figure 15-10. Accessing additional settings and tools

Clicking Microsoft SpyNet lists Microsoft SpyNet features and options that allow you to join this service offered by Microsoft. Microsoft SpyNet is an online community that helps users determine how to respond to potential threats to their computers. You have three options to choose from: join with a basic membership, join with an advanced membership, or not join at all.

A basic membership sends very little information to Microsoft about the software Windows Defender detects and the alert actions the computer uses. Advanced membership sends more information to Microsoft about spyware and other potentially unwanted programs encountered on the computer. Microsoft does not send any personal identification information in these updates. Of course, the "do not join" option does not send any information to Microsoft, but you also do not get the benefits of using SpyNet. Make sure you click the Save button to allow Windows to update your profile for future use of Windows Defender.

The Tools area gives you features for managing quarantined items, using Software Explorer, defining allowed items on your computer, and visiting the Windows Defender web site. Each feature allows you to define and act against different dimensions of protection within Windows Defender. Take the time to become familiar with the different aspects of these features and use them to your advantage.

"Quarantined items" lists the different programs and files Windows Defender has identified as threats against the computer. This feature also lists the default action taken against the listed objects, and the date the computer found the potentially unwanted program. You have three options for working with quarantined items:

Remove All
    Clicking Remove All permanently removes all quarantined items from your computer.

Remove
    Selecting a quarantined item and then clicking Remove removes the quarantined item from your computer.

Restore
    Selecting a quarantined item and then clicking Restore allows the item to run on your computer.

The top of the "Quarantined items" window lists the membership level if you have joined Microsoft SpyNet, and it allows you to change your membership level.

"Allowed items" lists the programs and files that you've allowed to run after Windows Defender alerted you about a potential threat. Each program or file is listed by name, alert level, and recommended action. If you want to remove a program or file from the "Allowed items" list, click it and then select "Remove from list." Windows Defender will then be able to monitor the program or file for potentially malicious activity. The top of the window also lists the membership level if you have joined Microsoft SpyNet, and it allows you to change your membership level.

Software Explorer allows you to manage security-related areas within the operating system. On the left side of the window are the options you can choose from, and on the right side are the properties of a selected item. Software Explorer offers you the ability to manage your startup programs, currently running programs, network-connected programs, and Winsock service providers.

Once you have identified the category you want to manage, click an item in the left pane to view its properties in the right pane. If you want to enable the item, click the Enable button. If you want to disable the item, click the Disable button. To remove the item, click the Remove button. You also can view items in the category list for the current user or for all users of the computer.

Selecting the link to the Windows Defender web site takes you directly to the official Windows Defender area of Microsoft's web site. The related pages have invaluable information concerning help and support using Windows Defender, as well as Microsoft's stance against spyware. You can find some wonderful information, in addition to an online community dedicated to helping users with problems using Windows Defender.

Troubleshooting Windows Defender

As with all programs associated with computers, you can sometimes have problems getting Windows Defender to work. The single most common problem with Windows Defender is it not starting at all. If this happens, you must make sure you have enabled Windows Defender to run on the computer. To check this setting, open the Security Center in the Control Panel. Under Malware Protection, you will see the Spyware and Other Malware Protection listing. Make sure you see "On" and a green circle identifying that Windows Defender protection is on.

If you do not see this listing, you will see "Off" and a button labeled "Turn on now." Click the button to turn on the Windows Defender feature and allow the program to scan the computer for spyware or malware infections. You will see the green light turn on, showing that the feature is enabled on the computer.

If you have problems turning on the Windows Defender feature, or if you receive an error stating that the Windows Defender service was unable to start, you can troubleshoot using Computer Management. To open Computer Management, click the Start button, right-click on the Computer icon, and then select Manage from the context menu provided.

Once you've opened Computer Management, click the Services and Applications node and then select Services. In the Services view, scroll down on the right side of the window until you see Windows Defender. Double-click the entry to view the properties of this service, as shown in Figure 15-11. If the service status is not listed as Started, click the Start button to start the service. If the Start button is dimmed, click the Stop button and then click the Start button. While you are working with the Windows Defender service, ensure that the "Startup type" is set to Automatic.

If you still cannot get the service to work correctly, you can check the event logs for additional information. In Computer Management, expand the Event View and Windows Logs nodes by double-clicking them and then selecting the System log. Look for stop errors listed with an X inside a red circle. If the stop error lists an unauthorized

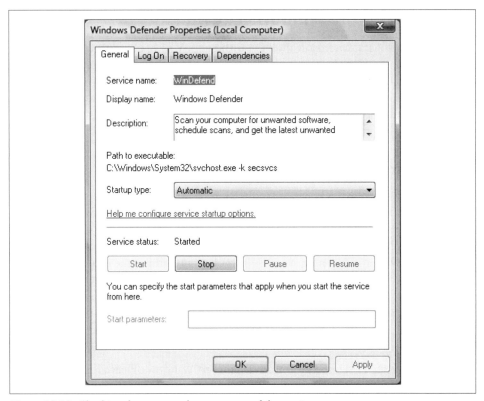

Figure 15-11. Checking the status and startup type of the service

account that is preventing the service from starting, access the Logon tab of the Properties dialog box for the Windows Defender service and verify that the "Log on as" option is set to "Local system account." If it isn't, select this option and then click Start on the General tab to start the service.

If you still cannot start the service, you can visit *http://support.microsoft.com* and enter the information from the Event Viewer as your search parameters to help you determine the source of the problem. Try using the Event ID number or error text as the search text. Usually you can find information on Microsoft's support pages to help identify existing problems and resolutions for errors on your computer. Other available options include checking for updates to Windows Defender on Microsoft's web site, or even reinstalling Windows Defender using the download link listed at the site. While these may not be the most appealing options, they do work from time to time.

If you continue to have problems getting Windows Defender to work correctly, you may need to run an antivirus program on the computer to determine if a computer file was corrupted, or you may need to contact a computer service company. Calling in a professional support representative is the most expensive option. Professional support would also be the last-ditch effort to fix the problem.

Working with the Windows Firewall

With Windows Vista, Microsoft offers you the ability to manage Windows Firewall in several different ways. You can manage the basic functionality of the firewall using the Windows Firewall dialog box, and the advanced functionality of the firewall using the Windows Firewall with Advanced Security console. This section looks at the basic Windows Firewall. You'll learn more about the advanced firewall in the next section.

Windows Firewall Features and Improvements

When Windows Firewall was first introduced, it enabled built-in exceptions for standard connections such as local computer connections, but it disallowed most other ports on the computer. In subsequent revisions, Microsoft added the ability to manage the firewall using Group Policy, enabling administrators to manage the feature throughout an enterprise. Later, Microsoft implemented the same changes into Windows Server 2003, which brought the same improvements to the server operating system. Unfortunately, in order to correct some of the problems associated with Windows Firewall, you often had to disable the product completely to make things work efficiently on your computer—and that definitely was not good for computer security.

Windows Vista offers significant improvements to Windows Firewall. Microsoft has included many different upgrades, including IPv6 support, outbound packet filtering, and a host of other improvements (see Table 15-3). Together, these features offer great improvements over the Windows Firewall that was first introduced with Windows XP. These new features also help alleviate the need to turn off Windows Firewall, as you had to do with previous offerings of the product.

Table 15-3. Windows Firewall improvements

Improvement	Description
IPv6 connection filtering	Allows filtering of connections using the IPv6 protocol, previously unsupported
Outbound packet filtering	Allows control of outbound ports, previously unsupported
Advanced packet filtering	Allows filtering rules specified by source and destination IP addressing, or complete port ranges
IPSec integration	Manages connections through the use of IP Security (IPSec) and a certificate
Encryption requirement	Manages connections through the ability to require encryption
Separate firewall policies for domains, private, and public network enrollment	Manages rule enforcement based on the network enrollment of the computer
Management Console (MMC)	New MMC snap-in, called Windows Firewall with Advanced Security

IPv6 connection filtering enables you to use the IPv6 protocol in a secure fashion. This ability did not exist under Windows XP or subsequent versions of the firewall product, including Windows Server 2003. With this improvement, you can migrate to IPv6 without the security implications previously associated with this task. Now the process should be considerably more secure thanks to Microsoft's effort to improve the quality of its firewall product.

Firewall rules for inbound packet filtering make up the majority of configuration efforts on firewalls. These rules determine how network traffic flows through the computer. You manage the flow of inbound and outbound traffic through these rules. The firewall inspects the packets as the computer receives them, and then determines based on the configured rules—how the computer will handle a particular packet. If Windows Firewall determines that the packet should be accepted, it passes the packet along internally to the computer. If the packet does not meet the requirements of the rule set, it discards the packet.

Outbound packet filtering enables you to manage outbound connections from your computer. This option did not exist as part of the Windows Firewall in previous versions. Outbound packet filtering lets you keep spyware or malware from uploading personal data that's been collected. To use this type of functionality in the past, you had to purchase a third-party application. Microsoft now offers this ability inherently in the operating system. When the computer encounters a packet requesting outbound access, Windows Firewall inspects the packet to determine its purpose, verifies the packet against the firewall rules, and then either allows the packet to be delivered or discards it completely.

Advanced packet filtering allows you to create rules associated with multiple IP addresses. This feature gives you greater flexibility in managing connections using a source or destination IP address. You even can manage a range of IP addresses for connectivity to the computer. Before, you could filter with only a single IP address, never a range of IP addresses. This is a marked improvement over previous versions of the product.

IPSec integration arguably offers the greatest improvement in Windows Firewall. Now you can manage connections using encryption. With IPSec integration, you can require that a connection have the proper certificate in order to connect to the computer. This allows for incredibly strong security and much greater flexibility when transferring data among computers.

 IPSec requires the use of certificates to transfer data. These certificates use public and private keys to determine whether the connecting entity has authorization to transfer data. This option makes transferring data much more secure among computers than before, especially among computers connected across the Internet.

Separating policies by network enrollment enables you to manage how your computer reacts to requests in different network environments. You can associate a very hardened security policy when you are using an insecure network, a fairly open security policy when connected to your corporate network, and a moderately secure policy when connected to your home network. The beauty of this feature is that you do not have to configure the settings over and over; Windows Vista allows you to create a profile for each type of environment and forget it. You specify the type of environment when you create the network connection.

The new management console offers the greatest flexibility in managing the advanced security options of Windows Firewall with Advanced Security. You now can manage the different types of connections and rules through a single interface. And administrators can easily manage the Windows Firewall connections and associate the settings with Group Policy.

Overall, Microsoft brings a very capable firewall into Windows Vista with the new offering of Windows Firewall. It offers considerably better security features, and truly supplements a network perimeter firewall. While you may have more difficulty configuring some of the advanced features of Windows Firewall, you will find considerably fewer intrusions and false positives on your computer when the firewall is configured correctly.

Configuring Security for the Basic Windows Firewall

The basic Windows Firewall provides essential firewall security for your computer. You can use the basic firewall to protect your computer from many types of attacks. In the Windows Security Center, you can start the basic firewall by clicking Windows Firewall in the left pane.

As Figure 15-12 shows, the main page in Windows Firewall provides an overview of the firewall configuration and status. You can use this information to tell at a glance whether the firewall is on or off, whether notifications are displayed when a program is blocked, and to which type of network you are currently connected. The network type, set as private, public, or domain, determines which firewall profile is currently being applied. Clicking "Change settings," or either of the links provided in the left pane, opens the Windows Firewall Settings dialog box.

In the Windows Firewall Settings dialog box, you can use the options on the General tab to turn the firewall on or off (see Figure 15-13). To turn the firewall on, click "On (recommended)." This setting allows the firewall to block incoming connections. To turn the firewall off, click "Off (not recommended)." This setting turns the firewall off and makes your computer vulnerable to remote attacks through network and Internet connections.

When you are connecting to networks that are less secure, you may want to turn the firewall on and block all incoming connections to your computer. To do this, select

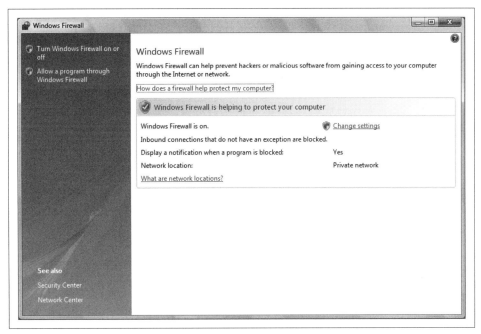

Figure 15-12. Viewing the status of Windows Firewall

the On option and the "Block all incoming connections" checkbox. This setting ignores all settings in the firewall configuration and blocks every connection to your computer. This setting also turns off notifications.

On the Exceptions tab, shown in Figure 15-14, you can control how programs communicate through Windows Firewall. Many Windows components commonly used for networking have exceptions listed in the Program or Port list. To enable an exception for a program, simply select the related checkbox. To disable an exception, clear the related checkbox. Using the "Add program," "Add port," and "Properties" buttons, you can add new programs to the exception list, add new ports to the exception list, and view the specific configuration properties of any program or port on the exception list. You can also enable Windows to notify you when Windows Firewall blocks a new program, giving you greater control over your computer's security parameters.

On the Advanced tab, shown in Figure 15-15, you can control which network connections use Windows Firewall. If you want to turn off Windows Firewall's association with a specific network connection, simply uncheck the box associated with this connection, and Windows will turn the feature off. By default, Windows Vista turns Windows Firewall on for all network connections associated with the operating system.

 Keep in mind that changing or disabling the default configuration of Windows Firewall may leave your computer in a vulnerable state. Take considerable care when changing these configuration settings.

Figure 15-13. Turning the firewall on or off

Troubleshooting the Basic Windows Firewall

Like Window Defender, Windows Firewall runs as a service on your computer. Because of this, you can use procedures similar to those discussed in the "Troubleshooting Windows Defender" section, earlier in this chapter, to troubleshoot Windows Firewall. If you begin to experience problems connecting to your network or you cannot connect to a specific computer or resource on the network, you may be experiencing problems associated with Windows Firewall. Other telltale signs of firewall problems include other computers failing to connect to your computer or the inability to ping, Tracert, or access network resources even though you have an IP address.

As with Windows Defender, start your troubleshooting by making sure Windows Firewall is on. If the firewall is on and you are blocking all incoming connections, you might want to clear this setting for your troubleshooting. Next, you should verify that the Windows Firewall service is running through the Services node in Computer

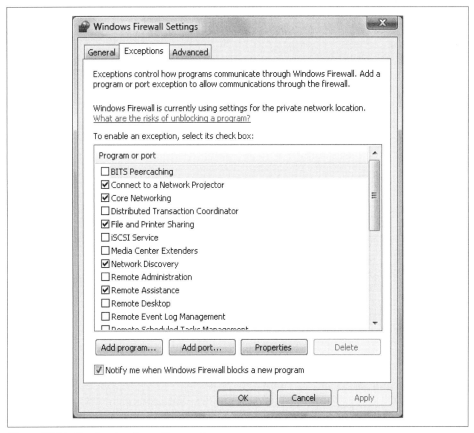

Figure 15-14. Configuring firewall exceptions

Management. Verify that the service status is listed as Started, and make sure the "Startup type" is set to Automatic. If the service is not listed as Started, click the Start button to start the service. Also, verify the logon credentials using the Log On tab associated with the service's Properties dialog box. You should see "Local service" as the selected account.

If the firewall still isn't working properly, you need to verify the network location. When you click the Windows Firewall option in the Windows Security Center, the main firewall window shows the network location. If you are on a private or domain network, other computers should be able to connect to you by default. If you are on a public network, most types of connections to your computer are disabled. If the wrong location type is listed, you can change the location type in the Network and Sharing Center by clicking the network's Customize link, selecting the desired location type, clicking Next, and then clicking Finish. Don't change the location type without first considering the possible ramifications of doing so. If you are on a public network and you specify that you are on a private network, you will open your computer to attack.

Figure 15-15. Selecting connections that should use the firewall

If the firewall still isn't working properly, check the exceptions that are listed on the Exceptions tab of the Windows Firewall Settings dialog box. By default, a private network should have the following exceptions enabled:

- Core Networking
- File and Printer Sharing
- Network Discovery
- Remote Assistance
- Windows Peer to Peer Collaboration Foundation

You might also have exceptions for:

- Connect to a Network Projector
- Windows Media Player
- Windows Media Player Network Sharing Service
- Windows Meeting Space

If you believe the appropriate exceptions are enabled and you still have problems, you can click the Restore Defaults button on the Advanced tab to go back to the original post-installation Windows Firewall settings and remove any changes you have made to these settings since installing the operating system. Keep in mind that this will also disable any custom exceptions you have created, possibly causing certain programs to function incorrectly. This is especially true for games, so you will need to reenable your custom settings after verifying that your network connections work correctly after resetting the default configuration. If you continue to have problems with connections, refer to the "Troubleshooting Advanced Firewall Problems" section, later in this chapter, for more information.

Configuring Advanced Firewall Security

In addition to the basic Windows Firewall, Windows Vista includes Windows Firewall with Advanced Security. At home, you probably won't work much with this feature. At the office, however, especially if you work in a medium-size to large organization, you may find it critical to know how the advanced firewall works.

Windows Firewall with Advanced Security allows you to open a custom management console for use in managing advanced firewall features. As Figure 15-16 shows, this console gives you direct control over inbound, outbound, and connection security rules for the firewall's domain profile, private profile, and public profile. To open the new management console, follow these steps:

1. Click Start and then click Control Panel.
2. In the Control Panel, click System and Maintenance. Scroll down and then click Administrative Tools.
3. In Administrative Tools, double-click Windows Firewall with Advanced Security.

Figure 15-16. Configuring advanced firewall settings using Windows Firewall with Advanced Security

Windows Firewall with Advanced Security gives you a host of new features and management options versus previous versions of Windows Firewall. You have object classes on the left side of the window, and their associated properties on the right side of the window. This follows the classic design of Microsoft products, making management very intuitive. To configure specific settings, simply click the desired object from the left and manage it from the right. You also have right-click context menus available on the objects selected. Table 15-4 provides the specific listings and their associated properties from the Windows Firewall with Advanced Security management console.

Table 15-4. Windows Firewall with Advanced Security features

Feature	Associated properties
Windows Firewall with Advanced Security	Provides an overview of the firewall profiles associated with the local computer as well as Getting Started options.
Inbound Rules	Provides an at-a-glance listing of the inbound packet filtering rules. Lists the associated inbound rules created on the computer according to the rule name, associated program group, profile, enabled status, action, and more.
Outbound Rules	Provides an at-a-glance listing of the outbound packet filtering rules. Lists the associated outbound rules created on the computer according to the rule name, associated program group, profile, enabled status, action, and more.
Connection Security Rules	Provides an at-a-glance listing of the IPSec rules. Lists the associated connection rules created on the computer according to the rule name, enabled status, endpoints, authentication mode, authentication method, and associated program group.
Monitoring	Provides a detailed summary of the firewall's domain profile, private profile, and public profile according to the firewall state, general settings, and logging settings.
Monitoring\Firewall	Lists the standard inbound and outbound connection settings and their associated status, giving you one place to look for monitoring the currently active inbound and outbound rules.
Monitoring\Connection Security Rules	Lists the status of connection security rules.
Monitoring\Security Associations	Lists the security associations for Main Mode and Quick Mode as well as their status.

Windows Firewall with Advanced Security maintains a separate firewall profile for each type of network to which you can connect. For each profile, you can manage settings for the firewall state, inbound connections, outbound connections, notification, unicast response, and logging. As Table 15-5 shows, the default configuration for each setting is the same for each profile.

Table 15-5. Default configuration for Windows Firewall with Advanced Security

Setting	Domain profile	Private profile	Public profile
Firewall State	On	On	On
Inbound Connections	Block	Block	Block

Table 15-5. Default configuration for Windows Firewall with Advanced Security (continued)

Setting	Domain profile	Private profile	Public profile
Outbound Connections	Allow	Allow	Allow
Notification	Yes	Yes	Yes
Unicast Response	Yes	Yes	Yes
Log Dropped Packets	No	No	No
Log Successful Connections	No	No	No

You can configure the settings for the domain, public, and private profiles by completing these steps:

1. In Windows Firewall with Advanced Security, select the Windows Firewall with Advanced Security node.

2. In the main pane, click the Windows Firewall Properties link. You'll find this link in the Overview section below the profile status listings. This opens the management dialog box, shown in Figure 15-17.

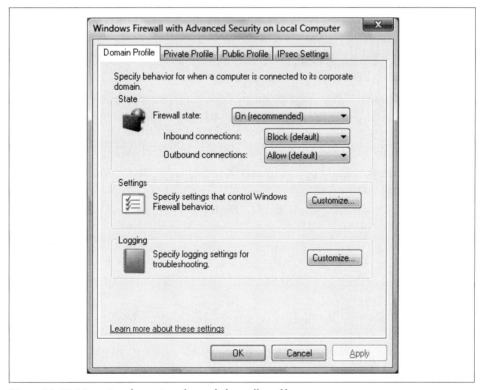

Figure 15-17. Managing the settings for each firewall profile

3. Select the tab for the profile type you want to manage.

4. Use the "Firewall state" list to turn the firewall on or off for the selected profile.

5. Use the "Inbound connections" list to allow or block inbound connections when using this profile. You can also specify that you want to override the profile settings and block all connections when using this profile.

6. Under Settings, you may also elect to customize the specific settings of a profile by selecting the Customize button. Settings customization allows you to turn notifications on or off, and to allow or disallow unicast responses to multicast or broadcast traffic.

7. Under Logging, you may also elect to customize the logging options of a profile by selecting the Customize button. Logging customization allows you to enable or disable logging of dropped packets and successful connections. When you use logging, you can also set the location and size of the firewall log.

8. Click OK to save your settings.

You can configure the default IPSec settings by completing these steps:

1. In Windows Firewall with Advanced Security, select the Windows Firewall with Advanced Security node.

2. In the main pane, click the Windows Firewall Properties link. You'll find this link in the Overview section below the profile status listings. This opens the management dialog box.

3. On the IPSec tab, click the Customize button. This displays the Customize IPSec Settings dialog box, shown in Figure 15-18.

4. In the Customize IPSec Settings dialog box, you can specify key exchange settings, including the security methods applied. These include SHA1 AES-128 and SHA1 3DES by default, with Kerberos V5 for authentication.

5. If you want to add a method for key exchange, do the following:

   a. Click the Advanced option under "Key exchange" and then click the related Customize button.

   b. In the Customize Advanced Key Exchange Settings dialog box, shown in Figure 15-19, click Add.

   c. Select the encryption algorithm and the related integrity algorithm to use and then click OK. Your options for encryption algorithms are AES-256, AES-192, AES-128, 3DES, and DES. Your options for integrity algorithms are SHA1 and MD5.

   d. In the "Security methods" list, use the options provided to set the relative priority of each configured algorithm. As the security method listed first is tried first, you'll usually want the strongest supported encryption method to be listed first.

   e. Use the "Key exchange algorithm" option to select the desired key exchange algorithm. The default algorithm is Diffie-Hellman Group 2. Your other options are to select Elliptic Curve Diffie-Hellman P-384, Elliptic Curve Diffie-Hellman P-256, Diffie-Hellman Group 14, and Diffie-Hellman Group 1.

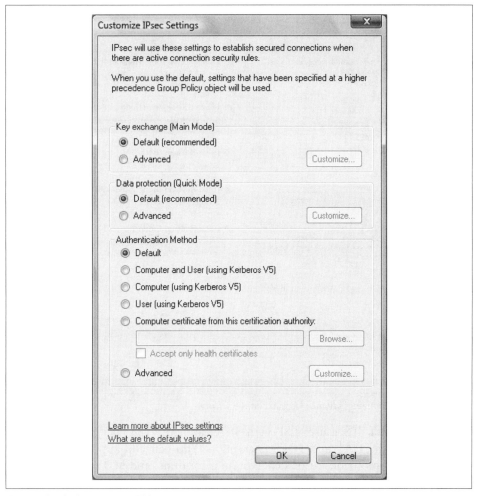

Figure 15-18. Customizing IPSec

6. If you want to require encryption for all connection security rules or add data integrity and encryption algorithms, do the following:

   a. Click the Advanced option under "Data protection" and then click the related Customize button.

   b. In the Customize Data Protection Settings dialog box, shown in Figure 15-20, select the "Require encryption…" checkbox if you want to require encryption for all connection security rules.

   c. By default, IPSec uses ESP with SHA1 and AH with SHA1 for data integrity. You can also use ESP and AH with MD5, but this configuration is not recommended. To do this, click Add under "Data integrity," select the desired security protocol and the desired integrity algorithm, and then click OK.

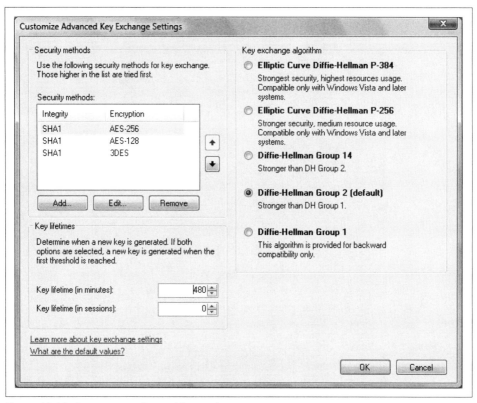

Figure 15-19. Customizing advanced key exchange settings

    d. By default, IPSec uses ESP with SHA1 and AES-128 encryption as well as ESP with SHA1 and 3DES encryption. You can add support for the AH security protocol, various encryption algorithms, and MD5 integrity checking if desired. To do this, click Add under "Data integrity and encryption," select the desired security protocol, the desired encryption algorithm, and the desired integrity algorithm, and then click OK.

    e. Select the encryption algorithm and the related integrity algorithm to use, and then click OK. Your options for encryption algorithms are AES-256, AES-192, AES-128, 3DES, and DES. Your options for integrity algorithms are SHA1 and MD5.

    f. In the Algorithms list, use the options provided to set the relative priority of each configured algorithm. As the security method listed first is tried first, you'll usually want the strongest supported encryption method to be listed first.

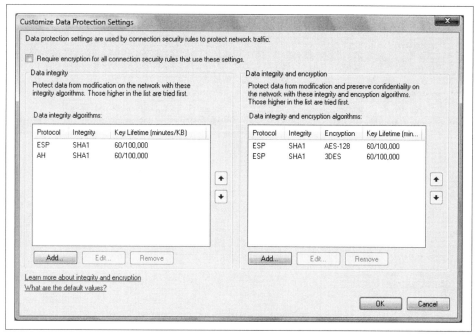

Figure 15-20. Customizing data protection settings

7. If you want to configure the authentication mechanism to use, do the following:

   a. Click the Advanced option under Authentication Method and then click the related Customize button.

   b. In the Customize Authentication Methods dialog box, shown in Figure 15-21, Kerberos V5 is listed as the first authentication method. You can also use NTLMv2, computer certificates, and preshared keys for authentication.

   c. To add an authentication method for use in authenticating your computer, click Add under "First authentication methods," select the desired authentication method, provide additional information as necessary, and then click OK.

   d. To add an authentication method for use in authenticating your user account, click Add under "Second authentication methods," select the desired authentication method, provide additional information as necessary, and then click OK.

   e. In the Methods lists, use the options provided to set the relative priority of each configured authentication method. As the method listed first is tried first, you'll usually want the strongest supported authentication method to be listed first.

8. Be sure to click OK to save your changes, or click Cancel to avoid changing these options if you are unsure of the implications.

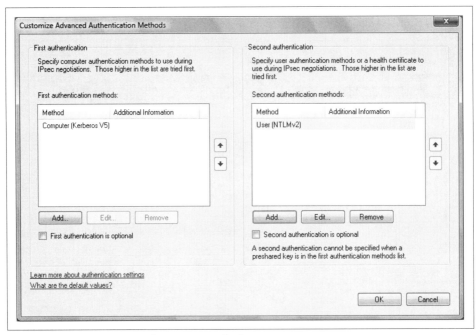

Figure 15-21. Customizing authentication methods

To create inbound or outbound rules, right-click the selection you desire and select New Rule from the context menu provided. You have the option of choosing a program, port, predefined selection, or custom rule. You must then determine the action taken by the rule, the profile with which to associate the rule, and the name you want to give the rule. Managing existing rules only requires you to double-click the rule to view the properties and manage the settings associated with the rule.

Numerous feature sets are available for each rule, allowing you to configure the associated users or computers, protocols and ports, scope of the rule, standard enablement, and allow or block action. You may select which program or service to associate with a rule. You also can change the profile associations, interface types, and edge traversal with the advanced feature options. Edge traversal allows traffic to and from the Internet to bypass specified devices, including Network Address Translation (NAT) routers, as may be necessary when using IPSec in a rule.

Windows Firewall with Advanced Security also offers you the ability to filter rules by profiles or state. You can manage the stopping, starting, and disablement of rules using the options on the Action menu. You can import and export rules by selecting the desired operation from the Action menu. This makes managing multiple computers a snap. You can create the rules you desire for all your computers on a single computer, export those settings, and then use them in Group Policy to manage your entire network.

Troubleshooting Advanced Firewall Problems

Troubleshooting advanced firewall configurations can become very complicated in a hurry. This is true especially if you have created customized authentication methods, applied certificate-based communications, or edited the standardized listings available within the management console. You must be methodical and patient when pursuing these problems in some cases. Do not become discouraged because you can always fall back to the post-installation configuration by restoring the default settings.

When you are experiencing problems with advanced firewall configurations, the first thing to set is the logging feature for each profile associated with Windows Firewall. Although you must enable logging separately for each profile, the firewall records all logged activities—dropped packets, successful connections, or both—in a central logfile. The default location for the firewall log is *%SystemRoot%\System32\logfiles\ firewall\pfirewall.log*. This log can help you diagnose problems, and offers some insight into additional issues associated with the advanced firewall features.

If you are having problems with inbound or outbound connections, refer to the profile settings for the active profile. When you select the Monitoring node in Windows Firewall with Advanced Security, the active profile is listed as such. Check the status of your current profile. If the firewall is on and you are blocking all incoming connections, select Block instead of Block All Connections. If the firewall is on and you are blocking outgoing connections, select Allow instead of Block.

If you have created IPSec policies for specific connection types or you require IPSec for communications, verify that you have the correct certificate installed or make sure the certificate has not expired or become untrusted. You will also want to verify that the remote computer has the same authentication methods set to allow proper authentication among them. You may also want to enable IPSec exemptions to allow ICMP traffic to flow regularly with IPSec. This can save a lot of time when determining specific network issues without IPSec blocking echo requests.

If a specific program does not work, make sure you have not created a customized rule that denies the desired behavior. Look in the inbound and outbound rules to make sure the settings are correct for the port, protocol, and IP address requirements as well as associated computers or users. Make sure you have enabled or disabled the rule, depending on your specific situation. You should also try to determine the correct ports and protocols in use for the program to operate correctly. Once you have the correct information, ensure that you have either created the custom rule for inbound and outbound traffic, or changed the predefined listing to work correctly according to your information.

Sometimes it helps to restart the Windows Firewall service to make sure something has not ended up in an unusable state due to configuration changes. Also, confirm that the desired functionality works with the firewall disabled. This can help to determine if you have a separate issue besides the firewall configuration.

You may also want to check Event View in Computer Management to determine whether errors are being logged for Windows Firewall. If you find a stop error, use the specified information to look up errors with Microsoft's Support site to determine how to fix your specific problem.

When all else fails, you may consider restoring the default settings. To do so, follow these steps:

1. In Windows Firewall with Advanced Security, select the Windows Firewall with Advanced Security node.
2. On the Action menu, select Restore Defaults.
3. When prompted to confirm the action, click Yes to change Windows Firewall back to the default settings when first installed. Keep in mind that this will also disable any custom exceptions you have created, possibly causing certain programs to function incorrectly. This is especially true for games, so you will need to reenable your custom settings after verifying that your network connections work correctly once you've reset the default configuration.

When all else fails, you can either consult with a professional computer repair service, contact your network administrator, consult with the Microsoft online forum for specific answers to detailed questions, or use any errors you find in the Event Viewer to determine whether someone else has this problem by searching for it online. Microsoft offers a diagnostic and troubleshooting link in the default listing of the management console. Clicking this link opens the Microsoft web site, which provides specific troubleshooting methods for different products.

CHAPTER 16

Using Windows Mail, Calendars, and Contacts

Windows Vista includes many programs designed to help you communicate with other people and share information, but few are as important to your everyday life as Windows Mail, Windows Contacts, Windows Calendar, and Windows Meeting Space. For many people, sending email is the most important thing they do on a computer. As popularity and importance of email have grown over the years, some serious risks have emerged. Windows Mail includes features that help you reduce the risks, while enjoying the many benefits of email.

While you may spend a lot of time with Windows Mail, don't overlook the benefits of Windows Contacts, Windows Calendar, and Windows Meeting Space. To help you keep track of all the people in your life, Windows Vista introduces Windows Contacts. Using Windows Contacts, you can create a virtual address book with the names, email addresses, and other contact information for friends, coworkers, business connections, and more. When you have appointments or tasks to track, Windows Calendar is there to help you. You can even use Windows Calendar to track other people's appointments and tasks. At school or at work, you may also want to use Windows Meeting Space to have virtual meetings that allow you to have a shared whiteboard and multiuser chat while sharing documents and programs.

Using Windows Mail

Windows Mail replaces Outlook Express as the standard email program included with the operating system. If you haven't purchased Microsoft Office Outlook, you can use Windows Mail to send and receive email. For connecting to email servers and receiving email, Windows Mail supports Post Office Protocol 3 (POP3) and Internet Message Access Protocol 4 (IMAP4). For sending email, Windows Mail supports Simple Mail Transfer Protocol (SMTP).

Getting to Know Windows Mail

To start Windows Mail, click Start, click All Programs, and then click Windows Mail. As Figure 16-1 shows, Windows Mail has an interface similar to earlier versions of Outlook Express. From the deceptively similar interface, you might think Windows Mail is essentially Outlook Express with a face-lift. The truth is, however, that Windows Mail is dramatically different from Outlook Express.

Figure 16-1. Creating and managing your email

While Outlook Express stores all email messages in a database, Windows Mail stores email messages as separate Email Message (*.eml*) files. The *.eml* file format is a raw email message file format that includes the routing information for the message. This is the same email message file format used by email servers, such as Exchange Server 2007. Storing your email in individual message files should provide improved stability and help to resolve those problems of corruption and lost email we experienced occasionally with Outlook Express.

If you browse your personal folders, you'll find the folders Windows Mail uses under *AppData\Local\Microsoft\Windows Mail\Local Folders*. The available folders are:

Inbox
> Stores individual *.eml* files for email you've received from other people

Outbox
> Stores individual *.eml* files for email you are sending while it is waiting to be delivered

Sent Items
> Stores individual *.eml* files for email you've sent to other people

---

Deleted Items
> Stores your deleted email messages as individual *.eml* files until you empty the Deleted Items folder

Drafts
> Stores individual *.eml* files for messages you've drafted but have not sent

Junk E-mail
> Stores junk email you've received as individual *.eml* files

 AppData and all the folders and files it contains are stored on your computer as hidden folders and files. See the "File Attributes" section of Chapter 11 for details on displaying hidden files.

Within these folders, you'll find a *Winmail.fol* file. This file tracks the folder location and the email items within the folder. Windows Mail uses this file to help manage your email. Because of how *.fol* and *.eml* files work, at a very basic level Windows Mail is really just an organizer and viewer for your email. Whether you are working with the Search Results window or the individual Windows Mail folder, you can:

- Open an email by double-clicking it.
- Forward an email to someone else by right-clicking it and selecting Forward.
- Reply to an email by right-clicking it and selecting Reply or Reply All as appropriate.

Not only is this a new and exciting way to work with your email, but it's also a great timesaver.

In the left pane of Windows Mail, you'll find the same folder structure, starting with a Local Folders node that includes subnodes for Inbox, Outbox, Sent Items, Deleted Items, Drafts, and Junk E-mail. In Windows Mail, you can search your email by selecting the starting folder and typing your search text into the Search box provided. If you select the Local Folders node, you can search all of the email folders at once.

Even more exciting is that you can search your email and read email returned in search results without ever having to open Windows Mail. You can do so by following these steps:

1. Click Start and then click Search.
2. In the Search Results window, select Email as the Show Only option.
3. In the Search box, type the text you want to search for within your email. In the search results, you'll see a list of emails that match your search text by the sender's email address and message subject.
4. When you click an email that you want to view, you'll see the complete text of the email in the Preview Pane.

As discussed in Chapter 6, the Windows Search service automatically indexes email folders used with Office Outlook and Windows Mail. This means you also can use this technique with Office Outlook.

The Windows Mail team has also devised a much easier way for you to back up your email. The previous Outlook Express clients did not make it very easy to back up and restore your email repository. Now that email storage is file-based, however, backing up and restoring your email is easy. You really need to back up only one folder, and that's the *AppData\Local\Microsoft\Windows Mail* folder.

Setting Up Windows Mail and Configuring Email Accounts

When you first start using Windows Mail, the Internet Accounts Wizard will guide you through the process of configuring your email account. Using this wizard, you can set up your default email account by completing the following steps:

1. On the Your Name page, shown in Figure 16-2, enter the display name for the email account and then click Next. The display name is the name that will appear in the From field when you send email to other people.

2. On the Internet E-Mail Address page, shown in Figure 16-3, type the email address for the account you are configuring. To successfully send and receive email, you must use the email address the email server expects—either the email address you've been assigned or the one you selected to use when initially setting up your email account.

Figure 16-2. Setting the display name for your account

Figure 16-3. Setting the email address for your account

3. On the "Set up e-mail servers" page, shown in Figure 16-4, select the incoming email server type as either POP3 or IMAP4. POP3 and IMAP4 are the only email protocols that you can use to receive Internet mail. Windows Mail doesn't support HTTP or other types of email protocols.

4. In the "Incoming e-mail (POP3 or IMAP) server" text box, type the fully qualified domain name of the incoming email server, such as *mail.microsoft.com*. The incoming email server is the POP3 or IMAP4 server from which you receive email.

5. In the "Outgoing e-mail server (SMTP) name" text box, type the fully qualified domain name of the outgoing email server, such as *smtp.microsoft.com*. The outgoing email server is the SMTP server to which you submit email that you want to send to other people. Just about every email server in the world uses SMTP for submitting messages.

6. Most SMTP servers require users to be authenticated before they will accept and route email for delivery. If your outgoing email server requires a username and password to send email, select the "Outgoing server requires authentication" checkbox. Click Next.

7. On the "Internet mail logon" page, type your email username and password, and then click Next. Typically, but not always, your email username is the name portion of your email address. For example, if your email address is *Williams@microsoft.com*, your email username typically would be Williams. If you've specified that your email server requires authentication, this account information is used whenever you send and receive email. Otherwise, the account information is used only when you receive email.

8. Click Finish to complete the account setup process.

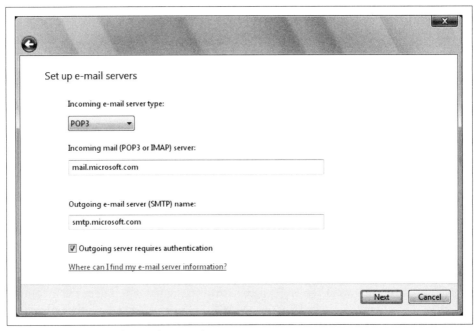

Figure 16-4. Specifying the email servers for your account

You can set up additional email accounts by following these steps:

1. In Windows Mail, click Tools, and then click Accounts.
2. In the Internet Accounts dialog box, click Add.
3. On the Select Account Type page, select Email Account and then click Next.
4. Follow steps 1–8 of the previous procedure to complete the account configuration.

Once you configure your email accounts, you'll be able to send and receive email using the configured accounts. As necessary, you can modify the settings of an email account by following these steps:

1. In Windows Mail, click Tools, and then click Accounts.
2. Under the Mail heading, click your account, and then click Properties.
3. As necessary, change the email account settings, including the user information, server information, and type of connection.
4. Click OK to save your settings.

Creating, Sending, and Receiving Email

In Windows Mail, you can create and send an email simply by clicking the Create Mail button on the toolbar, entering the necessary email addresses in the To field, typing a message subject, typing your message text, and clicking Send. That's it; it's that easy. When you want full control over the way your message is created and sent, however, you'll want to follow these steps:

1. To create an email message using your default stationery, click the Create Mail button on the toolbar. Alternatively, you can click the Create Mail options button to the right of the Create Mail button and select the stationery style for your email, such as Soft Blue.

2. The From field of your message is set to your default email address and your email will be routed through the outgoing email server associated with this account. If you've configured multiple email accounts, the From field becomes a selection list from which you can select the email address and email server to use (see Figure 16-5).

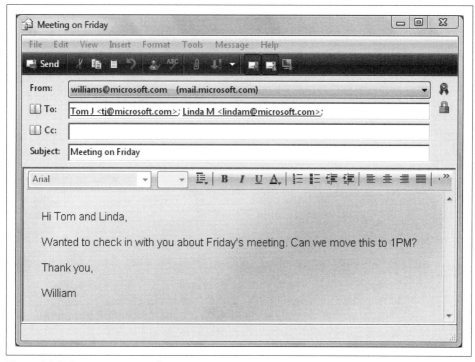

Figure 16-5. Creating your email message

3. In the To field, and optionally the Cc field, enter the email addresses for the people to whom you are sending the message. If you've created contacts or contact groups, these are available as well by clicking the Address Book button to the left of the To or Cc field. Alternatively, you can enter part of a name or email address and then click the Check Names button on the toolbar to fill in the contact information automatically.

4. In the Subject field, type the message subject.

5. Click in the message body and then use the Font and Font Size lists to set the desired font. After you type the text of your message, click the Spelling button on the toolbar to check the spelling.

6. To attach a file to the message, click the Attach File to Message button on the toolbar. Use the Open dialog box to locate the file to attach, and then click Open.

7. If your computer has a digital certificate, such as may be installed for you by your workplace, you can digitally sign your message before sending it. Click the Digitally Sign Message button to digitally sign your message. Your digital signature is used as proof of your identity.

8. Other people you contact through email can have digital certificates and signatures as well. If these people have shared their digital IDs with you and you've stored them as part of their contact details, you can encrypt messages before sending them by clicking the Encrypt Message button. When you encrypt an email only the intended recipients can open the email.

9. Click Send to send your email.

When you click Send, Windows Mail will always try to send your email immediately. It won't necessarily check for new email as quickly as you might like, however. By default, Windows Mail will:

- Send and receive messages when you start the program.
- Send messages when you click Send after drafting an email message.
- Check for new messages every 30 minutes and play a sound when they arrive.

You can change the way Windows Mail sends and receives messages by following these steps:

1. In Windows Mail, click Tools, and then click Options.

2. On the General tab, shown in Figure 16-6, you can control the way Windows Mail sends and receives email using the following options:

   Play sound when new messages arrive
   Clear this checkbox if you don't want Windows Mail to play a sound when new email arrives. Otherwise, select this checkbox and Windows Mail will alert you when new email arrives by playing a sound.

   Send and receive messages at startup
   Clear this checkbox if you don't want Windows Mail to send and receive messages at startup. Otherwise, select this option to allow Windows Mail to check for new email and send email in your Outbox at startup.

   Check for new messages every
   Clear this checkbox if you don't want Windows Mail to check for new messages automatically. Otherwise, select this checkbox and enter the desired interval to allow Windows Mail to check for new email sent to your configured email accounts.

3. Click OK to save your settings.

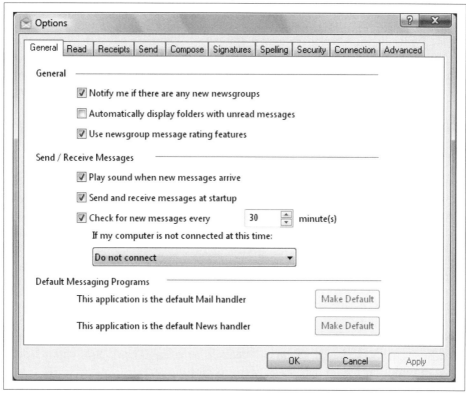

Figure 16-6. Configuring email options

You can manually send and receive messages for all configured accounts by clicking the Send/Receive button on the toolbar, or by pressing Ctrl-M. To send and receive email for a specific account only, click the Send/Receive Options button to the right of the Send/Receive button and then select the account to use.

Protecting Yourself from Junk Email

Unwanted junk email (spam) is annoying and disruptive, forcing us to wade through huge amounts of useless or offensive messages just to find the ones we need. To help reduce this problem, Windows Mail includes a built-in filter that automatically screens email to identify and separate the junk email from legitimate email. Unlike other filters that require you to "train" the filter to identify junk email correctly, Windows Mail automatically identifies many types of junk email from the first use, often without the need for feedback from you. It does this by using a version of filtering called *Bayesian spam filtering*.

Bayesian spam filtering is the process of using Bayesian statistical methods to classify documents into categories. Particular words have particular probabilities of occurring in spam email and in legitimate email. For instance, most email users will frequently encounter the word *Viagra* in spam email but will seldom see it in other email. Typically, the filter doesn't know these probabilities in advance and must first be trained so that it can build them up. To train the filter, you generally must indicate manually whether a new email is spam. For all words in each email you've identified as junk, the filter adjusts the probabilities that each word will appear in spam or legitimate email in its database. For instance, Bayesian spam filters typically will have learned a very high spam probability for the words *Viagra* and *refinance*, but a very low spam probability for words seen only in legitimate email, such as the names of friends and family members.

Fortunately, you do not have to have a degree in mathematics or programming skills to use this feature or to change the filtering to be more effective. Windows Mail comes ready with an initial database that you can use to distinguish between spam and legitimate email. You can choose to adjust the sensitivity of the filter to block more email or to block less email, depending on your needs. You can also specifically designate senders as either safe or blocked.

By default, Windows Mail moves any email identified as junk to the Junk E-mail folder. This ensures that you don't have to wade through junk email but can review the messages before deleting them as necessary. Checking your Junk E-mail folder periodically for regular email that has been incorrectly filtered is important to optimize junk email filtering. If an email is marked as junk but isn't junk, right-click it, point to Junk E-mail, and then select Mark As Not Junk.

You can set the filter level for junk email as well as safe senders and blocked senders by following these steps:

1. In Windows Mail, click Tools, and then click Junk E-mail Options.

2. In the Junk E-mail Options dialog box, shown in Figure 16-7, you can set the filter level for junk email on the Options tab. Choose one of the following filter levels:

   No Automatic Filtering
       Turns off automatic filtering. Only email addresses on your Blocked Senders list are filtered.

   Low
       Ensures that only email with the highest probability of being junk is filtered.

   High
       Uses rigid screening to detect the highest number of junk email possible, but may also incorrectly flag regular email as junk.

   Safe List Only
       Filters all email except for recipients specifically designed as Safe Senders.

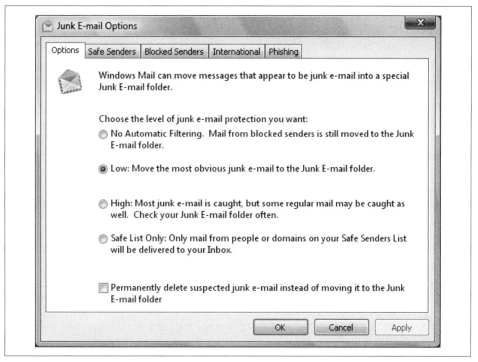

Figure 16-7. Configuring junk email options

3. You can permanently delete suspected junk email rather than moving it to the Junk E-mail folder by selecting the "Permanently delete..." checkbox. If you do this, keep in mind that legitimate email could also be deleted automatically.

4. Messages from email addresses designated as safe senders will never be treated as junk email. Use the following options on the Safe Senders tab to manage your Safe Senders list:

Add

Allows you to add a safe sender. Click Add, type the email address or Internet domain to add to the Safe Senders list, and then click OK.

Edit

Allows you to edit an existing safe sender entry. Click the entry you want to edit and then click Edit. As necessary, edit the email address or Internet domain and then click OK.

Remove

Allows you to remove a safe sender entry. Click the entry you want to remove and then click Remove.

5. Messages from email addresses designated as blocked senders are always treated as junk email. Use the following options on the Blocked Senders tab to manage your Blocked Senders list:

   Add

   > Allows you to add a blocked sender. Click Add, type the email address or Internet domain to add to the Blocked Senders list, and then click OK.

   Edit

   > Allows you to edit an existing blocked sender entry. Click the entry you want to edit and then click Edit. As necessary, edit the email address or Internet domain and then click OK.

   Remove

   > Allows you to remove a blocked sender entry. Click the entry you want to remove and then click Remove.

6. Click OK to save your settings.

Protecting Yourself from Phishing Links

Phishing is a type of fraud designed to steal your identity. In phishing scams, scam artists try to get you to disclose valuable personal data such as credit card numbers, passwords, account data, or other information. They usually do this by convincing you to provide the information under false pretenses. Phishing emails claim to be from a trusted party, such as a financial institution or online service, but they aren't. By including links to fraudulent web sites, these email messages can trick you into providing your personal information to sites you wouldn't normally use. Windows Mail has a phishing filter that analyzes email to help detect these fraudulent links and help protect you from these online scams. Although links in suspected phishing emails are blocked automatically, phishing emails are not moved automatically to the Junk E-mail folder.

You can configure phishing filtering by completing the following steps:

1. In Windows Mail, click Tools, and then click Junk E-mail Options.

2. In the Junk E-mail Options dialog box, select the Phishing tab, as shown in Figure 16-8.

3. To block links in phishing emails so that they cannot be clicked, select the "Protect my Inbox from messages with potential Phishing links" checkbox.

4. To move suspected phishing emails to the Junk E-mail folder, select the "Move phishing e-mail to the Junk Mail folder" checkbox.

5. Click OK to save your settings.

Figure 16-8. Setting phishing filter options

Changing Windows Mail Security Settings

By default, to protect you from viruses, Windows Mail treats all email as though it is from a restricted site. As discussed in the "Restricting Permissions Using Security Zones" section of Chapter 7, this setting ensures that Windows Mail uses the maximum safeguards and disables all types of potentially unsafe content. To prevent certain types of phishing and marketing scams as well as nefarious programs, Windows Mail also blocks images and other types of external content in HTML email automatically. In most cases, this is the best configuration to safeguard your computer and your data. With these settings, very few viruses can slip through. Plus, if you are sure an email is from a safe sender, you can right-click an image or other type of blocked external content in a message and then select Download to display the blocked contents.

You can use the Security tab in the Windows Mail Options dialog box to change settings for virus protection and secure email. To access and configure the Security tab options, follow these steps:

1. In Windows Mail, click Tools, and then click Options.

2. In the Options dialog box, click the Security tab, as shown in Figure 16-9.

3. For virus protection, select either the less secure Internet zone or the highly secure Restricted sites zone as the Internet Explorer security zone to use.

4. By default, Windows Mail warns you whenever another program tries to send email as you. This option is designed to protect other people from a virus that has infected your computer and is trying to spread itself through email. Clear the "Warn Me..." option if you don't want to be warned when other applications

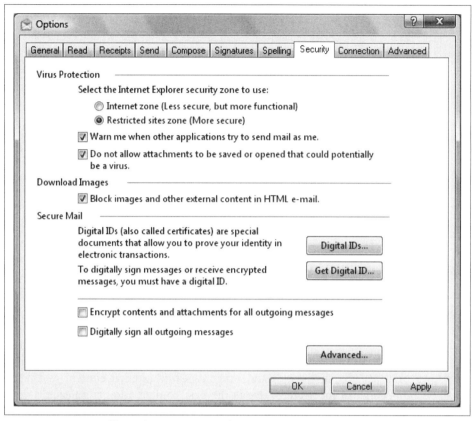

Figure 16-9. Setting additional security options for Windows Mail

try to send email as you. Otherwise, leave this option selected to help protect other people from viruses that spread themselves through email.

5. By default, any suspect attachments in messages are blocked so that they can't be saved or opened. Clear the "Do not allow attachments…" checkbox if you want to allow all attachments to be saved and opened. Otherwise, leave this option selected to help protect your computer and your data.

6. By default, images and other external content are blocked to help protect your computer. Clear the "Block images…" checkbox if you always want images and other external content to be displayed. Otherwise, leave this option selected to help protect your computer and your data.

7. Click OK to save your settings.

Secure Mail is the last set of security options on the Security tab. To use Secure Mail as it is offered here, you will have to acquire a digital certificate that you will need to import and configure. The digital certificate has settings that determine how you can use it. Some certificates are used just for SSL encryption, others for IPSec or network encryption, and some can be used for both of these purposes, and more. If you already have a digital certificate that is enabled for email encryption and/or digital signing, you can choose whether you want all emails to be encrypted and/or digitally signed automatically using the "Encrypt" and "Digitally sign" checkboxes. If you don't already have a digital certificate, Windows Mail gives you a few places you can enroll for one. Just click the Get Digital ID button and follow the prompts.

Using Windows Contacts

One of the early promises Microsoft made about Windows Vista was that it would include a deeply integrated contacts store that would replace the old Windows Address Book (WAB), which has been around for years. Microsoft delivered on this promise by including Windows Contacts with Windows Vista. You can use Windows Contacts to create a virtual address book of individual contacts and groups of contacts.

Any contact you create can have a picture, name, and email address associated with it as well as full details on home and work contact information. You can also add personal and family information, such as birthdays, anniversaries, and the names of a contact's children. When you use Windows Contacts to create groups of contacts, you can send email to everyone in the contact group simply by specifying the name of the contact group in your email message.

Getting to Know Windows Contacts

To start Windows Contacts, click Start, click All Programs, and then click Windows Contacts. Alternatively, you can start Windows Contacts from within Windows Mail by clicking the Contacts button on the toolbar. As Figure 16-10 shows, Windows Contacts is integrated into Windows Explorer. Similar to Windows Mail, Windows Contacts stores each contact and group you create as a separate file. Contact files for individuals are saved as *.contact* files. Contact files for groups are saved as *.group* files. In your profile, you'll find these files in the Contacts folder. As with Windows Mail, this allows you to easily access, modify, and back up contacts in ways that weren't possible previously. This new approach simplifies the way you work with and manage contacts.

Figure 16-10. Creating and managing your contacts

From within Windows Contacts, you can use the new Windows Explorer view styles to organize your contacts, add new contacts and contact groups, import contacts (from CSV, LDIF, vCard, and WAB), and export contacts (to CSV and vCard). You display and configure individual contacts using a dialog box that is actually quite similar to the old WAB Contacts Properties dialog box. The only big change is that you can now add a picture to represent each contact. When you add a picture to a contact, Windows Vista optimizes the picture for the small size Windows Contact uses, and then changes the contact's icon to match the picture. As discussed previously, several other features in Windows Vista use the picture associated with contacts, including People Near Me and the Start Menu for contacts that have user accounts on your computer.

Windows Contacts is designed to replace other storage mechanisms for personal contacts. You can use Windows to keep track of people and organizations by creating contacts for them in Windows Contacts. Each contact contains the information for one person or organization. When you need to look up a friend's email address or phone number, you can open your Contacts folder and find it there. When you want to take notes about a business contact, you can store the notes along with the contact in the Contacts folder. No matter what type of contact information you want to remember about someone, you can put it in the Contacts folder.

The Contacts folder also functions as the address book for Windows Mail. When you create an email message in Windows Mail, you select recipients from your Contacts folder. Even if you don't use Windows Mail as your email program, you can still use Windows Contacts to store information about people and organizations. Use Windows Contacts to keep track of all the people and organizations with which you communicate.

What's in a Contact?

You can store as much or as little information as you like about each contact. Windows Mail offers you the ability to store email addresses, a picture of your contact, phone numbers, addresses, family information, web site addresses, and notes, all associated with your contact.

You can store as many email addresses as you want for a contact, and set a single email address as the preferred address for your contact. The preferred email address is the one Windows Mail uses when you want to send someone an email quickly, without selecting from the different email addresses stored for the contact you selected.

Adding pictures of your contact can help you to remember the person you are trying to contact. Since most people occasionally have difficulty remembering some of their contacts, this can help jog your memory when browsing your contact list.

You can store separate home and work contact numbers for phone, fax, and cell/pager. Windows Mail also offers you the ability to store family information about your contact. The categories include a contact's spouse, children, gender, birthday, and anniversary information. This can help you considerably if you try to keep track of your contact's personal information for sending cards or gifts, or for other personal reasons. You also have the ability to keep notes associated with a contact, making it easy to find specific information you have noted about a particular contact.

Creating Contacts for Individuals

You can create a contact for an individual by completing these steps:

1. Click Start, click All Programs, and then click Windows Contacts.
2. Click New Contact on the toolbar. This opens a Properties dialog box like the one shown in Figure 16-11.
3. On the Name and E-mail tab, type the name and title information for the contact. Pay particular attention to the Full Name. This value is set based on the first, middle, and last name entries and is the name under which the contact file will be saved and the display name will be used in Windows Mail. If you don't like the default entry, click the Options button to display variations of the Full Name and then select the entry you want to use.

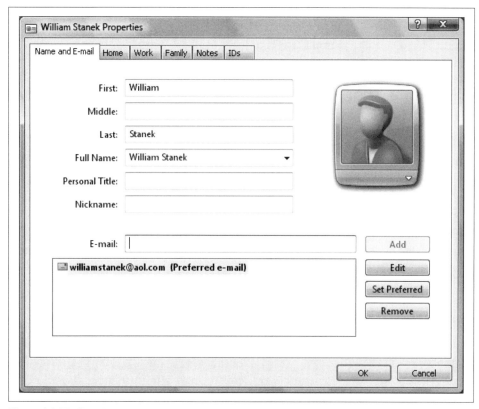

Figure 16-11. Creating a new contact

4. In the E-mail text box, type an email address for the contact and then click Add. The first email address you add is set automatically as the preferred email address. The preferred email address is the default for Windows Mail. If you add multiple email addresses to a contact, you can set the preferred email address by selecting the address to designate as preferred and then clicking Set Preferred.

5. On the Home tab, use the options provided to enter the home contact information, including the street address, city, state, and postal code, as well as phone, fax, and cell numbers. You can also enter the contact's personal web site address.

6. On the Work tab, use the options provided to enter the work contact information, including the street address, city, state, and postal code, as well as phone, fax, and cell numbers. You can also enter the contact's business web site address.

7. On the Family tab, use the options provided to track your contact's personal information, including spouse, children, gender, birthday, and anniversary.

8. On the Notes tab, enter any additional notes about the contact.

9. Click OK to create the contact.

Adding or Removing Contact Pictures

When you create a contact, Windows Vista adds a default image for each contact, which you can change to any picture or graphic you want. To add or remove a contact picture, follow these steps:

1. Click Start, click All Programs, and then click Windows Contacts.
2. Double-click the contact you want to work with.
3. On the Name and E-mail tab, click the contact picture, and then do one of the following:
   - To add a new picture, click Change Picture, locate the picture you want to use for the contact, click it, and then click Set.
   - To remove an existing picture, click Remove Picture. The picture will revert to the default contact image used by Windows.
4. Click OK to save your changes.

 Pictures can be in any of the following formats: BMP, GIF, JPEG, PNG, or ICO. Most pictures are optimized to a file size of 50 KB or less—even high-resolution pictures—before being saved as part of the contact information.

Creating Contact Groups

In addition to creating contacts for individuals, you can create contact groups, which combine multiple individual contacts into a single group. Creating a contact group enables you to send email to many people at once. If you send an email message to a contact group, it will be sent to everyone you added to the group. In this way, sending email to a contact group can be a lot easier than adding names one at a time to an email message, especially if you often send messages to the same group of people.

You can create a contact group by following these steps:

1. Click Start, click All Programs, and then click Windows Contacts.
2. Click New Contact Group on the toolbar. This opens a Properties dialog box like the one shown in Figure 16-12.
3. In the Group Name text box, type a name for the group.
4. To add existing contacts to the group, click Add to Contact Group, select the contact or contacts to add, and then click Add.
5. To create a new contact and add it to the group, click Create New Contact, provide the details for the group, and then click OK.
6. On the Contact Group Details tab, type any additional information for the group. This could include a meeting or office location, notes, and web site information.
7. Click OK to create the contact group.

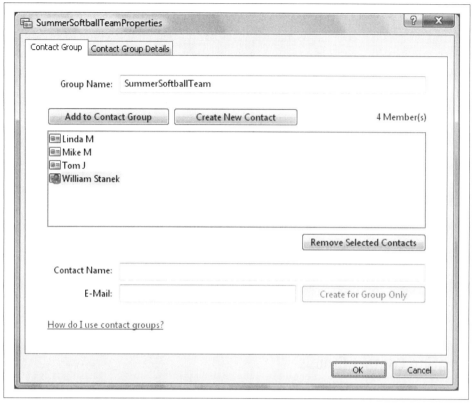

Figure 16-12. Creating a contact group

   Contact groups are meant to be used with Windows Mail. Keep in mind that Windows Mail will list each individual email address, so there is no way to hide the email addresses of the recipients.

Sending Contacts to Other People

In addition to using Windows Contacts to address email messages and store information about people and organizations, you can also send contacts to other people. This is useful if you want to send someone contact information about yourself or someone else. There is no need to type a bunch of phone numbers, addresses, and other contact information into an email message—just send them a contact with the information you want to share by right-clicking the contact, pointing to Send To, and selecting Mail Recipient.

   To send a contact to someone who is not using this version of Windows, you may first need to export the contact to another format. If you upgrade to Windows Vista from Windows XP, each contact in your Windows Address Book will be automatically stored as a contact in Windows Contacts.

Using Windows Calendar

Windows Calendar represents the biggest change in calendaring and scheduling since Microsoft released Schedule Plus. Windows Calendar lets you schedule appointments, create to-do lists, send meeting invitations, and share your calendar with others—all from one easy-to-use application that is included with Windows Vista. The Windows Calendar team designed Windows Calendar to be used with Windows Mail and Windows Contacts, allowing you to share and coordinate calendar information with family and friends.

Getting to Know Windows Calendar

One of Windows Calendar's most useful features is the ability to create multiple calendars for different people or different purposes. Because calendars and their respective appointments and tasks are color-coded, you can quickly and easily differentiate between one person's appointments and tasks and another's. Windows Calendar also makes it easy for you to access any available calendars and for you to allow others to access your calendars. If you want to access someone else's calendar, you can ask that person to publish the calendar so that you can subscribe to it. If you want others to be able to access your calendar, you can publish your calendar as a shared calendar.

To start Windows Calendar, click Start, click All Programs, and then click Windows Calendar. Alternatively, you can start Windows Calendar from within Windows Mail by clicking the Windows Calendar button on the toolbar. As Figure 16-13 shows, Windows Calendar is organized into three panes. On the left, the Navigation Pane shows the current month, calendars, and to-do tasks. The main window in the center displays the current view of the active calendar. On the right, the Details Pane is where you add and edit details for appointments, tasks, and other calendar management features.

You can use the toolbar in the main Calendar window to navigate the calendar, change views, and perform essential tasks. From left to right, the buttons on the toolbar are:

New Appointment
    Creates a new appointment in the selected calendar.

New Task
    Creates a new task in the selected calendar.

Delete
    Deletes a selected appointment or task.

Today
    Accesses the current date in the calendar.

Figure 16-13. Setting up your calendar

View

Provides options that set the calendar to the Day, Work Week, Week, or Month view. Also includes options for displaying or hiding the Navigation Pane and the Details Pane.

Subscribe

Allows you to subscribe to a calendar.

Print

Prints the Day, Work Week, Week, or Month view of the dates you select as the start and end dates under Print Range.

When you are working with the Date section of the Navigation Pane, you can use the Month view of the calendar to select individual dates to view in the main window. Highlighted (bold) dates represent dates with appointments or meetings. Using the Previous Month and Next Month buttons on the calendar, you can navigate to previous and next months. Other techniques to navigate the calendar are as follows:

- While viewing a particular month, you can navigate to previous or next months by clicking the month and year entry to display the 12 months of the year (see Figure 16-14). You can then select any month to view by clicking it.

- While viewing the 12 months of the year, you can navigate among years in the current decade by clicking the year entry (see Figure 16-15). You can then select a year to view by clicking it.

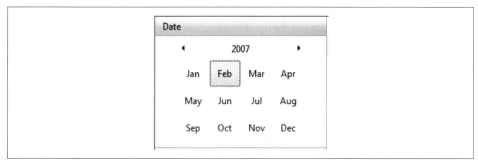

Figure 16-14. Viewing the months in a year

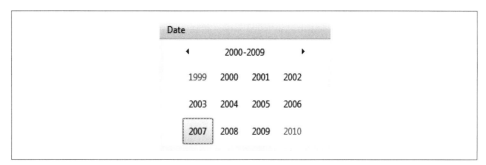

Figure 16-15. Viewing the years in a decade

- While viewing the 10 years of a decade, you can navigate among decades by clicking the decade entry (see Figure 16-16). You can then select a decade to view by clicking it.

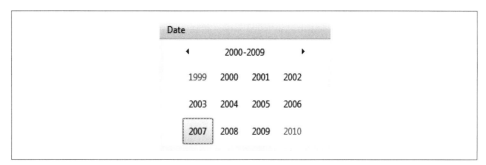

Figure 16-16. Viewing the decades in the current century

In Windows Calendar, the Day, Work Week, Week, and Month views in the main window show appointments and meetings associated with all the calendars you've created or to which you've subscribed. When you are working with the Calendars section of the Navigation Pane, you can select the calendar you want to work with to make it the active calendar for when you are creating appointments and tasks, or setting calendar properties.

When you are working with the Tasks section of the Navigation Pane, you can select a task to view the related details in the Details Pane. If the Details Pane is not displayed currently, you can display it by clicking View and then clicking Details Pane, or by pressing Ctrl-D. Since tasks are tied to particular calendars, clicking a task also switches to the related calendar.

Creating and Using Calendars

The true power of Windows Calendar is its capacity for creating and managing multiple calendars. If you would like to have separate calendars for work and play, or perhaps you would like to manage the calendars for each of your family members and see them all together at a glance to avoid conflicts, you can do this by creating multiple calendars. Because each calendar has a separate color code, it is easy to tell which appointments, meetings, and tasks are related to which calendar.

To create a new calendar, all you need to do is click File → New → Calendar or right-click an open area under the Calendars headings and select New → Calendar. A New Calendar entry is then added under the Calendars heading. The entry is selected and highlighted so that you can set the name of the new calendar by typing the desired name and then pressing Enter.

When you are creating appointments and tasks in Windows Calendar, the calendar you've selected under the Calendars heading becomes the active calendar. When you create tasks and appointments, Windows Calendar adds them to the active calendar by default. Calendars have two key properties that you can manage: a title and an associated color. You can edit calendar details by clicking the calendar name under the Calendars heading and displaying the Details view. If the Details view is hidden, pressing Ctrl-D opens the Details view. In the Details view, you can then set the calendar name and color (see Figure 16-17).

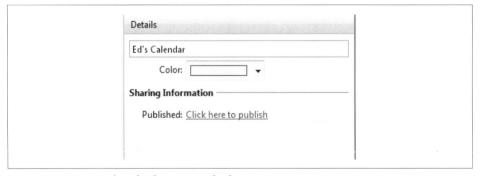

Figure 16-17. Setting the calendar name and color

When selecting a color to associate with a calendar's appointments and tasks, use a unique color for each calendar so that it is easy to distinguish the owner of appointments and tasks listed in the master calendar. For example, you might want to use red, blue, green, yellow, and orange as the colors for five different calendars.

In the Calendars area of the Navigation Pane, you can set the order of calendars by clicking and dragging the calendar to the desired position in the Calendars list. By default, items for all calendars are shown on the master calendar and on the Tasks list. To hide a calendar's items and tasks, clear the related checkbox under the Calendars heading. If you later want to display the calendar's items and tasks, select the related checkbox under the Calendars heading.

If you no longer need a calendar, you can permanently delete the calendar and all related appointments, meetings, and tasks. To delete the calendar, right-click it under the Calendars heading, and then select Delete. When prompted to confirm that you want to delete the calendar, click Yes.

Creating and Using Calendar Groups

You can group sets of related calendars together into calendar groups. To create a calendar group, click File → New → Calendar Group or right-click an open area under the Calendars headings and select New → Calendar Group. A New Calendar Group entry is then added under the Calendars heading. The entry is selected and highlighted so that you can set the name of the new calendar group by typing the desired name and then pressing Enter.

Once you've created a calendar group, you can add new calendars to the group by selecting the group name before creating the calendar. Using the Calendars area of the Navigation Pane, you can add an existing calendar to a group by dragging the calendar and dropping it beneath the group name.

One of the key reasons for grouping sets of calendars together is to be able to manage all items for all calendars with the click of a button. To hide all items for all calendars in a group, clear the checkbox for the group under the Calendars heading. To display all items for all calendars in a group, select the checkbox for the group under the Calendars heading.

Sharing Your Calendars with Others

Windows Calendar gives you two ways to share your calendars with others. You can send an entire calendar or calendar group to someone via email. Or you can publish a calendar or calendar group to a web site so that anyone with a calendar client that supports the iCalendar format can sync with your calendar.

To email a calendar or calendar group to someone, right-click the calendar under the Calendars heading and then select Send via E-mail. This opens a new email message in your default email program with the calendar or calendar group added as an attachment. The attachment is created as an iCalendar (*.ics*) file that anyone with a calendar client that supports the iCalendar format can view. All the recipient needs to do is to save the file and then double-click the file to open it for viewing.

You can publish any calendars and calendar groups you've created to a web server or an iCalendar site, such as Yahoo! or Google, so that other users can access and subscribe to them. To publish a calendar for sharing, follow these steps:

1. In Windows Calendar, click the calendar you want to work with under the Calendars heading. If the Details view is hidden, press Ctrl-D to display it.

2. Under the Sharing Information heading, select "Click here to publish."

3. In the Publish Calendar Wizard, shown in Figure 16-18, type a descriptive name for the calendar or calendar group you are publishing.

Figure 16-18. Publishing your calendar

4. In the "Location to publish calendar" text box, type the file location or web address to which you want to publish the calendar.

 If you have an account with Yahoo!, Google, or another web service that offers shared calendaring, you'll need to enter the URL to your shared calendar or the URL the service provided to you. Keep in mind that you can also publish to a file location, such as the Public folder. Once your calendar is published to the Public folder, anyone who logs on to your computer locally can access your calendar simply by double-clicking the calendar file.

5. Select the "Automatically publish changes..." checkbox if you want to ensure that the calendar or calendar group is kept up-to-date without you having to publish the calendar periodically.

6. Select the calendar details to include. You can include notes, reminders, and tasks.

7. Click Publish. Once your calendar is published, you'll see a confirmation page like the one shown in Figure 16-19. Congratulations, you have just published a shared calendar. It was that easy.

8. On the confirmation page, you can choose to click Finish to complete the process or Announce to announce your shared calendar via email. If you click Announce, Windows Calendar opens a new email message in your default email program with a link to your calendar to help you distribute news about your calendar to those to whom you want to allow access (see Figure 16-20).

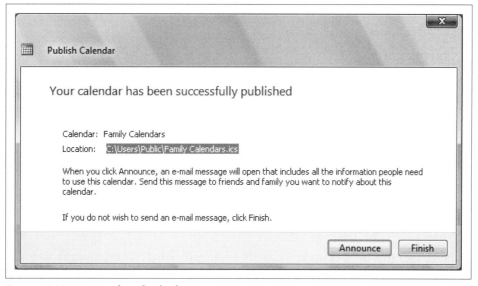

Figure 16-19. Viewing the calendar location

Calendars are published in the .ics format so that recipients that use a number of time management programs, including Microsoft Office Outlook, can open them. If you no longer want to publish a calendar, you can stop publishing it. To do so, follow these steps:

1. In Windows Calendar, select the applicable calendar or calendar group, and then select "Stop publishing" on the Share menu.

2. You'll see a confirmation prompt, shown in Figure 16-21. By default, the "Delete calendar on server?" checkbox is selected to ensure that the .ics file for the calendar is removed from the publish location. When you click Unpublish, other users will no longer be able to subscribe to the calendar or calendar group.

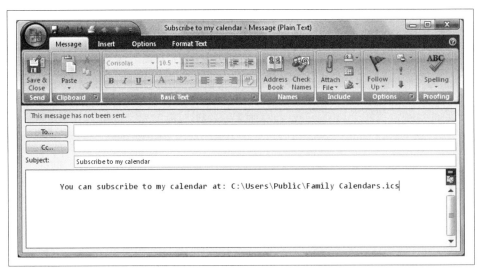

Figure 16-20. Announcing your calendar

Figure 16-21. Unpublishing the calendar

Being able to publish a calendar is pretty cool, but we haven't even begun to touch upon the new features Windows Vista has to offer. Now, keeping with our scenario, we just published a calendar, so your next task is to subscribe to someone else's calendar so that it will appear in Windows Calendar. Once you've subscribed to a calendar, you can get automatic updates to keep your view of the calendar in sync with the published view.

To subscribe to a calendar that someone else has published (including *.ics* calendars used on some web sites), follow these steps:

1. In Windows Calendar, click Subscribe on the Share menu. This starts the Subscribe to a Calendar Wizard.

2. In the "Calendar to subscribe to" text box, type the path to the calendar to which you want to subscribe and then click Next. This can be any iCalendar formatted

and published calendar. It can even be a calendar published by another user on your computer. If so, simply enter a file path instead of a web address, such as *C:\Users\Public\Family Calendars.ics*.

3. On the "Calendar subscription settings" page, shown in Figure 16-22, type the display name you want to use for the calendar or calendar group to which you are subscribing. This doesn't have to be the same as the name used when publishing the calendar or calendar group.

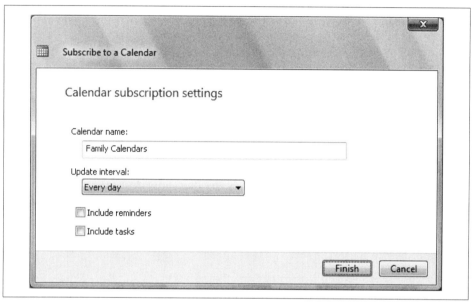

Figure 16-22. Subscribing to a calendar

4. Use the "Update interval" list to select the update interval. Your options are No update, Every 15 minutes, Every hour, Every day, and Every week.

5. If reminders and tasks have been published with the calendar, you can get this information as well by selecting the "Include reminders," "Include tasks," or both checkboxes.

6. Click Finish to complete the procedure.

Once you've subscribed to a calendar, you can update the calendar manually by right-clicking the subscribed calendar under the Calendars heading and selecting Sync. If there are updates, Windows Mail will retrieve and display them. If you subscribe to multiple calendars, you can update all subscribed calendars manually by right-clicking in the Calendars heading and selecting Sync All.

To unsubscribe from a calendar, right-click the calendar under the Calendars heading and select Delete. When prompted to confirm, click Yes.

Synchronizing Google Calendar with Windows Calendar

You can subscribe to Yahoo! and Google calendars, too. For Google, the steps you use should be similar to the following:

1. In Internet Explorer, browse to the Google calendar to which you want to subscribe, and log on.

2. At the main menu, select Manage Calendars in the lower-lefthand corner.

3. Under Sharing, click on "Share this calendar." Although there are a lot of sharing options, let's focus on what we need to get this Google calendar published and subscribed to in Windows Calendar. Be careful of what you select for the "Share with everyone" option. If you select "Share all information," everyone that has access to the shared calendar (including Internet search engines) can see all the details.

4. After you select the sharing options for this calendar, click Save.

5. On the main menu, click Manage Calendars in the lower-left pane.

6. When you click "Calendar details," you'll see several different calendar formats next to the calendar address. You should be interested in only iCalendar for now. Right-click on iCalendar under "Calendar address," and then click "Copy shortcut." This is the shortcut you use to synchronize your Google Calendar with Windows Calendar (or another iCalendar-enabled calendar).

7. In Windows Calendar, click Subscribe on the toolbar. This opens the Subscribe to a Calendar Wizard.

8. Click in the "Calendar to subscribe to" text box and then press Ctrl-V to paste in the web address of your Google calendar. Click Next.

9. On the "Calendar subscription settings" page, set the subscription options as discussed previously and then click Finish.

Because web interfaces tend to change more frequently than program interfaces, I won't repeat the example for Yahoo!. However, you'll use a similar procedure to share your Yahoo! calendar so that you can subscribe to it in Windows Calendar.

Scheduling Appointments and Meetings

Windows Calendar can help you track appointments for yourself and any calendars to which you've subscribed. All appointments can have a title and location associated with them. On the master calendar, the title is shown first, followed by the location in parentheses. When you create an appointment, you can specify start and end times or you can specify that an appointment lasts all day. Windows Calendar also allows you to specify whether appointments are recurring and to add reminders to appointments so that you are notified a specified amount of time prior to an appointment.

Because a meeting is essentially an appointment with invited participants, Windows Calendar doesn't try to distinguish between the two. This is why you can also list and invite attendees to scheduled appointments based on your configured contacts and contact groups. Invitations are sent by email to attendees.

 Windows Calendar is not unique in the fact that it doesn't try to distinguish between appointments and meetings; most calendaring and scheduling programs do not. This is because with both appointments and meetings, you must be somewhere at a particular time to meet someone or do something, and programmatically it doesn't make sense to create separate sets of features that do essentially the same thing.

You can create an appointment by following these steps:

1. In Windows Calendar, select the calendar you want to work with in the Navigation Pane.

2. In the Navigation Pane, use the Date options to navigate to the month, day, and year of the appointment.

3. In the main window, right-click the date and time the appointment starts, and then select New Appointment.

4. If the Details view is hidden, press Ctrl-D to display it, as shown in Figure 16-23.

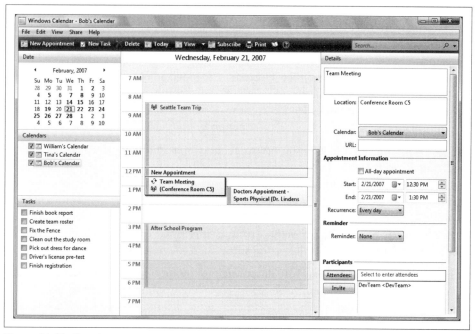

Figure 16-23. Creating your appointment

5. In the text box provided at the top of the Details Pane, type a title for the appointment.

6. In the Location text box, type the location for the appointment.

7. Use the Appointment Information options to see the start and end times for the appointment. Or for an all-day appointment, select the "All-day appointment" checkbox.

8. If the appointment should repeat, use the Recurrence list to select the interval at which the appointment repeats, such as Weekly, Monthly, or Yearly. If you want to use a recurrence schedule other than the default, select the Advanced option. You can then set the appointment to repeat every nth day, week, month, or year.

9. To have Windows Mail remind you prior to the appointment, use the Reminder list options to set the amount of time prior to the appointment to display a reminder. For example, if you select 1 hour, Windows Mail will remind you 1 hour before the appointment.

If you're creating an appointment, you don't need to do anything more. On the other hand, if you are creating a meeting request, you'll want to list and invite attendees. To do so, use the following techniques:

- To specify participants, such as for a meeting, click the Attendees button. Select a contact or contact group that should be listed as an attendee, and then click the To button to add the attendee to the Attendees list, as shown in Figure 16-24. Repeat this procedure to add other attendees, and then click OK.

- When all attendees appear in the invitation list, click Invite to generate an email message with the invitation attached. Edit the message if needed, and then click Send. The invitation will be attached as an *.ics* file, so users with iCalendar clients, such as Microsoft Office Outlook, can open it. When a recipient double-clicks on the attachment, the appointment information will be added to his calendar. Because Windows Calendar uses the popular iCalendar format, you can share information with a variety of calendaring programs across multiple platforms.

On the master calendar, it is important to note that different icons are added to recurring appointments and meetings with invited attendees to help distinguish them from standard appointments. If you want to remove an appointment from a nonsubscribed calendar, you can do so by right-clicking the appointment and selecting Delete. You cannot delete appointments from subscribed calendars. If you no longer want to see appointments from a subscribed calendar, clear the related checkbox under Calendars or delete the subscribed calendar.

With recurring appointments, you cannot delete the first occurrence of the appointment without deleting the entire series of recurring appointments. Because of this, you'll be prompted to delete the series or cancel the deletion. If you try to delete subsequent appointments in a recurring series, you'll be given the opportunity to delete the series, delete the selected occurrence, or cancel the deletion. Both related dialog boxes are shown in Figure 16-25.

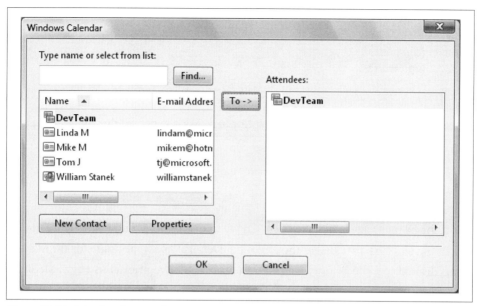

Figure 16-24. Selecting the attendees

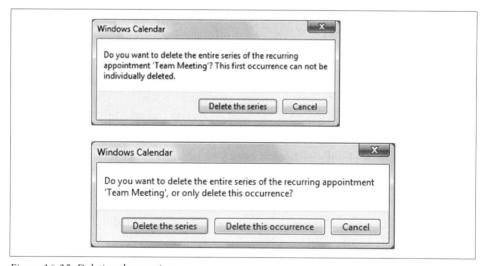

Figure 16-25. Deleting the meeting

Creating To-Do Lists

Windows Calendar can help you manage to-do lists for yourself and any calendars to which you've subscribed. In Windows Calendar, tasks are listed under the Tasks heading. Tasks have two basic states:

Unchecked (open)
  An open task that has not yet been completed

Checked (completed)
  A completed task

When you create a task, you can specify a priority to indicate the task's relative importance. You can set start and due dates. You can also add reminders so that you are notified a specified amount of time prior to a task's expected due date.

You can create a task by following these steps:

1. In Windows Calendar, select the calendar you want to work with in the Navigation Pane.

2. Click the New Task button on the toolbar.

3. If the Details view is hidden, press Ctrl-D to display it, as shown in Figure 16-26.

4. In the text box provided at the top of the Details Pane, type a title for the task.

5. If desired, use the Priority list to set the task's relative priority as High, Medium, or Low.

6. Use the Start options to set the task's expected start date.

7. Use the "Due date" options to specify the date when the task must be completed.

8. If you want to be reminded prior to the task's expected due date, select "On date" on the Reminder list and then set a reminder date. The default date for the reminder is the due date.

Any tasks created on your personal calendar or other calendars are displayed under the Tasks heading. You can mark a task as completed by selecting the checkbox provided under the Tasks heading. In the Details Pane, you can also mark a task as completed by selecting the Completed checkbox under Task Information.

You can send a task to another person via email by right-clicking the task and then selecting Send via E-mail to generate an email message with the task attached. Edit the message if needed, and then click Send. The task will be attached as an *.ics* file, so users with iCalendar clients, such as Microsoft Office Outlook, can open it. When a recipient double-clicks on the attachment, the task will be added to her calendar.

When you complete tasks, you may want to delete them. You can delete tasks by right-clicking them and selecting Delete. However, rather than deleting tasks, you may want to hide them from the calendar view, which would allow you to review completed tasks at a later date. You can also configure a regular reminder time and a color for overdue tasks. To customize the way tasks are handled, follow these steps:

1. In Windows Calendar, select Options on the File menu.

2. In the Options dialog box, shown in Figure 16-27, use the "Number of days before hiding completed tasks" list to specify whether and when completed tasks are hidden from the calendar view automatically. You can select Never, 1 day, 2 days, 4 days, 1 week, or 2 weeks.

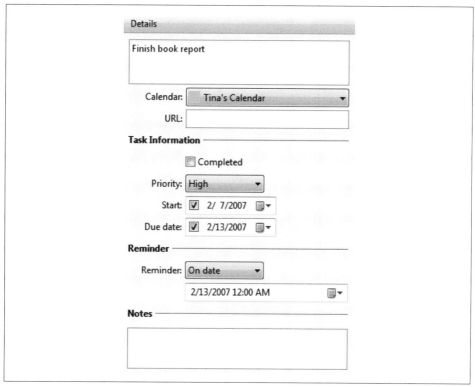

Figure 16-26. Configuring your task

3. To designate a specific time of day for the task reminder to be displayed, use the options on the "Reminder time" list.

4. The default color of overdue tasks is red. You can set a different color by clicking the current overdue color, selecting the desired color, and then clicking OK.

5. Click OK to save your settings.

Using Windows Meeting Space

Windows Meeting Space allows you to make virtual presentations over the network, share handouts, and collaborate with coworkers. To work properly, Windows Meeting Space requires that you use the Peer To Peer Foundation, Distributed File System Replication, and Network Projection services. Windows Meeting Space also uses the People Near Me feature for sharing information, requires that you enable file synchronization, and configures a Windows Firewall exception for communications with remote users. The first time you run Windows Meeting Space, you are prompted to allow Windows to enable the required services and configure the required options automatically.

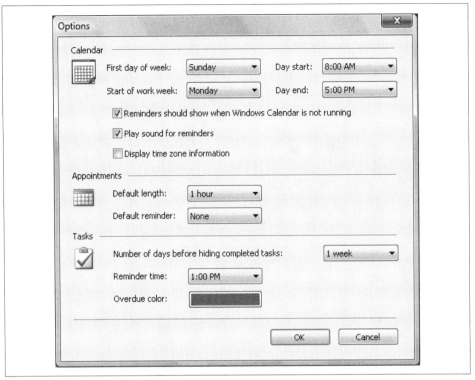

Figure 16-27. Customizing the way tasks are handled

Getting Started with Windows Meeting Space

Windows Meeting Space uses the concept of sessions to define the virtual space in which you hold your online gathering. To control entry into a Windows Meeting Space session, each session has a session name and a session password. You must know the session name and the session password to join a session.

The People Near Me feature is used to control session visibility. Typically, users with computers on the same network are considered to be nearby and are listed in the People Near Me window. The default new session options allow people who are nearby to see collaboration sessions. Users can then join a nearby meeting if they know the session password.

You can start and configure Windows Meeting Space for first use by following these steps:

1. Click Start, click All Programs, and then click Windows Meeting Space.

2. In the Windows Meeting Space Setup dialog box, click "Yes, continue setting up Windows Meeting Space" to allow automatic configuration to continue.

3. In the Set up People Near Me dialog box, type the display name you want to use, and then click OK. The default display name is your Windows logon display name.

4. The main Windows Meeting Space window appears, in which you can start a new session, join a session near you, or open an invitation file.

You can start a new Windows Meeting Space session by completing these steps:

1. Start Windows Meeting Space.

2. Click "Start a new meeting" in the main window.

3. In the "Session name" text box, type a meeting name or accept the default value. The default meeting name is your display name and the current time.

4. In the Password text box, enter a password for the session that is at least eight characters long. If you want to view the characters in the password, select the "Show characters" checkbox.

5. If you click the Options link before creating a new session, you can elect to hide the session from People Near Me by selecting "Do not allow people near me to see this meeting." When a meeting is hidden in this way, people who want to join must know both the session name and the session password to access the session.

6. Click the "Create a meeting" button. Windows Meeting Space then creates the session, and you can create presentations, share handouts, write on the whiteboard, and chat with participants.

Holding a Virtual Gathering

After Windows Meeting Space creates a session, you can use the options in the main window, shown in Figure 16-28, to invite people to the meeting, start a presentation, and share handouts. When you invite people to the meeting, you can choose people to invite from a list of those nearby by clicking the person's name in the Name list and then clicking "Send invitations." If you click the "Invite others" option, you can invite people via email or by creating an invitation file and saving it in a location others can access.

When you click "Share a program or your desktop," you can share programs running on your computer, or your entire desktop, with other people. In most cases, it is better to limit the presentation to a specific application. For example, if you have a document open in Microsoft Office PowerPoint, you can click "Share a program or your desktop," click the PowerPoint presentation in the list of open programs, and then click Share. During the meeting, other users could take control of PowerPoint as well to add notes, share their slides, and so on. Generally, only one person at a time can control the shared application. An additional option for presentations is to select Desktop as the program to share. If you select Desktop and then click Share, participants can see all running applications and items on your desktop.

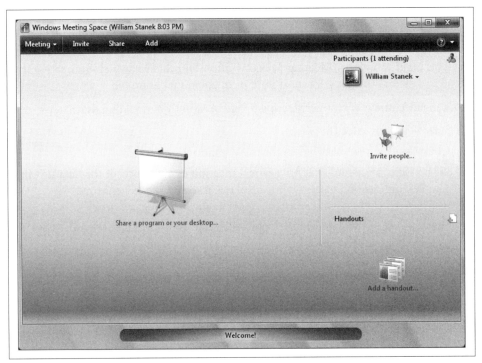

Figure 16-28. Holding a virtual meeting

You can also share handouts during the meeting. When you share handouts, a selected file is copied to each participant's computer. One participant at a time can then make changes to the copy of the handout, and those changes will be made to all participants' handouts. The original file will not be changed, however. To share a handout, click "Add a handout." If you see a warning prompt, click OK. In the "Select files to add" dialog box, select the file or files to share, and then click Open.

Joining a Windows Meeting Space Session

You can join a Windows Meeting Space session in several different ways. When the person holding the meeting is on the same LAN as you, you can join a Windows Meeting Space session by completing these steps:

1. Start Windows Meeting Space.
2. Click "Join a meeting near me" in the main window.
3. Click the meeting to join.
4. In the Password field, enter a password for the meeting.
5. Click the "Join a meeting" button.

If you've received an invitation from a person holding a meeting, you can join the session by double-clicking the invitation file and then providing the required password for the session when prompted. In Windows Meeting Space, you can open an invitation file by clicking the "Open an invitation file" link, selecting the invitation in the Open dialog box, and then clicking Open.

Once you join a Windows Meeting Space session, you can begin participating. As with other participants, you can start a presentation, share a handout, and invite others to join the session.

Participating in a Windows Meeting Space Session

When you join a session, you are listed as an available participant. If you need to work on something else or step away from your computer, you can change your participant status to let other participants know you are busy or away. To set a busy, away, or be right back status, click your name under the Participants heading, and then select the Busy, Be Right Back, or Away option. Your status is then updated in the Participants list.

When you are free or you return to your computer, you can change your status back to Available. To do this, click your name under the Participants heading, and then select the Available option. Your name in the Participants list will then reflect a normal status.

During a meeting, you can send notes to other participants. To send a note to a participant, follow these steps:

1. Right-click the participant's name, and then select "Send a note."
2. In the Send a Note dialog box, type the text of the note.
3. Click Send.

The recipient sees the note in a "You received a note" dialog box. To reply to the note, the recipient can:

1. Click Reply.
2. In the "Send a note" dialog box, type the text of the note.
3. Click Send.

Windows Meeting Space creates copies of shared files on each participant's computer. Any one participant can make changes to a shared copy of a file, and these changes will be made on all shared copies of the file on other participants' computers. The original file remains untouched in its original location.

When you leave a Windows Meeting Space session by clicking File and then selecting Leave Session, copies of shared files on your computer are not saved. If you want to save the copies of the shared files, you must do so before leaving the session. To save the copies of the shared files on your computer, click File, and then select Save Shared Files. Use the Browse for Folder dialog box to select the save location and then click OK. The shared files are then saved to the designated location.

CHAPTER 17

Mastering Dial-Up, Broadband, and On-the-Go Networking

As our need for information increases, our use of networks and communications has become increasingly important. Windows Vista allows greater flexibility and options for managing network infrastructure, and gives more flexible options to access networks than were previously available. This flexibility enhances support for standard networking and wireless technologies, and fully supports the next generation of networks.

Many of us spend time on the road trying to make connections to the corporate network, or even to our home network, to get information or files we need while away. While some of us are not as well connected as the quintessential road warrior, many of us require Virtual Private Network (VPN) connections, WiFi hotspot connectivity, or dial-up connections to get our email or download that specific information from a file server located remotely. This chapter discusses the different aspects of mobile computing with Windows Vista.

Configuring Dial-Up, Broadband, and On-the-Go Networking

Do you remember the last time you were sitting in a hotel room trying to make a remote connection to your corporate or home network? Windows Vista has eased the pain of making remote connections to your network by offering much greater flexibility in the ability to network. Windows Vista also offers many updated security measures to protect your data when connecting to remote networks or when gaining access to your critical data on an unsecured network.

Windows Vista allows you to make VPN connections, dial-up connections, wireless connections, and broadband connections. When working with the network features of your computer, you need to start with the Network and Sharing Center. You can easily access the Network and Sharing Center by following these steps:

1. Click Start, and then click Control Panel.
2. In the Control Panel, click Network and Internet and then click Network and Sharing Center. This opens the Network and Sharing Center, shown in Figure 17-1.

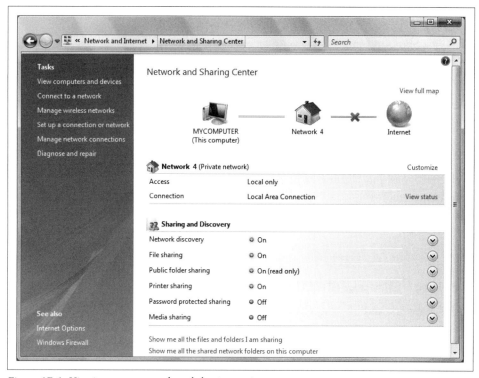

Figure 17-1. Viewing your network and sharing settings

After you have opened the Network and Sharing Center, you can use the console to manage your network settings, view your network status, and get an overview of your networking configuration. The left pane of the console offers you different tasks to choose from when managing your network features.

Your choices are:

- View computers and devices
- Connect to a network
- Manage wireless networks
- Set up a connection or network
- Manage network connections
- Diagnose and repair

The Network and Sharing Center houses the main features for managing your computer's networking capabilities. When you need to create, connect, or manage your network, this console offers you the ability to handle all of the management aspects available in Windows Vista.

You can determine the network devices and connections associated with your current network and personalize them by following these steps:

1. Click Start, and then click Control Panel.

2. In the Control Panel, under the Networking and Internet heading, click "View network status and tasks."

3. If you have a valid connection to a network, click Customize under Network Details.

4. Use the options in the Set Network Location dialog box to set the network name, location type, and network icon. Click Next and then click Finish.

In the Network and Sharing Center, you can create network connections by clicking "Set up a connection or network" in the left pane. This opens the "Set up a connection or network" Wizard, shown in Figure 17-2. You can use this wizard to create connections to the Internet and set up wireless networks and access points, ad hoc wireless networks, dial-up connections, and VPN connections to your workplace.

Creating Dial-up Connections

In the Network and Sharing Center, you can set up a dial-up connection by following these steps:

1. Click "Set up a connection or network" in the left pane. This opens the "Set up a connection or network" Wizard.

2. In the wizard, click "Set up a dial-up connection," and click the Next button.

3. The "Set up a dial-up connection" window appears and asks for specific information to configure your dial-up connection. See Figure 17-3 for an example.

4. In the "Dial-up phone number" text box, type the telephone number provided by your ISP or network administrator.

5. In the "User name" text box, type the username provided by your ISP or network administrator.

6. In the Password text box, type the password provided by your ISP or network administrator.

7. As necessary, select the "Show characters" checkbox when you are typing your password to view your entry. This will help eliminate any typing mistakes. Also, uncheck this selection after you confirm the correct spelling of your password to eliminate the possibility of anyone else seeing your password later.

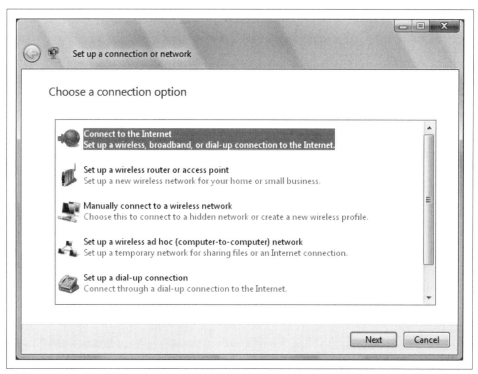

Figure 17-2. Setting up a network connection

8. In the "Connection name" text box, type a descriptive name for the connection. The default name is Dial-up Connection.

9. Select the "Remember this password" checkbox to save your password for future connections. If you do not check this box, you will have to enter your password every time you use your dial-up connection.

10. Select the "Allow other people to use this connection" checkbox if you want to allow anyone with access to your computer to use this connection.

11. Click Create to create the connection.

If you haven't previously set up a dialing location, the wizard will prompt you to provide the specific location information for your connection, as seen in Figure 17-4. When prompted, enter your country/region, area code, carrier code, and dial-out number as necessary. Click "Tone dialing" or "Pulse dialing" to identify your phone type. Windows Vista saves this information into My Location for future use. You have the option to change this information by clicking Dialing Rules from the wizard. Please see the next section for Dialing Rules configuration.

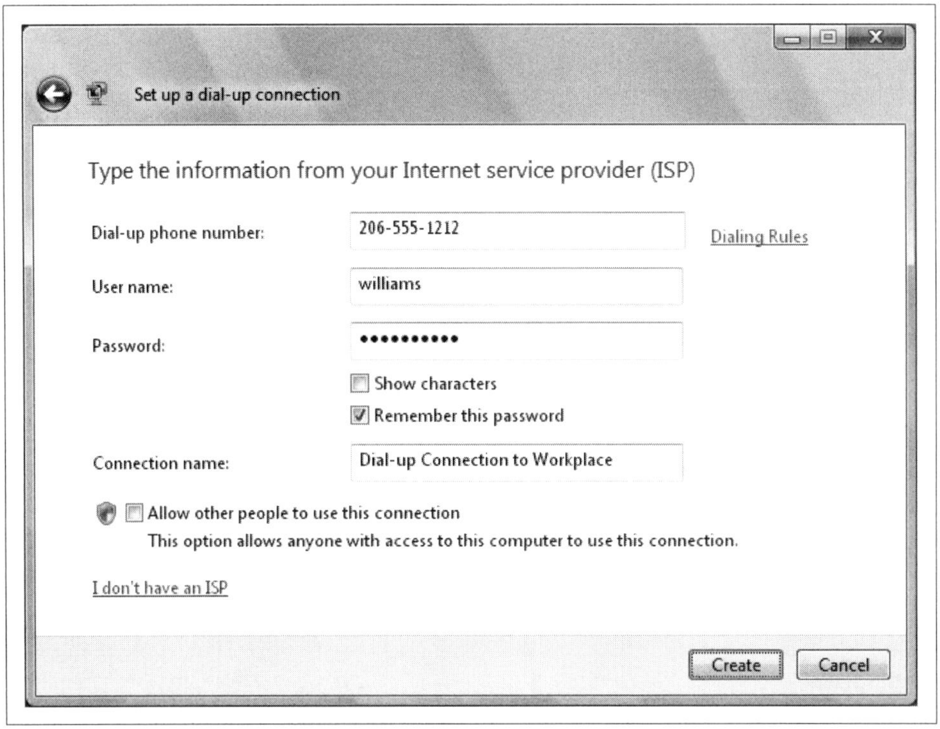

Set up a dial-up connection

Type the information from your Internet service provider (ISP)

Dial-up phone number: 206-555-1212   Dialing Rules

User name: williams

Password: ••••••••••

☐ Show characters
☑ Remember this password

Connection name: Dial-up Connection to Workplace

☐ Allow other people to use this connection
    This option allows anyone with access to this computer to use this connection.

I don't have an ISP

Create   Cancel

Figure 17-3. Setting up a dial-up connection

Setting a connection to use dialing rules

Dialing Rules, as seen in Figure 17-5, offers you the ability to control how your dial-up connections function in defined locations. These rules apply to outgoing phone calls from your modem. When you specify the phone number to dial, the dialing location determines whether the area code applies to the current call, and whether a calling card applies. To configure Dialing Rules, you must open the Phone and Modem Options dialog box.

To open the Phone and Modem Options dialog box, use the following steps:

1. Click Start and then click Control Panel.

2. In the Control Panel, click Hardware and Sound.

3. Click Phone and Modem Options.

If you have never opened the Phone and Modem Options dialog box, you will have to provide the default location information for your connections. When prompted, enter your area code, country/region, carrier code, and dial-out number, if you have one. Click "Tone dialing" or "Pulse dialing" to identify your phone type.

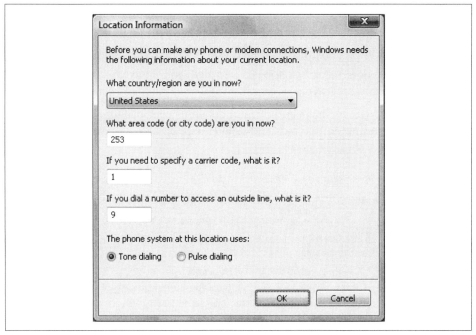

Figure 17-4. Configuring your location information

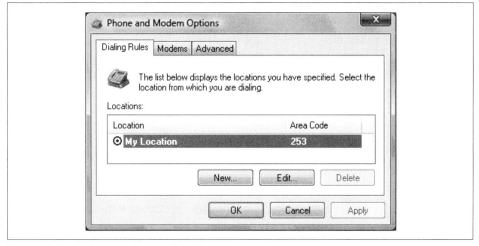

Figure 17-5. Configuring phone and modem options

To configure Dialing Rules for your connection, use the following steps:

1. In the Phone and Modem Options dialog box, click the Dialing Rules tab.
2. Click My Location to highlight the selection, and then click Edit.
3. The Edit Location dialog box appears and gives you three tabs to customize your rules. These tabs are listed as General, Area Code Rules, and Calling Card.

The General tab contains the basic information about your dialing rule. You have six areas to enter information that aids and defines aspects of your rule. See Table 17-1 for a detailed list of the areas covered.

Table 17-1. General information for dialing rules

Options	Description
Location Name	The name you have given your location. The default name is My Location.
Country/Region	The country or region you live in. The default is based on the information provided during setup and stored in your system.
Area Code	This field holds the area code in which you currently reside.
Dialing Rules	This heading allows you to change multiple details. You can quickly change settings for the number you use to dial a local outside call, the number you dial for a long-distance call, the carrier code used to make a long-distance call, and the carrier code to make international calls.
Disable Call Waiting	Check this option and enter the specific sequence to disable your call-waiting feature. Your options are *70, 1170, and 70#.
Tone/Pulse Dialing	Select the appropriate radio button for either tone or pulse dialing.

The Area Code Rules tab provides options for creating and managing area code rules. These rules determine how phone numbers are dialed from your current area code to different area codes. These settings also determine how numbers are dialed within your current area code. To create a new area code rule, follow these steps:

1. Click New. This displays the New Area Code Rule dialog box shown in Figure 17-6.
2. In the "Area code" text box, type the area code to which you want the rule to apply.
3. Use the Prefixes options to set the desired prefixes to use in the current area code rule. You can specify to use all of the prefixes or you can enter specific prefixes.
   - To use all prefixes, select the "Include all the prefixes within this area code" option.
   - To specify prefixes to use with this rule, select the "Include only the prefixes in the list below" option and then click Add. In the Add Prefix dialog box, enter one or more prefixes separated by commas or spaces, and then click OK.

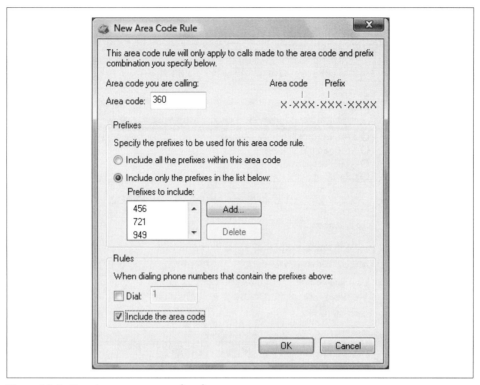

Figure 17-6. Creating a new area code rule

4. When dialing phone numbers that contain the prefixes you've selected, you have the option to set the number to dial, as in dialing a 1 to call a long-distance number. Select the Dial checkbox and then enter the number to dial.

5. To include the area code when dialing the call, select the "Include the area code" checkbox.

When gaining access to the Internet, you may find that you need to use a calling card for long-distance expenses. Windows Vista supports the use of calling cards within the dialing rules associated with your dial-up connection. The Calling Card tab, as shown in Figure 17-7, allows you to enter information about a predefined calling card you use. Windows Vista supplies a prepopulated list of common calling cards. If you cannot find your calling card company, you can create a new entry for it.

To create a new calling card entry, click New, and the New Calling Card window appears. There are four tabs with which to define your new calling card. The four tabs are listed in Table 17-2.

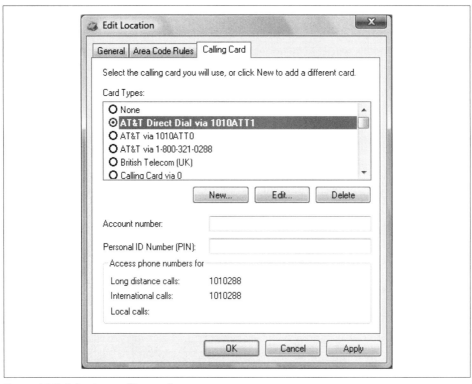

Figure 17-7. Selecting a calling card to use

Table 17-2. Calling card information for dialing rules

Tab	Related options
General	This tab allows you to name your new calling card settings, letting you assign an easy-to-remember name. In the "Account number" box, type your calling card account number. In the "Personal Identification Number (PIN)" box, type your PIN.
Long Distance	This tab provides the options required to dial a long-distance call, and allows you to specify the steps required to make a connection using the card. Enter the number required for long-distance calls into the "Access phone number for long distance calls" field. Use the buttons provided to sequence the steps required to dial a call. Use the Move Up, Move Down, and Delete buttons for your sequencing needs.
International	This tab provides the options required to dial an international call, and allows you to specify the steps to make a successful connection using the calling card. Enter the number required for the call into the "Access phone number for international calls" field provided. Use the buttons provided to sequence the steps required to dial a call. Use the Move Up, Move Down, and Delete buttons for your sequencing needs.
Local	This tab provides the options required to dial a local call. Enter the number to dial for a local call into the "Access phone number for local calls" field. Use the buttons provided to sequence the different aspects for a successful call. Use the Move Up, Move Down, and Delete buttons to move your sequence into the desired arrangement.

Configuring dial-up connection properties

When connecting using a dial-up connection, you may need to configure additional options for your connection. Windows Vista enables you to change the properties of your dial-up connection to alter your phone numbers, manage redial attempts, and manage your personal security settings. You can also configure the network protocol options and network sharing options.

To change the properties of your network connection, you need to open the Network Connections window and the Dial-up Connection Properties dialog box by using the following steps.

1. Click Start and then click Control Panel.
2. In the Control Panel, click Network and Internet and then click Network and Sharing Center.
3. In the Network and Sharing Center, click "Manage network connections" in the left pane, under Tasks.
4. Right-click the entry for your dial-up connection and then select Properties.

The Dial-up Properties window gives you five tabs of features to configure. The different tabs are labeled General, Options, Security, Networking, and Sharing. Each tab enables you to manage the different features available for use with your modem and dial-up connections. Table 17-3 shows the different tabs available and the features you can manage through the Dial-up Properties window.

Table 17-3. Dial-up connection properties feature settings

Tab	Related options
General	Modem device configuration
	Phone number to dial
	Alternative phone numbers to dial
	Associate dialing rules with this dial-up connection
Options	Dialing options
	Redialing options
	PPP settings
Security	Security options
	Interactive logon and scripting options
Networking	Internet Protocol Version 6 (TCP/IPv6)
	Internet Protocol Version 4 (TCP/IPv4)
	File and Printer Sharing for Microsoft Networks
	QoS Packet Scheduler
	Client for Microsoft Networks
Sharing	Internet Connection Sharing

The General tab of the Dial-up Properties dialog box allows you to manage the device configuration of your modem by clicking the Configure button. See Figure 17-8 for an example. The Modem Configuration dialog box allows you to change the maximum transfer speed of your modem and the hardware features available for your modem. Using the "Hardware features" options, you can turn a feature on or off by checking the associated checkbox for each feature listed:

- Enable hardware flow control
- Enable modem error control
- Enable modem compression
- Enable modem speaker

Figure 17-8. Optimizing the modem configuration

From the General tab, you can also edit the phone number to dial for calls. Editing the "Phone number" field allows you to change the stored phone number to dial. If you have multiple numbers to choose from through your service provider or VPN provider, you can add these phone numbers using the Alternates button. Clicking the Alternates button provides you with the ability to add new numbers, change their dialing priority, and use error checking to go to the next number in the list.

The Options tab allows you to configure the dialing options available for your dial-up connection. You can have Windows Vista display progress while connecting by checking the box next to this feature. You can have Windows prompt for a name and password, certificate, and so on, by checking the box for this feature. You can also turn on the "Include Windows logon domain" feature by checking its associated checkbox, and the "Prompt for phone number" feature, which opens a dialog box for you to fill in the appropriate phone number to dial. See Figure 17-9 for an example of the Options tab.

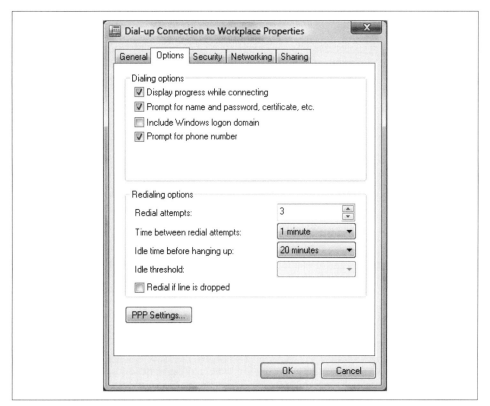

Figure 17-9. Configuring additional modem options

The Options tab also allows you to configure the options used to redial a connection. Use the "Redial attempts" text box to set the number of attempts Windows Vista makes to dial a connection. You can also use the "Time between redial attempts" listbox to change the behavior Windows Vista uses between call attempts. Setting the "Idle time before hanging up" feature allows you to turn off a connection automatically when you are no longer using the connection for active data transfers on the network. This feature can save you money if you are using a calling card or if long-distance charges apply to your dial-up connection.

As Figure 17-10 shows, typical settings on the Security tab allow you to validate your identity with secured and unsecured password use. You also have the option to choose a smart card for authentication purposes when connecting to your dial-up connection. With a secured password, you can specify that you want to use your Windows logon name and password automatically and that data encryption is required. With a smart card, you can specify that data encryption is required as well.

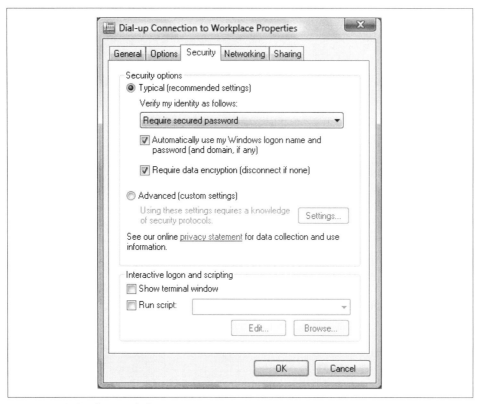

Figure 17-10. Configuring dial-up security

If the typical settings don't meet your needs, click the Advanced option and then click the Settings button. Using the options shown in Figure 17-11, you can then configure data encryption and logon security. With logon security, you can choose to use the Extensible Authentication Protocol (EAP) or other security protocols.

As shown in Figure 17-12, the Networking tab gives you the ability to configure the protocols associated with your dial-up connection. You can enable or disable a protocol by checking its associated checkbox. To configure the individual protocol properties, you may either double-click the desired protocol or highlight the protocol and choose the Properties button to open the dialog box associated with its properties. By default, dial-up connections have file and printer sharing as well as Client for Microsoft Networks disabled. If you are connecting directly to your workplace using dial-up, you'll want to enable these protocols.

Figure 17-11. Configuring advanced security settings as necessary

Figure 17-12. Configuring the networking protocols to use with the dial-up connection

The Sharing tab allows you to configure the Internet Connection Sharing feature of Windows Vista, as seen in Figure 17-13. To enable this feature, check the associated box. This will allow other users to connect to the connection you define from the drop-down menu. You have the option to associate any network connection defined to your system with this feature.

Figure 17-13. Configuring Internet Connection Sharing as necessary

Creating Broadband Connections

Most people have a broadband connection to the Internet these days. Broadband connections are defined by their bandwidth and fall into five categories: cable, ADSL, SDSL, fiber to the premises, and broadband wireless. Any of these types of connections provides high-speed access to the Internet. Each connection requires service from an ISP. If the ISP allows you to connect without having to provide a username and password, such as with cable modem service, you typically don't need to establish a separate broadband connection. Instead, you simply need to connect your computer to the cable modem provided by the cable provider. On the other hand, if your broadband provider requires you to use a username and password it has assigned, you'll need to create a broadband connection that sets the username and password for you.

In the Network and Sharing Center, you can set up a broadband connection by following these steps:

1. Click "Set up a connection or network" in the left pane. This opens the "Set up a connection or network" Wizard.

2. In the wizard, click Connect to the Internet, and click the Next button.

3. If your computer has existing connections that could be used to connect to the Internet, you'll see a list of the existing connections. Select "No, create a new connection" and then click Next.

4. The wizard gives you three selections from which to choose. The choices are Wireless, Broadband (PPPoE), and Dial-up. Click Broadband (PPPoE).

5. On the "Type the information…" page, shown in Figure 17-14, type the username and password provided by your ISP in the text boxes provided. As necessary, select the "Show characters" checkbox to see your password and verify the correct syntax.

6. Select the "Remember this password" checkbox to save your password for future use.

7. Windows Vista also enables you to share your connection with anyone with access to your computer. If you want other users to have access to this connection, check "Allow other people to use this connection."

8. Click Connect to create the connection and establish a connection to the ISP.

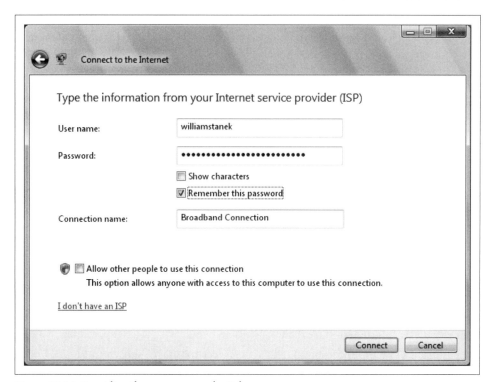

Figure 17-14. Providing the necessary credentials

Creating VPN Connections

Many organizations use VPN connections to gain access to their networks. These connections use encryption to secure the transmitted data between the user and the network. They also provide remote connectivity to a network so that you can access network resources, such as file shares, email servers, and terminal service connections.

Most organizations use Internet connections to allow VPN client connections to their network. If you do not have the correct information to connect to the VPN service, contact your network administrator for specific information on how to connect to the network. Some organizations use specific VPN client applications, which require the installation of a separate VPN client application. To determine whether the default VPN client included in Windows Vista will work with your VPN connection, contact your network administrator. If your organization is running Microsoft's Routing and Remote Access Service (RRAS), the VPN client in Windows Vista will work by default.

In the Network and Sharing Center, you can set up a VPN connection by following these steps:

1. Click "Set up a connection or network" in the left pane. This opens the "Set up a connection or network" Wizard.

2. In the wizard, click "Connect to a workplace," and click the Next button.

3. If your computer has existing connections that could be used to connect to your workplace, you'll see a list of the existing connections. Select "No, create a new connection" and then click Next.

4. On the "How do you want to connect?" page, you have two choices:

    Use my Internet connection
    This feature connects you to a workplace using a VPN connection through the Internet. It requires a username and password for connecting to your VPN server.

    Dial directly
    This feature connects you to a workplace using a VPN connection with a modem by directly dialing a phone number to your workplace without going through the Internet.

To use an existing Internet connection for a VPN connection, follow these steps:

1. Click "Use my Internet connection (VPN)" to use an Internet connection for a VPN connection.

2. If you aren't currently connected to the Internet, you'll see the "Before you connect" page. On this page, choose the connection that you want to use to connect to the Internet, and then click Next.

3. On the "Type the Internet address to connect to" page, shown in Figure 17-15, type the IP address provided by your network administrator. This is the IP address of your organization's remote access server.

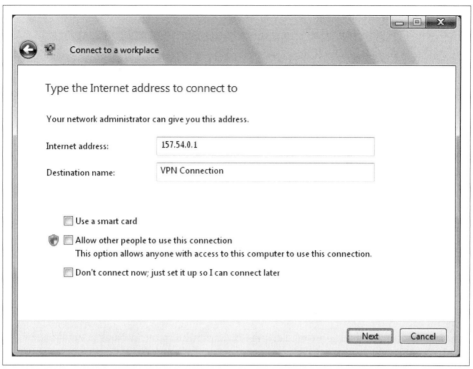

Figure 17-15. Configuring the connection address and options

4. In the "Destination name" text box, type a name for the connection. The default name is VPN Connection.

5. Check "Use a smart card" if you have a smart card for use in authenticating you to your VPN connection.

6. Check "Allow other people to use this connection" if you want anyone with access to your computer to be able to use this VPN connection.

7. Check "Don't connect now; just set it up so I can connect later" if you want to create the VPN connection, but not actually connect to it.

8. Click Next. On the "Type your user name and password" page, the wizard prompts you to enter your username and password. In the "User name" text box, enter the domain username for your workplace. In the Password text box, enter the password for your domain user account. As necessary, click "Show characters" to view your password. This helps you identify the correct syntax and find typos.

9. Click "Remember this password" to save your password for future use.

10. As necessary, enter the name of the domain at your workplace into the Domain text box. This setting is optional, but it remembers your domain so that you do not have to type it in each time you use the connection.

11. After entering the correct data into the fields provided by the wizard, click the Connect button to create and establish your broadband VPN connection.

To use a dial-up connection for a VPN connection, follow these steps:

1. Click "Dial directly" to use your modem to make the VPN connection.

2. On the "Type the telephone number" page, enter the phone number provided by your network administrator.

3. Complete steps 4–10 of the previous procedure. After providing the necessary information, click Create to create the dial-up VPN connection.

Configuring Proxy Settings for Mobile Connections

Many organizations today use proxies to protect their users from intrusion and to use smaller amounts of publicly routed IP addresses. A *proxy* is a server that sits between you and the Internet. It receives all client requests to the Internet, fulfills the request itself, and then sends the information to the client. When creating network connections, you may need to configure a proxy in order to gain access to the Internet or other external servers.

Windows Vista offers support for adding proxies inside Internet Explorer's settings. You can configure the proxy server and port to support the different protocols you use for accessing services that require a proxy within your organization.

You can enable or disable proxy settings on a per-connection basis as well as for the LAN. You should enable proxy settings only when using a proxy is required. If you enable proxy settings and a proxy is not required, you won't be able to use the related connection to access the Internet or resources on your network. This happens because your computer will look for a proxy that isn't there. Malware programs sometimes target your proxy settings, and you may have to enable or disable these settings as a result.

You can configure a proxy for a LAN connection by completing these steps:

1. Click Start, and then click Internet Explorer.

2. Click Tools from the menu bar, and then click Internet Options.

3. In the Internet Options dialog box, click the Connections tab.

4. Click the LAN Settings button listed under the Local Area Network (LAN) Settings heading.

5. To enable the use of a proxy server, check the box for "Use a proxy server for your LAN (These settings will not apply to dial-up or VPN connections)," as shown in Figure 17-16.

6. Enter the IP address of the proxy in the Address text box.

7. Enter the port number of the proxy in the Port text box.

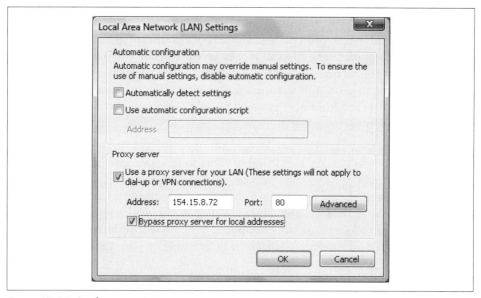

Figure 17-16. Configuring LAN proxy settings as necessary

8. If you want to bypass the proxy server for local IP addresses, select the "Bypass proxy server for local addresses" checkbox.

9. Click OK to complete the proxy configuration process.

You can configure a proxy for a dial-up or VPN connection by completing these steps:

1. Click Start, and then click Internet Explorer.

2. Click Tools from the menu bar, and then click Internet Options.

3. In the Internet Options dialog box, click the Connections tab.

4. Under Dial-up and Virtual Private Network Settings, click the connection you want to work with and then click Settings.

5. In the Connection Settings dialog box, enable the use of a proxy server by checking the box for "Use a proxy server for your LAN (These settings will not apply to dial-up or VPN connections)."

6. Enter the IP address of the proxy in the Address text box.

7. Enter the port number of the proxy in the Port text box.

8. Click OK to complete the proxy configuration process.

Whenever you change network connection settings, you should verify that you can establish a connection and access resources. If you are having difficulty connecting to the Internet after changing your connection settings, check your proxy settings in Internet Explorer to enable or disable your proxy configuration as appropriate for each connection.

Enabling and Disabling Windows Firewall

Windows Firewall helps prevent hackers and malicious programs from gaining access to your computer. The firewall blocks access to your computer through network or Internet connections. The firewall can also block packets being sent by your computer, helping to protect others from malicious content on your computer, such as a virus or worm. The firewall is essential to help protect your computer and your data, and you will want to enable it.

If you enable Windows Firewall, make sure you do not run other software firewalls on your computer, as it takes considerable effort to troubleshoot networking issues when you have multiple firewalls enabled on your computer. If you are using an Ethernet router, you should enable the firewall on the router as well, as this will also help block attacks against your computer. While no firewall has the capability to stop all harmful attacks against your computer, it is well worth the time to configure Windows Firewall and any firewall that may be available on your Ethernet router.

Windows Vista offers you the ability to configure the options of the Windows Firewall feature by giving you an easy-to-use interface. You can determine the status of Windows Firewall by following these steps:

1. Click Start, and then click Control Panel. In the Control Panel, click the Network and Internet heading and then click Windows Firewall.

2. As shown in Figure 17-17, you'll see a summary of the firewall status and configuration. To change the firewall settings, click "Change settings."

3. In the Windows Firewall Settings dialog box, you can then use the option on the General tab to turn the firewall on or off. To turn the firewall on, click "On (recommended)." This setting allows the firewall to block incoming connections. To turn the firewall off, click "Off (not recommended)." This setting turns the firewall off and makes your computer vulnerable to remote attacks through network and Internet connections.

4. When you are connecting to networks that are less secure, you may want to block all incoming connections to your computer. To do this, select the "Block all incoming connections" checkbox. This setting ignores all settings in the firewall configuration and blocks every connection to your computer. This setting also turns off notifications.

5. Once you have completed making changes to the firewall settings, complete the steps by clicking OK, and Windows Vista applies your changes to the system. If you are a member of a domain and you cannot change some of your firewall configuration options, your network administrator may be controlling the settings through Group Policy. You also need the correct credentials to change your firewall settings. If you do not have local administrative rights, the advanced features of Windows Firewall are unavailable for your configuration.

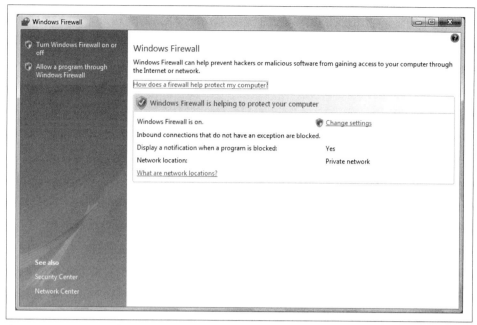

Figure 17-17. Viewing the status of Windows Firewall

Establishing Network Connections

Network connections are the actual settings that allow you to connect to a network. They require several configurations in order to work. First, you must have a hardware device offering you connectivity to the network. You also need a profile associated with the network connection, and you must configure the network protocols to use on the related network adapter. Each setting is required for any connection to work properly.

You must have a connection defined in order to establish a connection to a network. To verify that you have a connection defined, you can use the Network Connections window, as shown in Figure 17-18. The Network Connections window holds all of the network connections defined for your computer. When you install network hardware in your computer, Windows Vista creates a connection in the Network Connections window. If you install an Ethernet card, Windows Vista creates a Local Area Connection in the Network Connections window. If you install a wireless network adapter, Windows Vista creates a Wireless Network Connection in the Network Connections window.

To open the Network Connections window, follow these steps:

1. Click Start and then click Control Panel.

2. In the Control Panel, click Network and Internet and then click Network and Sharing Center.

3. In the Network and Sharing Center, click "Manage network connections" in the left pane, under Tasks.

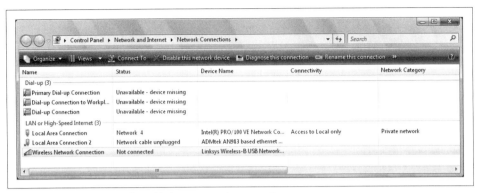

Figure 17-18. Viewing and establishing network connections

In the Network Connections window, you will see the status of each connection. If a connection is active, you will see a standard icon and a status entry that shows the name of the connected network. For an error status, you will see the adapter icon with a red *X* and a related error in the Status column, such as "Not connected," "Network cable unplugged," or "Unavailable – Device Missing." Once you've verified that you have a network connection, you will want to connect to a network or the Internet using dial-up, broadband, or VPN.

To activate a connection that is not connected, right-click the connection and then select Connect/Disconnect. This starts the Connect to a Network Wizard. On the "Select a network to connect to" page, click the network you want to connect to and then click Connect. Windows Vista will establish a connection to the network using the connection settings you previously defined. Click Close when the connection process completes.

Alternatively, you can establish a connection using the following steps:

1. Click Start and then click Connect To. This starts the Connect to a Network Wizard.

2. On the "Select a network to connect to" page, click the network you want to connect to and then click Connect.

3. Windows Vista will establish a connection to the network using the connection settings you previously defined. Click Close when the connection process completes.

If your connection fails, Windows Vista will show you a troubleshooting dialog box, which gives you the following options:

Diagnose the problem
The wizard goes through a check of the connection properties and tries to diagnose the problem with your connection. If Windows Vista does not find a problem, you are prompted to report the problem to Microsoft.

Try again

The wizard attempts to make the dial-up connection again, using the same settings as your previous attempts.

Try a different connection

The wizard takes you back to the "Select a network to connect to" page, allowing you to choose a different connection.

Wireless Networking

If you travel frequently, chances are you are quite familiar with the existence of wireless networks. Most hotels, coffee shops, airports, and libraries offer WiFi or 802.11 networks. Many cities are beginning to offer WiFi connections also, offering low-cost Internet access to residents. Eventually wireless networks may become so prevalent that we'll be able to connect to the Internet from just about anywhere. With this in mind, Windows Vista makes creating and connecting to wireless networks very easy. With Windows Vista, Microsoft has taken the time to revamp the wireless networking interface, making it considerably easy to create and connect to wireless networks.

The beauty of wireless networking correlates directly to the word *wireless*. Wireless networks allow you the freedom to move about, whether in your home or on the road, which can make your life considerably easier when you need to connect to a network. With wireless networking, you gain the complete functionality of a standard network without the need for any cables to connect the computers or devices. This eases the requirements and restrictions of regular networks, but it adds some complexity and additional pitfalls to the networking process.

Wireless Network Technologies

The most common wireless network technologies fall under the Institute of Electrical and Electronics Engineers (IEEE) 802.11 specification. Although other wireless technologies exist, they are not as prevalent as 802.11 (WiFi) networks. WiFi networks transmit radio waves between devices to allow network communications. WiFi uses the 2.4 GHz and 5 GHz spectrums. There are three major standards within the WiFi designation. See Table 17-4 for a listing of the major standards and their specifications.

Table 17-4. Common wireless networking technologies

Version	Transmission frequency	Transmission rate
802.11a	5 GHz	Up to 54 Mbps
802.11b	2.4 GHz	Up to 11 Mbps
802.11g	2.4 GHz	Up to 54 Mbps

The 802.11b specification was the first WiFi technology introduced to the market. It uses the 2.4 GHz spectrum to transmit data at 11 Mbps. The 802.11b specification uses Complimentary Code Keying (CCK) coding to transmit data. While 802.11b has enjoyed the most widespread use, the lowering costs of faster technologies are rapidly replacing it with newer technologies.

The 802.11a specification transmits in the 5 GHz spectrum at a transmission rate of 54 Mbps. This specification uses Orthogonal Frequency-Division Multiplexing (OFDM) to transmit data, which is considerably better than the CCK coding standard. This gives 802.11a a considerably faster transmission rate.

The 802.11g specification transmits in the 2.4 GHz spectrum at a transmission rate of 54 Mbps. This specification also uses OFDM to transmit data, and it enjoys the most widespread use of the newer technologies.

These technologies fall under the WiFi designation, since they transmit in the 2.4 GHz and 5 GHz spectrums. Windows Vista supports each of these wireless technologies and the devices used to make connections to these types of networks.

New networking standards are also in the marketplace today. It bears noting that early adoption of new technologies does not always favor the consumer, because some products in the market may support early adoption of a standard that is not yet finalized. Therefore, if you purchase products too early you may have to purchase additional hardware to support the additional features defined in the final version of the standard. While this is not always true, be wary of purchasing the latest and greatest wireless products. Take some time to research the technology before buying equipment on impulse.

Newer 802.11 transmission specifications include 802.11n, which offers up to 540 Mbps while using Multiple-Input-Multiple-Output (MIMO) technology. Essentially this means that the client computer and the wireless access point will use multiple receivers and multiple transmitters to achieve improved performance.

Not all 802.11 specifications are about transmission speed and rate, however. The 802.11i specification offers enhanced security. The 802.11h specification offers frequency and power control management. The 802.11e specification offers quality of service enhancements. The 802.11x specification provides a framework for authenticating users and controlling their access to a protected network.

Another emerging wireless technology is Worldwide Interoperability for Microwave Access (WiMax). WiMax is not really a technology, but a stamp of approval for use with the 802.16 specification in broadband wireless deployments in metropolitan areas. WiMax-certified equipment usually uses the 2.5 GHz spectrum, but the 3.5 GHz, 2.3 GHz, and 5 GHz spectrums are available in other countries. Currently, a movement exists to use the 700 MHz spectrum for future WiMax deployments.

Wireless Network Devices

Wireless devices come in different shapes and sizes. A wireless device is the network adapter used to make the connection to wireless networks. A wireless network adapter is the actual hardware device you install into a slot or port in your computer. You must have a wireless network adapter to create a wireless network connection, which in turn allows you to connect to a wireless network.

Most new portable computers offer integrated wireless networking adapters. Older PCMCIA cards are available for older laptops that go into the PC slot and have a dongle, but these are increasingly less common to find. PCI cards exist for the desktop and workstation. USB adapters are now more prevalent in the market, and they will work in all computers with a USB slot.

You can find wireless network adapters at just about any store that carries electronics. Most office supply, electronics, and retail stores offer you the ability to purchase wireless adapters for your computer. Make sure that you purchase the correct card for the type of wireless technology you are using. If you are in doubt, buy an 802.11g adapter, since it can use both 802.11a and 802.11b technologies to communicate.

The device to which your wireless adapter connects is a wireless router or a wireless access point. At the office or out on the town, you may be able to use someone else's wireless router or wireless access point to access the Internet. At home, however, you must purchase the necessary wireless router or a wireless access point. Several manufacturers produce wired/wireless router combinations. A wired/wireless router, such as the LinkSys Wireless G Broadband router, has ports for network cables that use wired communications as well as receivers for receiving wireless communications.

Installing and Configuring a Wireless Adapter

You must have a wireless adapter or chip in your computer in order to create a wireless connection. You can see the devices installed in your computer using Device Manager. Device Manager allows you to manage the different devices in your system from a single console. You have the ability to enable or disable devices, update or roll back the device drivers, and uninstall devices.

You can open the Computer Management console to use Device Manager by following these steps:

1. Click Start, right-click Computer, and then select Manage.

2. In the Computer Management console, click Device Manager in the left pane.

3. Your computer's wired and wireless adapters should be listed under the Network Adapters node. Expand this node by double-clicking it.

If you have a PCI card to install, install it as discussed in Chapter 5. If you have a PCMCIA card or a USB adapter, slide the card into the appropriate slot in your computer. Once you have installed the PCMCIA card or USB adapter into your computer, Windows Vista should automatically see the device and install a driver for the adapter or ask you to install a driver for the adapter. See Chapter 5 for details on installing the device driver.

If you are using an integrated wireless network card in your computer and this card is not enabled, reboot the computer into the BIOS. (Most OEM manufacturers use the Delete key. Press the Delete key every second or so after the reboot to enter the main BIOS screen.) Usually, you can find the network card settings under Integrated Devices. Once you have found the wireless network card settings in your BIOS, select and enable the device. After you have enabled the device, save the changes in the BIOS and reboot your computer into the operating system.

When you have completed the setup process, you will need to open Device Manager to verify that the installation of the wireless adapter finished correctly. In Device Manager, right-click on the adapter you previously installed or enabled and select Properties from the context menu. On the Driver tab, verify that the details for the Driver Provider listing are correct. If you see Microsoft listed, you should go to your network adapter manufacturer's web site and download the latest driver for your network card. This allows you to use the entire functionality of the card. Microsoft drivers usually allow you only the lowest common features of the card.

If you do not see a network adapter listed in the Device Manager screen under Network Adapters, you should verify that the device does not show up under Other Devices as a network controller. If this happens, you should go to your network adapter manufacturer's web site and download the latest driver for your network card. If you continue to have problems installing the network card, refer to the networking troubleshooting section in Chapter 14.

Creating Wireless Connections

To connect to a wireless network, you must create a wireless network connection. Windows Vista makes this process very intuitive. You can create wireless network connections by following these steps:

1. Click Start and then click Control Panel. In the Control Panel, click Network and Internet and then click Network and Sharing Center.
2. In the Network and Sharing Center, click "Manage wireless networks" in the left pane.
3. In the "Manage wireless networks" window, shown in Figure 17-19, you'll see a list of any currently defined wireless network connections.
4. Click Add. This starts the "Manually connect to a wireless network" Wizard, as shown in Figure 17-20.

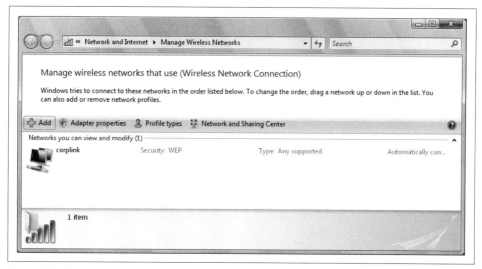

Figure 17-19. Viewing wireless connections

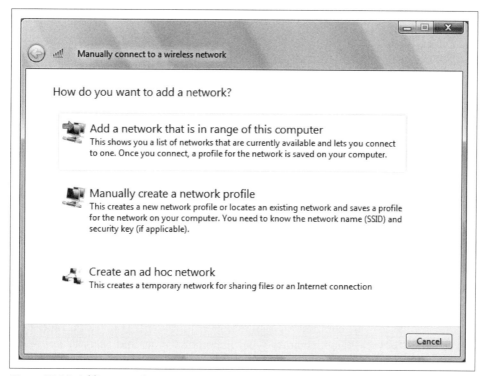

Figure 17-20. Adding a wireless connection

5. Select one of the following options:

Add a network that is in range of this computer

Making this selection shows you a list of networks within range of your computer and allows you to connect to them (see Figure 17-21). Click the name of the wireless connection you want to use and then click Connect. If the network requires a security key or pass phrase and you haven't previously provided and saved this information, enter the required credentials when prompted. If the network is unsecured, the wizard will prompt you to authorize this connection. Once you have completed the connection, you are prompted to define the network type as Home, Work, or Internet. Selecting Home or Work implies that the network is secure and that you can share resources with other computers on the network. If you select Internet, this implies that the network is unsecured, or in a public place, and Windows Vista locks down the ability to share resources with other computers on the network.

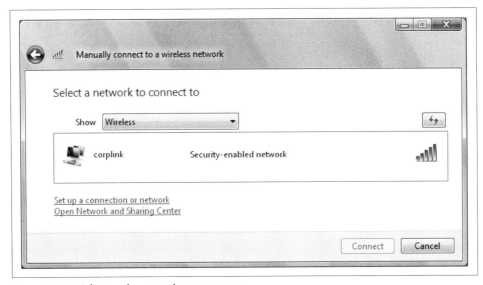

Figure 17-21. Selecting the network to connect to

Manually create a network profile

Making this selection creates a new wireless network profile and saves the profile to your computer. As shown in Figure 17-22, you are prompted for the Network name, Security type, Encryption type, and Security Key/Passphrase for access to the wireless network. Select the "Start this network connection automatically" checkbox if you want to connect to this network without prompting. Click "Connect even if the network is not broadcasting" if you have a stealth wireless network. When you click Next, the wizard adds the network to your list and prompts you to connect or change the settings.

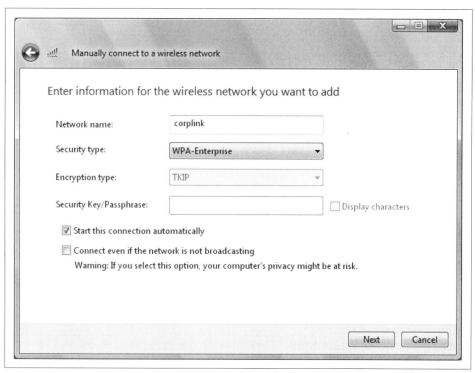

Figure 17-22. Entering the necessary connection information

Create an ad hoc network

Making this selection allows you to create a computer-to-computer network with other computers using only the wireless network adapters installed in your computer. You can use these types of connections to share files or share Internet connections with other computers. Devices in ad hoc networks must be within 30 feet of one another. When making the connection to the ad hoc network, you may lose connectivity to an active Internet connection. Click Next. As shown in Figure 17-23, enter the name of the network, select a security type, and then enter the security key or pass phrase to use. You have the option to save this network for future use, allowing you to keep your settings without prompting during future use. When you click Next, the wizard tells you the network is ready to use.

Connecting to and Configuring Available and Preferred Wireless Networks

You can connect to and configure wireless networks using the Network and Sharing Center. You have the option of setting the preferences of wireless networks defined to your computer and the order in which you connect to the available networks. You can even set your network connections to start automatically.

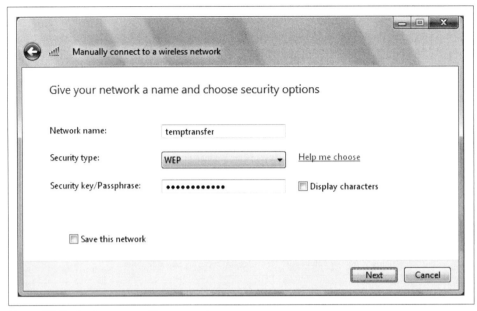

Figure 17-23. Setting up an ad hoc network

You can manage wireless network connections by following these steps:

1. Click Start and then click Control Panel. In the Control Panel, click Network and Internet and then click Network and Sharing Center.

2. In the Network and Sharing Center, click "Manage wireless networks" in the left pane. This opens the "Manage wireless networks" window.

In the "Manage wireless networks" window, you will see the wireless networks defined for your computer. You also have a toolbar with different options for managing your wireless networks. Table 17-5 lists the options available for your use.

Table 17-5. Properties for managing wireless networks

Option	This feature allows you to...
Add	Add wireless network connections to your computer.
Remove	Remove a selected wireless network connection from your computer.
Move Down	Change the connection preference of a wireless network to a lower state. This will allow other wireless connections to connect before this one.
Move Up	Change the connection preference of a wireless network to a higher state. This will allow the selected connection to connect before other connections you've created.
Adapter Properties	Open the properties window of your wireless network adapter. The properties window allows you to change the network protocol definitions and services available.

Table 17-5. Properties for managing wireless networks (continued)

Option	This feature allows you to...
Profile Types	Change the way profiles are handled on the computer. You can use all-user profiles, or all-user and per-user profiles. All-user profiles apply to all users of the computer. Per-user profiles apply only to the logged-on user.
Network and Sharing Center	Open the Network and Sharing Center, allowing you to manage more of your network settings.

Setting Up a Wireless Router or Access Point

You can set up a wireless router or wireless access point by completing these steps:

1. Click Start and then click Control Panel. In the Control Panel, click Network and Internet and then click Network and Sharing Center.

2. In the Network and Sharing Center, click "Set up a connection or network" in the left pane. This opens the "Set up a connection or network" Wizard.

3. In the wizard, click "Set up a wireless router or access point," and click the Next button.

4. Read the introductory text. The wizard allows you to configure a wireless router or access point, set up the properties of file and printer sharing, save the network configuration for future use, and make the network a private network. If you have all of the required information to set up your wireless network, click the Next button and follow the steps provided by the wizard.

5. The wizard starts by detecting network hardware and settings. If you have an access point, Windows Vista discovers it, and if the device allows automatic configuration, it will connect to the device. If your device does not allow automatic configuration, you have the option to "Configure this device manually," or "Create wireless network settings and save to USB flash drive." Selecting the first choice opens an authentication dialog window for connecting to your device. This allows you to configure the access point or router manually by following the information in the user manual associated with the network device.

6. The latter choice allows you to copy network settings and transfer the settings to multiple computers. This feature also allows you to share the settings across the network after configuration of the central connection for hosts associated with the network. You must input the network name (SSID), and click the Next button. You must then enter the pass phrase for network connections, and click the Next button. Next, select the file and printer sharing options, consisting of "Do not allow file and printer sharing," "Allow sharing with anyone with a user account and password for this computer," and "Allow sharing with anyone on the same network as this computer." After selecting the properties of file and printer sharing, click the Next button, and identify the USB key or path where you want to save the network settings for future use.

PART IV

Managing and Supporting Windows Vista

CHAPTER 18

Managing User Accounts and Parental Controls

In Windows Vista, you use user accounts to manage access to your computer and parental controls to manage the types of content users can access while logged on. User accounts and parental controls are the two main areas of the operating system where you'll have entirely different sets of features and functions at home and at the office. At home, you'll use local accounts on your computer and you'll have full access to parental controls. While you are logged on to your computer with a local account, local computer security is applied to your account through Local Group Policy and through other local computer security components.

On the other hand, at the office, your computer will typically be a member of a domain and you'll typically use domain accounts to log on to computers and the network. While you are logged on to the network with a domain account, domain security is applied to your account through Active Directory Group Policy and through other domain security components. Although you can log on to a domain computer using a local account, some of the domain security changes will still affect what you can do and how you can work with user accounts.

When working with domain computers, one of the biggest changes you'll notice is that there are no parental controls, and this remains true whether you log on with a local account or a domain account. Another big change is in the available options for managing local computer accounts. Local computer account options for domain computers are completely different from the options for managing local computer accounts on nondomain computers.

Managing Access to Your Computer

Windows Vista provides user accounts and group accounts. User accounts are designed for individuals. Group accounts, usually referred to as *groups*, have users as members and are used to manage the file access permissions and privileges of multiple users. Although you can log on to a user account, you can't log on to a group account.

At the office, your IT administrators will create and manage the user account you need to log on to the network. You can use the techniques discussed in the "Logging On, Switching, Locking, Logging Off, and Shutting Down" section of Chapter 1 to log on to the network and access your account. If you have a problem with your account, you can ask your IT administrators to help you resolve it.

At home, you have complete control over your computer. During installation, you created the user account that you need to log on to your computer. When you are logged on with an Administrator account rather than a standard user account, you can create other accounts to allow other people to log on to your computer. You can also manage user account settings as necessary.

While the user and group names are what Windows Vista displays to you, these names aren't the actual identifiers Windows Vista uses. Behind the scenes, when you create a user or group account, Windows Vista assigns each user or group a unique security identifier (SID). The SID consists of a computer or domain security ID prefix combined with a unique relative ID for the user or group. The SID allows Windows Vista to track an account independently from its display name. Windows Vista does this to enable you to easily change account names, and delete accounts without worrying that someone might gain access to resources simply by re-creating an account with the same name as one you've deleted.

Thus, when you change a username or group name, you tell Windows Vista to map a particular SID to a new display name. When you delete a user or group, you tell Windows Vista that a particular SID is no longer valid. If you later were to create an account with the same username or group name, the new account would not have the same privileges and permissions as the previous one. This occurs because the new account will have a new SID.

When you install Windows Vista, the operating system installs several types of default accounts. The default user accounts are Administrator and Guest. The default system accounts include LocalSystem, LocalService, and NetworkService. You use these accounts as follows:

Administrator

A standard account that provides complete access to your computer. To protect your computer, the Administrator account should have a secure password.

Guest

A standard account that provides limited privileges on your computer. Because this account can potentially put your computer at risk, the Guest account is disabled by default.

LocalSystem

A system account for running system processes and handling system tasks. The operating system manages this account.

LocalService

A system account for running services with fewer privileges and logon rights than the LocalSystem account. The operating system manages this account.

NetworkService

A system account for running services that need network access privileges. The operating system manages this account.

In most cases, you don't need to modify these or other default accounts. While you can configure Administrator and Guest so that you can use them for logon, in most cases you should use a user account with administrator privileges instead. An administrator user account is one of two types of user accounts you can create. You can also create standard user accounts. When a user needs the highest level of permissions possible, create his account as an administrator user account. Otherwise, create his account as a standard user account.

Managing Your User Account

Your user account has many properties associated with it. These properties include a password, picture, account name, and account type designation. At home, you can manage the properties associated with your user account by following the techniques discussed in this section. Most account management tasks require you to have an Administrator account or the username and password of an Administrator account.

 At the office, you won't be able to use these techniques to manage your account, even if you log on to your computer using a local account. As discussed previously, when your computer is a member of a domain, different security components and features are in effect.

Changing Your Account Name

Because your computer tracks your account with an SID, you can safely change your account name at any time without worrying that this will cause problems with your access permissions or privileges. If you want to change your account name, follow these steps:

1. Click Start and then click Control Panel.

2. In the Control Panel, click the User Accounts and Family Safety heading and then click User Accounts.

3. On the User Accounts page, click "Change your account name."

4. On the Change Your Name page, shown in Figure 18-1, type the new name for your account and then click Change Name.

Figure 18-1. Changing your account name

Changing Your Account Picture

Your account picture is displayed on the logon screen and on the Start menu. If you want to change your account picture, follow these steps:

1. Click Start and then click Control Panel.
2. In the Control Panel, click the User Accounts and Family Safety heading and then click User Accounts.
3. On the User Accounts page, click "Change your picture."
4. On the Change Your Picture page, shown in Figure 18-2, click the picture you want to use, or click the "Browse for more pictures" link to select any BMP, GIF, JPEG, PNG, DIB, or RLE picture to use.
5. Click Change Picture.

When you use a picture other than a default picture provided by Microsoft, Windows Vista automatically optimizes the picture and saves the optimized copy as part of your personal Contact entry in Windows Contacts. While it may seem strange to save the picture as part of your personal *.contact* file, doing so is a quick and easy shortcut for the operating system. Most pictures are optimized to a file size of 50 KB or less—even high-resolution pictures.

Changing Your Account Type

You can configure your user account as a standard user account or as an administrator user account. If you are logged on with a standard user account, you can change the account type to Administrator. If you are logged on with an Administrator account, you can change the account type to Standard User.

Figure 18-2. Changing your account picture

You can change the account type by following these steps:

1. Click Start and then click Control Panel.
2. In the Control Panel, click the User Accounts and Family Safety heading and then click User Accounts.
3. On the User Accounts page, click "Change your account type."
4. On the "Select your new account type" page, shown in Figure 18-3, set the account type as either Standard user or Administrator.
5. Click Change Account Type.

Creating Your Password

To protect your computer, your user account should have a strong password. You can create a password for your account by completing the following steps:

1. Click Start and then click Control Panel.
2. In the Control Panel, click the User Accounts and Family Safety heading and then click User Accounts.
3. On the User Accounts page, click "Create a password for your account."
4. On the "Create a password for your account" page, shown in Figure 18-4, type a password and then confirm it.
5. Afterward, type a unique password hint. The password hint is a word or phrase that can help you remember the password if you forget it. This hint is visible to anyone who uses your computer, so be careful what you use.
6. Click "Create password."

Figure 18-3. Changing your account type

Figure 18-4. Creating your account password

Changing Your Password

You should periodically change your password to help protect your computer. You can change the password on your account by completing the following steps:

1. Click Start and then click Control Panel.

2. In the Control Panel, click the User Accounts and Family Safety heading and then click User Accounts.

3. On the User Accounts page, click "Change your password."

4. On the "Change your password" page, shown in Figure 18-5, type your current password in the first text box.

5. Type your new password in the second text box.

6. Confirm your new password by retyping it in the third text box.

7. Afterward, type a unique password hint. The password hint is a word or phrase that can help you remember the password if you forget it. Because this hint is visible to anyone who uses your computer, you'll want to be careful what you use as the hint.

8. Click "Change password."

Figure 18-5. Changing your account password

Storing Your Password for Recovery

You can store your password in a secure, encrypted file on a floppy disk or USB flash key, and then use this file to recover your password if you forget it.

To store your password for recovery, complete these steps:

1. Press Ctrl-Alt-Delete and then click the Change a Password option.

2. Click "Create a password reset disk" to start the Forgotten Password Wizard.

3. In the Forgotten Password Wizard, read the introductory message and then click Next.

4. You can use a floppy disk or a USB flash key as your password key disk. To use a floppy disk, insert a blank, formatted disk into the A: drive and then select Floppy Disk Drive (A:) in the drive list. To use a USB flash key, select the device you want to use on the drive list. Click Next.

 If you insert a USB flash device, it won't be displayed on the list automatically. Click Back and then click Next to update the list to include the device you just inserted.

5. Type your current password in the text box provided and then click Next.

6. After the wizard creates the password reset key, click Next and then click Finish.

7. Remove the disk or USB flash key and store it in a safe location. Anyone who has this disk or key can use it to access your account.

Recovering Your Password

Windows Vista provides two ways for recovering passwords: password hints and password reset disks. You can access your password hint or recover your password by completing the following steps:

1. On the logon screen, click your username to display the Password prompt.

2. Click the button to the right of the password text box without entering a password.

3. When you click OK, the password hint for your account is displayed on the logon screen.

4. Type your password and click the logon button. If you log on successfully, skip the remaining steps. Otherwise, click OK and continue with password recovery.

5. On the logon screen, click Reset Password.

6. When the Reset Password Wizard starts, click Next.

7. Insert the disk into the A: drive or the USB flash key containing your password recovery file, and then click Next.

8. Type a new password in the first text box.

9. Confirm your new password by retyping it in the second text box.

10. Type a new password hint in the third text box.

11. Click Next to log on with your new password.

Managing Other People's User Accounts

You can allow other people to log on to your computer by creating a user account for them. As with your user account, you can create the account for other people as a standard user account or as an administrator user account. Both account types have passwords, pictures, account names, and account type designations associated with them. At home, you can manage the properties associated with other people's accounts by following the techniques discussed in this section. You must have an Administrator account to manage other people's accounts, or the username and password of an Administrator account.

At the office, you won't be able to use these techniques to manage other people's accounts, even if you log on to your computer using a local account. As discussed previously, when your computer is a member of a domain, different security components and features are in effect.

Creating User Accounts for Other People

Your computer can, and probably should, have multiple user accounts configured as administrators. However, not everyone who logs on to your computer should be configured with an Administrator account. Remember, anyone with administrator privileges can read any file on your computer and make changes to your computer's configuration. If you're in doubt as to whether a person needs an Administrator account, create her account as a standard user account first. When she is trying to perform tasks that require administrator privileges and cannot, you should encourage her to ask you for help. You can then type in your username and password to allow her to perform the task, or explain to her why she shouldn't be trying to perform this type of task on your computer.

Before other people can log on to your computer, you'll need to create a user account for them. You can create a local user account on a computer by following these steps:

1. Click Start and then click Control Panel.

2. In the Control Panel, click the User Accounts and Family Safety heading and then click User Accounts.

3. On the User Accounts page, click "Manage another account."

4. On the "Choose the account you would like to change" page, you'll see a list of existing accounts on the computer. If an account has a password, it is listed as being password-protected. If an account is disabled, it is listed as being off.

5. Click "Create a new account." This displays the Create New Account page shown in Figure 18-6.

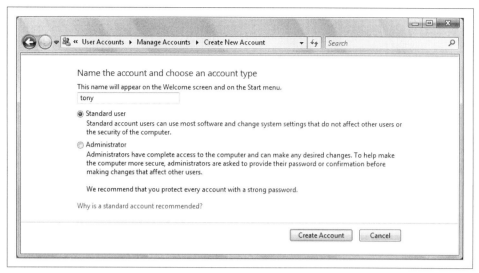

Figure 18-6. Creating a new account

6. Type the name of the local account. This name is displayed on the Welcome screen and Start menu.

7. Set the type of account as either Standard user or Administrator.

8. Click Create Account.

Windows Vista will create a user profile and personal desktop for this user the first time she logs on to your computer.

Changing User Account Names for Other People

Your computer tracks account names with SIDs. This allows you to safely change account names at any time without worrying that this will cause problems with access permissions or privileges. If you want to change someone else's account name, follow these steps:

1. Click Start and then click Control Panel.

2. In the Control Panel, click the User Accounts and Family Safety heading and then click User Accounts.

3. On the User Accounts page, click "Manage another account."

4. On the "Choose the account you would like to change" page, you'll see a list of existing accounts on the computer. Click the account you want to work with.

5. On the "Make changes to…" page, click "Change the account name."

6. On the "Type a new account name for…account" page, shown in Figure 18-7, type the new name for the account and then click Change Name.

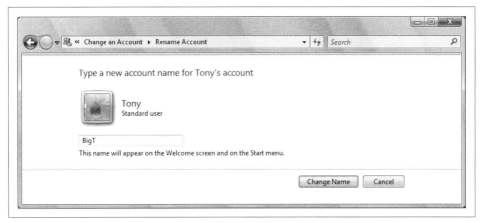

Figure 18-7. Changing the account name

Changing the Account Picture for Other People

Every user account can have a unique picture associated with it. This picture is displayed on the logon screen and on the Start menu. If you want to change the picture associated with another person's account, follow these steps:

1. Click Start and then click Control Panel.
2. In the Control Panel, click the User Accounts and Family Safety heading and then click User Accounts.
3. On the User Accounts page, click "Manage another account."
4. On the "Choose the account you would like to change" page, you'll see a list of existing accounts on the computer. Click the account you want to work with.
5. On the "Make changes to…" page, click "Change the picture."
6. On the "Choose a new picture for…account" page, shown in Figure 18-8, click the picture you want to use, or click the "Browse for more pictures" link to select any BMP, GIF, JPEG, PNG, DIB, or RLE picture to use.
7. Click Change Picture.

 If the user for whom you are setting the picture hasn't logged on to the computer yet, the picture data is saved temporarily in your profile. When the user logs on, Windows Vista will create the user's profile and copy the picture you've assigned into this profile. Most pictures are optimized to a file size of 50 KB or less—even high-resolution pictures.

Figure 18-8. Changing the account picture

Changing the Account Type for Other People

You can create user accounts as standard user or Administrator accounts. You can change the account type at any time by following these steps:

1. Click Start and then click Control Panel.
2. In the Control Panel, click the User Accounts and Family Safety heading and then click User Accounts.
3. On the User Accounts page, click "Manage another account."
4. On the "Choose the account you would like to change" page, you'll see a list of existing accounts on the computer. Click the account you want to work with.
5. On the "Make changes to…" page, click "Change the account type."
6. On the "Choose a new account type for…" page, shown in Figure 18-9, set the account type as either Standard user or Administrator.
7. Click Change Account Type.

Creating a Password for Other People's Accounts

To protect your computer, every user account should have a strong password. You can create a password for someone else's account by completing the following steps:

1. Click Start and then click Control Panel.
2. In the Control Panel, click the User Accounts and Family Safety heading and then click User Accounts.

Figure 18-9. Changing the account type

3. On the User Accounts page, click "Manage another account."

4. On the "Choose the account you would like to change" page, you'll see a list of existing accounts on the computer. Click the account you want to work with.

5. On the "Make changes to…" page, click "Create a password."

6. On the "Create a password for…account" page, shown in Figure 18-10, type a password for the account and then confirm the password by retyping it in the second text box.

7. Afterward, type a unique password hint. The password hint is a word or phrase that can help this person remember the password if he forgets it. Because this hint is visible to anyone who uses the computer, you'll want to be careful what you use as the hint.

8. Click "Create password."

Create a password for an account only if this person doesn't have encrypted files, personal certificates, or stored passwords for web sites. If he does have these items and you create a password, he will lose all the associated data. To keep this from happening, simply ask him to log on to his account and create his own password. Alternatively, you can log on as this person and create the password for the account. Follow the instructions discussed in the "Creating Your Password" section, earlier in this chapter.

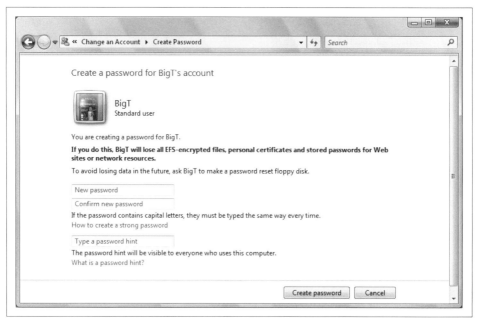

Figure 18-10. Creating the account password

Changing the Password on Other People's Accounts

Everyone who logs on to your computer should periodically change his password to help protect your computer. The best way to change passwords is to have the person log on and change the password himself. This way, he won't lose any encrypted files, personal certificates, or stored passwords for web sites. Alternatively, you can log on as this person and change his password for him by following the instructions discussed in the "Changing Your Password" section of this chapter.

If a user loses his password and you have no password recovery file, you can change the password on that person's account by completing the following steps:

1. Click Start and then click Control Panel.
2. In the Control Panel, click the User Accounts and Family Safety heading and then click User Accounts.
3. On the User Accounts page, click "Manage another account."
4. On the "Choose the account you would like to change" page, you'll see a list of existing accounts on the computer. Click the account you want to work with.
5. On the "Make changes to…" page, click "Change the password."
6. On the "Change…password" page, shown in Figure 18-11, type the new password for this user's account in the first text box.
7. Confirm the new password by retyping it in the second text box.
8. Afterward, type a unique password hint and then click "Change password."

Figure 18-11. Changing the account password

Storing Another Person's Password for Recovery

To ensure that another person can recover her password if she forgets it, you can store her password in a secure, encrypted file on a floppy disk or USB flash key, and then use this file to recover her password if she forgets it. To store another person's password for recovery, have the person log on to the computer. Follow the steps discussed in the "Storing Your Password for Recovery" section, earlier in this chapter. In step 5, be sure to have the other person type her password and not your current password.

Recovering Another Person's Password

To help another person remember or recover his password, complete the following steps:

1. On the logon screen, click this person's username to display the Password prompt.

2. Click the button to the right of the password text box without entering a password.

3. When you click OK, the password hint for the account is displayed on the logon screen.

4. Have the other person type his password if he remembers it, and click the logon button. If he logs on successfully, skip the remaining steps. Otherwise, click OK and continue with password recovery.

5. On the logon screen, click Reset Password.

6. When the Reset Password Wizard starts, click Next.

7. Insert the disk into the A: drive or the USB flash key containing the other person's password recovery file, and then click Next.

8. Have the other person type a new password in the first text box.

9. Have him confirm his new password by retyping it in the second text box.

10. Have him type a new password hint in the third text box.

11. Have him click Next to log on with his new password.

Enabling Local User Accounts

User accounts on your computer can become disabled for several reasons. If a user forgets her password and tries to guess it, she might exceed the security settings for bad logon attempts. Another person with an Administrator account could have disabled the account as well. When an account is disabled or locked out, you can enable it by following these steps:

1. Click Start and then click Control Panel.

2. In the Control Panel, click System and Maintenance.

3. On the System and Maintenance page, scroll down and then select Administrative Tools.

4. On the Administrative Tools page, double-click Computer Management.

5. In Computer Management, double-click Local Users and Groups under System Tools and then select the Users node.

6. Right-click the account name and then select Properties. This displays a Properties dialog box for the account, as shown in Figure 18-12.

7. Clear the "Account is disabled" checkbox if selected.

8. Clear the "Account is locked out" checkbox if selected.

9. Click OK.

Controlling the Way Account Passwords Are Used

User accounts can have three flags that control the way passwords are used with the account. You can specify that a particular person:

- Must change his password the next time he logs on
- Cannot change his password
- Has a password that never expires

To manage these settings for passwords for a user account, follow these steps:

1. Click Start and then click Control Panel.

2. In the Control Panel, click System and Maintenance.

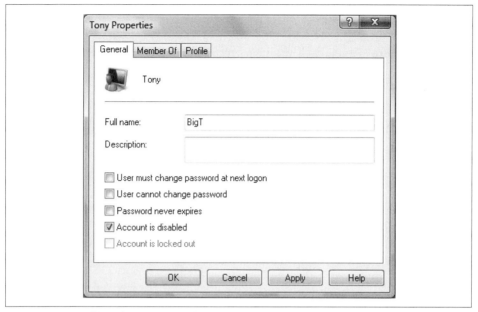

Figure 18-12. Enabling the account for logon

3. On the System and Maintenance page, scroll down and then select Administrative Tools.

4. On the Administrative Tools page, double-click Computer Management.

5. In Computer Management, double-click Local Users and Groups under System Tools and then select the Users node.

6. Right-click the account name and then select Properties. This displays a Properties dialog box for the account, as shown previously in Figure 18-12.

7. If you want this person to have to change his password the next time he logs on, select the "User must change password at next logon" checkbox.

8. If you don't want this person to be able to change his password, select the "User cannot change password" checkbox.

9. If you don't want this person's password to expire, select the "Password never expires" checkbox.

10. Click OK.

Deleting Local User Accounts

Every account has a user profile and personal folders associated with it. The user profile stores the desktop configuration and preferences as well as other settings and data. When an account is no longer needed and you are sure the user has no settings or personal data that is needed, you can delete the account.

To a delete a person's account, follow these steps:

1. Click Start and then click Control Panel.

2. In the Control Panel, click the User Accounts and Family Safety heading and then click User Accounts.

3. On the User Accounts page, click "Manage another account."

4. On the "Choose the account you would like to change" page, you'll see a list of existing accounts on the computer. Click the account you want to delete.

5. On the "Make changes to…" page, click "Delete the account."

6. On the "Do you want to keep…files?" page, shown in Figure 18-13, you have two options. You can:

   • Click Keep Files to create a folder on your desktop containing a copy of the user's personal data, and then delete the account.

   • Click Delete Files to delete all personal settings and personal data for this account, and then delete the account.

 Regardless of which option you choose, the user's email, preferences, and other settings are deleted with the account.

Figure 18-13. Deleting the user account

Managing Access Permissions with Group Accounts

At home, the best and easiest way to share files with other people who log on to your computer is to simply copy or move files you want to share to the Public folder or a related subfolder. If you use this technique, you don't have to worry about file access permissions or privileges because Windows Vista sets the access permissions for you. As discussed in Chapter 11, if you configure password-protected sharing, you can be sure that only people with accounts on your computer can access your shared data. For folders other than your personal folders, the personal folders of other people, or Public folders, you can set access permissions to control who has access. As also discussed in Chapter 11, you can assign access permissions to individual users or groups.

Every Windows Vista computer has the same set of default groups, which includes groups for performing administrative and maintenance tasks. If you're using an Administrator account, your account is a member of the Administrators group. If you're using a standard user account, your account is a member of the Users group. For most at-home uses of Windows Vista, these are the only groups you'll ever need to use.

Although all Windows Vista computers have the same set of default groups, each computer sees its groups as being different from the local groups on any other computer. This occurs because computers track groups with unique SIDs rather than display names. At the office, your network will have its own unique groups, which are also different from your computer's groups.

Creating Local Groups

If you find that you need additional groups beyond the Administrators and Users groups, you can create local groups on your computer. You create local groups by completing the following steps:

1. Click Start and then click Control Panel.
2. In the Control Panel, click System and Maintenance.
3. On the System and Maintenance page, scroll down and then select Administrative Tools.
4. On the Administrative Tools page, double-click Computer Management.
5. In Computer Management, double-click Local Users and Groups under System Tools.
6. Select the Groups node to display a list of the current groups on your computer, as shown in Figure 18-14.
7. Right-click Groups and then select New Group. This opens the New Group dialog box, shown in Figure 18-15.
8. Type a name and description for the group.
9. Click the Add button.
10. In the Select Users dialog box, shown in Figure 18-16, type the name of a user you want to add to the group. This must be the username rather than the full name of the account.
11. Click Check Names and then do one of the following:
    - If a single match is found for each entry, the dialog box is automatically updated as appropriate and the entry is underlined.
    - If multiple matches are found, you'll see an additional dialog box that allows you to select the name or names you want to use, and then click OK.
    - If no matches are found, you've probably entered an incorrect name. Modify the name in the Name Not Found dialog box and then click Check Names again.

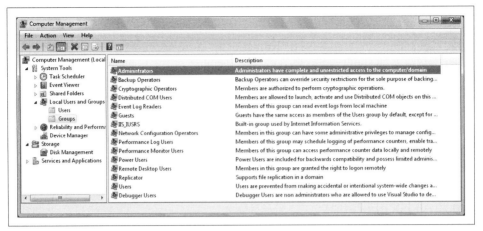

Figure 18-14. Viewing the groups on your computer

Figure 18-15. Creating a group and adding members

You must enter the username rather than the full name of the account. If you changed the username by following the directions in the "Changing Your Account Name" or "Changing User Account Names for Other People" sections, earlier in this chapter, you actually changed the full name associated with the account rather than the username. To view the usernames associated with accounts on your computer, open Computer Management. Double-click Local Users and Groups under System Tools. Select the Users node and then double-click the user account.

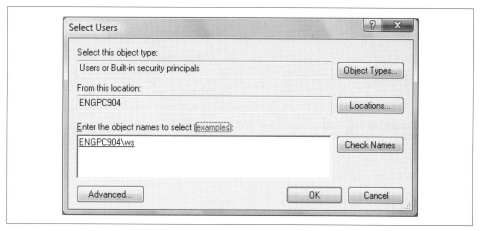

Figure 18-16. Selecting users to add to the group

12. Repeat step 11 as necessary. When you are finished selecting names, click OK to close the Select Users dialog box.

13. The New Group dialog box is updated to reflect your selections. If you made a mistake, select a name and remove it by clicking Remove.

14. Click Create when you're finished adding or removing group members.

Adding and Removing Local Group Members

You add and remove local group members using Local Users and Groups. Complete the following steps:

1. Click Start and then click Control Panel.

2. In the Control Panel, click System and Maintenance.

3. On the System and Maintenance page, scroll down and then select Administrative Tools.

4. On the Administrative Tools page, double-click Computer Management.

5. In Computer Management, double-click Local Users and Groups under System Tools.

6. Select the Groups node to display a list of the current groups on your computer.

7. Double-click the group with which you want to work.

8. Use the Add button to add user accounts to the group via the Select Users dialog box, as discussed previously.

9. Use the Remove button to remove user accounts from the group. Simply select the user account you want to remove from the group and then click Remove.

10. Click OK when you are finished.

Renaming Local User Accounts and Groups

Because your computer tracks users and groups with SIDs, you can safely change account names at any time without worrying that this will cause problems with access permissions or privileges. While you can rename any user and group accounts you've created, you shouldn't rename the default user and group accounts without considering the impact these changes may have on other users. For example, if you change the name of the Administrators group to HeadHonchos, you may be the only person who knows that this group was originally the Administrators group. If a year or so from now you forget that you renamed Administrators, you may think this group has mysteriously disappeared from your computer.

To rename a user or group account, complete the following steps:

1. Open Computer Management.
2. In Local Users and Groups, select the Users or Groups folder as appropriate.
3. Right-click the account name and then select Rename.
4. Type the new account name and then click a different entry.

Deleting Groups

Deleting a group permanently removes it. Once you delete a group, you can't create another group with the same name to get the same permissions because the SID for the new group won't match the SID for the old group. Deleting built-in accounts can have far-reaching effects on your computer, so don't do it.

To delete a group, complete the following steps:

1. Open Computer Management.
2. In Local Users and Groups, select the Users or Groups folder as appropriate.
3. Right-click the group and then select Delete.
4. When prompted to confirm, click Yes.

Keeping Your Family Safe While Using Your Computer

As a parent, teacher, or librarian, you'll want to use parental controls to help keep young people safe when they are on the Internet and to prevent them from accessing types of content they shouldn't be accessing. Parental controls enable you to manage four broad categories of Windows settings:

Web restrictions
> Block access to web sites either automatically or based on a specific list you've configured, and block file downloads.

Time restrictions
Control the times when a user can use the computer by blocking or allowing specific hours of the day.

Game restrictions
Control whether a user can play games and the types of games this person can play.

Application restrictions
Control the types of applications a user can run while using the computer.

When parental controls are turned on, you can also collect information about computer usage, select a game rating system, and configure reminders about activity reports.

Turning On Parental Controls

You can set parental controls for standard user accounts on the local computer only. You cannot set parental controls for administrators, and you cannot set parental controls at the office for domain user accounts. Any user designated as an administrator on the local computer can configure parental controls and view activity reports for users subject to parental controls.

You can turn on parental controls by completing the following steps:

1. Click Start and then click Control Panel.

2. In the Control Panel, click the User Accounts and Family Safety heading and then click User Accounts.

3. On the User Accounts page, click "Manage another account."

4. Click "Set up Parental Controls." On the "Choose a user and set up Parental Controls" page, shown in Figure 18-17, you'll see a list of all users on the computer and a summary of their current account configuration. Any account that has parental controls turned on is listed as such.

5. All Administrator accounts on your computer should have a password to prevent your kids or other people with standard user accounts from bypassing or turning off parental controls. If there are Administrator accounts on your computer that have no password, you'll see a warning on the "Choose a user and set up Parental Controls" page.

6. To clear the password warning if displayed, click the warning text to display the Ensure Administrator Passwords page shown in Figure 18-18. On this page, the "Force all administrator accounts to set a password at logon" checkbox is selected by default. To force all users with an Administrator account to set a password the next time they log on, accept this setting and click OK.

7. Click the account for which you want to turn on parental controls.

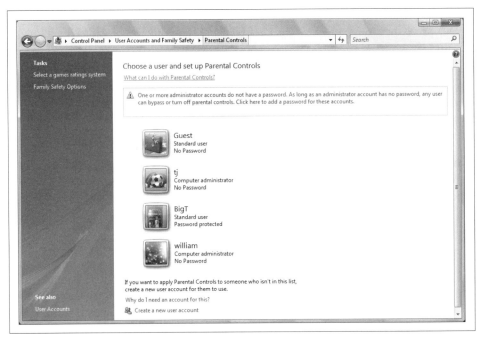

Figure 18-17. Setting up parental controls

Figure 18-18. Ensuring that administrators have passwords

8. On the "Set up how…will use the computer" page, shown in Figure 18-19, click "On, enforce current settings" under Parental Controls to turn on parental controls.

9. To turn on activity reporting, click "On, collect information about computer usage" under Activity Reporting.

10. Click OK to apply these settings and then configure the Windows settings to control, as discussed in the sections that follow. Be sure to select a game rating system and configure activity report reminders as appropriate.

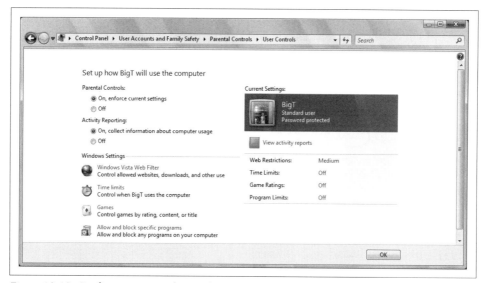

Figure 18-19. Configuring parental controls

Selecting a Game Rating System

Game rating systems, such as those used by the Entertainment Software Ratings Board (ESRB), are meant to help protect young people from specific types of mature content in computer games and on the Internet. You can learn more about the available rating systems and select a default rating system to use by completing these steps:

1. Click Start and then click Control Panel.

2. In the Control Panel, click the User Accounts and Family Safety heading and then click User Accounts.

3. On the User Accounts page, click "Manage another account."

4. Click "Set up Parental Controls."

5. In the left panel of the main Parental Controls page, click "Select a game rating system."

6. On the "Which games rating system do you want to use?" page, shown in Figure 18-20, you can review the game rating systems available. The default rating system used depends on the country or region settings for your computer.

7. If you want to change the default rating system, click the rating system you want to use. Beneath each option, you'll find a link to the home page for the game rating organization. If you have questions about a rating system, click this link to open the home page in Internet Explorer. You can then read about the organization and the related rating system.

8. Click OK to apply your changes and go back to the Parental Controls page in the Control Panel.

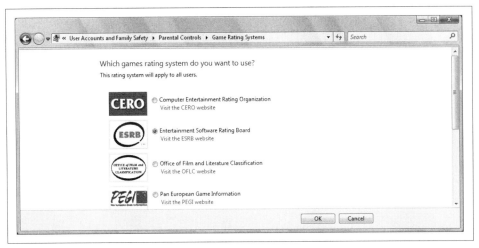

Figure 18-20. Choosing a game rating system

Configuring Reminders for Parental Controls

By default, when you configure parental controls, you are reminded weekly to read activity reports. If you want to change the way reminders are used, follow these steps:

1. Click Start and then click Control Panel.
2. In the Control Panel, click the User Accounts and Family Safety heading and then click User Accounts.
3. On the User Accounts page, click "Manage another account."
4. Click "Set up Parental Controls."
5. In the left panel of the main Parental Controls page, click "Family safety options."
6. On the Family Safety Options page, shown in Figure 18-21, specify how often you would like to be reminded to read activity reports. You can specify that you want to be notified weekly, daily, or never.
7. Click OK.

Configuring Web Restrictions

Web restrictions determine what web sites and what types of content to allow. If you've turned on parental controls, some web restrictions are already enforced automatically. To configure other restrictions or to change how web restrictions are used, follow these steps:

1. Click Start and then click Control Panel.
2. In the Control Panel, click the User Accounts and Family Safety heading and then click User Accounts.

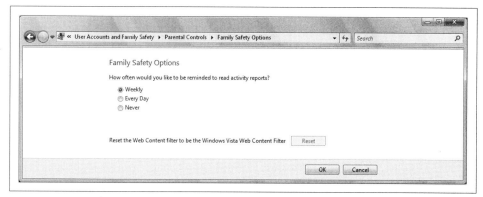

Figure 18-21. Configuring reminders for activity reports

3. On the User Accounts page, click "Manage another account."

4. Click "Set up Parental Controls" and then click the account you want to restrict.

5. On the "Set up how...will use the computer" page, click Windows Vista Web Filter under Windows Settings.

6. On the "Which parts of the Internet can...visit?" page, shown in Figure 18-22, the "Block some websites or content" option is selected automatically. When this setting is selected, you can use the additional options to manage the level of restriction. If you don't want to restrict web access, select "Allow all websites and content," click OK, and skip the remaining steps.

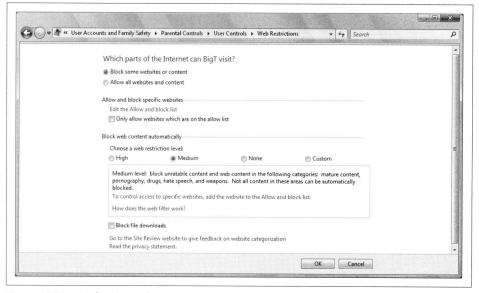

Figure 18-22. Configuring web restrictions

7. By default, when parental controls are turned on, Windows Vista blocks certain types of web content automatically, based on the web restriction level. You can choose one of the following web restriction levels:

High
> Blocks all web content except web sites approved for children. Your child can then access only children's web sites and web sites you specifically designated as allowed.

Medium
> Attempts to block automatically unratable content and web sites that include mature content, pornography, drugs, hate speech, and weapons. You can also block or allow specific sites.

None
> No web content is blocked automatically. You can block specific sites by adding them to the block list.

Custom
> Allows you to choose the categories of content that Windows Vista should attempt to block automatically. Categories you can select for blocking include pornography, mature content, unratable content, sex education, hate speech, bomb making, weapons, drugs, alcohol, tobacco, and gambling. You can also block or allow specific sites.

8. To designate a site as blocked or allowed, click the "Edit the Allow and Block list" link. To allow a site, type the web address and then click Allow. To block a site, type the web address and then click Block. Click OK.

9. File downloads can include malicious programs or types of content you don't want your children to access. To block file downloads, select the "Block file downloads" checkbox.

10. Click OK to save your settings.

Configuring Time Restrictions

Time restrictions control the times when a user can use the computer by blocking or allowing specific hours of the day. If you've turned on parental controls, allow hours are permitted by default. You can configure time restrictions by completing the following steps:

1. Click Start and then click Control Panel.

2. In the Control Panel, click the User Accounts and Family Safety heading and then click User Accounts.

3. On the User Accounts page, click "Manage another account."

4. Click "Set up Parental Controls" and then click the account you want to restrict.

5. On the "Set up how...will use the computer" page, click "Time limits" under Windows Settings.

6. On the "Control when...will use the computer" page, shown in Figure 18-23, you can specify what times you allow and what times you block.

7. Click and drag over allowed hours to change them to blocked hours.

8. Click and drag over blocked hours to change them to allowed hours.

9. Click OK to save your settings.

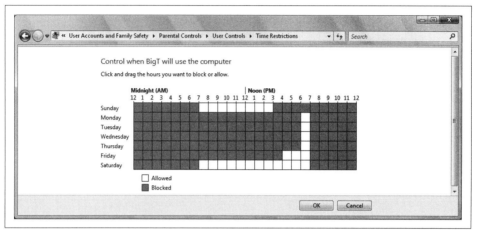

Figure 18-23. Configuring time restrictions

Configuring Game Restrictions

Game restrictions control whether a user can play games and the types of games that this person can play. If you've turned on parental controls, users are allowed to play games and no types of games are blocked by default. You can configure game restrictions by completing these steps:

1. Click Start and then click Control Panel.

2. In the Control Panel, click the User Accounts and Family Safety heading and then click User Accounts.

3. On the User Accounts page, click "Manage another account."

4. Click "Set up Parental Controls" and then click the account you want to restrict.

5. On the "Set up how...will use the computer" page, click Games under Windows Settings.

6. On the "Control which types of games...can play" page, shown in Figure 18-24, "Can...play games?" is set to Yes by default and the user is allowed to play games. To block game playing, click No under "Can...play games?," click OK, and skip the remaining steps.

7. To block or allow games by rating and content type, click "Set game ratings," choosing which game ratings are OK for the user to play, and then click OK.

8. To block or allow games installed on the computer by name, click "Block or Allow specific games," choose allowed or blocked games, and then click OK.

9. Click OK to save your settings.

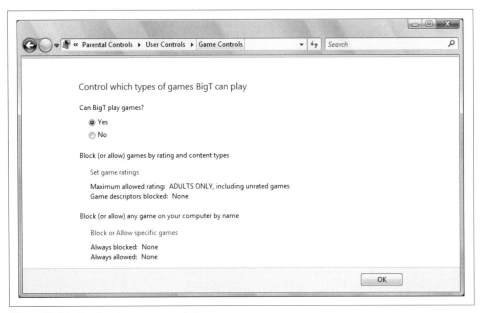

Figure 18-24. Configuring game restrictions

Configuring Application Restrictions

Application restrictions control the types of applications a user can run while using the computer. If you've turned on parental controls, users are allowed to run any programs installed on the computer by default, and no programs are restricted. You can configure application restrictions by completing these steps:

1. Click Start and then click Control Panel.

2. In the Control Panel, click the User Accounts and Family Safety heading and then click User Accounts.

3. On the User Accounts page, click "Manage another account."

4. Click "Set up Parental Controls" and then click the account you want to restrict.

5. On the "Set up how…will use the computer" page, click "Allow or Block specific programs" under Windows Settings.

6. On the "Which programs can...use?" page, the "Use all programs" option is selected by default. To restrict program use so that only programs specifically allowed can be run, select the "...can only use the programs I allow" option. You'll then see a list of every program installed on the computer, as shown in Figure 18-25.

7. You can now control the allowed programs. Select the checkbox for a program you want the user to run. Clear the checkbox for a program you don't want the user to run. Alternatively, click Check All to select all programs and then selectively clear the programs the user shouldn't be able to run.

8. Click OK to save the settings. Whenever you install new programs on the computer that you want the user to be able to run, you'll need to repeat this procedure to allow running the program and its related executable files.

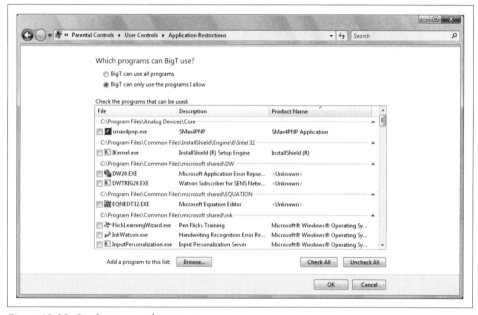

Figure 18-25. Configuring application restrictions

Accessing Activity Reports

When you turn on parental controls, you can view activity reports that provide complete details about the user's activities while using your computer.

You can turn on activity reporting by completing these steps:

1. Click Start and then click Control Panel.

2. In the Control Panel, click the User Accounts and Family Safety heading and then click User Accounts.

3. On the User Accounts page, click "Manage another account."

4. Click "Set up Parental Controls" and then click the account you want to work with.

5. On the "Set up how…will use the computer" page, click "On, collect information about computer usage" under Activity Reporting.

6. Click OK to save your settings.

You can view activity reports for a user by following these steps:

1. Click Start and then click Control Panel.

2. In the Control Panel, click the User Accounts and Family Safety heading and then click User Accounts.

3. On the User Accounts page, click "Manage another account."

4. Click "Set up Parental Controls" and then click the account you want to work with.

5. Click "View activity reports" to access the Activity Viewer page, shown in Figure 18-26. By default, Activity Viewer provides summary details for all categories of information tracked. To view more detailed information, expand the Account Activity, General System, or both nodes.

6. Access summary details for each major category by selecting the category heading in the left pane.

7. Access detailed information for subcategories by selecting the subcategory headings in the left pane.

Computer usage details fall into the following categories:

Web Browsing

Websites Visited
   A date/time list of web sites the user visited

Websites Blocked
   A date/time list of web sites the user tried to visit, but were blocked

Web Overrides
   A date/time list of web sites the user was initially blocked from visiting, but that were allowed to be visited by someone else with an Administrator account

File Downloads
   A date/time list of files downloaded

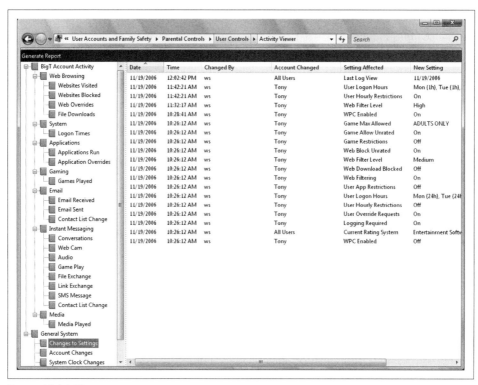

Figure 18-26. Viewing activity reports

System

Logon Times

A date/time list of when the user logged on and how long she was logged on for each session

Applications

Applications Run

A date/time list of the applications the user started or was blocked from starting. For applications started, the length of time the programs were used is also provided.

Application Overrides

A date/time list of programs the user was initially blocked from running, but that were allowed to be run by someone else with an Administrator account.

Gaming

Games Played

A date/time list of the games the user started or was blocked from starting. For games started, the length of time the games were played is also provided.

Email

Email Received

A date/time list of emails received as well as who those emails were from, the subject of the email, and the list of attachments to the email messages (if any)

Email Sent

A date/time list of emails sent as well as to whom those emails were sent, the subject of the email, and the list of attachments to the email messages (if any)

Contact List Change

A date/time list of email contacts changed as well as details on who changed the contact and what type of change was made

Instant Messaging

Conversations

A date/time list of instant messaging according to the participants involved

Web Cam

A date/time list of web cam use according to the participants involved

Audio

A date/time list of instant messaging that used voice or audio according to the participants involved

Game Play

A date/time list of instant messaging games played according to the participants involved

File Exchange

A date/time list of files exchanged during instant messaging according to the filenames and participants involved

Link Exchange

A date/time list of files exchanged during instant messaging according to the link address and participants involved

SMS Message

A date/time list of SMS messages exchanged according to the message text and participants involved

Contact List Change

A date/time list of instant messaging contacts changed as well as details on who changed the contact and what type of change was made

Media

Media Played

A date/time list of the media the user played by type, title, album, and media player. If the media had explicit lyrics, this is also listed.

General System

Changes to Settings

A date/time list of the setting changes on the computer according to who made the change and the account affected.

Account Changes

A date/time list of the accounts changed according to who made the change and the account affected.

System Clock Changes

A date/time list of changes to the computer time according to who made the change as well as the new date and new time set. If you think your child is changing the computer time to get around time restrictions, this is where you'd check to see if this is the case.

Failed Logon Attempts

A date/time list of failed logon attempts according to the account and the reason for the failed logon.

CHAPTER 19

Managing Disks and Drives

The disks and drives configured within or attached to your computer provide storage for the operating system and your personal files. You use internal storage devices and external storage devices in different ways. You use internal storage devices for the operating system and your primary storage. You use external storage devices for you secondary storage only.

Disks and drives are one area of computer configuration that you won't work with often. Primarily, this is because disks and drives are something you need to prepare only one time, and once you've prepared a disk, you perform maintenance tasks on it rather than configuration tasks. Preparing a disk for use involves three main tasks:

- Partitioning the disk with volumes
- Formatting the disk volume
- Mounting the disk volume

You can partition a disk into one or more volumes. You then format the volumes with the File Allocation Table (FAT) or FAT32 filesystem, or with the NT File System (NTFS), as appropriate. Finally, you mount the volume to a drive letter or file path. When you format volumes with NTFS, you can use compression to reduce the disk space used, or encryption to add an extra layer of protection to your data.

Configuring Disks and Drives

Like filesystems, disks have a particular formatting that determines how you can use the disk. Windows Vista allows you to configure disks to be either the basic disk type or the dynamic disk type. Basic disks are the traditional disk type Windows has used since it was first introduced. Dynamic disks are a newer disk type that was introduced with Windows 2000.

The differences between the two disk types largely concern what you can do with the disks. Consider the following:

- With basic disks, Windows Vista supports both primary and extended partitions. A primary partition is used to start the operating system. You access a primary partition directly by its drive designator. You cannot subdivide a primary partition. In contrast, an extended partition is designed to be subdivided. After you create an extended partition, you must divide it into one or more logical drives. You can then access the logical drives independently of each other.
- With dynamic disks, Windows Vista supports several different types of volumes. A simple volume is a volume on a single disk that can be used to start the operating system and for general data storage. A spanned volume is a volume that you extend across several disks. A striped volume uses free space on multiple disks and stripes the data as it is written to give you faster read/write access.

Dynamic disks have several advantages over basic disks, including improved error detection and error handling. Volumes on dynamic disks can also be expanded or reduced in size. However, when you boot your computer to a non-Windows operating system, such as Linux, you'll usually want to have a basic disk. Further, you cannot create dynamic disks on any removable-media drives (such as ZIP, Jazz, and CD-ROM) or any disk on portable computers. While you can convert external disks attached via FireWire or USB to dynamic disks in some cases, you typically don't want to use dynamic disks with external disks.

Using Disk Management

Your primary tool for working with your computer's disks is Disk Management. You will use Disk Management to partition disks, format disk volumes with filesystems, and mount disk volumes. You can also use Disk Management to convert a disk from the basic disk type to the dynamic disk type and vice versa. However, while you can convert from a basic disk type to the dynamic disk type without losing data, you must remove disk volumes on a dynamic disk before you can convert the disk to the basic disk type.

Using an Administrator account, you can start and work with Disk Management by completing the following steps:

1. Right-click Computer on the Start menu.
2. On the shortcut menu, choose Manage to start Computer Management.
3. In the left pane of the Computer Management window, select Disk Management under Storage.

As Figure 19-1 shows, Disk Management provides an overview of the storage devices configure within or attached to your computer. By default, Disk Management's main windows show the Volume list view in the upper panel and the Graphical view in the lower panel. The third view available but not displayed is the Disk List view.

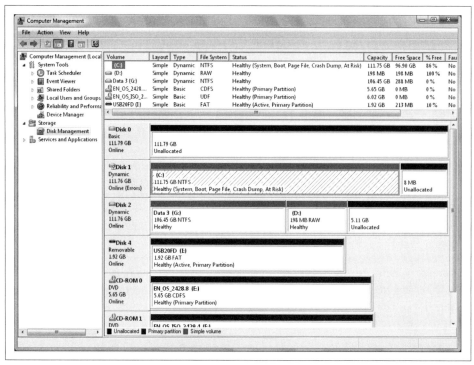

Figure 19-1. Managing your computer's disks

You can set the view for the top or bottom pane using options from the View menu. To change the top view, select View, choose Top, and then select the view you want to use. To change the bottom view, select View, choose Bottom, and then select the view you want to use.

Volume list view provides a detailed summary of internal drives and external devices with removable storage. Devices with removable media, such as CD-ROM and DVD-ROM drives, are listed only if you've inserted a CD or DVD. The volume details provide the following information:

Volume
> The drive letter or the volume name and drive letter, such as C: or Primary (C:)

Layout
> The layout type of the volume, such as simple

Type
> The drive type, such as basic or dynamic

File System
> The filesystem type, such as FAT or NTFS

Status
> The status of the volume, as well as any relevant volume designations, such as Healthy (Active, Primary Partition)

Capacity
    The amount of data the volume can store

Free Space
    The amount of free space in megabytes (MB) or gigabytes (GB)

% Free
    The amount of free space as a percentage of total volume capacity

Fault Tolerance
    An indicator as to whether the volume uses fault tolerant features

Overhead
    The total additional disk space required because of the fault tolerant feature used
    (if applicable)

The Graphical view provides a graphical overview of internal drives, external drives
with removable storage, and devices with removable media. This is the view you use
to partition, format, and mount disks.

In the Graphical view, you can see the individual areas of allocated and unallocated
space on internal disks and disks with removable storage. An allocated area of a disk
has a volume. An unallocated area of a disk is free space that's not being used.

As Figure 19-2 shows, the summary information regarding disks and devices with
removable storage includes the disk number, drive type, disk capacity, and overall
status. For each volume allocated on a disk, you'll see the volume name, drive designator, volume capacity, filesystem type, and status as well.

Figure 19-2. Viewing disk and volume details

Although Disk Management can show only two view panes at a time, you can display the Disk List view in either the upper or the lower pane of the main window. As
Figure 19-3 shows, the Disk List view provides summary information about physical
drives. This information includes:

Disk
    The disk designator and number, such as Disk 0 or CD-ROM 1.

Type
    The drive or media type, such as basic, dynamic, removable, CD, or DVD.

Capacity
    The amount of data the drive, device, or media can store.

Unallocated Space
    The amount of space that hasn't been allocated (if any).

Status

The drive or device status, as either online, online (errors), or offline.

Device Type

The device interface type, such as Integrated Device Electronics (IDE), Small Computer System Interface (SCSI), USB, or FireWire (1394).

Partition Style

The partition style of the disk or device. Windows Vista supports both Master Boot Record (MBR) and GUID Partition Table (GPT) partition styles. For the most part, the partition style used is determined by your computer's processor architecture and the type of device.

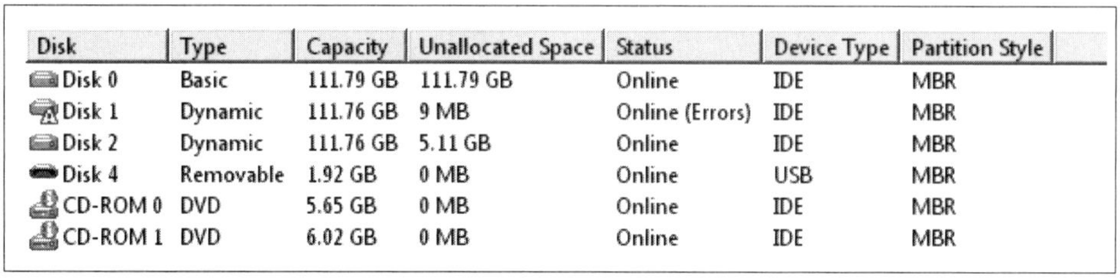

Disk	Type	Capacity	Unallocated Space	Status	Device Type	Partition Style
Disk 0	Basic	111.79 GB	111.79 GB	Online	IDE	MBR
Disk 1	Dynamic	111.76 GB	9 MB	Online (Errors)	IDE	MBR
Disk 2	Dynamic	111.76 GB	5.11 GB	Online	IDE	MBR
Disk 4	Removable	1.92 GB	0 MB	Online	USB	MBR
CD-ROM 0	DVD	5.65 GB	0 MB	Online	IDE	MBR
CD-ROM 1	DVD	6.02 GB	0 MB	Online	IDE	MBR

Figure 19-3. Viewing a list of disks

When you are working with basic or dynamic disks, you should note the special designations assigned to drive sections. Drive sections can have one or more of the following designations:

Active

The drive section used for system cache and startup. Some devices with removable storage may be listed as having the active partition, such as when you use ReadyBoost.

System

The drive section containing the boot manager files needed to load the operating system. A drive section with this designation can't be part of a striped or spanned volume.

Boot

The drive section containing the operating system and its related files.

Page File

A drive section containing a paging file used by the operating system.

Crash Dump

The drive section to which the computer attempts to write dump files in the event of a system crash.

Your computer has one active, one system, one boot, and one crash dump drive section. The page file designation is the only drive designation you might see on multiple drive sections.

Depending on the disk type and status, you might also see the following designations:

At Risk
> A drive section with this designation is at risk of failing, and probably also has an error status, such as Online (Errors). See the "Recovering Volumes" section, later in this chapter, for details on how to resolve the problem.

Primary Partition
> A drive section that is designated as a primary partition. Although this designation isn't usually displayed for fixed disks, you'll see this designation on devices with removable storage and on devices with removable media.

Installing and Initializing New Disks

With the dramatic increase in the quality and capacity of external disk drives, there aren't many good reasons to bother going inside your computer to install an internal disk anymore. In fact, if you follow the tips and advice in Chapter 5 regarding USB and FireWire devices, you can have an external hard disk up and running in five minutes or less.

With that said, if you want to install a disk inside your computer, you'll also find tips and advice for doing so in Chapter 5. When you are finished installing the disk inside your computer and you turn your computer on, you need to log on and start Disk Management. If the new disks have already been initialized with disk signatures by the manufacturer, they should be brought online automatically if you select Rescan Disks from the Action menu. If you are working with new disks that have not been initialized with disk signatures by the manufacturer, Disk Management will start the Initialize and Convert Disk Wizard as soon it detects the new disk.

In this case, you can use the Initialize and Convert Disk Wizard to initialize the disk by completing these steps:

1. Read the introductory text and then click Next.

2. On the Select Disks to Initialize page, the disk you added should be selected for initialization automatically. If it isn't, select it for initialization. Click Next.

3. On the Select Disks to Convert page, you'll see a list that includes the new disk as well as any nonsystem or boot disks that can be converted to dynamic disks. If you want to convert the new disk or other disks from the basic disk type to the dynamic disk type, select the disk or disks to convert and then click Next.

4. Review the actions that will be performed on each disk. If the options are correct, click Finish to allow Disk Management to perform the listed actions, which can include initializing the new disk, converting the new disk, and converting other disks.

Converting a Basic Disk to a Dynamic Disk

Windows Vista allows you to convert a basic disk to a dynamic disk. Moving from a basic disk to a dynamic disk is considered an upgrade. When you upgrade to a dynamic disk, partitions become volumes of the appropriate type.

To upgrade successfully to a dynamic disk, keep the following caveats in mind:

- There must be at least 1 MB of free space at the end of the disk. Disk Management reserves this free space automatically, but other disk management tools might not.
- Drives that use sector sizes larger than 512 bytes can't be converted. If the drive has large sector sizes, you'll need to reformat before upgrading.
- Devices with removable media or removable storage can't be converted. In most cases, these devices can be configured only as basic drives with primary partitions.
- Disks with the system, boot, or both partitions can't be converted if they are part of a spanned or striped volume. You'll need to stop the spanning or striping before you perform the conversion.

You can convert a basic disk to a dynamic disk by completing the following steps:

1. In Disk Management, right-click the disk designator for the basic disk that you want to convert in the Graphical view and then select Convert to Dynamic Disk.
2. In the Convert to Dynamic Disk dialog box, the disk you selected is listed, as shown in Figure 19-4.

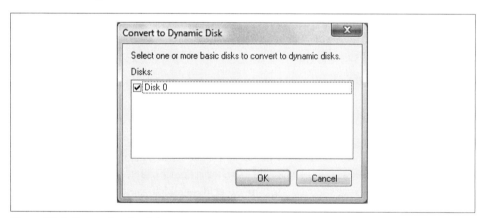

Figure 19-4. Converting the disk

3. If the disk you are converting has no formatted volumes, the disk is automatically selected for conversion and clicking OK converts the disk. You do not need to follow the remaining steps.

4. If the disk you are converting has formatted volumes, you must select the disk and then click OK. Continue with the remaining steps to complete the conversion.

5. As shown in Figure 19-5, the Disks to Convert dialog box shows the disk you're converting so that you can confirm the conversion. The value in the Will Convert column should be Yes as long as the disk meets the conversion criteria.

Figure 19-5. Checking the disk's associated volumes

6. Click the disk and then click Details to see the volumes on the selected disk. When you are ready to continue, click OK to close the Convert Details dialog box.

7. Click Convert. Disk Management warns you that once you convert the disk, you won't be able to boot other operating systems from volumes on the selected disk. Click Yes to continue.

8. If disks are mounted and active, Disk Management warns you that it needs to dismount the disk to convert its volumes. Click Yes to continue.

9. If a selected drive contains the boot partition, the system partition, or a partition in use, Disk Management will need to restart the computer and you will see another prompt.

Converting a Dynamic Disk to a Basic Disk

Downgrading to the basic disk type from the dynamic disk type is not so easy. Before you convert a dynamic disk to a basic disk, you must delete all the volumes on the disk. This results in the loss of all data in those volumes if you do not back up or move the data to another disk beforehand.

You can convert a dynamic disk to a basic disk by completing the following steps:

1. In Windows Explorer, copy or move all data on all the disk's volumes to another disk. Confirm that all data has been copied or moved before continuing.

2. In Disk Management, delete all volumes on the dynamic disk by right-clicking and selecting Delete Volume. Because this destroys all the data on the volumes,

Disk Management displays a warning prompt (see Figure 19-6). If you are sure you want to delete the volume, click Yes.

3. In Disk Management, right-click the disk you want to convert and select Convert to Basic Disk. This changes the dynamic disk to a basic disk, and you can then partition and format the disk for use.

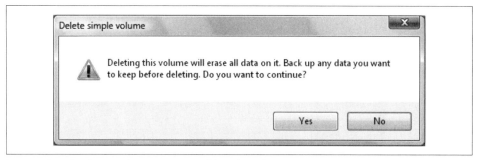

Figure 19-6. Confirming that you want to delete the volume

Preparing Disks for Use

Disk Management uses the same set of dialog boxes and wizards whether you are partitioning basic disks or dynamic disks. By default, the first three volumes on a basic drive are created automatically as primary partitions. If you try to create a fourth volume on a basic drive, the remaining free space on the drive is converted automatically to an extended partition with a logical drive that is the same size as the extended partition. Any subsequent volumes are created in the extended partitions as logical drives automatically.

In Disk Management, you create partitions, logical drives, and simple volumes on an internal or external hard disk drive by completing the following steps:

1. In Disk Management's Graphical view, right-click an unallocated or free area and then choose New Simple Volume.

2. In the New Simple Volume Wizard, click Next.

3. On the Specify Volume Size page, shown in Figure 19-7, size the volume within the maximum and minimum size limits. If you want the volume to use all the space available, set the volume size equal to the value shown for the maximum disk space in MB. Click Next.

4. On the Assign Drive Letter or Path page, shown in Figure 19-8, use the "Assign the following drive letter" list to assign a drive letter to the volume, and then click Next.

On most systems, the drive letter B and drive letters E through Z are available, with drive letter A reserved for a floppy disk, C assigned to the primary disk, and D assigned to the CD/DVD drive. If your computer has a secondary hard disk, a secondary CD/DVD drive, or both, you may find that drive letter E or the drive letters E and F are already assigned as well.

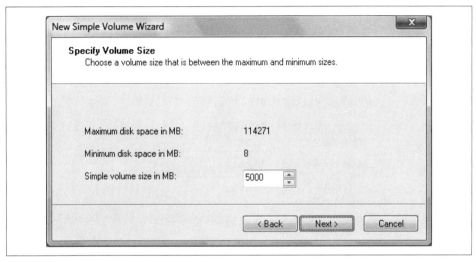

Figure 19-7. Setting the volume size

Figure 19-8. Assigning a drive letter

On the Format Partition page, shown in Figure 19-9, use the "File system" list to set the filesystem type. The options you have depend on the size of the volume and type of device, and they include FAT, FAT32, and NTFS. NTFS is selected by default in most cases. If you create a filesystem as FAT or FAT32, you can later convert it to NTFS. However, you can't convert NTFS partitions to FAT or FAT32.

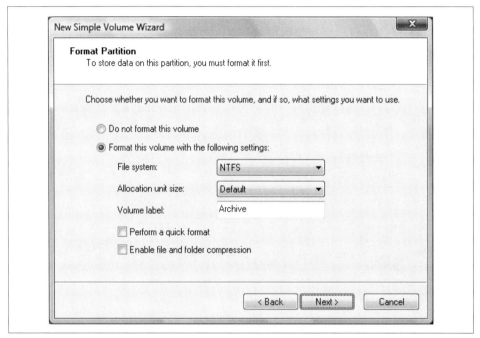

Figure 19-9. Setting the formatting options

1. The "Allocation unit size" list sets the cluster size for the filesystem. A cluster is a logical grouping of file sectors. In most cases, you'll want the "Allocation unit size" list to be set to Default. This allows Windows Vista to optimize the cluster size based on the volume size.

 On the Windows operating system, most disk drives use a fixed sector size of 512 bytes, and because of this, a cluster is typically made up of multiple sectors. For example, if the cluster size is 4,096 bytes, there will be four 512-byte file sectors per cluster. If you create large quantities of small files, you might want to use a smaller cluster size, such as 512 or 1,024 bytes. With these settings, small files use less disk space. With that said, it is important to point out that the disk drive industry is transitioning to large-sector disks. See *http://support.microsoft.com/kb/923332/en-us* for more information.

2. The "Volume label" text box sets a text label for the volume. By default, the label is set to "New volume."

3. The "Perform a quick format" checkbox allows Windows Vista to format the volume without checking the partition for errors. While this option can save you a few minutes, it's usually better to allow Disk Management to check for errors and mark any bad sectors it finds on the disk so that they aren't used.

4. The "Enable file and folder compression" checkbox turns on compression for the disk. Built-in compression is available only for NTFS. If you select this option, files and folders on the volume are compressed automatically. See the "Compressing Drives" section, later in this chapter, for more information.

5. Click Next and then click Finish. Disk Management will create and format the new volume.

Creating Spanned or Striped Volumes

When you are partitioning and formatting dynamic disks in Disk Management, you can create spanned and striped volumes as well as simple volumes. If you have unallocated space on two or more dynamic disks, you can combine this space to create a spanned volume or a striped volume.

With spanned volumes, the only benefit is being able to combine multiple disks to create a single volume. Files are written to the entire spanned volume randomly and there are no read/write benefits. There is a huge downside, however. If any disk in a spanned volume fails, the entire volume fails as well, and all data will be lost.

With striped volumes, you also can combine multiple disks to create a single volume. You get faster read/write access to data because data is read from and written to multiple disks. For example, with a three-disk striped volume, data from a file will be written to Disk 1, then to Disk 2, and then to Disk 3 in 64 KB blocks. However, like a spanned volume, a striped volume has no fault tolerance. If any disk in a striped volume fails, the entire volume will fail as well, and all data will be lost. Additionally, although you can extend simple and spanned volumes to increase their volume size, you cannot extend striped volumes.

In Disk Management, you create spanned or striped volumes on dynamic disks by completing the following steps:

1. In Disk Management's Graphical view, right-click an unallocated area and then choose New Spanned Volume or New Striped Volume as appropriate. When the wizard starts, click Next.

2. On the Select Disks page, shown in Figure 19-10, available dynamic disks are shown in the Available listbox. Select a disk in this listbox and then click Add to add the disk to the Selected listbox. If you make a mistake, you can remove disks from the Selected listbox by selecting the disk and then clicking Remove.

3. The "Maximum available space" text box shows you the largest area of free space that can be used on a selected disk; the "Total volume size" text box shows you the total disk space currently allocated to the volume.

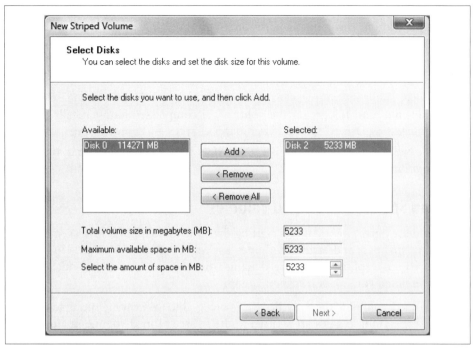

Figure 19-10. Selecting the disks to span or stripe

4. Specify the space that you want to use on each disk by selecting each disk in the Selected listbox and then using the "Select the amount of space in MB" listbox to specify the amount of space to use on the selected disk. While spanned volumes can use all available space on any selected dynamic disk, striped volumes must use an equal amount of space on each disk.

5. Follow steps 4–10 in the preceding section, "Preparing Disks for Use."

Shrinking or Extending Volumes

In Disk Management, you can change the size of simple volumes and spanned volumes. When you reduce the size of a volume, you shrink the volume to free up available space. When you increase the size of a volume, you extend the volume into unallocated space. For spanned volumes on dynamic disks, the space can come from any available dynamic disk, not only those on which the volume was originally created. This enables you to combine areas of free space on multiple dynamic disks and use those areas to increase the size of an existing volume.

You can extend simple and spanned volumes only if they are formatted and the file-system uses NTFS. You can't shrink or extend striped volumes.

You can shrink a simple or spanned volume by completing the following steps:

1. In Disk Management's Graphical view, right-click the volume that you want to shrink and then select Shrink Volume. This displays the Shrink dialog box shown in Figure 19-11.

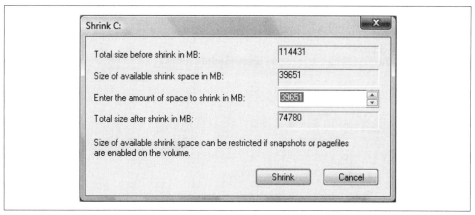

Figure 19-11. Shrinking the volume

The Shrink dialog box provides the following information:

Total size before shrink in MB
Shows the current capacity of the volume in MB. This is the formatted size of the volume.

Size of available shrink space in MB
Shows the maximum amount by which you can shrink the volume. This doesn't represent the total amount of free space on the volume. Instead, it represents the maximum amount of space that can be removed safely.

Enter the amount of space to shrink in MB
Shows the total amount of space that will be removed from the volume. The initial value defaults to the maximum amount of space that you can remove from the volume.

Total size after shrink in MB
Shows what the total capacity of the volume in MB will be after the shrink. This is the new formatted size of the volume.

2. Enter the amount of space to shrink the volume and then click Shrink to shrink the volume.

You can extend a simple volume or a spanned volume by completing the following steps:

1. In Disk Management's Graphical view, right-click the volume that you want to extend and then select Extend Volume.

2. When the Extend Volume Wizard opens, read the introductory message and then click Next.

3. On the Select Disks page, shown in Figure 19-12, the disk you right-clicked is listed in the Selected list with all of its remaining unallocated space selected for use in extending the volume.

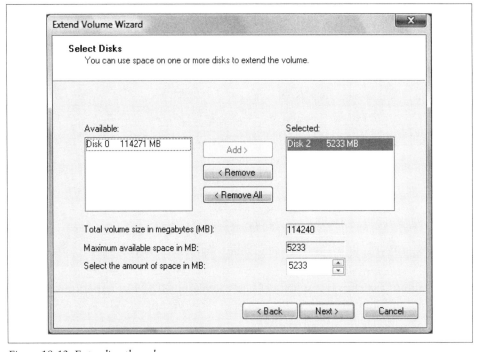

Figure 19-12. Extending the volume

4. In the Available list, you'll see available space on other dynamic disks. If you add one or more of these additional disks to the Selected list, you'll be able to use the free space on these disks as well. However, doing so will create a spanned volume with no fault tolerance.

5. Click Next and then click Finish. Disk Management will extend the volume.

Formatting Volumes

Formatting a volume creates a filesystem that you can use to store your data. If you format an existing volume that you've already used, you will permanently delete any existing data. You can format a volume by following these steps:

1. In Disk Management's Graphical view, right-click the volume that you want to format and then select Format. This displays the Format dialog box shown in Figure 19-13.

2. In the "Volume label" text box, type a text label for the volume.

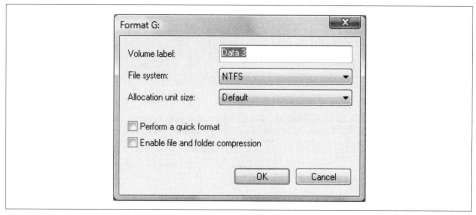

Figure 19-13. Formatting the volume

3. Use the "File system" list to set the filesystem type. The options you have depend on the size of the volume and type of device, but they include FAT, FAT32, and NTFS.

4. The "Allocation unit size" list sets the cluster size for the filesystem. A cluster is a logical grouping of file sectors. In most cases, you'll want the "Allocation unit size" list to be set to Default. This allows Windows Vista to optimize the cluster size based on the volume size.

5. The "Perform a quick format" checkbox allows Windows Vista to format the volume without checking the partition for errors. While this option can save you a few minutes, it's usually better to allow Disk Management to check for errors and mark any bad sectors it finds on the disk so that they aren't used.

6. The "Enable file and folder compression" checkbox turns on compression for the disk. Built-in compression is available only for NTFS. If you select this option, files and folders on the volume are compressed automatically. See the "Compressing Drives" section of this chapter for more information.

7. Click OK to continue. Because formatting a volume destroys any existing data, Disk Management displays a warning. Click OK to start formatting the volume or Cancel to cancel.

Changing Drive Letters

Assigning a drive letter to a volume is the fastest and easiest way to access and work with a volume. On most systems, the drive letter B and drive letters E through Z are available, with drive letter A reserved for a floppy disk, C assigned to the primary disk, and D assigned to the CD/DVD drive. If your computer has a secondary hard disk, a secondary CD/DVD drive, or both, you may find that drive letter E or the drive letters E and F are already assigned as well.

To prevent potential startup problems, you should rarely if ever change the drive letter for the system and boot volumes. However, you can change the drive letters for other volumes at any time. To change a drive letter, follow these steps:

1. In Disk Management's Graphical view, right-click the volume that you want to work with and then select Change Drive Letter and Path. This displays the Change Drive Letter and Paths for... dialog box shown in Figure 19-14.

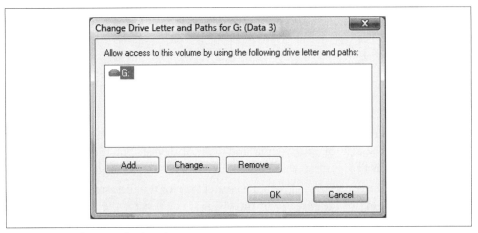

Figure 19-14. Changing the drive letter

2. To change the drive letter, select the current drive letter and then click Change. In the Change Drive Letter or Path dialog box, choose a different letter to assign to the drive. Only those drive letters that aren't currently assigned will be available.

 Although volumes can have multiple drive letters or be mounted to file paths instead of drive letters, I recommend that you avoid these options. You'll prevent possible confusion and it always will be clear how your drives are accessed.

3. Click OK twice to save your settings.

Changing Volume Labels

The *volume label* is a text descriptor for a volume that is displayed when the volume is accessed in Windows Explorer and other Windows programs. If your computer has multiple volumes, giving each volume a descriptive label will help you easily navigate between volumes. For example, you might have a volume named Documents and a volume named Archive.

To change or set a volume label, follow these steps:

1. In Disk Management's Graphical view, right-click the volume that you want to work with and then select Properties.
2. On the General tab of the Properties dialog box, use the Label field to type a new label for the volume.
3. Click OK.

Converting a Volume to NTFS

Windows Vista provides the Convert utility for converting FAT or FAT32 volumes to NTFS. Convert is a command-line utility that requires administrator privileges to run. When you convert a volume, Convert preserves the file and folder structure and no data is lost.

Windows Vista does not provide a utility for converting NTFS to FAT or FAT32. The only way to go from NTFS to FAT or FAT32 is to delete the volume and then re-create the volume with FAT or FAT32 as the filesystem format.

You can convert any volume to NTFS, including the active, boot, and system volumes. If you try to convert the boot or system volume, Windows Vista displays a prompt asking whether you want to schedule the volume to be converted the next time you start your computer. If you click Yes, you can restart the system to begin the conversion process. In most cases, it will take several restarts to convert the boot or system volume. Don't interrupt the conversion process and don't attempt to shut down your computer during the conversion process.

Convert needs a block of free space that's approximately equal to 25 percent of the total space used on the drive. For example, if the drive stores 5 GB of data, Convert needs about 500 MB of free space. If there isn't enough free space, Convert will not convert the volume and will instead tell you that you need to free up disk space.

You can convert a volume by following these steps:

1. Click Start → All Programs → Accessories.
2. Right-click Command Prompt and then select Run As Administrator.
3. At the command prompt, use the following syntax to convert the volume:

```
convert volume /FS:NTFS
```

where *volume* is the drive letter followed by a colon (:). For example, if you wanted to convert the H volume to NTFS, you would use the following command:

```
convert H: /FS:NTFS
```

Deleting Volumes

Occasionally, you may need to delete volumes that you no longer need. You might also need to delete a volume if you want to extend or reconfigure another volume on the same disk drive. Because deleting a volume erases all data on the volume, you will want to copy or move all data on the volume and then verify the copy or move prior to deleting the volume.

 You can't delete the system or boot volume. However, Windows Vista will let you delete the active volume if it isn't also designated as boot, system, or both. Always check to ensure that the volume that you are deleting doesn't contain important data or files.

You can delete a volume by following these steps:

1. In Disk Management's Graphical view, right-click the volume that you want to delete and then select Delete Volume.
2. When prompted to confirm that you want to delete the volume, click Yes.

Recovering Volumes

As part of routine preventive maintenance for your disks, you should periodically check disks for errors, defragment volumes, and clean up unnecessary temporary files. Windows Vista provides separate utilities for each of these tasks; they are discussed in Chapter 20.

When you experience problems with a disk, you can use Disk Management to help you troubleshoot. In most cases, simple volumes are easier to troubleshoot and recover than spanned and striped volumes. With simple volumes, only one disk is involved. If a disk with a simple volume has problems, you might see the Failed, Online (Errors), or Unreadable status. You can correct most error status flags simply by right-clicking the volume and selecting Reactivate Disk. If this doesn't work, click Rescan Disks on the Action menu. If a disk is listed as Failed or Unreadable and won't return to a Healthy status, you should replace the volume. If a disk is listed as Online (Errors) and won't return to an Online status without errors, you should check the disk for errors, as discussed in Chapter 20.

Sometimes you might need to reboot your computer to get a disk back online. The Online (Errors) status can also be an indicator of a failing disk, so if you see this status several times on the same disk, check for problems with the drive, its controller, and its cables. A bad power supply could also be the source of the problem, so make sure that the drive has power. If you can't fix the problem, you'll need to replace the disk. Shut down your computer before you try to examine your computer's hardware.

With disks that have striped and spanned volumes, the drive status might show as Failed, Online (Errors), or Unreadable. In many cases, you can resolve these problems using the same techniques as with simple volumes. Right-click the volume and select Reactivate Disk. If this doesn't work, click Rescan Disks on the Action menu. You might also see the Missing or Offline status if drives have been disconnected or powered off. In this case, you can try to reactivate or rescan, but this probably won't work. To resolve the problem, you may need to check the disk to ensure that it is connected and that its power supply is connected. If you can't fix the problem, you'll need to replace the disk. Shut down your computer before you try to examine your computer's hardware.

Using Compression and Encryption

When you format volumes with NTFS, you can use compression to reduce the disk space used or encryption to add an extra layer of protection to your data. Because these two options are mutually exclusive, a file or folder can be either compressed or encrypted, not both. While you can compress or encrypt entire drives, you can also compress or encrypt individual files and folders.

 In Windows Explorer, compressed or encrypted NTFS files and folders are shown in color by default. Compressed files and folders are shown in blue. Encrypted files and folders are shown in green.

Compressing Drives

When you format a volume with NTFS, Windows Vista allows you to turn on compression for the entire disk. With compression enabled, any files created on or moved to the disk are compressed automatically. When you open files or access folders, Windows Vista expands the files or folders for viewing as well. This behind-the-scenes compression and expansion makes NTFS compression completely transparent, but it does use some of your computer's processing power. With that said, there's an enormous benefit: you can store much more information on a compressed drive.

 You cannot compress encrypted data. If you try to do so, Windows Vista automatically decrypts the data and then compresses it. Likewise, if you try to encrypt compressed data, Windows Vista expands the data and then encrypts it.

Compressing a drive

You can compress a drive and all its data by completing these steps:

1. In Windows Explorer or Disk Management, right-click the drive that you want to compress and then select Properties.

2. On the General tab, select "Compress drive to save disk space" and then click OK.

3. In the Confirm Attribute Changes dialog box, shown in Figure 19-15, specify whether you want to compress only the top-level folder of the drive or the entire drive:

    • To compress only the drive's top-level folder, select "Apply changes to drive... only."

    • To compress the drive's top-level folder, subfolders, and files, select "Apply changes to drive ..., subfolders and files."

4. Click OK.

Any files or folders you create on a compressed drive are compressed automatically.

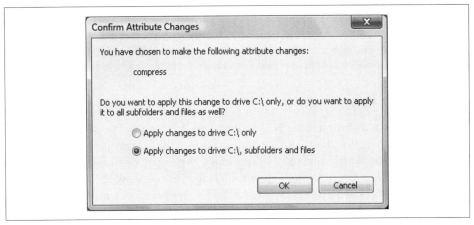

Figure 19-15. Confirming the compression options

Expanding a drive to remove compression

If you later decide that you no longer want to compress a drive, you can remove compression from the drive. However, before you do this, you should ensure that the drive has adequate free space to accommodate the expanded files. Typically, you'll need at least 50 percent more free space on the disk to expand its contents successfully. If a compressed disk currently uses 40 GB of space, this means you'd probably need about 20 GB of free space to expand the disk successfully.

You can expand a disk by completing these steps:

1. In Windows Explorer or Disk Management, right-click the drive that contains the disk that you want to expand and then select Properties.
2. On the General tab, clear the "Compress drive to save disk space" checkbox and then click OK twice.
3. In the Confirm Attribute Changes dialog box, shown in Figure 19-16, specify whether you want to expand only the top-level folder of the drive or the entire drive:
   - To expand only the drive's top-level folder, select "Apply changes to drive… only."
   - To expand the drive's top-level folder, subfolders, and files, select "Apply changes to drive…, subfolders and files."
4. Click OK.

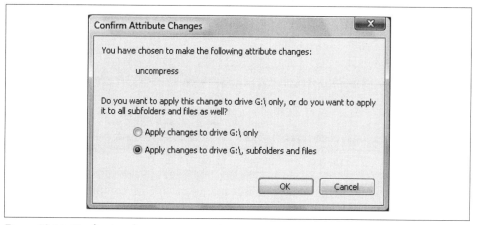

Figure 19-16. Confirming the uncompress options

Compressing Files and Folders

Instead of compressing an entire drive, Windows Vista allows you to compress files and folders selectively. When you compress a folder, you can elect to compress only the folder and the files it contains, or the folder, its subfolders, and all related files.

Compressing a file or folder

Any files or folders you create in a compressed folder are compressed automatically. When you move an uncompressed file or folder to a compressed drive or folder, the file or folder is compressed automatically when you are moving between drives. However, if you move an uncompressed file or folder to a compressed folder on the same NTFS drive, the file or folder isn't compressed automatically and you will need to compress the file or folder manually.

You can compress a file or folder by completing these steps:

1. In Windows Explorer, right-click the file or folder that you want to compress and then select Properties.
2. On the General tab of the Properties dialog box, click Advanced.
3. In the Advanced Attributes dialog box, shown in Figure 19-17, select the "Compress contents to save disk space" checkbox and then click OK.

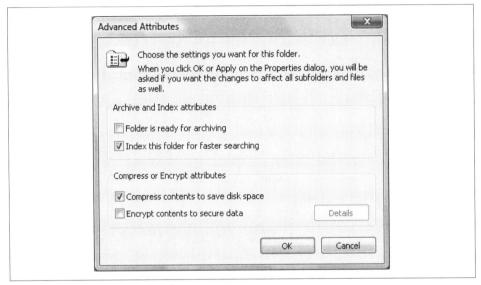

Figure 19-17. Compressing the disk

4. For an individual file, Windows Vista marks the file as compressed and then compresses it. For a folder, Windows Vista marks the folder as compressed and then compresses all the files in it. If a folder contains subfolders, Windows Vista displays the Confirm Attribute Changes dialog box, shown in Figure 19-18:

   - To compress only the folder and the files it contains, select "Apply changes to this folder only" and then click OK.
   - To compress the folder, subfolders, and all related files, select "Apply changes to this folder, subfolders and files" and then click OK.

Expanding a file or folder to remove compression

If you later decide that you no longer want to compress a folder or file, you can remove compression. Before you do this, you should ensure that the drive has adequate free space to accommodate the expanded files. Typically, you'll need at least 50 percent more free space on the disk to expand its contents successfully. If a compressed folder currently uses 2 GB of space, this means you'd probably need about 1 GB of free space to expand the folder successfully.

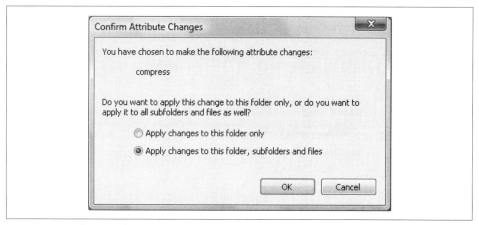

Figure 19-18. Choosing the compression options

You can expand a file or folder by completing these steps:

1. In Windows Explorer, right-click the file or folder that you want to expand and then select Properties.

2. On the General tab of the related property dialog box, click Advanced.

3. In the Advanced Attributes dialog box, clear the "Compress contents to save disk space" checkbox and click OK twice.

4. For a file, Windows Vista removes compression and expands the file. For a folder, Windows Vista expands all the files within the folder. If the folder contains subfolders, Windows Vista displays the Confirm Attribute Changes dialog box, shown in Figure 19-19:

   - To expand only the folder and the files it contains, select "Apply changes to this folder only" and then click OK.

   - To expand the folder, subfolders, and all related files, select "Apply changes to this folder, subfolders and files" and then click OK.

Encrypting Files and Folders

You can use encryption to protect your files and folders so that only you can access them regardless of the NTFS permissions assigned to those files or folders. The first time you encrypt a file or folder, Windows Vista creates a personal certificate containing your encryption key. A personal certificate is similar to other types of certificates used by computers in that it contains both private key and public key encryption data. The certificate is extremely important. If it is damaged or removed from your computer, you won't be able to access your encrypted data.

Unlike NTFS compression, you can't encrypt entire drives. You can't encrypt compressed files, system files, or read-only files either. If you try to encrypt compressed

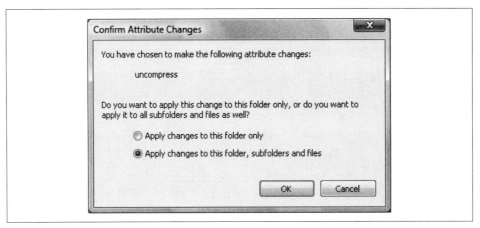

Figure 19-19. Choosing the uncompress options

files, they are automatically uncompressed and then encrypted. If you try to encrypt system files, you'll get an error message.

The Windows Vista component that handles encryption is called the Encrypting File System (EFS). EFS encrypts files and folders using an encryption key that is automatically generated and unique for each person that uses encryption on your computer. When you encrypt a file or folder, the associated data is converted to an encrypted format so that only you can access the file or folder.

By default, you are the only person who can access your encrypted files and folders. However, as you might expect there are some caveats. If your computer has any assigned recovery agents, those recovery agents have the authority to decrypt any encrypted files and folders on your computer. You can think of a recovery agent as having a master key. Additionally, you can grant a person the right to access your encrypted files and folders. When you do this, this person's encryption key is added to the file or folder's encryption data, allowing the person to access the file or folder just like you can.

Encrypting a file or folder

You can encrypt a file or folder by completing these steps:

1. In Windows Explorer, right-click the file or folder that you want to encrypt and then select Properties.

2. On the General tab of the related property dialog box, click Advanced.

3. In the Advanced Attributes dialog box, select the "Encrypt contents to secure data" checkbox and then click OK.

4. For an individual file, Windows Vista marks the file as encrypted and then encrypts it. If the file is in a folder that is not encrypted, Windows Vista displays the Confirm Attribute Changes dialog box:

- To encrypt the file and its parent folder, select "Encrypt the file and its parent folder" and then click OK.
- To encrypt the file only, select "Encrypt the file only" and then click OK.

5. For a folder, Windows Vista marks the folder as encrypted and then encrypts all the files in it. If the folder contains subfolders, Windows Vista displays the Confirm Attribute Changes dialog box:
  - To encrypt only the folder and the files it contains, select "Apply changes to this folder only" and then click OK.
  - To encrypt the folder, subfolders, and all related files, select "Apply changes to this folder, subfolders and files" and then click OK.

Before other people can access your encrypted data, you must decrypt the file or you must grant special access permission. Once you encrypt a file or folder, you can work with it just like any other file or folder. You can copy, move, and rename an encrypted file or folder just like any other files or folders. However, if you move an encrypted file to a disk or device formatted using FAT, the file is decrypted automatically.

Removing encryption from files and folders

If you later decide that you no longer want to encrypt a folder or file, you can remove encryption by completing the following steps:

1. In Windows Explorer, right-click the file or folder you want to decrypt and then select Properties.
2. On the General tab of the related property dialog box, click Advanced.
3. In the Advanced Attributes dialog box, clear the "Encrypt contents to secure data" checkbox and then click OK twice.
4. For a file, Windows Vista decrypts the file and restores it to its original format. For a folder, Windows Vista decrypts all the files within the folder. If the folder contains subfolders, Windows Vista displays the Confirm Attribute Changes dialog box:
  - To decrypt only the folder and the files it contains, select "Apply changes to this folder only" and then click OK.
  - To decrypt the folder, subfolders, and all related files, select "Apply changes to this folder, subfolders and files" and then click OK.

Sharing encrypted files

If you want other people to be able to access an encrypted file, you must either remove encryption or grant the person special access to the file. When you grant a person special access to the file, this person's encryption key is added to the file encryption data, allowing the person to access the file just like you can.

The person to whom you are granting access must have an encryption key on your computer. The easiest way to get an encryption key is to have the person log on and then encrypt a file. Because Windows Vista generates an encryption key automatically the first time a person encrypts a file, this person will then have an encryption key.

You can grant access to an encrypted file by completing the following procedure:

1. In Windows Explorer, right-click the file for which you are granting access and then select Properties.
2. On the General tab of the related property dialog box, click Advanced. The Advanced Attributes dialog box appears.
3. Click Details. In the User Access dialog box, shown in Figure 19-20, users who have access to the encrypted file are listed by name.

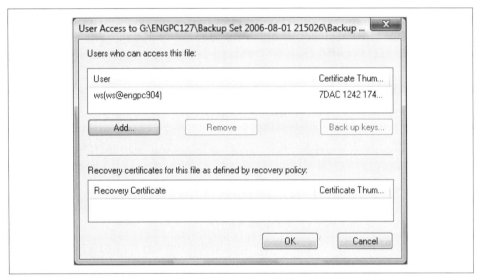

Figure 19-20. Viewing users who can access the encrypted file

4. To allow another user access to the file, click Add.
5. In the Encrypting File System dialog box, shown in Figure 19-21, you'll see a list of every user who has an encryption key on your computer.
6. Select the user's name in the list provided and then click OK three times.

Backing up your encryption keys

As discussed previously, the first time you encrypt a file or folder, Windows Vista creates an encryption key for you. This key is critically important because if it becomes damaged or is removed, you won't be able to access your encrypted files or folders ever again. Several safeguards are put in place to prevent catastrophic data loss. The first is a feature called the *recovery agent*. A recovery agent is a person who

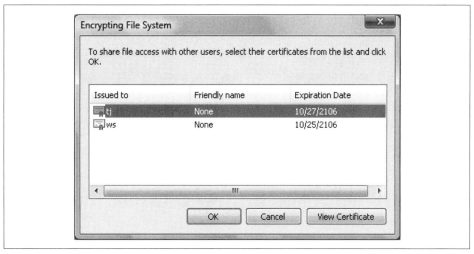

Figure 19-21. Sharing file access with another person

is issued a master key for all encrypted data on a computer. While recovery agents cannot use their master keys to open and read files and folders, they can use their master keys to decrypt files and folders. Once decrypted, the files and folders can be accessed according to their NTFS permissions. If you are using encryption at work, your IT administrators will create and manage recovery agents for you. At home (and at the office as a supplement to recovery agents), you can back up your encryption key to a USB flash drive.

The first time you create an encryption key, Windows Vista will display a notification icon in the System Tray telling you to back up your encryption key. If you click this icon and then click "Back up now," you'll start the Certificate Export Wizard. You can use this wizard to back up your encryption key by completing the following steps:

1. In the Certificate Export Wizard, shown in Figure 19-22, read the introductory message and then click Next twice.

2. To help safeguard your encryption key, you must protect it with a password. This password should not be the same one you use to log on to your computer, but it should be one you can easily remember. On the Password page, type a password and then confirm it by typing it again. Click Next.

3. As necessary, connect a USB flash device to your computer.

4. On the File to Export page, click Browse.

5. Use the Save As dialog box to select the USB flash device as the save location.

6. Type a name for the encryption key file and then click Save.

7. Click Next and then click Finish. If the export was successful, you'll see a dialog box confirming this. Click OK.

Figure 19-22. Backing up your encryption key by exporting it

If your encryption key is damaged or you need to recover encrypted files moved to a new computer, you can do so by completing the following steps:

1. Connect the USB flash device containing the encryption key file.

2. Click Start. On the Start menu, type **MMC** in the search box and then press Enter.

3. In the Console window, click Add/Remove Snap-in on the File menu. In Add or Remove Snap-ins, select Certificates under Available Snap-ins and then click Add.

4. In the Certificates Snap-in window, select My User Account and then click Finish. Click OK. The Certificates snap-in is now added to the console.

5. In the left pane, double-click Certificates → Current User, right-click Personal, point to All Tasks, and then select Import. This starts the Certificate Import Wizard. Click Next.

6. On the File to Import page, shown in Figure 19-23, click Browse. Use the Open dialog box to select the location where you previously saved the key file.

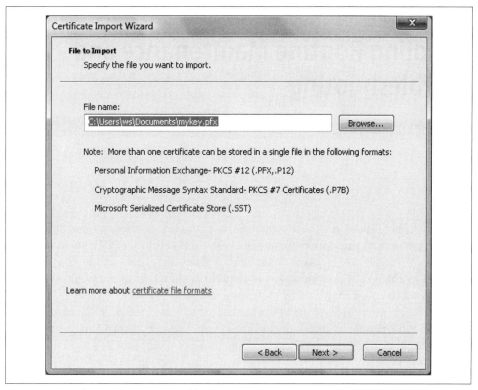

Figure 19-23. Selecting the encryption file to import

7. Your key file is saved as a Personal Information Exchange file. You won't see this file type until you use the "File type" list to the right of the "File name" text box to select Personal Information Exchange as the file type.

8. Click your key file and then click Open.

9. Click Next. Type the password you assigned to the key file.

10. Click Next twice and then click Finish.

You can now decrypt any files that were encrypted using this encryption key.

CHAPTER 20

Handling Routine Maintenance and Troubleshooting

Often when people ask me to help them solve computer problems, I ask them when they last performed preventive maintenance on their computers. The most common responses I receive are a blank stare and a sheepish grin—sort of like it never occurred to them that a computer was something they had to maintain, or they're embarrassed to admit they don't do anything to maintain their computers. The problem is that a computer—just like a home or a car—needs to be maintained. Although most people wouldn't neglect their homes or cars, a surprisingly high number of people neglect their computers. They think of a computer as something they turn on and off, like a car stereo. They forget about the computer's dozens of interconnected components, such as the hard disk they're filling up with data, the programs they're installing and uninstalling, and all the other processes that must work together to make their computer operate normally. They don't realize that a poorly maintained computer is a computer that doesn't run as efficiently as it should, or that the problems they're experiencing with long startup times, slow responsiveness, and delays when performing tasks have everything to do with the fact that they're not maintaining their computer.

Sometimes, though, it's not a matter of neglecting your computer, but of knowing where to start. Most people who have told me they don't maintain their computers have also told me they just don't know where to start or what to do. Your new car comes with an owner's manual and on page 62 or thereabouts it says to change the oil every 3,000 miles, rotate the tires every 10,000 miles, get this maintenance done at 30,000 miles, and get that maintenance done at 60,000 miles. Your computer, on the other hand, doesn't come with an owner's manual that spells out the specific maintenance tasks you should perform—but maybe it should. Maybe if a computer came with a maintenance checklist we'd all have far fewer problems with our computers. Until that happens, though, you can use this chapter and the next chapter as your guide to practically everything you need to know to perform routine and not-so-routine maintenance on your computer.

Maintaining Your System Configuration

As part of routine maintenance, you should periodically review your computer's core configuration. You control many of your computer's core configuration properties through the System Properties dialog box. You use the System Properties dialog box to manage settings for your computer's network identity, environment variables, user profiles, and much more. The System Properties dialog box has five tabs:

- Computer Name
- Hardware
- Advanced
- System Protection
- Remote

The sections that follow discuss how to use the related options to configure the computer name, view hardware settings, set advanced options, and manage remote access. Chapter 21 covers how to configure system protection options.

Configuring the Computer Name

Whenever you access resources on another computer, you do so using the computer's name. Generally, when computers are in the same domain or workgroup, you'll have an easier time accessing and working with them. When your computer is a member of a domain, it uses a different naming scheme than when it is a member of a workgroup. At the office, the full computer name is essentially the Fully Qualified Domain Name (FQDN) of the computer, which identifies the computer's name as well as its place on the network. At home, your computer has a computer name and a workgroup associated with it.

As Figure 20-1 shows, you can determine the domain or workgroup membership for your computer on the Computer Name tab in the System Properties dialog box. If you have appropriate permissions, you can also use this tab to modify the computer's name and its domain or workgroup membership.

You can access the Computer Name tab in the System Properties dialog box by completing these steps:

1. Click Start and then click Control Panel.
2. In the Control Panel, click System and Maintenance and then click System.
3. In the System Console, click "Change settings" under "Computer name, domain, and workgroup settings." Alternatively, click Advanced System Settings in the left pane.
4. Click the Computer Name tab.

Figure 20-1. Viewing the computer name

You can use the options on the Computer Name tab to join a computer to a domain or to change a computer's name. To join a computer to a domain, follow these steps:

1. On the Computer Name tab of the System Properties dialog box, click Network ID to start the Join a Domain or Workgroup Wizard.

2. Click Next three times to accept the default options.

3. As shown in Figure 20-2, enter the name of your domain user account, the password for this account, and the name of the domain. You will use this account to connect to the domain.

4. When you click Next, the wizard will search for a computer account in your user account domain. If the wizard can't find a computer account, you'll need to specify the computer name and computer domain to use, and then click Next.

5. As necessary, type the domain username, password, and domain of an account with permission to join the computer to the previously specified domain, and then click OK.

6. Click Finish and then click OK.

7. You'll see a prompt stating that you need to restart the computer. Click Restart Now to restart the computer.

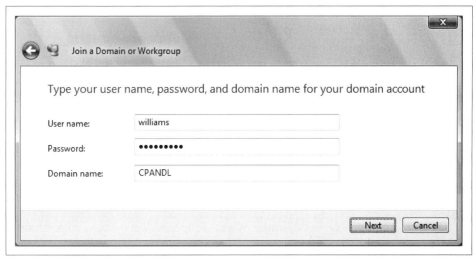

Figure 20-2. Providing your credentials for connecting to the domain

You can move a computer from a domain to a workgroup by following these steps:

1. On the Computer Name tab of the System Properties dialog box, click Change. This displays the Computer Name/Domain Changes dialog box, shown in Figure 20-3.

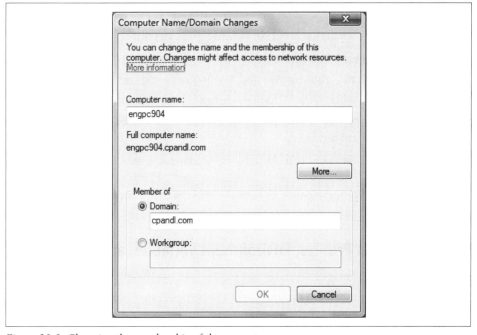

Figure 20-3. Changing the membership of the computer

2. If you want to change the computer name, type the new name for the computer in the Computer Name text box.

3. Select the Workgroup option and then type the name of the workgroup to join.

4. When you click OK, you'll see a Windows Security prompt. Enter the name and password of an account with permission to remove the computer from the domain, and then click OK.

5. When prompted that your computer has joined the previously specified workgroup, click OK.

6. You'll see a prompt stating that you need to restart the computer. Click OK.

7. Click Close and then click Restart Now to restart the computer.

You can change the computer name by following these steps:

1. On the Computer Name tab of the System Properties dialog box, click Change. This displays the Computer Name/Domain Changes dialog box.

2. Type the new name for the computer in the Computer Name text box.

3. You'll see a prompt stating that you need to restart the computer. Click OK.

4. Click Close and then click Restart Now to restart the computer.

Viewing Hardware Settings

You can use the Hardware tab in the System Properties dialog box to access Device Manager and Windows Update (see Figure 20-4). You can access the Hardware tab in the System Properties dialog box by following these steps:

1. Click Start and then click Control Panel.

2. In the Control Panel, click System and Maintenance and then click System.

3. In the System console, click "Change settings" under "Computer name, domain, and workgroup settings." Or click Advanced System Settings in the left pane.

4. Click the Hardware tab.

I discuss Device Manager and Windows Update Driver Settings options in Chapter 5. See the "Learning About Your Computer's Hardware Devices" and the "How Does the Operating System Obtain Driver Updates?" sections in that chapter for more information.

Configuring User Profiles, Environment Variables, and Startup and Recovery

You can use the Advanced tab in the System Properties dialog box to configure application performance, virtual memory usage, user profiles, environment variables, and startup and recovery. I cover configuring application performance and virtual memory in the "Optimizing Performance" section of Chapter 3. This section looks at options related to user profiles, environment variables, and startup and recovery.

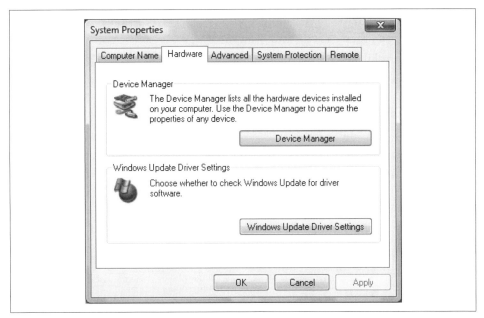

Figure 20-4. Viewing hardware settings

User profiles

When you create a user account on a computer, your computer creates a user profile for that account the first time the user logs on. A user profile contains the global settings and configuration options that are unique to a particular user account. Anytime you make changes to your desktop or other settings that affect only you rather than everyone who logs on to your computer, the changes are saved in your user profile. This is also where your computer stores all your personal files. Any documents, music, or other files you've put into your personal folders are actually stored within your profile.

While I could easily spend 50 pages extolling the details of profiles, what you really need to know is this:

- At the office, your IT administrators will largely control the ways you can use your profile. If your IT administrators create a special type of profile, called a *roaming profile,* for your account, you can use the same profile on every computer you use, and this would ensure that you always have a consistent user environment. When you have a roaming profile, your profile is stored on a Windows server and a cached copy is stored on your computer.

- At home, you are in complete control of your profile. Your profile contains your desktop settings and user-specific configuration settings. Your profile contains all the files and folders listed when you click Start and then click your username on the Start menu. Because your account settings and your personal data are stored in your profile, any problems with your profile could prevent you from logging on and could result in catastrophic data loss.

You can view the profiles on your computer by following these steps:

1. Click Start and then click Control Panel.
2. In the Control Panel, click System and Maintenance and then click System.
3. In the System console, click "Change settings" under "Computer name, domain, and workgroup settings." Alternatively, click Advanced System Settings in the left pane.
4. On the Advanced tab, click Settings under User Profiles.
5. In the User Profiles dialog box, shown in Figure 20-5, you'll see a list of profiles stored on your computer according to the associated account name, size, type, status, and date last modified.

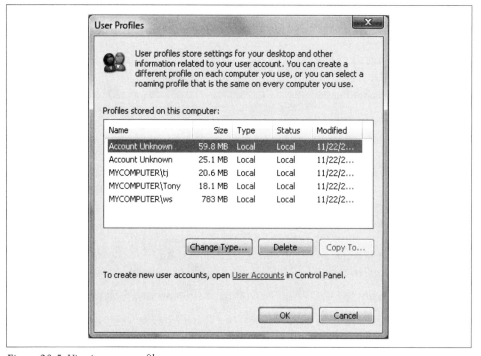

Figure 20-5. Viewing user profiles

As you can see from the list of profiles, profiles can grow quite large. On this computer, my profile is 783 MB in size. On my primary computer, my profile is a whopping 5.2 GB in size. That's a lot of data for the computer to drag around. In the profile list shown in Figure 20-5, you should also note that several names are listed as "Account Unknown." These entries aren't for corrupt profiles or necessarily for profiles that should be deleted. Rather, these entries are typically for profiles created when a computer was a member of a domain, and since the computer was removed from the domain, it no longer recognizes the related accounts to which the profiles belong.

In the User Profiles dialog box, you can:

Change the type of profile

At the office, your IT administrators may use the Change Type option to change your profile from the default profile type—local profile—to a roaming profile or vice versa. Other settings you must configure in your user properties to ensure that you get the correct environment when you log on.

Create a copy of a profile

Use the Copy To option to create a copy of a profile and all its related data. You cannot copy a profile that is currently logged on. If you want to copy your own profile, you'll need to log on using a different account.

Delete a profile

Use the Delete option to delete a profile that is no longer needed. You cannot delete a profile that currently is logged on. If you delete a profile from an account that is still being used, the computer will create a new profile the next time the other person logs on.

Because so much of your important personal data is stored in your user profile, you might want to create a backup copy of your profile. As long as you aren't logged on to an account using a profile, you can copy a profile to a folder by completing these steps:

1. In Windows Explorer, create a new folder for storing the profile data.

2. In the User Profiles dialog box, click the profile you want to copy and then click Copy To.

3. In the Copy To dialog box, shown in Figure 20-6, click Browse, locate the folder you created for storing the profile data, and then click OK.

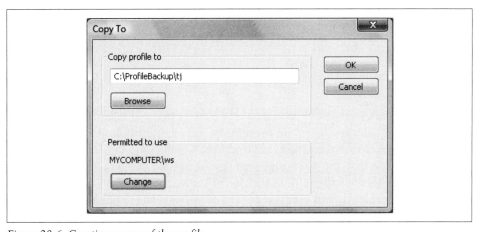

Figure 20-6. Creating a copy of the profile

4. Under "Permitted to use," click Change. Use the Select User or Group dialog box to specify the user or group who should be granted the Full Control permission for the profile data and then click OK. No other user or group will be granted access to the profile data.

5. In the Copy To dialog box, click OK.

6. In the Confirm Copy dialog box, click Yes to confirm that you want to delete the contents of the new folder you created and store the profile in this location.

7. You'll now have a complete backup copy of the profile.

To ensure that a corrupt profile can't prevent you from logging on, you should create at least one additional Administrator account on your computer. If you find that you can't log on to your primary account due to a profile or other problem, you can log on to the backup Administrator account to try to resolve the problem. When you are logged on to the backup Administrator account, you can try to use System Restore, as discussed in Chapter 21, to restore your computer to a previous point in time. While the restore may cause you to lose your most recent setting changes, you won't lose all the data in your user profile. If you find that you aren't able to restore your computer with a working profile for your primary account, you can try to restore your computer from backup, also discussed in Chapter 21. Alternatively, you can do the following to restore logon:

1. Log on to your computer with the backup Administrator account.

2. Create a copy of your profile in a working folder, or create copies of your profile folders in Windows Explorer.

3. Delete your profile. When you delete your profile, all your personal data will be permanently lost if you haven't backed it up or copied it.

4. Log off the backup Administrator account.

5. Log on to your primary account. When you log on, Windows Vista will create a new profile for you. You can then copy your personal data back into your personal folders.

Environment variables

Your computer uses environment variables to track many different aspects of the computer configuration—from the location of your user profile, to the computer name, to the processor architecture. Environment variables are divided into two general classes: those that the operating system uses, called *system environment variables*; and those that are specially related to the currently logged on user, called *user environment variables*. If you access a command prompt and type **set**, you'll see all the environment variables that are currently being used.

In the System Properties dialog box, you can view and configure environment variables by completing these steps:

1. Click Start and then click Control Panel.

2. In the Control Panel, click System and Maintenance and then click System.

3. In the System console, click "Change settings" under "Computer name, domain, and workgroup settings." Alternatively, click Advanced System Settings in the left pane.

4. On the Advanced tab, click Environment Variables. This displays the Environment Variables dialog box shown in Figure 20-7.

5. You can now configure environment variables using the following techniques:

   • To create an environment variable, click New under "User variables" or under "System variables," whichever is appropriate. In the New Variable dialog box, type the variable name and value in the fields provided and then click OK.

   • To edit an existing environment variable, select the variable in the "User variables" or "System variables" listbox. Click Edit under "User variables" or under "System variables," whichever is appropriate. In the Edit Variable dialog box, type a new value in the Variable Value field and then click OK.

   • To delete an environment variable, select it and click Delete.

When you create or edit system environment variables, the changes take effect when you restart the computer. When you create or edit user environment variables, the changes take effect the next time you log on.

Startup and recovery

Startup and recovery options control the way Windows Vista starts and handles failures. You can view and configure startup and recovery options by completing these steps:

1. Click Start and then click Control Panel. In the Control Panel, click System and Maintenance and then click System.

2. In the System console, click "Change settings" under "Computer name, domain, and workgroup settings." Alternatively, click Advanced System Settings in the left pane.

3. On the Advanced tab, click Settings under Startup and Recovery. This displays the Startup and Recovery dialog box shown in Figure 20-8.

4. If your computer has multiple bootable operating systems, you can set the default operating system by selecting one of the operating systems on the "Default operating system" list. These options change the configuration settings that Windows Boot Manager uses.

Figure 20-7. Configuring your computer's environment variables

5. At startup of a computer with multiple bootable operating systems, Windows Vista displays the startup configuration menu for 30 seconds by default. To boot immediately to the default operating system, clear the "Time to display list of operating systems" checkbox. To display the available options for a specific amount of time, select the "Time to display list of operating systems" checkbox and then set the desired time delay in seconds.

6. When the system is in a recovery mode and is booting, a list of recovery options might be displayed. To boot immediately using the default recovery option, clear the "Time to display recovery options when needed" checkbox. To display the available options for a specific amount of time, select the "Time to display recovery options when needed" checkbox and then set a time delay in seconds.

7. System Failure options control what happens when the system encounters a fatal system error (also known as a STOP error). The available options for the System Failure area are used as follows:

Write an event to the system log
Logs the error in the system log, which allows you to review the error later using the Event Viewer.

Automatically restart
Check this option to have the system attempt to reboot when a fatal system error occurs.

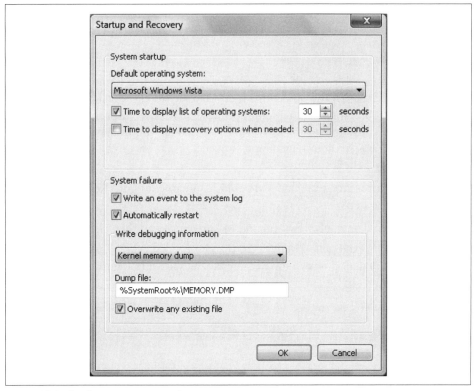

Figure 20-8. Configuring startup and recovery options

Write debugging information
Choose the type of debugging information to write to a dump file if a fatal error occurs. You can then use the dump file to diagnose system failures.

Dump file
Sets the location for the dump file. The default dump locations are *%SystemRoot%\Minidump* for small memory dumps and *%SystemRoot%\ MEMORY.DMP* for all other memory dumps.

Overwrite any existing file
Ensures that any existing dump files are overwritten if a new STOP error occurs.

8. Click OK to save your settings.

Configuring Remote Access

The Remote tab in the System Properties dialog box controls Remote Assistance invitations and Remote Desktop connections. With Remote Assistance, you can send invitations to support technicians, enabling them to service your computer remotely.

With Remote Desktop, you can connect remotely to another person's computer and access its resources.

Remote Assistance

When you have a problem with your computer, you can use Remote Assistance to ask an expert for help. At the office, this is an easy way to allow a support technician either to guide you through a configuration task or to solve a problem for you. At home, if you have a home network, you can use this feature to ask a trusted person to do the same. You should rarely, if ever, however, ask others to help you when they are connecting over the Internet.

Remote Assistance is not enabled by default. You can configure Remote Assistance by following these steps:

1. In the Control Panel, click System and Maintenance and then click System.
2. On the System page, click Remote Settings in the left pane. This opens the System Properties dialog box to the Remote tab, as shown in Figure 20-9.

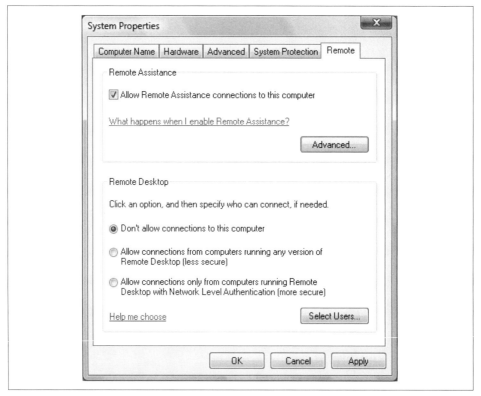

Figure 20-9. Viewing remote access options

3. To disable Remote Assistance, clear the "Allow Remote Assistance connections to this computer" checkbox, and then click OK. Skip the remaining steps.

4. To enable Remote Assistance, check the "Allow Remote Assistance connections to this computer" checkbox.

5. Click Advanced. This displays the Remote Assistance Settings dialog box shown in Figure 20-10.

Figure 20-10. Configuring Remote Assistance options

6. To allow assistants to view and control the computer, select the "Allow this computer to be controlled remotely" checkbox. To provide view-only access to the computer, clear this checkbox.

7. By default, Remote Assistance invitations are valid for six hours and then expire. The helper must initiate a Remote Assistance session within this time limit. As necessary, use the Invitations options to set a different time limit.

8. Because Windows Vista offers improved security and enhanced management, you might want to create invitations that only computers running Windows Vista or later can answer. If so, select the related checkbox.

9. Click OK to save your settings. See Chapter 21 for details on getting help.

Remote Desktop access

Remote Desktop is a feature you can use to connect to your home computer when you are at work or to your work computer when you are at home. Unlike Remote Assistance, this feature is not designed to allow someone to use a computer locally while the computer is being access remotely. If someone is currently logged on to the desktop locally and then you try to log on remotely, the local desktop locks automatically and the remote user can then access all of the currently running applications just as if she were sitting at the keyboard. If no one is logged on locally and you try to log on remotely, Windows creates a new user session and you are then able to work with the computer remotely just as if you were sitting at the keyboard.

Remote Desktop is not enabled by default. You can configure Remote Desktop access by completing these steps:

1. In the Control Panel, click System and Maintenance and then click System.

2. On the System page, click Remote Settings in the left pane. This opens the System Properties dialog box to the Remote tab.

3. To disable Remote Desktop, select "Don't allow connections to this computer" and then click OK. Skip the remaining steps.

4. To enable Remote Desktop, you can select "Allow connections from computers running any version of Remote Desktop" to allow connections from any version of Windows, or you can select "Allow connections only from computers running Remote Desktop with network level authentication" to allow connections only from Windows Vista or later computers (and computers with secure network authentication).

5. By default, only users who have Administrator accounts on your computer can connect remotely to your computer. You can manage access for other users using the following techniques:

   • To allow users with standard user accounts to connect remotely to your computer, click "Select users." In the Remote Desktop Users dialog box, shown in Figure 20-11, click Add. Use the Select User or Group dialog box to specify the user or group who should be granted remote desktop access and then click OK.

   • To revoke remote access permissions for a user account, click "Select users." In the Remote Desktop Users dialog box, select the account to remove and then click Remove.

6. Click OK to save your settings.

General Maintenance Tools

Windows Vista provides a wide range of tools to help you maintain your computer. They include the following:

Automatic Updates
> Allows you to keep your computer up-to-date with the latest hot fixes and security updates

Disk Cleanup
> Allows you to check disk drives for files that aren't needed

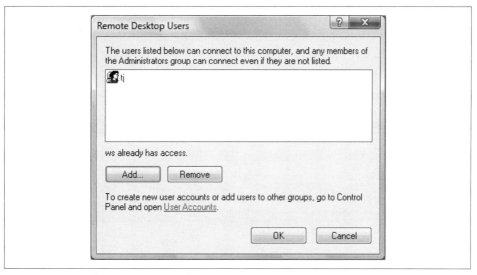

Figure 20-11. Configuring Remote Desktop users

Check Disk
> Allows you to check disks for errors in the filesystem and on the disk volume itself

Disk Defragmenter (Dfrg.msc)
> Allows you to optimize disk performance by reducing fragmentation of files

The sections that follow discuss how you can use each tool to perform preventive maintenance and routine checkups on your computer.

Updating Your Computer

Ensuring that your computer is up-to-date with the most recent hot fixes, security updates, and service packs is the most important preventive maintenance task you can perform. The great news is that you can completely automate the update process so that as updates become available, you can have your computer automatically download and install them.

The feature in Windows Vista that handles updates is called Windows Update. Windows Update is an enhanced version of the standard automatic update feature included in earlier releases of Windows. With Windows Update, you can be sure that all operating system components and related programs that ship with the operating system, such as Internet Explorer 7, are updated automatically.

You can even take this process a step further by having your computer download and install updates for related Microsoft products, including Microsoft Office. To do this, you need to install Microsoft Update. Microsoft Update extends Windows Update to provide a total update shield for your computer and key Microsoft products.

Configuring Automatic Updates

You can configure Automatic Updates by completing these steps:

1. Click Start → All Programs → Windows Update. This displays the Windows Update page in the Control Panel.

2. In the left panel, click "Change settings." This displays the Change Settings page, shown in Figure 20-12.

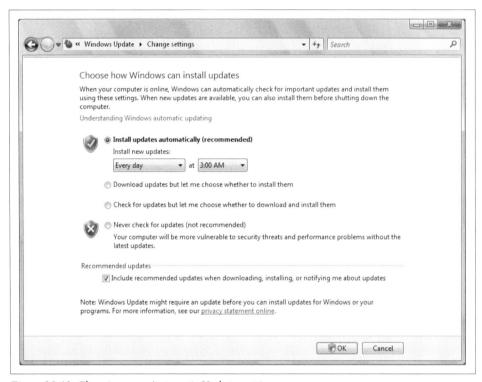

Figure 20-12. Changing your Automatic Updates settings

3. You can now specify whether and how updates should occur. To download and install updates automatically, select "Install updates automatically" and then set the interval for installing updates. By default, your computer periodically checks for and downloads updates when you are connected to the Internet. However, updates are installed only on the specific days and times you set. If you shut down your computer after updates have been downloaded, the updates are installed automatically before the computer shuts down, unless you elect to shut down without installing updates.

4. To ensure that recommended updates for device drivers included with the operating system and other optional updates are downloaded when they are available, select the "Include recommended updates" checkbox. Recommended updates

are not installed automatically. Instead, you are notified when recommended updates become available.

5. Click OK to save your settings.

Installing Microsoft Update

When you are using Microsoft Office, related Office applications, Visual Studio, and some other Microsoft products, you might want to install Microsoft Update to ensure that your computer downloads and installs updates for these programs according to your Automatic Updates settings. Because Windows Defender is also updated through Microsoft Update, this will help to consolidate your computer's updates into one central update process.

You can install Microsoft Update by completing these steps:

1. Click Start → All Programs → Windows Update. This displays the Windows Update page in the Control Panel.

2. Click the "Get updates for more products" link. This opens the Windows Update page at the Microsoft web site in Internet Explorer (see Figure 20-13).

3. After you read about Microsoft Update, scroll down, select "I accept the Terms of Use," and then click Install.

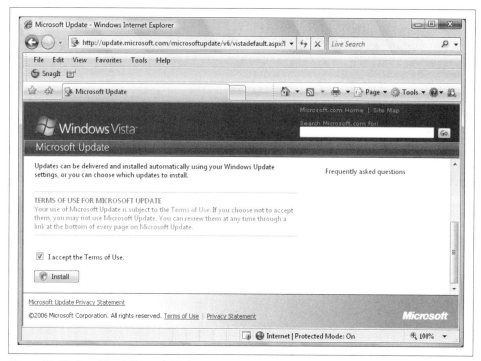

Figure 20-13. Installing Microsoft Update

Your computer will then download Microsoft Update as an automatic update for your computer, display the Windows Update page, as shown in Figure 20-14, and then begin to install Microsoft Update. You can install any other updates that are available by clicking "Install updates." Otherwise, your computer will automatically start checking for updates to other Microsoft programs.

You can determine whether your computer is using Microsoft Update by following these steps:

1. Click Start → All Programs → Windows Update. This displays the Windows Update page in the Control Panel.

2. If your computer is configured to use Microsoft Update, you'll see the following message in the lower portion of the page:

   You receive updates: For Windows and other products from Microsoft Update.

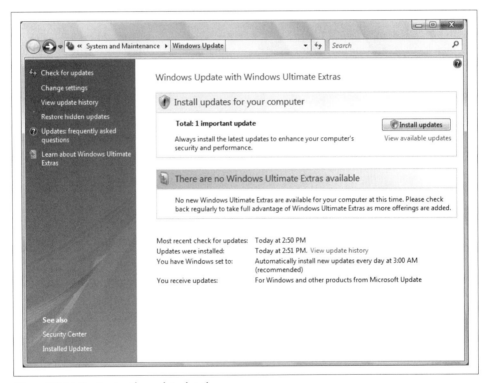

Figure 20-14. Reviewing the update details

Checking for updates

You can check for and install updates manually at any time by following these steps:

1. Click Start → All Programs → Windows Update. This displays the Windows Update page in the Control Panel.

2. Statistics are provided regarding the most recent check for updates, the last time updates were installed, and the current update configuration. If you want to check manually for updates, click "Check for updates."

3. If updates are available, they are downloaded. To install downloaded updates, click "Install updates."

Viewing update history

You can view a detailed update history and a list of both successful and failed updates by following these steps:

1. Click Start → All Programs → Windows Update. This displays the Windows Update page in the Control Panel.

2. In the left panel, click "View update history." This displays the History page shown in Figure 20-15.

3. On the History page, updates listed with a Successful status were downloaded and installed. Updates listed with an Unsuccessful status were downloaded but failed to install.

4. To remove an update while accessing the History page, click Installed Updates. Then on the Installed Updates page, right-click the update that you do not want and select Uninstall.

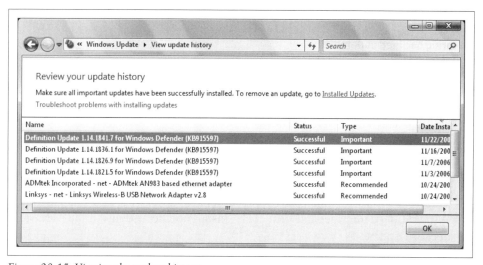

Figure 20-15. Viewing the update history

Removing updates and resolving update problems

Occasionally your computer may experience problems due to installing updates. Although this happens rarely, it does happen. You can remove updates if you need to by following these steps:

1. Click Start → All Programs → Windows Update. This displays the Windows Update page in the Control Panel.

2. In the left panel, click "View update history" and then click Installed Updates.

3. Select the update you want to modify or remove and then click Change or Remove as appropriate.

A problem I've experienced several times with Automatic Updates occurs due to a conflict between McAfee Security Center and Automatic Updates. As this is an equal opportunity conflict, I've also seen it occur due to a conflict between Norton Security and Automatic Updates. Normally, when you shut down your computer and there are updates to install, these updates are installed automatically. The problem I've experienced is that the update process gets locked when I shut down my computer, and there are multiple updates that affect components protected by McAfee or Norton as part of their antivirus or anti-malware protection.

To shut down my computer, I had to press and hold the power button—something you should never do when updates are being installed. When I later started my computer, the computer froze as soon as either McAfee or Norton started, and I was at a complete standstill. If you experience this problem, too—and you might—you'll need to boot your computer to Safe Mode, as discussed in Chapter 21, and restore your computer to a previous point in time using System Restore, which is also discussed in Chapter 21.

Restoring declined updates

If you decline an update that you later want to install, you can restore the update so that you can install it by completing these steps:

1. Click Start → All Programs → Windows Update. This displays the Windows Update page in the Control Panel.

2. In the left pane, click "Restore hidden updates."

3. On the Restore Hidden Updates page, select an update you want to install and then click Restore.

4. Windows Vista will unhide the declined update. Click Back to display the main Windows Update page, and then click "Install updates" to install the previously declined update.

Cleaning Up Your Disk Drives

Over time, the many types of temporary files created when you browse the Internet, install programs, or update your computer can eat up the free space on your computer's disks. As your computer's primary disk fills to 85 percent or more of its total capacity, you may start to notice that it's not as responsive as it used to be. Your computer may slow down as its primary disk fills to capacity, because it depends on this free space to write the page file and other temporary files it needs to use. To help prevent performance problems due to your primary disk being too full, you should periodically clean up your computer's disks using Disk Cleanup. Table 20-1 provides a summary of the types of temporary files Disk Cleanup can help you track down and remove.

Table 20-1. Temporary files that you can clean up

Type of temporary file	Description
Downloaded program files	Contains programs downloaded for use by your browser, such as ActiveX controls and Java applets. These files are temporary, and you can delete them.
Hibernation file cleaner	Contains the hibernation file used when your computer enters sleep mode. You can delete this file, but it will be re-created the next time your computer enters sleep mode.
Microsoft Office temporary files	Contains logfiles Office created as well as other temporary files Office uses. These files are temporary, and you can delete them.
Offline files	Contains local copies of network files that you've designated for offline use. These files are stored to enable offline access, and you can delete them.
Recycle Bin	Contains files that have been deleted from the computer but not yet purged. Emptying the Recycle Bin permanently removes the files.
Setup logfiles	Contains logfiles Windows created during setup. If your computer is fully installed and you have no problems with the installation, you can delete the setup logfiles.
System error memory dump files	Contains dump files Windows created because of a STOP error. If you've resolved the problem that caused the STOP error or do not plan to send the dump file to Microsoft or another support technician, you can delete the dump files.
Temporary files	Contains information stored in the Temp folder. These files are primarily temporary data or work files for applications.
Temporary Internet files	Contains web pages stored to support browser caching of pages. These files are temporary, and you can delete them.
Temporary offline files	Contains temporary data and work files for recently used network files. These files are stored to enable working, and you can delete them.
Thumbnails	Contains thumbnails of pictures, videos, and documents Windows Vista has created. When you access a folder the first time, Windows Vista creates thumbnails of pictures, videos, and documents. These thumbnails are saved so that they can be quickly displayed the next time you access a folder. If you delete thumbnails, they are re-created the next time you access a folder.
Windows Error Reporting	Windows Error Reporting creates several types of temporary files that are used for error reporting and solution checking. Once you've resolved any problems or if there are no current problems, you can delete these temporary files.

You can clean up temporary files by completing the following steps:

1. Click Start → All Programs → Accessories → System Tools. Then select Disk Cleanup.

2. In the Disk Cleanup Options dialog box, shown in Figure 20-16, you can choose to clean up only your files or files from all users on your computer. Most of the time, you'll want to clean up files from all users to ensure that you free up all the space that's being wasted.

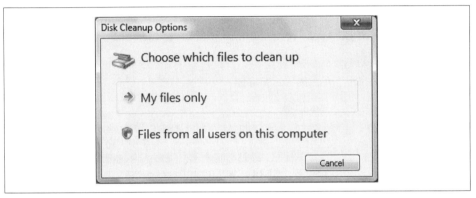

Figure 20-16. Choosing the files to clean up

3. In the Disk Cleanup: Drive Selection dialog box, shown in Figure 20-17, select the primary system disk as the drive you want to clean up and then click OK. The primary system disk is the disk with the Windows logo.

4. Disk Cleanup then examines the selected drive, looking for temporary files that can be deleted and files that are candidates for compression. The more files on the drive, the longer the search process takes.

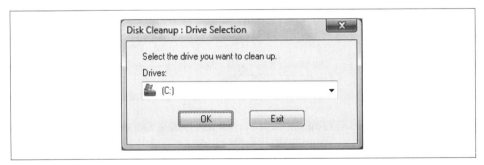

Figure 20-17. Selecting the drive to clean up

5. When Disk Cleanup finishes, you'll see a list of files that can be deleted, similar to the list shown in Figure 20-18. Only a few types of temporary files are selected

by default. Because of this, you'll want to carefully review the other types of temporary files that you can delete. As shown in the example, only 684 MB of data was selected for deletion by default, but I was able to increase this to 3.31 GB by selecting other types of unnecessary files.

6. After you select additional checkboxes as necessary, click OK. When prompted to confirm the action, click Yes.

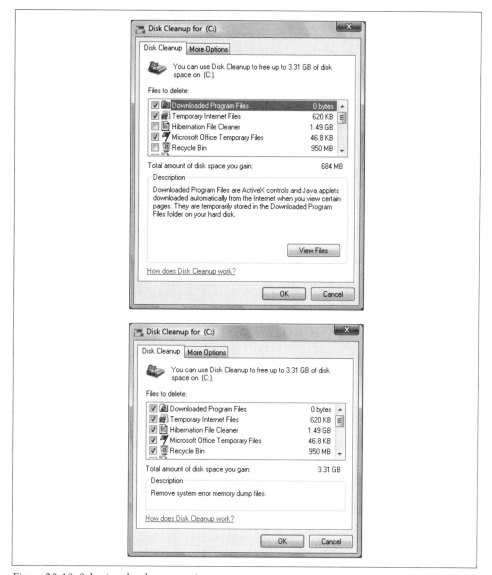

Figure 20-18. Selecting the cleanup options

When Disk Cleanup finishes, I recommend that you restart your computer and consider the two additional options it provides:

Program Clean Up
Helps you free up space by removing programs that you do not use

System Restore and Shadow Copy Clean Up
Helps you free up space by removing all but the most recent restore point and shadow copy

I recommend backing up and restarting your computer before using these cleanup options to ensure that your computer is in a bootable state, that no updates need to be applied, and that no current errors need to be resolved. You can use Disk Cleanup to help you clean up programs, as well as system restore and shadow copies, by completing these steps:

1. Click Start, type `cleanmgr` in the Search box, and then press Enter.
2. In the Disk Cleanup Options dialog box, select "Files from all users on this computer."
3. Select a disk to clean up and then click OK.
4. In the Disk Cleanup dialog box, select the More Options tab, as shown in Figure 20-19.
5. To remove all system restore and shadow copies except for the current restore point, click "Clean up" under System Restore and Shadow Copies. When prompted to confirm that you want to delete this data, click Delete.
6. To find programs to clean up, click "Clean up" under Programs and Features. On the Programs and Features page in the Control Panel, select a program that you want to remove and then click Uninstall.

Checking Your Disks for Errors

Your primary disk is one of the most-used pieces of hardware on your computer. Your computer is constantly reading and writing data. If it experiences the slightest hiccup, the wrong data can be written to parts of the disk. If a particular sector or cluster on a disk is damaged or otherwise cannot be written to, your computer will experience problems whenever it tries to read or write data to this sector or cluster. While Windows Vista and hardware controllers on the disk drives themselves both do a good job of correcting problems, neither one can correct all disk problems. To keep your computer's disks running optimally, you need to check your computer's disks periodically for errors and correct any errors found.

You can check disk drives for errors and correct any errors found by following these steps:

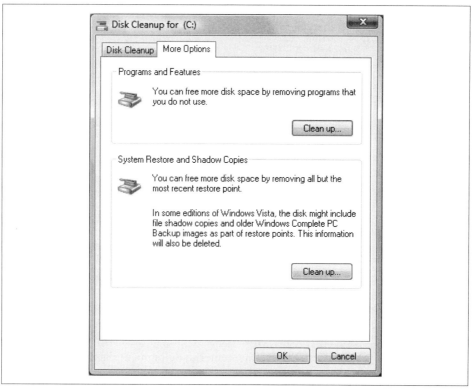

Figure 20-19. Cleaning up programs and other files as necessary

1. Click Start and then click Computer. Under Hard Disk Drives, right-click the drive you want to check and then select Properties.

2. On the Tools tab, click Check Now. This displays the Check Disk dialog box, shown in Figure 20-20.

Figure 20-20. Checking your disk for errors

3. To check for errors and attempt to resolve them, select either or both of the following options, and then click Start:

   Automatically fix file system errors
   > When this is selected, Windows Vista fixes any filesystem errors it finds.

   Scan for and attempt recovery of bad sectors
   > When this is selected, Windows Vista checks for bad sectors and attempts to recover readable information from them.

4. With the primary disk or other disks that are in use, Check Disk displays a prompt that asks whether you want to schedule the disk to be checked the next time you restart the system. Click Yes to schedule this check.

5. When Check Disk finishes analyzing and repairing the disk, click OK.

Optimizing Disk Performance

Another problem that causes disk drives to perform poorly is fragmentation. Fragmentation occurs when a file can't be written to a single contiguous area on the disk, and the operating system often must write a single file to several smaller areas on the disk. Having to seek different parts of the disk slows down not only the write process, but also the read process. Because fragmentation is the number-one cause of disk performance problems (second only to disks being packed with too much information), Windows Vista uses Disk Defragmenter to defragment disks automatically.

Windows Vista runs Disk Defragmenter automatically at 4:00 a.m. every Sunday by default. As long as the computer is on at the scheduled runtime, automatic defragmentation will occur. You can cancel automatic defragmentation or modify the defragmentation schedule by following these steps:

1. Click Start and then click Computer. Under Hard Disk Drives, right-click a drive and then select Properties.

2. On the Tools tab, click Defragment Now. This displays the Disk Defragmenter dialog box, shown in Figure 20-21.

3. To cancel automated defragmentation, clear "Run on a schedule" and then click OK twice. Skip the remaining steps.

4. To modify the defragmentation schedule, ensure that "Run on a schedule" is selected and then click "Modify schedule." Use the Modify Schedule dialog box, shown in Figure 20-22, to set the desired run schedule. For example, you might want to schedule automatic defragmentation to occur every Thursday at 9:00 a.m. during your weekly staff meeting.

5. Click OK twice to save your settings.

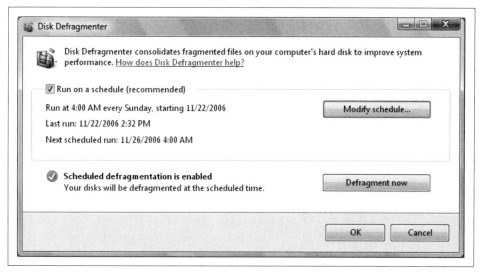

Figure 20-21. Viewing the Disk Defragmenter configuration

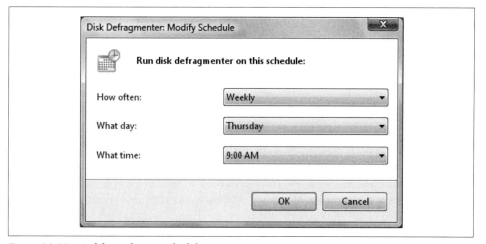

Figure 20-22. Modifying the run schedule

Windows Vista will defragment your disks only if the computer is on, meaning that the computer isn't sleeping or powered off. To ensure that your computer's disks are defragmented periodically, you'll want to use a time when you know you'll be in the office or at home on the computer. Because of performance improvements to Windows Vista, you might not even notice defragmentation is running. Why? Well, unlike Windows XP and other earlier releases of Windows, Windows Vista gives whatever programs you are running priority over background housekeeping tasks such as disk defragmentation.

When you access Disk Defragmenter, the last runtime and next runtime are listed. If your computer hasn't been automatically defragmented in several weeks or months, you can defragment a disk manually by completing the following steps:

1. Click Start and then click Computer. Under Hard Disk Drives, right-click a drive and then select Properties.

2. On the Tools tab, click Defragment Now.

3. In the Disk Defragmenter dialog box, click "Defragment now."

4. Defragmentation can take several hours. You can click "Cancel defragmentation" at any time to stop defragmentation.

Scheduling Maintenance Tasks

You can automate any routine task that you perform. To do this, you can use the Task Scheduler service to schedule the task to run automatically. Not only can you schedule tasks to run once or periodically, but you can also schedule them to run when the computer starts, when you log on, or when a specific event occurs.

Getting Started with Task Scheduling

You use the Task Scheduler to view and work with scheduled tasks. To access the Task Scheduler, click Start and then click Control Panel. In the Control Panel, click System and Maintenance and then click the Schedule Tasks link under Administrative Tools.

As Figure 20-23 shows, scheduled tasks are stored in the Task Scheduler Library. Task Scheduler displays tasks created by you or other users when you select the Task Scheduler Library node in the left pane. Unlike earlier versions of Windows, Windows Vista makes extensive use of scheduled tasks. In the Task Scheduler Library, you'll find system tasks under *Microsoft\Windows* and *Microsoft\Windows Defender*. Tasks under *Microsoft\Windows* handle many of the background housekeeping tasks on your computer. Tasks under *Microsoft\Windows Defender* are used to automate malware scans.

 To ensure that you don't accidentally delete or modify system tasks, most system tasks are locked so that you cannot edit them. Some system tasks are also hidden. In Task Scheduler, you can view hidden tasks by selecting Show Hidden Tasks on the View menu.

Tasks can have many properties associated with them, including:

• Triggers that specify the circumstances under which a task begins and ends

• Actions that define the action a task performs when it is started

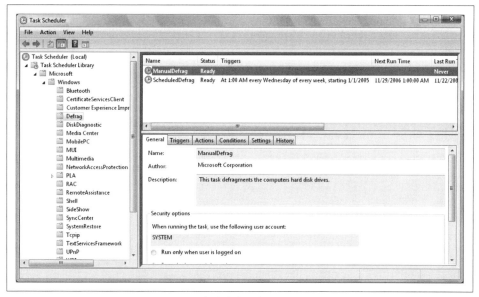

Figure 20-23. Viewing your computer's scheduled tasks

- Conditions that qualify the conditions under which a task is started or stopped
- Settings that affect the behavior of the task

Based on these properties, you can use Task Manager to create two types of tasks: basic tasks and advanced tasks. Basic tasks have only triggers and actions, and are meant to help you quickly schedule a common task. Advanced tasks have triggers, actions, conditions, and settings, and are meant to be used by advanced users or administrators.

Creating Basic Tasks

You can create a basic task by completing these steps:

1. Click Start and then click Control Panel. In the Control Panel, click System and Maintenance and then click the Schedule Tasks link under Administrative Tools.

2. Right-click the Task Scheduler node and then select Create Basic Task. This starts the Create Basic Task Wizard.

3. On the Create a Basic Task page, type a name and description of the task. Click Next.

4. On the Task Trigger page, select a run schedule for the task. You can schedule tasks to run periodically (daily, weekly, or monthly), or when a specific event occurs, such as when the computer starts or when the task's user logs on. Click Next. The next page you see depends on when the task is scheduled to run.

5. If you've selected a daily running task, the Daily page appears, as shown in Figure 20-24. Configure the task using these fields and then click Next:

Start
    Use the Start options to set a start date and time.

Recur every
    Allows you to run the task every day, every other day, or every *n*th day, beginning with the start date you set. For example, if you want the task to run every other day, you'd set the "Recur every...days" text box to 2 days.

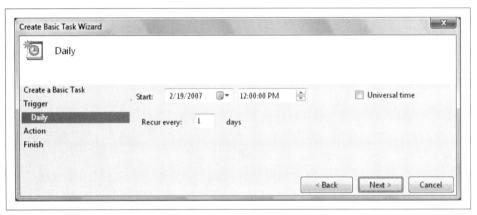

Figure 20-24. Configuring a daily scheduled task

6. If you've selected a weekly running task, the Weekly page appears, as shown in Figure 20-25. Configure the task using these fields and then click Next:

Start
    Use the Start options to set a start date and time.

Recur every
    Allows you to run the task every week, every other week, or every *n*th week.

Days of the week
    Sets the day(s) of the week when the task runs, such as on Tuesday or on Tuesday and Friday.

7. If you've selected a monthly running task, the Monthly page appears, as shown in Figure 20-26. Configure the task using these fields and then click Next:

Start
    Use the Start options to set a start date and time.

Months
    Use this selection list to choose which months the task runs. You can select all months or months individually.

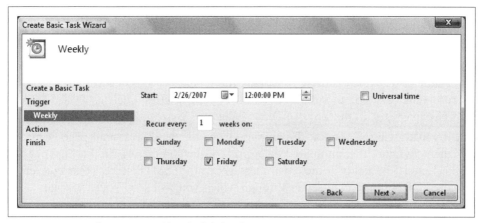

Figure 20-25. Configuring a weekly scheduled task

Days

Sets the day(s) of the month the task runs. For example, if you select 2 and 8, the task runs on the second and eighth days of the month.

On

Sets the task to run on the *n*th occurrence of a day in a month, such as the second Monday or the third Tuesday of every month.

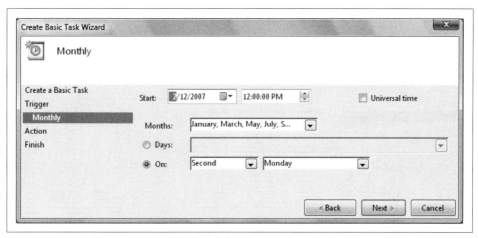

Figure 20-26. Configuring a monthly scheduled task

8. If you've selected "One time only" for running the task, the "One time" page is displayed. Use the Start options to set a start date and time. Click Next.

9. If you've selected "When a specific event is logged," the "When a specific event is logged" page is displayed. You'll need to select the event log to monitor and the specific event source, event ID, or both. Click Next.

10. On the Action page, specify the task to perform. You can start a program, send an email, or display a message. Click Next. The next page you see depends on the action you selected.

11. If you've selected Start a Program, you'll see the Start a Program page, shown in Figure 20-27. Click Browse to display the Open dialog box and then select the program or script to run. You'll find system utilities, such as Disk Cleanup (*cleanmgr.exe*), in the *%SystemDrive%\Windows\System32* folder. Click Next.

12. If you've selected Send an E-mail, you'll see the Send an E-mail page. You can then configure the automated email to send by completing the From, To, Subject, and Text fields of the email message. In the "SMTP server" text box, enter the FQDN of the mail server through which you will send your message. Click Next.

13. If you've selected Display a Message, you'll see the Display a Message page. You can then configure the message to display on the desktop when the task is started. Enter the title and text of your message in the text boxes provided. Click Next.

14. On the Summary page, review the task details and then click Finish. By default, basic tasks you create run under your logon account and will run only when you are logged on.

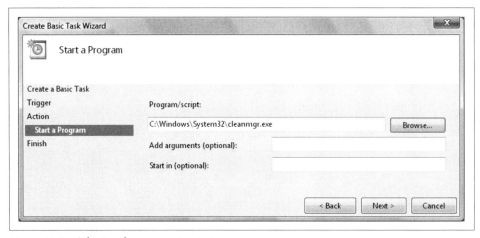

Figure 20-27. Selecting the program to start

Creating Advanced Tasks

You can create an advanced task by completing these steps:

1. Click Start and then click Control Panel. In the Control Panel, click System and Maintenance and then click the Schedule Tasks link under Administrative Tools.

2. Right-click the Task Scheduler node and then select Create Task. This opens the Create Task dialog box.

---

3. On the General tab, shown in Figure 20-28, type a name and description for the task you are creating. By default, the task runs only when you are logged on. If you want to run the task regardless of whether you are logged on, select "Run whether user is logged on or not." You can also elect to run with highest privileges and configure the task for earlier releases of Windows.

4. On the Triggers tab, create and manage triggers using the options provided. Using triggers, you can schedule tasks to run periodically (daily, weekly, or monthly), or when a specific event occurs, such as when the computer starts or when the task's user logs on. To create a trigger, click New, use the options provided to configure the trigger, and then click OK.

5. On the Actions tab, create and manage actions using the options provided. You can start a program, send an email, or display a message. To create an action, click New, use the options provided to configure the action, and then click OK.

6. On the Conditions tab, specify any limiting conditions for starting or stopping the task.

7. On the Settings tab, choose any additional optional settings for the task.

8. Click OK to create the task.

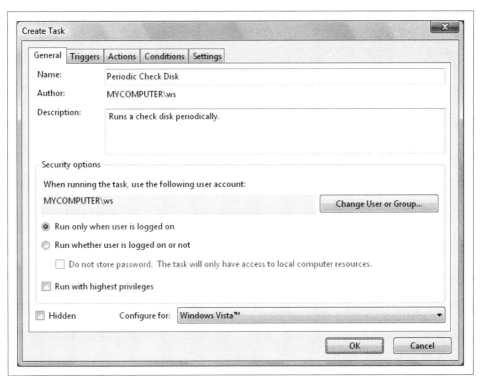

Figure 20-28. Configuring the settings for the task

Managing and Troubleshooting Tasks

You can access the current tasks configured on your computer through the Task Scheduler. You can view and manage scheduled tasks you or other people created by completing the following steps:

1. Click Start and then click Control Panel. In the Control Panel, click System and Maintenance and then click the Schedule Tasks link under Administrative Tools.

2. In the left pane, select the Task Schedule Library node to display tasks created by you or other people.

3. Select a task to view its properties using the tabs provided. Note the task status, last runtime, and last run result. If a task has a status of Queued, it is waiting to run at a scheduled time. If a task has a status of Ready, it is ready to run on its next runtime. If a task should be running automatically but has a Last Run Time of Never, you'll need to check the task's properties to determine why it isn't running. If the Last Run Result is an error, you'll need to resolve the referenced problem so that the task can run normally.

4. On the History tab, as shown in Figure 20-29, you'll see a detailed history of the task from its creation to its last runtime. Use the history information to help you resolve problems with the task.

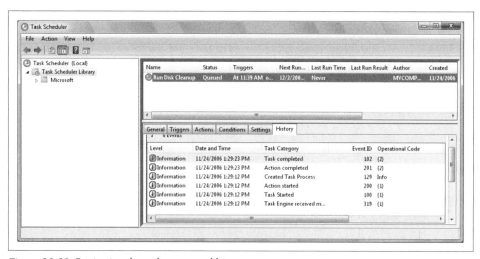

Figure 20-29. Reviewing the task status and history

5. If you want to manage the task, right-click the task and then:
   - Select Delete to delete the task.
   - Select Disable to disable the task so that it doesn't run.
   - Select Properties to edit the task's properties.
   - Select Run to run the task.
   - Select End to stop a running task.

When checking for problems with tasks, keep in mind that a task that is listed as Running might not in fact be running, but instead might be a hung process. You can check for hung processes using Last Run Time, which tells you when the task was started. If a task has been running for more than 24 hours, there is usually a problem. To stop the task, right-click it in the Task Scheduler and then select End.

CHAPTER 21

Getting Help and Handling Advanced Support Issues

Computers have dozens, and in some cases hundreds, of different devices, services, and applications configured on them. Keeping all these components working properly is a big job that Windows Vista handles aptly with your help. Still, it's a fact of life that stuff happens: computers crash, services and applications stop working, and devices fail. Fortunately, Windows Vista includes many features to help ensure that your computer keeps running optimally and to help you resolve any problems you may encounter. In addition to the traditional tools available in earlier releases of Windows, you'll find a new diagnostics framework that can detect problems as they occur, new tools for helping you recover your computer and data, and more.

While the built-in diagnostics features attempt to provide solutions to problems, not all problems can be diagnosed automatically, and you'll often need to work to resolve problems on your own. This is why Windows Vista includes a variety of troubleshooting tools as well as tools for backing up and restoring your computer. Because it's too late when disaster strikes to configure these tools, you'll need to ensure that your computer's backup and restore features are configured properly as part of your periodic preventive maintenance.

Detecting and Resolving Computer Problems

Windows Vista includes an extensive diagnostics and problem resolution architecture. Although earlier versions of Windows include some help and diagnostics features, those features are, for the most part, not self-correcting or self-diagnosing. Windows Vista, on the other hand, can detect many types of hardware, memory, and performance issues and can either resolve them automatically or help users through the process of resolving them. When the automated features are unable to resolve problems for you, you may have to do more extensive troubleshooting by using the event logs and checking the status of essential services.

Throughout this book, you'll find troubleshooting tips and techniques for specific components, features, and applications as well. Don't overlook these additional resources in your troubleshooting. If you have problems that you can't resolve yourself and you are able to load the operating system, you can also use Remote Assistance to get help from other people, regardless of where they may be located. See the "Getting Help and Giving Others Assistance" section, later in this chapter, for details.

Solving the Tough Problems Automatically (and Sometimes with a Little Help)

Windows Vista's built-in diagnostics framework is designed to monitor the operating system and your computer's hardware components. The diagnostics framework has many components, including:

- Application compatibility alerts to warn you about possibly incompatible programs
- Disk fault monitoring to alert you about a disk that is failing and may need to be replaced
- Corrupt file monitoring to detect and recover corrupted system files
- Memory leak detection to detect memory allocation problems caused by programs or components, and to automatically free memory
- Boot performance monitoring to detect and alert you about conditions that affect startup
- Standby/resume performance monitoring to detect and alert you about conditions that affect standby/resume
- Shutdown performance monitoring to detect and alert you about conditions that affect shutdown
- System performance monitoring to detect and alert you about conditions that affect system responsiveness
- Virtual memory monitoring to detect and alert you about low memory conditions that affect system performance

All these diagnostics components work together to help ensure that your computer runs as smoothly and efficiently as possible. The alerts and notifications these components generate are displayed on the screen in dialog boxes and are recorded in the event logs. While the alerts and notifications vary depending on the type of performance problem, most alerts provide you with a diagnosis and a possible resolution. For example, if your computer is running low on available virtual memory, you'll see the "Close programs to prevent information loss" dialog box. This dialog box will alert you about the low memory condition and provide options for closing the biggest resource hogs to free up memory.

With disk faults, hardware diagnostics alerts you about a disk that is failing and helps guide you through the process of backing up your computer. Performance problems addressed by built-in diagnostics include slow application startup, slow boot, slow standby/resume, and slow shutdown. If a computer is experiencing degraded performance, performance diagnostics can detect the problem and provide possible solutions for resolving it.

Some of the more serious problems you may be alerted to are memory leaks and failing memory. Memory leaks are caused by applications or system components that don't free up memory they've previously allocated, and this can cause your computer to run out of available memory. Failing memory can also be exceptionally difficult to troubleshoot. To detect system crashes possibly caused by failing memory, memory diagnostics works with the Microsoft Online Crash Analysis tool. If your computer crashes due to failing memory and memory diagnostics detects this, you are prompted to schedule a memory test the next time the computer is restarted. If you suspect that your computer has a memory problem, you can run Windows Memory Diagnostics manually as well by completing these steps:

1. Click Start → All Programs → Accessories.
2. Right-click Command Prompt and then select Run As Administrator.
3. At the command prompt, type **mdsched.exe**.
4. Choose whether to restart the computer and run the tool immediately or schedule the tool to run at the next restart.
5. Windows Memory Diagnostics runs automatically after the computer restarts and performs a standard memory test automatically. If you want to perform fewer or more tests, press F1, use the Up and Down arrow keys to set the Test Mix as Basic, Standard, or Extended, and then press F10 to apply the desired settings and resume testing.
6. When testing is completed, the computer restarts automatically. You'll see the test results when you log on.

Built-in diagnostics is only one part of a comprehensive overhaul of the operating system. Windows Vista:

- Prevents many common causes of hangs and crashes by using more reliable and better performing device drivers. Improved input/output (I/O) cancellation for device drivers ensures that there are fewer blocking disk I/O operations and that Windows Vista can recover gracefully from any blocking calls that do occur.

- Reduces downtime and restarts required for application installations and updates by marking in-use files for update and then automatically replacing the files the next time the application is started. In some cases, Windows Vista can save the application's data, close the application, update the in-use files, and then restart the application.

- Improves the overall system performance and responsiveness by using memory more efficiently. Windows Vista provides ordered execution for groups of threads, and provides new process scheduling mechanisms. By optimizing memory and process usage, Windows Vista ensures that background processes have less impact on system performance.

- Provides improved guidance on the causes of unresponsive conditions. Windows Vista makes it easier to identify and resolve problems by including additional error reporting details in the event logs.

- Attempts to resolve the issue of unresponsive applications by using Restart Manager. Restart Manager can shut down and restart unresponsive applications automatically. This means you might not have to intervene to try to resolve issues with frozen applications.

Windows Vista also tracks failed installation and nonresponsive conditions of applications and drivers through the Problem Reports and Solutions console. Should an installation fail or an application become nonresponsive, the built-in diagnostics displays a Check for Solutions balloon message. If you click the balloon, Windows Vista opens the Problem Reports and Solutions console, which enables you to check the Internet for solutions to selected problems. You can view a list of current problems at any time by following these steps:

1. Click Start and then click Control Panel.

2. In the Control Panel, click System and Maintenance and then click Problem Reports and Solutions.

3. In the Problem Reports and Solutions console, click "See problems to check" in the left pane to display a list of known problems.

4. Select the checkbox for a problem and then click "Check for solutions" to search the Microsoft web site for possible solutions.

Tracking Errors in the Event Logs

Windows Vista stores errors generated by processes, services, applications, and hardware devices in logfiles. Two general types of logfiles are used:

Windows logs
Logs that the operating system uses to record general system events related to applications, security, setup, and system components

Applications and services logs
Logs that specific applications or services use to record application-specific or service-specific events

You can access event logs using the Event Viewer node in Computer Management. To open Computer Management, click Start. Then select All Programs → Administrative Tools → Computer Management. If the Administrative Tools menu isn't accessible, you can access this tool by clicking Start and then selecting Control Panel. In the Control Panel, click System and Maintenance → Administrative Tools → Computer Management.

You can access the event logs by completing the following steps:

1. Open Computer Management. You are connected to the local computer by default. If you want to view logs on a remote computer, right-click the Computer Management entry in the console tree (left pane) and then select Connect to Another Computer. Then, in the Select Computer dialog box, enter the name of the computer that you want to access and click OK.

2. Expand the Event Viewer node and then expand the Windows Logs node, the Applications and Services Logs node, or both to view the available logs.

3. Select the log that you want to view.

As shown in Figure 21-1, Windows Vista records entries in logfiles according to the activity date, time, and warning level. The various warning levels you'll see are as follows:

Information
> An informational event, which is generally related to a successful action

Audit Success
> An event related to the successful execution of an action

Audit Failure
> An event related to the failed execution of an action

Warning
> A warning about a component, service, or application that can be useful in resolving current problems or preventing future problems

Error
> An error that you should examine, such as the failure of a service to start

In addition to the date, time, and warning level, the summary and detailed event entries provide the following information:

Source
> The application, service, or component that logged the event

Event ID
> An identifier for the specific event

Task Category
> The category of the event, which is sometimes used to further describe the related action

User
> The user account or system process that was logged on when the event occurred or that caused the event to occur

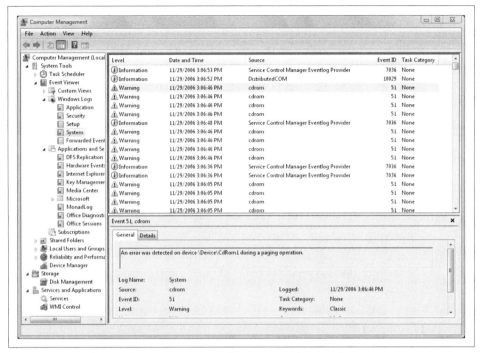

Figure 21-1. Tracking and reviewing errors and warnings in the event logs

Computer
The name of the computer where the event occurred

Details
A text description of the event followed by any related data or error output

You can examine events by double-clicking the entry to view the detailed event description. Use the information provided to help you resolve problems. To learn more about the error or warning, you can click the link provided in the error description or search the Microsoft Knowledge Base for the event ID or part of the event description.

Resolving Problems with System Services

Just about every advanced facet of the operating system runs as a system service. If an essential service stops, the related functionality will not be available and your computer won't work as expected. When you are troubleshooting problems, you'll want to ensure that essential services are running as expected early in your troubleshooting process. To manage system services, you'll use the Services entry in the Computer Management console. You can start Computer Management and access the Services entry by completing the following steps:

1. Click the Start button, right-click on the Computer icon, and then select Manage from the context menu provided.

2. In Computer Management, double-click the Services and Applications node and then select Services.

3. As Figure 21-2 shows, you'll now see the available services. Services are listed by:

   Name
   > The name of the service.

   Description
   > A short description of the service and its purpose.

   Status
   > The status of the service. If the entry is blank, the service is stopped.

   Startup Type
   > The startup setting for the service.

   Log On As
   > The account the service logs on as. The default in most cases is the local system account.

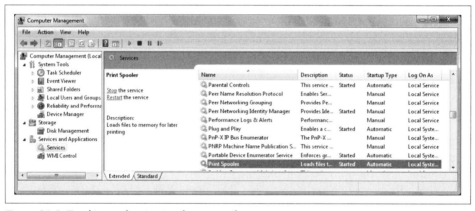

Figure 21-2. Tracking and reviewing the status of services

Once you've accessed the Service node in Computer Management, you can work with services by completing the following steps:

1. In the Services view, scroll down on the right side of the window until you see the service you want to work with. Double-click the entry to view the properties of this service (see Figure 21-3).

2. If the service startup type is listed as Automatic and the service status is not listed as Started, click the Start button to start the service.

3. If the Start button is dimmed, click the Stop button and then click the Start button.

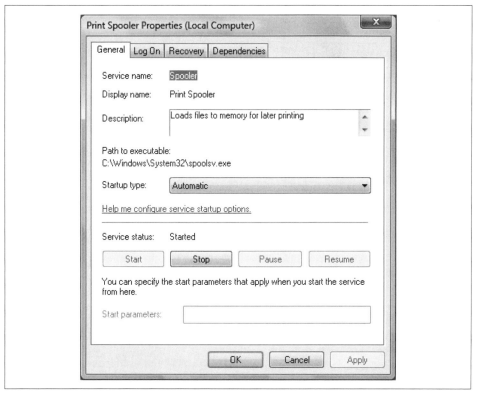

Figure 21-3. Checking the properties of the service

4. If a service that should have a startup type of Automatic has a different configuration, set the startup type as Automatic.

5. Click OK.

As part of the comprehensive overhaul of the Windows operating system, essential services in Windows Vista are set to restart automatically if they fail. You can review and configure the restart settings for a service by following these steps:

1. In the Services view, scroll down on the right side of the window until you see the service you want to work with. Double-click the entry to view the properties of this service.

2. On the Recovery tab, the first, second, and third restart actions are listed as shown in Figure 21-4. Restart actions you'll see include Take No Action, Restart the Service, and Restart the Computer.

3. As necessary, use the "First failure" list to set the first failure option.

4. As necessary, use the "Second failure" list to set the second failure option.

5. As necessary, use the "Subsequent failures" list to set the third failure option.

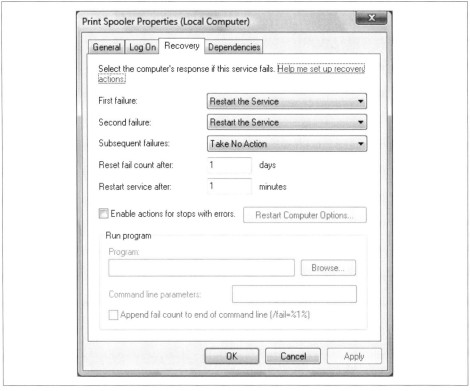

Figure 21-4. Setting recovery options for the service

6. Use the "Reset fail count after" text box to set the expiration period for the failure count. The default value is 1 day.

7. Use the "Restart service after" text box to set how long Windows Vista waits to restart a failed service after detection.

8. Click OK to save your settings.

Creating Backups and Preparing for Problems

Windows Vista includes a number of backup features that can help safeguard your computer against disaster. The ones you'll want to use are as follows:

System Restore
> Used to back up the configuration and settings of your computer for easy restoration without having to reinstall the operating system

Previous Versions
> Used to back up previous versions of files and folders so that you can easily recover your data

Automated Backup
   Used to back up your personal data automatically so that you can recover it easily

Complete PC Backup
   Used to back up your entire computer so that you can recover it from a backup image

None of these features is meant to be used in lieu of the other; you should configure and use all four backup features. As part of periodic maintenance, you should also regularly check the status of these features.

Configuring System Restore

You use System Restore to fix problems and undo changes to Windows. With System Restore enabled, your computer makes periodic snapshots of the system configuration. These snapshots are called *restore points*.

Restore points include Windows settings, device settings, and program settings. Restore points are intended to be used to recover your computer to the state it was in prior to performing a task that changed the configuration of the operating system, devices, or programs. If your computer has problems starting or isn't working properly because of a configuration change, you can use a restore point to restore the computer to the point at which the snapshot was made. For example, suppose your computer is working fine until you install a security patch or a service pack. Although you uninstall the update, your computer still doesn't work correctly, so you decide to use System Restore to restore the computer using a snapshot taken prior to the update.

System Restore can provide several different types of restore points. One type, System Checkpoint, is scheduled by the operating system and occurs at regular intervals. Another type of snapshot, Installation Restore Point, is created automatically based on events that the operating system triggers when you install applications. Other snapshots, known as Manual Restore Points, are ones you create manually. You should create a Manual Restore Point prior to performing any operation that might cause problems on your computer.

You can restore your computer when it is running in normal mode or safe mode. In normal mode, a restore point is created prior to restoration of the computer. But in safe mode, a restore point is not created because changes you make in safe mode aren't tracked and you can't undo them using restore points. However, you can use safe mode to restore any previously created restore point.

You control how System Restore works using the System Restore tab of the System Properties dialog box. System Restore saves system checkpoint information for all monitored drives and requires at least 300 MB of disk space on the System volume to save restore points. System Restore reserves additional space for restore points as necessary—up to 15 percent of the total disk capacity—but this additional space is always available for user and application storage. If System Restore needs to create a restore point and has no more allocated space, the operating system overwrites previously created restore points. You cannot configure the amount of disk space System Restore uses.

You can manage System Restore monitoring of your computer by completing these steps:

1. Click Start and then click Control Panel.
2. In the Control Panel, click System and Maintenance and then click System.
3. In the System console, click System Protection under Tasks in the left pane.
4. System Restore is enabled on the System disk by default (see Figure 21-5). You should enable system restore on all disks that store system, program, and personal files:
   - To enable System Restore for a disk, select the disk's checkbox. When you enable System Restore, restore points are created automatically, as discussed previously.
   - To disable System Restore for a disk, clear the disk's checkbox and then confirm the action by clicking Yes. When you disable System Restore, all restore points on that disk are removed and you cannot undo this action.
5. When you are finished making configuration changes, click OK.

You can create a manual restore point by following these steps:

1. Open the Backup and Recovery Center. Click Start, click Control Panel, and then click the "Back up your computer" link under the System and Maintenance heading.
2. In the Backup and Restore Center, click "Create a restore point or change settings" under Tasks.
3. Select the disk for which you want to create the restore point and then click Create.
4. Enter a description for the restore point and then click Create.
5. When your computer finishes creating the restore point, click OK.

Configuring Previous Versions

System Restore does not affect personal data. You can recover your computer to a restore point without affecting your application data, cached files, or documents. System Restore doesn't write any information to any of your personal document folders, either. However, as a new feature in Windows Vista, restore points include previous versions of your data. Because of this, you should enable System Restore for all disks on your computer that store system and program data as well as disks that store personal data. If you've configured System Restore only for the System disk, you should update the configuration to include any disks that store personal data as

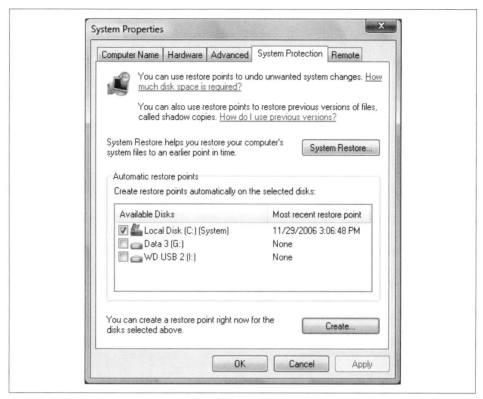

Figure 21-5. Configuring System Restore

well. See the "Restoring Previous Versions of Files" section, later in this chapter, for more information on Previous Versions.

Scheduling Automated Backups

As a new feature, Windows Vista is capable of automatically backing up your personal data. While you cannot use automated backups to back up system and program files, you can use automated backups to create periodic backups of pictures, music, videos, email, documents, and other types of important files. You can write your automated backups to internal or external disks, CD/DVD drives, and network locations.

When you are working with automated backups, keep the following in mind:

- The computer must be turned on at the scheduled runtime for automated backups to work. You cannot save backups to the system disk, the boot disk, tape, or USB flash drives. Only files on NTFS disks can be backed up. System files, program files, and temporary files will not be backed up.

- When you use CD/DVD drives, you'll need to make sure that you remove the CD or DVD from the previous backup and insert a new CD or DVD prior to the scheduled backup. For best results, keep in mind the size of the data you are backing up and use the appropriate media. Most CDs can store up to 700 MB of data, and most single-sided single-layered DVDs can store 4.7 GB of data. If the backup doesn't fit on one disk, you'll need to be available to insert disks when prompted to do so.

If you haven't previously configured automated backups, you can do so by following these steps:

1. Click Start → All Programs → Accessories → System Tools → Backup Status and Configuration.

2. In the Backup Status and Configuration dialog box, click "Set up automatic file backup."

3. On the "Where do you want to save your backup?" page, shown in Figure 21-6, use the options provided to specify a backup location on a local disk, a CD/DVD drive, or the network, and then click Next.

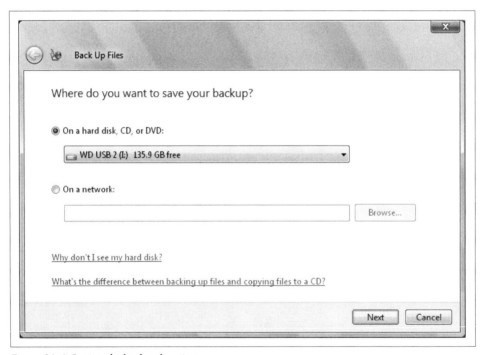

Figure 21-6. Setting the backup location

4. On the "Which disks do you want to back up?" page, select the disks that you want to back up and then click Next. Only personal data is included in the backup. System and program files are skipped.

5. On the "Which file types do you want to back up?" page, shown in Figure 21-7, select the types of files to back up. You can configure backing up pictures, music, videos, email, documents, TV shows, or compressed files by selecting or clearing the related checkboxes. Select "Additional files" to back up any additional files that do not fit in the defined categories. System files, program files, and temporary files are never backed up regardless of your selections.

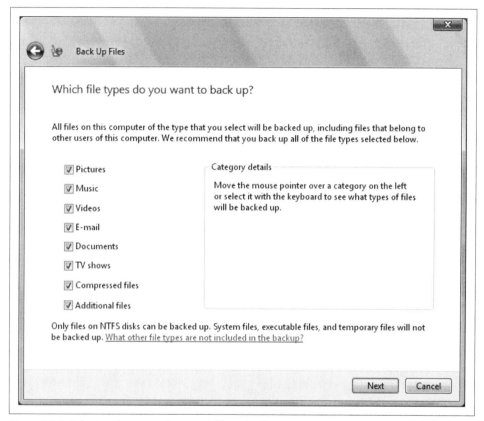

Figure 21-7. Selecting the types of personal files to back up

6. On the "How often do you want to create a backup?" page, shown in Figure 21-8, use the options provided to set the desired backup schedule. The "How often" selection list lets you choose Daily, Weekly, or Monthly as the run schedule. If you choose a weekly or monthly run schedule, you'll need to set the day of the week or day of the month using the "What day" selection list. Finally, the "What time" selection list lets you set the time of the day when automated backup should occur. Be sure to pick a time when your computer will typically be on, and a time that the backup process will cause the least disruption to your work.

7. To save the backup schedule and create the first backup set, click Save Settings and Start Backup. When prompted to confirm, click Yes.

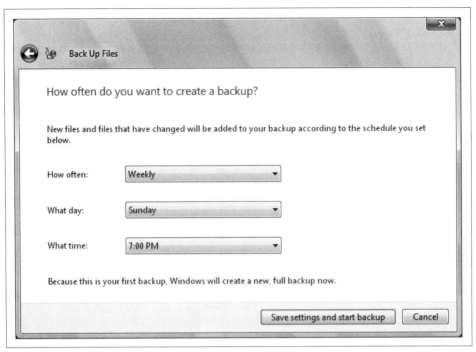

Figure 21-8. Setting how often backups should be created

To modify the backup schedule or configuration, follow these steps:

1. Click Start → All Programs → Accessories → System Tools → Backup Status and Configuration.

2. In the Backup Status and Configuration dialog box, click "Change backup settings."

3. If you want to change the backup settings, select "Change backup settings" and then complete steps 3–7 of the previous procedure.

Once you've configured automated backups, you can run a backup manually to add new or updated files to your backup. To do this, complete the following steps:

1. Click Start → All Programs → Accessories → System Tools → Backup Status and Configuration.

2. In the Backup Status and Configuration dialog box, click "Backup now."

You can turn automated backups on and off by following these steps:

1. Click Start → All Programs → Accessories → System Tools → Backup Status and Configuration.

2. If automated backups are on and you want to turn them off, click the "Turn off" button. To protect your personal data, you'll need to create backups manually or reenable automated backups.

3. If automated backups are off and you want to turn them on, click the "Turn on" button. The settings you configured previously are used for automated backups.

When you are using automated backups, you can view the status of the last backup in the Backup Status and Configuration dialog box. If an error occurs, such as the one shown in Figure 21-9, click the Details link to view detailed information about the error. One of the most common errors you'll see pertains to insufficient storage space. You'll see this error if the backup device you've selected doesn't have enough free space to either start or complete the backup. For example, while the backup program will let you use a device with removable storage as a backup location, the device might not have enough free space to start or complete the backup.

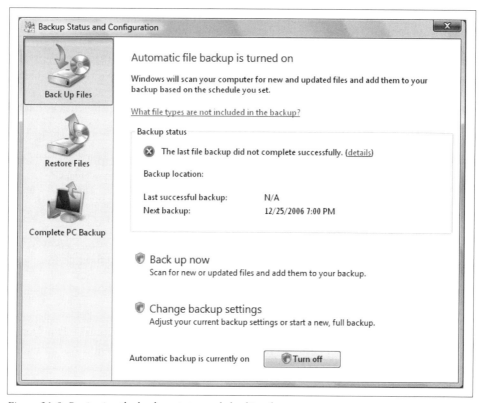

Figure 21-9. Reviewing the backup status and checking for errors

Performing Complete Computer Backups

Complete PC Backup creates a backup image of the entire computer and everything needed to restore it completely. If you haven't previously used image-based backups, you'll find that you can create and restore image-based backups much faster than you can file-based backups. Unlike file-based backups, you can't choose individual files to restore with image-based backups. With image-based backups, you must restore your entire computer, and all the associated programs, system settings, and files. Additionally, when you are using the Complete PC Backup feature, you need to keep the following in mind:

- Backups can only be made to internal or external hard disks, CDs, or DVDs.
- Disks must be formatted with NTFS and cannot be compressed.
- While you can back up dynamic disks, you cannot create a backup on a dynamic disk.

When you create a Complete PC Backup, you should back up all disks that contain Windows files, programs, and your personal data. If you choose to back up to a hard disk, you cannot include that disk in the backup. In addition, when you are backing up dynamic disks, you should back up all dynamic disks together.

Because compression is not used with Complete PC Backup, the backup image will be the same approximate size as the size of the data you are backing up. For fast backups on a medium that is portable, I recommend using an external disk drive. With my external disk drive, I can create a complete backup image at a rate of about 20 GB every 10 minutes. In contrast, using a $16 \times$ DVD-R drive requires three to four DVDs and 30 to 45 minutes to back up 20 GB.

 Because backup images create an actual duplicate of a disk, you should check for and fix disk errors prior to running Complete PC Backup. You should also defragment the disks prior to the complete backup. Performing both of these maintenance tasks will help ensure that disk recovery works smoothly and that your computer operates smoothly after disk recovery. If a disk that you want to back up has been flagged as having errors or has a pending check disk, Complete PC Backup will not continue until you've checked for and fixed disk errors.

You can start a Complete PC Backup by following these steps:

1. Open the Backup and Recovery Center. Click Start, click Control Panel, and then click the "Back up your computer" link under the System and Maintenance heading.
2. In the Backup and Recovery Center, click "Back up computer." Windows Complete PC Backup will then examine your computer's disks and attached devices, looking for compatible backup devices.
3. On the "Where do you want to save the backup?" page, shown in Figure 21-10, use the options provided to specify a backup location, preferably on removable media, and then click Next.

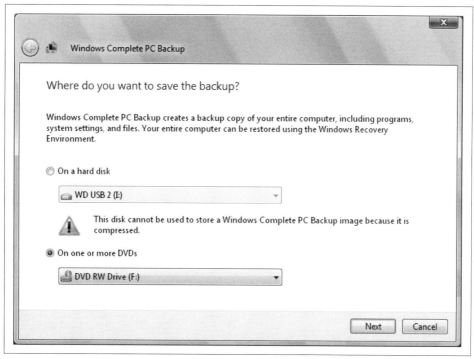

Figure 21-10. Selecting the complete PC backup location

4. On the "Which disks do you want to include in the backup?" page, shown in Figure 21-11, the computer's system drive is selected by default. You cannot change this selection, but you can add other drives to the backup image by selecting the related checkboxes. Click Next to continue.

5. Confirm the backup settings. If you are writing the backup to CD or DVD, you'll see the approximate number of CDs or DVDs required for the backup. Click Start Backup to start the backup.

Recovering After a Crash or Other Problem

Windows Vista includes a number of features to help you recover your computer and your data in case disaster strikes. The recovery features you'll want to use are as follows:

Restore points
> Use restore points to fix problems and undo changes to the operating system, programs, and devices.

Previous versions
> Use previous versions of files to help you recover files that were accidentally deleted or incorrectly edited.

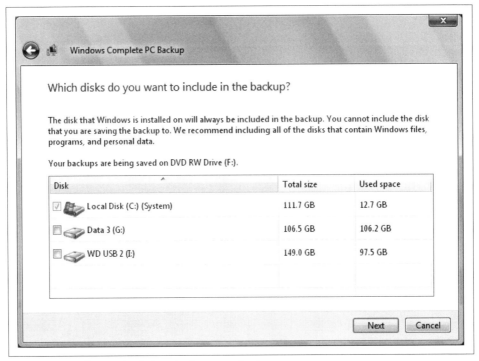

The disk that Windows is installed on will always be included in the backup. You cannot include the disk that you are saving the backup to. We recommend including all of the disks that contain Windows files, programs, and personal data.

Your backups are being saved on DVD RW Drive (F:).

Figure 21-11. Selecting the disks to back up completely

File recovery from backup
Use file recovery from backup to recover files when previous versions aren't available.

Force restart or shutdown
Use this technique to recover after your computer hangs so that you can restart or shut down.

Failed resume recovery
Use this technique to recover after a failed resume.

Startup repair
Use this technique to repair system files so that you can start the operating system.

Complete PC recovery
Use this technique to recover your computer completely in the event that restore points and startup repair do not resolve your problem.

Operating system reinstall
Use this technique to reinstall the operating system in the event that no other recovery technique works.

Table 21-1 provides an overview of problems you may have that force you to use recovery techniques, and the techniques you should use to resolve the problem.

Table 21-1. Recovery techniques

Issue	Recovery technique
Need to recover pictures, music, videos, email, documents, and other types of important personal files	1. Use Previous Versions. 2. Use File Recovery from Backup.
Need to resolve resume, restart, or shutdown issues	Use Force Restart or Shutdown, or use Failed Resume Recovery.
Need to resolve startup problem due to corrupt system files	1. Use Startup Repair. 2. Use Complete PC Recovery. 3. Use operating system reinstall.
Need to recover by undoing changes to the operating system, programs, and devices	1. Use Restore Points. 2. Use Complete PC Recovery. 3. Use operating system reinstall.

Recovering Using Restore Points

You use restore points to fix problems and undo changes to the operating system, programs, and devices. Using a restore point does not affect personal data. If the restore point doesn't resolve your problem, you can undo it or choose another restore point.

If you can start your computer and log on, you can try to recover the computer using a restore point by following these steps:

1. Open the Backup and Recovery Center. Click Start, click Control Panel, and then click the "Back up your computer" link under the System and Maintenance heading.

2. Select "Repair Windows using System Restore" under Tasks. This starts the System Restore Wizard. Click Next.

3. On the "Choose a restore point" page, shown in Figure 21-12, click the restore point you want to use. Restore points you've created are prefixed with the keyword *Manual*. Restore points created by Windows Vista are prefixed with the keyword *System*.

4. Click Next and then click Finish. When prompted, click Yes to confirm that you want to restore the computer's system files and settings using the selected restore point. Do not interrupt the restore process once it has started.

5. System Restore will then prepare to restore your computer. During the restoration, System Restore restarts your computer. During startup, System Restore uses the settings from restore points you've selected.

6. After your computer restarts, the System Restore dialog box is displayed again. Read the message provided and then click Close. If Windows Vista isn't working properly, you can apply a different restore point or reverse the restore operation by repeating this procedure and selecting the restore operation that was created prior to applying the current system state.

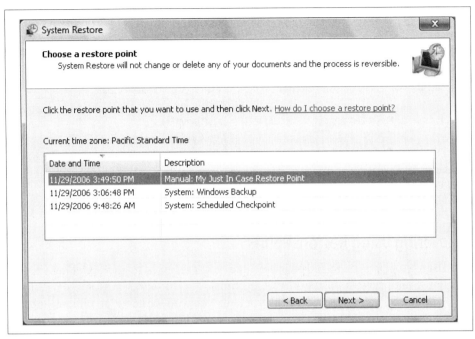

Figure 21-12. Choosing a restore point

If you cannot start your computer, you can try to recover the computer using a restore point by following these steps:

1. Insert the Windows Vista installation disc and then restart the computer. When prompted, press a key to boot from the installation disc. Setup will then load the operating system from the disc.

2. When prompted, choose your language settings and then click Next. On the installation screen, do not click "Install now." Instead, click the "Repair your computer" link in the lower-left corner of the screen.

3. In the System Recovery Options dialog box, select the operating system to repair and then click Next.

4. In the System Recovery Options dialog box, choose System Restore. Follow the prompts to recover the system using the selected recovery tool.

Restoring Previous Versions of Files

Windows Vista tracks changes in files and folders using Previous Versions. When you configure System Restore for a disk, System Restore creates previous versions of files and folders automatically as part of restore points. Any personal file or folder that was modified since the last restore point is saved and made available as a previous version.

 Previous versions are created for pictures, music, videos, email, documents, and other types of personal files. Previous versions are not created for files and folders that the operating system uses.

You can use previous versions of files to restore files that were inadvertently changed, deleted, or damaged. While System Restore creates previous versions daily for all drives being monitored by System Restore, only those versions of files that are actually different from the current version are stored as previous versions. You can enable or disable previous versions by enabling or disabling System Restore on a particular drive.

Accessing previous versions of files and folders is a snap. To view previous versions of a file or folder, right-click the file or folder and then select "Restore previous versions." This opens the file or folder's Properties dialog box to the Previous Versions tab. Your computer will then search the available restore points for previous versions of the selected folder or file. When previous versions are available, the Previous Versions tab lists the previous versions of the file or folder by name and date. Select the previous version you want to work with and then click:

- Open to open the selected previous version
- Copy to create a copy of the selected previous version
- Restore to revert the file or folder to the selected previous version

If no previous versions are found, you'll see a message stating this, as shown in Figure 21-13. In this case, you may need to check your computer's configuration to ensure that System Restore is monitoring the related disk. Keep in mind that System Restore does not create previous versions of offline files cached on your computer or system files. For offline files, previous versions may be available on the server where the file is stored. Changes made to system files are tracked as part of restore points, and you must recover the computer to the restore point to go back to a previous state.

 If the folder in which the file was stored has been deleted, you must open the Properties dialog box for the folder that contained the file or folder that was deleted. Use this folder's Previous Versions tab to restore the folder and then access the file or folder to recover the previous version of the file you are looking for.

Figure 21-13. Checking for previous versions

Recovering Files from Backup

You can recover files you've backed up by following these steps:

1. Open the Backup and Recovery Center. Click Start, click Control Panel, and then click the "Back up your computer" link under the System and Maintenance heading.

2. In the Backup and Recovery Center, click "Restore files."

3. On the "What do you want to restore?" page, shown in Figure 21-14, select "Files from the latest backup" or "Files from an older backup" as appropriate, and then click Next.

4. If you selected "Files from an older backup," select the date to restore and then click Next.

5. On the "Select the files and folders to restore" page, shown in Figure 21-15, use the following techniques to select the files and folders to restore, and then click Next:

   - To restore individual files, click the "Add files" button. In the "Add Files to Restore" dialog box, you'll see a list of all the folders and files in the backup. Select files to restore and then click Add. Repeat this process to select other individual files to restore.

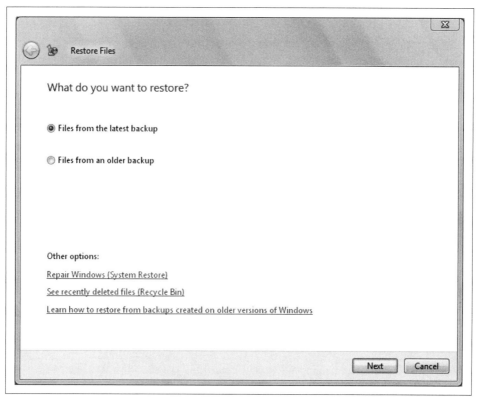

Figure 21-14. Selecting what you want to restore

- To restore folders and all their contents, click the "Add folders" button. In the "Add folder to restore" dialog box, you'll see a list of all the folders in the backup. Select a folder to restore and then click Add. Repeat this process to select other folders to restore.

- To search for a particular file or folder, click the Search button. In the "Search for files to restore" dialog box, type all or part of the filename or folder to search for, and then click Search. In the Search results, select the files or folders to restore, and then click Add. Repeat this process to search for other files and folders to restore.

6. On the "Where do you want to save the restored files?" page, the "In the original location" option is selected by default. You use this option to restore files to their original location. To restore files and folders to an alternative location, select "In the following location," click Browse, select a restore location, and then click OK.

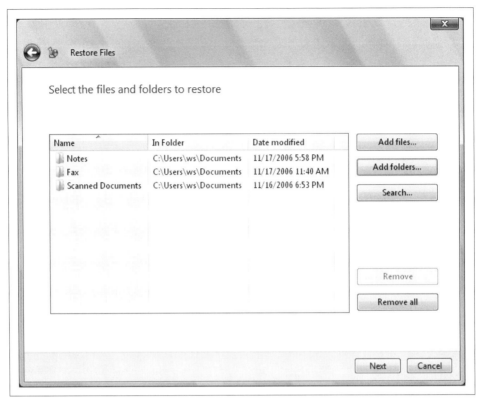

Figure 21-15. Selecting the files and folders to restore

7. Click Start Restore to restore the selected files and folders. If there is already a file or folder with the same name in the location you've selected, you can:

- Overwrite the current version with the restored version by clicking Copy and Replace.
- Keep the current version and discard the restored version by clicking "Don't copy."
- Keep both versions by clicking the "Copy, but keep" option. The new file-name will be the same as the old filename, but with a numeric suffix, indicating the version increment.

 If you want to use the same response for all conflicts, select the "Do this for all conflicts" checkbox before you click an option.

8. Your files and folders are restored as appropriate. Click Finish.

Resolving Restart or Shutdown Issues

The normal way to shut down or restart Windows Vista is to click Start, click the Options button to the right of the power and lock buttons, and then click Restart or Shut Down as appropriate. There are times, however, when Windows Vista won't shut down or restart normally and you must resolve the problem that is preventing the operating system from shutting down or restarting. To resolve shutdown or startup problems, follow these steps:

1. Press Ctrl-Alt-Delete to display the Windows screen and then click Start Task Manager. If your computer doesn't respond and you've waited a sufficient amount of time for it to recover by itself or complete any pending tasks, press and hold the computer's power button to force a shutdown.

2. In Task Manager, click the Application tab. Look for an application that is not responding. If all programs appear to be running normally, skip to step 5.

3. Click the application that is not responding, and then click End Task.

4. If the application fails to respond to the request, you'll see a prompt that allows you to end the application immediately or cancel the end-task request. Click End Now.

5. Try shutting down or restarting the computer. Press Ctrl-Alt-Delete, click the Options button to the right of the power and lock buttons, and then click Restart or Shut Down as appropriate.

6. If the preceding steps don't work, perform a hard shutdown by pressing and holding the computer's power button or by unplugging the computer.

If you force the computer to shut down, Check Disk will probably run the next time you start the computer. This allows the computer to check for errors and problems that might have been caused by the hard shutdown. If Check Disk doesn't run automatically, you should run it manually.

Recovering from a Failed Resume

When your computer enters sleep mode or hibernates, Windows Vista creates a snapshot of the current state of the computer. With sleep mode, this snapshot is created in memory and then read from memory when you wake the computer. With hibernate mode, this snapshot is written to disk and then read from disk when you wake the computer. Windows Resume Loader handles both the sleep and the hibernate operations.

Your computer may have a problem with resume for a variety of reasons, including errors in the snapshot, physical errors in memory, and physical disk errors. If there is a problem resuming after waking the computer, Windows Resume Loader will prompt you with a warning message similar to the following:

```
Windows Resume Loader
The last attempt to restart the system from its previous location failed. Attempt to
restart again?

Continue with system restart
Delete restoration data and proceed to system boot.

Enter=choose
```

This prompt gives you two options for resuming:

- Continue with system restart.
- Delete restoration data and proceed to system boot.

If you select "Continue with system restart," Windows Resume Loader will attempt to reload the system state again. If you select "Delete restoration data and proceed to system boot," Windows Resume Loader will delete the saved state of the computer and restart the computer. Although a full restart will typically resolve any problem, you'll lose any work you hadn't saved before the computer entered sleep or hibernate mode.

Repairing a Computer to Enable Startup

Windows Vista includes the Startup Repair tool (StR) to automatically detect corrupted system files during startup and guide you through automated or manual recovery. Once started, StR attempts to determine the cause of the startup failure by analyzing startup logs and error reports, then attempts to fix the problem automatically. If StR is unable to resolve the problem, it restores the system to the last known working state and then provides diagnostics information and support options for further troubleshooting.

You can run StR from the Windows Vista installation disk by following these steps:

1. Insert the Windows Vista installation disc and then restart the computer. When prompted, press a key to boot from the installation disc. Setup will then load the operating system from the disc.

2. When prompted, choose your language settings and then click Next. On the installation screen, do not click Install Now. Instead, click the Repair Your Computer link in the lower-left corner of the screen.

3. In the System Recovery Options dialog box, select the operating system to repair and then click Next.

4. In the System Recovery Options dialog box, choose Startup Repair. Startup Repair will then check for and fix any startup problems. Follow the prompts to recover the system.

Corrupted system files aren't the only types of problems that can prevent proper startup of the operating system. Many other types of problems can occur, but most of these problems occur because something on the system has changed. Often you can resolve startup issues using safe mode to recover or troubleshoot system problems. When you are finished using safe mode, be sure to restart the computer using a normal startup. You will then be able to use the computer as you normally would.

You can restart a system in safe mode by completing the following steps:

1. If the computer is running but has started with errors, click Start, then click the Options button to the right of the power and lock buttons, and click Shut Down.

2. Start the computer. During startup, press F8 to access the Advanced Options screen.

3. Use the arrow keys to select the safe mode you want to use and then press Enter. The safe mode option you use depends on the type of problem you're experiencing. In most cases, you'll want to use one of the following options:

   Safe Mode
   > Windows loads only basic files, services, and drivers during the initialization sequence. The drivers loaded include the mouse, monitor, keyboard, mass storage, and base video. No networking services or drivers are started.

   Safe Mode with Networking
   > Windows loads only basic files, services, and drivers during the initialization sequence. The drivers loaded include the mouse, monitor, keyboard, mass storage, and base video. After the initialization sequence, Windows loads the networking components.

   Safe Mode with Command Prompt
   > Windows loads basic files, services, and drivers, and then starts a command prompt instead of the Windows Vista graphical interface. No networking services or related drivers are started.

   Last Known Good Configuration
   > Windows starts the computer in Safe Mode using registry information that Windows Vista saved at the last shutdown. Only the HKEY_CURRENT_CONFIG (HKCC) hive is loaded. This registry hive stores information about the hardware configuration with which you previously and successfully started the computer.

4. If a problem doesn't reappear when you start in Safe Mode, you can eliminate the default settings and basic device drivers as possible causes. If a newly added device or updated driver is causing problems, you can use Safe Mode to remove the device or reverse the update.

5. If you are still having a problem starting the computer normally and you suspect that problems with hardware, software, or settings are to blame, remain in Safe Mode and then try using System Restore to undo previous changes.

Recovering Your Computer from Backup

Complete PC Backup creates a backup image of the entire computer and everything needed to restore it completely. All system, program, and personal data included in the backup is completely restored, overwriting any existing data. You can recover your computer completely by following these steps:

1. Insert the Windows Vista installation disc and then restart the computer. When prompted, press a key to boot from the installation disc. Setup will then load the operating system from the disc.

2. When prompted, choose your language settings and then click Next. On the installation screen, do not click Install Now. Instead, click the "Repair your computer" link in the lower-left corner of the screen.

3. In the System Recovery Options dialog box, select the operating system to repair and then click Next.

4. In the System Recovery Options dialog box, choose Windows Complete PC Restore. Follow the prompts to recover the system.

Reinstalling Windows Vista

When all else fails and you cannot recover Windows in any other way, you can reinstall Windows Vista. This procedure follows the same steps you would follow if performing a clean install of the operating system. Reinstalling Windows Vista will result in the loss of all user settings and programs. After reinstalling the operating system, you will need to reconfigure the computer and reinstall your applications.

Getting Help and Giving Others Assistance

Windows Vista offers two similar features for getting help and remotely accessing computers: Remote Assistance and Remote Desktop. When you have a problem with your computer, you can use Remote Assistance to ask an expert for help. You can also use Remote Assistance to give others assistance. Remote Desktop is a feature you can use to connect to a computer from another location and then work with the computer as though you were sitting at the keyboard.

Getting Help from Another Person

When you want to get help from others, you must create a Remote Assistance invitation and then make this invitation available to the person from whom you want help. The easiest way to do this is to create an email invitation.

You can create a Remote Assistance invitation and send it to your helper by following these steps:

1. Click Start and then click Help and Support.

2. In Windows Help and Support, click Windows Remote Assistance under Ask Someone. This starts the Windows Remote Assistance Wizard.

3. On the "How do you want to invite someone to help you?" page, shown in Figure 21-16, click "Invite someone you trust to help you" and then click "Use e-mail to send an invitation."

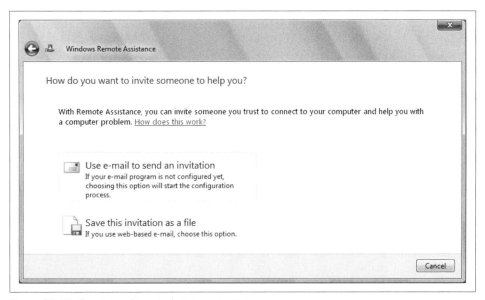

Figure 21-16. Creating a Remote Assistance invitation

4. On the "Choose a password" page, enter and confirm a secure password that is at least six characters long. This password is used by the person you are inviting and is valid only for this Remote Assistance session.

5. When you click Next, Windows Vista starts your default mail program and creates an email message with the invitation, as shown in Figure 21-17.

6. In the To field, type the email address of the person you are inviting and then click Send.

Once you've sent the invitation via email, the Windows Remote Assistance dialog box is displayed, as shown in Figure 21-18. This dialog box provides the following options:

Cancel
Cancels the Remote Assistance request by not allowing the invitation to be used.

Start/Stop sharing
Starts or stops sharing control of the computer with the helper.

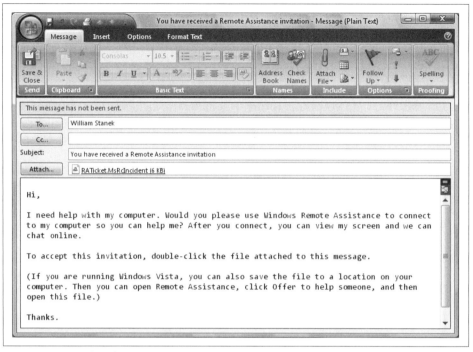

Figure 21-17. Sending the invitation to your helper

Pause/Resume
Pause temporarily hides your computer's screen from the helper. Resume restores the helper's view of your computer screen.

Settings
Allows you to configure the session settings.

Chat
Opens a chat window for sending messages between you and the helper.

Send file
Transfers a file to the helper's computer.

Figure 21-18. Controlling the Remote Assistance session

As long as you've allowed remote control of your computer, the helper will have a similar set of controls and will be able to access your desktop and Start menu, allowing her to fix your computer much like she could if she were sitting at the keyboard. If you haven't allowed remote control of your computer, the helper will only be able to view your desktop and guide you through chat.

 For Windows Vista, Remote Assistance has been enhanced in several ways. First, two people can now simultaneously connect to a computer for troubleshooting. Second, if troubleshooting requires that the computer be restarted, the Remote Assistance session is reestablished automatically after the computer reboots.

Giving Other People Assistance

Just as you can use Remote Assistance to get help, you can use Remote Assistance to help other people. Have the person send you a Remote Assistance invitation via email. When you receive the email, double-click the invitation attached to the message. You'll then see a Windows Remote Assistance dialog box with a view of the other person's computer. As long as the person has allowed remote control, the view will have a similar set of controls as previously discussed, and will provide complete access to the person's desktop and Start menu, allowing you to fix the person's problem much like you could if you were sitting at the keyboard.

If you know that a user is having problems with her computer, you can follow these steps to offer remote assistance rather than waiting for an invitation:

1. Click the Help and Support Home button on the toolbar and then click Remote Assistance under Ask Someone.

2. In the Remote Assistance Wizard, click "Offer to help someone."

3. Type the name or IP address of the computer you want to assist. The computer must be configured to accept Remote Assistance offers.

4. Click Finish.

Connecting to Your Computer Remotely

Sometimes you may want to be able to connect remotely to your computer. For example, if you are at home, you may want to be able to access files on your work computer. Or if you are at work, on vacation, or out wherever, you may want to be able to access files on your home computer. To access your computer remotely, you can use Remote Desktop.

You can make a Remote Desktop connection to your computer by following these steps:

1. Click Start → All Programs → Accessories → Remote Desktop Connection. This displays the Remote Desktop Connection dialog box, shown in Figure 21-19.

Figure 21-19. Connecting to a remote computer

2. In the Computer field, type the name of the remote computer or its IP address. For a connection over the Internet, you'll need to use the IP address in most cases (when connecting to your home computer from other places, this is the public IP address assigned by your ISP).

3. Click Connect. Your screen will go black for a moment except for a title bar at the top.

4. When you see the logon dialog box, enter the username and password of an account that is a member of the Remote Desktop Users group, and then click OK.

5. If the account is already logged on to the remote computer, the desktop on the computer will lock and you'll then see the current desktop as though you were sitting at the keyboard.

6. If someone is already logged on to the remote computer, you'll see a prompt telling you that the other person will be disconnected. Click Yes to continue. The user will then see a prompt asking if she wants to allow the connection. If she clicks Yes, she'll be logged off similar to what happens when you use fast user switching. The user can resume her logon session later.

When you've connected successfully, you'll see the Remote Desktop window on the selected computer, and you'll be able to work with resources on the computer. While you are using the remote computer, the remote computer shows the welcome screen with your account listed as being logged on and locked. A person with physical access to the remote computer cannot see what you're doing at the local computer. Keep in mind that firewalls can prevent successful remote desktop connections. Transmission Control Protocol (TCP) port 3389 must be open to any firewall between your local computer and the remote computer.

Troubleshooting Windows Vista Programs and Features

Windows Vista has so many features and components that you are bound to run into problems occasionally that I don't address in other sections of this book. When you run into these problems, please refer to this section for possible solutions for everything from installation to playback in Windows Media Player.

Resolving Problems with Programs and Features

Table 21-2 provides an extensive list of problems you may encounter while working with Windows Vista. The table is organized alphabetically by program or issue, followed by details on problems you may encounter and possible resolutions to those problems. In some cases, the resolution details will also point to a specific page within the Microsoft Knowledge Base where you can look to find more information.

Table 21-2. Troubleshooting Windows Vista programs and features

Program/Issue	Problem/Resolution
16-bit DOS-based programs	Some 16-bit DOS-based programs and the Command Prompt will not run in full-screen mode in Windows Vista. This issue occurs because Windows Vista device drivers do not support running all of the DOS video modes. The Vista device drivers are based on the Windows Vista Display Driver Model (WDDM). To resolve this problem, you may need to install a Windows XP version of the video drivers for your video adapter.
Activation expires	You see an error stating "Your activation period has expired" or that you have a "non-genuine version of Windows Vista installed." If you have not activated Windows Vista in the time allowed or you are running a nongenuine version of Windows Vista, Windows Vista will run in a reduced functionality mode. If you modify the computer hardware so that Windows Vista determines that it is running on a different computer, Windows Vista will also run in a reduced functionality mode. You'll need to activate and validate Windows Vista as necessary to resume full functionality mode. See *http://support.microsoft.com/kb/925582/en-us* for more information.
Activation fails	Activation of Windows Vista fails over the Internet. If you connect to the Internet through a proxy server where Basic authentication is enabled, you will not be able to activate Windows Vista. Change the authentication method or see KB. Alternatively, when the Windows Activation Wizard prompts you, click Use the Automated Phone System and then activate Windows Vista over the telephone. See *http://support.microsoft.com/kb/921471/en-us* for more information.
Administrator account	The Administrator account does not appear on the Windows Vista Welcome screen. In Windows Vista, the built-in Administrator account is disabled by default and you cannot use it to log on to the computer in safe mode. However, during an upgrade, if the built-in Administrator account is the only active local Administrator account, Windows Vista leaves the built-in Administrator account enabled and puts this account into Admin Approval mode. See *http://support.microsoft.com/kb/926183/en-us* for more information.
ATM network adapters	You receive an error message when you start Windows Vista after you install an ATM network adapter. This error occurs because Windows Vista does not support ATM.

Table 21-2. Troubleshooting Windows Vista programs and features (continued)

Program/Issue	Problem/Resolution
Audio playback	You lose audio playback after you unplug a USB audio device, such as a microphone or headphones. This problem occurs because Windows Media Player does not detect that the USB audio device has been removed. To resolve this issue, stop and restart the media player or restart the computer after you unplug a USB audio device.
BitLocker Drive Encryption	You see a "BitLocker Drive Encryption key needed" error message when your computer resumes from hibernation. This occurs because the BitLocker Drive Encryption feature expects the USB key to be inserted prior to you waking the computer. As prompted, insert the USB key and then press the Esc key to reboot. To avoid this problem in the future, insert the USB key prior to waking the computer.
Burning discs	When you try to burn a disc, Windows Media Player doesn't recognize your DVD-RAM. This error occurs because you can't use Windows Media Player to burn DVD-RAM discs. You'll need to use Windows Explorer to burn DVD-RAM discs.
Computer names	After you change the name of a computer, other computers can continue to access the computer by using the previous name of the computer. This occurs because the computer name is stored in the DNS cache. At an elevated command prompt, flush the DNS cache by typing `ipconfig /flushdns`.
Connecting computers	You cannot use a serial cable connection to connect a Windows XP-based computer to a Windows Vista-based computer. To work around this issue, connect the computers using a network connection with Ethernet cables.
DHCP	Windows Vista cannot obtain an IP address from a router or non-Microsoft Dynamic Host Configuration Protocol (DHCP) server. This can occur due to a design difference in the way DHCP is implemented. See *http://support.microsoft.com/kb/928233/en-us* for more information.
Digital still cameras	A digital still camera is not recognized. Windows Vista uses the Windows Image Acquisition (WIA) standard instead of the Windows Portable Devices (WPD) standard to import pictures and videos. To resolve this problem, configure the camera to use the Picture Transfer Protocol (PTP) standard instead of the WIA standard. See the owner's manual for the camera to configure the camera to use the PTP standard.
Digital video cameras	When you are changing modes, Windows Movie Maker incorrectly detects the mode of a digital video camera. This can occur if you quickly switch between the Camera, Off, VCR, and Memory modes. To avoid this problem, pause momentarily after switching from one mode to another and before switching to another mode.
Disk drives with large sectors	Windows Vista supports large-sector hard disk drives. Newer hard disk drives may contain physical sector sizes that are larger than the traditional 512 bytes per sector. If the drive uses an emulation mode to support these large-sector sizes, your applications should continue to work without problems. If the drive doesn't use an emulation mode, some of your applications may not work. See *http://support.microsoft.com/kb/923332/en-us* for more information.
EAP-MD5	Extensible Authentication Protocol-Message Digest 5 (EAP-MD5) doesn't work. In Windows Vista, EAP-MD5 has been deprecated and is not enabled. You can reenable support for EAP-MD5. See *http://support.microsoft.com/kb/922574/en-us* for more information.
Favorites in Internet Explorer	In Internet Explorer, Windows Vista does not let you type a favorite name that is longer than 221 characters. Make sure that the name of the new favorite is no longer than 221 characters.
Fingerprint readers	You cannot use a fingerprint reader or another biometric device to log on after you upgrade to Windows Vista. Windows Vista does not support the Graphical Identification and Authentication (GINA) components that the device requires. Install drivers for the device that are compatible with Windows Vista.

Program/Issue	Problem/Resolution
FireWire devices	In Windows Explorer or other interfaces, you cannot see a specific FireWire (IEEE 1394a) device that you've connected to the computer. To resolve this issue, see *http://support.microsoft.com/kb/927827/en-us* for more information.
GINA/biometrics	Custom GINA modules do not work after you upgrade your computer to Windows Vista. This occurs because GINA functionality that existed in earlier versions of Windows is replaced by a credential provider model in Windows Vista. See *http://support.microsoft.com/kb/925520/en-us* for more information.
Help (*.hlp*) files	Windows Vista won't display Help (*.hlp*) files. The Windows Help program (WinHlp32.exe) is not included in Windows Vista. Windows Help is no longer supported. See *http://support.microsoft.com/kb/917607/en-us* for more information.
Hosts and Lmhosts	You cannot modify the Hosts or Lmhosts file in Windows Vista. This occurs because the program you are using must be in elevated mode to save the edited files. Before opening the Hosts or Lmhosts file, right-click the program shortcut and then select Run As Administrator.
Installation	Installation media is not recognized when you try to install Windows Vista. If the media is damaged, you'll need to obtain replacement media. Otherwise, make sure that the CD or DVD drive is configured as a startup device in the BIOS and that you are inserting the media into the appropriate CD or DVD drive.
Installation	During installation, you are unable to select the hard disk you want to use. This issue can occur if the hard disk partition contains an invalid byte offset value. To resolve this issue, you'll need to follow the procedure discussed in the "Removing Disk Partitions During Installation" section, later in this chapter.
Installation	During installation of Windows Vista, you see an "Error: uncaught exception" message. This error can occur if there are problems with the selected disk partitions. To resolve this problem, you'll need to remove the partitions, as discussed previously.
Installation	During installation of Windows Vista, you cannot select or format a hard disk partition. If the partition is formatted with FAT32 or has other incompatible settings, this may be causing the problem. To work around this issue, you may want to boot to the current operating system, convert the partition to NTFS, and then restart the installation. As this could also be due to a problem with the drivers for the hard disk, you may need to boot to the current operating system, update the disk drivers, and then restart the installation.
Installation	During installation, you see a "This computer's hardware may not support booting to this disk" message. This can occur if the disk has not been initialized for use or if the BIOS of the computer does not support starting the operating system from the selected disk. To resolve this problem, create one or more partitions on all the hard disks that are not initialized and then restart the installation.
Language/Keyboard	Only one keyboard layout is available during installation. If your keyboard language and the language edition of Windows Vista you are installing are different, you may see unexpected characters as you type. Ensure that you select the correct keyboard language to avoid this.
Language/Keyboard	Some user interface items are not displayed in the correct language after you change the display language. This occurs because Windows Vista cannot update language settings for currently running processes. To resolve this problem, restart your computer.
Language/Keyboard	You see an incorrect display language when you use elevated permissions to open a dialog box. This can occur because Windows Vista uses the preferred user interface language of the administrator whose credentials you provide. This language may differ from your preferred user interface language.

Table 21-2. Troubleshooting Windows Vista programs and features (continued)

Program/Issue	Problem/Resolution
Live File System	The available space on a Live File System disc is less than the capacity of the disc. This issue occurs because the Live File System reserves a small amount of disc space to accommodate link-loss area. In contrast, the Universal Disc Format (UDF) file system reserves at least 10 percent of the reported capacity of the disc for sparing. See *http://support.microsoft.com/kb/928353/en-us* for more information.
Mf.sys devices	You cannot install a device that requires the Mf.sys device driver in Windows Vista. The Mf.sys device driver is not installed in Windows Vista by default. See *http://support.microsoft.com/kb/926171/en-us* for more information.
Network Map	In Windows Vista, Network Map does not display computers that are running Windows XP. This occurs because the Link-Layer Topology Discovery (LLTD) Responder component is not installed on most Windows XP-based computers. You can download and install this component from the Microsoft web site. See *http://support.microsoft.com/kb/922120/en-us* for more information.
Networking programs	Third-party networking programs that use NDIS drivers no longer function after you upgrade to Windows Vista. To resolve this issue, you must reinstall the networking program. This will ensure that the third-party NDIS driver is installed and configured correctly.
Playing DVDs	A DVD+RW or DVD-RW video disc that was formatted on a Windows Vista-based computer is not recognized by a DVD player that supports DVD+RW or DVD-RW video discs. This problem can occur if Windows Vista uses a version of the UDF that the DVD player does not support. See Chapter 9 for details on how to set the UDF version used by Windows Vista.
Playing DVDs	A video DVD does not appear in the correct aspect ratio in Windows Media Player on a Tablet PC. This problem may occur when you view the DVD in portrait mode. To resolve the problem, set the display to landscape mode.
RAW image files	You cannot view RAW image files after you copy them from a camera to your computer. This issue occurs if you do not have a RAW image codec for your camera model installed in Windows Vista. To resolve this issue, install a Windows Vista-compatible RAW image codec that either supports the camera model or is from the camera manufacturer.
Recording DVDs	You cannot record more data to a recordable DVD after you format and then eject the disc. This issue occurs because Windows Vista automatically closes a disc when you eject it. Closing a disc lets you use it in another computer or device. If you don't want Windows Vista to automatically close sessions, see the "Changing Disc Close on Eject Settings" section, later in this chapter, for a workaround.
Slide show playback	On a Tablet PC, the screen goes black when you switch the screen orientation during slide show playback. To resolve this problem, exit the slide show before you change the screen orientation, and then restart the slide show. Or press the Esc key to restore the original screen orientation.
Sound Recorder	You do not hear any sound when you play back a recording that was recorded with the Sound Recorder. This can occur because the default volume of microphones is 0 dB. To resolve this problem, adjust the volume for the microphone, as discussed in Chapter 5.
Speech Recognition	Speech Recognition does not appear to be using the correct language. Speech Recognition is only available in U.S. English, U.K. English, French, German, Spanish, Japanese, and Chinese versions of Windows Vista. Because of the way Speech Recognition is integrated into the operating system, the feature cannot be removed from versions of Windows Vista for which Speech Recognition is unavailable.

Program/Issue	Problem/Resolution
Speech Recognition commands	You cannot use Speech Recognition in Windows Vista to select commands on floating toolbars in Microsoft Office. With Speech Recognition, you can select commands on docked toolbars in Microsoft Office. Dock the toolbars to resolve the problem.
USB audio devices	You are unable to hear the audio from a newly connected USB audio device in Windows Media Player 11. To resolve this issue, restart Windows Media Player 11.
USB drives	A USB drive does not appear in the Windows Connect Now window. This behavior occurs if the USB drive uses the NTFS filesystem format and you do not have permission to write to the root directory of the drive. To avoid this problem, use a device that uses the File Allocation Table (FAT) filesystem format.
USB storage devices	A connected USB storage device does not appear when you click the Safely Remove Hardware icon in the notification area in Windows Vista. This problem can occur if the USB device has an embedded USB hub. In this case, you may be able to manage the device in the Computer console or you may need to shut down the computer before removing the device.
User Account Control	You encounter an unexpected error or behavior when you try to perform a task that requires elevated privileges. This issue can occur if UAC is turned off. To resolve this issue, turn UAC on, as discussed in Chapter 18.
Windows Complete PC Restore	You receive a version error message when you use the Windows Complete PC Restore program to restore a computer. If you try to restore a computer using a 64-bit version of Windows Vista using a 32-bit installation disc, you will see an error stating "This version of System Recovery Options is not compatible with the version of Windows you are trying to repair. Try using a recovery disc that is compatible with this version of Windows." To resolve this issue, start recovery using a 64-bit installation disc.
Windows Explorer menu bar	When you view files and folders by using Windows Explorer, the Windows Explorer menu bar is not displayed. To display the menu bar, press the Alt key. Press the Alt key again to hide the menu bar.
Windows Media Player	You see an "Invalid File Format" error message when you play a file in Windows Media Player. This can occur if you are trying to play a file type that Windows Media Player doesn't support. It can also occur if the file is damaged. See Chapter 8 for more information on Windows Media Player's supported file formats. If the file is in a supported format and is not damaged, you may need to reinstall Windows Media Player and then reinstall or upgrade to the latest version of Microsoft DirectX. See *http://support.microsoft.com/kb/924073/en-us* for more information.
Windows Movie Maker	You receive a "Movie Maker has stopped working" error message when you try to start Windows Movie Maker. An incompatible video filter is installed on the computer. Resolve this problem using the techniques discussed in the "Removing an Incompatible Video Filter" section, later in this chapter.
Windows Movie Maker	A file you've imported into Windows Movie Maker does not play correctly in Windows Vista. This issue can occur if the video codec that is required to play the file is not installed on the computer. To resolve this problem, install the program used to create the file or install the related codec.
Windows startup	In a dual-boot configuration, Windows XP does not start if you subsequently format or delete the partition on which Windows Vista is installed. This occurs because Windows Vista uses a different startup method than Windows XP does. To resolve this problem, you'll need to repair your Windows XP installation by starting an installation and selecting the Repair option. See *http://support.microsoft.com/kb/922809/en-us* for more information.

Table 21-2. Troubleshooting Windows Vista programs and features (continued)

Program/Issue	Problem/Resolution
Windows Vista startup	Windows Vista won't start after you install an earlier version of the Windows operating system in a dual-boot configuration. See the next section, "Restoring the Windows Vista Boot Sector" for more information.
Wireless adapters	When running on battery, you experience connectivity or performance issues when you connect to a wireless access point. This can occur if the wireless access point doesn't support the 802.11 power save protocol. To resolve this issue, connect the computer to a power source or change the power saving options for the wireless adapter to use the Maximum Performance power saving mode.

Restoring the Windows Vista Boot Sector

Windows Vista won't start after you install an earlier version of the Windows operating system in a dual-boot configuration. This occurs because Windows Vista uses a different startup method than earlier versions of Windows do. You must restore the Windows Vista boot sector and allow dual boot by following these steps:

1. Click Start, click Accessories, right-click the command prompt, and then click Run As Administrator.

2. Restore the Windows Vista boot code by typing the following command at a command prompt: **DriveLetter:\boot\Bootsect.exe –NT60 All**, where **DriveLetter** is the actual letter of the drive on which Windows Vista is installed.

3. Allow booting of the earlier operating system by typing the following commands at a command prompt, where *DriveLetter* is the actual letter of the drive on which Windows Vista is installed:

   ```
   DriveLetter:\Windows\system32\Bcdedit –create {ntldr} –d "Description for earlier
       Windows version."
   DriveLetter:\Windows\system32\Bcdedit –set {ntldr} device partition=DriveLetter:
   DriveLetter:\Windows\system32\Bcdedit –set {ntldr} path \ntldr
   DriveLetter:\Windows\system32\Bcdedit –displayorder {ntldr} –addlast
   ```

4. Restart the computer.

Removing an Incompatible Video Filter

If you are unable to start Windows Movie Maker, you may see a "Movie Maker has stopped working" error message. In this case, an incompatible video filter probably is installed on the computer. To resolve this problem, start Movie Maker in safe mode, and then remove the incompatible video filter. To do this, follow these steps:

1. Click Start → All Programs → Accessories, and then click Command Prompt.

2. At the command prompt, type **CD "c:\program files\movie maker"**, and then press Enter.

3. Type **moviemk.exe /safemode**, and then press Enter.

4. When Movie Maker starts, click Tools, and then click Options.

5. On the Compatibility tab in the Options dialog box, clear the checkboxes of any third-party video filters that are not required, and then click OK.

Changing Disc Close on Eject Settings

In Windows Vista, closing a disc session lets you use it in another computer or device. If you don't want Windows Vista to automatically close sessions, follow these steps:

1. Click Start and then click Computer.

2. Right-click the writable DVD drive, and then click Properties.

3. In the Properties dialog box, click the Recording tab, and then click Global Settings.

4. Clear the "Automatically close the current UDF session when the disc is ejected" checkbox and then click OK twice.

Removing Disk Partitions During Installation

During installation, you may be unable to select the hard disk you want to use. This issue can occur if the hard disk partition contains an invalid byte offset value. To resolve this issue, you'll need to remove the partitions on the hard disk (which destroys all associated data) and then create the necessary partition using the advanced options in the Setup program. During installation on the "Where do you want to install Windows?" page, you can remove unrecognized hard disk partitions by following these steps:

1. Press Shift-F10 to start a command prompt.

2. At the command prompt, type **diskpart**.

3. To view a list of disks on the computer, type **list disk**.

4. Select a disk by typing select **disk *DiskNumber*** where ***DiskNumber*** is the number of the disk you want to work with.

5. To permanently remove the partitions on the selected disk, type **clean**.

6. When the cleaning process finishes, type **exit** to exit the DiskPart tool.

7. Type **exit** to exit the command prompt.

8. Restart the computer, and then start the Windows Vista installation.

PART V

Advanced Tips and Techniques

CHAPTER 22

Installing and Running Windows Vista

Windows Vista is the latest version of the Windows operating system for personal computers. Unlike earlier releases of Windows, Windows Vista is hardware-independent and ships on media as a modular disk image.

Thanks to Windows Vista's new hardware-independent architecture, all editions of Windows Vista except the Starter Edition support both 32-bit and 64-bit hardware. This means that you can use every product edition except the Starter Edition with computers that have 32-bit x86, 64-bit (IA-64), and 64-bit extension architectures. During installation, the setup program detects your computer's architecture and installs the components appropriately.

Thanks to Windows Vista's modular disk image, all editions of Windows Vista ship on the same media. This means that you can use any Windows Vista media disk to install any Windows Vista edition. The product key you provide during installation is what determines the edition and the features of Windows Vista that are installed.

Comparing Windows Vista Features and Versions

Windows Vista is available in six main editions:

Windows Vista Starter
    A budget edition of Windows Vista for emerging markets

Windows Vista Home Basic
    A budget edition of Windows Vista for home users with basic entertainment features

Windows Vista Home Premium
    An enhanced edition of Windows Vista with premium entertainment features

Windows Vista Business
    A basic edition of Windows Vista for use in Windows domains

Windows Vista Enterprise
> An enhanced edition of Windows Vista for use in Windows domains with extended management features

Windows Vista Ultimate
> An enhanced edition of Windows Vista with all the available home user and business user features

Only Business, Enterprise, and Ultimate have the components needed to join a Windows domain. Table 22-1 provides an overview of the differences among these editions. Supported features are listed with a "Yes" entry. Standard features that all Windows Vista editions support are not listed.

Table 22-1. Differences among Windows Vista editions

Windows Vista feature	Windows Vista edition				
	Home Basic	Home Premium	Business	Enterprise	Ultimate
All worldwide user interface languages				Yes	Yes
Backup of user files to network device		Yes	Yes	Yes	Yes
BitLocker Drive Encryption				Yes	Yes
Centralized power management through Group Policy			Yes	Yes	Yes
Client-side caching			Yes	Yes	Yes
Control over installation of device drivers			Yes	Yes	Yes
Desktop deployment tools for managed networks			Yes	Yes	Yes
Encrypting File System (EFS)			Yes	Yes	Yes
Folder redirection			Yes	Yes	Yes
Group Policy support			Yes	Yes	Yes
Integrated smart card management			Yes	Yes	Yes
Internet Information Server			Yes	Yes	Yes
Join a Windows domain			Yes	Yes	Yes
Maximum RAM on 32-bit systems	4 GB	4 GB	4 GB	4 GB	4 GB
Maximum RAM on 64-bit systems	8 GB	16 GB	128+ GB	128+ GB	128+ GB
Multiple user interface languages				Yes	Yes
Network Access Protection Client Agent			Yes	Yes	Yes
Network projection		Yes	Yes	Yes	Yes
Offline file and folder support			Yes	Yes	Yes
PC-to-PC sync		Yes	Yes	Yes	Yes
Pluggable logon authentication architecture			Yes	Yes	Yes
Policy-based quality of service for networking			Yes	Yes	Yes
Presentation settings		Yes	Yes	Yes	Yes

Table 22-1. Differences among Windows Vista editions (continued)

Windows Vista feature	Windows Vista edition				
Remote desktop	Client only	Client only	Client and host	Client and host	Client and host
Rights Management Services Client			Yes	Yes	Yes
Roaming user profiles			Yes	Yes	Yes
Scheduled backup of user files		Yes	Yes	Yes	Yes
Small-business resources			Yes		Yes
Subsystem for Unix-based applications				Yes	Yes
Support for Media Center Extenders					
System image-based backup and recovery			Yes	Yes	Yes
Themed slide shows		Yes			Yes
Two-processor support			Yes	Yes	Yes
Virtual PC Express				Yes	Yes
Windows Aero		Yes	Yes	Yes	Yes
Windows Anytime Upgrade	Yes	Yes	Yes		
Windows DVD Maker		Yes			Yes
Windows Fax and Scan			Yes	Yes	Yes
Windows Media Center		Yes			Yes
Windows Meeting Space	View only	Yes	Yes	Yes	Yes
Windows Mobility Center	Partial	Partial	Yes	Yes	Yes
Windows Movie Maker	Yes	Yes			Yes
Windows Movie Maker HD		Yes			Yes
Windows Shadow Copy			Yes	Yes	Yes
Windows SideShow		Yes	Yes	Yes	Yes
Windows Tablet PC support		Yes	Yes	Yes	Yes
Wireless network provisioning			Yes	Yes	Yes
Xbox 360		Yes			Yes

Installing Windows Vista

You can install Windows Vista on new hardware or as an upgrade. When you install Windows Vista on a computer with an existing operating system, you can perform either a clean installation or an upgrade. With a clean installation, the Windows Vista Setup program completely replaces the original operating system on the computer, and all user or application settings are lost. With an upgrade, the Windows Vista Setup program performs a clean installation of the operating system followed by a migration of user settings, documents, and applications from the earlier version of Windows.

Before you install Windows Vista, you should make sure that your computer meets the minimum requirements of the edition you plan to use. Microsoft provides both minimum requirements and recommended requirements. If your computer doesn't meet the minimum requirements, you will not be able to install Windows Vista. If your computer doesn't meet the recommended requirements, you will experience performance issues.

Windows Vista Starter and Home Basic editions require a minimum of 512 MB of RAM, an 800 MHz or higher processor, and a graphics processor that supports DirectX 9. For Windows Vista Home Premium, Business, Enterprise, and Ultimate editions, you'll have a better experience and get better performance if the computer has at least 1 GB of RAM, a 1.0 GHz 32-bit (x86) or 64-bit (x64) processor, and a graphics processor with 128 MB of graphics memory that supports DirectX 9. Although Business, Enterprise, and Ultimate provide two-processor support, Home Basic and Home Premium do not.

Windows Vista requires 4 GB or more of disk space. Additional features, such as protection points that include previous versions of files and folders that have been modified, can increase the size of the installation over time. You'll also want at least 10 percent of free space on your disk at all times.

You can run Windows Vista on any computer that meets or exceeds these requirements. If you run into problems during installation, see the section, "Troubleshooting Windows Vista Programs and Features," in Chapter 21, for possible solutions. During installation on the "Where do you want to install Windows?" page, you can display a command prompt by pressing Shift-F10.

Performing a Clean Installation

To perform a clean installation of Windows Vista, complete the following steps:

1. Start the Setup program using one of the following techniques:

   - For a new installation, turn on the computer and insert the Windows Vista distribution media into the computer's CD-ROM or DVD-ROM drive. Press a key to start Setup from your media when prompted.

   - For a clean installation over an existing installation, start the computer and log on using an account with administrator privileges. Insert the Windows Vista distribution media into the computer's CD-ROM or DVD-ROM drive. Setup should start automatically. If it doesn't, use Windows Explorer to access the distribution media and then double-click Setup.exe.

2. When prompted, choose your language, time and currency format, and keyboard layout. Click Next.

3. Start the installation by clicking Install Now. If you are starting the installation from an existing operating system and are connected to a network or the Internet,

choose whether to get updates during the installation. Click either "Go online to get the latest updates for installation" or "Do not get the latest updates for installation."

4. If prompted for a product key, enter the product key and then click Next.

5. Read the license terms. Click "I accept the license terms (required to use Windows)" and then click Next.

6. Since you are performing a clean installation over an existing installation, select "Custom (advanced)" as the installation type.

7. Choose the disk drive on which you want to install the operating system and then click Next.

8. If the disk you've selected contains a previous Windows installation, Setup provides a prompt stating that existing user and application settings will be moved to a folder named *Windows.old* and that you must copy these settings to the new installation to use them. Click OK.

9. Setup starts the installation of the operating system. During this procedure, Setup copies the full disk image of Windows Vista to the location you've selected and then expands it. Afterward, Setup installs features based on the computer's configuration and detected hardware. This process requires several automatic restarts. When Setup finishes the installation, the operating system will be loaded and you can complete the installation.

10. You must next create a local machine account that will be created as a computer administrator account. Enter a username. Type and then confirm a password. Enter an optional password hint and then choose a picture for the account. Click Next.

11. Type a computer name and select a desktop background. Click Next.

12. Select a Windows Update option for the computer. Usually, you'll want to use the recommended settings to allow Windows Vista to automatically install all available updates and security tools as they become available. Choose "Ask me later" only if you want to disable Windows Update.

13. Setup displays the date and time settings, and then makes changes as necessary. Click Next.

14. If a network card was detected during setup, networking components were installed automatically. Because of this, you'll need to configure each detected network connection:

   • Depending on the type of location and connection, click Home for a home network, Work for a network in a workplace, or Public Location for a public network. Windows Vista will then configure networking as appropriate for this location.

   • If there are multiple networks, you'll see a prompt for each network. You can configure each detected network in a different way.

15. Click Start. Windows Vista will check the computer performance and assign a performance rating.

16. When the operating system starts, you'll see the Welcome Center.

Performing an Upgrade Installation

Although Windows Vista provides an upgrade option during installation, an upgrade with Windows Vista isn't what you think it is. With an upgrade, the Windows Vista Setup program performs a clean installation of the operating system followed by a migration of user settings, documents, and applications from the earlier version of Windows.

During the migration portion of the upgrade, Setup moves folders and files for the previous installation to a folder named *Windows.old*. As a result, the previous installation will no longer run. Settings are migrated because Windows Vista doesn't store user and application information in the same way as earlier versions of Windows do. See Chapter 1 for more information on where Windows Vista stores user data.

To perform an upgrade installation of Windows Vista, complete the following steps:

1. Start the computer and log on using an account with administrator privileges. Insert the Windows Vista distribution media into the computer's CD-ROM or DVD-ROM drive. Setup should start automatically. If Setup doesn't start automatically, use Windows Explorer to access the distribution media and then double-click Setup.exe.

2. Start the installation by clicking Install Now.

3. Choose whether to get updates during the installation. Click either "Go online to get the latest updates for installation" or "Do not get the latest updates for installation."

4. If prompted for a product key, enter the product key and then click Next.

5. Read the license terms. Click "I accept the license terms (required to use Windows)" and then click Next.

6. Since you are performing a clean installation over an existing installation, select the installation type as Upgrade.

7. Setup will start the installation. During this process, Setup copies the full disk image of Windows Vista to the disk you've selected and then expands it. Afterward, Setup installs features based on the computer's configuration and detected hardware. When Setup finishes the installation, the operating system will be loaded and you can complete the installation.

8. Select a Windows Update option for the computer. Typically, you'll want to use the recommended settings to allow Windows Vista to automatically install all

available updates and security tools as they become available. If you choose "Ask me later," Windows Update will be disabled.

9. Review the date and time settings, and then make changes as necessary. Click Next.

10. If a network card was detected during setup, networking components were installed automatically. Depending on the type of location you are at, click Home, Work, or Public Location. Windows Vista will then configure networking for this location.

11. Click Start. Windows Vista will check the computer performance and assign a performance rating.

12. When the operating system starts, you'll see the Welcome Center.

Upgrading Your Windows Vista Edition

You can easily upgrade Windows Vista editions from one edition to another. Table 22-2 provides an overview of the upgrade paths you can use to upgrade from basic editions to the enhanced editions.

Table 22-2. Upgrade options for Windows Vista editions

Windows Vista Edition	Upgrades to...
Windows Vista Home Basic	Windows Vista Home Premium, Windows Vista Ultimate
Windows Vista Home Premium	Windows Vista Ultimate
Windows Vista Business	Windows Vista Enterprise, Windows Vista Ultimate
Windows Vista Enterprise	Windows Vista Ultimate

You can upgrade the edition installed on a computer by clicking Start → Control Panel → System and Maintenance. On the System and Maintenance page, click "Find which version of Windows you are using" under Welcome Center. Once you've determined the Windows Vista edition you are running and have determined that an edition upgrade is possible, you can begin your upgrade.

You can perform an edition upgrade using the built-in Windows Anytime Upgrade feature or a Windows Anytime Upgrade disk:

- To start an upgrade using the built-in Windows Anytime Upgrade feature, click Start and then click Control Panel. In the Control Panel, click System and Maintenance and then click Windows Anytime Upgrade. To complete the upgrade, you'll access the Microsoft web site, where you can purchase the upgrade and find instructions for upgrading. You'll need the Windows Vista distribution media. The distribution media contains the components for all Windows Vista versions, and it is the product key you provide to unlock and install the features for a specific version.

- To start an upgrade using a Windows Anytime Upgrade disk, start your computer and then insert the upgrade disk you've purchased. You'll need the Windows Vista distribution media. The distribution media contains the components for all Windows Vista versions, and it is the product key you provide to unlock and install the features for a specific version.

Once you've completed the upgrade, your computer will be running the new edition and will have all the features of this edition.

CHAPTER 23

Exploring the Windows Boot Environment

Unlike earlier releases of Windows, Windows Vista uses a preoperating system boot environment. At the core of this boot environment is the Boot Configuration Data (BCD) data store, which contains boot configuration parameters and controls how the operating system is started. The preboot environment provides a fundamental change in the way computers running Windows Vista are started. If you understand how this preboot environment works, you'll be better prepared to work with and troubleshoot Windows Vista installations. Be sure to read this chapter before you install an earlier version of Windows on a computer running Windows Vista.

Introducing the Windows Vista Boot Environment

Windows computers can use several different processor architectures and several different disk partitioning styles. Generally, computers with x86-based processors use the MBR disk partitioning style and BIOS. Computers with x64-based processors use the GUID Partition Table (GPT) disk partitioning style and Extensible Firmware Interface (EFI):

- BIOS-based computers use *Ntldr* and *Boot.ini* to boot into the operating system. *Ntldr* handles the task of loading the operating system. *Boot.ini* contains the parameters that enable startup, including identity of the boot partitions. Through *Boot.ini* parameters, you can add options that control the way the operating system starts, the way computer components are used, and the way operating system features are used.

- EFI-based computers use *Ia64ldr.efi*, *Diskpart.efi*, and *Nvrboot.efi* to boot into the operating system. *Ia64ldr.efi* handles the task of loading the operating system. *Diskpart.efi* identifies the boot partitions. *Nvrboot.efi* contains the parameters that enable startup.

Through *Boot.ini* or *Nvrboot.efi* parameters, you can add options that control the way the operating system starts, the way computer components are used, and the way operating system features are used. Windows Vista doesn't use these boot facilities. Instead, startup is controlled using the parameters in the BCD data store:

- Entries in the BCD data store identify the boot manager to use during startup and the specific boot applications available.
- Windows Boot Manager controls the boot experience and enables you to choose which boot application is run.
- Boot applications load a specific operating system or operating system version. For example, a Windows Boot Loader application loads Windows Vista.

Because BCD abstracts the underlying firmware, you can boot BIOS-based and EFI-based computers in much the same way—just as you can computers based on other firmware models. The BCD store is contained in a file called the *BCD registry*. On BIOS-based operating systems, the BCD registry file is stored in the *\Boot\Bcd* directory of the active partition. On EFI-based operating systems, the BCD registry file is stored on the EFI system partition.

The BCD store contains multiple entries. On a BIOS-based computer, you'll see the following entries:

- One Windows Boot Manager entry. There is only one boot manager, so there is only one boot manager entry.
- One or more Windows Boot Loader application entries, with one for each Windows Vista operating system or later versions of Windows installed on the computer.
- One legacy operating system entry. The legacy entry is not for a boot application. This entry is used to initiate *Ntldr* and *Boot.ini* so that you can boot into a pre-Windows Vista operating system. If the computer has more than one pre-Windows Vista operating system, you'll be able to select the operating system to start after selecting the legacy operating system entry.

Working with Boot Configuration Data

Several tools are available to work with and manage the BCD, including the following:

- Startup and Recovery
- System Configuration utility
- BCD Editor

The sections that follow discuss how these tools are used.

Using the Startup and Recovery Dialog Box

The Startup and Recovery dialog box enables you to select the default operating system to start if you have multiple operating systems installed on your computer. You can also specify timeout values for operating system selection lists and recovery options.

You can access the Startup and Recovery dialog box by following these steps:

1. Click Start → Control Panel. In the Control Panel, click System and Maintenance and then click System.

2. In the System utility, click "Advanced system settings" in the left pane.

3. On the Advanced tab of the System properties dialog box, click Settings under Startup and Recovery. This displays the Startup and Recovery dialog box, as shown in Figure 23-1.

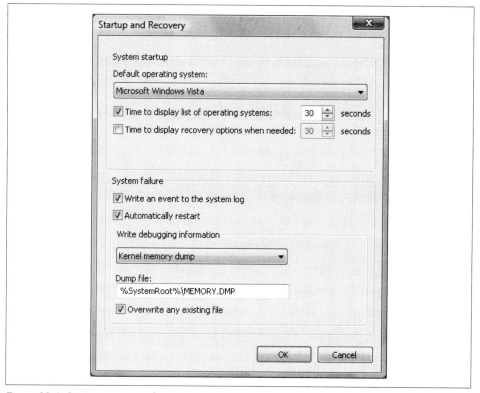

Figure 23-1. Setting startup and recovery options

4. Use the "Default operating system" drop-down list to specify the default operating system.

5. Set the timeout interval for the operating system list by selecting the "Time to display list of operating systems" checkbox and specifying a timeout in seconds in the field provided.

6. Set the timeout interval for the recovery options list by selecting the "Time to display recovery options when needed" checkbox and specifying a timeout in seconds in the field provided.

7. Click OK.

Using the System Configuration Utility

Using the System Configuration utility (*Msconfig.exe*), you can set the default operating system and control the way your computer starts. For example, you can configure the computer to start in Safe Mode or force the computer to use standard VGA display settings.

The basic steps for starting and using the System Configuration utility are as follows:

1. Click Start, type **msconfig.exe** in the Search box, and press Enter.
2. Select the Boot tab, as shown in Figure 23-2.

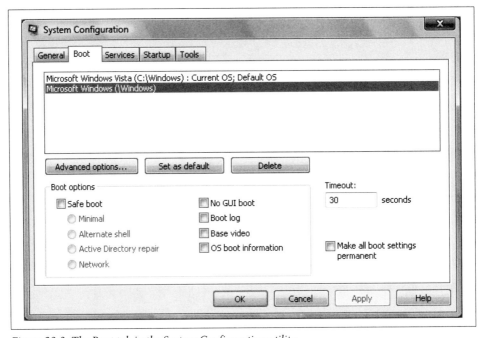

Figure 23-2. The Boot tab in the System Configuration utility

3. To set the default operating system, click the operating system you want to use and then click "Set as default."
4. To start the operating system in Safe Mode for troubleshooting, select the "Safe boot" checkbox and then set other troubleshooting options as appropriate.
5. Click OK to apply your changes.

If you are using the System Configuration utility for troubleshooting, you must later remove your selective startup options. After you restart the computer and resolve any problems, access the System Configuration utility again, select Normal Startup on the General tab, and then click OK.

Using the BCD Editor

The BCD Editor (*BCDEdit.exe*) is the only tool that gives you direct access to view and manage the BCD data store. You can use *BCDEdit* to view the entries in the BCD store by following these steps:

1. Click Start, click All Programs, and then click Accessories.
2. Right-click Command Prompt and then select Run As Administrator.
3. Type **bcdedit** at the command prompt.

Example 23-1 shows an example of the output from *BCDEdit*. As the listing shows, the BCD store for this computer has three entries: one for the Windows Boot Manager, one for the Windows Legacy OS Loader, and one for the Windows Boot Loader.

Example 23-1. Examining the contents of the BCD data store

```
Windows Boot Manager
--------------------
Identifier:          {bootmgr}
Type:                10100002
Device:              partition=C:
Description:         Windows Boot Manager
Locale:              en-US
Inherit options:     {globalsettings}
Boot debugger:       No
Default:             {current}
Resume application:  {23432149-a32e-132a-ba28-ed8322b34395}
Display order:       {ntldr}
                     {current}
Timeout:             30

Windows Legacy OS Loader
------------------------
Identifier:          {ntldr}
Type:                10300006
Device:              partition=C:
Path:                \ntldr
Description:         Legacy (pre-Longhorn) Microsoft Windows Operating System
Boot debugger:       No

Windows Boot Loader
-------------------
Identifier:          {current}
Type:                10200003
Device:              partition=D:
Path:                \Windows\system32\winload.exe
Description:         Microsoft Windows
Locale:              en-US
Inherit options:     {bootloadersettings}
```

Example 23-1. Examining the contents of the BCD data store (continued)

```
Boot debugger:          No
Windows device:         partition=D:
Windows root:           \Windows
Resume application:     {23432149-a32e-132a-ba28-ed8322b34395}
No Execute policy:      OptIn
No integrity checks:    Yes
Kernel debugger:        No
EMS enabled in OS:      No
```

The Windows Boot Loader entry has parameters that track the status of the No Execute (NX) policy, integrity checking, kernel debugger mode, and Emergency Management Services (EMS). Although the Windows Boot Manager, Windows Legacy OS Loader, and Windows Boot Loader are the primary types of entries that control startup, the BCD also stores information about preoperating system boot environment utilities and settings. If you want to view the BCD entries for utilities and settings, you use the following command line:

```
bcdedit /enum all /v
```

This command line enumerates all BCD entries, regardless of their current state, and lists them in Verbose Mode. Example 23-2 shows the verbose entries. It is important to note that Verbose Mode provides the actual value of the Globally Unique Identifiers (GUIDs) needed to manipulate entries in the BCD data store.

Example 23-2. Viewing extended BCD entries

```
Windows Boot Manager
--------------------
identifier              {9dea862c-5cdd-4e70-acc1-f32b344d4795}
device                  partition=C:
description             Windows Boot Manager
locale                  en-US
inherit                 {7ea2e1ac-2e61-4728-aaa3-896d9d0a9f0e}
bootdebug               No
default                 {263bf496-4ab4-11db-b478-c0671802252f}
resumeobject            {263bf497-4ab4-11db-b478-c0671802252f}
displayorder            {263bf496-4ab4-11db-b478-c0671802252f}
                        {0c728e1b-d009-11da-b18b-9dc1d02cdda0}
toolsdisplayorder       {b2721d73-1db4-4c62-bf78-c548a880142d}
timeout                 30

Windows Boot Loader
-------------------
identifier              {0c728e1b-d009-11da-b18b-9dc1d02cdda0}
device                  unknown
path                    \Windows\system32\winload.exe
description             Microsoft Windows
locale                  en-US
inherit                 {6efb52bf-1766-41db-a6b3-0ee5eff72bd7}
bootdebug               Yes
osdevice                unknown
```

Example 23-2. Viewing extended BCD entries (continued)

```
systemroot          \Windows
resumeobject        {0c728e1c-d009-11da-b18b-9dc1d02cdda0}
nx                  OptIn
quietboot           No
debug               No
ems                 No

Windows Boot Loader
-------------------
identifier          {263bf496-4ab4-11db-b478-c0671802252f}
device              partition=C:
path                \Windows\system32\winload.exe
description         Microsoft Windows Vista
locale              en-US
inherit             {6efb52bf-1766-41db-a6b3-0ee5eff72bd7}
osdevice            partition=C:
systemroot          \Windows
resumeobject        {263bf497-4ab4-11db-b478-c0671802252f}
nx                  OptIn

Resume from Hibernate
---------------------
identifier          {0c728e1c-d009-11da-b18b-9dc1d02cdda0}
device              unknown
path                \Windows\system32\winresume.exe
description         Windows Resume Application
locale              en-US
inherit             {1afa9c49-16ab-4a5c-901b-212802da9460}
bootdebug           Yes
filedevice          unknown
filepath            \hiberfil.sys
pae                 No
debugoptionenabled  No

Resume from Hibernate
---------------------
identifier          {263bf497-4ab4-11db-b478-c0671802252f}
device              partition=C:
path                \Windows\system32\winresume.exe
description         Windows Resume Application
locale              en-US
inherit             {1afa9c49-16ab-4a5c-901b-212802da9460}
filedevice          partition=C:
filepath            \hiberfil.sys
pae                 No
debugoptionenabled  No

Windows Memory Tester
---------------------
identifier          {b2721d73-1db4-4c62-bf78-c548a880142d}
device              partition=C:
path                \boot\memtest.exe
```

Example 23-2. Viewing extended BCD entries (continued)

```
description             Windows Memory Diagnostic
locale                  en-US
inherit                 {7ea2e1ac-2e61-4728-aaa3-896d9d0a9f0e}
badmemoryaccess         Yes
bootdebug               No

Windows Legacy OS Loader
------------------------
identifier              {466f5a88-0af2-4f76-9038-095b170dc21c}
device                  partition=C:
path                    \ntldr
description             Legacy (pre-Longhorn) Microsoft Windows Operating System

bootdebug               No

EMS Settings
------------
identifier              {0ce4991b-e6b3-4b16-b23c-5e0d9250e5d9}
bootems                 Yes

Debugger Settings
-----------------
identifier              {4636856e-540f-4170-a130-a84776f4c654}
debugtype               Serial
debugport               1
baudrate                115200

RAM Defects
-----------
identifier              {5189b25c-5558-4bf2-bca4-289b11bd29e2}

Global Settings
---------------
identifier              {7ea2e1ac-2e61-4728-aaa3-896d9d0a9f0e}
inherit                 {4636856e-540f-4170-a130-a84776f4c654}
                        {0ce4991b-e6b3-4b16-b23c-5e0d9250e5d9}
                        {5189b25c-5558-4bf2-bca4-289b11bd29e2}

Boot Loader Settings
--------------------
identifier              {6efb52bf-1766-41db-a6b3-0ee5eff72bd7}
inherit                 {7ea2e1ac-2e61-4728-aaa3-896d9d0a9f0e}

Resume Loader Settings
----------------------
identifier              {1afa9c49-16ab-4a5c-901b-212802da9460}
inherit                 {7ea2e1ac-2e61-4728-aaa3-896d9d0a9f0e}
```

As you can see from the listing, there are a number of additional entries. Each entry has a specific purpose, and lists values that you can set, including the following:

Resume from Hibernate

The Resume from Hibernate entry shows the current configuration for the resume feature in Windows Vista. The preoperating system boot utility that controls resume is *Winresume.exe*, which in this example is stored in the *C:\ Windows\system32* folder. The hibernation data, as specified in the filepath parameter, is stored in the *Hiberfil.sys* file in the root folder on the osdevice (c: in this example). Because the resume feature works differently if the computer has Physical Address Extension (PAE) and debugging enabled, these options are tracked by the PAE and Debugoptionenabled parameters.

Windows Memory Test

The Windows Memory Test entry shows the current configuration for the Windows Memory Diagnostics utility. The preoperating system boot utility that controls memory diagnostics is *Memtest.exe*, which in this example is stored in the *C:\boot* folder. Because the memory diagnostics tool is designed to detect bad memory by default, the badmemoryaccess parameter is set to yes by default. Because the memory diagnostics tool works differently if the computer has debugging enabled, Bootdebug is used to track the status of boot debugging.

EMS Settings

The EMS Settings entry shows the configuration used when booting with Emergency Management Services. Individual Windows Boot Loader entries control whether EMS is enabled.

Debugger Settings

The Debugger Settings entry shows the configuration used when booting with the debugger turned on. Individual Windows Boot Loader entries control whether the debugger is enabled. When debug booting is turned on, Debugtype sets the type of debugger as SERIAL, 1394, or USB. With SERIAL debugging, Debugport specifies the serial port being used as the debugger port and Baudrate specifies the baud rate to be used for debugging. With 1394 debugging, you can use Channel to set the debugging channel. With USB debugging, you can use Targetname to set the USB target name to be used for debugging.

Managing the BCD Data Store

You can use the BCD Editor to add, modify, and delete entries in the BCD data store. Although I discuss related tasks in the sections that follow, only experienced users should attempt to modify the BCD data store. If you make a mistake, your computer may end up in a nonbootable state.

Changing the Default Operating System

To change the default operating system entry, you can use the /Default parameter for *BCDEdit*. The syntax for this parameter is:

```
Bcdedit /default bootldrid
```

where *bootldrid* is the GUID of the boot loader to use. You can boot to a particular installation of Windows Vista or a later Windows operating system by specifying the identifier for the related boot loader. When you view verbose details for the BCD data store, the identifiers for a particular Windows Boot Loader are listed with its entry, such as:

```
Windows Boot Loader
-------------------
identifier          {0c728e1b-d009-11da-b18b-9dc1d02cdda0}
device              unknown
path                \Windows\system32\winload.exe
description         Microsoft Windows
locale              en-US
inherit             {6efb52bf-1766-41db-a6b3-0ee5eff72bd7}
bootdebug           Yes
osdevice            unknown
systemroot          \Windows
resumeobject        {0c728e1c-d009-11da-b18b-9dc1d02cdda0}
nx                  OptIn
quietboot           No
debug               No
ems                 No
```

The Windows Boot Manager entries also list each Windows Vista or later operating system by its identifier in the displayorder field:

```
Windows Boot Manager
-------------------
identifier          {9dea862c-5cdd-4e70-acc1-f32b344d4795}
device              partition=C:
description         Windows Boot Manager
locale              en-US
inherit             {7ea2e1ac-2e61-4728-aaa3-896d9d0a9f0e}
bootdebug           No
default             {263bf496-4ab4-11db-b478-c0671802252f}
resumeobject        {263bf497-4ab4-11db-b478-c0671802252f}
displayorder        {263bf496-4ab4-11db-b478-c0671802252f}
                    {0c728e1b-d009-11da-b18b-9dc1d02cdda0}
toolsdisplayorder   {b2721d73-1db4-4c62-bf78-c548a880142d}
timeout             30
```

You could set one of the related operating systems as the default for the computer, as shown in this example:

```
bcdedit /default {0c728e1b-d009-11da-b18b-9dc1d02cdda0}
```

If you want to use a pre-Windows Vista operating system as the default, you'd use the identifier for the Windows Legacy OS Loader. The related BCD entry looks like this:

```
Windows Legacy OS Loader
------------------------
identifier              {466f5a88-0af2-4f76-9038-095b170dc21c}
device                  partition=C:
path                    \ntldr
description             Legacy (pre-Longhorn) Microsoft Windows Operating System
```

Following this, you could set *Ntldr* as the default by entering:

```
bcdedit /default {466f5a88-0af2-4f76-9038-095b170dc21c}
```

Changing the Default Timeout

You can change the timeout value associated with the default operating system using the /timeout parameter. Set the /timeout parameter to the desired wait time in seconds, such as:

```
bcdedit /timeout 30
```

If you set the timeout to zero seconds, the system will boot automatically to the default operating system.

Enabling Physical Address Expansion

Physical Address Expansion (PAE) is a feature that allows x86-based computers to support more than 4 GB of physical memory, effectively expanding the number of addressable bits from 32 to 36. Physical memory in addresses above the first 32 bits is accessed as regular 4 KB memory pages.

If you want to enable PAE through the BCD, you can use the command syntax:

```
bcdedit /set bootldrid pae paeState
```

where *bootldrid* is the identifier for the operating system that should use PAE and *paeState* specifies how you want PAE to be used:

Default
:   If you set *paeState* to Default, the operating system will use the default configuration for PAE.

ForceEnable
:   If you set *paeState* to ForceEnable, the operating system will use PAE.

ForceDisable
:   If you set *paeState* to ForceDisable, the operating system will not use PAE.

This means you could enable PAE for the operating system identified by this boot loader identifier:

```
Windows Boot Loader
-------------------
identifier              {0c728e1b-d009-11da-b18b-9dc1d02cdda0}
```

using the following command:

```
bcdedit /set {0c728e1b-d009-11da-b18b-9dc1d02cdda0} pae forceenable
```

Changing the Operating System Display Order

You can change the display order of boot managers associated with a particular Windows Vista or later operating system using the /Displayorder parameter. Follow the parameter with the operating system identifiers in the desired display order.

This means you could change the display order of the operating systems identified in these BCD entries:

```
Windows Boot Loader
-------------------
identifier              {0c728e1b-d009-11da-b18b-9dc1d02cdda0}

Windows Boot Loader
-------------------
identifier              {263bf496-4ab4-11db-b478-c0671802252f}
```

using the following command:

```
bcdedit /displayorder {263bf496-4ab4-11db-b478-c0671802252f} {0c728e1b-d009-11da-
b18b-9dc1d02cdda0}
```

You can set a particular operating system as the first entry by using /addfirst with /displayorder, such as:

```
bcdedit /displayorder {263bf496-4ab4-11db-b478-c0671802252f} /addlast
```

You can set a particular operating system as the last entry by using /addlast with /displayorder, such as:

```
bcdedit /displayorder {263bf496-4ab4-11db-b478-c0671802252f} /addlast
```

Changing the Restart Boot Sequence

If you'd like to boot to a particular operating system one time and then revert to the default boot order, you can use the /bootsequence parameter to do this. Follow the parameter with the operating system to which you want to boot after restarting the computer, such as:

```
bcdedit /bootsequence {0c728e1b-d009-11da-b18b-9dc1d02cdda0}
```

Now when you restart the computer, the computer will set the specified operating system as the default for that restart only. If you restart the computer again, the computer will use the default boot order.

Managing the Boot Sector for Hard Disk Partitions

The Boot Sector Configurator (*Bootsect.exe*) is a tool you can use to manage the master boot sector on computers running Windows Vista. Before you try to install an earlier version of Windows on a computer running Windows Vista, you should familiarize yourself with this tool.

Bootsect is provided as part of the Windows Automated Installation Kit (Windows AIK), which is available as a free download from the Microsoft Download web site. Visit *http://download.microsoft.com* and search for "Windows AIK."

Using the Boot Sector Configurator

You use *Bootsect* to modify the master boot code for a designated hard disk partition so that either Boot Manager or *Ntldr* is used to boot the operating system. You also can use *Bootsect* to restore the boot sector on your computer if it has been corrupted or accidentally overwritten. This tool replaces *FixNTFS*.

The hard disk partition that you want to modify is identified using one of the following identifiers:

- `DriverLetter:`, where `DriveLetter` identifies the letter of the drive to modify, followed by the colon, such as `C:`. The drive letter must be for a connected, bootable volume.

- `SYS` specifies that you want to modify the system partition used to boot Windows Vista.

- `ALL` specifies that you want to modify all partitions that could be used as Windows boot volumes and exclude those that cannot be used as boot volumes.

To create a boot sector for *Ntldr* and a pre-Windows Vista operating system, you use the `/nt52` parameter followed by the identifier for the disk partition you want to modify, such as:

```
bootsect /nt52 SYS
```

To create a boot sector for Boot Manager and Windows Vista or later, you use the `/nt60` parameter followed by the identifier for the disk partition you want to modify, such as:

```
bootsect /nt60 D:
```

Bootsect will always try to lock and dismount the partition before updating it. If *Bootsect* cannot gain exclusive access to the drive, the drive's boot sector is modified the next time the computer is started.

 You can attempt to force a partition to dismount using the `/force` parameter. However, this causes all open file handles to become invalid, which may cause programs to lock or fail.

Installing a Previous Version of Windows on a Computer Running Windows Vista

One scenario where *Bootsect* is particularly handy is when you are installing a previous version of Windows on a computer running Windows Vista. Normally, Windows Vista won't let you install and then run a previous version of Windows. You can work around this issue using *Bootsect* and *BCDedit*.

To install a previous version of Windows onto a computer running Windows Vista, follow these steps:

1. Insert the media for the previous version of Windows into your CD-ROM or DVD-ROM drive.

2. Restart the computer and start Setup for the previous version of Windows.

3. Log on to the previous version of Windows and restore the Windows Vista boot manager. You must specify the partition where Windows Vista is installed. If Windows Vista was installed on C:, you'd use the following command:

   ```
   bootsect /nt60 c:
   ```

4. Create a BCD entry for the pre-Windows Vista operating system you just installed using *BCDedit*. *BCDedit* is located in the *\Windows\System32* directory of the Windows Vista partition. Type the following commands exactly as shown, where *Windows_Version* is the version of Windows you installed:

   ```
   Bcdedit /create {legacy} /d "Windows_Version"
   Bcdedit /set {legacy} device boot
   Bcdedit /set {legacy} path \ntldr
   Bcdedit /displayorder {legacy} /addlast
   ```

5. Restart the computer to apply the BCD changes.

CHAPTER 24

Understanding Windows Vista Security Changes

The baseline security configuration of a computer running Windows Vista is different from that of a computer running Windows XP Professional. In Windows Vista, baseline computer security is enhanced by several key modifications to the security settings for local policies. You can manage security settings for local policies on an organization-wide basis using Active Directory Group Policy or for individual computers using Local Group Policy.

To manage Active Directory Group Policy, you can use the Group Policy Object Editor (GPOE) or the Group Policy Management Console (GPMC). To manage Local Group Policy on a local computer, you can access security settings using the Local Security Policy console. The sections that follow look at security changes that affect Password Policy, User Rights Assignment, and Security Options.

Identifying Password Policy Changes

Password policies control security for passwords. You can follow these steps to access Password Policy in the Local Security Policy console:

1. Click Start, and then click Control Panel.
2. In the Control Panel, click System and Maintenance and then click Administrative Tools.
3. Double-click Local Security Policy.
4. As shown in Figure 24-1, expand the Account Policies node in the left pane and then click the Password Policy node.

Table 24-1 compares the default Password Policy in Windows Vista with the policy assigned in Windows XP. The default settings for Windows Vista are set for all computers that are part of a domain. Likewise, the default settings for Windows XP are for all computers that are part of a domain.

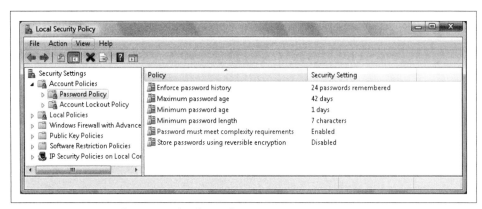

Figure 24-1. Accessing the Password Policy node

Table 24-1. Default Password Policy in Windows XP and Windows Vista

Password Policy	Default setting in Windows XP	Default setting in Windows Vista
Enforce Password History	3 passwords remembered	24 passwords remembered
Maximum Password Age	42 days	42 days
Minimum Password Age	0 days	1 days
Password Must Meet Complexity Requirements	Enabled	Enabled
Store Passwords Using Reversible Encryption	Disabled	Disabled

An important change to note is that Windows Vista requires secure, complex passwords by default. All passwords must have a minimum length of seven characters, a user must keep a new password for at least one day, and the password must meet the minimum complexity requirements.

Identifying User Rights Assignment Changes

User Rights Assignment policies determine what a user or group can do on a computer. You can follow these steps to access User Rights Assignment policies in the Local Security Policy console:

1. Click Start, and then click Control Panel.
2. In the Control Panel, click System and Maintenance and then click Administrative Tools.
3. Double-click Local Security Policy.
4. As shown in Figure 24-2, expand the Local Policies node in the left pane and then click the User Rights Assignment node.

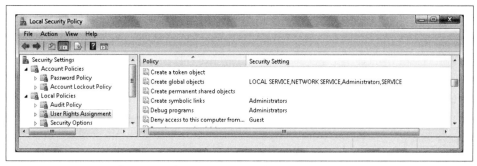

Figure 24-2. Accessing the User Rights Assignment node

Several new user rights are available in Windows Vista. These user rights are:

Access Credential Manager as a trusted caller
> This privilege controls whether an application that a user or member of a particular group is running can establish a trusted connection to Credential Manager. In Windows Vista, you use Credential Manager to manage a user's credentials. Credentials provide identification and proof of identification. Examples of credentials are usernames and passwords, smart cards, and certificates.

Allow log on locally
> This privilege controls whether a user or member of a particular group can log on at the keyboard. This user right was originally named Log On Locally and is renamed in Windows Vista so that there are now both "allow logon locally" and "deny logon locally" user rights.

Create symbolic links
> This privilege controls whether an application that a user or member of a particular group is running can create a symbolic link from the computer to which she is logged on. Symbolic links make it appear as though a document or folder is in a specific location when it actually resides in another location. Because malicious users can exploit symbolic links, use of symbolic links is limited by default.

Change the time zone
> This privilege allows a user or member of a particular group to change the time zone. As all members of the Users group have this right by default, all users are able to change the computer's time zone without requiring administrator privileges.

Increase a process working set
> This privilege allows an application that a user or member of a particular group is running to increase the memory that a process working set uses. A *process working set* is the set of memory pages currently visible to a process in physical memory (RAM). As these pages are resident in memory, they are available for an application that a user is running without triggering a page fault. The size of the working sets used by processes a user is running affects the virtual memory paging. This privilege is added to Windows Vista to allow standard user applications to request additional memory for process working sets, and it is the desired behavior.

Modify an object label

This privilege allows a process that a user or member of a particular group is running to modify the integrity label of objects, such as files, registry keys, or processes owned by other users. You can use this privilege to lower the priority of other processes. Processes running under a user account can modify the label of any object owned by that user without requiring this privilege.

Table 24-2 compares the user rights assigned in Windows Vista with those assigned in Windows XP. An important change to note is that Windows Vista phased out the Power Users group and maintains this group only for backward compatibility with legacy applications. As a result, the Power Users group is not granted user rights in Windows Vista.

Table 24-2. User Rights Assignment in Windows XP and Windows Vista

User right	Default setting in Windows XP	Default setting in Windows Vista
Access Credential Manager As a Trusted Caller	Not applicable	
Access This Computer from the Network	Everyone, Administrators, Users, Power Users, Backup Operators	Everyone, Administrators, Users, Backup Operators
Act As Part of the Operating System		
Add Workstations to Domain		
Adjust Memory Quotas for a Process	LOCAL SERVICE, NETWORK SERVICE, Administrators	LOCAL SERVICE, NETWORK SERVICE, Administrators
Allow Logon Locally	Not applicable	Guest, Administrators, Users, Backup Operators
Allow Logon Through Terminal Services	Administrators, Remote Desktop Users	Administrators, Remote Desktop Users
Back Up Files and Directories	Administrators, Backup Operators	Administrators, Backup Operators
Bypass Traverse Checking	Everyone, Administrators, Users, Power Users, Backup Operators	Everyone, LOCAL SERVICE, NETWORK SERVICE, Administrators, Users, Backup Operators
Change the System Time	Administrators, Power Users	LOCAL SERVICE, Administrators
Change the Time Zone	Not applicable	LOCAL SERVICE, Administrators, Users
Create a Pagefile	Administrators	Administrators
Create a Token Object		
Create Global Objects	Administrators, INTERACTIVE, SERVICE	LOCAL SERVICE, NETWORK SERVICE, Administrators, SERVICE
Create Permanent Shared Objects		
Create Symbolic Links		Administrators
Debug Programs	Administrators	Administrators

User right	Default setting in Windows XP	Default setting in Windows Vista
Deny Access to This Computer from the Network	SUPPORT, Guest	Guest
Deny Logon As a Batch Job		
Deny Logon As a Service		
Deny Logon Locally	SUPPORT, Guest	Guest
Deny Logon Through Terminal Services		
Enable Computer and User Accounts to Be Trusted for Delegation		
Force Shutdown from a Remote System	Administrators	Administrators
Generate Security Audits	LOCAL SERVICE, NETWORK SERVICE	LOCAL SERVICE, NETWORK SERVICE
Impersonate a Client After Authentication	Administrators, SERVICE	LOCAL SERVICE, NETWORK SERVICE, Administrators, IIS_IUSRS SERVICE
Increase a Process Working Set		Users
Increase Scheduling Priority	Administrators	Administrators
Load and Unload Device Drivers	Administrators	Administrators
Lock Pages in Memory		
Log On As a Batch Job	SUPPORT, Administrator	Administrators, Backup Operators, IIS_IUSRS
Log On As a Service	NETWORK SERVICE	NETWORK SERVICE
Log On Locally	Guest, Administrators, Users, Power Users, Backup Operators	Not applicable
Manage Auditing and Security Log	Administrators	Administrators
Modify an Object Label	Not applicable	
Modify Firmware Environment Values	Administrators	Administrators
Perform Volume Maintenance Tasks	Administrators	Administrators
Profile Single Process	Administrators, Power Users	Administrators
Profile System Performance	Administrators	Administrators
Remove Computer from Docking Station	Administrators, Users, Power Users	Administrators, Users
Replace a Process Level Token	LOCAL SERVICE, NETWORK SERVICE	LOCAL SERVICE, NETWORK SERVICE
Restore Files and Directories	Administrators, Backup Operators	Administrators, Backup Operators
Shut Down the System	Administrators, Users, Power Users, Backup Operators	Administrators, Users, Backup Operators
Synchronize Directory Service Data		
Take Ownership of Files or Other Objects	Administrators	Administrators

Identifying Security Options Changes

Security Options enable or disable security settings for a computer. You can follow these steps to access Security Options in the Local Security Settings console:

1. Click Start, and then click Control Panel.

2. In the Control Panel, click System and Maintenance and then click Administrative Tools.

3. Double-click Local Security Policy.

4. As shown in Figure 24-3, expand the Local Policies node in the left pane and then click the Security Options node.

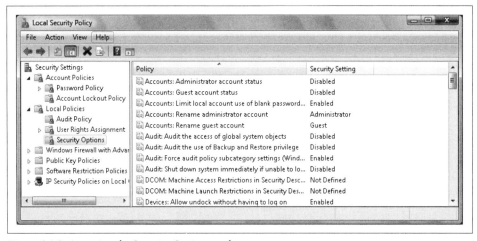

Figure 24-3. Accessing the Security Options node

Table 24-3 compares the default Security Options settings in Windows XP and Windows Vista. Most new Security Options changes pertain to UAC. In Windows Vista, UAC is used to enhance security and restrict what applications can be run. In particular, UAC is designed to block installation of spyware and other types of malicious programs or at least make the user aware that these programs are trying to install themselves.

Table 24-3. Comparing Security Options in Windows XP and Windows Vista

Security option	Default setting in Windows XP	Default setting in Windows Vista
Accounts: Administrator Account Status	Not applicable	Disabled
Accounts: Guest Account Status	Not applicable	Disabled
Accounts: Limit Local Account Use of Blank Passwords to Console Logon Only	Enabled	Enabled
Accounts: Rename Administrator Account	Administrator	Administrator
Accounts: Rename Guest Account	Guest	Guest

Security option	Default setting in Windows XP	Default setting in Windows Vista
Audit: Audit the Access of Global System Objects	Disabled	Disabled
Audit: Audit the Use of Backup and Restore Privilege	Disabled	Disabled
Audit: Shut Down System Immediately If Unable to Log Security Audits	Disabled	Disabled
DCOM: Machine Access Restrictions in Security Descriptor Definition Language (SDDL) Syntax	Not defined	Not defined
DCOM: Machine Launch Restrictions in Security Descriptor Definition Language (SDDL) Syntax	Not defined	Not defined
Devices: Allow Undock Without Having to Log On	Enabled	Enabled
Devices: Allowed to Format and Eject Removable Media	Administrators	Not defined
Devices: Prevent Users from Installing Printer Drivers	Disabled	Disabled
Devices: Restrict CD-ROM Access to Locally Logged-On User Only	Disabled	Not defined
Devices: Restrict Floppy Access to Locally Logged-On User Only	Disabled	Not defined
Devices: Unsigned Driver Installation Behavior	Warn but Allow Installation	Not applicable
Domain Controller: Allow Server Operators to Schedule Tasks	Not defined	Not defined
Domain Controller: LDAP Server Signing Requirements	Not defined	Not defined
Domain Controller: Refuse Machine Account Password Changes	Not defined	Not defined
Domain Member: Digitally Encrypt or Sign Secure Channel Data (Always)	Enabled	Enabled
Domain Member: Digitally Encrypt Secure Channel Data (When Possible)	Enabled	Enabled
Domain Member: Digitally Sign Secure Channel Data (When Possible)	Enabled	Enabled
Domain Member: Disable Machine Account Password Changes	Disabled	Disabled
Domain Member: Maximum Machine Account Password Age	30 days	30 days
Domain Member: Require Strong (Windows 2000 or Later) Session Key	Disabled	Disabled
Interactive Logon: Do Not Display Last User Name	Disabled	Disabled
Interactive Logon: Do Not Require CTRL+ALT+DEL	Not defined	Not defined
Interactive Logon: Message Text for Users Attempting to Log On		
Interactive Logon: Message Title for Users Attempting to Log On		

Table 24-3. Comparing Security Options in Windows XP and Windows Vista (continued)

Security option	Default setting in Windows XP	Default setting in Windows Vista
Interactive Logon: Number of Previous Logons to Cache (in Case Domain Controller Is Not Available)	10 logons	10 logons
Interactive Logon: Prompt User to Change Password Before Expiration	14 days	14 days
Interactive Logon: Require Domain Controller Authentication to Unlock Workstation	Disabled	Disabled
Interactive Logon: Require Smart Card	Not defined	Disabled
Interactive Logon: Smart Card Removal Behavior	No action	No action
Microsoft Network Client: Digitally Sign Communications (Always)	Disabled	Disabled
Microsoft Network Client: Digitally Sign Communications (If Server Agrees)	Enabled	Enabled
Microsoft Network Client: Send Unencrypted Password to Third-Party SMB Servers	Disabled	Disabled
Microsoft Network Server: Amount of Idle Time Required Before Suspending Session	15 minutes	15 minutes
Microsoft Network Server: Digitally Sign Communications (Always)	Disabled	Disabled
Microsoft Network Server: Digitally Sign Communications (If Client Agrees)	Disabled	Disabled
Microsoft Network Server: Disconnect Clients When Logon Hours Expire	Enabled	Enabled
Network Access: Allow Anonymous SID/Name Translation	Not applicable	Disabled
Network Access: Do Not Allow Anonymous Enumeration of SAM Accounts	Enabled	Enabled
Network Access: Do Not Allow Anonymous Enumeration of SAM Accounts and Shares	Disabled	Disabled
Network Access: Do Not Allow Storage of Credentials or .NET Passports for Network Authentication	Disabled	Disabled
Network Access: Let Everyone Permissions Apply to Anonymous Users	Disabled	Disabled
Network Access: Named Pipes That Can Be Accessed Anonymously	COMNAP, COMNODE, SQL\QUERY, SPOOLSS, LLSRPC, browser	netlogon, lsarpc, samr, browser
Network Access: Remotely Accessible Registry Paths	(Multiple paths defined as accessible)	(Multiple paths defined as accessible)
Network Access: Remotely Accessible Registry Paths and Subpaths	Not applicable	(Multiple paths defined as accessible)
Network Access: Restrict Anonymous Access to Named Pipes and Shares	Not applicable	Enabled

Security option	Default setting in Windows XP	Default setting in Windows Vista
Network Access: Shares That Can Be Accessed Anonymously	COMCFG,DFS$	Not defined
Network Access: Sharing and Security Model for Local Accounts	Guest only—local users authenticate as Guest	Classic—local users authenticate as themselves
Network Security: Do Not Store LAN Manager Hash Value on Next Password Change	Disabled	Enabled
Network Security: Force Logoff When Logon Hours Expire	Disabled	Disabled
Network Security: LAN Manager Authentication Level	Send LM and NTLM responses	Send NTLMv2 response only
Network Security: LDAP Client Signing Requirements	Negotiate signing	Negotiate signing
Network Security: Minimum Session Security for NTLM SSP Cased (Including Secure RPC) Clients	No minimum	No minimum
Network Security: Minimum Session Security for NTLM SSP Based (Including Secure RPC) Servers	No minimum	No minimum
Recovery Console: Allow Automatic Administrative Logon	Disabled	Disabled
Recovery Console: Allow Floppy Copy and Access to All Drives and All Folders	Disabled	Disabled
Shutdown: Allow System to Be Shut Down Without Having to Log On	Enabled	Enabled
Shutdown: Clear Virtual Memory Pagefile	Disabled	Disabled
System Cryptography: Force Strong Key Protection for User Keys Stored on the Computer	Not applicable	Not defined
System Cryptography: Use FIPS Compliant Algorithms for Encryption, Hashing, and Signing	Disabled	Disabled
System Objects: Default Owner for Objects Created by Members of the Administrators Group	Object creator	Not applicable
System Objects: Require Case Insensitivity for Non-Windows Subsystems	Enabled	Enabled
System Objects: Strengthen Default Permissions of Internal System Objects (e.g., Symbolic Links)	Enabled	Enabled
System Settings: Optional Subsystems	Not applicable	POSIX
System Settings: Use Certificate Rules on Windows Executables for Software Restriction Policies	Not applicable	Disabled
User Account Control: Admin Approval Mode for the Built-in Administrator Account	Not applicable	Disabled
User Account Control: Behavior of the Elevation Prompt for Administrators	Not applicable	Prompt for consent
User Account Control: Behavior of the Elevation Prompt for Standard Users	Not applicable	Prompt for credentials

Security option	Default setting in Windows XP	Default setting in Windows Vista
User Account Control: Detect Application Installations and Prompt for Elevation	Not applicable	Enabled
User Account Control: Only Elevate Executables That Are Signed and Validated	Not applicable	Disabled
User Account Control: Only Elevate UIAccess Applications That Are Installed in Secure Locations	Not applicable	Enabled
User Account Control: Run All Administrators in Admin Approval Mode	Not applicable	Enabled
User Account Control: Switch to the Secure Desktop When Prompting for Elevation	Not applicable	Enabled
User Account Control: Virtualize File and Registry Write Failures to Per-User Locations	Not applicable	Enabled

As Table 24-3 shows, new Security Options for Windows Vista are as follows:

Accounts: Administrator Account Status
   This security option determines whether the local Administrator account is enabled or disabled. When enabled, you can use the built-in Administrator account for logon. When disabled, you cannot use the built-in Administrator account for logon. If you disable Administrator and later try to enable it, you must use a secure password. In some cases, the Administrator account may become locked and a member of the Administrators group may need to reset it. You can resolve some problems by booting to Safe Mode. In Safe Mode, the Administrator account is always enabled regardless of this setting.

Accounts: Guest Account Status
   This security option determines whether the local Guest account is enabled or disabled. When enabled, you can use the Guest account for logon. When disabled, you cannot use the guest account for logon. If you disable the guest account, and Network Access: Sharing and Security Model for Local Accounts is set to Guest-only, local users authenticate as guests and some network logons may fail.

Audit: Force audit policy subcategory settings
   This security option determines the behavior of the audit policy. When it is enabled, it forces affected computers to use audit policy subcategory settings rather than category settings. Subcategory settings provide finer control over what is audited than broad category settings.

Network Access: Allow anonymous SID/Name translation
   This security setting determines whether an anonymous user can request security identifier (SID) attributes for another user. When enabled, a user with knowledge of an administrator's SID could contact a computer that has this policy enabled

and use the SID to get the administrator's name. Enabling this option can possibly open the computer to exploitation by malicious users. Generally, only domain controllers need to have this option enabled.

Network Access: Remotely access registry paths and subpaths
This security setting determines which registry paths and subpaths can be accessed over the network, regardless of the users or groups listed in the access control list (ACL) of the Winreg registry key. A number of default paths are set, and you should not modify these default paths without carefully considering the damage that changing this setting may cause.

Network Access: Restrict anonymous access to named pipes and shares
This setting determines whether named pipes and shares can be accessed anonymously. When enabled, this security setting restricts anonymous access to named pipes and shares to those listed under "Network access: Named pipes that can be accessed anonymously," and "Network access: Shares that can be accessed anonymously."

System Cryptography: Force strong key protection for user keys stored on the computer
This security setting determines whether a user's private keys require a password to be used. When defined, the options are "user input is not required when new keys are stored and used," "user is prompted when the key is first used," and "user must enter a password each time they use a key."

System Settings: Optional subsystems
This security setting determines which subsystems are used to support your applications. With this security setting, you can specify additional subsystems to support as your application requires. The default subsystem available is POSIX.

System Settings: Use certificate rules on Windows executables for software restriction policies
This security setting determines whether digital certificates are processed when a user or process attempts to run software with an *.exe* filename extension. You use this security setting to enable or disable software restriction rules. With software restriction policies, you can create a certificate rule that will allow or disallow software that is signed by Authenticode to run, based on the digital certificate that is associated with the software. In order for certificate rules to take effect, you must enable this security setting.

User Account Control: Admin approval mode for the built-in administrator account
This security option determines the behavior of Admin Approval mode for the built-in Administrator account. When enabled, the built-in Administrator account will log on in Admin Approval mode. This means that prior to performing any operation that requires elevation of privileges, the user logged on as the built-in administrator will be prompted for consent. When disabled, the built-in administrator runs in Windows XP-compatible mode and all applications run with full administrative privileges by default.

User Account Control: Behavior of the elevation prompt for administrators in admin approval mode

This security setting determines the behavior of the elevation prompt for administrators. You can set this option to one of three values: "Prompt for consent," "Prompt for credentials," or "Elevate without prompting." With "Prompt for consent," an operation that requires elevation of privileges will prompt an administrator for consent to either permit or deny the operation. If the administrator selects Permit, the operation will continue with the highest available privilege. With "Prompt for credentials," an operation that requires elevation of privileges will prompt the administrator to enter his username and password. If the user enters valid credentials, the operation will continue with the applicable privilege. With "Elevate without prompting," administrators can perform an operation that requires elevation without consent or credentials. Using "Elevate without prompting" is a poor security practice which circumvents the protections of UAC.

User Account Control: Behavior of the elevation prompt for standard users

This security setting determines the behavior of the elevation prompt for standard users. You can set this option to "Prompt for credentials" or "Automatically deny elevation requests." With "Prompt for credentials," an operation that requires elevation of privileges will prompt the user to enter an administrative username and password. If the user enters valid credentials, the operation will continue with the applicable privilege. With "Automatically deny elevation requests," an access denied error message is displayed when a nonadministrator user tries to perform an operation that requires elevation of privileges.

User Account Control: Detect application installations and prompt for elevation

This security setting determines the behavior of application installation detection for the computer. You can enable or disable this option. When enabled, application installation packages that require an elevation of privileges to install will be detected and will trigger the configured elevation prompt. When disabled, users will not be prompted for consent if an application is trying to install itself. If you use Group Policy Software Install (GPSI) or SMS, installer detection is unnecessary and you can disable this feature.

User Account Control: Only elevate executables that are signed and validated

This security setting determines whether untrusted applications can run using elevated privileges. When enabled, this security setting forces checks of the digital signatures on any interactive application that requests elevation of privileges, and only applications with valid digital signatures are allowed to run using administrator privileges.

User Account Control: Only elevate UIAccess applications that are installed in secure locations

This security setting determines whether applications that request execution with a UIAccess integrity level (via a marking of UIAccess=true in their application manifests) must reside in a secure location on the filesystem. Secure locations are limited to the subdirectories of *Program Files* and *Windows\System32*. When enabled, an application will launch with UIAccess integrity only if it resides in a secure location in the filesystem. When disabled, an application will launch with UIAccess integrity regardless of whether it does not reside in a secure location in the filesystem. If signed and validated signatures are required, Windows checks the digital signature regardless of the setting for this option.

User Account Control: Run all administrators in Admin Approval Mode
This security setting determines the behavior of UAC for all users including standard users and administrators. When enabled, you can use and enforce Admin Approval Mode and all other UAC policies. When disabled, "Disabled: Admin Approval Mode" and all other UAC policies are disabled, reducing the overall security of the operating system.

User Account Control: Switch to the secure desktop when prompting for elevation
This security setting determines whether the elevation request will prompt on the interactive users desktop or the secure desktop. When enabled, the operating system switches to the secure desktop prior to displaying elevation requests. Switching to the secure desktop isolates the process so that other processes cannot affect it, and protects the computer by preventing malicious misuse. When disabled, the operating system does not switch to the secure desktop prior to displaying elevation prompts, which opens the elevation process to possible attack and abuse.

User Account Control: Virtualize file and registry write failures to per-user locations
This security setting enables the redirection of legacy application write failures to defined locations in the registry and filesystem. This feature is designed to allow legacy programs that require administrator privileges to run. If you are running only Windows Vista-compliant applications, you may want to disable this feature. When enabled, this setting allows redirection of application write failures to defined user locations for both the filesystem and the registry. When disabled, applications that write data to protected locations will silently fail.

Some of the subtler security changes in Windows Vista have to do with remote registry access, the way local accounts are used, how LAN Manager stores passwords, and how LAN Manager Authentication works:

- In Windows XP, multiple registry paths are remotely accessible by default. In Windows Vista, no areas of the registry are remotely accessible by default. This change improves registry security. Additionally, Windows Vista includes a new security option to manage access to registry subpaths.

- In Windows XP, the default sharing and security model for local accounts is to authenticate local users as guests. In Windows Vista, local users are authenticated as themselves. This change enhances security by ensuring that users must have appropriate permissions to access all areas of the filesystem.

- In Windows XP, when a user changes a password, the LAN Manager hash value can be stored on the computer. Windows Vista ensures that these hash values are not stored on the computer. This improves security by requiring a user to obtain a new hash value anytime a password is changed.

- In Windows XP, client computers use LM and NTLM authentication and never use NTLM Version 2 session security. In Windows Vista, client computers use NTLM Version 2 authentication only and can also use NTLM Version 2 session security if the server supports it. As NTLM Version 2 is more secure than LM and NTLM, this makes the authentication process more secure.

As you can see, the many Security Options changes substantially alter the way default security is applied and enforced in Windows Vista.

CHAPTER 25

Mastering Windows Media Center

Microsoft introduced Windows Media Center Edition (MCE) with Windows XP. The company has followed through and added the functionality of MCE to Windows Vista. In Windows Vista, Windows Media Center gives you a "living room" computer that will connect to your home entertainment system and allow you to manage your media easily without the need for a keyboard, mouse, or monitor. You can connect directly to your television for a display, and you can use an optional remote control with Windows Media Center.

Windows Media Center allows you to control how you watch television by letting you record programs and schedule content, and it gives you an easy-to-use scheduling window so that you can view programming many days in advance. You can also use Windows Media Center to play your digital music, watch movies, and even burn a DVD, so you can share your content or archive it for later use. This chapter discusses the different features of Windows Media Center and gives you detailed information on how to set it up and purchase the correct hardware to make Windows Media Center come alive for your entertainment.

Understanding Windows Media Center Requirements

Only computers running Windows Vista Home Premium or Windows Vista Ultimate have Windows Media Center. When considering using Windows Media Center, you should ask yourself the following questions:

- What type of entertainment equipment do I want to connect to my computer?
- What type of network bandwidth will I need for media services?
- Where do I want to locate my computer?

Each question leads to different requirements for using Windows Media Center and each feature that Windows Media Center provides requires different software and hardware.

If you want to use Windows Media Center to watch TV, you must have a TV tuner card. If you want to use Windows Media Center to manage recorded TV programs, you need to install a video capture card. Listening to music with the music library or watching a movie requires that you install a sound card. If you want to use Windows Media Center to download album and additional online content, you need a connection to the Internet. To make it easier to navigate the TV functions and movie library features, you should purchase a programmable remote control. Table 25-1 summarizes Windows Media Center functionalities and their respective requirements for successful use.

Table 25-1. Windows Media Center functionalities and requirements

Functionality	Requirement
Watch TV	TV tuner card
Record TV	Video capture card
Listen to music or watch a movie	Sound card
Download online content	Internet connection
Access via remote control	Windows Media Center IR remote control
Listen to radio stations	Radio tuner card

Selecting the Correct Hardware for Windows Media Center

As with all other operating systems, purchasing the correct hardware for use with Windows Media Center can mean the difference between using something that merely works and having a great experience while using it. Microsoft has gone to great lengths to increase the reliability of video functions within Windows Vista. Drivers for the video card work differently than they did in previous operating systems. The kernel mode drivers and their functions in previous operating systems do not exist in Windows Vista.

Video Cards

Windows Vista uses a fully rendered 3D accelerated desktop called Windows Vista Display Driver Model (WDDM), which offers greater flexibility than previous Windows display models. WDDM moved most of the driver components out of the kernel environment and into the user environment. This driver arrangement isolates the graphics driver from the operating system and additional applications.

You should take the time to look for the best hardware available for Windows Vista. Spending the time upfront will improve your experience with Windows Vista as a whole, as well as with Windows Media Center. Currently the two hardware manufacturers writing Windows Vista drivers and video capture drivers are ATI and NVIDIA. These manufacturers are the largest in the industry, and while others create video cards that work with Windows Vista, it is in your best interest to decide between these two manufacturers. They have taken considerable time to develop new drivers in conjunction with Microsoft to offer premium services to their customers.

Visit the manufacturers' web sites and research the hardware they currently offer that works with Windows Vista. Each offers tables that give you choices on price versus performance on each card they deliver for different needs. The professional-level cards will always cost considerably more than cards at the novice or enthusiast level. So, research the available hardware when you are ready to move to Windows Vista. It will pay dividends in the end. For a list of the video cards available for use in Windows Vista at the time of this writing, see Tables 25-2 and 25-3.

Table 25-2. ATI video cards and chipsets

Types of card/chipset	Card series
ATI cards	ATI Radeon X1900 Series
	ATI Radeon X1800 Series
	ATI Radeon X1600 Series
	ATI Radeon X1300 Series
	ATI Radeon X850 Series
	ATI Radeon X800 Series
	ATI Radeon X700 Series
	ATI Radeon X600 Series
	ATI Radeon X550 Series
	ATI Radeon X300 Series
	ATI Radeon 9800 Series
	ATI Radeon 9700 Series
	ATI Radeon 9600 Series
	ATI Radeon 9550 Series
	ATI Radeon 9500 Series
ATI chipsets	ATI CrossFire Xpress 3200
	ATI Radeon Xpress 1150
	ATI Radeon Xpress 200
	ATI CrossFire Xpress 1600
	ATI Radeon Xpress 200M

Table 25-2. ATI video cards and chipsets (continued)

Types of card/chipset	Card series
ATI mobile	ATI Radeon Xpress 200M
	ATI Mobility Radeon X1800 Series
	ATI Mobility Radeon X1600 Series
	ATI Mobility Radeon X1400 Series
	ATI Mobility Radeon X1300 Series
	ATI Mobility Radeon X800 Series
	ATI Mobility Radeon X700 Series
	ATI Mobility Radeon X600 Series
	ATI Mobility Radeon X300 Series
	ATI Mobility Radeon 9800 Series
	ATI Mobility Radeon 9700 Series
	ATI Mobility Radeon 9600 Series
	ATI Mobility Radeon 9500 Series
	ATI Mobility FireGL V5200
	ATI Mobility FireGL V5000
	ATI Mobility FireGL V3200
	ATI Mobility FireGL V3100
ATI multimedia	ATI All-in-Wonder X1900 Series
	ATI All-in-Wonder X1800 Series
	ATI All-in-Wonder 2006 Edition
	ATI All-in-Wonder X800 Series
	ATI All-in-Wonder X600 Series
	ATI Theater 550 PRO
	ATI TV Wonder Elite
	ATI All-in-Wonder 9800 Series
	ATI All-in-Wonder 9600 Series

Table 25-3. NVIDIA cards and chipsets

Types of card/chipset	Card series
NVIDIA desktop GPUs	GeForce 7900 GPUs
	GeForce 7800 GPUs
	GeForce 7600 GPUs
	GeForce 7300 GPUs
	GeForce 6800 GPUs
	GeForce 6600 GPUs
	GeForce 6500 GPUs
	GeForce 6200 GPUs
	GeForce 6100/6150 GPUs
	GeForce FX 5900 GPUs
	GeForce FX 5700 GPUs
	GeForce FX 5600 GPUs
	GeForce FX 5500 GPUs
	GeForce FX 5200 GPUs
	GeForce PCX GPUs
NVIDIA notebook GPUs	GeForce Go 7800 GPUs
	GeForce Go 7600 GPUs
	GeForce Go 7400 GPUs
	GeForce Go 7300 GPUs
	GeForce Go 7200 GPUs
	GeForce Go 6800 GPUs
	GeForce Go 6600 GPUs
	GeForce Go 6400 GPUs
	GeForce Go 6200 GPUs
	GeForce Go 6100 GPUs
	GeForce FX Go5700 GPUs
	GeForce FX Go5650 GPUs
	GeForce FX Go5600 GPUs
	GeForce FX Go5200 GPUs
	GeForce FX Go5100 GPUs
	NVIDIA Quadro NVS 120M GPUs
	NVIDIA Quadro NVS 110M GPUs

Table 25-3. NVIDIA cards and chipsets (continued)

Types of card/chipset	Card series
NVIDIA workstation GPUs	NVIDIA Quadro FX 5500 GPUs
	NVIDIA Quadro FX 5500 SDI GPUs
	NVIDIA Quadro FX 4500 X2 GPUs
	NVIDIA Quadro FX 4500 GPUs
	NVIDIA Quadro FX 4500 SDI GPUs
	NVIDIA Quadro FX 4400 GPUs
	NVIDIA Quadro FX 4000 SDI GPUs
	NVIDIA Quadro FX 4000 GPUs
	NVIDIA Quadro FX 3500 GPUs
	NVIDIA Quadro FX 3450 GPUs
	NVIDIA Quadro FX 3400 GPUs
	NVIDIA Quadro FX 3000G GPUs
	NVIDIA Quadro FX 3000 GPUs
	NVIDIA Quadro FX 1500 GPUs
	NVIDIA Quadro FX 1400 GPUs
	NVIDIA Quadro FX 1300 GPUs
	NVIDIA Quadro FX 1100 GPUs
	NVIDIA Quadro FX 1000 GPUs
	NVIDIA Quadro FX 560 GPUs
	NVIDIA Quadro FX 550 GPUs
	NVIDIA Quadro FX 540 GPUs
	NVIDIA Quadro FX 350 GPUs
	NVIDIA Quadro FX 2500M GPUs
	NVIDIA Quadro FX 1500M GPUs
	NVIDIA Quadro FX 350M GPUs

Sound Cards

Sound cards are also essential to enjoying Windows Media Center. The best advice on purchasing a sound card is similar to the advice on finding a good video card. Assess your sound needs. Do you require digital output? Are you using this professionally, or are you just an enthusiast who wants to listen to your music? If you require excellent sound, research what's available and make your decision based on how the products meet your needs.

Installing and Configuring Windows Media Center Using the Wizard

Windows Vista offers a Setup wizard to help you configure Windows Media Center. To install Windows Media Center, click Start → All Programs, and then click Windows Media Center. The initial installation screen appears, as shown in Figure 25-1, requesting that you choose between Express and Custom setup.

Figure 25-1. Selecting a setup option

Express setup offers the default settings most people use. If you click "Express setup," Windows Vista tries to automatically configure everything you need to use Windows Media Center. Therefore, if you click "Express setup," you are done as far as the initial configuration is concerned and you can skip the rest of this section.

Custom setup allows you to select specific applications installed on your computer, and then customize their settings for use with Windows Media Center. With the wizard, you can configure your video settings, TV signal, and other settings for optimal use. To get started, click the "Custom setup" option, read the Welcome screen, and then click Next twice. Setup asks you to join the Microsoft Customer Experience Improvement Project, which helps Microsoft determine how you use Windows Media Center, and periodically asks you to fill out surveys. Joining this program is optional, but it does help Microsoft improve product use and enjoyment. Once you have chosen whether to join the program and you click Next, you are asked for permission to connect to the Internet to retrieve album art information, additional music information including artist and composer, and other assorted pieces of information about the media you have listed for use in Windows Media Center. Click Yes and then click Next twice. The wizard will inform you that the required part of the setup is complete.

At this point, you have four options from which to choose (see Figure 25-2):

Optimize how Windows Media Center looks on your display
> Selecting this option brings up the Display Configuration screen. Click the "Watch video" button, and then click either Yes or No to watch a video that explains the benefits of display configuration. Although you don't have to watch the video, doing so will teach you how to eliminate moiré patterns, optimize the colors on your screen, and overcome contrast or brightness issues with your display.
>
> The next section requests information about the display device connected to your machine. You have several choices: Monitor, Flat panel, Projector, Television, and Built-in display. Select the correct device from the list, and select the correct cable used to connect the device to your machine. You have three options to choose from: Composite or S-Video; DVI, VGA, or HDMI; and Component cable. Selecting the proper connection helps Windows Media Center optimize itself to your system by using the best settings for each type of cable and device connected to your system.
>
> Once you have selected the correct cable type, you must supply information concerning the display width of your computer. You can select from standard or widescreen format. The standard format uses a ratio of 4:3. The widescreen format uses a ratio of 16:9, which is the same format as a movie screen. These choices enable you to optimize your display settings based on the media formats and device configurations available. After you make your choices, Windows Media Center displays a final screen listing the settings you have chosen and saved in your custom configuration.

Set up your speakers
> Select this option to set up your speakers for use with Windows Media Center. You must know how many speakers connect to your system, and then you must test your speakers. Three speaker selections are available for use with Windows Media Center: two speakers, 5.1 surround speakers, and 7.1 surround speakers.

Once you have identified the type of speakers connected to your computer, click Next and then select the Test button. If you heard sound from all of your speakers, click "I heard the sound from all of my speakers," click Next, and then click Finish. If you didn't hear sound from all of your speakers, click "I did not hear sound from all of my speakers," click Next, review the troubleshooting advice, and then click Finish.

Set up your Music, Pictures, and Videos Libraries

Choosing this option allows you to tell Windows Media Center about folders that contain your media. Use the "Add folder to watch" option to identify folders in which your music, movies, or other media types reside. Windows Media Center will then scan these folders for media and add it to your library. Windows Media Center will then monitor the folders you selected for new media as well, and will automatically make them available for your use.

I am finished

Choose this option when you have finished the setup process and you're ready to begin using Windows Media Center. Click "I am finished," click Next, and then click Finish.

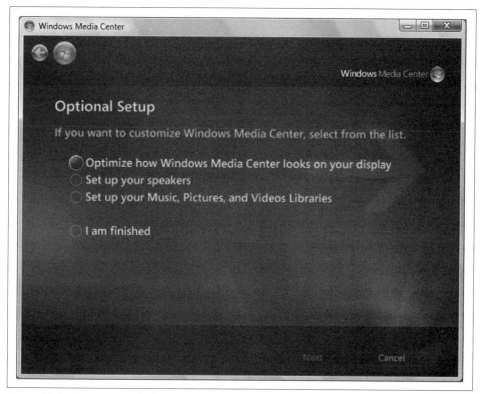

Figure 25-2. Continuing with the optional setup as necessary

Navigating Windows Media Center

Once you have completed setup, you will see the main screen for Windows Media Center, as shown in Figure 25-3. The main menu works a little differently than most Windows menus. It scrolls up and down, and when you make a selection, you see the options of a related submenu on which you can scroll left to right to view and select the available options. Once you get started, the menu is rather intuitive, but it can be a bit confusing at first.

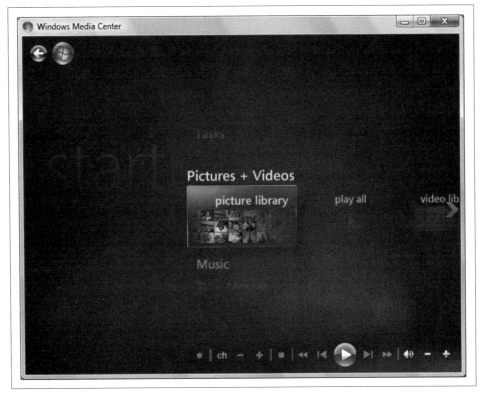

Figure 25-3. Navigating the main menu

Working with Pictures + Videos

The Pictures + Videos menu allows you to play pictures and videos saved to folders that Windows Media Center is monitoring. On this menu, you have a Play All option for playing all available pictures and videos, as well as Picture Library and Video Library options, which let you select individual pictures and videos to view.

As Figure 25-4 shows, the options are similar to those in Windows Media Player. When you are working with pictures, you can even select Play Slideshow to play a slide show of all your pictures or of pictures in a selected folder. To go up to the next level of the menu system from a submenu, move the pointer around the screen and then click the Back button.

Figure 25-4. Selecting a folder and viewing your pictures

Using the Picture Library option you can view pictures saved in the Picture folder within your profile, and any other folders monitored by Windows Media Center that contain pictures. The following menu offers you thumbnail images of the pictures available for viewing. You have different choices from the menus provided. Menus include date taken, tags, and folders. You also have the option to play a slide show, which scrolls through each picture associated with Windows Media Center using different special effects and cinematic techniques.

You can view pictures associated with the picture library using a Folder view, which shows you thumbnails of the pictures available in each folder. You can also view pictures by selecting the Tag option, which allows you to select pictures to which you have added a tag for easier management. In addition, you can select pictures by the date they were taken to make it easier to manage large numbers of photos, or if you have forgotten their specific locations.

Selecting the Video Library option brings you to a screen where you can sort your videos by date recorded or title. You can view pictures saved in the Videos folder within your profile, and any other folders monitored by Windows Media Center that contain videos. The options allow you to manage your media by name or date.

Both the Picture Library and the Video Library make it easy to manage your collections. You can view your content by selecting the Folders option. To add picture or video folders to monitor, click Tasks → Settings → Library Setup.

Working with Music

From the Music menu, you can play music saved to folders being monitored by Windows Media Center, and access Internet radio stations. You must have a sound card to play music. Additionally, you must have an Internet connection in order to use the radio management functionality. Table 25-4 lists Windows Media Center music functionality and requirements.

Table 25-4. Music and radio functionalities and requirements

Functionality	Requirement
Listen to music	Sound card
Download online updates to album information	Internet connection
Listen to Internet radio	Internet connection

On the Music menu, you have a Play All option for playing all available music, as well as Music Library, Radio, and Search options. If you select Music Library, you will see a list of albums and other audio files that are available. As Figure 25-5 shows, your music is organized in much the same way as it is in Windows Media Player. You can play all your music, or select albums or individual songs to play. You can also create playlists that work just like Windows Media Player playlists.

Using the Music Library option you can access music saved in the Music folder within your profile, and any other folders monitored by Windows Media Center that contain music. From the main menu, click Tasks → Settings → Library Setup to specify additional music folders that should be monitored.

The Music Library section lets you view your music library by the following categories:

- Albums
- Artists
- Genres
- Songs
- Playlists
- Composers
- Years

These categories make it very simple to find the music you want to play. You also have the option to play all of the music in your library, by selecting the Play All button.

Figure 25-5. Viewing your music

When you select an album within your music library, as shown in Figure 25-6, you have the following options:

Play Album
Plays the selected album from the beginning.

Add to Queue
Adds the album to the active playlist where it is queued to play after any previously queued music.

Burn
Burns the album to an audio CD or a data CD/DVD. See "Burning Disks," later in this chapter, for more information.

Edit Info
Allows you to edit the album details downloaded from the Internet.

Delete
Permanently deletes the album from your computer.

Figure 25-6. Selecting an album within your library

If you select the Radio option from the Music menu, you can manage the different aspects of Internet radio, including adding new stations, managing how you sort them, and listening to the different stations you add. Clicking the Sources selection opens the Showcase menu. Selecting the Music and Radio option takes you to a screen listing the preset options available to you—among them VH1 and XM satellite radio. You must have Adobe Flash Player to view some content in the Showcase menu subsection. You can either click the installation selection available on the screen provided, or download Flash Player directly from the Adobe web site (*http://www.adobe.com*).

You can select many different radio stations from any of these predefined selections. You can choose by genre or specific radio station listed. Some of the different genres available are jazz, Latin, metal, new age, oldies, pop, country, and blues. Each genre has numerous sites to choose from, and offers endless hours of music entertainment.

If you select the Search option from the Music menu, you can search your music by keyword to find a song, album, artist, and so on. As Figure 25-7 shows, matches for text you enter are returned as you type, and you can click on a selection to view more details. To go up to the next level of the menu system from a submenu, move the pointer around the screen, and then click the Back button.

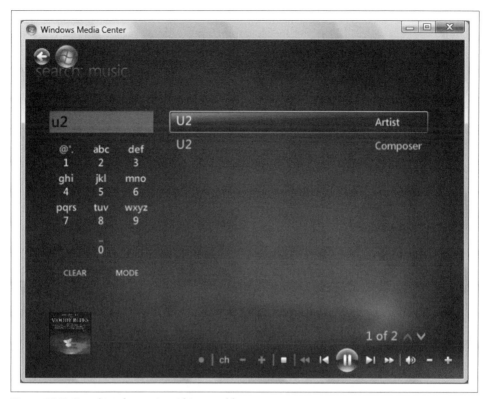

Figure 25-7. Searching for music within your library

Working with Now Playing + Queue

When you are playing media, you will have the Now Playing + Queue option on the main menu for accessing media that is currently playing or is queued to play. You can think of the queue as the active playlist. When you select Now Playing + Queue, you will see the Now Playing screen shown in Figure 25-8. The main options for Now Playing + Queue are as follows:

View Queue

Displays the current queue and provides options for editing and clearing the queue, saving the current queue as a playlist, shuffling the queue to create a random play order, and setting the queue to repeat automatically. The final option allows you to burn the playlist to an audio CD or a data CD/DVD. The process of burning a disk is similar to that of burning a disk in Windows Media Player.

Visualize

Displays a graphical depiction of the music being played called a visualization. Visualizations work just as they do in Windows Media Player. Use the channel +/− buttons to change the visualization.

Play Slide Show

Plays a slide show using pictures in monitored folders. When you play a slide show, any selected and queued music will continue to play. Use the channel +/– buttons to move forward and backward through your pictures. Use the Stop button to exit the slide show.

Shuffle

Shuffles the play order of items in the Now Playing queue.

Repeat

Sets the Now Playing queue to repeat automatically.

Buy Music

Allows you to buy music from your default online store.

Figure 25-8. Viewing music that is playing and queued to play

Working with TV + Movies

The TV + Movies menu allows you to play recorded TV shows saved to folders that Windows Media Center is monitoring. You can set up TV options, and by clicking Play DVD, you can play a DVD inserted into your computer's DVD drive. If your computer has two DVD drives, you can insert a DVD into either drive. However, if

DVDs are inserted into multiple drives, Windows Media Center plays the DVD in the primary DVD drive. The primary DVD drive is determined according to the drive letter, meaning that the DVD in drive D will play if drives D and E both have DVDs inserted into them.

As Figure 25-9 shows, your recorded TV content is organized in much the same way as it is in Windows Media Player. When you select a recorded TV show by clicking it, you have the following options:

Play
>   Plays the recorded TV show. When the show is playing, you can use the controls to manage playback. Click the Stop button to stop playing the show and go back to the main menu.

Cast + More
>   Displays information about the cast and the show.

Delete
>   Permanently deletes the recorded TV show from your computer.

Burn CD/DVD
>   Burns the recorded TV show to a data CD/DVD or a Video DVD. See the "Burning Disks" section for more information.

The Recorded TV option lets you view and manage your favorite recorded TV content, as well as add TV content to your collection. You can also watch live TV from this menu. To configure these options, you must have the required hardware. You need a TV tuner card to watch live TV and a video capture card to record and manage your favorite TV shows.

When working with Recorded TV and Live TV, you can add recorded content already scheduled and recorded for you to use. Each selection offers you the ability to view the desired content by date recorded and by title. You may also want to view the scheduled content to be recorded by the system so that you can see what program will be recorded and the date and time of the scheduled recording for editing or configuration.

Microsoft was nice enough to include some sample recorded content for you to view. You can also add content you want to record, view scheduled recordings, and view your collection of recorded content. You can view your content by thumbnails, the date of the video recording, or the title of the content. Selecting any one of the thumbnails listed will bring up the Movie Details menu, which allows you to play the recorded show, view information about the cast, delete the recorded show, or burn the recorded show to a CD/DVD.

The Live TV menu allows you to view live TV. If you want to use this feature, you must have a TV tuner card installed in your machine. The submenu options available in this section include Recorded TV, Live TV, Guide, and Movie Guide, all of which give you flexibility when managing and searching your TV content.

Figure 25-9. Viewing recorded TV

Once you have chosen a channel to watch, you can change channels just as though you are watching a regular television. If you have purchased an optional remote control, you can even select the Up and Down Channel options to change channels. If you select Up or Down, you will change to other channels. If you select Left or Right, you will change to other content on that channel. From here, you can also record the channel you are watching, pause live TV, rewind, or fast-forward.

With the Guide option, you can search live TV content just as though you are watching satellite dish or cable programming guides on your regular TV. The Guide refreshes periodically to update content made available to Windows Media Center. Using the Guide you can browse based on channel, categories, date, or time.

If you have purchased a remote control, finding content really does not get much easier. You can choose from the available content, record shows, or just browse the different channels available to you. The Guide content does not require any additional licensing or fee-based utilities, making recording your favorite programs easy and affordable.

If you decide not to purchase a remote control, you can still easily find, record, and browse content via the keyboard or mouse. Select the Arrow menu in the bottom-right corner to change the direction in which you want to scroll. Up and Down move you in the corresponding directions, and Left and Right do the same. You can also click the red button on the Play menu to record live TV.

The Movie Guide option allows you to search for movies only. You can view thumbnails of movie jackets, and filter the Movie Guide based on top-rated movies, what's on at the moment, what's on next, or different predefined genres. Remember, these are just movies, not general TV content. The movie list is based on the downloaded TV guide.

The Movie Guide makes finding movies a breeze, because it lets you search by predefined criteria. You can use the keyboard, mouse, or optional remote control to access the Movie Guide as well as all aspects of Windows Media Center.

As noted earlier, once you have selected the Movie Guide option, you can view available movies based on the following criteria:

- Top Rated
- On Now
- On Next
- Genres

After you have selected a method to sort the content, you are presented with a picture representing the movie, based on the original movie poster or DVD cover. Highlighting a movie brings up the title of the movie, the year it was released, and the channel and time it is available to watch.

Working with Online Media

The Online Media menu allows you to access your computer's program library so that you can play games on your TV rather than on your computer. When you click Online Media and then click Program Library, you will see a list of available games, as shown in Figure 25-10. Click the game you want to play, such as Chess Titans or Purble Place.

Burning Disks

Burning disks in Windows Media Center is similar to burning disks with Windows Media Player and Windows DVD Maker, but with fewer options. To burn a DVD, click Tasks and then click Burn CD/DVD. With CDs, Windows Media Center helps you burn audio and data CDs. With DVDs, it helps you burn a data DVD, Video DVD, or DVD slide show. Start by inserting the CD or DVD and then selecting the disk format, such as Video DVD, when prompted (see Figure 25-11).

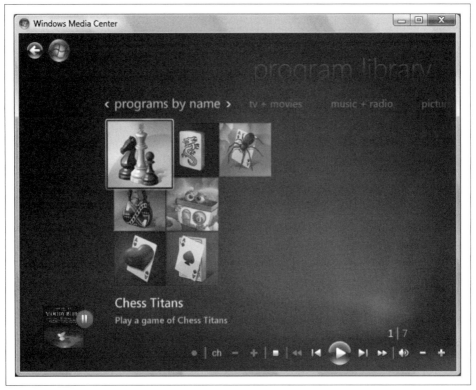

Figure 25-10. Viewing your program library

Next, provide a title for the disk and select a media location to browse for media:

- If you selected Data DVD as the disk format, you will be able to select from Recorded TV, Music Library, Picture Library, and Video Library options.

- If you selected Video DVD as the disk format, you will be able to select from Recorded TV and Video Library options.

- If you selected DVD Slide Show as the disk format, you will be able to select from Music Library and Picture Library options.

When creating your disk, you can mix and match different types of content from available categories by selecting a category, adding items, clicking the Back button, selecting a different category, and then adding items from that category. Only categories for the selected type of disk are available, however. If you decide to go back and change the disk type, you will have to start all over again with the media item selection.

With Recorded TV, you can select the recorded TV shows to add to your disk. With Music Library, you can select albums and songs to add. With Picture Library, you can select pictures to add as a slide show, and with Video Library, you can select videos to add. The process of burning a disk is similar to that of burning a disk in Windows Media Player.

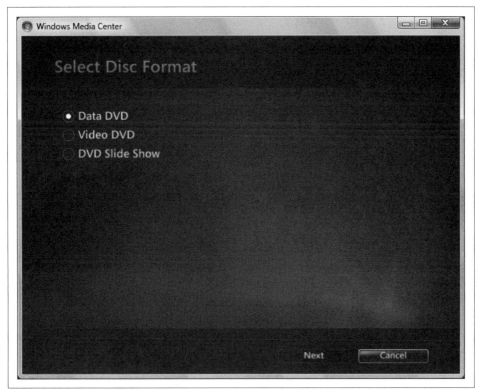

Figure 25-11. Selecting the disk format

On the Review & Edit List page, shown in Figure 25-12, you can set the play order of media items you have selected. When you are ready to create the DVD, click Burn DVD.

Working with Tasks

You use the options on the Tasks menu to manage Windows Media Center settings and perform management tasks. Your options are as follows:

Shutdown
> Provides options for closing Windows Media Center, logging off your computer, shutting down your computer, restarting your computer, and putting your computer in sleep mode.

Burn CD/DVD
> Burns recorded TV, pictures, and videos to a data CD/DVD or Video DVD. See "Burning Disks" for more information.

Sync
> Syncs media content to a device with removable storage. This process works much like it does with Windows Media Player.

Figure 25-12. Using the options provided to set the play order and burn your disk

Add Extender

Helps you set up your computer to work with a Windows Media Center extender configured on your home network. You can use extenders to allow Windows Media Center to work with other devices, such as the Xbox 360.

Media Only

Turns the Media Only mode on and off. In Media Only mode, Windows Media Center is displayed in full screen mode and the Minimize and Close buttons are hidden.

Settings

Allows you to manage Windows Media Center configuration. The main options let you configure settings for TV, Pictures, Music, DVD, and Extender. If you select Library Setup, you can change the folders that Windows Media Center monitors for media. If you select General, you will have a completely new set of option categories. I discuss these additional options in the section that follows.

Fine-Tuning the Settings for Windows Media Center

Selecting the Tasks list, clicking Settings, and then clicking General brings you to Windows Media Center's main configuration section (see Figure 25-13). You should take advantage of the ability to customize Windows Media Center so that you can optimize its use, as well as optimize the settings of your sound, display, and video.

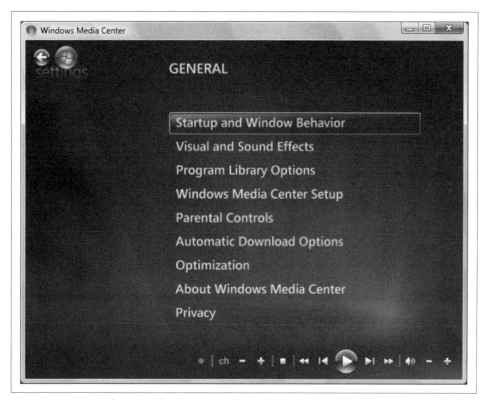

Figure 25-13. Using the General options to configure Windows Media Center

Configuring Window Behavior

When you click Tasks → Settings → General → Startup and Window Behavior, you will see the Startup and Window Behavior screen shown in Figure 25-14. From this screen, you can choose how your Windows Media Center windows behave in conjunction with other windows. You can tell Windows Media Center to always be on top of other windows on your desktop by checking the box next to this setting. You can also have Windows Media Center display the "Not designed for Windows Media Center" dialog box by checking the box next to this setting.

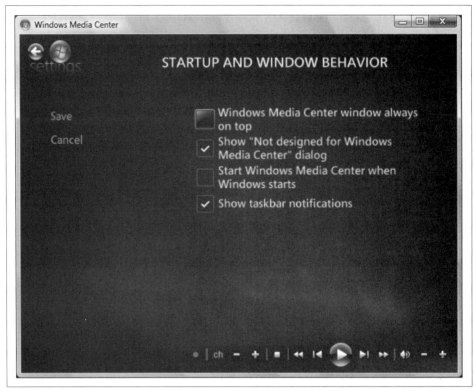

Figure 25-14. Configuring startup and window behavior

Selecting the checkbox next to "Start Windows Media Center when Windows starts" will allow Windows Media Center to open on the desktop display before anything else opens. This enables you to work with Windows Media Center as the main focal point of the operating system, and controlling it via a remote control allows you to use it like you would use your TV.

The last setting available, "Show taskbar notifications," allows Windows Media Center to notify you with issues or settings you need to look at in Windows Media Center. Once you have made your desired selections, click or select Save to save the settings into your profile.

Configuring Visual and Sound Effects

When you click Tasks → Settings → General → Visual and Sound Effects, you'll see the Visual and Sound Effects screen shown in Figure 25-15. From this screen, you can control the visual and sound behavior of Windows Media Center. You can customize the behaviors of transition animations by selecting the "Use transition animations" checkbox. Checking the "Play sounds when navigating Windows Media Center" checkbox allows you to control how sound is used with Windows Media Center. If you want to hear sounds when you select menus or files, you should leave this setting checked, as it is a default setting.

Figure 25-15. Configuring visual and sound effects

Selecting the best color scheme for Windows Media Center is simple. Leave the "Windows Media Center standard" checkbox selected if you do not want to change the color scheme. If you want a higher-contrast color scheme so that you can view Windows Media Center better, select either "High contrast white" or "High contrast black" from the menu.

Additionally, you can change the video background color by selecting the – or + sign available under "Video background color." This changes the black settings from 100 percent black to different shades of gray. This can help with specific types of eyestrain. Once you have made your desired selections, select or click the Save button to update the settings in your profile.

Configuring Additional Program Library Options

When you click Tasks → Settings → General → Program Library Options, you'll see the Program Library Options screen shown in Figure 25-16. From this screen, you can allow applications in the program library to control the Windows Media Center experience. By selecting the related checkbox, you allow other programs to control how Windows Media Center looks and acts. This is a default setting for Windows Media Center, and unless you have reason to change it, it is best to leave it checked.

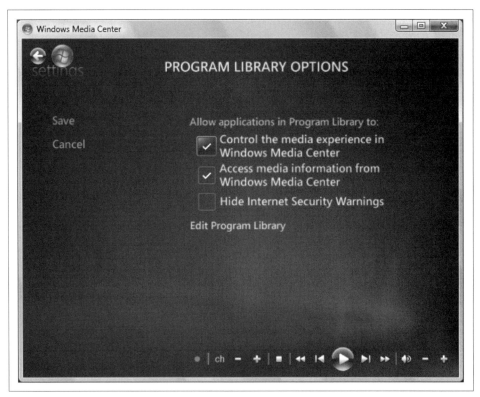

Figure 25-16. Configuring program library options

You can also select the "Access media information" from Windows Media Center checkbox to allow other applications to retrieve and use the information that Windows Media Center collects.

The next selection available allows you to hide security warnings in Windows Media Center. If you do not want to see the security dialog messages concerning security issues with Windows Media Center, you can check the box next to this setting to stop them from appearing.

The Edit Program Library option allows you to customize how applications interact with Windows Media Center. Click or select the Edit Program Library option and then choose specific applications to show or hide within Windows Media Center.

Choices available include Burn CD/DVD as well as other programs. Then click or select the Save button to save these settings in your profile.

Configuring Parental Controls

Selecting Tasks → Settings → General → Parental Controls allows you to customize how you view specific content within Windows Media Center. These settings work similarly to adding access codes to your TV, cable, or satellite device. Once you have selected the Parental Controls option, you must enter a new four-digit access code to begin the process, and then confirm the access code to ensure that you did not mistype it. Make sure you write down and memorize this code. After completing this step, you are allowed access to the content menu shown in Figure 25-17.

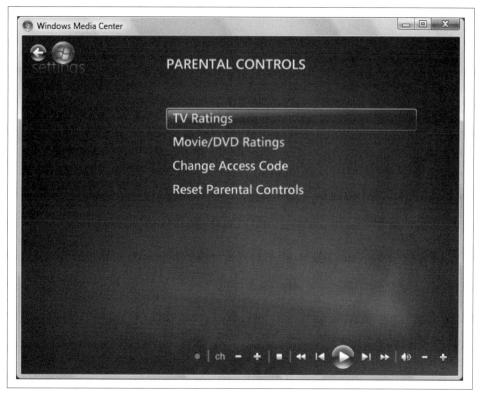

Figure 25-17. Setting parental controls to restrict usage

The content menu allows you to control specific content related to TV ratings and movie/DVD ratings, manage and reset the access code, and reset the default parental controls. For example, select TV Ratings to turn on the TV blocking attributes based on standard TV rating scales. You can select from the following choices: TV-MA, TV-14, TV-PG, TV-G, TV-Y7, TV-Y, and None. Table 25-5 provides more information concerning these settings.

Table 25-5. TV ratings

TV rating	Description
TV-MA	Mature audience only. This program selection is designed specifically to be viewed by adults and, therefore, may be unsuitable for children under 17.
TV-14	Parents strongly cautioned. This program contains some material that many parents would find unsuitable for children less than 14 years of age.
TV-PG	Parental guidance suggested. This program contains material that parents may find unsuitable for younger children.
TV-G	General audience. Most parents would find this program suitable for all ages.
TV-Y7	Directed to older children. This program selection is designed for children ages 7 and older.
TV-Y	All children. This program selection is designed to be appropriate for all children.
None	All rated programs will be blocked.

Within the selection of each setting, you can use the Advanced Options button to configure your system further. The available options are:

- Fantasy
- Violence
- Suggestive
- Dialogue
- Offensive Language
- Sexual Content

This allows parents even greater flexibility in rating content specific to their children's needs or desires.

You can select the Movie/DVD Ratings option to control viewing of specific movie and DVD content. By turning on movie blocking, you can control movies available for viewing based on their ratings. Selections include NC-17, R, PG-13, PG, G, and None. Table 25-6 summarizes these settings and their meanings.

Table 25-6. Movie ratings

Movie rating	Description
NC-17	Not intended for anyone 17 and under.
R	Restricted. Children under 17 require an accompanying parent or adult guardian.
PG-13	Parents strongly cautioned. Some material may be inappropriate for children under 13.
PG	Parental guidance suggested. Some material may not be appropriate for children.
G	General audience. Appropriate for all ages.
None	All rated movies will be blocked.

After you have selected the settings you feel are appropriate for viewing on your system, click or select the Save button to save your settings into your profile. Failure to save the settings will leave the previous settings selected and saved to your profile.

Configuring Automatic Download Options

Selecting Tasks → Settings → General → Automatic Download Options allows you to turn on or off the capability of Windows Media Center to connect to the Internet to retrieve information as it pertains to your CDs, DVDs, and movies. If you do not want Windows Media Center to connect to the Internet to retrieve this information, you need to uncheck the box next to the "Retrieve CD album art…" checkbox (see Figure 25-18). By default, Windows Media Center will automatically try to connect to the Internet to retrieve this information, with the belief that it gives you a better user experience within Windows Media Center. Once you have made your desired selection, click or select the Save button to save these settings to your profile. You can also set the download method for the Media Guide and other information to "Download when connected" or "Manual download." If you want to use manual downloads, you must remember to access this screen periodically and then click "Download now" to retrieve media information.

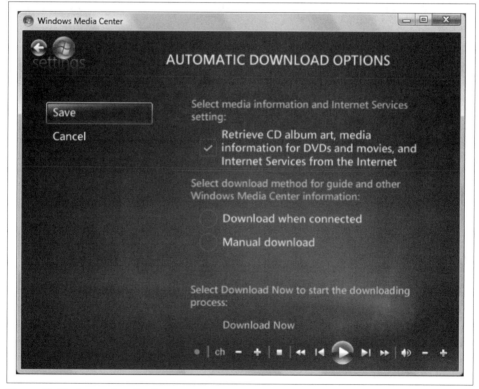

Figure 25-18. Setting download options

Configuring Optimization

Selecting Tasks → Settings → General → Optimization allows you to turn on and configure automatic optimization (see Figure 25-19). When optimization is enabled, your computer will periodically optimize your media to work more smoothly with Windows Media Center. Windows Media Center will perform specific optimization tasks that make it easier to use, such as reindexing your media content for faster content retrieval.

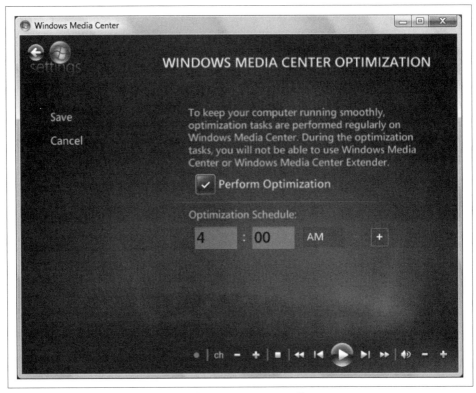

Figure 25-19. Optimizing Windows Media Center automatically

When you select the Perform Optimization checkbox, you must choose a time for optimization to start. You can select any time during a 24-hour period, but keep in mind that during the optimization process, you will be unable to use Windows Media Center. Standard times are after 11 p.m. for most people, but if you require a different time, you can select it here. Once you have made the desired selection, click or select the Save button to save your configuration settings into your profile.

Using the About Windows Media Center Menu

Selecting Tasks → Settings → General → About Windows Media Center provides you with critical information concerning Windows Media Center. Within this section, you can view the software version of the application by selecting the Software Version button. The About Windows Media Center menu also allows you to view the terms of service when using the program. Finally, you can select Data Provider Credits to open a listing of the content providers for media information, allowing you to see where Windows Media Center retrieves its online content.

Viewing Privacy Information in Windows Media Center

Selecting Tasks → Settings → General → Privacy allows you to view the online Windows Media Center privacy statement, privacy settings, and customer experience settings. Clicking on the Online Windows Media Center Privacy Statement opens a window showing you the updated privacy available from Microsoft's web site. To view the specific content from your browser, go to *http://go.microsoft.com/fwlink/?LinkId=41386*.

From the Privacy Settings option, you can change the Guide and Most Viewed settings available in Windows Media Center. The Guide selection allows you to turn on or off the ability for Windows Media Center to send anonymous information to Microsoft, which helps Microsoft improve the quality and accuracy of the services available within Windows Media Center. The Most Viewed selection turns on or off the favorites filter in the Windows Media Center guide. Once you have made your selections, click or select the Save button to update your local profile.

The Customer Experience Settings option lets you select whether you want to send anonymous usage and reliability information to Microsoft. When you experience an error within the program, you are asked whether to send a report to Microsoft, which helps Microsoft determine specific problems with the product and its interaction with additional programs. If you want to send this information to Microsoft, leave the checkbox selected, as it is a default setting within Windows Media Center. After you have completed your selection, click or select the Save button to save your preferences.

Using Windows Media Center Setup

If you did not use the Startup Wizard to configure your hardware and customized settings in the initial startup screen, you can select Tasks → Settings → General → Windows Media Center Setup to configure your hardware and network settings. You also can run the entire Setup Wizard again. Even if you did use the wizard to set up Windows Media Center, you can use these menu options to add new hardware or change the configuration settings.

When you select Tasks → Settings → General → Windows Media Center Setup, you will have the following additional options:

- Set Up Internet Connection
- Set Up TV Signal
- Set Up Your Speakers
- Configure Your TV or Monitor
- Join Wireless Network
- Run Setup Again

The sections that follow discuss using these options.

Configuring your Internet connection

If you have not previously configured an Internet connection for your computer, the Set Up Internet Connection option allows you to configure an Internet connection. Click Next on the first screen of the wizard. When prompted as to whether you have an always-on connection, click Yes or No as appropriate. If you are using a cable model or DSL, select Yes and then click Next. If you are using dial-up, click No, click Next, select the dial-up connection to use with Windows Media Center, and then click Next again. If you choose a wrong selection, you can always select the Back button to change your settings.

Click the Test button to see whether you can connect to the Internet. If you can successfully connect to the Internet, you will see Connection Working listed under the test button. If you are unsuccessful, click the Back button to change your settings. If you are still having problems connecting to the Internet, refer to the "Troubleshooting Problems with Windows Media Center" section, later in this chapter.

Once you have resolved any problems and can successfully complete the connection, click the Next button to proceed to the "You are done" window. Click the Finish button to complete setup of your Internet connection.

Configuring your TV signal

The Set Up TV Signal option allows you to configure your TV tuner card. Click Next on the first screen in the wizard, and then confirm your respective region. If the region selected matches your desired region, click the "Yes, use this region to configure TV services" radio button. If the settings listed do not match your region, click the "No, I want to select a different region" radio button. After making your selection, click the Next button to proceed. This section moves forward on the assumption that your region is now correct. Next, you see the Download TV Setup Options screen. Windows Media Center will download the TV options available for your region. Once this section completes, click the Next button to proceed.

It is recommended that you use the "Configure my TV signal automatically" selection, which will load the most common default settings available for your TV settings. You do have the option to configure your TV signal manually, but you will have to have specific information to provide to the wizard, including region and local information. Next, you are brought to the "Examining your TV signal setup" window. Windows Media Center scans your TV antenna signal to find the relevant TV information available to your hardware. Once this section completes, select the Next button to begin setting up your TV program guide.

You are presented with a menu selection asking you to agree to the licensing information provided to you. To proceed, you must select "I agree" and the Next button. Then enter your zip code in the text box provided, and click Next. Windows Media Center will download the guide information and show you a status of either Downloading or Download Complete. Once you see the Download Complete status, click the Next button to proceed. Congratulations, you have successfully installed and configured your TV signal and guide options.

Configuring your speakers

Use the Set Up Your Speakers option to configure your speakers within Windows Media Center. Click Next on the first screen of the wizard. You need to select the proper speaker configuration for Windows Media Center to test. Selections available include two speakers, 5.1 surround speakers, and 7.1 surround speakers. Table 25-7 provides more information concerning these configurations.

Table 25-7. Speaker selections available in Windows Media Center

Speaker setting	Description
Two speakers	Two individual speakers connected via a single cable to your system. The main speaker has the master volume, and the other connects to the main speaker.
5.1 surround sound	Composed of a subwoofer, center channel, and four satellite speakers connected to your system via a single connection managed through the subwoofer.
7.1 surround sound	Composed of a subwoofer, center channel, and six satellite speakers connected to your system via a single connector managed through the subwoofer.

After you have chosen the correct speaker configuration for your system, click the Next button to proceed to the Speaker Connection Type window. In this window, you need to select the type of connection you use to connect your speaker to the system. Table 25-8 lists the types of connections available for use in Windows Media Center.

Table 25-8. Cable connection types in Windows Media Center

Connector	Description
Mini-plug	A single stereo jack connected to your computer
Dual RCA	Two RCA connectors colored red and white
Single RCA	A single RCA connector colored yellow
Fiber	A single fiber-optic connector with a predominantly square connector and a shaft containing the filament for light connectivity on the end, usually colored white
Built-in	Laptop integrated speakers

Once you have selected the correct cable type, click the Next button to proceed, and then click the Test button to test your settings. If you heard the sound provided by Windows Media Center, select the "I hear sound from all of my speakers" option. If you did not hear the sound, select the "I do not hear sound from all of my speakers" option, or click the Back button to change your speaker selection. If you continue having problems hearing sound from your speakers, refer to the "Troubleshooting Problems with Windows Media Center" section for more information on how to fix this issue.

Configuring your TV or monitor

Selecting the Configuring Your TV or Monitor option runs the Display Wizard. The first screen allows you to watch a video to help you configure the display settings available in Windows Media Center. Clicking the "Watch video" button plays the video. During the video, you can adjust your monitor or TV settings, including color, brightness, and geometric aspects of your display device. To continue using the wizard, click Next on the first screen to begin your configuration. You need to tell Windows Media Center whether your preferred display is connected to your system. Make sure you are watching the wizard from your preferred display to configure the correct settings. If you are viewing on your desired display, click the "Yes, I see the wizard on my preferred display" selection. If you are not, select "No, I want to use a different display" option. Click Next to proceed to the next screen, where you are asked to identify the correct display device connected to your system. Choices include Monitor, Built-in display, Flat panel, Television, and Projector. Table 25-9 provides information about each device type.

Table 25-9. Display types available in Windows Media Center

Display type	Description
Monitor	A single CRT-type monitor with an SVGA connector connected to your video card
Built-In Display	A laptop screen or all-in-one PC unit
Flat Panel	A flat panel screen with a digital connector connected to your video card

Table 25-9. Display types available in Windows Media Center (continued)

Display type	Description
Television	A television set connected to your system, usually with an S-Video connector cable
Projector	A device with a lens and separate lighting source used to project a picture onto a wall or screen, connected to your system with an SVGA connection, S-Video connection, or additional connectors

Once you have selected the correct display type for use on your system, click the Next button to proceed. You need to tell Windows Media Center the display width of your display. Only two formats are available: standard (4:3) and widescreen (16:9). Select the appropriate display ratio for your system and click Next. The next screen asks you to confirm your display resolution, and asks you to either keep or discard your current settings. Click the desired selection and then click the Next button. Once you have completed this task, you are finished setting up your display device.

Joining a wireless network with Windows Media Center

Using the Join a Wireless Network option allows you to connect Windows Media Center directly to your wireless network. If you have previously set up your wireless network settings, do not use this menu, as it will overwrite your existing settings. If you have not completed the setup of a wireless network, you can use this wizard to configure the use of a wireless network on your system.

 Your wireless network must be working in order to use this wizard. If you do not have a wireless network card, or any other wireless devices, this wizard will not work correctly.

If you have a wireless network set up, click the Yes radio button to connect the system to your wireless network, and then click the Next button. The next screen shows you the wireless networks available to your system. Choose your desired option and click Next. Windows Media Center will attempt to connect to your wireless network. Once this task completes, you are finished setting up your wireless network. Click Next and then click Finish to complete this wizard. If you continue having problems connecting to your wireless network, see the "Troubleshooting Problems with Windows Media Center" section of this chapter to help alleviate this issue.

Running the Windows Media Center Setup Wizard again

The last menu selection under Tasks → Settings is "Run Windows Media Center setup again." This selection will actually run the original Setup Wizard again, allowing you to reconfigure your system using the wizard. If you either did not initially run the wizard or did not feel comfortable going through the different setup menus, this option will help you add new hardware and change specific settings relevant to your system.

Before running the Setup Wizard again, Windows Media Center prompts you to confirm that you really want to do this. If you click Yes to continue, you will lose all current preferences and settings. If you click No, you will exit Setup.

Troubleshooting Problems with Windows Media Center

The options under Tasks → Settings → General offer the greatest flexibility in managing and troubleshooting Windows Media Center. This section provides detailed troubleshooting information with devices in Windows Media Center.

Troubleshooting with the Windows Media Center Setup Menu

Selecting Tasks → Settings → General → Windows Media Center Setup allows you to configure your options as you did during initial installation of the product. This enables you to set up your Internet connection using the same menu as the original installation wizard. Setting up your TV signal brings up the wizard to install the TV tuner card, which you need in order to watch TV and record desired shows. Using the Set Up Your Speakers option allows you to configure the sound within Windows Media Center, or change the settings previously input into the application during the initial installation, which may be necessary when you update your sound system or have trouble with sound working correctly in Windows Media Center.

Selecting Tasks → Settings → General → Program Library Options allows you to control how applications control the media experience, access media information, and set the Windows Media Center Internet security settings. You also can edit programs and how they interact with Windows Media Center. Clicking the "Edit more programs" button lists the different programs that can connect to Windows Media Center. Checking or unchecking a particular application allows or disallows the application to connect to Windows Media Center for content. These settings can help you diagnose problems with other applications and with Windows Media Center.

Selecting Tasks → Settings → General → Startup and Windows Behavior allows you to manage Windows Media Center startup behavior. You can have Windows Media Center start automatically during Windows startup, or leave it in the default mode, requiring you to start the program manually from the Start menu.

Selecting Tasks → Settings → General → Visual and Sound Effects allows you to manage transition animations and navigational sounds. You can also manage the Windows Media Center color scheme and contrast.

Selecting Tasks → Settings → General → Windows Media Setup → Configure Your TV or Monitor allows you to adjust your display settings within Windows Media Center for optimal viewing.

Selecting Tasks → Settings → General → Windows Media Setup → Join Wireless Network allows you to add a wireless network to your installation. The wizard can automatically detect wireless networks within your area and configure them for use in Windows Media Center. This option helps when you lose wireless connectivity or need to set up a new wireless network connection.

The Microsoft web site offers additional information on troubleshooting Windows Media Center. Visit *http://www.microsoft.com/windowsxp/mediacenter/default.mspx* for more information. Many different web sites and blogs versed in troubleshooting Windows Media Center problems exist on the Web and are easy to access using an online search engine.

Troubleshooting Windows Media Center Networking Issues

If you have problems with network settings and configuration during the Setup Wizard, this section describes how to overcome common obstacles and get your networking issues corrected. First, you need to know what type of network card you have installed in your system. Second, you need to have the latest driver from the manufacturer.

Once you have the items you need to find your way around Device Manager in Windows Vista, you can open Device Manager by selecting the Start menu, right-clicking on the Computer icon, and selecting Manage. This opens Computer Management. In Computer Management, double-click the Device Manager node in the left pane. Then, in the right pane, click the + sign next to Network Adapters. This will show you the networking devices connected to your system. Once you have identified that a network card exists, right-click the appropriate icon and select Properties from the context menu.

Under the General tab listing, you'll see the device type, manufacturer, and location of the device. You also should see the Device Status listing, which should say "This device is working properly." If you do not see that the device is working properly, you need to click the Driver tab. The Driver tab has several buttons available for use. You need to click the "Update driver" button for this example. Once you have clicked this button, select "Browse my computer for driver software." Select the path to the driver you have for the network card and click the Next button. Windows Vista automatically installs the driver from the listing you gave and updates the driver on your system. Most of the time this will fix any problems you have with a network card.

If this procedure does not fix the problem, you may need to verify that the hardware actually works. You can do this by inserting a second network card, or running utilities available online. If you continue to have problems when you add a new card, you need to determine whether the slot in the motherboard is working correctly. Move the card into a new slot and see if Windows Vista picks it up after you reboot. Make sure to turn off the system completely by unplugging the computer from the wall outlet before you attempt to remove or install any hardware devices. Chapter 5 provides additional information on device troubleshooting.

Troubleshooting TV Tuner and Video Capture Problems

If you have problems with your video card or video capture card during Windows Media Center configuration, you need to verify that you have the latest driver available from the manufacturer. You need to know the manufacturer of the card first, and then download the driver file from the company's web site. Once you have retrieved the files, open Device Manager in Windows Vista and update the driver for the card, as discussed previously for network cards.

This procedure fixes the majority of issues you'll find with video cards. However, if you continue to have problems, you will need to verify that the card works correctly. Usually when you have video problems, you can identify them well before you load the operating system. If a video card fails to work correctly, you will not see any POST information from the system. If you are using a video capture or TV tuner card, this does not always stand true, however. If you have problems with these types of cards after updating the drivers in the operating system, you will need to move the card to a different slot to verify that the problem follows the card. If the card works in another slot, you need to check your motherboard for problems with the PCI bus. Make sure to turn off the system completely by unplugging the computer from the wall outlet before you attempt to remove or install any hardware devices. Chapter 5 provides additional information on device troubleshooting.

Troubleshooting Sound Problems

If you have problems with network settings and configuration during the Setup Wizard, this section describes how to overcome common obstacles and correct your sound issues. First, you need to know what type of sound card you have installed on your system. Second, you need to have the latest driver from the manufacturer. Once you have retrieved the files, you need to open Device Manager in Windows Vista and update the driver for the card, as discussed previously for network cards and video cards.

Most of the time this will fix any problems you have with a network card. If this procedure does not fix the problem, you may need to verify that the hardware actually works. You can do this by inserting a second sound card, or by running utilities available online. If you continue to have problems when you add a new card, you need to determine whether the slot in the motherboard is working correctly. Move the card into a new slot and see if Windows Vista picks it up after you reboot. Make sure to turn off the system completely by unplugging the computer from the wall outlet before you attempt to remove or install any hardware devices. Chapter 5 provides additional information on device troubleshooting.

CHAPTER 26

Using Group Policy with Windows Vista

Whether you are working with your computer at home or at the office, your computer is affected by Group Policy. Group Policy is a collection of policy settings that simplify management of a computer's configuration. Two general types of Group Policy are available: Active Directory Group Policy and Local Group Policy. As Active Directory Group Policy applies to all computers that are part of a Windows domain, a computer being used on a business network is affected by Active Directory Group Policy. As Local Group Policy applies to all computers regardless of their configuration, your computer—whether on a home network or a business network—is affected by Local Group Policy.

Whether you are a home user or an office user, policy settings are important because you can use them to manage a great many operating system features. Policy settings also typically control the things you can and cannot do with your computer. For example, the default policy configuration doesn't allow a nonadministrator user to install device drivers, but if you know how to work with policies you could modify this behavior to allow certain types of devices to be installed by users with standard user accounts. Also, as a broad set of policies known as Administrative Templates is used to configure registry settings, Group Policy has become the preferred way to manage a computer's registry settings. Collectively, the Administrative Templates settings expose hundreds of registry settings, making it much easier to manipulate operating system configuration.

Windows Vista features several fundamental changes to the way Group Policy works. This chapters looks at these features and discusses how they affect the way Group Policy is used. Chapters 27 and 28 provide comprehensive references for new policies included in Windows Vista.

Exploring Group Policy in Windows Vista

In Windows Vista, the overall architecture of Group Policy has changed in several fundamental ways. Windows Vista:

- Includes a new Group Policy Client service
- Makes multiple Local Group Policy Objects (LGPOs) available
- Integrates Group Policy with Network Location Awareness
- Features updated management tools and policy file formats

I discuss each enhancement in the sections that follow.

Introducing the Group Policy Client Service

One of the most significant changes is the introduction of the Group Policy Client service to completely isolate Group Policy notification and processing from the Windows logon process. Separating Group Policy from the Windows Logon process:

- Ensures that a single service can deliver the needed Group Policy functionality
- Enables more dynamic control over how policy settings are applied, maintained, and updated
- Reduces the resources used for background processing of policies while increasing overall performance
- Allows delivery of new Group Policy files as part of the update process and application of those updates without restart

The Group Policy Client service is a standalone service that runs under the Svchost process and no longer uses the trace logging functionality in *userenv.dll*. As a result, Group Policy event messages are now written to the system log with the event source of Microsoft-Windows-GroupPolicy, and the Group Policy Operational log replaces previous Userenv logging. The operational event log provides detailed event messages specific to Group Policy processing. When troubleshooting Group Policy issues, you'll use this log rather than *userenv.log* in the *%WINDIR%\Debug\ Usermode* folder.

Using Multiple Local Group Policy Objects

Unlike earlier implementations of Group Policy, Group Policy in Windows Vista allows the use of multiple LGPOs on a single computer. Previously, computers had only one LGPO. Windows Vista allows you to assign a different LGPO to each local user or group. This allows the application of a policy to be more flexible and support a wider array of implementation scenarios.

Multiple LGPOs are particularly useful when computers are being used in a standalone configuration rather than a domain configuration, because local administrator users no longer have to explicitly disable or remove settings that interfere with their ability to manage a computer before performing administrator tasks. Instead, an administrator user can implement one LGPO for administrators and another LGPO for nonadministrators.

 Administrator and nonadministrator LGPOs are the two standard types of LGPOs available. See "Working with Multiple Local Group Policy Objects," later in this chapter, for more information.

Enhancing Group Policy Application

Thanks to the Network Location Awareness feature in Windows Vista, Group Policy can respond better to changing network conditions and no longer relies on ICMP (ping) for policy application. Network Location Awareness ensures that a computer is aware of the type of network to which it is currently connected—in other words, whether the computer is on a private, public, or work network—and is responsive to changes in the system status or network configuration. This gives Group Policy access to the resource detection and event notification capabilities in the operating system, allowing Group Policy to determine when a computer is in standby mode or resuming from hibernation, as well as when a network connection has been disabled or disconnected. In cases where the network isn't available, Group Policy won't wait for the network, allowing for faster startup.

Because ICMP (ping) is no longer used for slow link detection, business networks can filter this protocol on their firewalls. Group Policy in Windows Vista uses Network Location Awareness to determine the network bandwidth. When mobile users connect to a business network, Group Policy can detect the availability of a domain controller and initiate a background refresh of policy over the VPN connection.

Improving Group Policy Management

Windows Vista includes the Group Policy Management Console (GPMC) and Group Policy Object Editor (GPOE) for managing Group Policy. While GPMC was previously provided as a separate download from Microsoft, it is now integrated directly into the operating system.

Using the GPMC, shown in Figure 26-1, you can manage Active Directory Group Policy in an enterprise environment. To open the GPMC, follow these steps:

1. Log on to a computer running Windows Vista with an administrative user account.

2. Click Start, type **mmc** into the Search box, and then press Enter.

3. In the Microsoft Management Console, click File → Add/Remove Snap-in.

4. In the Add or Remove Snap-ins dialog box, click Group Policy Management Console, click Add, and then click OK.

5. You can now navigate through the forest and domains in the organization to view individual Group Policy Objects (GPOs).

6. If you expand the site, domain, or organizational unit node in which a related policy object is stored, you can right-click the policy object and then choose Edit. This opens the object for editing in the GPOE.

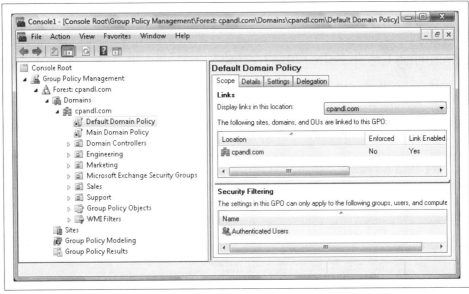

Figure 26-1. Accessing Active Directory Group Policy

Using the GPOE, shown in Figure 26-2, you can manage individual GPOs. To open the GPOE, follow these steps:

1. Log on to a computer running Windows Vista with an administrative user account.

2. Click Start, type **mmc** into the Search box, and then press Enter.

3. In the Microsoft Management Console, click File → Add/Remove Snap-in.

4. In the Add or Remove Snap-ins dialog box, click Group Policy Object Editor and then click Add.

5. In the Select Group Policy Object dialog box, the default object is the Local Computer Group Policy Object. If this is the object you want to work with, click Finish. If this isn't the object you want to work with, click Browse, select the object you want to work with, and then click OK.

6. Click OK to close the Add or Remove Snap-ins dialog box.

7. You can now work with the GPO you've opened.

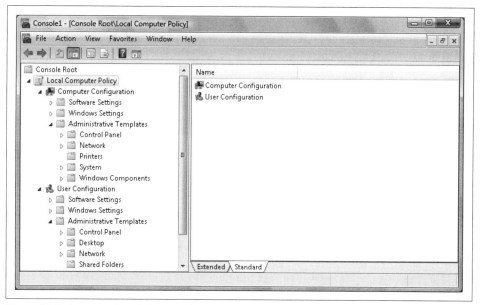

Figure 26-2. Accessing Local Group Policy

The included versions of the GPMC and GPOE have been updated to work with the new XML-based Administrative Templates implemented in Windows Vista and later versions of Windows. The new format is referred to as ADMX. These tools can also work with the previous ADM format.

ADMX files are divided into language-neutral and language-specific file sets. The language-neutral files ensure that a GPO has the same core policies. The language-specific files allow policies to be viewed and edited in multiple languages. Since the language-neutral files store the core settings, policies can be edited in any language for which a computer is configured, thus allowing one user to view and edit policies in English and another to view and edit policies in Spanish. The mechanism that determines which language is used is the language pack installed on the computer.

In domains, ADMX files are stored in a central store—the domain-wide directory created in the Sysvol. Previously, Administrative Templates were stored with each GPO. In the new implementation, only the current state of the setting is stored in the GPO and the ADMX files are stored centrally. As a result, this reduces the amount of storage space used as the number of GPOs increases, and it reduces the amount of data being replicated throughout the enterprise. As long as you edit GPOs using Windows Vista, new GPOs will not contain either ADM or ADXM files inside the GPO.

 The next server version of Windows after Windows Server 2003 will also implement a new replication mechanism for Group Policy—Distributed File System (DFS) Replication Service. With DFS replication, only the changes in GPOs are replicated, thereby eliminating the need to replicate an entire GPO when there is a change.

Editing Group Policy

After you access a policy for editing, you can use the GPOE to work with group policies. The GPOE has two main nodes:

Computer Configuration
    Enables you to set policies that are applied to computers, regardless of who logs on

User Configuration
    Enables you to set policies that are applied to users, regardless of which computer they log on to

The Computer Configuration and User Configuration nodes have subnodes for the following:

Software Settings
    Enables you to set policies for software settings and software installation

Windows Settings
    Enables you to set policies for folder redirection, scripts, and security

Administrative Templates
    Enables you to set policies for the operating system, Windows components, and programs

The policy settings you'll work with the most are those found under Administrative Templates. You can enable, disable, and configure policy settings for Administrative Templates by completing the following steps:

1. Open the policy object you want to edit. Access the GPOE for the resource you want to work with.

2. Expand Computer Configuration → Administrative Templates or User Configuration → Administrative Templates as appropriate for the type of policy you want to set.

3. After you expand the policy subfolders as appropriate, double-click or right-click a policy and select Properties to display its Properties dialog box.

4. Click the Explain tab to see a description of the policy, if one is available.

5. On the Setting tab, use the following buttons to change the state of the policy:

    Not Configured
        The policy is not configured.

    Enabled
        The policy is enabled.

    Disabled
        The policy is disabled.

6. If you enabled the policy, set any additional parameters specified on the Setting tab and then click Apply.

7. Click OK to save your settings.

Policy changes are applied when Group Policy is refreshed. Windows automatically refreshes policy periodically. However, with some types of policies you may need to log off and then log back on, or restart the computer.

Working with Multiple Local Group Policy Objects

As discussed previously, computers running Windows Vista can have multiple LGPOs. The way you use and work with multiple LGPOs is explored in this section.

Understanding Multiple Local Group Policy Object Usage

Multiple LGPOs increase flexibility when applying policy settings and allow home and workgroup users to gain some of the benefits and controls previously available only in Windows domains. They do this by allowing a policy to be uniquely tailored to users based on the logon account and their membership in specific groups.

Windows Vista has three layers of LGPOs:

1. Local Group Policy
2. Administrators and Non-Administrators Local Group Policy
3. User-specific Local Group Policy

These layers of LGPOs are processed in order. Local Group Policy is applied first. Administrators and Non-Administrators Local Group Policy is applied second. User-specific Local Group Policy is applied third.

Local Group Policy is the only LGPO that allows both computer configuration and user configuration settings to be applied. User configuration settings applied through the LGPO apply to all users of the computer, even the built-in Administrator account. Local Group Policy works the same as it did in Windows XP.

Administrators and Non-Administrators Local Group Policy contains only user configuration settings and is applied based on whether the user account being used is a member of the local Administrators group. A user is either an administrator or a nonadministrator. If the user is a member of the Administrators group, Administrators Local Group Policy is applied to the user at logon. If the user is not a member of the Administrators group, Non-Administrators Local Group Policy is applied to the user at logon.

User-specific Local Group Policy contains only user configuration settings and is applied based on whether an additional policy object has been created and applied to a user's account. In this way, you use User-specific Local Group Policy to apply policy settings to one specific user.

The available user settings are the same among all LGPOs. Because of this, it is possible that a setting in one GPO may conflict with a setting in another GPO. Windows

Vista resolves conflicts in settings by overwriting any previous setting with the last read and most current setting. The final setting is the one Windows Vista uses. Because of this, the processing order is extremely important: it determines which user settings are actually applied when there are conflicting settings.

 Only the enabled or disabled state of a setting matters. If a setting is set as Not Configured, this has no effect on the state of the setting from a previous policy application.

To see how setting overwriting works, consider the following examples:

- Jim is a member of the local Administrator account and has a user-specific GPO. When Jim logs on to his computer, Local Group Policy is applied, then Administrators Local Group Policy, and then his User-specific Local Group Policy. Thus, if Local Group Policy disabled a setting, then Administrators Local Group Policy enabled a setting, and then User-specific Local Group Policy disabled the setting, the setting would be disabled.

- Tina is not a member of the local Administrator account and has a user-specific GPO. When Tina logs on to her computer, Local Group Policy is applied, then Non-Administrators Local Group Policy, and then her User-specific Local Group Policy. Thus, if a setting is disabled in Local Group Policy, then enabled in Administrators Local Group Policy, and then not configured in User-specific Local Group Policy, the setting would be enabled.

As you can see, using multiple LGPOs in a standalone configuration allows you to control precisely how policy settings are applied to users based on their logon account and group membership. In a domain configuration, however, you might not want to use multiple LGPOs because in domains, most computers and users already have multiple GPOs applied to them, and adding multiple LGPOs to this already varied mix can make it confusing to manage Group Policy.

In a domain, computers apply local policy first and then domain policy. Because domain policy is applied last, domain policy settings overwrite any conflicting settings from local policy. Further, to simplify administration, domain administrators can disable processing of LGPOs on computers running Windows Vista by enabling the "Turn off Local Group Policy objects processing" policy setting in a domain GPO. In Group Policy, this setting is located under *Computer Configuration\Administrative Templates\System\Group Policy*.

Creating Multiple Local Group Policy Objects

Using the GPOE, you can easily create and manage multiple LGPOs. By default, the only local policy object that exists on a computer is the LGPO. You can, however, create other local objects as necessary. Other objects are created when you access them in the GPOE.

Accessing the top-level LGPO

The way you create or access a particular LGPO depends on the object you want to work with. You can access the top-level LGPO by completing the following steps:

1. Log on to a computer running Windows Vista with an administrative user account.
2. Click Start, type **mmc** into the Search box, and then press Enter.
3. In the Microsoft Management Console, click File → Add/Remove Snap-in.
4. In the Add or Remove Snap-ins dialog box, click Group Policy Object Editor and then click Add.
5. In the Select Group Policy Object dialog box, click Finish because this is the default object.
6. Click OK.

 You can use the same Microsoft Management Console to manage more than one LGPO. In the Add or Remove Snap-ins dialog box, you simply add one instance of the GPOE for each object you want to work with.

Accessing the Administrators Local Group Object or the Non-Administrators Local Group Object

You can create or access the Administrators Local Group Object or the Non-Administrators Local Group Object by completing the following steps:

1. Log on to a computer running Windows Vista with an administrative user account.
2. Click Start, type **mmc** into the Search box, and then press Enter.
3. In the Microsoft Management Console, click File → Add/Remove Snap-in.
4. In the Add or Remove Snap-ins dialog box, click Group Policy Object Editor and then click Add.
5. In the Select Group Policy Object dialog box, click Browse.
6. In the Browse for a Group Policy Object dialog box, click the Users tab, as shown in Figure 26-3. Note that the entries in the Group Policy Object Exists column specify whether a particular local policy object has already been created.
7. Select Administrators to create or access the Administrators Local Group Object. Select Non-Administrators to create or access the Non-Administrators Local Group Object.
8. Click OK.

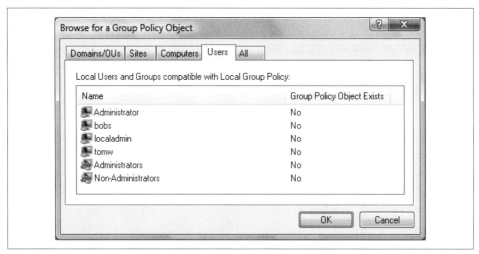

Figure 26-3. Creating or accessing the desired object

In the Microsoft Management Console, the policy is listed as *Local Computer\ Administrators Policy* or *Local Computer\Non-Administrators Policy* (see Figure 26-4). As discussed previously, only the top-level LGPO has both computer configuration and user configuration settings. Other types of local policy objects have only user configuration settings.

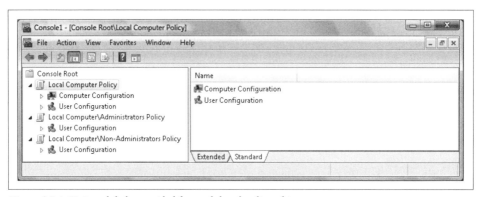

Figure 26-4. Unique labels provided for each local policy object

Accessing a user-specific local group object

You can create or access a user-specific local group object using the procedure outlined in the preceding section. The only change is that in step 7, you select the local user whose user-specific local group object you want to create or work with. If this object doesn't already exist, it will be created. Otherwise, you'll open the existing object for review and editing.

Deleting Local Group Policy Objects

All computers have an LGPO. You cannot delete this top-level policy object. You can, however, set each policy setting to Not Configured to ensure that no related policy settings are applied.

While you cannot delete this object, you can delete other LGPOs that you have created. When you delete an LGPO, the object and all its related settings are removed from the computer.

You can delete the Administrators Local Group Object, Non-Administrators Local Group Object, or User-specific Local Group Object by following these steps:

1. Log on to a computer running Windows Vista with an administrative user account.

2. Click Start, type **mmc** into the Search box, and then press Enter.

3. In the Microsoft Management Console, click File → Add/Remove Snap-in.

4. In the Add or Remove Snap-ins dialog box, click Group Policy Object Editor, and then click Add.

5. In the Select Group Policy Object dialog box, click Browse.

6. In the Browse for a Group Policy Object dialog box, click the Users tab, as shown in Figure 26-3.

7. Right-click the name of the policy you want to remove and then select Remove Group Policy Object.

8. When prompted to confirm, click Yes.

9. Click Cancel three times to exit all open dialog boxes.

10. In the Microsoft Management Console, click File → Exit. If prompted to save the console, click No.

11. Log off the computer to ensure that the policy object can be removed.

Updating Active Directory Group Policy Objects for Windows Vista

On a Windows Vista computer, you'll automatically see the Windows Vista policies as well as the other policies when you work with LGPOs. The same is not true automatically, however, if you try to use the Windows Vista policies in a domain. This is because Active Directory Group Policy objects must be updated to include Windows Vista policies. A similar update is required to apply any additional policies defined in service packs or later Windows releases. Once you've performed the update and made any necessary changes, you can perform basic management, such as policy linking or blocking, using any computer. However, it is recommended that the actual policy editing be done on a computer running Windows Vista or later.

Each Active Directory Group Policy object that should include Windows Vista policies must be updated separately. You update an individual GPO by following these steps:

1. Log on to a computer running Windows Vista with an administrative user account.

2. Click Start, type **mmc**, and then press Enter. This starts the Microsoft Management Console.

3. On the File menu, click Add or Remove Snap-in. This opens the Add or Remove Snap-ins dialog box.

4. In the Add or Remove Snap-ins dialog box, click Group Policy Management Console. Click Add and then click OK.

5. In the Microsoft Management Console, expand the Group Policy Management node.

6. Expand the Forest node. This node represents the current forest to which you are connected.

7. When you expand the Forest node, you'll see Domains and Sites nodes. Expand these nodes and their subnodes to work your way to the GPO you want to work with.

8. When you find the GPO you want to work with, right-click it and then select Edit to open the GPOE.

9. In the GPOE, select the Computer Configuration node by clicking it and then select the User Configuration node by clicking it.

When you select the Computer Configuration and User Configuration nodes, the current administrative templates are read and applied to the GPO you've selected. Once Group Policy is refreshed, you can modify policy settings as necessary, and the changes will be updated as appropriate in the selected site, domain, or organizational unit. Repeat this procedure to update the GPO for other sites, domains, or organizational units.

CHAPTER 27

Navigating Windows Vista Policy Changes

Each policy setting has a specific requirement for the operating system or systems it will work with. Some policies require at least Windows XP Professional or a later version of Windows. Others require at least Windows Vista or later. The exact requirements are listed in the explanatory text when you select a policy in the GPOE.

Since Group Policy was introduced with Windows 2000, every version of Windows and just about every service pack includes policy settings that extend the set of available policies. In its original implementation, Windows Vista has more than 2,400 policies—about 700 of which are new.

Navigating Windows Vista Policy Changes

The 700 new policies in Windows Vista can be grouped into a few dozen broad categories, summarized in Table 27-1. Use the details provided to help you understand what additional features and components can be managed using Group Policy for Windows Vista. The "Scope" column tells you which portion or portions of a policy are used for configuration—either User Configuration, Computer Configuration, or both. The "Group Policy location" column tells you where the related policies are located within User Configuration, Computer Configuration, or both.

Table 27-1. New areas of management in Group Policy for Windows Vista

Group Policy category	Scope	Group Policy location	Description
Antivirus	User Configuration	*Administrative Templates\ Windows Components\ Attachment Manager*	Sets the behavior for evaluating high-risk attachments.
Background Intelligent Transfer Service (BITS)	Computer Configuration	*Administrative Templates\ Network\Background Intelligent Transfer Service*	Manages the new BITS Neighbor Casting feature which facilitates peer-to-peer file transfer within a domain.

Table 27-1. New areas of management in Group Policy for Windows Vista (continued)

Group Policy category	Scope	Group Policy location	Description
Deployed Printer Connections	Computer Configuration, User Configuration	*Windows Settings\Deployed Printers*	Connects printers automatically by deploying a printer connection to a computer. This is useful when the computer is shared in a locked-down environment, such as a school, or when a user roams to different locations.
Device Installation	Computer Configuration	*Administrative Templates\System\Device Installation*	Permits or denies a device installation based on the device class or device ID.
Disk Troubleshooting and Diagnostics	Computer Configuration	*Administrative Templates\System\Troubleshooting and Diagnostics\Disk Diagnostic*	Manages automated disk diagnostics and controls the level of information displayed by the disk failure diagnostics.
DVD Video Burning	Computer Configuration, User Configuration	*Administrative Templates\Windows Components\Import Video*	Manages the way videos can be imported and burned to disk.
Enterprise Quality of Service (QoS)	Computer Configuration	*Windows Settings\Policy-based QoS*	Allows prioritization of network traffic to alleviate network congestion.
Hybrid Hard Disk	Computer Configuration	*Administrative Templates\System\Disk NV Cache*	Configures the hybrid hard disk with nonvolatile cache properties. This allows you to manage nonvolatile cache, startup and resume optimizations, solid state mode, and power savings mode.
Internet Explorer 7	Computer Configuration, User Configuration	*Administrative Templates\Windows Components\Internet Explorer*	Allows configuration of Internet Explorer registry-based values through Group Policy.
Network Quarantine	Computer Configuration	*Windows Settings\Security Settings\Network Access Protection*	Manages Health Registration Authority (HRA), Internet Authentication Service (IAS), and Network Access Protection (NAP).
Online Assistance	Computer Configuration,	*Administrative Templates\Windows Components\Online Assistance*	Controls where your users access Help content.
Power Management	Computer Configuration	*Administrative Templates\System\Power Management*	Makes it possible to configure all system-configurable power management options.

Table 27-1. New areas of management in Group Policy for Windows Vista (continued)

Group Policy category	Scope	Group Policy location	Description
Removable Storage	Computer Configuration, User Configuration	*Administrative Templates\ System\Removable Storage Access*	Protects data by limiting the data that can be read from and written to removable storage devices. Administrators can enforce restrictions on specific computers or users through policy settings.
Shell Application Management	User Configuration	*Administrative Templates\ Start Menu and Taskbar*	Manages access to the toolbar, taskbar, Start menu, and icon displays.
User Profiles	Computer Configuration, User Configuration	*Administrative Templates\ Windows Components\User Profiles*	Configures the logon experience to include expanded Group Policy settings in roaming user profiles, redirected folders, and logon dialog screens.
Auto Run, Auto Play	Computer Configuration, User Configuration	*Administrative Templates\ Windows Components\ AutoPlay Policies*	Customizes Autorun for different devices and media, creation and removal of partnerships, synchronization schedule and behavior, and creation and access to workspaces.
Shell Visuals	Computer Configuration, User Configuration	*Administrative Templates\ Windows Components\Desktop Windows Manager*	Configures the desktop display to include new graphics features, including flip views and live thumbnails.
Tablet PC	Computer Configuration, User Configuration	*Administrative Templates\ Windows Components\Input Personalization, Pen Training, TabletPC\Tablet PC Input Panel, TabletPC\Touch Input*	Configures Tablet PC features.
Terminal Services	Computer Configuration, User Configuration	*Administrative Templates\ Windows Components\Terminal Services*	Provides security and ease-of-use enhancements for Terminal Services. You can allow or prevent redirection of additional supported devices to the remote computer in a Terminal Services session. You can require the use of Transport Layer Security (TLS) 1.0 or native Remote Desktop Protocol (RDP) encryption, or negotiate a security method. You can also require the use of a specific encryption level (FIPS Compliant, High, Client Compatible, or Low).

Table 27-1. New areas of management in Group Policy for Windows Vista (continued)

Group Policy category	Scope	Group Policy location	Description
Troubleshooting and Diagnostics	Computer Configuration	*Administrative Templates\ System\Troubleshooting and Diagnostics*	Controls the diagnostics level, from automatically detecting and fixing problems to indicating to the user that assisted resolution is available for application issues, leak detection, and resource allocation.
User Account Control (UAC)	Computer Configuration	*Windows Settings\Security Settings\Local Policies\Security Options*	Determines behavior for the elevation prompt, automated application install, and file and registry virtualization.
Windows Error Reporting	Computer Configuration, User Configuration	*Administrative Templates\ Windows Components\Windows Error Reporting*	Allows you to disable Windows Feedback. By default, Windows Feedback is turned on for all Windows components.
Windows Firewall	Computer Configuration	*Windows Settings\Security Settings\Windows Firewall with Advance Security*	Provides integrated management of advanced firewall features and IP Security (IPSec).

CHAPTER 28

Navigating Internet Explorer 7 Policies

Internet Explorer 7 is included with Windows Vista. For the first time since Group Policy was introduced, you can fully manage Internet Explorer 7's registry-based settings using Group Policy. This means you can manage most features of Internet Explorer in one place without having to use the Internet Explorer Maintenance (IEM) extension or the Internet Explorer Administration Kit (IEAK). Not only does this give you a consistent way to manage the configuration of Internet Explorer 7 for both users and computers, but it also makes managing the configuration of Internet Explorer 7 much easier. This chapter provides a quick reference to the approximately 200 policy settings for Internet Explorer 7.

Getting Started with Internet Explorer 7 Policy Settings

Internet Explorer 7 is the version of Internet Explorer that ships with Windows Vista. To apply changes to Internet Explorer-related settings in policy, you must refresh policy, but no reboot or logoff is required.

Internet Explorer 7 policy settings are located in *Computer Configuration\Administrative Templates\Windows Components\Internet Explorer*, and in *User Configuration\ Administrative Templates\Windows Components\Internet Explorer*.

Using Internet Explorer 7 Policy Settings

Internet Explorer 7 settings can be divided into two broad categories:

Policy settings with exclusions
> Policy settings with exclusions apply only when Internet Explorer 7 is used with certain operating systems and configurations.

Policy settings without exclusions
> Policy settings without exclusions apply only to Windows operating systems running Internet Explorer 7.

Table 28-1 lists policies with specific exclusions. The "Scope" column specifies whether the policy setting is found under Computer Configuration, User Configuration, or both.

Table 28-1. Internet Explorer 7 policies and their applicable configurations

Scope	Policy setting	Description	Applicable configuration
Computer/ User	Turn on Protected Mode	When enabled, Protected Mode is turned on to protect Internet Explorer from exploited vulnerabilities by reducing the locations that Internet Explorer can write to in the registry and the filesystem. When disabled, Protected Mode will be turned off. When not configured, users will be able to turn Protected Mode on and off.	Applicable when Internet Explorer 7 is running on Windows Vista or later
User	Turn on Internet Connection Wizard Auto Detect	When enabled, the Internet Connection Wizard is launched automatically if it was not completed previously. The user cannot prevent the wizard from launching. When disabled, the Internet Connection Wizard is not launched automatically. The user can launch the wizard manually. If not configured, the user will have the freedom to decide whether the Internet Connection Wizard should be launched automatically.	Not applicable when Internet Explorer 7 is running on Windows Vista
Computer/ User	Prevent participation in the Customer Experience Improvement Program	When enabled, this prevents users from participating in the Customer Experience Improvement Program (CEIP) and removes the Customer Feedback Options menu item from the Help menu. When disabled, users must participate in the CEIP. It also removes the Customer Feedback Options menu item from the Help menu. If not configured, users can choose to participate in the CEIP.	Not applicable when Internet Explorer 7 is running on Windows Vista

Table 28-2 lists policies applicable regardless of which version of Windows is running Internet Explorer 7. The "Scope" column specifies whether the policy setting is found under Computer Configuration, User Configuration, or both.

Table 28-2. Internet Explorer 7 policies for all operating systems

Scope	Policy setting	Description
Computer/ User	Add a specific list of search providers to the user's search provider list	When enabled, the user can add and remove search providers, but only from the set of search providers specified in the list of search provider policy keys (found under *[HKCU or HKLM\Software\policies\Microsoft\Internet Explorer\Search-Scopes]*). If disabled or not configured, the user will be able to configure his search provider list unless another policy setting is restricting such configuration.
Computer/ User	All Processes	When enabled, a script running in any of the processes on the machine can perform a clipboard operation without prompting. This means that if the zone behavior is currently set to Prompt, it will be bypassed and enabled. When disabled, a script running in any of the processes on the machine cannot bypass the prompt for cut, copy, or paste operations from the clipboard. If not configured, current values of the URL action for the application/processes on the machine prevail.

Scope	Policy setting	Description
Computer/ User	Allow scriptlets	When enabled, users will be able to run scriptlets. When disabled, users will not be able to run scriptlets. If not configured, users can enable or disable scriptlets.
Computer/ User	Allow status bar updates via script	When enabled, a script is allowed to update the status bar. When disabled, a script is not allowed to update the status bar. If not configured, status bar updates via scripts will be disabled.
User	Allow the display of image download placeholders	When enabled, placeholders will be drawn for graphical images while the images are downloading. Users cannot change this policy setting. The "Turn off picture display" policy setting must be disabled if this policy setting is enabled. When disabled, placeholders will not be drawn for graphical images while the images are downloading. Users cannot change this policy setting. If not configured, users can allow or prevent the display of placeholders for graphical images while they are downloading.
User	Allow the printing of background colors and images	When enabled, Internet Explorer prints background colors and images when users print a web page. Users cannot change this policy setting. When disabled, Internet Explorer will not print background colors and images when users print a web page. Users cannot change this policy setting. If not configured, users can turn the ability to print background colors and images on and off.
Computer/ User	Allow video and animation on a web page that does not use an external media player (through the dynsrc attribute)	When enabled, video and animation can be played through the img/dynsrc tag in the zones chosen. When disabled, video and animation cannot be played through the img/dynsrc tag. If not configured, video and animation can be played through the img/dynsrc tag in the zones chosen.
Computer/ User	Customize User Agent string	When enabled, Internet Explorer will send the specified custom string in the version portion of the User Agent header. If disabled or not configured, Internet Explorer will send the current Internet Explorer version in the User Agent header (for example, "MSIE 7.0").
Computer/ User	Disable WinFX Runtime Components Setup	When enabled, WinFX Runtime Components Setup will be disabled. Users will not be able to change this behavior. When disabled, WinFX Runtime Components Setup will be enabled. Users will not be able to change this behavior. If not configured, WinFX Runtime Components Setup will be enabled by default. Users will have the freedom to change this behavior.
Computer/ User	Do not allow resetting Internet Explorer settings	When enabled, users will not be able to use Reset Internet Explorer Settings. If disabled or not configured, users will be able to use Reset Internet Explorer Settings.
Computer/ User	Enable Native XMLHttp Support	When enabled, users will be allowed to use natively implemented scriptable XMLHttp. When disabled, users will be prevented from running scriptable native XMLHttp. If not configured, users can choose to run scriptable native XMLHttp.
Computer/ User	Enforce full screen mode	When enabled, the navigation bar, command bar, and menu bar will not be visible and users will not be able to access them. If disabled or not configured, users will be able to view and access the navigation bar, command bar, and menu bar.
User	Help menu: Remove "Tour" menu option	When enabled, the Tour command is removed from the Help menu. When disabled or not configured, users can run the tour from the Help menu.
Computer/ User	Internet Explorer processes	When enabled, a script running in the Internet Explorer process can perform a clipboard operation without prompting. In the Internet Explorer process, if the zone behavior is currently set to Prompt it will be bypassed and enabled. When disabled, the script cannot bypass the prompt for cut, copy, or paste operations from the clipboard in the Internet Explorer process. When not configured, current values of the URL Action for the Internet Explorer process will prevail.

Scope	Policy setting	Description
Computer/ User	Loose or uncompiled .xaml files	When enabled and the drop-down box is set to Enable, .xaml files will be auto-matically loaded inside Internet Explorer 7. Users will not be able to change this behavior. If the drop-down box is set to Prompt, users will receive a prompt for loading .xaml files. When disabled, .xaml files will not be loaded inside Internet Explorer 7. Users will not be able to change this behavior. When not configured, users can decide whether to load .xaml files inside Internet Explorer 7.
User	Moving the menu bar above the navigation bar	When enabled, the menu bar will be above the navigation bar. Users will not be able to interchange positions of the menu and navigation bars. When disabled, the menu bar will be below the navigation bar. Users will not be able to inter-change positions of the menu and navigation bars. When not configured, users will be able to interchange positions of the menu and navigation bars.
Computer/ User	Prevent "Fix settings" functionality	When enabled, users cannot use the "Fix settings" functionality. When disabled, users can use the "Fix settings" functionality. When not configured, users will be able to use the "Fix settings" functionality. When this policy setting is enabled, the "Fix setting" option in the Information bar shortcut menu should be disabled.
User	Prevent configuration of search from the Address bar	When enabled, you must specify what action should be performed when search-ing from the Address bar. Users cannot change this setting. If you disable or do not configure this policy setting, users can specify what action should be per-formed when searching from the Address bar.
Computer/ User	Prevent ignoring certifi-cate errors	When enabled, users are not permitted to continue navigation if certificate errors occur. When disabled or not configured, users may elect to ignore certificate errors and continue navigation.
Computer/ User	Prevent performance of First Run Customize settings	When enabled, users must make one of two choices the first time they use Inter-net Explorer: skip Customize Settings and go directly to their home page, or skip Customize Settings and go directly to the Welcome to Internet Explorer web page. If disabled or not configured, users go through the regular first run process.
Computer	Prevent setting of the code download path for each machine	This policy setting prevents the setting of the code download path for each machine. When the Internet Component Download service is enabled, users can-not specify the download path for the code of an OLE component. You must spec-ify the download path. If disabled or not configured, users can specify the download path for the code.
Computer	Prevent the configuration of cipher strength update information URLs	This policy setting prevents the configuration of cipher strength update informa-tion URLs. When enabled, users will not be able to configure the cipher strength update information URL. You must specify the cipher strength update informa-tion URL. If disabled or not configured, users can configure the cipher strength update information URL.
Computer/ User	Prevent the Internet Explorer Search box from displaying	When enabled, the Search box in Internet Explorer will be disabled and will not appear in the Internet Explorer frame. If disabled or not configured, the Search box will appear in the Internet Explorer frame by default.
User	Prevent the use of Win-dows colors	When enabled, Windows colors will be turned off. Users cannot turn them on. When disabled, Windows colors will be turned on. Users cannot turn them off. When not configured, users will have the freedom to turn Windows colors for dis-play on and off.
User	Prevent users from choos-ing default text size	When enabled, users cannot choose the default text size in Internet Explorer. You must specify the default text size. If disabled or not configured, users can choose the default text size in Internet Explorer.

Scope	Policy setting	Description
User	Prevent users from configuring background color	When enabled, users cannot choose the background color in Internet Explorer. You must specify the background color. If disabled or not configured, users can choose the background color in Internet Explorer.
User	Prevent users from configuring text color	When enabled, users cannot choose the text color in Internet Explorer. You must specify the text color. If disabled or not configured, users can choose the text color in Internet Explorer.
User	Prevent users from configuring the color of links that have already been clicked	When enabled, users cannot configure the color of links that have already been clicked in Internet Explorer. You must specify the link color. If disabled or not configured, users can choose the color of links that have already been clicked.
User	Prevent users from configuring the color of links that have not yet been clicked	When enabled, users cannot configure the color of links that have not yet been clicked in Internet Explorer. You must specify the link color. If disabled or not configured, users can choose the color of links that have not yet been clicked.
User	Prevent users from configuring the hover color	When enabled, users cannot configure the hover color. You must specify the hover color. If disabled or not configured, users can configure the hover color.
Computer/ User	Process List	This policy setting allows administrators to define applications for which they want this feature to be prevented or allowed. When enabled for the application process in the list, a script can perform a clipboard operation without prompting. This means that if the zone behavior is currently set to Prompt, it will be bypassed and enabled. When disabled for the application/process in the list, a script running in the application/process in the list cannot bypass the prompt for clipboard operations. When not configured, current values of the URL Action for the application/process in the list are used.
Computer/ User	Restrict changing the default search provider	When enabled, users will not be able to change the default search provider. If disabled or not configured, users will have the freedom to change the default search provider.
Computer/ User	Restrict search providers to a specific list of providers	When enabled, users will not be able to configure the list of search providers on their computer, and any default providers installed will not appear (including providers installed from other applications). The only providers that will appear will be those in the list of search provider policy keys (found under *[HKCU or HKLM\Software\policies\Microsoft\Internet Explorer\SearchScopes]*). If disabled or not configured, users will be able to configure their list of search providers.
Computer/ User	Send internationalized domain names	When enabled, you must specify when Unicode domain names in IDN format should be sent. If disabled or not configured, users can control this setting by using Advanced Options in the Internet Control Panel. By default, domain names will be converted to IDN format only for addresses that are not in the intranet zone.
Computer/ User	Turn off Delete Browsing History functionality	When enabled, users cannot perform the Delete Browsing History action in Internet Options for Internet Explorer 7. If disabled or not configured, users can perform the Delete Browsing History action in Internet Options for Internet Explorer 7.
Computer/ User	Turn off Delete Forms functionality	When enabled, users cannot delete form entries from the browsing history. If disabled or not configured, users can delete form entries from the browsing history.
Computer/ User	Turn off Delete Passwords functionality	When enabled, users cannot delete passwords from the browsing history. If disabled or not configured, users can delete passwords from the browsing history.

Scope	Policy setting	Description
Computer/ User	Turn off addition and removal of feeds	This policy setting prevents users from subscribing to a feed or deleting a sub-scribed feed. When enabled, the menu item to subscribe to the feed and the menu item to delete the feed are disabled. If disabled or not configured, users can add a feed through the Subscribe button in Internet Explorer and delete a feed through the feed list control.
User	Turn off automatic image resizing	This policy setting specifies whether you want Internet Explorer to automatically resize large images so that they fit in the browser window. When enabled, auto-matic image resizing is turned off. Users cannot change this setting. When dis-abled, automatic image resizing is turned on. Users cannot change this setting. When not configured, users can turn automatic image resizing on and off.
Computer/ User	Turn off background sync for feeds	This policy setting controls whether feeds are synced in the background. When enabled, the ability to sync feeds in the background is disabled. If disabled or not configured, users are allowed to sync their feeds in the background.
Computer	Turn off changing the URL to be displayed for check-ing updates to Internet Explorer and Internet Tools	When enabled, users will not be able to change the URL to be displayed for checking updates to Internet Explorer and Internet Tools. You must specify the URL to be displayed for checking updates to Internet Explorer and Internet Tools. If disabled or not configured, users will be able to change the URL to be displayed for checking updates to Internet Explorer and Internet Tools.
Computer/ User	Turn off ClearType	When enabled, applications hosting MSHTML will not render text using the Microsoft ClearType rendering engine. If disabled or not configured, applications hosting MSHTML will render text using the Microsoft ClearType rendering engine.
Computer/ User	Turn off configuration of default behavior of new tab creation	This policy setting allows you to configure the default behavior of new tab cre-ation in Internet Explorer. When enabled, users will not be able to configure tab behavior. You must specify whether tabs should open in the foreground or back-ground. Users will not be able to open the tabs in the background by pressing Ctrl-Shift-Select or open the tabs in the foreground by pressing Ctrl-Shift-Select. If disabled or not configured, users will be able to control tab opening behavior.
Computer/ User	Turn off configuration of tabbed browsing pop-up behavior	This policy setting allows you to define the user experience related to pop-up windows and tabbed browsing in Internet Explorer. When enabled, users will not be able to configure the tabbed browsing pop-up behavior. You will have to specify the behavior desired. If you disable or do not configure this setting, the users' settings for tabbed browsing pop-up behavior will be used.
Computer/ User	Turn off configuration of window reuse	This policy setting allows you to configure the behavior of new windows in Inter-net Explorer. When enabled, users will not be able to configure the behavior of window reuse. You must specify the behavior. If tabbed browsing is enabled, a new tab will be created in this scenario. If disabled or not configured, users will be able to change window reuse.
Computer	Turn off configuring the update check interval (in days)	The default update check interval is 30 days. When enabled, users will not be able to configure the update check interval. You will have to specify the update check interval. If disabled or not configured, users will have the freedom to con-figure the update check interval.
User	Turn off configuring underline links	This policy setting specifies how you want links on web pages to be underlined. When enabled, users cannot select when to underline links. You must specify when to underline links. If disabled or not configured, users can choose when to underline links.

Scope	Policy setting	Description
Computer/ User	Turn off displaying the Internet Explorer Help menu	When enabled, users will not be able to use the Internet Explorer Help menu. If disabled or not configured, the Internet Explorer Help menu will be available to users, and they can also use F1 to access help.
Computer/ User	Turn off downloading of enclosures	When enabled, the setting to download a file attachment in a feed is disabled. When disabled, users can set the Feed Sync Engine to download a file attachment through the Feed property page. When not configured, users can set the Feed Sync Engine to download a file attachment through the Feed property page.
Computer/ User	Turn off Feed Discovery	When enabled, users do not get notification on the toolbar that a feed is available. If disabled or not configured, users can see when a feed is available and click on the Feed Discovery button.
Computer/ User	Turn off First-Run Opt-In	When users encounter a new control that has not previously run in Internet Explorer, they may be prompted to approve the control. When enabled, the prompt will be turned off in the corresponding zone. When disabled, the prompt will be turned on in the corresponding zone. When not configured, the first-run prompt is turned off by default.
User	Turn off friendly HTTP error messages	When enabled and there is a problem connecting with an Internet server, users will not get a detailed description or hints about how to correct the problem. Users cannot change this policy setting. When disabled and there is a problem connecting with an Internet server, users will get a detailed description with hints about how to correct the problem. Users cannot change this policy setting. When not configured, users can turn friendly HTTP error messages on and off.
Computer/ User	Turn off managing phishing filter	When enabled, the user will not be prompted to enable the phishing filter. You must specify which mode the phishing filter uses. If disabled or not configured, users will be prompted to decide the mode of operation for the phishing filter.
Computer/ User	Turn off managing Allow Pop-up Exceptions list	You can allow pop ups from specific web sites by adding the site to the exceptions list. When enabled, users will not be able to add web sites to or remove web sites from the exceptions list. If disabled or not configured, users will be able to specify web sites in the Allow Pop-Up Exceptions list.
Computer/ User	Turn off managing pop-up filter level	When enabled, users will not be able to change the filter levels for blocking pop ups. You can specify the pop-up filter level by importing Privacy settings from your machine under Internet Explorer Maintenance. If you disable or do not configure this policy, users will be able to manage pop ups based on filter levels. You may also want to enable the "Turn off managing pop-up Allow list" and "Turn off pop-up management policies" to disable users from configuring pop-up behavior.
User	Turn off page transitions	When enabled, page transitions will be turned off. Users cannot change this behavior. When disabled, page transitions will be turned on. Users cannot change this behavior. When not configured, users can turn page transitions on and off.
Computer/ User	Turn off page zooming functionality	When enabled, applications hosting MSHTML will not respond to user input that causes the content to be rerendered at a scaled size. When disabled, applications hosting MSHTML will respond to user input that causes the content to be re-rendered at a scaled size. Note: this policy setting is disabled by default.
User	Turn off picture display	When enabled, images are not shown. Users can still display an individual image by right-clicking the icon that represents the image and then clicking Show Picture. When disabled, pictures are shown. Users cannot change this setting. When not configured, users will have the freedom to turn the ability to display pictures on and off.

Scope	Policy setting	Description
Computer/User	Turn off Quick Tabs functionality	When enabled, the entry points to Quick Tabs will be removed from the Internet Explorer user interface. If disabled or not configured, Quick Tabs will not be affected by this setting.
User	Turn off sending URLs as UTF-8 (requires restart)	When enabled, Internet Explorer does not allow sending URLs as UTF-8. Users cannot change this policy setting. When disabled, Internet Explorer allows sending URLs as UTF-8. Users cannot change this policy setting. When not configured, users can allow or prevent the sending of URLs as UTF-8.
User	Turn off smart image dithering	When enabled, images will not be smoothed for display. Users cannot change this policy setting. When disabled, images will be smoothed for display. Users cannot change this policy setting. When not configured, users can turn smart image dithering on and off.
User	Turn off smooth scrolling	When enabled, smooth scrolling will be turned off. Users cannot change this behavior. When disabled, smooth scrolling will be turned on. Users cannot change this behavior. When not configured, users can turn smooth scrolling on and off.
Computer/User	Turn off tabbed browsing	When enabled, tabbed browsing and related entry points will be disabled and users cannot change this setting. When disabled, tabbed browsing and related entry points will be enabled and users cannot change this setting. When not configured, users will be able to enable or disable tabbed browsing.
Computer/User	Turn off the feed list	This policy setting prevents users from using Internet Explorer as a feed reader. This setting has no impact on the RSS platform. When enabled, users cannot access the feed list located in the Favorites Center. If disabled or not configured, users can access the feed list in the Favorites Center.
Computer/User	Turn off the Security Settings Check feature	This policy setting turns off the Security Settings Check feature, which checks Internet Explorer security settings to determine when the settings put Internet Explorer at risk. When enabled, the security settings check will not be performed. If disabled or not configured, the security settings check will be performed.
Computer/User	Turn off toolbar upgrade tool	The toolbar upgrade tool checks to see if incompatible toolbars or browser helper objects are installed when Internet Explorer is started. If so, users will be prompted to update or disable the toolbar. Specific toolbars or browser helper objects that are enabled or disabled via policy will not undergo this check. If this policy is enabled, the toolbar upgrade tool will not check for incompatible toolbars and incompatible toolbars will run unless previously disabled through policy or the user. If this policy is disabled or not configured, the toolbar upgrade tool will check for incompatible toolbars and give users the option to enable or disable incompatible toolbars. Toolbars that are enabled or disabled via policy will not undergo these checks.
Computer/User	Turn on automatic detection of the intranet	This policy setting enables intranet mapping rules to be applied automatically when the computer belongs to a domain. When enabled, intranet automatic detection will be enabled and the intranet mapping rules will be applied automatically if the computer belongs to a domain. When disabled, intranet automatic detection will be disabled and the intranet mapping rules will be applied however they are configured. If this policy setting is not configured, users can choose whether to automatically detect the intranet through the intranet settings dialog shown in the Control Panel.

Scope	Policy setting	Description
User	Turn on Automatic Signup	When enabled, Internet Explorer is launched automatically to complete the signup process after the branding is complete for ISPs using the IEAK. Users cannot change this behavior. When disabled, Internet Explorer will not be launched automatically. Users cannot change this behavior. When not configured, users can control whether Internet Explorer is started.
Computer/ User	Turn on Compatibility Logging	When enabled, users will be able to log information blocked by new Internet Explorer features. Users cannot turn off logging. When disabled, users will not be able to log information blocked by new Internet Explorer features. Users cannot turn on logging. When not configured, users can change the logging settings.
Computer/ User	Turn on Information bar notification for intranet content	When enabled, an Information bar notification will be shown whenever a user navigates to a page that loads content from an intranet site. When disabled, no Information bar notification will be shown when users load content from an intranet site that is being treated as though it is in the Internet zone. If this policy setting is not configured, the Information bar will be shown for intranet content loaded in a browser on a computer that is part of a workgroup.
User	Turn on inline AutoComplete for web addresses	When enabled, the AutoComplete feature for web addresses is turned on. Users cannot turn it off. When disabled, the AutoComplete feature for web addresses is turned off. Users cannot turn it on. When not configured, users can turn the AutoComplete feature for web addresses on and off.
Computer/ User	Turn on menu bar by default	When enabled, the menu bar will appear in Internet Explorer by default and users cannot turn it off. When disabled, the menu bar will not appear in Internet Explorer by default and users cannot turn it on. When not configured, the menu bar will be turned off by default. Users are free to turn the menu bar on and off.
User	Turn on script debugging	When enabled, script debugging will be turned on. Users cannot change the Disable Script Debugging option. When disabled, script debugging will be turned off. Users cannot change the Disable Script Debugging option. When not configured, users can turn the Disable Script Debugging option on and off.
User	Turn on the display of a notification about every script error	When enabled, users are shown the actual script errors when a page does not appear properly because of problems with scripting. Users cannot change this policy setting. When disabled, users are not shown the actual script errors when a page does not appear properly because of problems with scripting. Users cannot change this policy setting. When not configured, users can turn the display of a notification about every script error on and off.
User	Turn on the hover color option	This policy setting is used to make hyperlinks change color when the mouse pointer pauses on them. When enabled, the hover color option will be turned on. Users cannot turn it off. When disabled, the hover color option will be turned off. Users cannot turn it on. When not configured, users will have the freedom to turn the hover color option on and off.
Computer/ User	Use UTF-8 for mailto links	When enabled, Internet Explorer will encode mailto links in UTF-8. When disabled, Internet Explorer will send mailto links encoded through the current user's code page as per Internet Explorer 6 and earlier. When not configured, Internet Explorer will send mailto links encoded through the current user's code page. Users can change this behavior in the Internet Explorer Tools menu: click Internet Options, click the Advanced tab, and under International, select the "Use UTF-8 for mailto links" checkbox.

Table 28-2. Internet Explorer 7 policies for all operating systems (continued)

Scope	Policy setting	Description
Computer/ User	Web Browser Applications	Controls browser-hosted, ClickOnce-deployed applications built using WinFX. When enabled and the drop-down box is set to Enable, *.xbap*s will be automatically loaded inside Internet Explorer 7. Users will not be able to change this behavior. If the drop-down box is set to Prompt, users will receive a prompt for loading *.xbap*s. When disabled, *.xbap*s will not be loaded. Users will not be able to change this behavior. When not configured, users can decide whether to load *.xbap*s inside Internet Explorer 7.
Computer/ User	XPS files	Controls files using the XML Paper Specification (XPS) document format. These files contain a fixed-layout representation of a document. When enabled and the drop-down box is set to Enable, *.xps* files will be automatically loaded inside Internet Explorer 7. Users will not be able to change this behavior. If the drop-down box is set to Prompt, users will receive a prompt for loading *.xps* files. When disabled, *.xps* files will not be loaded inside Internet Explorer 7. Users will not be able to change this behavior. When not configured, users can decide whether to load *.xps* files inside Internet Explorer 7.

Desktop Tips and Tricks with Keyboard Shortcuts

Programmable keyboards are fantastic. I love mine because it allows me to start my favorite programs and perform common tasks, such as copying, cutting, and pasting, with the click of a button. As wonderful as programmable keyboards are, no programmable keyboard is a substitute for the raw power of the keyboard shortcuts that are built into Windows Vista and all Windows programs. A *keyboard shortcut* is a combination of two or more keys that you can use to perform a task that would otherwise require using a mouse or other pointing device.

In this chapter, I'll discuss desktop tips and tricks you can perform with keyboard shortcuts. I'll also provide lists of shortcuts for Windows Vista and other Windows programs.

Using and Creating Keyboard Shortcuts

Keyboard shortcuts are meant to save you time and effort. Since literally hundreds of shortcuts are available, don't try to memorize them all. Instead, select and memorize the ones you'll use the most and the ones that'll save you the most time and effort.

Some Windows programs have navigation shortcuts for their menus and menu options. When you are working with a program, check the menu for shortcuts. If a letter is underlined in a menu, you can usually press the Alt key and the underlined letter in combination to display the menu. If a letter is underlined in a menu option, you can then press Alt and the underlined letter in combination to perform the related task and display a submenu.

All Windows programs have keyboard shortcuts for performing common tasks. When you display a menu by clicking it, the keyboard shortcut sometimes is listed after the name of the menu option. Increasingly, though, the trend is to streamline menus and menu options by removing the lists of shortcuts, and you'll find this to be true in many of the programs that ship with Windows Vista. For this reason, in this chapter I've included guides to the available shortcuts for Windows Vista and some other Windows programs.

With Windows Vista, you can create keyboard shortcuts to open programs, which is often simpler than opening programs using the Start menu. All keyboard shortcuts that open programs require that you use Ctrl-Alt in combination with another key. For example, rather than clicking Start → All Programs → Microsoft Office → Microsoft Office Outlook, you could create a keyboard shortcut that opens Microsoft Office Outlook by clicking Ctrl-Alt-O.

To create a keyboard shortcut for opening a program, you must modify the properties of a menu item, a desktop shortcut, or other shortcut that opens the program. If no shortcut is available for opening the program, you must create one by completing the following steps:

1. In Windows Explorer, browse to the folder that contains the program. The program file will have a *.exe* extension.

 If you cannot see file extensions, click Organize and then select Folder and Search Options. This displays the Folder Options dialog box. On the View tab, clear "Hide extensions for known file types" and then click OK.

2. Right-click the program file and then click Create Shortcut.
3. If prompted to create the shortcut on the desktop, click Yes.

Once you've created the required shortcut or located a shortcut to the program, you can create a keyboard shortcut that opens the program by completing the following steps:

1. Right-click the shortcut, and then click Properties.
2. In the Shortcut Properties dialog box, click the Shortcut tab, and then click the Shortcut Key box.
3. Press the key on your keyboard that you want to use in combination with Ctrl-Alt to open the program. Usually, you'll want to use a letter or a number in combination with Ctrl-Alt. You cannot use the Esc, Enter, Tab, Space bar, Print Screen, Shift, or Backspace key.
4. Click OK to save your settings.

You can now use the keyboard shortcut to open the program when you're working with the desktop. Although the shortcut will also open the program from within some other programs, this won't always work because the program might use this shortcut.

Keyboard Shortcuts for Windows Vista

Shortcut keys are available for many of the commands in Windows Vista. Using shortcut keys, you can quickly accomplish common tasks. Table 29-1 lists keyboard shortcuts for accessibility.

Table 29-1. Ease-of-access keyboard shortcuts

To do this...	Use this keyboard shortcut...
Open the Ease of Access Center	Windows logo key-U
Turn filter keys on and off	Right-Shift for 8 seconds
Turn High Contrast on or off	Left Alt-left Shift-Print Screen (or PrtScn)
Turn mouse keys on or off	Left Alt-left Shift-Num Lock
Turn Sticky Keys on or off	Shift five times
Turn toggle keys on or off	Num Lock for 5 seconds

Table 29-2 lists general keyboard shortcuts for when you are working with Windows Vista and Windows programs.

Table 29-2. General keyboard shortcuts

To do this...	Use this keyboard shortcut...
Activate the menu bar in the active program	F10
Cancel the current task	Esc
Close the active document when multiple documents are open	Ctrl-F4
Close the active item or exit the active program	Alt-F4
Copy the selected item	Ctrl-C
Cut the selected item	Ctrl-X
Cycle through items in the order in which they were opened	Alt-Esc
Cycle through screen elements in a window or on the desktop	F6
Delete the selected item and move it to the Recycle Bin	Delete
Delete the selected item without moving it to the Recycle Bin first	Shift-Delete
Display properties of the selected item	Alt-Enter
Display the address history list	F4
Display the shortcut menu for the selected item	Shift-F10
Flip 3D through open items	Windows logo key-Tab
Flip 3D through open items	Ctrl-Windows logo key-Tab
Flip between open items	Ctrl-Alt-Tab

Table 29-2. General keyboard shortcuts (continued)

To do this...	Use this keyboard shortcut...
Move the cursor to the beginning of the next paragraph	Ctrl-down arrow
Move the cursor to the beginning of the next word	Ctrl-right arrow
Move the cursor to the beginning of the previous paragraph	Ctrl-up arrow
Move the cursor to the beginning of the previous word	Ctrl-left arrow
Open Task Manager	Ctrl-Shift-Esc
Open the next menu to the left, or close a submenu	Left arrow
Open the next menu to the right, or open a submenu	Right arrow
Open the shortcut menu for the active window	Alt-Space bar
Open the Start menu	Ctrl-Esc
Paste the selected item	Ctrl-V
Prevent the CD from automatically playing	Shift-insert a CD
Refresh the active window	F5
Rename the selected item	F2
Search for a file or folder	F3
Select a block of text	Ctrl-Shift-any arrow key
Select all items in a document or window	Ctrl-A
Select more than one item	Shift-any arrow key
Switch between open items	Alt-Tab
Undo an action	Ctrl-Z
View the folder one level up in Windows Explorer	Alt-up arrow

Table 29-3 lists keyboard shortcuts for when you are working with dialog boxes.

Table 29-3. Dialog box keyboard shortcuts

To do this...	Use this keyboard shortcut...
Click the mouse	Enter
Display Help	F1
Display the items in the active list	F4
Move back through options	Shift-Tab
Move back through tabs	Ctrl-Shift-Tab
Move forward through options	Tab
Move forward through tabs	Ctrl-Tab
Open a folder one level up if a folder is selected in the Save As or Open dialog box	Backspace
Perform the command or select an option	Alt-underlined letter
Select a button if the active item is a group of option buttons	Arrow keys
Select or clear the checkbox if the active item is a checkbox	Space bar

Table 29-4 lists keyboard shortcuts for keyboards with the Windows logo key.

Table 29-4. Windows logo key shortcuts

To do this...	Use this keyboard shortcut...
Bring all gadgets to the front and select Windows Sidebar	Windows logo key-Space bar
Cycle through programs on the taskbar	Windows logo key-T
Cycle through Sidebar gadgets	Windows logo key-G
Display the desktop	Windows logo key-D
Display the System Properties dialog box	Windows logo key-Break
Flip 3D through open items	Windows logo key-Tab or Ctrl-Windows logo key-Tab
Lock your computer if you are connected to a network domain, or switch users if you're not connected to a network domain	Windows logo key-L
Minimize all windows	Windows logo key-M
Open Computer	Windows logo key-E
Open Ease of Access Center	Windows logo key-U
Open or close the Start menu	Windows logo key
Open the Run dialog box	Windows logo key-R
Open Windows Mobility Center	Windows logo key-X
Restore minimized windows to the desktop	Windows logo key-Shift-M
Search for a file or folder	Windows logo key-F
Search for computers if you are on a network	Ctrl-Windows logo key-F

Keyboard Shortcuts for Windows Explorer and Windows Sidebar

Shortcut keys are available for some common tasks in Windows Explorer and Windows Sidebar. Using these shortcut keys, you can more easily navigate through the available options. Table 29-5 lists keyboard shortcuts for when you are working with Windows Explorer.

Table 29-5. Keyboard shortcuts for Windows Explorer

To do this...	Use this keyboard shortcut...
Collapse the current selection if it is expanded, or select the parent folder	Left arrow
Collapse the selected folder	Num Lock-minus sign (−) on numeric keypad
Display all subfolders under the selected folder	Num Lock-asterisk (*) on numeric keypad
Display the bottom of the active window	End
Display the contents of the selected folder	Num Lock-plus sign (+) on numeric keypad

Table 29-5. Keyboard shortcuts for Windows Explorer (continued)

To do this...	Use this keyboard shortcut...
Display the current selection if it is collapsed, or select the first subfolder	Right arrow
Display the top of the active window	Home
Select the Address bar	Alt-D
View the next folder	Alt-right arrow
View the previous folder	Alt-left arrow

Table 29-6 lists keyboard shortcuts for when you are working with Windows Sidebar.

Table 29-6. Keyboard shortcuts for Windows Sidebar

To do this...	Use this keyboard shortcut...
Bring all gadgets to the front and select Sidebar	Windows logo key-Space bar
Cycle through Sidebar controls	Tab
Cycle through Sidebar gadgets	Windows logo key-G

Keyboard Shortcuts for Windows Photo Gallery

Shortcut keys are available for many of the commands in Windows Photo Gallery. Using shortcut keys, you can quickly accomplish common tasks and manage videos. Table 29-7 lists general keyboard shortcuts for when you are working with Windows Photo Gallery.

Table 29-7. General keyboard shortcuts for Windows Photo Gallery

To do this...	Use this keyboard shortcut...
Collapse node	Left arrow
Expand node	Right arrow
Go back	Alt-left arrow
Go forward	Alt-right arrow
Move the selected item to the Recycle Bin	Delete
Open or close the Details Pane	Ctrl-I
Open or close the Fix Pane	Ctrl-F
Permanently delete the selected item	Shift-Delete
Print the selected picture	Ctrl-P
Rename the selected item	F2
Rotate the picture clockwise	Ctrl-period (.)

To do this...	Use this keyboard shortcut...
Rotate the picture counter-clockwise	Ctrl-comma (,)
Search for an item	Ctrl-E
Select the first item	Home
Select the last item	End
Select the next item or row	Down arrow
Select the previous item	Left arrow
View next screen	Page Down
View picture with best fit	Ctrl-B
View previous item or row	Up arrow
View previous screen	Page Up
View the selected picture at a larger size	Enter
Zoom in or resize the picture thumbnail	Plus sign (+)
Zoom out or resize the picture thumbnail	Minus sign (−)

Table 29-8 lists keyboard shortcuts for when you are working with videos in Windows Photo Gallery.

Table 29-8. Keyboard shortcuts for working with videos in Windows Photo Gallery

To do this...	Use this keyboard shortcut...
Advance to the next frame	Alt-right arrow
Go back to the previous frame	Alt-left arrow
Move back one frame	J
Move forward one frame	L
Move to the start trim point	Home
Move to the end trim point	End
Pause the playback	K
Play from the current location	Ctrl-P
Seek to nearest split point after the current location	Page Down
Seek to nearest split point before the current location	Page Up
Set the end trim point	O
Set the start trim point	I
Split a clip	M
Stop and rewind playback	Ctrl-K
Stop and rewind to the start trim point	Home

Keyboard Shortcuts for Windows Media Center

Just about every common command you'll use when working with Windows Media Center has a keyboard shortcut. Using shortcut keys, you can quickly accomplish any common task, view pictures, and control radio, TV, audio, and video. Table 29-9 lists general keyboard shortcuts for when you are working with Windows Media Center.

Table 29-9. General keyboard shortcuts in Windows Media Center

To do this...	Use this keyboard shortcut...
Accept the selection	Enter
Close Windows Media Center	Alt-F4
Go back to the previous screen	Backspace
Go in and go out of windowed mode	Alt-Enter
Go to the first item in a list	Home
Go to the last item in a list	End
Go to the next page	Page Down
Go to the previous page	Page Up
Move left, right, up, or down	Arrow keys
Open Windows Media Center or return to the Windows Media Center Start screen	Windows key-Alt-Enter

Table 29-10 lists keyboard shortcuts for when you are working with audio in Windows Media Center.

Table 29-10. Audio controls in Windows Media Center

To do this...	Use this keyboard shortcut...
Display the context menu	Ctrl-D
Fast-forward a song	Ctrl-Shift-F
Go to Music	Ctrl-M
Mute volume	F8
Pause or resume an audio file or song	Ctrl-P
Play an audio file or song	Ctrl-Shift-P
Replay an audio file or song	Ctrl-B
Rip a CD	Ctrl-R
Skip to the next song	Ctrl-F
Turn down volume	F9
Turn on or turn off closed captioning	Ctrl-Shift-C
Turn up volume	F10

Table 29-11 lists keyboard shortcuts for when you are working with TV in Windows Media Center.

Table 29-11. TV controls in Windows Media Center

To do this...	Use this keyboard shortcut...
Display the context menu	Ctrl-D
Fast-forward live TV or recorded TV	Ctrl-Shift-F
Go to live TV	Ctrl-T
Go to recorded TV	Ctrl-O
Go to the Guide	Ctrl-G
Go to the next channel	Page Up
Go to the previous channel	Page Down
Pause or resume live TV or recorded TV	Ctrl-P
Record a TV show	Ctrl-R
Resume playing a TV show	Ctrl-Shift-P
Rewind live TV or recorded TV	Ctrl-Shift-B
Skip back	Ctrl-B
Skip forward	Ctrl-F
Stop recording or stop playing a TV show	Ctrl-Shift-S

Table 29-12 lists keyboard shortcuts for when you are working with radio in Windows Media Center.

Table 29-12. Radio controls in Windows Media Center

To do this...	Use this keyboard shortcut...
Display the context menu	Ctrl-D
Go to Radio	Ctrl-A
Pause or resume live radio	Ctrl-P
Resume playing radio	Ctrl-Shift-P
Skip back	Ctrl-B
Skip forward	Ctrl-F
Stop live radio	Ctrl-Shift-S

Table 29-13 lists keyboard shortcuts for when you are viewing pictures in Windows Media Center.

Table 29-13. Picture viewing options in Windows Media Center

To do this...	Use this keyboard shortcut...
Display the context menu	Ctrl-D
Go to Pictures	Ctrl-I

Table 29-13. Picture viewing options in Windows Media Center (continued)

To do this...	Use this keyboard shortcut...
Pause a slide show	Ctrl-P
Play a slide show	Ctrl-Shift-P
Skip back to the previous picture	Up arrow or left arrow
Skip forward to the next picture	Down arrow or right arrow
Stop a slide show	Ctrl-Shift-S
Zoom a picture in Picture Details	Enter

Table 29-14 lists keyboard shortcuts for when you are viewing recorded videos in Windows Media Center.

Table 29-14. Video viewing options in Windows Media Center

To do this...	Use this keyboard shortcut...
Fast-forward	Ctrl-Shift-F
Go to Videos	Ctrl-E
Pause	Ctrl-P
Play	Ctrl-Shift-P
Rewind	Ctrl-Shift-B
Skip back	Ctrl-B
Skip forward	Ctrl-F
Stop	Ctrl-Shift-S

Table 29-15 lists keyboard shortcuts for when you are playing DVDs in Windows Media Center.

Table 29-15. DVD playing options in Windows Media Center

To do this...	Use this keyboard shortcut...
Change the DVD angle	Arrow keys
Change the DVD audio selection	Ctrl-Shift-A
Change the DVD subtitles selection	Ctrl-U
Fast-forward	Ctrl-Shift-F
Go to the DVD menu	Ctrl-Shift-M
Go to the next chapter	Ctrl-F
Go to the previous chapter	Ctrl-B
Pause	Ctrl-P
Play	Ctrl-Shift-P
Rewind	Ctrl-Shift-B
Stop	Ctrl-Shift-S

Keyboard Shortcuts for Windows Media Player

As Table 29-16 shows, shortcut keys are available for many of the commands in Windows Media Player. Using these shortcut keys, you can quickly accomplish common tasks when working with Windows Media Player.

Table 29-16. Windows Media Player keyboard shortcuts

To do this…	Use this keyboard shortcut…
Access the Search box	Ctrl-E
Add media files to the library	F3
Close or stop playing a file	Ctrl-W
Create a new playlist	Ctrl-N
Decrease size of album art	Shift-F6
Decrease volume	F8
Display Windows Media Player Help	F1
Edit media information on a selected item in the library	F2
Eject CD or DVD (on a computer with one CD or DVD)	Ctrl-J
Fast-forward through video or music	Ctrl-Shift-F
Go to next item or chapter	Ctrl-F
Go to previous item or chapter	Ctrl-B
Increase size of album art	F6
Increase volume	F9
Mute volume	F7
Open a file	Ctrl-O
Play at normal speed	Ctrl-Shift-N
Play or pause playing	Ctrl-P
Rate an item that is playing as five stars	Ctrl-Windows logo key-5
Rate an item that is playing as four stars	Ctrl-Windows logo key-4
Rate an item that is playing as three stars	Ctrl-Windows logo key-3
Rate an item that is playing as two stars	Ctrl-Windows logo key-2
Rate an item that is playing as one star	Ctrl-Windows logo key-1
Rate an item that is playing as zero stars	Ctrl-Windows logo key-0
Refresh information in the panes	F5
Retrace steps back through your recent views	Alt-left arrow
Retrace steps forward through your recent views	Alt-right arrow
Return to full mode from full screen	Esc
Rewind video	Ctrl-Shift-B
Show or hide the Classic menus (in full-mode)	Ctrl-M
Show the Classic menus (menu bar)	F10

Table 29-16. Windows Media Player keyboard shortcuts (continued)

To do this...	Use this keyboard shortcut...
Specify a URL or path to a file	Ctrl-U
Stop playing	Ctrl-S
Switch to full mode	Ctrl-1
Switch to skin mode	Ctrl-2
Switch to the first view in a media category after Recently Added	Ctrl-7
Switch to the second view in a media category after Recently Added	Ctrl-8
Switch to the third view in a media category after Recently Added	Ctrl-9
Switch the view of items in the Details Pane	F4
Toggle display for full-screen video	Alt-Enter
Turn captions and subtitles on or off	Ctrl-Shift-C
Turn repeat on or off in audio playback	Ctrl-T
Turn shuffle on or off	Ctrl-H
Use a fast play speed	Ctrl-Shift-G
Use a slow play speed	Ctrl-Shift-S
Zoom to 100 percent	Alt-2
Zoom to 200 percent	Alt-3
Zoom to 50 percent	Alt-1

Keyboard Shortcuts for Internet Explorer 7

Shortcut keys are available for many of the commands in Internet Explorer 7. Using these shortcut keys, you can quickly accomplish common tasks. Table 29-17 lists general keyboard shortcuts for when you are working with Internet Explorer 7.

Table 29-17. General keyboard shortcuts in Internet Explorer 7

To do this...	Use this keyboard shortcut...
Activate a selected link	Enter
Click the Information bar	Space bar
Close the current tab or window	Ctrl-W
Display a shortcut menu for a link	Shift-F10
Display Help	F1
Find on this page	Ctrl-F

Table 29-17. General keyboard shortcuts in Internet Explorer 7 (continued)

To do this...	Use this keyboard shortcut...
Force refresh of the current web page	Ctrl-F5
Go to the next page	Alt-right arrow
Go to the previous page	Alt-left arrow or Backspace
Go to your home page	Alt-Home
Move back through the items	Shift-Tab
Move backward between frames (works only if tabbed browsing is disabled)	Ctrl-Shift-Tab
Move focus to the Information bar	Alt-N
Move forward through frames and browser elements (works only if tabbed browsing is disabled)	Ctrl-Tab or F6
Move forward through items	Tab
Move to the beginning of a document	Home
Move to the end of a document	End
Open a new web site or page	Ctrl-O
Open a new window	Ctrl-N
Open Favorites	Ctrl-I
Open Feeds	Ctrl-J
Open History	Ctrl-H
Open the Help menu on the classic menu bar	Alt-H
Open the Help menu on the standard toolbar	Alt-L
Open the Home menu	Alt-M
Open the Page menu	Alt-P
Open the Print menu	Alt-R
Open the RSS menu	Alt-J
Open the Tools menu on the classic menu bar	Alt-T
Open the Tools menu on the standard toolbar	Alt-O
Page down	Page Down
Page up	Page Up
Print the current page or active frame	Ctrl-P
Refresh the current web page	F5
Save the current page	Ctrl-S
Scroll down	Down arrow
Scroll up	Up arrow
Stop downloading a page	Esc
Toggle between full-screen and regular viewing modes	F11

Table 29-18 lists keyboard shortcuts for when you are working with tabbed browsing in Internet Explorer 7.

Table 29-18. Keyboard shortcuts for tabbed browsing in Internet Explorer 7

To do this...	Use this keyboard shortcut...
Close current tab or window	Ctrl-W
Close other tabs	Ctrl-Alt-F4
Jump to a specific tab number	Ctrl-*N* (where *N* is a number between 1 and 8)
Jump to the last tab	Ctrl-9
Open a new tab in the foreground	Ctrl-T
Open a new tab in the foreground from the Address bar	Alt-Enter
Open links in a new tab in the background	Ctrl-click
Open links in a new tab in the foreground	Ctrl-Shift-click
Switch between tabs	Ctrl-Tab or Ctrl-Shift-Tab
Toggle Quick Tabs on or off	Ctrl-Q

Table 29-19 lists keyboard shortcuts for when you are working with zoom, search, preview, and print in Internet Explorer 7.

Table 29-19. Keyboard shortcuts for zoom and search in Internet Explorer 7

To do this...	Use this keyboard shortcut...
Decrease zoom (– 10%)	Ctrl-minus sign
Go to the Search box	Ctrl-E
Increase zoom (+ 10%)	Ctrl-plus sign
Open the search provider menu	Ctrl-down arrow
Open your search query in a new tab	Alt-Enter
Zoom to 100%	Ctrl-0

Table 29-20 lists keyboard shortcuts for when you are working with Print Preview in Internet Explorer 7.

Table 29-20. Keyboard shortcuts for Print Preview in Internet Explorer 7

To do this...	Use this keyboard shortcut...
Change page setup	Alt-U
Close Print Preview	Alt-C
Configure printing for pages with frames	Alt-F
Display a list of zoom percentages	Alt-Z

Table 29-20. Keyboard shortcuts for Print Preview in Internet Explorer 7 (continued)

To do this...	Use this keyboard shortcut...
Display the first page to be printed	Alt-Home
Display the last page to be printed	Alt-End
Display the next page to be printed	Alt-right arrow
Display the previous page to be printed	Alt-left arrow
Go to page in preview	Alt-A and then type the page number to display
Zoom in	Alt-plus sign
Zoom out	Alt-minus sign

Table 29-21 lists keyboard shortcuts for when you are working with addresses, feeds, history, and favorites in Internet Explorer 7.

Table 29-21. Keyboard shortcuts for addresses, feeds, history, and favorites in Internet Explorer 7

To do this...	Use this keyboard shortcut...
Add *www.* to the beginning and *.com* to the end of the text typed (when working with addresses)	Ctrl-Enter
Add the current page to your favorites	Ctrl-D
Display address history list	F4
Display all feeds (when in Feed view)	Alt-I
Mark a feed as read (when in Feed view)	Alt-M
Move back through the list of AutoComplete matches	Down arrow
Move forward through the list of AutoComplete matches	Up arrow
Move selected item down in the Favorites list in the Organize Favorites dialog box	Alt-down arrow
Move selected item up in the Favorites list in the Organize Favorites dialog box	Alt-up arrow
Move the cursor left to the next logical break in the address (when working with addresses)	Ctrl-left arrow
Move the cursor right to the next logical break in the address (when working with addresses)	Ctrl-right arrow
Open Add to Favorites menu	Alt-Z
Open and dock the Favorites Center and display your feeds	Ctrl-Shift-J
Open Favorites Center and display your favorites	Alt-C
Open Favorites Center and display your feeds	Ctrl-J
Open Favorites Center and display your history	Ctrl-H
Open the Organize Favorites dialog box	Ctrl-B
Select the text in the Address bar	Alt-D

Keyboard Shortcuts for Windows Movie Maker

As Table 29-22 shows, shortcut keys are available for many of the commands in Windows Movie Maker. Using these shortcut keys, you can quickly accomplish common tasks.

Table 29-22. Keyboard shortcuts for Windows Movie Maker

To do this...	Use this keyboard shortcut...
Add selected clips to the storyboard or timeline	Ctrl-D
Back	Ctrl-Alt-left arrow
Clear the storyboard/timeline	Ctrl-Delete
Clear trim points	U
Collapse the Video track when it is selected in the timeline	–
Combine contiguous clips	N
Copy selected item	Ctrl-C
Create a new project	Ctrl-N
Cut selected item	Ctrl-X
Delete selected item	Delete
Display Help topics	F1
Expand the Video track when it is selected in the timeline	+
Forward	Ctrl-Alt-right arrow
Go to the first item	Home
Go to the last item	End
Import an existing digital media file	Ctrl-I
Import video from a digital video camera	Ctrl-R
Next frame	L
Nudge clip to the left	Ctrl-Shift-B
Nudge clip to the right	Ctrl-Shift-N
Open an existing project	Ctrl-O
Paste previously cut or copied item	Ctrl-V
Play content on the storyboard or timeline	Ctrl-W
Play or pause clip	K
Play video in full-screen mode	Alt-Enter
Previous frame	J
Publish a movie	Ctrl-P
Redo the last undone action	Ctrl-Y
Rename a collection or clip	F2
Rewind and go to the beginning of the storyboard or timeline	Ctrl-Q
Save a project	Ctrl-S

Table 29-22. Keyboard shortcuts for Windows Movie Maker (continued)

To do this...	Use this keyboard shortcut...
Save a project with a new name	F12
Select all clips	Ctrl-A
Select clip trim handle	Alt-Shift-up/down arrow
Select item above	Up arrow
Select item below	Down arrow
Select next item	Right arrow
Select previous item	Left arrow
Set end trim point	O
Set start trim point	I
Split a clip	M
Stop playback on the storyboard or timeline	Ctrl-K
Switch between the storyboard and the timeline	Ctrl-T
Trim clip edge left	Alt-Shift-left arrow
Trim clip edge right	Alt-Shift-right arrow
Undo the last action	Ctrl-Z
Zoom in on the timeline	Page Down
Zoom out on the timeline	Page Up
Zoom the timeline to fit on the screen	F9

Index

We'd like to hear your suggestions for improving our indexes. Send email to *index@oreilly.com*.

E

Ease of Access, 444
    Explore All Settings, 466
    Get Recommendations, 466
    Quick Access to Common Tools, 466
elevation, 64
email (see Windows Mail)
Email Message (.eml) files, 556
email viruses, 516
Encrypting File System (EFS), 688
encryption
    drives, 687
    files and folders, 687–693
        removing, 689
        sharing, 689
    keys, backing up, 690
end user license agreement (EULA), 521
English domain names, 223
Enhanced Integrated Drive Electronics
    (EIDE), 133
Enterprise edition, 5, 774
    upgrade options, 6
Enterprise Quality of Service (QoS) (Group
    Policy category), 860
Entertainment Software Ratings Board
    (ESRB), 653
environment variables, 702
errors, tracking in event logs, 733–735
Ethernet router
    installing, 478
    versus hub or switch, 476
Ethernet standard, 476
event logs
    accessing, 733
    information
        computer, 735
        details, 735
        Event ID, 734
        source, 734
        task category, 734
        user, 734
    tracking errors, 733–735
    types of, 733
    warning levels
        Audit Failure, 734
        Error, 734
        Information, 734
        Warning, 734

Event Viewer node in Computer
    Management, 733
explicit consent and browser cookies, 228
Extensible, 13
Extensible Firmware Interface (EFI), 13

F

Failed, Online (Errors), or Unreadable
    status, 682
FAT versus NTFS, 384
fax machines (see printers, scanners, and fax
    machines)
features
    ActiveX Installer Services, 129
    adding and removing, 129–131
    Games, 129
    Indexing Service, 129
    Internet Information Services, 129
    Microsoft .NET Framework 3.0, 129
    Microsoft Message Queue (MSMQ)
        Server, 129
    Print Services, 130
    Remote Differential Compression, 130
    Removable Storage Management, 130
    RIP Listener, 130
    Services for N, 130
    Simple TCPIP Services, 130
    Tablet PC Optional Component, 130
    Telnet Client, 130
    Telnet Server, 130
    TFTP Client, 130
    Windows DFS Replication Service, 130
    Windows Fax and Scan, 130
    Windows Meeting Space, 131
    Windows Process Activation Service, 131
    Windows Ultimate Extras, 131
Feed Headlines gadget, 40
File and Printer Sharing for Microsoft
    Networks, 496
file attributes, 384–386
    Hidden, 385
    Read-only, 385
    System, 385
    viewing or changing, 385–386
file sharing (see sharing data)
File Sharing Panel, 400

transport encryption mechansim, 502
Trojans, 517
troubleshooting programs and
    features, 763–769
  DVDs
    playing, 766
    recording, 766
  installation, 765
  Internet Explorer 7 problems, 248
  language/keyboard, 765
  Live File System, 766
  manufacturer system devices, 766
  Network Map, 766
  networking programs, 766
  RAW image files, 766
  removing partitions, 769
  restoring boot sector, 768
  sessions, closing, 769
  Slide show playback, 766
  Sound Recorder, 766
  Speech Recognition, 766
    commands, 767
  USB
    audio devices, 767
    drives, 767
    storage devices, 767
  User Account Control, 767
  video filter, 768
  Windows Complete PC Restore, 767
  Windows Explorer menu bar, 767
  Windows Media Center
    Microsoft web site, 845
    network settings, 845
    sound, 846
    TV tuner and video capture, 846
  Windows Media Center Setup, 844
  Windows Media Player, 767
  Windows Movie Maker, 767
  Windows startup, 767
  Windows Vista startup, 768
  wireless adapters, 768
trusted sites, configuring, 241
tunneling encryption mechanism, 502
turn, 659
turning off and shutting down, 17
TV library, 263
TV ratings (Windows Media Center Parental
    Controls), 836

U

UAC, 800
UDF 1.5 format, 326
UDF 2.0 format, 326
UDF 2.01 format, 326
UDF 2.5 format, 326
Ultimate edition, 5, 774
    upgrade options, 6
Universal Resource Locators (URLs), 223
Universal Serial Bus (USB), 134
  adapters, 619
  audio devices, 767
  devices, 148
    storage, 767
  drives, 767
  ports, 135
  ReadyBoost and, 97
update history, viewing, 713
upgrading, 6
User Account Control (UAC), 62–65, 383,
    767
  elevation and security, 64
  enabling and disabling, 65
  permission and consent prompting, 62
  standard and administrator user
    accounts, 62
user account settings, 9
user accounts, 629–646
  changing account name, 631
  changing account picture, 632
  changing account picture for other
    people, 639
  changing account type, 632
  changing account type for other
    people, 640
  changing for other people, 638
  creating for other people, 637
  enabling local user accounts, 644
  local user accounts
    deleting, 645
    renaming, 650
  managing access, 629–631
    Administrator, 630
    Guest, 630
    LocalService, 631
    LocalSystem, 630
    NetworkService, 631
    SID, 630

About the Author

William R. Stanek (*http://www.williamstanek.com*) has more than 20 years of hands-on experience with advanced programming and development. He is a leading technology expert, an award-winning author, and a pretty darn good instructional trainer. His 63 books include *Microsoft Windows Vista Administrator's Pocket Consultant*, *Windows Server 2003 Inside Out*, *Microsoft Exchange Server 2007 Administrator's Pocket Consultant*, and *Microsoft IIS 7.0 Administrator's Pocket Consultant* (all from Microsoft Press). For O'Reilly, he wrote *MCSE Core Exams in a Nutshell*, in addition to the book you hold in your hands.

Mr. Stanek has been involved in the commercial Internet community since 1991. His core business and technology experience comes from more than 11 years of military service. He has substantial experience developing server technology, encryption, and Internet solutions. He has written many technical white papers and training courses on a wide variety of topics. He is widely sought after as a subject matter expert.

Mr. Stanek has an MS (with distinction) in information systems and a BS (magna cum laude) in computer science. He is proud to have served in the Persian Gulf War as a combat crewmember on an electronic warfare aircraft. He flew on numerous combat missions into Iraq and was awarded nine medals for his wartime service, including one of the United States of America's highest flying honors, the Air Force Distinguished Flying Cross. Currently, he resides in the Pacific Northwest with his wife and children. For fun he used to spend a lot of time mountain biking and hiking, but now his adventures in the great outdoors are mostly restricted to short treks around the Pacific Northwest.

Colophon

The animal on the cover of *Windows Vista: The Definitive Guide* is a European common frog (*Rana temporaria*), also known as the "brown frog" or "grass frog." This species inhabits Europe from the Pyrenees to the Urals and West Siberia. It can be found in just about any damp habitat within this range, including lowland and mountain forests, meadows, swamps, ponds, lakes, rivers, gardens, backyards, and parks.

The European common frog has a small, squat body and a wide, flat head. The frog is typically brown or grayish in color but can also have yellowish or red hues. The lower segments of its backbone are fused into a stiff rod called the urostyle, which, along with its strong pelvic bones, helps provide strength and firmness to the rear of the body. The frogs have powerful hind legs and webbed feet, which contribute to their excellent jumping and swimming abilities.

The males of the species tend to be slightly smaller than the females and are identifiable by whitish swellings on the inner digits of their front feet. During breeding season, these swellings support dark "nuptial pads" that enable the male to grasp the female more effectively. The male can be very vocal when trying to attract a mate, even croaking underwater. Once he has attracted a female, he climbs on her back and embraces her in a tight, sometimes suffocating grip called amplexus, which can last up to two days. He fertilizes the eggs as the female lays them. In recent years, scientists researching the species in the Pyrenees have discovered a behavior known as "clutch piracy," in which gangs of males search for newly laid eggs to fertilize them again. The researchers have found evidence of fertilization from as many as four males in a single clutch of eggs.

Although huge numbers of eggs are laid, few frogs survive to adulthood. Tadpoles are preyed upon by both terrestrial and aquatic animals, and adult frogs count grass snakes, kingfishers, and herons among their many predators. Additionally, many frogs are caught by humans for the purposes of education, medicine, and science. Overall, however, this particular species is neither declining nor threatened.

The cover image is from Wood's *Reptiles, Fishes, Insects, &c.* The cover font is Adobe ITC Garamond. The text font is Linotype Birka; the heading font is Adobe Myriad Condensed; and the code font is LucasFont's TheSans Mono Condensed.

Better than e-books

Buy *Windows Vista: The Definitive Guide* and access
the digital edition FREE on Safari for 45 days.

Go to www.oreilly.com/go/safarienabled
and type in coupon code HLNVHXA

Search
thousands of
top tech books

Download
whole chapters

Cut and Paste
code examples

Find
answers fast

Search Safari! The premier electronic reference
library for programmers and IT professionals.

The O'Reilly Advantage

Stay Current and Save Money